RUSSIA AND IRAN

NICOLE GRAJEWSKI

Russia and Iran

Partners in Defiance from Syria to Ukraine

HURST & COMPANY, LONDON

First published in the United Kingdom in 2026 by
C. Hurst & Co. (Publishers) Ltd.,
New Wing, Somerset House, Strand,
London, WC2R 1LA

Printed in Scotland.

A Cataloguing-in-Publication data record for this book is available from the British Library.

ISBN: 9781911723738

EU GPSR Authorised Representative
Easy Access System Europe Oü, 16879218
Address: Mustamäe tee 50, 10621, Tallinn, Estonia
Contact Details: gpsr.requests@easproject.com, +358 40 500 3575

This book is printed using paper from registered sustainable and managed sources.

Printed and bound in Great Britain by Bell & Bain Ltd, Glasgow

www.hurstpublishers.com

To my parents

CONTENTS

LIST OF MAPS

INTRODUCTION

"Death to Russia" (*Marg bar Rusiyeh*) echoed among the crowd at a Friday sermon in Tehran—a stark departure from the state-sanctioned mantra of "Death to America" (*Marg bar Amrika*). The chants emerged as a direct consequence of Russia's swift endorsement of incumbent President Mahmoud Ahmadinejad's contested election in June 2009. Widespread allegations of electoral fraud triggered nationwide protests known as the Green Movement, with Iranians taking to the streets to challenge the election's legitimacy and demand Ahmadinejad's resignation. These demonstrations, which continued throughout the summer of 2009, represented the largest display of civil unrest in Iran since the 1979 Islamic Revolution. Most states refrained from recognizing the results of the election. Russia, however, did not.

Not only did Moscow become the first government to recognize the disputed June 2009 election, but it also hosted the contested winner, Ahmadinejad, at the Shanghai Cooperation Organization (SCO) summit in Yekaterinburg just days later. Behind the scenes, Russian security services assisted Iran's riot police and Islamic Revolutionary Guard Corps (IRGC) by sharing tactics to suppress mass movements. The outbursts of "Death to Russia" by Green Movement protestors highlighted societal frustration towards Russia's stifling of democratic dissent. The Iranian popular mistrust of Russia notably diverged from the government's policy, which used Moscow's recognition as a testament to the election's legitimacy.

For many Iranians, Russia's actions in 2009 were not an isolated incident but rather the latest chapter in a long history marked by mistrust and betrayal. The roots of this fraught relationship can be traced back centuries, to the eighteenth-century wars of territorial expansion that saw Iran cede significant portions of its land to imperial Russia. Throughout the nineteenth and twentieth centuries, Tsarist Russia repeatedly meddled in Iran's internal affairs, obstructing attempts at political reform while continuing to eye further territorial gains. In the early twentieth century, Russia and Britain divided Iran into spheres of influence, with Russia controlling the north and Britain the south, undermining Iran's sovereignty. Later, the Soviet Union fostered further Iranian enmity by supporting separatist movements and providing arms to Iraq during the devastating Iran-Iraq War of the 1980s.

The tumultuous history of the Russia-Iran relationship, marked by periods of cooperation punctuated by episodes of tension and mistrust, carried over into the post-Soviet era. In the years leading up to the Green Movement, Russia's cancellations of arms sales to Iran, combined with Moscow's support for United Nations (UN) sanctions on Iran's nuclear program, further deepened Iran's mistrust. Typically, Iran's reformists, a faction advocating gradual socio-political reforms while maintaining the country's Islamic governance structure, have been vocal critics of cooperation with Russia. However, conservatives like Ahmadinejad have also lodged critiques of Russia. Indeed, one year after Russia lent its backing to his contested election, Ahmadinejad warned that Russia's approval of new UN sanctions over Iran's controversial nuclear program could turn Moscow into "an enemy of the Iranian people."[1] Moscow's eventual support for these sanctions in 2010 would thrust the relationship between Russia and Iran to the lowest point in modern history, with President Ahmadinejad describing Russia as caving in to "Satan."

The chasm between Iran's historical grievances and the extent of Russia-Iran cooperation would dramatically narrow within two years of the Green Movement. In 2011, a confluence of sweeping regional shifts in the Middle East, coupled with domestic changes in Russia, precipitated closer collaboration between Moscow and Tehran.

The Arab Spring uprisings, followed by the North Atlantic Treaty Organization (NATO) intervention in Libya, stoked fears in both capitals about Western-led regime change. These events resonated particularly strongly in Russia, where protests over the 2011 parliamentary elections echoed the specter of Color Revolutions that had long haunted the Kremlin. Meanwhile, following a brief interlude as Prime Minister, Vladimir Putin returned to the presidency in 2012. Under Putin's renewed leadership, Moscow pursued a more vigorous and unyielding diplomatic course, openly challenging Western dominance—a posture that strongly aligned with Iran's long-standing defiance of American influence. This convergence of interests laid the groundwork for a new era of partnership between Russia and Iran, transcending their historical animosities and setting the stage for unprecedented cooperation.

The most striking manifestation of this newfound cooperation came in 2015 with Russia and Iran's joint military campaign to support the beleaguered Syrian dictator Bashar Assad in the face of a popular uprising that had turned into a civil war. Seven years later, Vladimir Putin's full-scale invasion of Ukraine in 2022 cast a spotlight on Russia's partnership with Iran as Moscow looked to Tehran to provide drones and ammunition for its so-called "special military operation." Historically, Russia has held a dominant position in its relationship with Iran, a dynamic particularly visible in the arms trade, where Russia was the primary supplier of military equipment to Iran. The prolonged conflict in Ukraine and Western sanctions, however, impaired Russia's ability to replenish certain weapons reliant on Western components. This new reality compelled Moscow to seek assistance from Tehran, reversing the usual flow of military technology between the two countries.

'In the wake of Russia's February 2022 invasion of Ukraine, the diplomatic and economic ties between Tehran and Moscow dramatically expanded—evidenced by new arms deals, rising trade flows, and a surge in high-level delegations between the two capitals. Yet, whereas the Ukraine war injected fresh impetus into their partnership, the sudden collapse of Bashar Assad's regime in late 2024 demonstrated that the joint project originally uniting Russia and Iran could not endure indefinitely.

Paradoxically, Assad's downfall served as a stark testament to the evolution of their "partnership of defiance"—one born out of mutual antagonism toward the liberal international order and bolstered by an unwavering commitment to protecting their respective regimes. Originally forged in Syria, then strengthened by the war in Ukraine, Moscow and Tehran's shared strategic, military, and economic interests endured well beyond the end of the very regime they had once fought to save.

* * *

A partnership between Russia and Iran was far from inevitable. Long-lasting mistrust, unmet expectations, and weak economic ties have historically marred the Russia-Iran relationship. The question that emerges from this complex history is how two countries with such a contentious past, marked by deep-seated mistrust and conflicting interests, could come to forge a partnership.

Political scientists have long studied the reasons for state cooperation, using complex datasets and variables to find a "one-size-fits-all theory" to explain state behavior.[2] Some theories posit that states balance against military power or common military threats.[3] Others suggest that shared norms and values like democracy drive states to cooperate.[4] Theories about interstate cooperation tend to privilege one explanation over others rather than treating cooperation as a dynamic process with twists, turns, and contradictions.[5] This book deliberately does not restrict itself to abstract political science variables and theoretical models to uncover the textured reality of how Russia and Iran's partnership unfolded. Drawing on extensive Russian and Persian sources and interviews, it reveals how their cooperation emerged through cycles of engagement and distrust, eschewing neat theoretical explanations or predictive frameworks.

While Russia and Iran have long shared an antipathy towards the so-called "collective West" and a common concern with the threat of domestic upheavals, these factors alone were not sufficient to overcome the barriers that once divided them. It was the outbreak of the Syrian Civil War that transformed their ties from sporadic collaboration and recurrent tensions into a nascent alignment. Working together in Syria not only solidified operational and tactical coordination between Russian and Iranian forces but also laid the groundwork for a broader partnership that would persist even after the fall of the Assad regime in late 2024. In fact, the shared experience in Syria enabled Russia and Iran to expand their cooperation into areas such as sanctions evasion and more assertive challenges to Western influence within international organizations. The war in Ukraine not only intensified the shared threat perceptions and anti-Western sentiments that had long underpinned the Russia-Iran relationship but also created a new set of imperatives and opportunities for cooperation.

A Partnership of Defiance

For decades, Russia and Iran had independently harbored a profound sense of marginalization and alienation from the Western-led liberal international order, perceiving it as a system that disproportionately favors the interests and values of the United States and its allies at the expense of their own. Domestically, Moscow and Tehran shared a deep-seated belief that they were perennial targets of Western interference, facing concerted efforts to undermine their regimes and foment internal unrest. Despite these shared grievances, Russia and Iran had struggled to translate their conceptual alignment into tangible cooperation on specific issues. While they occasionally found common ground in their critiques of the U.S.-led international system, their partnership remained largely confined to the realm of discourse rather than action.

If the Syrian Civil War served as the initial catalyst for the deepening of the Russia-Iran partnership, it was Russia's 2022 invasion of Ukraine that cemented the relationship into one of necessity and mutual dependence. The invasion plunged Moscow into a steep downturn in relations with the West, triggering unprecedented sanctions and diplomatic isolation. Under these circumstances, Iran's long-cultivated expertise in evading international sanctions proved indispensable to Russia, offering valuable insights into alternative financial channels, illicit trade networks, and economic resiliency strategies. At the same time, Russia's protracted military campaign in Ukraine severely strained its defense capabilities, creating a dire need for new sources of armaments, ammunition, and other materiel. Iran emerged as one of the few actors not only willing but also equipped to meet this demand, supplying drones and ammunition that played a key role in bolstering Moscow's war effort. In turn, Iran benefited by securing advanced Russian technology and deepening its access to vital military know-how. Rather than simply deepen existing ties, the Ukraine war entrenched Russia and Iran's cooperation to a degree neither could easily abandon.

Russia and Iran's partnership has been shaped by a series of reactive measures—diplomatic, economic, and military—aimed at preserving their sovereign interests in defiance of perceived Western encroachments.[6] The reactive nature of this partnership, coupled with a degree of enforced necessity due to a lack of alternatives, has defined the contours of their relationship. While Russia and Iran found common cause in opposing Western dominance, this stance served more as a foundation for dialogue than a catalyst for substantial collaboration.[7] The mere alignment of views, though persistent, fell short of creating the comprehensive partnership needed to effectively pursue their objectives on the global stage.[8] With the Syrian Civil War, the partnership of defiance was institutionalized through formal mechanisms and informal structures that provided for the expansion of cooperation beyond the battlefield.

Throughout this book, I deliberately avoid describing the relationship as an alliance because it implies a binding agreement to provide military support and assistance in the event of an attack, such as Article V of NATO. It is more appropriate to describe the Russia-Iran relationship as a partnership or alignment, both of which imply informal cooperation to pursue common interests. Russia and Iran have evolved into partners in defiance—an alignment initially forged through shared opposition to U.S. dominance and Western norms, but one that has since become deeply institutionalized. At its core, the Russia–Iran relationship is animated by a logic of defiance: defiance of Western liberal order, defiance of democratization, defiance of U.S.-led security arrangements, and defiance of international expectations.

Disgruntled and Discontented

With the Soviet Union's dissolution in 1991, the bipolar Cold War order gave way to a unipolar world with the U.S. as the single superpower, possessing unmatched military, economic, and diplomatic influence. The enthusiasm that pervaded the West rested on the conviction that democracy and liberal values would be widely embraced. A world that, in theory, would thrive through "open markets, international institutions, cooperative security, democratic community, progressive change, collective problem solving, shared sovereignty, [and] the rule of law."[9] Within the West, the optimism about the wider acceptance of democracy and liberal values often overshadowed the discontent from states outside and on the periphery of the liberal international order.

Russia and Iran's shared experiences under the shadow of American global primacy laid a crucial foundation for their collaboration. Despite marked differences in culture, governance, and regional goals, both nations harbored a deep-seated resentment of Western hegemony—a conviction that the post-Cold War order was skewed in favor of U.S. interests. Their encounters with American power, whether through sanctions, diplomatic isolation, or perceived intrusion into their spheres of influence, solidified this mutual antagonism. Over time, it evolved into a shared resolve to reshape global power, transcending even periods of serious diplomatic rifts.

For Vladimir Putin and much of the Russian elite, the Soviet collapse and the perceived weakness of the Russian state under Boris Yeltsin were seen as profound deviations from Russia's longstanding identity as a great power or "great powerness" (*derzhavnost*).[10] This sense of lost status and influence was deeply felt across the Russian political spectrum as the country grappled with economic turmoil, social upheaval, and a diminished role on the global stage in the 1990s. The consensus around Russian self-perception as an independent "great power" (*velikaya derzhava*) emerged as a reaction to the perceived failure of Yeltsin's pro-Western foreign policy, which many Russian elites believed had led to the country's marginalization and subordination to Western interests.[11] This sentiment intensified during the Putin era, as Russia's international position strengthened, bolstered by rising oil prices and a more assertive foreign policy. It also led to a domestic focus on a "strong state" (*sil'noye gosudarstvo*) or "state power" (*derzhavstvo*), which was often used to justify political repression and interference in neighboring states.[12]

Great power status has not only been integral to Russia's understanding of itself but also how it expects to be treated. Russia has coveted the hallmarks of great power status through its possession of nuclear weapons, permanent membership in the United Nations Security Council (UNSC), and an imperialistic entitlement to a sphere of influence. Viewed from Russia, the promises of treatment as an "equal" partner in the post-Cold War international system rang hollow. In response to this perceived marginalization, Russia began promoting the concept of multipolarity (*mnogopolyarnost*) as an alternative to the Western-led liberal international order. Emerging from the ruins of the Soviet collapse and confronting diminished global influence, Russia found profound appeal in the vision of a multipolar world—one where power would be distributed among several major actors rather than concentrated in a single superpower's grasp. This conception of global order promised to restore Russia's standing, while simultaneously embodying a broader repudiation of the Western-imposed norms and values that defined the liberal international order.

Iran's initial encounters with unipolarity differed significantly from Russia's. Tehran's revolutionary slogan of "neither East nor West" (*na sharghi, na gharbi*), emblematic of Iran's aspiration for political and ideological autonomy, was conceived in a bipolar world where aligning with either superpower bloc was seen as forsaking national sovereignty. The emergence of a unipolar world order ostensibly threatened this ideological equilibrium, as the United States' singular preeminence posed a new kind of imperial exertion. In this context, the U.S. policy of "dual containment" emerged in the 1990s, chiefly under the Clinton administration. This policy sought to isolate both Iran and Iraq through sanctions, export controls, and diplomatic pressure, effectively curbing their regional influence and cutting off access to military technology. Instead of compelling Iran to align with the Western-led order, however, dual containment hardened Tehran's determination to defy what it saw as American hegemony. It drove Iran to look for partners beyond the West who shared its quest to counterbalance U.S. preeminence, laying the groundwork for deeper ties with powers like Russia.

Tehran's emphasis on independence (*esteghlal*) and counter-hegemonic resistance to great powers not only led to critiques of the United States but also of Russia. Iran saw the very existence of great powers as a "completely private club whose walls are so high that no other country can pass through."[13] However, over time, Iran's worldview began to gravitate closer to the Russian perspective on multipolarity. As discussed in Chapters 1 and 7, Iran increasingly emphasized strengthening ties with Eastern powers—Russia and China—as a means to counterbalance U.S. influence and build alternative centers of power.

Over the years, Russia and Iran cultivated narratives of victimhood, portraying themselves as beleaguered actors in an often hostile international system. In reality, Russia's and Iran's own foreign policy decisions, internal governance, and aggressive ambitions have contributed to this sense of marginalization. By framing themselves as perennial victims, Russia and Iran have sought to divert attention from their own actions, including infringements of other nations' sovereignty and the pursuit of patrimonial policies. Yet, these narratives of victimhood have been heavily internalized within the Russian and Iranian foreign policy establishments, creating a degree of empathy between the leaderships, who see themselves as facing similar constraints.

Each country had its own distinct motivations for challenging the liberal international order, but the underlying grievances they articulated—such as objections to perceived Western dominance or constraints imposed by U.S.-led institutions—were *generalizable* in nature. In other words, these concerns transcended the specific historical and political contexts of Russia and Iran, resonating with other states that also felt marginalized or threatened by the prevailing global system. This broad applicability made it easier for Russia and Iran to identify common ground, even though their immediate contexts and goals diverged. Although their overlapping experiences fostered a mutual understanding of global affairs, it did not, by itself, generate the robust bureaucratic ties or institutional frameworks needed to sustain a deepening partnership. Instead, the practical institutionalization of their relationship—accelerated by the Syrian Civil War and reinforced by the willingness of both leaderships to pursue collaboration—was what turned this conceptual alignment into tangible diplomatic and military engagements.

Deep State and Regime (in)Security

The domestic decision-making apparatuses in Russia and Iran have played a crucial role in their partnership. Domestically, the prioritization of regime security and sovereignty in both political systems has not only cultivated mutual empathy but also served as a critical basis for their partnership. Conservative elements in both nations, including the influential *siloviki* in Russia and hardline conservatives in Iran, continue to wield substantial power and shape the political discourse. These domestic elites harbor deep-seated concerns about foreign interference and externally orchestrated regime change.

In Russia, under President Vladimir Putin's leadership, the centralization of power and the reliance on personal networks have increased the importance of Putin himself and the Russian Security Council in the decision-making process.[14] Headed by the president, the Security Council serves as the primary conduit for foreign policy formulation, with key government members such as the Prime Minister, Minister of Defense, Minister of Foreign Affairs, and the heads of the security and intelligence agencies as its members. The Russian Security Council is influenced by a faction known as the *siloviki*, a prominent cohort of influential officials and politicians in Russia whose professional experience lies predominantly within the realm of the country's security structures. Advocating for a strong state and centralized control, the *siloviki* prioritize domestic stability and are skeptical of Western democracy, often suppressing political opposition and enforcing media censorship in Russia. This faction's influence has been evident in actions like Putin's 2007 Munich address, the overseas assassination of dissidents, restrictive Non-Government Organization (NGO) laws, and the annexation of Crimea in 2014.[15]

In Iran, the Supreme Leader wields ultimate authority over foreign policy, setting broad directives and serving as the country's top arbitrator. His office, the Office of the Supreme Leader (OSL), actively orchestrates foreign affairs through high-level oversight of various government institutions. Meanwhile, the Supreme National Security Council (SNSC) takes the lead on matters affecting national security. Decisions concerning Russia ultimately fall under the Supreme Leader's purview, with input from the IRGC, the General Staff, the Ministry of Defense, and intelligence agencies.[16] Iran's military and security elites, many of whom play a direct role in shaping foreign policy, share a worldview similar to Russia's *siloviki*. These elites often favor deeper collaboration with Russia to enhance Iran's technological and military capabilities.[17] In both countries, leading figures see themselves as guardians of traditional values and national sovereignty, pushing back against the spread of Western-style liberal democracy, which they view as a threat to their political systems and cultural identities.

For Russia and Iran alike, the U.S. democratization agenda and the promotion of human rights are interpreted as intrusions on sovereignty, part of a broader effort by Washington to universalize its own values.[18] Russia and Iran framed Western criticism of authoritarian practices of the collective non-West within the context of a broader U.S.-led campaign to eliminate challenges to unipolarity. Russia's response to the coercive nature of liberal internationalism was most clearly articulated through the concept of "sovereign democracy," first promulgated by Putin's Deputy Chief of Staff Vladislav Surkov in 2006. Sovereign democracy was based on the idea that

> the form of democracy appropriate to Russian society, and by extension to other modernizing societies, is one where the state has the primary role in managing the transition to democracy, ensuring that the resulting societal transformation does not lead to disorder and conflict but preserves social stability and economic reform.[19]

Tehran also criticized Western efforts to promote democracy, describing it as a "soft war" (*jang-e narm*) in reference to the perceived cultural, media-driven, and psychological warfare waged against Iran, primarily by Western powers, especially the United States. From the perspective of the Iranian leadership, the "soft war" is a series of coordinated efforts by external actors aimed at weakening Iran from within, by targeting its societal values, national identity, and public opinion.[20] The Iranian government has repeatedly accused Western media of spreading misinformation, propaganda, or content that is harmful to the principles of the Islamic Republic. In response, the Iranian regime has invested heavily in counterpropaganda and internet censorship tools—often looking to Russia for assistance.

Russia and Iran have long challenged the universal applicability of democracy, human rights, and liberal norms by framing them as Western impositions incompatible with their civilizational identities. Both regimes contend that these concepts stem from Western history, culture, and interests rather than representing globally valid principles.[21] By insisting that each society possesses its own distinct values and governance traditions, they cast liberal democracy as a foreign construct inherently at odds with their domestic systems. In practice, however, these civilizational claims serve as a convenient veneer for authoritarianism, enabling both regimes to consolidate power while deflecting international criticism of their human rights records.

A shared sense of grievance over perceived Western efforts to sideline them solidified the bond between Russia and Iran. Both countries believed that the U.S.-dominated unipolar system aimed to diminish their influence and deny them a meaningful role on the global stage.[22] The unipolar world order galvanized Russia and Iran's desire to stand in opposition, offering a clearly defined set of Western-centric norms and values they could actively challenge. In this perceived marginalization, they found not only a common adversary but also a rallying point for cooperation.

Ties that Bind

The Syrian Civil War provided more than just a theater for Russian and Iranian cooperation— it emerged as the defining moment that crystallized their shared vision of resistance and reshaped their relationship from opportunistic cooperation to institutionalized defiance. While both countries' foreign policy establishments had previously shown inclinations toward cooperation, the joint campaign to preserve Assad's rule catalyzed unprecedented coordination across their military, intelligence, and diplomatic institutions. The demands of managing a complex military intervention forced Moscow and Tehran to develop integrated command structures, joint military commissions, and robust intelligence-sharing arrangements. These newly formed frameworks were further reinforced by personal connections cultivated among top-level defense and security officials in both countries. The result was the creation of durable channels of engagement that would endure well beyond their initial wartime purpose.

In many ways, Russian and Iranian cooperation in Syria was remarkable due to the lack of interoperability between their forces. Interoperability—the capacity of different militaries to coordinate operations effectively despite variations in equipment, tactics, and command structures—is usually honed over time.[23] Alliances, bound by a commitment to mutual defense, focus on ensuring the interoperability of forces before battle through military exercises and joint training. For example, NATO's military exercises serve the purpose of ensuring that Estonian troops can work alongside French or Italian soldiers. In stark contrast, Russia and Iran had neither a history of joint military training nor an institutionalized commitment to mutual defense.

The absence of prior military-to-military cooperation between Russia and Iran, as discussed in Chapter 4, inevitably led to significant challenges on the Syrian battlefield. Chief among these were communication barriers, difficulties in synchronizing missions, and occasional confusion over the chain of command. The stark differences between their respective militaries further heightened these frictions. Russia fielded technologically sophisticated aircraft—most notably the Tu-22M strategic bomber and advanced fighter-bombers such as the Su-34 and Su-35—which operated from airbases like Khmeimim under Russia's tightly centralized command-and-control apparatus. Iran, by contrast, relied heavily on ground forces, especially the IRGC and its network of affiliated militias, whose equipment, tactics, and battlefield culture diverged sharply from Russia's. These challenges were compounded by structural differences in their armed forces: Russia's rigid hierarchy, with regional commands reporting directly to the General Staff, contrasted sharply with Iran's bifurcated system, where the Artesh and the IRGC often operated under separate command philosophies. Yet over time, these obstacles were mitigated through the expansion of liaison mechanisms and high-level coordination bodies that institutionalized wartime cooperation.

Within Russia, the Ministry of Defense assumed a central role in orchestrating defense cooperation with Iran. The Department for International Military-Technical Cooperation was tasked with broader bilateral military ties, while the General Staff of the Russian Armed Forces oversaw the operational aspects of the Syrian campaign. Simultaneously, the Federal Service for Military-Technical Cooperation and Rosoboronexport acted as facilitators, brokering arms deals that provided Russia with a lasting foothold in Iran. On the Iranian side, the General Staff took the lead in implementing military cooperation with Russia and managing various aspects of the relationship, from day-to-day engagements to joint production efforts and intelligence sharing. The involvement of Iran's General Staff and the SNSC helped navigate the overlapping command structures between the IRGC and the regular military, enabling Russia to engage with both entities across a full spectrum of military activities.

The mechanisms developed in Syria—joint operations centers, intelligence cells, and logistical networks—outlasted their initial wartime rationale. They evolved into enduring instruments of collaboration, extending into domains such as cyber defense, internal security, and space cooperation. Syria also became an experimental laboratory for new technologies and tactics, fostering cross-pollination in electronic warfare and unmanned systems. Russia's provision of GPS jamming and electronic warfare expertise, for example, directly informed Iran's subsequent advances in these fields, establishing a technical foundation for future joint operations.

By the time of Russia's invasion of Ukraine in 2022, these wartime habits of coordination had hardened into institutional routines. The bureaucratic scaffolding built in Syria facilitated rapid adaptation: joint command structures and logistical routes were repurposed for the Ukrainian theater, where Iranian drones became integral to Moscow's war effort. Even after the collapse of the Assad regime in late 2024, the partnership endured—its vitality no longer dependent on the Syrian front but on the shared imperative to resist Western pressure and reinforce regime security. In the process, Russia and Iran discovered, and ultimately solidified, each other as partners in defiance.

The View from Russia and Iran

This book goes into the heart of how Russian and Iranian interactions are perceived, understood, and communicated within the domestic settings of *both* countries. It draws from various Russian and Persian sources, including official government and diplomatic statements, academic literature, news articles, archival documents, and memoirs.[24] The use of Russian- and Persian-language sources is, first and foremost, important for comprehending the internal views, policy debates, and broader foreign policies of Russia and Iran. It also distinguishes this book from previous studies of contemporary Russia-Iran relations that have not only failed to engage with Russian and Persian sources but have also offered limited insight into the internal factors driving the relationship.[25] Simply put, bilateral relations are two-sided, and as such, it is difficult to truly grasp bilateral dynamics without a deeper examination of how each country views the other and what truly matters to them both on a mutual level.

The book is further enriched by interviews conducted in Moscow from 2017 to 2019 and a series of online interviews conducted from 2020 to 2023 with Russian and Iranian experts and elites. My interviewees included current and former presidential advisors, diplomats, ambassadors, deputy foreign ministers, military officials, experts, and academics.[26] The interviews, particularly those conducted in Moscow, offer a rare glimpse into Russia's internal calculations about Iran—a level of access unlikely to be given to Western researchers in the near future. While in Russia, I was also able to meet with Iranians visiting Russia for conferences and business.

Throughout the chapters, the book seeks to accurately represent the views of Russia and Iran. This is not an endorsement of either country's position. The value of understanding Russian and Iranian perspectives goes beyond storytelling. It provides crucial insight into a relationship that is often the subject of intrigue but seldom fully understood.

About This Book

Russia and Iran opens with an expansive overview of the historical shifts in Russia-Iran relations, laying the groundwork for understanding the complexities that shape their interactions today. Chapter 1 delves into the often tense history between the two nations, highlighting how past events have informed Iran's enduring mistrust of Russia. It explores critical moments like the 19th-century treaties that resulted in Persia's significant territorial losses and Soviet interventions during World War II. The chapter proceeds to trace the evolution of their relationship through the Soviet era, the Cold War, and the 1979 Islamic Revolution in Iran. It details the shift in ties under Mikhail Gorbachev, during the waning days of the Soviet Union, and the thaw that culminated in Gorbachev's 1989 meeting with Iranian parliamentary speaker and future president Akbar Hashemi Rafsanjani.

Chapter 1 then transitions to the post-Soviet period, chronicling the development of Russia-Iran relations from the tumultuous Boris Yeltsin era through Vladimir Putin's first two presidential terms. In the immediate aftermath of the Soviet collapse, Russia struggled with severe political instability and economic turmoil, leading to heavy dependence on Western economic aid and political support. Although Moscow recognized Iran as a potential market for civilian nuclear cooperation and arms sales, American pressure limited Russia's ability to fully develop this partnership. When Vladimir Putin assumed the presidency in 1999, Russian foreign policy became increasingly focused on restoring state authority and reasserting Russia's position as a global power. Initially, Putin viewed Iran as a crucial partner in counterbalancing Western influence, particularly following NATO's campaign against Serbia. This stance was exemplified when Putin publicly denounced the previous agreement with Washington that had restricted arms sales to Iran, marking a clear departure from Yeltsin's more conciliatory approach to Western demands. However, the landscape shifted dramatically after the 9/11 attacks, as Russia prioritized its role as a counterterrorism partner with Washington over its relationship with Iran.

As Putin's second term progressed, Russia's mounting frustrations over NATO expansion and U.S. unilateral actions in Iraq began to mirror Iran's own dissatisfaction with Western dominance. Chapter 1 concludes by analyzing how shared grievances over the Iraq War, Color Revolutions, and NATO expansion provided common ground for Moscow and Tehran's mutual opposition to the U.S.-led international order. Nevertheless, despite these aligned perspectives, a combination of historical mistrust, competing regional interests, and Russia's reluctance to completely alienate the West prevented the relationship from achieving its full potential.

The constraints on Russia-Iran relations became particularly evident during the presidency of Putin's successor, Dmitry Medvedev. Chapter 2 begins in 2009, when Russia initiated a "reset" with Washington, aiming to improve bilateral relations and collaborate on shared challenges. As Russia-U.S. relations improved, Russia-Iran ties correspondingly deteriorated. Washington's growing concern over Iranian nuclear activities presented an opportunity for Russian-American rapprochement, given Moscow's influence over Iran's civilian nuclear program. Russian frustration with Iranian nuclear activities intensified, prompted by Iran's covert enrichment operations at Fordow and Tehran's rejection of a Russian-brokered fuel swap agreement. Increasingly dissatisfied with Tehran's intransigence and eager to improve relations with the United States, Russia supported new sanctions against Iran in June 2010. Moscow further demonstrated its commitment by canceling the lucrative S-300 air defense contract with Iran, citing the UN arms embargo on Iran—a decision that deepened Tehran's sense of betrayal. However, Moscow's reset with Washington proved short-lived as emerging geopolitical dynamics soon drove Russia and Iran closer together once again.

As Chapter 2 progresses, it shifts the focus to a series of domestic and international developments that would lead to the improvement of Russia-Iran relations. The Arab Spring protests of 2010-2011 initially elicited different responses: Russia viewed them as internal matters, while Iran characterized them as an "Islamic Awakening" against Western-backed regimes. The 2011 NATO intervention in Libya, which resulted in Muammar Qaddafi's overthrow, profoundly influenced both Russian and Iranian foreign policy.[27] The fallout from NATO's intervention reinforced a shared conviction in Moscow and Tehran that Western-led humanitarian interventions were merely disguised attempts at regime change—a perspective that would later shape their unified defense of Bashar Assad's regime during the Syrian crisis. Meanwhile, within Russia, the 2011-12 domestic protests around electoral fraud in the Duma elections further hardened Moscow's international posture, creating a siege mentality among the country's leadership. Chapter 2 concludes with Vladimir Putin's return to the presidency, marked by an increasingly aggressive stance toward the West that converged with Iran's worldview.

As Putin pursued his more aggressive stance toward the West, the outbreak of the Syrian Civil War provided new grounds for Russian-Iranian convergence in Chapter 3. From 2011 to 2014, shared anxieties over potential regime change in Syria prompted both Moscow and Tehran to emerge as principal supporters of the Assad regime. The chapter opens with the March 2011 outbreak of the Syrian Civil War, as multiple external powers vied to influence the conflict's trajectory. Initially, while both Russia and Iran supported Assad, they pursued largely independent policies with minimal coordination. Russia's early involvement focused primarily on diplomatic efforts to prevent Western intervention, leveraging its veto power in the UNSC while providing military support to the Syrian government. Iran, drawing on its longstanding alliance with Syria, offered more substantial material assistance, including military advisors, financial aid, and weapons shipments.

The latter half of Chapter 3 places the growing Russian and Iranian convergence in Syria within the context of broader changes to Moscow's foreign policy after its February 2014 annexation of Crimea and subsequent proxy war in Eastern Ukraine. These actions triggered a marked decline in Russia's relationship with the West, resulting in the imposition of severe sanctions on Russia. The resultant isolation drove Russia towards an even more assertive foreign policy approach, marked by heightened involvement in regional conflicts like Syria and a strengthened partnership with nations that were similarly isolated internationally, particularly Iran. By the end of Chapter 3, the rise of the Islamic State not only threatened Assad's control over Syrian territory but also created urgent new imperatives for Russian-Iranian collaboration that would lead to the Kremlin's first direct military intervention outside of the former Soviet space.

Chapter 4 opens with the decisive shift in Russian policy in early 2015, when a series of setbacks threatened the Assad regime's survival. Although Moscow initially rebuffed Iranian requests for military support, the rapid erosion of the Assad regime's control—marked by rebel advances in northwest and southern Syria and an Islamic State offensive in the northeast—forced a recalculation. These mounting pressures ultimately led to Russia's direct military intervention in September 2015.

With Russia's intervention in Syria, it became an overnight partner with Tehran. Chapter 4 analyzes how these two militaries with no prior experience in joint operations and significant differences in equipment, tactics, and command structures managed to forge a battlefield partnership. It provides an in-depth examination of the resulting Russian-Iranian military cooperation in Syria, analyzing the deliberations in both Moscow and Tehran that shaped the course of their campaign. Chapter 4 concludes with the battle for Aleppo, which not only consolidated Assad's control over Syria's major population centers but also ushered in a new phase of regional dynamics as Turkey entered the fray. Despite numerous challenges, detailed throughout the chapter, Russian-Iranian military collaboration proved decisive in reversing the war's trajectory in Assad's favor, establishing a new era of cooperation between Moscow and Tehran that would extend well beyond Syria's borders.

Following the success in Aleppo, Russia and Iran were confronted with a series of escalating challenges ranging from tensions over Syrian reconstruction to the involvement of external powers. Chapter 5 examines the evolving dynamics of Russia-Iran relations in the aftermath of the Aleppo campaign, beginning with the inception and implementation of the Astana Process with Russia, Iran, and Turkey. The Astana Process demonstrated the ability of Russia and Iran to jointly sponsor a negotiating framework that could marginalize Western influence and promote their interests. However, it also exposed the divergent priorities and competing visions that Moscow and Tehran held for Syria's future. Russia prioritized stability and a political settlement that would preserve its influence, while Iran was more invested in the long-term entrenchment of its military presence and the consolidation of a friendly regime in Damascus.

Against this backdrop of emerging tensions, Chapter 5 traces the final major military campaigns that consolidated Assad's control over Syria. These campaigns include the offensive to break the Islamic State's control of Deir ez-Zor to secure crucial oil-rich territories near the Iraqi border as well as Assad's 2018 campaign in southern Syria to eliminate the rebel presence along the Jordanian border and Golan Heights. However, these successes brought new complications, particularly as Israel increased its airstrikes against Iranian assets in Syria, which thrust Russia into the role of an imperfect mediator between the two rivals. Throughout Chapter 5, Russia's fraught balancing act in the Middle East is brought to the fore as Moscow sought to maintain its partnership with Iran while also managing relationships with other key players, including Israel, Turkey, and the United States.

The challenges in Syria gradually became overshadowed by external developments, as the election of Donald Trump in 2016 catalyzed a deeper convergence between Moscow and Tehran. Chapter 6 examines how the Trump presidency entrenched Russia and Iran's common cause, driving them to coordinate their positions more actively in opposition to U.S. unilateralism. Trump's withdrawal from the Iran nuclear deal and subsequent "maximum pressure" campaign had the unintended consequence of elevating Russia's importance as a partner for Tehran. Simultaneously, the deterioration of U.S.-Russia relations under Trump, marked by successive rounds of sanctions and diplomatic tensions, created additional common ground between Moscow and Tehran.

Chapter 6 details how both countries, finding themselves increasingly isolated by Washington, discovered new avenues for mutual support. Faced with significant domestic unrest during this period, Moscow and Tehran began sharing expertise in monitoring and controlling online spaces, which they viewed as critical battlegrounds for thwarting both foreign interference and domestic opposition. The Trump administration's policies ultimately prompted a broader reorientation of Russian and Iranian foreign policy, setting the stage for Iran's deeper integration into Russia's vision for Eurasia.

For Iran, the Trump administration's pressure campaign catalyzed a decisive shift toward the "Eastern vector" of its foreign policy, with Iranian elites increasingly emphasizing ties with Russia and China while seeking deeper participation in non-Western multilateral initiatives like China's Belt and Road Initiative (BRI), the Eurasian Economic Union (EAEU), and Shanghai Cooperation Organization (SCO).[28] Chapter 7 examines how this Iranian reorientation coincided with Russia's growing interest in expanding its vision for Eurasian integration. As Moscow distanced itself farther away from Europe, the leadership pursued a policy known as the "turn to the East" (*Povorot na Vostok*) and later the notion of Greater Eurasia. Increasingly, Iran formed a critical junction in Moscow's vision for Eurasian integration and a like-minded partner who sought to induce a more transition to the East.[29]

Chapter 7 broadens the scope to examine Russia and Iran's relationship within the context of their mutual efforts to contest the nature of international order and facilitate the rise of the East. It explores how the ideas of multipolarity and the "East" have provided a powerful narrative for Moscow and Tehran to frame their partnership and challenge Western hegemony. Both countries envision an international system free from Western dominance and have sought to position themselves as vanguards of an emerging non-Western coalition. This ambition, while often more rhetorical than substantive, would gain unprecedented momentum in the years ahead

Russia's full-scale invasion of Ukraine in 2022 ushered in a maelstrom that would fundamentally transform Russia-Iran relations. As one of the few nations to openly endorse Russia's actions, Iran's support for Moscow took on new significance in the context of the Ukrainian conflict. Chapters 8 and 9 detail the ascendance of the Russia-Iran relationship since the War in Ukraine, focusing on military and political cooperation as well as strategies of resistance against Western sanctions.

Chapter 8 traces how Iran emerged as a crucial military supplier to Moscow within months of its invasion. Leveraging the networks and procurement channels established during their joint campaign in Syria, Iran began supplying Russia with much-needed drones for its Ukraine campaign, eventually expanding into joint production facilities on Russian territory. Meanwhile, Russia gravitated closer to Iran politically. This shift was symbolized by Putin's June 2022 visit to Tehran, where Russia finally embraced the "strategic" nature of ties with Iran—a designation it had deliberately avoided for decades despite Iran's eagerness to elevate ties.

The deepening of this partnership manifested not only in military cooperation but also in internal security matters. Chapter 8 details how Iran's widespread protests following Mahsa Amini's death in September 2022 spurred further cooperation in internal security matters, with both countries signing agreements to share expertise between their domestic security agencies. What began as ideological alignment against Western influence rapidly evolved into a partnership of necessity: Iran provided Russia with essential military hardware and expertise while gaining battlefield insights and advanced repression technology in return.

Chapter 9 examines how the war in Ukraine catalyzed cooperation between Moscow and Tehran against what they euphemistically call 'unilateral coercive measures.' As Russia found itself encumbered by sanctions, it turned to Iran, seeking to learn from Tehran's decades of experience in sanctions evasion. Iran's strategy of "resistance economics"—focused on fostering domestic production, reducing import dependence, and promoting self-reliance—provided a valuable blueprint for Russia. Chapter 9 details how Russia and Iran have developed shadow networks of banking, shipping, and trade to sustain their economies outside the Western-dominated financial system. However, their economic partnership faced significant structural challenges. Despite rhetoric about de-dollarization and plans for increased bilateral trade, their economies proved poorly matched for integration, sharing similar export products and maintaining dependency on dollar-based transactions. As a result, cooperation flourished primarily in grey areas like sanctions evasion techniques, parallel imports, and black-market oil sales, though they sometimes found themselves competing in these shadowy domains.

The shared experience of economic pressure catalyzed new opportunities for collaboration between their military-industrial complexes, space technology programs, and cyber capabilities, as examined in the second part of Chapter 9. Russia increasingly provided Iran with sophisticated weaponry and assistance with satellite launches while helping Tehran develop advanced surveillance tools and "sovereign internet" infrastructure. This technological cooperation served both countries' goals of resisting Western restrictions while strengthening their authoritarian governance models. However, their partnership of necessity highlighted both opportunities and constraints—while sanctions drove them closer together, their cooperation remained fundamentally reactive, unified more by shared opposition to Western pressure than by a coherent joint vision.

Chapter 10 chronicles how the interconnected conflicts in Syria and Ukraine profoundly reshaped the Russia-Iran partnership, ultimately solidifying it even beyond Bashar Assad's downfall. It opens with the sudden death of Iranian President Ebrahim Raisi in a helicopter crash, prompting Masoud Pezeshkian to assume office. Despite Raisi's demise and a sweeping reshuffle in Moscow's leadership, Russia and Iran continued to cultivate tighter ties, building on the institutional frameworks they had honed during their joint military intervention in Syria. This collaboration soon spilled into more volatile arenas: as the October 2023 Hamas attack on Israel ignited a regional conflict, Iran found itself battling devastating Israeli strikes, and Russia, increasingly reliant on Iranian drones for its war in Ukraine, tilted further toward Tehran's Axis of Resistance.

Yet the most consequential episode of Chapter 10 is the rapid collapse of the Assad regime in late 2024. Weakened by Israeli strikes on Iranian-backed forces and deprived of robust Russian reinforcements, Damascus fell in a whirlwind opposition offensive. Even as Assad fled to Russia, the underlying Russia-Iran relationship endured and even grew stronger. Their years of military cooperation in Syria had already expanded to Ukraine, ensuring that the hard-won synergy between Moscow and Tehran would outlast Assad's regime. Far from fracturing over the fall of their original client, Russia and Iran emerged with a partnership of defiance that transcended the Syrian battlefield, bound by a common drive to challenge Western power and insulate their regimes at home.

Throughout this book, several key themes emerge that characterize the evolution and nature of the Russia–Iran relationship. One central theme is the concept of a "partnership of defiance"—the idea that both nations have forged common ground through their shared opposition to Western hegemony and perceived interference in their domestic and regional affairs. This defiance has taken many forms, ranging from diplomatic coordination in multilateral forums to intelligence and military collaboration in conflict zones such as Syria. It has been a consistent driving force in transforming what was once a historically mistrustful relationship into a strategic alignment.

Another core theme is the influence of domestic politics and regime security on foreign policy behavior. The book explores how internal political conservative factions such as the siloviki in Russia and hardline clerical and security elements in Iran have reinforced the logic of alignment. Both regimes perceive themselves as targets of externally engineered destabilization, especially in the context of Western support for protest movements and so-called "Color Revolutions." This shared sense of vulnerability has fostered a deeper understanding between Moscow and Tehran, underpinned by the belief that regime survival is best secured through mutual reinforcement and resistance to liberal international norms.

The book also highlights the theme of pragmatic cooperation under conditions of international isolation. Facing overlapping sanctions regimes and constrained access to Western markets and technology, Russia and Iran have increasingly looked to one another as partners in resilience. They have shared expertise in sanctions circumvention, expanded energy and arms cooperation, and worked to establish parallel financial structures to reduce reliance on the Western-dominated global system. This pragmatism is not merely transactional—it reflects a strategic calculus aimed at enhancing autonomy in a hostile international environment.

A final overarching theme is the structural limits of this partnership. While Russia and Iran have deepened cooperation across multiple domains, their relationship falls short of a formal military alliance. Divergent geopolitical interests, asymmetries in power, and lingering mistrust—rooted in both history and strategic culture—continue to shape the contours of their engagement. Moscow remains cautious about overcommitting to Tehran, especially when it might jeopardize ties with other regional actors or major powers. Similarly, Iranian officials are aware of Russia's tendency to prioritize its own flexibility, even at the expense of its partners. Thus, while the Russia–Iran relationship has become more institutionalized and multifaceted, it remains defined as much by its constraints as by its convergence.

1

THE WEIGHT OF HISTORY

RUSSIA, IRAN, AND THE LEGACIES OF THE PAST

To mark the Islamic Revolution's fortieth anniversary in 2019, the Institute of the Compilation and Publication of Imam Khomeini's Works initiated an "international contest on Imam Khomeini's historic letter to Gorbachev," inviting scholars from various disciplines—including theology, history, and political science—to explore the profound messages and ideological underpinnings of Khomeini's outreach to the then-Soviet leader. Emblematic of the various attempts to nurture a cult of personality around the late Ayatollah Khomeini, the contest sought to illuminate "the enlightened thought and dynamic ideals of the late founder of the Islamic Republic," as contained in his letter to Gorbachev.[1] The letter in question, sent in January 1989, was an attempt to mend ties between Iran and the Soviet Union after years of acrimony surrounding the Soviet invasion of Afghanistan, Iran's prosecution of communists, and Soviet arms sales to Iraq during the Iran-Iraq War.[2]

Ayatollah Ruhollah Khomeini saw the slow unraveling of the Soviet bloc as the perfect moment to pen an unsolicited piece of advice to Mikhail Gorbachev, the man helming the staggering behemoth that was the Soviet Union.[3] With the confidence of a cleric who had seen his revolution topple a monarchy, Khomeini informed Gorbachev that the days of Marxism-Leninism were over. The grand experiment in state control and atheism had, according to Khomeini, been a dismal failure. Khomeini suggested that the Soviet Union, a bastion of state atheism and scientific socialism, should consider Islam as a panacea for its woes. Khomeini advanced the proposition that Islam could offer a redemptive path for the Soviet Union, which he perceived to be in a spiritual and ideological crisis, epitomized by the "absence of True faith in God."[4] While the letter did not convert Gorbachev to Islam, it laid the groundwork for a thaw in the relationship between the two states. Within the Soviet Union, Khomeini's letter to Gorbachev, irrespective of its philosophical undertones, was viewed as an attempt to bridge the chasm that had widened between Iran and the Soviet Union due to a host of contentious issues.

The late 1980s were a period of introspection and recalibration for both countries. The Soviet Union was grappling with internal challenges and looking to reduce tensions with the West, while Iran, emerging from the tumult of the Islamic Revolution and the protracted Iran-Iraq War, was exploring avenues to break its own diplomatic isolation. It was in this context that Khomeini's letter, as audacious as it was, became an unlikely catalyst for dialogue. The eventual collapse of the Soviet Union in 1991 did not derail this nascent collaboration—if anything, it opened new commercial, political, and military possibilities. Under Boris Yeltsin, the newly formed Russian Federation inherited the Soviet Union's relationship with Iran, and both countries found ample reason to deepen it, particularly in areas such as arms deals and nuclear cooperation.

This chapter traces the historical relationship between Russia and Iran from imperial conflicts through the Soviet era into the post-Cold War period. It examines how Russian-Iranian relations evolved through distinct phases—from imperial expansion and Soviet intervention to post-Soviet realignment and Putin's revival of Russian great power ambitions. Despite centuries of territorial disputes, broken agreements, and mutual suspicion, Russia and Iran found pragmatic reasons to cooperate in arms sales, nuclear technology, and regional security while harboring deep-seated reservations about each other's reliability. The track record of Russia-Iran relations is laden with oscillations and contradictions. For this reason, their historical evolution remains relevant not as a deterministic force but as a crucial context for understanding how both have overcome past challenges to forge their current partnership.

The Trappings of History

History has cast a long shadow over Russia and Iran. As explained by Russian scholars Elena Dunaeva and Lyudmila Kulagina, the historical evolution of relations between Russia and Iran has been characterized by "long-lasting wars over spheres of influence, seizure of territories, and the struggle for existence."[5] Russia earned a reputation as a predatory imperial power due to recurrent instances of interference in Iranian internal affairs and Persian concessions (*imtiyazat*) associated with economic capitulation and the loss of territory.[6] Iranian leaders have not forgotten how the Soviet Union occupied Iran during World War II, refused to leave promptly afterward, and armed Baghdad during the brutal Iran-Iraq War. Russia, for its part, is mindful of Iran's occasional swings toward the West, whether during the Pahlavi era or at times after the revolution when Tehran flirted with Western diplomatic overtures.

After the Soviet collapse, Iranian scholars continued to suggest that the historical memory of Russia's interference (*modakheleh*) and exploitation of Iran remain a source of resentment and bitterness in Iran's historical consciousness. Jahangir Karami, director of the Russian Department at the University of Tehran, hailed the collapse of the Soviet Union for returning "Russia to the borders of the eighteenth century," meaning that "the ominous shadow of Moscow ... moved back 2,250 km from the common border [with Iran]."[7] Similarly, Mandana Tishehyar, professor at Allameh Tabataba'i University of Tehran, reflected on the "Death to Russia" chants in the 2009 Iran's Green Movement protests which demonstrated that "historic negativity still remains in Iranian society with regard to Russia."[8] Yet this deep-seated public wariness often contrasts sharply with the strategic posture adopted by Iran's political elite. The Supreme Leader, senior military officials, and hardline parliamentarians have consistently viewed cooperation with Moscow as a pragmatic tool for advancing regime security and countering Western pressure.

Some scholars contend that the legacy of imperial wars, betrayals, and ideological rivalry has placed structural limits on the relationship, fostering mutual hesitation and undermining the durability of cooperation. From this view, any alignment between Tehran and Moscow is inherently fragile—vulnerable to collapse under the weight of lingering mistrust. However, historical memory, while influential, does not constitute an insurmountable barrier. It shapes elite perceptions and domestic debates, informs strategic culture, and conditions diplomatic engagement—but it does not determine outcomes. In the case of Iran and Russia, history has acted both as a constraint and a condition to be managed, a burden to be acknowledged and, at times, deliberately set aside in pursuit of shared geopolitical interests.

From Tsar to Commissar

From the sixteenth century onward, Russia's transformation from a minor principality to a vast empire inevitably influenced its relationship with the dynasties governing Persia.[9] The Safavids (1501-1736) had to contend with Russia's incremental expansion eastward, but it was under the Qajar dynasty (1794-1925) that Iran faced a series of humiliating defeats. Throughout the eighteenth and nineteenth centuries, Russia pressed into the Caucasus region—a zone that had been, to varying degrees, in the Persian sphere of influence for centuries. Repeated Iranian attempts to defend or reclaim these territories met with failure, culminating in defeats that produced the infamous treaties of Gulistan and Turkmenchay. These campaigns capitalized on Persia's military setbacks, which left it susceptible to external aggression. In the end, Russia's triumphs redrew Persia's northern boundary far closer to its present-day parameters, foreshadowing a turbulent relationship that would intensify over the next two centuries.[10]

In 1813, Tehran was compelled to sign the Treaty of Gulistan under the duress of military defeat. The treaty saw Iran relinquish control over strategically important regions, including Tbilisi and Baku, along with numerous other Caucasian territories and khanates, to Russian dominion. The situation worsened for Persia with the 1828 Treaty of Turkmenchay, which severed its control over its Azerbaijani lands, granting Russia authority north of the Aras River.[11] The treaty not only cemented Russian dominance by awarding it exclusive rights to the Caspian Sea's navigation, trade, and naval presence—reversing the parity Persia enjoyed under the 1732 Treaty of Rasht—but also imposed heavy financial reparations on Iran, diminished its sovereignty through extraterritorial rights for Russian nationals, and marked the beginning of a deep-seated resentment towards Russia.

The treaties of Gulistan and Turkmenchay underscored a period of severe loss and compromise for Persia. Within a year of the Turkmenchay Treaty, a mob in Tehran brutally assassinated the treaty's primary negotiator, Ambassador Alexander Griboyedov, a thirty-four-year-old diplomat who is now widely recognized as the author of the play *Woe from Wit*.[12] Griboyedov became an enduring symbol of the acrimonious relations between the two nations, occasionally appearing in Russian critiques about the untrustworthy nature of Iran. The resentment fostered by Persia's losses to imperial Russia has persisted over the centuries, resurfacing in contemporary Iran's disputes with Russia over the Caspian Sea's resources and diplomatic confrontations over Iran's nuclear ambitions.[13]

As the nineteenth century progressed, the regional dynamics in and around Persia became even more fraught with the emergence of a new power struggle that involved not only Russia but also the British Empire. The end of the Napoleonic Wars in 1815 did not herald a period of peace but rather the beginning of a new chapter of foreign interference in Persia, characterized by Russian and British rivalry for regional influence. This Russian and British rivalry for influence in Persia often infringed on the country's sovereignty and ingrained the popular notion of the "deceitful English" (*Inglis-e portadlis*) and "ominous Russia" (*Rus-e manhus*).[14]

Throughout the nineteenth and early twentieth centuries, Iran found itself caught between the British Empire in India and the Persian Gulf and Tsarist Russia's expanding empire in the Caucasus and Central Asia. The 1907 Anglo-Russian Convention formalized this competition by partitioning Persia into spheres of influence, undermining its sovereignty and establishing patterns of foreign intervention that would reverberate well into the twentieth century.[15] The Bolshevik Revolution of 1917 initially offered a glimmer of hope to Iranian nationalists to revisit territorial disputes that had been simmering since the nineteenth century. Vladimir Lenin and his associates railed against imperialism, formally renouncing many Tsarist-era privileges and stoking Iranian aspirations to reclaim territories lost in the Caucasus. For instance, during the Paris Peace Conference of 1919, in the aftermath of World War I and amid the Russian Civil War, Iran asserted formal claims to territories that had historically been part of its sphere of influence but had been lost through the treaties of Gulistan and Turkmenchay.[16]

The inception of the Soviet Union did not lead to a territorial reconsolidation for Iran. Instead, the Soviet-Persian Treaty signed on 26 February 1921 effectively reaffirmed the borders established by the Treaty of Turkmenchay with additional concessions. Notably, while the treaty officially renounced the Treaty of Turkmenchay, it maintained the demarcations that had been set nearly a century earlier. A silver lining for Iran was that this new treaty restored equal navigation rights on the Caspian Sea, revitalizing Iran's ability to freely access this crucial body of water for trade and transportation. An additional, and perhaps more ominous provision within the 1921 treaty was the allowance for Soviet troop intervention in Iran should a hostile third party pose a threat.[17] This clause, while seemingly a gesture of Soviet support for Iran's sovereignty, foreshadowed future interventions that would undermine Soviet-Iranian diplomatic ties.

During World War II, the Soviet Union occupied Iran under the pretext of securing supply lines to the Allied forces.[18] Following the cessation of hostilities, the Soviet Union did not withdraw its forces in compliance with the Tehran Conference agreements but instead fostered separatist movements within Iran.[19] One such movement, the Azerbaijan People's Government, sought to carve out a Soviet-aligned Azerbaijani state within Iran's territory, aspiring to unite it with the Azerbaijani Soviet Socialist Republic. Parallel to these endeavors, the Soviet Union also provided support to the Kurdish Democratic Party of Iran, aiming to establish an independent Kurdish state in northwestern Iran.[20] Soviet-backed attempts at secession marked one of the early crises of the Cold War. The situation exacerbated tensions not just on a bilateral level but also positioned Iran as a frontier in the broader struggle between the United States and the Soviet Union. While the direct Soviet threat to Iran's territorial integrity eventually receded, the legacy of these interventions had a lasting impact on Iran's foreign policy for decades to come.

During the Cold War, Iran initially aligned itself with the Western bloc, exemplified by its participation in the 1955 Baghdad Pact—a military alliance between Iran, Iraq, Pakistan, Turkey, and the United Kingdom designed to prevent Soviet expansion into the Middle East. The United States became a crucial ally, providing substantial military aid and economic support for Iran's modernization initiatives. This partnership included intelligence gathering facilities near the Soviet border, which Moscow viewed as a direct threat to its security interests, particularly concerning the potential establishment of American military installations along its southern frontier. Despite the ideological gulf between Iran and the Soviet Union, their relationship evolved into one marked by pragmatic cooperation, particularly after the normalization in 1962.

In 1962, the Shah's decision to prohibit foreign military bases on Iranian soil, later enshrined in Iran's Constitution after the Islamic Revolution, alleviated Moscow's concerns about hostile military bases along its southern borders. The Soviet Union responded with substantial economic initiatives, beginning with the July 1963 agreement for a hydroelectric project on the Aras River along the Iran-Soviet border, followed by a November transit agreement that established regular trade routes. Most significantly, between 1965 and 1966, Moscow extended a $286 million credit to Iran primarily for the construction of the Isfahan Steel Mill and other industrial projects, to be repaid through Iranian natural gas supplies.[21] The Kremlin continued to remain wary of Iran's pro-Western orientation and its monarchical regime, which it critiqued as embodying "national-bourgeois" characteristics or "Oriental despotism," but the Soviets recognized the potential benefits of engagement with its southern neighbor.[22]

After the 1979 Islamic Revolution, the Soviet leadership appeared to greatly overestimate the extent to which Ayatollah Khomeini's fervent anti-Western rhetoric would result in an embrace of the Soviet Union.[23] Any hope was shattered when Khomeini, the Iranian revolutionary leader, proved to be as vehemently anti-Soviet as he was anti-American.[24] With the Soviet invasion of Afghanistan in 1979, Khomeini perceived the USSR as a foe, given the presence of Soviet troops on Iran's eastern border.[25] Moreover, in 1983, Khomeini launched a harsh crackdown on the Tudeh Party, the country's communist party. Many Tudeh members were imprisoned, tortured, or executed as part of a broader effort to suppress political opposition and consolidate power.

Moscow's supply of the bulk of Iraq's weapons in its eight-year war with Iran, from 1980 to 1988, would also damage relations. For Tehran, Soviet support for Baghdad was a major hindrance to developing ties with Moscow. The Iran-Iraq War, known in Persian as the Imposed War (*jang-e tahmili*), remains deeply embedded in the modern Iranian consciousness.[26] Even while supplying Iraq with arms, the Soviet Union continued to stress the need for a cessation of hostilities and sharply criticized Khomeini's refusal to agree to a ceasefire, since Moscow considered the continuation of fighting as detrimental to its national interests in the region.[27]

The cessation of the Iran-Iraq War in 1988, in tandem with the Soviet withdrawal from Afghanistan, marked the advent of a new epoch in Soviet-Iranian relations. Despite harboring reservations about communism and entertaining suspicions of the Soviet Union, Ayatollah Khomeini, in one of his final gestures, called for cordial and amicable relations in his letter to Gorbachev—one that is now consecrated in competitions within Iran.[28] After Khomeini's letter, a series of diplomatic overtures culminated in a summit between Gorbachev and Iranian Majlis Speaker Akbar Hashemi Rafsanjani in Moscow in June 1989. Khomeini himself would not live to see the realization of some of the hopes expressed in his letter, having died merely two weeks before the summit. Notwithstanding the forty-day mourning period after Khomeini's death, Rafsanjani, who was heir apparent as the next president of Iran, traveled to Moscow. The Gorbachev-Rafsanjani summit would form the basis for modern

Russia-Iran relations, with many of the deals and contracts continuing into the Yeltsin era following Soviet collapse.[29]

* * *

In the wake of the Soviet Union's collapse, Boris Yeltsin served as the first president of the Russian Federation (1991-9), steering the nation through a transformative period characterized by political uncertainty, economic collapse, and a fractured national identity. In the early years of Russian foreign policy, Yeltsin, along with his Foreign Minister Andrei Kozyrev, pursued a vision of aligning Russia closely with the West, aspiring for integration with what they termed the group of "civilized Western nations."[30] This pro-Western policy, however, faced internal opposition as critics argued that the leadership's almost unconditional pro-Western orientation jeopardized its national interests and influence, particularly in the post-Soviet space. The backlash intensified following the 1993 constitutional crisis and subsequent Duma elections, which empowered nationalist forces skeptical about Yeltsin's tilt to the West.[31] As the 1990s unfolded, Russia's initial optimism about its relations with the West began to dissipate, beset by the perceived betrayals of North Atlantic Treaty Organization (NATO) eastward expansion and airstrikes in Serbia.[32]

In the 1990s, Russia struggled to formulate a clear and coordinated policy on Iran across its various ministries and departments. Although partly endemic to the domestic challenges after the Soviet collapse, the inconsistency pointed to differences among the Russian elite on the scope of cooperation with Iran. Various intergovernmental agreements, contracts, and protocols between Russia and Iran were subject to delays in ratification. For example, in March 1993, a political document was initialed on the foundations of relations and principles of good-neighborly cooperation between Russia and Iran; however, the treaty itself was signed only in March 2001 under Putin.

In the aftermath of the devastating Iran-Iraq War and the death of Ayatollah Khomeini in 1989, Iran under President Akbar Hashemi Rafsanjani (1989-97) embarked on an ambitious program of post-war reconstruction and diplomatic reorientation. Rafsanjani sought to revitalize Iran's war-ravaged economy and end its international isolation. In this context, Russia emerged as an invaluable partner, particularly as Western sanctions continued to restrict Iran's access to military equipment and nuclear technology.

Arms and Influence

The growth of military-technical contacts between the Soviet Union and Iran in the late 1980s culminated in several intergovernmental agreements and lucrative arms contracts between 1989 and 1991.[33] Under these agreements, Moscow supplied Tehran with MiG-29 fighter jets, Su-24 combat aircraft, Kilo-class diesel-electric submarines, armored personnel carriers, tanks, and S-200 surface-to-air missile systems.[34] Iran paid only $1 billion in cash for the arms and military technology it purchased. The rest was settled by write-offs of outstanding Soviet debts to Iran and various barter deals, mostly Iranian oil handed over to Russia for resale.[35]

The Soviet Union's dissolution left Russia in search of markets for its military industry, while Iran, facing international sanctions and arms embargoes, found a willing supplier in Russia. As a means of maintaining some semblance of great power status, the Russian leadership saw Iran as a potential partner where it could exhibit its independence in foreign policy from the West and strengthen the power of the state through sales of arms and civilian nuclear energy. The United States, in particular, viewed the Russia-Iran arms trade with increasing concern, fearing it would alter the balance in the Middle East and potentially help Iran to develop military capabilities that could threaten U.S. interests and those of its allies in the region.

Throughout the 1990s, the Yeltsin administration's relationship with the U.S. often impeded Moscow's desire to assert an independent foreign policy and to stimulate economic growth through military exports to Iran.[36] The Clinton administration conducted consultations with the aim to persuade the Russian leadership to abandon arms sales and nuclear cooperation with Iran. Russian military-technical and civilian nuclear cooperation with Iran was elevated to one of the key issues discussed at bilateral summits, along with NATO expansion and the Balkan wars, where both the U.S. and Russia were actively engaged in mediating the conflict.

To assuage U.S. concerns, Russia signed a secret agreement between U.S. Vice President Al Gore and Russian Prime Minister Viktor Chernomyrdin, which placed a moratorium on Russian arms sales to Iran. The 1995 Gore-Chernomyrdin agreement prohibited additional arms agreements and stipulated that Russia complete its existing contracts with Iran by 2000. Whereas the Gore-Chernomyrdin agreement generated distrust among the Iranian elite, Moscow's failure to meet its obligations under the contracts signed with Tehran and the moratorium on further arms sales resulted in an estimated loss of $4 billion for Russia.[37]

Russia's civilian nuclear cooperation with Iran also faced pressure from Washington.[38] Tehran identified Moscow as a country that could help reconstruct the Bushehr Nuclear Power Plant, a civilian nuclear power plant in southern Iran that was abandoned by the German company Siemens after the Iran-Iraq War. In the 1990s, Russia viewed the agreement on constructing the Bushehr Nuclear Power Plant with Iran as a way to revive its domestic nuclear industry and provide employment. According to a former MinAtom official, for Russia, completing Bushehr was necessary for maintaining its business reputation in the broader civilian nuclear sector and to demonstrate that the Russians could complete a technologically complex project.[39] In August 1992, Russia and Iran signed long-term cooperation agreements on the peaceful use of atomic energy and on the construction of a power plant in Iran, which culminated in the January 1995 agreement on the construction of the Bushehr Nuclear Power Plant.[40] Due to U.S. pressure, Moscow decided to forgo several projects that could be used for the dual purpose of nuclear weapons technology, but remained adamant about the construction of a light-water reactor at Bushehr.[41]

Russia's comparative advantage in the Iranian arms and civilian nuclear energy markets, combined with Moscow's demand for hard currency, motivated the pursuit of such deals despite U.S. opposition. Russian foreign policy observers recalled that the humiliation experienced by Moscow due to the imposition of American economic sanctions in 1992 on Russian cryogenic rocket engines in India and the cancelation of the contract under insistence from Washington suggested that "none of the serious political forces can speak in favor of unilateral and unjustified U.S. concessions" that would harm its commercial interests and relations with neighboring Iran.[42] Some observers supported a policy of great power balancing in which "Russia would have the opportunity to further strengthen its ties with both Iran and the U.S., while maintaining the independence of its policy and the beneficial aspects of its cooperation with both states."[43]

During the 1990s and 2000s, Iran-Russia defense cooperation operated through multiple channels, ranging from official high-level agreements to more covert interactions. While the primary avenue was characterized by formal military commissions and bilateral accords, Iranian entities sought and received assistance from specific Russian organizations and individuals, sometimes with Moscow's tacit approval. More controversially, some Iranian entities allegedly acquired similar assistance by circumventing Russian export controls, either without Moscow's knowledge or with authorities deliberately turning a blind eye. The institutional disarray in Russia contributed to this situation, with several Russian institutions reportedly cooperating with Iran's missile and nuclear programs without full oversight from central authorities. Key institutions like Mendeleyev University were implicated in allegedly aiding Iran's pursuit of nuclear weapons capabilities. Additionally, the Moscow Aviation Institute faced allegations of contributing technical expertise to Iran's ballistic missile program, particularly in enhancing flight control systems. These activities drew the attention of U.S. policymakers, leading to sanctions against Russian entities accused of supporting Iran's missile and nuclear advancements, which in turn provoked a backlash in Russia and persisted as a sore spot in Moscow-Washington relations.[44]

The involvement of Russian expertise and technology in Iran's civilian nuclear and military sectors created operational dependencies. Nuclear power plants require a continuous exchange of technology, parts, and nuclear fuel, along with the need for ongoing maintenance, safety checks, and training for personnel. Meanwhile, the arms sales to Iran included repairs and maintenance for equipment. This ensured Russia's long-term presence in Iran's infrastructure, embedding Russian influence deeply within critical sectors of Iran's national development. It also placed Russia in a valuable position as a gatekeeper to Iran's access to essential civilian nuclear technology and more advanced military equipment, thereby rendering Iran dependent on Russia.

Iran on Russia's Periphery

The collapse of the Soviet Union prompted Russia to fear the prospects of growing Iranian or Turkish influence in the former Soviet republics in Central Asia and the South Caucasus.[45] Russia was primarily concerned with Iran's role along the periphery of its "near abroad" (*blizhnee zarubezh'e*), the region encompassing the Soviet successor states of the Commonwealth of Independent States (CIS). There were widespread concerns in Moscow that Russia's lack of attention to the post-Soviet space would lead to a vacuum for influence and pave the way for an "Islamic revival" in the former Soviet republics. For example, some argued that Moscow needed to pay attention to "the return of the 'Soviet' Islamic republics to the Islamic world, which could activate Islamic fundamentalism" along Russia's borders.[46] Such concerns were reflected in Russia's April 1993 Foreign Policy Concept, which envisioned the "near abroad" as a zone of Russia's privileged interests and explicitly identified Iran as "a source of dangerous unpredictability and instability in the region."[47]

In the early 1990s, ethnic tensions and separatist movements engulfed newly independent states such as Armenia, Azerbaijan, Tajikistan, Georgia, and Moldova. These conflicts threatened to create a belt of instability along Russia's southern periphery. Moscow feared not only the ramifications of regional turmoil but also the potential for external actors—especially Iran—to gain a foothold in what it considered its traditional sphere of influence. Contrary to Russian apprehensions, however, Iran largely prioritized regional stability and demonstrated notable strategic restraint. Rather than exploiting these upheavals to expand its reach, Tehran adopted a pragmatic approach that often aligned with Russia's interests.

When the Tajik Civil War erupted in 1992, Russia and Iran emerged as the primary external powers influencing both the unfolding of the conflict and the subsequent peace process. Although Iran was accused of providing limited military aid to the Islamic Renaissance Party of Tajikistan (IRPT)—part of the broader opposition coalition—its overarching stance gradually shifted toward de-escalation. Iran initially emphasized its close cultural, religious, and linguistic bonds with Tajikistan's Persian-speaking population *(farsi zabanan)* and seemed poised to expand its revolutionary ideals in Central Asia.[48] However, Tehran soon began to prioritize stability along its borders and the preservation of its relationship with Moscow over any notion of "exporting the revolution" (*sodur-e enghelab*).[49] Tehran's change in approach soon resulted in United Nations (UN)-sponsored peace talks in 1994 that eventually led to the Tajik Peace Accord in 1997. One former head of the Russian Foreign Ministry's department on the affairs of the post-Soviet states claimed that the Russians grew to see Iran as a constructive actor after Tehran used its influence over the Islamic opposition to help reach a solution through negotiations in Tajikistan.[50]

A similar convergence of interests emerged in the Nagorno-Karabakh conflict between Armenia and Azerbaijan. Early in the conflict, Iran attempted to mediate, even hosting negotiations between Armenian and Azerbaijani representatives in 1992. Although these diplomatic efforts showed initial promise, they were soon overshadowed by larger international processes, particularly the Minsk Group, which included Russia, the United States, and France, limiting Iran's direct role. Yet, Moscow and Tehran found common ground in their support of Armenia in its ongoing conflict with Azerbaijan, as well as their shared objective of counterbalancing American and Turkish influence in the Caucasus and Central Asia.[51]

Russia faced a major internal challenge in the 1990s as Chechnya, an autonomous republic situated in southern Russia between the Caspian and Black Seas, sought independence. The Chechen Wars, characterized by fierce resistance from Chechen fighters and heavy-handed Russian military responses, spotlighted Russia's struggles with regional separatism, human rights abuses, and the complexities of asserting federal control.[52] Like Tajikistan and Nagorno-Karabakh,

Iran adopted a cautious position on the Chechen issue that deferred to Russian interests. While there was a degree of religious and cultural sympathy in Iran towards the predominantly Muslim Chechens, Iran largely refrained from taking an explicit stance, aiming to balance its concern for Muslim populations with the priority of maintaining diplomatic relations with Russia.

As chair of the Organization of Islamic Cooperation (OIC) during the Second Chechen War (1999–2009), Iran led several delegations to Russia to assess the situation in the North Caucasus.[53] Tehran's chairmanship coincided with the conflict's bloodiest phase, yet instead of repeating the open censure that prevailed under Saudi leadership during the First Chechen War (1994-96), Iran described the violence as "terrorism suppression inside Russia." Iranian-led OIC fact-finding missions never met separatist representatives; instead, they typically accepted Russian military escorts and produced reports blaming "Wahhabi outsiders" for the violence. This helped thwart cohesion within the OIC on a response to the situation. Meanwhile, Iran publicly defended Russia's territorial integrity and condemned terrorism while calling for peaceful resolution, a rhetorical formula that provided Moscow with political cover without requiring Tehran to endorse the military campaign's brutality.[54]

By the mid-1990s, the experience of Russia-Iran cooperation during the civil war in Tajikistan, combined with Tehran's constructive position on the Nagorno-Karabakh conflict and recognition of Chechnya as Russia's internal affair, precipitated an evolution in Russia's understanding of Iranian foreign policy along its periphery. Some in Russia even argued that alignment with Iran would "prevent the transformation of Russia's near abroad to the south into the buffer zones of NATO."[55] Moreover, Tehran's implicit recognition of Moscow's privileged interests in Central Asia and the South Caucasus shaped the view of Iran as a stabilizing actor and bulwark against Western encroachment.[56]

How to Share the Caspian Sea

The Soviet collapse sparked a two-decade struggle among the five littoral states—Iran, Russia, Kazakhstan, Turkmenistan, and

Azerbaijan—over the legal status of the Caspian Sea. Under Soviet rule, the 1921 Friendship Treaty and 1940 Treaty of Commerce and Navigation had established the Caspian as a closed, jointly-managed domain where Moscow and Tehran enjoyed equal navigation rights and shared fishing privileges while excluding third parties. The emergence of three newly independent energy-rich republics immediately complicated this framework.

Initially, Russia and Iran presented a united front, insisting that the Soviet-era agreements remained valid until all five littoral states reached consensus. Both argued that any resource development required unanimous approval, effectively giving each nation veto power over Caspian projects. This position served their immediate interests: preventing Western oil companies from gaining unfettered access to Caspian energy reserves through partnerships with the newly independent republics.[57] However, Russia's stance began shifting as economic realities set in during the chaotic 1990s. While Iran continued demanding equal 20 percent shares for all five states, Russia grew increasingly attracted to a different formula. Moscow realized that dividing the seabed based on coastal length would grant it a much larger share while allowing profitable partnerships with Western energy firms. By 1997, Russia had abandoned Iran entirely, proposing to divide underwater resources into national sectors while keeping surface waters common for navigation. This shift culminated in Russia's bilateral delimitation agreements with Kazakhstan (1998) and Azerbaijan (2001-2003), effectively carving up the northern Caspian without Iranian consent.

Iran found itself diplomatically isolated, having initially insisted on equal 20 percent shares for each littoral state based on the historical Soviet-Iranian bilateral division.[58] With only 748 km of coastline—roughly 13 percent of the total shore—Iran recognized that Russia's preferred median-line formula would limit Tehran to approximately 11-13 percent of seabed resources. Iranian opposition peaked during the 2001 Araz-Alov-Sharg incident, when Iranian forces confronted an Azerbaijani survey vessel in disputed waters, demonstrating Tehran's willingness to use military force to protect its claims.[59]

Iran's estrangement deepened as multiple rounds of multilateral negotiations failed to bridge the fundamental gap between Tehran's demands and the other states' preferences. At a 2002 working group meeting, Iran again proposed its equal 20 percent formula, only to face Russia's counter-proposal offering Iran roughly 13 percent—a figure quickly rejected by Iranian negotiators. Meanwhile, Russia, Kazakhstan, and Azerbaijan proceeded to finalize their trilateral northern Caspian agreements by 2003, effectively settling approximately 64 percent of the seabed without Iranian participation. Yet, Iran's ability to sustain its opposition weakened considerably as international sanctions over its nuclear program severely limited foreign investment in Iranian energy projects and constrained Tehran's diplomatic options. Facing economic isolation and unable to develop its own Caspian offshore resources without Western technology and capital, Iranian leadership gradually adopted a less confrontational approach, prioritizing broader strategic cooperation with Russia over maximizing its Caspian share.

Despite their deepening disagreements over Caspian resource division, Russia and Iran discovered a shared strategic imperative that ultimately proved more important than their bilateral disputes: keeping Western military forces, particularly NATO and the United States, out of the Caspian basin entirely.[60] This convergence of interests emerged from concrete American initiatives in the early 2000s that alarmed both Moscow and Tehran. The U.S. "Caspian Guard" program sought to enhance maritime security capabilities among American partners Azerbaijan and Kazakhstan, while broader NATO outreach threatened to establish Western military infrastructure along the Caspian's shores. For Russia, such developments represented an unacceptable penetration of its traditional sphere of influence. For Iran, already facing American military presence in the Persian Gulf and Afghanistan, Western forces in the Caspian would complete a strategic encirclement.

Russia and Iran responded by jointly advocating an exclusive security framework for littoral states only. This cooperation produced tangible results: Iran enthusiastically supported Russia's proposal for KASFOR, a rapid-reaction naval force comprising all five Caspian states designed to coordinate security operations and manage threats from Afghanistan, including terrorism and narcotics trafficking.[61] At multiple summits throughout the 2000s, Putin and Iranian leaders publicly championed this "Caspian for Caspians" principle, conducting joint naval exercises and issuing statements declaring that no outside power should use Caspian territory for military operations against any littoral state. The two countries also found common cause in opposing trans-Caspian energy infrastructure projects that would diminish their strategic leverage. Russia and Iran successfully maintained that any underwater pipeline required unanimous consent from affected states, effectively giving both nations veto power over Western-backed projects like the proposed Trans-Caspian Gas Pipeline that would bypass their territories entirely.

These shared security concerns ultimately provided the foundation for the August 2018 Convention on the Legal Status of the Caspian Sea. After nearly three decades of negotiations following the Soviet collapse, the agreement codified the Russian-Iranian position by explicitly prohibiting military presence by non-littoral countries while establishing frameworks for navigation rights, environmental protection, and pipeline construction. However, the convention avoided the most contentious issue, the seabed boundary demarcation in the southern Caspian, for future bilateral negotiations between Iran, Azerbaijan, and Turkmenistan.

Discontent with Unipolarity

In the 1990s, Russia and Iran found alignment on several key issues, particularly their shared concerns over the unilateralism of the Western-led global order. The expectations of the Russian elite about partnership with the West proved overoptimistic, leading to unfulfilled hopes and disappointments.[62] Many Russian foreign policy experts pointed to one of the central contradictions of Western policy—the desire to deprive Russia of its traditional sphere of influence by binding it with new treaties limiting its activities, while the West and the United States practically continued the policy of a new division of the world without Russia's participation. While Russian frustration was rooted in the loss of its former superpower status and influence, Iran's discontent was driven by its adversarial relationship with the West, particularly the United States. In the

1990s, Western criticism of Iran's human rights record, attempts to impede Iran's development of technologies through export controls, and sanctions on its oil reserves contributed to the discontent.

By the mid-1990s, a domestic consensus had formed around Russia's self-perception as an independent great power (*velikaya derzhava*) as a reaction to the failure of its pro-Western foreign policy, which intensified into the Putin era.[63] For example, in December 1995, longtime Russian foreign policy experts lamented that NATO expansion, delays over Russia's membership in the Council of Europe due to "double standards," U.S. interference in the Russian-Iranian nuclear reactor deal, and NATO's role in Serbia had contributed to Moscow's drift away from the West.[64] In May 1995, Russian journalist Pavel Felgenhauer observed that "the ruling class already agrees that cooperation with Iran is important and necessary, that NATO expansion is bad, that the Chechen resistance must be ended, that the army must be strengthened." Felgenhauer added that "NATO's eastward expansion is forcing Russia to frantically look back in the search for at least some strategic allies. The anti-Western and anti-American Iranian regime would be natural in such a situation and a very important partner."[65]

In cultivating closer relations with Iran, Russia found a powerful means to articulate its grievances against the Western-led international order while reasserting its great power ambitions.[66] During the 1997 U.S.-Russia summit in Helsinki, Yeltsin warned Clinton that in the event of NATO expansion to the former Soviet Union, Russia would be forced to pay more attention to its policy in the East, and in particular to its relations with China, India, and Iran.[67] In a pointed rebuke to Washington, the Russian State Duma voted on a resolution on the promotion of bilateral relations with Iran in October 1998. The resolution declared that deepened ties with Iran were consistent with "the national interests of Russia," contributing "to the formation of a multipolar world."[68]

Russia and Iran converged in opposition to Washington's greater willingness to use military force for humanitarian aims, essentially undermining sovereignty.[69] The 1999 NATO airstrikes over Serbia's treatment of Kosovars received unequivocal condemnations from Russia and Iran.[70] As in Tajikistan and during the earlier Bosnian

Civil War, Russia and Iran found themselves on opposing sides of the conflict, with Moscow offering its support to Slobodan Milošević while Tehran lent its support to the Kosovar Albanians out of a sense of Islamic solidarity.[71] Moscow's and Tehran's condemnation of the prospects of military intervention over Kosovo seemed to indicate a greater concern for the precedent set by the prospects of intervention without United Nations Security Council (UNSC) approval, which "raised suspicions that the most powerful western states will flout Westphalian norms in pursuit of their special interests, and will use international law and organizations as a tool of those interests."[72]

The Kosovo conflict was a turning point in Russian foreign policy, epitomizing for Moscow the global ambitions of the U.S. and seen as an attempt to revive "the politics of force."[73] In Tehran, President Khatami claimed the military action was illegal, arguing it served major powers' interests in the Balkans rather than aiding the oppressed Muslims of Kosovo.[74] The Iranian Foreign Ministry, while blaming Serbian authorities for ignoring Kosovar rights, noted this negligence gave foreign powers an excuse to politically exploit the crisis, leading to "military operations … without the permission of the UN Security Council."[75] Russia portrayed Kosovo as a precedent that NATO could use to provoke "the disintegration of Russia, China, India, and Iran—that is, particularly inconvenient [*neudobnye*], unmanageable [*neupravliaemye*] countries."[76] Elites in Moscow underscored the imperative to contest unipolarity by forging new partnerships with states such as China and India as well as Iran.[77] Russian political scientist Aleksandr Lukin predicted that U.S. hegemony would "inevitably stimulate the creation of a broad coalition of various states with the sole purpose of opposing" U.S. hegemony, including Russia, China, India, Malaysia, Mexico, Brazil, Nigeria, Iran, and other countries trying to preserve their "own sovereignty from arbitrary interference" in "the struggle to preserve the international system, based on the principle of state sovereignty."[78]

The late 1990s saw a commonality in Russia's and Iran's resistance to Western criticism of their domestic policies and human rights records. Both nations shared a growing frustration over what they perceived as selective Western scrutiny, particularly regarding Russia's handling of the Chechen conflict and Iran's domestic repression. This synergy was reflected in the 1999 Russian and Iranian Declaration on Human Rights, which articulated their shared commitment to "preventing double standards, respecting national and historic peculiarities of each State … without imposing borrowed value systems" on any state.[79] The statement foreshadowed a recurring trend that when faced with domestic opposition or international criticism over human rights issues, both countries often attribute such criticisms to Western attempts to undermine their sovereignty under the guise of promoting democracy. Konstantin Shuvalov, the Russian ambassador to Tehran, stressed that for Russia and Iran "the most important thing" driving the relationship is the "views regarding general international affairs, including the issue of the future world order" since Moscow and Tehran are "opposed to a unipolar world order" and "support a democratic multipolar order which will guarantee the interests of all nations."[80]

Despite their shared antipathy towards Western dominance, Russian-Iranian cooperation remained constrained by practical realities. Russia's deep economic entanglement with the West, exacerbated by post-Soviet financial hardships, limited Moscow's ability to fully align with Tehran in challenging Western interests. This economic dependence meant that while Moscow could use its Iranian partnership to signal discontent with Western policies, it could not risk more substantive cooperation that might jeopardize its integration into the global economy.

* * *

Following Yeltsin's resignation in December 1999, Putin assumed office with the desire to restore authority through state power (*gosudarstvennost*) with the aim of maintaining internal order and asserting the country's interests abroad. In the aftermath of NATO's intervention in Serbia, Russian foreign policy was reevaluated as elites across the spectrum became more aware of the limits of equal partnership with the West. During the 2000s, Russia had to overcome the painful syndrome of "historical retreat" and proceed to the phase of "foreign policy concentration."[81]

From the outset, it appeared that Putin would strengthen relations with Iran. In late June 2000, Putin approved Russia's new Foreign Policy Concept, which identified "the growing trend towards the establishment of a unipolar world order" as the primary threat to global stability. The Concept stated that "it is important to develop further relations with Iran" to achieve a "multipolar system" that would "genuinely reflect the diversity of the contemporary world and its great variety of interests."[82]

Within Iran, the transition from Mohammad Khatami (1997-2005) marked a redirection from economic reconstruction to social and political reform. President Khatami's visit to Moscow in March 2001—the first by an Iranian head of state since 1974—appeared to indicate Putin's emphasis on the diversification of relations with states beyond the West.[83] During the visit, Khatami and Putin signed the Treaty on Mutual Relations which was intended to lead to extensive cooperation but fell short of the Iranian side's expectations.[84] The treaty emerged from nearly a decade of negotiations, starting with initial discussions in September 1992 and a draft agreement initialed by Foreign Ministers Kozyrev and Velayati in March 1993. While Iran sought a strategic partnership, Russia deliberately kept the agreement's military commitments vague, limiting it to basic non-aggression pledges and peaceful dispute resolution mechanisms.

Global developments further undermined the prospects of burgeoning Russia-Iran relations as the War on Terror and Russia's desire to be seen as an equal with the West in the struggle against terrorism took precedence in Russian foreign policy. Despite initial expectations, Russia pursued cooperative relations with the West, albeit inconsistently, for the better part of the decade. Still, glimpses of Russia's divergence from the West would also appear throughout the decade, particularly over NATO expansion and the Color Revolutions—a series of non-violent, pro-democracy movements that swept across several former Soviet republics in the early to mid-2000s.[85]

Meanwhile, the Russia-Iran relations entered a new phase with Mahmoud Ahmadinejad's presidency (2005-2013), characterized by Iran's more assertive nuclear policy and Russia's increasingly complex role as both partner and mediator. Throughout this period,

Russia maintained a delicate balance between developing ties with Iran and managing Western concerns, particularly regarding nuclear cooperation. Even while supporting sanctions on Iran's nuclear program, Moscow continued to pursue military cooperation with Tehran.

Resuming Arms Sales

In the autumn of 2000, Vladimir Putin's public repudiation of the 1995 Gore-Chernomyrdin agreement signaled Russia's intent to break from Yeltsin-era foreign policy commitments that were scorned for their concessions to Washington. Putin's repudiation transformed arms sales into a tool for challenging Western hegemony, with Iran emerging as a prime beneficiary of Moscow's newfound assertiveness in military-technical cooperation.[86] Between 2002 and 2007, Iran's procurement of Russian military hardware increased substantially, with transactions totaling around $2 billion. The surge in arms sales positioned Iran as the third-largest recipient of Russian arms, trailing only behind China and India. The acquisitions included a variety of advanced weaponry including Mi-171 and Mi-17V-5 helicopters, Su-25 close-combat aircraft, and Tor-M1 short-range surface-to-air missile systems.[87] At the time, defense analysts speculated that military sales to Iran—one of the few markets where the Russian defense industry faced no competition from the U.S.—could amount to $7 billion.[88]

The 2005 contract between Russia and Iran for 29 Tor-M1 units marked a milestone in military-technical cooperation. Financially valued at between $700 million and $1.4 billion, the Tor-M1 deal was paramount for Iran because it enhanced its air defense capabilities, enabling it to protect key sites against potential aerial threats. Later, against the backdrop of Russian discontent surrounding the Color Revolutions and European missile defense, Moscow's decision to provide Iran with the more sophisticated, long-range S-300 surface-to-air defense systems in 2007 was driven by politics as well as material gains. For Iran, the $800 million deal with Rosoboronexport for at least five S-300 air defense systems was another crucial agreement for the modernization of its defensive air capabilities and the protection of its nuclear, chemical, and energy facilities from high-precision attacks.[89]

While the period saw a notable increase in Iran's acquisition of Russian military hardware, it was not without its complications. The revelation of Iran's secret nuclear facilities in 2002 put Russia in a delicate position. Arms sales to Iran faced increasing scrutiny, with a series of U.S. sanctions on Rosoboronexport, Russia's state-owned arms exporter, in 2006, 2007, and 2008. Moreover, the U.S. withdrawal from the Anti-Ballistic Missile (ABM) Treaty in 2002 under the pretext of threats from "rogue states" like Iran and North Korea directly impacted Russia's own security posture.[90] No longer constrained by the ABM Treaty, the U.S. could now deploy advanced missile defense systems, which Russia viewed as undermining the deterrence provided by its nuclear arsenal. Moscow believed that the justification of threats from "rogue states" like Iran and North Korea was merely a pretext, with the true aim being to weaken Russia's strategic position and erode its ability to deter U.S. power.

The Nuclear Challenge

The 2002 revelations of Iran's clandestine uranium enrichment plant at Natanz and a heavy-water facility at Arak transformed international perceptions of Tehran's nuclear program and triggered intensified diplomatic efforts to contain its atomic ambitions. These undisclosed sites, exposed by Iranian opposition groups, contradicted Tehran's declarations to the IAEA and vindicated longstanding American suspicions. Russia had previously dismissed U.S. claims about Iran's weapons aspirations, insisting that Iranian leadership had provided assurances to Moscow of purely peaceful intent. However, the discovery of Natanz and Arak—facilities designed for fuel cycle activities with potential weapons applications—placed Moscow's continued involvement in the Bushehr Nuclear Power Plant under uncomfortable international scrutiny.[91]

The timing proved particularly awkward for the Kremlin, which had justified its nuclear cooperation with Iran on the grounds that Bushehr was a purely civilian light-water reactor incapable of producing weapons-grade material. The Bush administration, however, expressed persistent concerns about the spent nuclear fuel that Bushehr would generate. Though difficult to weaponize from light-water reactors, this radioactive byproduct could theoretically be reprocessed to extract plutonium. To address these proliferation concerns and salvage the diplomatic viability of the Bushehr project, Russia negotiated a fuel take-back agreement with Iran. Under this arrangement, Moscow committed to retrieving all spent fuel from Bushehr and transporting it back to Russia for reprocessing or long-term storage. It also ensured Moscow's continued role as the sole supplier of Iranian fuel for Iran's civilian nuclear program.

After Iran resumed its uranium enrichment activities in 2005—a move that raised alarm over the potential military dimensions of its nuclear ambitions—Moscow found itself in a difficult position.[92] Disillusioned by Iranian intransigence, Moscow sought to uphold the global nuclear nonproliferation regime without damaging its commercial interests in Bushehr.[93] Acknowledging the gravity of the situation, Russia supported the International Atomic Energy Agency's (IAEA) decision in February 2006 to refer Iran's nuclear dossier to the UNSC. Moscow often played a role in watering down the language in UNSC Resolutions against Iran, seeking to moderate global scrutiny on Iran. Even when supporting UNSC Resolutions 1696 and 1737 in 2006, Russia lobbied for exempting civilian nuclear energy and existing cooperation in light-water reactor technology, such as Bushehr.[94] The backlash within Iran over Russia's support for UNSC sanctions left Russian diplomats frustrated, with many privately complaining that Tehran failed to appreciate Moscow's behind-the-scenes efforts to soften the measures' economic impact.

Russia deliberately slowed construction at Bushehr to manage both leverage and optics. The delays prolonged Iran's dependence on Russian technology while easing U.S. nonproliferation concerns by projecting Moscow as a responsible intermediary.[95] This strategy gave Russia significant influence over Tehran, allowing it to condition progress on compliance with the IAEA and UNSC resolutions.[96] For example, in March 2007, Russia issued an ultimatum to Iran, stating that it would not provide fuel for Bushehr until the Iranian leadership complied with the requirements of the UNSC to stop uranium enrichment. Later, as discussed in Chapter 2, Russia's position on

Iran's nuclear program, including support for additional sanctions, became one of the major areas of contention between Russia and Iran, leading to one of the lowest points in modern Russia-Iran relations.

The Global War on Terror

The cataclysmic events of 11 September 2001 created a rare opening for Moscow to recast itself as an indispensable partner in the U.S.-led "War on Terror" and to pursue what it hoped would be an equal relationship with Washington.[97] Putin viewed the campaign through the lens of Russia's own counterinsurgency in the North Caucasus, interpreting the U.S. invasion of Afghanistan as an opportunity for Russia to be a key player in global security. This period briefly softened tensions that had been strained by NATO's 1999 airstrikes over Kosovo, as Russia acquiesced to the establishment of U.S. military bases in Central Asia and framed its cooperation as a pragmatic convergence of interests.[98]

Iran, for its part, initially responded to the 9/11 attacks with condemnation and a rare offer of assistance to the United States, including help with search and rescue operations and a proposal for a broader dialogue on combating terrorism. The reformist government under President Mohammad Khatami was keen on easing tensions with the West and pursuing a path of dialogue and cooperation. Iran played a constructive role in the Bonn Conference on Afghanistan, contributing to the establishment of a new Afghan government after the fall of the Taliban—a regime that Tehran had opposed due to its extreme interpretation of Sunni Islam and its support for groups hostile to Iran.

The War on Terror and the U.S.-led campaign in Afghanistan transformed the regional security order encompassing Russia's near abroad and Iran through the provision of foreign aid and the establishment of military bases. The presence of NATO forces restricted Tehran's mobility within its immediate neighborhood and limited the prospects of engagement at the regional level.[99] The Bush administration's designation of Iran as part of the "Axis of Evil" and its subsequent invasion of Iraq intensified Tehran's concern about its security and its antipathy towards the presence of hostile extra-regional powers in its neighborhood.[100] While Russia initially accommodated the US military presence in Central Asia after 11 September, Moscow came to share Iran's view that NATO forces posed a destabilizing threat to regional security.

The 2003 U.S.-led military campaign in Iraq, carried out without UNSC authorization, showcased Moscow's and Tehran's mutual disdain for U.S. dominance and the unilateral exercise of military force. Both nations harbored reservations towards externally enforced regime changes justified on the grounds of pre-emptive self-defense. However, the relationship between Moscow and Tehran experienced strain due to disagreements over the Caspian Sea and the unveiling of Iran's covert nuclear activities. At the time, the threat of a U.S. military intervention in Iraq prompted "Moscow to tone down its public skepticism and concern over Iran's nuclear fuel cycle program."[101]

In the diplomatic arena, Russia coordinated with France and Germany in the UNSC to form an anti-war coalition, while Iran engaged regional states like Turkey, Syria, and the Gulf monarchies. Bilateral consultations between Russian and Iranian officials were limited but underscored their shared commitment to a UN-centered resolution of the Iraq issue.[102] During a visit to Tehran in March 2003, Russian Foreign Minister Igor Ivanov stated that both Russia and Iran

> share a common commitment to the ideas of a multipolar world order and a dialogue of civilizations. They are in favor of strengthening the central role of the UN in world affairs [and] resolving conflicts in strict accordance with the UN Charter and international law. All this is especially true now, against the backdrop of a sharp deterioration of the situation around Iraq.[103]

The Iraq War provided insight into the period of early Putinism when Moscow's internal weakness and the desire for integration with the West tempered its discontent with U.S. unilateralism. Russian opposition to Operation Iraqi Freedom reflected Moscow's apprehension about the future of the UNSC and the use of preemptive self-defense for regime change. Russian discussions about U.S. intentions in Iraq were framed by a broader critique of the expanding tendency toward unilateral and interventionist behavior in American foreign policy. For Iran, Saddam Hussein's removal led to a significant expansion of Iranian influence in Iraq and the wider region, while the "presence of foreign forces" in Iraq became a focal point of Tehran's broader security concerns about external powers in the Middle East.[104] Whereas the U.S. presence in Iraq served as a balance against Iranian influence, Tehran increasingly sought to "change the balance of power in the region" through its ideological, political, and military support to non-state actors.[105]

One of the major consequences of the Iraq War was the rise in Iran's prominence as a major regional power. Some in Russia viewed the strengthening of the Iranian presence in the Middle East as a beneficial development, introducing another "independent" entity into a region formerly controlled by the United States. Russia believed that U.S. actions in Iraq had already helped Tehran become the strongest power in the Persian Gulf. One expert noted that Iran continued to increase its influence in Iraq, Palestine, and Afghanistan while asserting itself as "the center of power in the strengthening Shiite axis."[106] The war not only amplified Iran's regional standing but also solidified a shared Russian–Iranian determination to prevent similar regime-change operations elsewhere. Both powers internalized the lessons of Iraq's destabilization as evidence of the dangers of Western interventionism—a convergence that would resurface after the Arab Spring.

The Roots of Resistance

By the early 2000s, both Russia and Iran had grown increasingly disillusioned with the U.S.-led liberal international order. In Moscow, NATO's eastward expansion, Washington's withdrawal from the ABM Treaty, and the invasion of Iraq in 2003 hardened elite perceptions of American unipolarity and disregard for multilateral constraints. In Tehran, the rise of Mahmoud Ahmadinejad in 2005 marked a decisive turn toward defiance. His presidency coincided with the upheaval of the Iraq War and the reconfiguration of regional power dynamics, which Iran exploited to expand its influence through allied militias and political movements in Iraq and Lebanon.

Russia's aversion to the imposition of liberal norms was exacerbated amid a series of "Color Revolutions" in Georgia, Ukraine, and Kyrgyzstan, which Russian officials openly accused Washington of supporting.[107] Later, in Iran, the 2009 Green Movement protests evoked similar sentiments in the official discourse, which deemed Western efforts to promote democracy a "soft war."[108] Under Ahmadinejad, Tehran became more vocal in critiquing "U.S. attempts at unipolarity and domination" and "the cynical use of human rights for political purposes and the manufacturing of Color Revolutions" as grounds for closer alignment with states such as Russia and China.[109]

The Russian leadership was concerned that the Middle East and the near abroad had become more entwined in the U.S. democratization agenda, a sentiment that grew in the aftermath of the 2011 Arab Spring. The perception originated with the "Cedar Revolution" in Lebanon, which occurred immediately after Georgia's Rose and Ukraine's Orange Revolutions.[110] Russian and Iranian assertions in early 2005 that the U.S. was actively directing events in Beirut were reminiscent of the discourse around the Color Revolutions. According to Russia's former ambassador to Libya, officials in Tehran and Moscow shared a similar concern that developments in Lebanon and Syria "could trigger a domino effect, transforming the Middle East into a U.S.-dominated zone" akin to the Rose, Orange, and Tulip Revolutions in Russia's neighborhood.[111]

Under Putin, the Kremlin embarked on a deliberate effort to accelerate Russia's economic modernization, centralize political control, and expand its influence over states it regarded as part of its "sphere of influence while reclaiming Russia's position as an indispensable global power."[112] This posture was demonstrated forcefully in Putin's February 2007 Munich Security Conference speech. In the speech, Putin decried the U.S. for its "nearly uncontained hyper-use of force" to establish and exploit a unipolar world that destabilized the world under U.S. supremacy.[113] Putin's assertiveness represented the culmination of several factors that contributed to Moscow's new posture—a growing sense of Russian fragility in the face of political instability on its periphery following the Color Revolutions combined with the perception of strengthened state authority and improved economic conditions. At the time of the

2007 Munich speech, few observers viewed the remarks as heralding a new era in Russia's foreign policy, with many assuming they were more of an emotional response to a succession of setbacks extending to 1991 than a calculated appraisal of Russia's future. Over time, however, it became clear that the 2007 Munich speech heralded a new epoch in Moscow's foreign policy posture.

By the end of Putin's second term in office, Russian foreign policy had changed substantially from the period when Russia attempted to collaborate with the West on the War on Terror and integrate into the global economy. The events following 11 September 2001 represented Russia's desire to become an equal partner with the West—a partnership that never came to fruition. Putin's Munich speech and ensuing measures, such as increased air force patrols near U.S. and NATO borders and Russia's decision to suspend its participation in the Conventional Armed Forces in Europe Treaty, demonstrated the Kremlin's determination to coerce the West into accepting equal cooperation. This effort was unsatisfactory. In a final bid at cooperation, discussed in Chapter 2, Putin's successor, Dmitry Medvedev, would embark on a "reset" with Washington.

Medvedev's First Months

Putin's designation of Dmitry Medvedev as his preferred successor in 2008 was a carefully orchestrated transition that seemed to signal a potential shift in Russia's trajectory.[114] Facing constitutional term limits that prohibited more than two consecutive presidential terms, Putin chose this route rather than immediately amending the constitution, selecting a trusted protégé who would maintain his power behind the scenes. Medvedev was seen as a technocratic modernizer who might guide Russia toward greater economic liberalization and diplomatic engagement with the West. This perception was reinforced by Medvedev's early rhetoric emphasizing judicial reform, anti-corruption efforts, and technological innovation.

The first months of Medvedev's presidency were overshadowed by events that stoked resentment toward the United States. At the now-infamous April 2008 Bucharest summit, NATO welcomed Ukraine's and Georgia's aspirations of joining the NATO membership action plan. A few months later, in July 2008, the U.S. signed an agreement with the Czech Republic on the deployment of an advanced missile defense radar base, followed by an agreement in August with Poland on the deployment of an American missile defense base on Polish territory. The reaction in Russia was acute. Notably, several figures suggested pursuing relations with Iran in retaliation for NATO expansion and the West's policy on missile defense.

The major flashpoint came in August 2008 when Russia backed the independence of South Ossetia and Abkhazia, sparking the Russo-Georgia War.[115] The immediate catalyst for the war was Georgia's attempt to regain control over South Ossetia, launching a military offensive on 7 August 2008. Russia responded swiftly and forcefully, advancing beyond South Ossetia into Georgia proper, arguing it was protecting its citizens and peacekeepers in the area.[116] The conflict lasted for five days before a ceasefire was brokered by the French presidency of the European Union Council on 12 August.

Russia defended its actions, which breached Georgia's sovereignty, by presenting several quasi-legal arguments. These ranged from the need for an emergency humanitarian response to the principles of self-determination and self-defense. The war had significant consequences. Russia recognized the independence of South Ossetia and Abkhazia, which intensified tensions with Georgia and drew condemnation from the international community, including the United States and Europe.

Iran, under Ahmadinejad, capitalized on Russia's confrontation with the West to argue that Russia ought to respond to supposed U.S. and NATO plans to expand into the Caucasus by increasing military cooperation with Iran.[117] Ahmadinejad went as far as to justify Russian actions by suggesting that the conflict arose because of Georgia's acquiescence to foreign interference and Western pressure to join military blocs that exacerbated regional tensions. The Iranian president also pushed a claim that Tehran had "information that shows that Zionists have a role in the South Ossetia and Abkhazia case," including plans to promote terrorism and drug transit in the region.[118] However, Iran strayed from recognizing South Ossetia or Abkhazia due to its concerns about separatism with its Kurdish,

Baloch, and Ahvaz Arab minorities. Such a stance would similarly be expressed during Russia's 2014 annexation of Crimea and full-fledged invasion of Ukraine in 2022.

Despite initial hopes of exploiting the Russo-Georgia war, Iran's enthusiasm at the downturn in U.S.-Russia relations was short-lived, as the election of Barack Obama as U.S. president in November 2008 led to a shift in U.S. policy. The Obama administration introduced the "reset" concept, aiming to mend and fortify U.S.-Russia ties by centering their relationship on shared interests. During this period, Iran's accelerating nuclear program was a looming concern. As part of the "reset," the U.S. prioritized discussions about the Iranian nuclear dossier with Russia. In Chapter 2, we will see how Russia's inclination to leverage Iran in its negotiations with the West eventually exacerbated the strains in its relationship during Medvedev's tenure.

* * *

The course of Russia-Iran relations has been an extensive journey, fraught with numerous periods of intense tension along the way. Imperial legacies cast long shadows over this relationship. In the 19th century, successive Russo-Persian wars resulted in significant territorial losses for Iran, creating deep-seated grievances that would reverberate through generations of Iranian political thought. These historical wounds, however, tell only part of the story. Despite this troubled past, both nations have repeatedly demonstrated pragmatism in pursuing shared strategic interests, particularly when confronting common adversaries or external pressures.

The collapse of the Soviet Union in 1991 marked a crucial turning point. As Russia grappled with its diminished global status and Iran faced increasing international isolation, both nations discovered new grounds for cooperation and new areas of disagreement. For Russia, the Yeltsin era was dominated by efforts to align with the West, limiting the scope of its partnership with Tehran. The 1995 Gore-Chernomyrdin agreement exemplified these constraints, as Moscow halted new arms deals with Iran under U.S. pressure, frustrating Tehran and curtailing opportunities for deeper military-technical collaboration. For Iran, this agreement was particularly galling, as it reinforced perceptions that Russia's commitment to the partnership was transactional and secondary to its ties with the United States.

Under Putin, Russia began to prioritize its national interests over Western approval, leading to a revival of arms sales and expanded cooperation with Iran. The repudiation of the Gore-Chernomyrdin agreement in 2000 allowed for the sale of advanced weaponry like the S-300 air defense system. However, Moscow's deep economic interdependence with the West and its cautious stance on Iran's nuclear program continued to frustrate Tehran. While Iran welcomed Putin's more independent posture, the delays in fulfilling arms contracts and Russia's support for certain UN sanctions on Iran underscored the limitations of the partnership.

Despite persistent skepticism and underlying tensions, the 1990s and 2000s offered moments of potential synergy between Russia and Iran. Yet these opportunities largely went unrealized, constrained by deep-seated mistrust and Moscow's limited political will. These unresolved frictions came to a head during Medvedev's presidency, marking one of the most difficult periods in the bilateral relationship.

2

RETRENCHING AFTER THE RESET

PROTESTS AND THE SEEDS OF REALIGNMENT

In an address broadcast live across Iran on 3 November 2010, President Mahmoud Ahmadinejad stated that "some people who are under the influence of Satan [the U.S.] thought that if they can unilaterally and illegally cancel some defense agreements that they have with us, it will hurt the Iranian nation."[1] Ahmadinejad's accusation of caving in to "Satan" directly targeted Russia's cancellation of the contract for the S-300 surface-to-air defense system. The S-300, capable of intercepting aircraft and ballistic missiles at long ranges, was viewed in Tehran as essential for protecting its nuclear and military facilities from potential Israeli or U.S. strikes. Moscow had signed the contract in 2007 but froze the deal in 2010 following the adoption of new sanctions over Iran's nuclear program.

The cancelation of the S-300 deal and Ahmadinejad's criticism of Russia occurred against the backdrop of a period in U.S.-Russia relations coined the reset where Moscow and Washington sought to improve their relationship by working together on various issues, including how to handle Iran's controversial nuclear program. Improving U.S.-Russia relations during the "reset" era had unintended consequences for Moscow's dynamic with Tehran, introducing a phase fraught with perceived betrayals and heightened tensions.

This chapter explores the tumultuous period in Russia-Iran relations during the U.S.-Russia reset under President Dmitry Medvedev, spanning 2009 to Vladimir Putin's return to the presidency in 2012. The reset initiated by the Obama administration, aimed to repair the strained U.S.-Russia relationship that had deteriorated during the later years of the George W. Bush administration. As part of the reset, Russia made several concessions to rebuild ties with Washington. Among the most significant was Russia's agreement in 2010 to support stringent United Nations Security Council (UNSC) sanctions against Iran. Russia anticipated that these moves would be compensated, and, to an extent, they were. The mutual concessions led to two notable outcomes: the signing of an important arms control agreement aimed at reducing the strategic nuclear arsenals of the United States and Russia, and U.S. support for Russia's entry into the World Trade Organization (WTO).

However, the reset would prove to be temporary. Within a year of Russia endorsing sanctions against Iran, the Arab Spring and domestic protests in Russia led to a retrenchment that set the stage for Putin's return to the Russian presidency in the spring of 2012. Where Medvedev had supported international sanctions against Iran and cancelled arms deals, Putin brought a fundamentally different vision that would reshape Russia's approach to Tehran. Putin's concerns over perceived Western attempts at regime change steered Russian foreign policy towards a more bellicose posture that emphasized sovereignty and opposition to external interventions. This ideological shift positioned Iran, itself a target of Western pressure and regime change rhetoric, as a natural partner in opposing American hegemony and defending the principle that sovereign states should be free from external interference, regardless of their domestic political systems.

The Rise and Fall of the Reset

When Barack Obama assumed the U.S. presidency in January 2009, he inherited a strained relationship between the United

States and Russia.[2] The tensions were not born overnight but had been intensifying over the years, rooted in contentious issues such as strategic arms control, missile defense plans, and the North Atlantic Treaty Organization's (NATO) flirtations with further eastward expansion, particularly concerning Georgia and Ukraine. The situation reached a tipping point in August 2008 with the Russia-Georgia War, exacerbating the already tense U.S.-Russia relationship.[3]

A fraught U.S.-Russia relationship was not the only challenge Obama faced upon assuming office. Iran's nuclear program was growing rapidly.[4] Under the preceding Bush administration, U.S. policy towards Iran advocated for zero enrichment to halt Tehran's nuclear ambitions. Yet, Iran's efforts to enrich uranium and operate clandestine facilities continued unabated. Under hardline President Ahmadinejad, Tehran demonstrated little willingness to engage with international demands for transparency.

The Obama administration recognized that Russian cooperation was indispensable to resolving the Iranian nuclear impasse.[5] As a member of the UNSC, Russia had the ability to block multilateral UNSC sanctions on Iran. Starting in 2006, Russia supported several UNSC Resolutions that imposed graduated restrictions targeting Iran's nuclear and ballistic missile programs. These measures included prohibitions on the transfer of sensitive nuclear materials and technologies, asset freezes, and travel bans on individuals and entities involved in proliferation-related activities. Yet even as it endorsed these resolutions, Moscow consistently warned against applying excessive pressure. Russian officials argued that overly harsh sanctions would harden Tehran's defiance, reduce incentives for diplomatic compromise, and risk destabilizing a region already on edge.[6]

After the Russo-Georgia War, Moscow became reluctant to endorse further sanctions, even threatening to veto resolutions.[7] Russia's resistance to further UNSC sanctions was not just a procedural hurdle. Russia held a sizeable influence over Iran's nuclear program.[8] Though it continued to cooperate with Iran on the Bushehr Nuclear Power Plant, it often delayed its construction to pressure Iran to cooperate with the International Atomic Energy Agency (IAEA).[9]

The Bushehr project gave Russia unique insight into Iran's nuclear infrastructure and provided it with a degree of influence unmatched by other major powers. These ties positioned Moscow as a critical intermediary between Tehran and the international community, allowing it to mediate disputes and shape the contours of diplomatic engagement over Iran's nuclear activities.[10]

Acknowledging these complexities, the United States sought to navigate the dual challenges of Iran and Russia by identifying Iran's nuclear issue as a potential leverage point for improving U.S.-Russia relations.[11] Russia recognized that the Obama administration prioritized preventing a nuclear Iran. As a result, Russia aimed to secure the cooperation of the United States on issues such as European missile defense and Russia's bid to join the WTO. Moreover, Russia lobbied for the ratification of the 1-2-3 Nuclear Cooperation Agreement—a bilateral accord that would allow the Russian nuclear industry to access advanced U.S. nuclear technologies and expertise.[12] Diplomats with expertise in North America and arms control were moved into the Foreign Ministry's 2nd Asia Regional Department, which managed relations with Iran. Meanwhile, personnel changes were also made at the thematic department that dealt with nonproliferation and arms control, increasing its cadre of Persian speakers.[13]

Peregruzka or Perezagruzka?

The symbolic start of what would come to be known as the reset between the United States and Russia took place on 6 March 2009 during U.S. Secretary of State Hillary Clinton's visit to Geneva.[14] During this meeting with Sergey Lavrov, Clinton presented the Russian foreign minister with a red button that was meant to represent the reset of U.S.-Russia relations. This button bore the English word reset alongside the Russian word *peregruzka*. However, the intention to symbolize reset was lost in translation, as *peregruzka* actually translates to "overload" in English, not reset. The correct Russian word should instead have been *perezagruzka*.

The mistranslation of Clinton's reset button to Lavrov in March 2009 was an inadvertent yet poignant metaphor for the complexities and misunderstandings that have often characterized U.S.-Russia relations. Intended to symbolize a fresh start or a reset of the bilateral relationship, the error—translating "reset" to "overload"—instead underscored the broader challenges of navigating the U.S.-Russia relationship, marked by a history of mutual suspicion, strategic misalignments, and the perennial risk of intentions being lost in translation, both literally and figuratively.

Despite this initial misstep, the following year witnessed a period of increased cooperation between the United States and Russia, marking a temporary thaw in their traditionally frosty relations. This era of collaboration saw both countries working together on various issues, from arms control—epitomized by the signing of New START—to increased logistical support for American operations in Afghanistan through Russian territory. But this rapprochement came at a cost to the Russia-Iran relationship, especially as Moscow drifted closer to Washington's stance on the Iran nuclear issue.

Iran seemed concerned about the prospects of the U.S.-Russia reset, realizing its reliance on Russia to block UNSC Resolutions. The Iranian press closely monitored the developments in U.S.-Russia relations. Many observers cautioned against the unpredictability of U.S. foreign policy while expressing skepticism about Russia's engagement with Washington. For example, the Iranian newspaper *Jam-e Jam* featured an article suggesting that the budding friendship between the U.S. and Russia signaled that it was time for Tehran to reassess its diplomatic ties and strategies.[15] Some reformists suggested that U.S.-Russia diplomatic endeavors could unexpectedly force Iran into a corner, calling for a more flexible approach to negotiations with the West.[16] Iran's concerns were not unsubstantiated. Soon, Moscow would use the Iranian "bargaining chip" with the United States. But first, Russia would demonstrate its complex approach to Iranian affairs by supporting a regime facing internal turmoil—a pattern that would persist in the years to come.

The Color Revolution Comes to Iran

The reset coincided with mass protests in Iran, known as the Green Movement. The June 2009 Iranian presidential election saw

Ahmadinejad re-elected despite widespread allegations of voter fraud. The movement, named for the campaign color of opposition candidate Mir Hossein Mousavi, quickly grew beyond contesting election outcomes to symbolize a broader demand for political reform and civil liberties. The streets of major cities, especially Tehran, were flooded with millions of Iranians who hailed from diverse social strata to demand transparency, accountability, and a more open society.

The Green Movement protests over Ahmadinejad's contested re-election also coincided with the Shanghai Cooperation Organization (SCO) summit hosted by Russia in Yekaterinburg.[17] Though Ahmadinejad delayed his trip due to the protests, the decision to attend the summit amid internal upheaval indicated the Iranian regime's desire to secure international recognition and legitimacy. While most of the international community refrained from recognizing the elections, Russia offered its support. Russian Deputy Foreign Minister Sergey Ryabkov affirmed that "elections in Iran are an internal affair of the Iranian people" and noted that Ahmadinejad's decision to make "his first foreign trip after re-election to Russia is symbolic" of the countries' good neighborly relations.[18] Iran's state-led media portrayed the visit as an indication of the widespread recognition of Ahmadinejad's victory. Throughout the protests, Russia issued a series of statements supporting the election results.[19] Inside Iran, that posture backfired in the street: protesters chanted "Death to Russia," casting Moscow as an enabler of repression.

Russia's view of the Iranian Green Movement was shaped by its own experiences and perceptions of the Color Revolutions in the early 2000s. Having witnessed a series of popular movements ousting pro-Russian leaders in countries like Georgia, Ukraine, and Kyrgyzstan, Moscow developed a deep-rooted suspicion of mass protests. Russia often viewed protests as Western-engineered efforts aimed at destabilizing its partners and expanding Western influence at the expense of Russian interests.

In Iran, the official response to the Green Movement protests evoked similar sentiments to the Color Revolutions as Tehran criticized Western efforts to promote democracy, describing them as constituting a "soft war" (*jang-e narm*). By connecting the Green Movement to the Color Revolutions, the Iranian official and semi-official discourse appropriated the rhetoric used by Russia to describe the events in Ukraine, Georgia, and Kyrgyzstan. An article published by the Islamic Revolutionary Guard Corps (IRGC)-linked Fars News Agency accused the enemies of the Iranian nation of attempting to replicate the experiences of the Color Revolutions through externally funded efforts to propagate fallacious allegations of electoral fraud and to foment internal discord and disunion in society.[20] Similarly, an op-ed in *Iran*, the official daily newspaper of the Iranian government, argued that the enemies of Iran were seeking to replicate the experience of countries like Ukraine, Georgia, and Kyrgyzstan with the support of the "Western and Zionist media."[21] Narrative borrowing was matched by method borrowing: Iran's security services studied and adapted Russian tactics for information control and protest management.

The government's response was swift and severe, employing riot police and paramilitary forces to suppress the protests. Arrests, media censorship, internet blackouts, and violent crackdowns characterized the state's effort to quell the dissent. During the protests, allegations surfaced about Russia's assistance to the Iranian government, particularly in the realm of riot control and surveillance. A subsequent agreement published by Russia's and Iran's interior ministries indicated that assistance likely encompassed riot gear, surveillance technology, and advice on crowd control tactics.[22]

Russia's backing of the Iranian authorities during the protests was part and parcel of its opposition to domestic unrest, yet Moscow's support for Iran's suppression of the protests would not extend to Iran's nuclear program. Moscow had grown frustrated with Tehran's persistent advancement of its nuclear activities and hardened its position, supporting international sanctions.

Iran's Nuclear Deception

In September 2009, several months after Ahmadinejad's election, American officials shared information about Iran's construction of a covert underground enrichment facility in Fordow, near Qom. For the Russians, the intelligence about Iran's construction of Fordow was not only viewed as a surprise, but according to a former Russian diplomat, "it was a betrayal."[23] Having supported Iran's development of a nuclear program for peaceful purposes, Russia felt blindsided by the discovery of the covert underground facility.[24] Iran's deception over Fordow was compounded in November by Tehran's failure to accept a proposal to supply Iran with fuel for the Tehran Research Reactor (TRR), which had been discussed as a joint effort between the U.S. and Russia.

The TRR proposal emerged after Iran had essentially exhausted its fuel for its research reactor and requested potential suppliers to provide fuel rods for its operation. However, the U.S. feared Iran would use the fuel for military purposes. A proposal was devised by the United States, Russia, and France to reduce Iran's stockpile of low-enriched uranium while providing Iran with a legitimate avenue to obtain the fuel needed for its civilian purposes. In October 2009, after months of negotiations, Iran was presented with a tentative agreement. Under this proposal, Russia would enrich the uranium further to 19.75 percent and then transfer it to France to manufacture fuel rods for Iran. Basically, the proposal ensured international oversight and verification, minimizing the risk of diversion for military purposes by ensuring that the enrichment occurred outside Iranian territory. It was designed as a win-win: Iran would obtain its fuel, while the international community would not have to worry about its use for military purposes.

Iran initially seemed receptive, with Ahmadinejad even assuring Putin in Beijing that Tehran would accept the proposal. Tehran acknowledged the proposal's merit but sought to incorporate "several important technical and economic additions" to the plan.[25] While this approach drew criticism from some Russian analysts, who interpreted it as a delaying tactic, the official Russian stance remained patient and understanding of Iran's position. Even after Iran formally rejected the initial TRR proposal in November, Russia defended Iran's negotiation strategy, suggesting that it was reasonable for Iran to negotiate for the most favorable terms possible.[26]

At the end of 2009 and early 2010, reports indicated that the Iranian government might reconsider the TRR plan. In Moscow, this sparked a glimmer of hope for a potential breakthrough. But Russia's optimism was temporary. With Iran's announcement that it would resume uranium enrichment, a new perspective emerged in Moscow, fueled by pessimism towards Iran and a greater willingness to cooperate with Washington.[27]

Tested with Sanctions and Setbacks

In February 2010, Iran's announcement that it would begin enriching uranium to 20 percent—approaching levels considered weapons-grade—sparked alarm in Russia.[28] Iran's announcement followed revelations about the previously undisclosed Fordow enrichment facility and Iran's earlier rejection of the TRR proposal in November 2009, both of which had already tested Moscow's patience. Despite this, Russia had exercised notable restraint in supporting additional sanctions on Iran. However, Iran's move to enrich uranium to 20 percent contributed to doubts about the peaceful intentions of its nuclear program.[29] In response, Moscow began to demonstrate a greater willingness to collaborate with the United States in implementing multilateral sanctions against Iran.[30]

Starting in 2010, the U.S. began engaging Russia in discussions about a new UNSC sanctions resolution on Iran. By early April, these negotiations had advanced to the stage of drafting a resolution for consideration by the UNSC. The period also saw the signing of the New START Treaty, a major arms control treaty that limited the strategic nuclear arsenals of both the U.S. and Russia. Leveraging this positive momentum, the United States successfully garnered Russian support for a new sanctions resolution targeting Iran. Nevertheless, the achievement came with qualifications. Moscow worked the text to protect its commercial equities—carving out explicit exemptions for civilian nuclear projects, notably Bushehr—and to narrow enforcement, pressing for softer provisions on arms transfers and more cautious language on financial restrictions and cargo inspections.[31]

In the lead-up to the resolution vote, Iran issued a series of public threats to dissuade Russia from backing the sanctions.[32] In May 2010, Ahmadinejad personally criticized Russian President Medvedev, warning that Russia's stance on sanctions could turn Moscow into "an enemy of the Iranian people."[33] Kazem Jalali, a member of the Iranian parliament's National Security and International Policy Committee and the future ambassador to Russia, declared that if Russia keeps going along with the "extremist and radical" group that includes the U.S., then Iran "will be compelled to reevaluate the level of relations with [Russia]."[34]

Despite these threats and the charged rhetoric, Iran's attempts to sway the Russian position did not ultimately alter the course of the sanctions vote. In June 2010, with Russia's support, UNSC Resolution 1929 was passed. UNSC Resolution 1929 hindered Iran's access to international financial systems, impeded its trade activities, and imposed restrictions on key sectors of the Iranian economy, including its banking, shipping, and energy industries. The resolution also restricted arms transfers to Iran—a provision that Russia would invoke to cancel the sale of the S-300 air defense system to Iran. The Iranian media's reaction was unsurprisingly inflammatory.[35] In particular, many of the articles highlighted Russia's betrayal, with some even declaring that Russia had transformed into a puppet of the West.[36]

Russia, keen to navigate the balance between adhering to international sanctions against Iran and preventing the full deterioration of ties, initially signaled that UNSC Resolution 1929 left room to proceed with the S-300 sale. There was an overarching belief among many observers that the S-300 deal would be neatly sidestepped from the sanctions' grasp. The rationale behind Russia's initial promise that the S-300 missile system would not be impacted by sanctions stems from its classification as a defensive weapon. For example, Russian parliamentarian Konstantin Kosachev downplayed concerns that the resolution would hinder Russia-Iran defense cooperation.[37]

However, much to Iran's dismay and contrary to expectations, President Medvedev announced a ban on transferring S-300 systems to Iran.[38] The decision was justified by referencing UNSC Resolution 1929's broad prohibition on the sale of conventional weapons to Iran. What made this move especially perplexing and indeed controversial was that UNSC Resolution 1929 did, in fact, provide exemptions for defensive surface-to-air missiles, which ostensibly covered systems like the S-300. The discrepancy between the resolution's terms and Russia's subsequent interpretation of them sparked uproar in Iran. Iran interpreted Medvedev's decision as nothing short of a betrayal, with Ahmadinejad vocally criticizing Russia for succumbing to Western pressure, notably referring to Russia's actions as akin to caving in to "Satan."[39]

From Tehran's perspective, Russia's cancellation of the S-300 deal marked a stark departure from Moscow's typical approach to UNSC sanctions, where Russia often favored narrow interpretations that permitted continued military and economic engagements with Iran. In an escalation of the dispute, Iran proceeded to file a lawsuit against Rosoboronexport, Russia's state arms export agency, demanding $4 billion USD in compensation for the unfulfilled delivery of the S-300 systems at the International Court of Arbitration—a decision that prompted irritation in Russia.[40] Though Russia eventually resolved the dispute by delivering the S-300 systems years later, the episode underscored the deepening strains in the bilateral relationship. Yet this cooling proved fleeting: exogenous shocks and domestic transformations would soon pull the two nations into a deeper partnership that extended well beyond arms sales.

* * *

Russia's support for UNSC 1929 and the cancellation of the S-300 system represented a brief period of cooperation between Russia and the U.S., during which Moscow leveraged its relations with Tehran to improve relations with Washington. However, the reset was short-lived.

The relationship between Russia and the United States started to worsen in 2011, primarily due to disagreements over the Syrian Civil War and the implementation of UNSC Resolution 1973 on Libya. Months later, the 2011-12 protests surrounding the Duma elections—Russia's lower legislative body—further hardened Moscow's stance toward the West. Western leaders, particularly in Washington, voiced strong support for the protesters and openly criticized the election process, which the Kremlin characterized as foreign-manipulated interference designed to fuel public dissent.

Moscow interpreted these endorsements as a deliberate attempt to weaken Russian authority and destabilize the government under the pretense of promoting democratic values.

By autumn 2011, the once-promising reset in U.S.-Russia relations had unraveled completely, with cooperation giving way to mutual suspicion and hostility. The relationship fractured along two critical fault lines: profound disagreements over missile defense systems and escalating disputes concerning human rights practices. The formal collapse came in November 2011 when missile defense negotiations reached an impasse, but the diplomatic damage deepened significantly in 2012 through a consequential exchange of retaliatory measures. First, the U.S. Congress passed the Magnitsky Act, imposing targeted sanctions on Russian officials implicated in the death of tax lawyer Sergey Magnitsky, who had exposed alleged massive tax fraud before dying under suspicious circumstances in a Moscow prison. Moscow's response was swift and symbolic—the Russian Duma enacted legislation prohibiting American citizens from adopting Russian children, a move widely seen as using vulnerable orphans as political pawns. This bitter sequence not only extinguished the Obama administration's hopes for improved bilateral relations but established a pattern of tit-for-tat confrontation that would characterize U.S.-Russia dynamics for years to come.

Amid these tensions with the West, Russia found a renewed kinship with Iran. By the summer of 2011, international developments, particularly in the Middle East, had contributed to a "thaw" in Russia-Iran relations.[41] Notable exchanges and meetings between the two countries' officials underscored this warming of ties. Productive dialogues occurred at various international forums, such as the SCO summit, and were further exemplified by reciprocal visits from high-ranking officials. For example, in August, Russian Security Council Secretary Nikolai Patrushev went to Tehran, where he met with Ahmadinejad. Patrushev's trip coincided with Iranian Foreign Minister Ali Akbar Salehi's arrival in Moscow for talks with Russian Foreign Minister Lavrov. By the close of the summer of 2011, *Kommersant* journalist Elena Chernenko declared that Moscow's relations with Tehran had improved in proportion to the decline in U.S.-Russia relations.[42]

The improvement in Russia-Iran relations was driven not only by estrangement from the U.S. but also by the broader backdrop of the Arab Spring. The upheavals in Libya and Syria, in particular, highlighted shared concerns over Western-led regime change, prompting Moscow and Tehran to unite against what they saw as Western attempts to destabilize sovereign states under the guise of promoting democracy.

The Arab Spring and Libya

Sparked by the self-immolation of Mohamed Bouazizi, a young Tunisian street vendor, protesting against corruption and economic hardship in December 2010, a wave of protests, demonstrations, and uprisings spread throughout the Middle East. The regional upheaval became known collectively as the Arab Spring. Protests in Tunisia inspired similar movements in other countries, most notably Egypt, where mass protests erupted on 25 January 2011. After eighteen days of public pressure, President Hosni Mubarak resigned on 11 February, allowing the Supreme Military Council to take control. Given the disposition of long-term autocrats like Mubarak and Tunisia's Ben Ali, one would assume that Russia and Iran—two staunch defenders of regime stability—would look negatively on developments. However, it was not until the fallout from Libya that Russia and Iran began to coalesce over a much more negative view of the Arab Spring.

The Kremlin initially adopted a cautious approach, recognizing the situation's volatility and its potential implications for regional stability. Until the end of 2011, Russia's position on the Arab Spring "was not always consistent and clearly expressed," as official statements from the Foreign Ministry often contradicted statements from President Medvedev and other high-level Russian officials.[43] The early Russian discourse on the Arab Spring portrayed the protests as an internal phenomenon rather than a result of external interference. In early 2011, for example, Lavrov stated that there are "more differences than similarities between the so-called 'Color Revolutions' in the Commonwealth of Independent States (CIS) space and what is happening in the Middle East [which] is much more the result of internal events and processes, internal problems, internal dissatisfaction with unemployment, poverty, and lack of political pluralism."[44] As the Arab Spring evolved, particularly with the Libyan intervention and later the Syrian Civil War, Russia's stance shifted considerably.[45]

From Tehran's perspective, the uprisings provided an opportunity to reshape the power dynamics in the Middle East and expand its regional influence. Initially, Iran portrayed the Arab Spring as an Islamic Awakening, mirroring its own 1979 Islamic Revolution, against Western-backed autocratic regimes.[46] Iran particularly welcomed the uprisings in countries such as Egypt and Tunisia, hoping that the democratic movements would lead to the establishment of governments more aligned with its own ideological stance and less closely tied to the West.

When the uprising against Muammar Gaddafi's regime in Libya began in February 2011, Russia initially called for a peaceful resolution of the crisis, expressing its disapproval of any external interference in Libya's internal affairs.[47] This stance was underlined by Russia's support for UNSC Resolution 1970, which imposed an arms embargo on Libya and called for an end to the violence.[48] Despite Russian support for Resolution 1970, Foreign Minister Lavrov clarified that Moscow did not see "foreign intervention and even more so armed [intervention] as a means to resolve the crisis in Libya. The Libyans must solve their problems themselves."[49] Iran, still parroting the narrative of the uprisings in Libya as part of the larger Islamic Awakening, condemned the Gaddafi regime's brutal actions against its people. Tehran simultaneously expressed strong criticism of the hypocrisy of Western intervention in Libya, given the West's support for other authoritarian regimes in the region that also brutally suppressed protests, such as Bahrain.

The escalation of violence and the humanitarian crisis in Libya led to the passing of UNSC Resolution 1973, authorizing member states to establish a no-fly zone and take all necessary measures to protect civilians. In response, NATO launched Operation Unified Protector, conducting airstrikes against Gaddafi's forces and enforcing the no-fly zone over Libya. Rather than exercising its veto right, Russia abstained from the resolution due to questions over the enforcement of the no-fly zone, "rules of engagement," and the "limits on the use of force." Russia also argued that certain provisions in the resolution could "potentially open the door to a large-scale military operation" that could have "destabilizing" and "inevitable humanitarian consequences."[50] Iran's response to NATO's intervention in Libya included a condemnation of the Libyan government's actions against its people and its criticism of the military action taken by NATO. Supreme Leader Ali Khamenei stated that "Iran utterly condemns the behavior of the Libyan government against its people, the killings and pressure on people, and the bombing of its cities ... but it [also] condemns the military action in Libya."[51] An editorial in the conservative Iranian newspaper *Siyasat-e Ruz* questioned the rationale behind Russia's muted response to military intervention in Libya since Moscow has historically been "against ... interventionist policies and actions by the U.S. in the Middle East."[52]

To some extent, Russia's abstention on the Libya vote served as the final nail in the coffin for the waning "reset" in U.S.-Russia relations. It also illustrated a greater divide within the Russian elite. Whereas Medvedev supported the mission, an overwhelming majority of high-level officials questioned the permissibility of NATO's involvement, including Prime Minister Putin, UN Ambassador Vitaly Churkin, and Foreign Minister Lavrov.[53] Thus, Russia's abstention from the UNSC Resolution 1973 was "the result of a compromise between the centers of power of Russian foreign policy."[54] Prior to the vote on UNSC Resolution 1973, the dismissal of Russia's Ambassador to Libya, Vladimir Chamov, who opposed the intervention, underscored the internal divisions in Russian foreign policy. Chamov later compared the justifications used by NATO to those invoked "as a pretext for invading Iraq" and argued that supporting the intervention would equate to "betraying Russian interests."[55] A former intelligence officer in Russia with deep ties in Libya stated that "the Russian position was unexpected," considering the tendency of the Russian elite to oppose intervention against a "legally standing government."[56] The deep divisions over the Russian abstention were echoed in the Duma on 23 March, when all three opposition factions criticized President Medvedev for Russia's failure to use its veto on the 17 March Libya resolution.[57] For many in Russia, the main threat associated with the Libyan operation was the precedent of turning military intervention into a universal tool for overthrowing undesirable regimes.[58]

The operation to establish a no-fly zone devolved into a protracted conflict as NATO exceeded its mandate, eventually violating the arms embargo of Resolution 1970 as well as the limits and purpose stipulated in Resolution 1973.[59] In the aftermath of the intervention, a post-facto narrative that "Russia was deceived" by NATO's assurance that "it would limit itself to controlling Libyan airspace" seemed to be confirmed as the "external military intervention in Libya eventually led to the overthrow of Gaddafi's regime."[60] Within Russia, NATO's Libya intervention affirmed that attempts by extra-regional powers "to impose values by force, even under the most noble pretexts, are fraught with a slide towards instability in international affairs."[61] Vitaly Naumkin, Russia's leading expert on the Middle East, remarked that the results from the NATO campaign in Libya "sharpened the question of the legitimacy, permissibility, and conditions for intervention in internal conflicts by extra-regional forces, including those with the declared humanitarian goal of protecting the civilian population."[62]

NATO's campaign in Libya culminated in Gaddafi's violent overthrow, confirming Russian and Iranian suspicions that Western humanitarian rhetoric could mask a broader agenda of regime change in countries opposing their interests. As chronicled in Chapter 4, when the Arab Spring reached Syria in the spring of 2011, the widespread chaos resulting from the Libya intervention largely predetermined Moscow's negative attitude towards attempts to intervene in Syria.[63] With multiple Western countries demanding the resignation of Syrian President Bashar Assad due to his regime's repression, Russian elites grew inexorably vocal in their opposition to any Western-led regime change.[64] Similarly, Tehran's narrative about the Arab Spring took a sharp turn after the violence escalated in Syria. The possibility of intervention against the Syrian regime, Tehran's closest regional ally, sharpened the tension between Iran's revolutionary transnationalism and its concerns about regime survival.[65]

Concurrent with these developments, Russia's domestic political scene became a theater of mass protests following the 2011 Duma elections, the lower house of the Russian parliament. The protests, which became known as the Bolotnaya movement, erupted after Vladimir Putin's United Russia party secured a controversial victory in elections for the State Duma. Tens of thousands of citizens flooded the streets of Moscow and other major cities, with Bolotnaya Square emerging as the symbolic heart of the movement. While protesters primarily demanded electoral reform and challenged alleged voting irregularities, the Kremlin viewed these events through a different lens. Drawing parallels with the Color Revolutions in neighboring states and the Arab Spring, Russian authorities interpreted the protests not merely as expressions of domestic discontent but as evidence of a Western-orchestrated strategy to foment regime change.

Regime Security and Power Transitions

In 2012, Putin's four years as prime minister—a scheme designed to maintain a veneer of democracy by formally adhering to the constitutional limit of two consecutive presidential terms—were over. As prime minister, Putin had sat back and watched his handpicked protégé, Dmitry Medvedev, attempt a reset with the West. This reset ultimately failed. In Putin's eyes, what emerged from the reset was a further sense of Western betrayal, rampant instability in the Middle East, and a Russia still considered weak on the international stage. The provision within the Russian Constitution preventing two consecutive presidential terms no longer constrained Putin. In September 2011, when Medvedev revealed his decision not to pursue re-election, he recommended that his mentor, Putin, should once again vie for the presidency. In a move that surprised no one, Putin heeded Medvedev's suggestion and declared his candidacy for the 2012 presidential election.

The declaration of Putin's return to the presidential race triggered a chain reaction, intensifying perceptions of electoral malpractices that emerged during the December legislative elections for the Russian State Duma. Public grievances over electoral fraud, political corruption, and the erosion of civil liberties culminated in a series of anti-government protests in Moscow and St. Petersburg, spanning 2011-12. Putin was particularly critical of the United States and Western countries, accusing them of interference and meddling in Russia's internal affairs under the pretext of supporting democracy. In the wake of the protests, the Russian political discourse gravitated towards a fortified interpretation of "sovereign democracy"—a concept that originally emerged in the early 2000s under the tutelage of political strategist Vladislav Surkov. Rooted in the principle of national sovereignty, the concept of "sovereign democracy" argues for a model of governance tailored to Russia's unique historical, cultural, and political context rather than adhering to what is perceived as Western democratic norms and values.[66]

The convergence of Russia's 2011-12 electoral protests, the Arab Spring upheavals, and the looming threat of Western military intervention in Syria crystallized the Kremlin's fears of coordinated regime change operations targeting Moscow and its allies.[67] Russian officials began drawing parallels between the Arab Spring and the 2011-12 Bolotnaya protests, framing both as examples of Western interference akin to the Color Revolutions. This narrative later served to justify Russia's support for Assad in Syria, portraying him as a bastion of state sovereignty against foreign intervention.[68]

Ahead of the presidential election in March 2012, Putin penned a detailed exposition of his foreign policy vision in *Moskovskie Novosti*, foreshadowing Russia's future foreign policy path. Putin's article reflected key elements of Russian foreign policy: a vigorous defense of Russian sovereignty, resistance to foreign meddling, and concerns over Western efforts to isolate Moscow internationally.[69] He argued forcefully for a formidable and autonomous Russia, suggesting that "respect and consideration for Russia manifest only when it demonstrates strength and steadfast independence."[70] Expressing his long-held skepticism towards the West, Putin declared that "the Americans have become obsessed with the idea of becoming absolutely invulnerable."[71] Putin declared that "we cannot allow anyone to realize the 'Libya scenario' in Syria."[72]

The violent and undignified manner of Gaddafi's demise had a profound impact on Putin, resonating with him personally.[73]

Widespread dissemination of the images and videos of Gaddafi's brutal end, having been beaten and humiliated by his captors, elicited further concerns about external interference. As prime minister, Putin did not shy away from expressing his disagreements with Medvedev. After Medvedev decided not to veto the Libya resolution, Putin voiced his disagreement publicly, comparing the resolution to a "medieval call to the crusades." With his impending return to power, Putin would follow through with the promise of preventing a "Libya scenario" in Syria.

* * *

Under Medvedev, the Russia-Iran relationship entered one of its most challenging phases in contemporary times. The downturn can largely be attributed to Moscow's endorsement of UN sanctions against Iran in 2010, compounded by Russia's decision to cancel the delivery of the S-300 air defense system. Under Medvedev's tenure as president, Russia was perceived, especially in Tehran, as leaning towards the West, which was evident in Moscow's decisions that adversely impacted its relations with Iran.

The eruption of the Arab Spring in early 2011 transformed the region and redefined both states' foreign policy priorities. Both Russia and Iran, albeit for different reasons, approached the Arab Spring with caution. The perceived threats of externally driven regime change, sparked by the events of the Arab Spring, NATO intervention in Libya, and suspicions surrounding the Duma protests, formed the backdrop against which Russia and Iran found themselves drawn closer together. Simultaneously, the downfall of previously stable regimes in the Middle East during the Arab Spring underscored the critical importance of Russia-Iran relations in countering Western interventionism.[74]

With Putin's return to the presidency in May 2012, Russian foreign policy towards Iran changed significantly. Putin's assertiveness would define Moscow's foreign policy in the coming years, creating an additional incentive for cooperation. In Iran, the election of Hassan Rouhani in 2013 provided Moscow with a more congenial partner than the Ahmadinejad administration. Much like their Iranian counterparts, Russia's leadership began to value the significance of the two nations' bilateral ties. Putin's return to office signaled a potential shift away from Medvedev's approach. With Putin at the helm, a renewed opportunity emerged to recalibrate and strengthen military-technical ties with Tehran, setting the stage for a collaborative phase in Russia-Iran relations.

3

SYRIA DEVOLVES INTO CIVIL WAR

In March 2011, in the southern Syrian city of Daraa, a group of teenagers was arrested and tortured for spray-painting the phrase "Your turn, Doctor" on the walls of their school. Emboldened by the revolutionary tide of the Arab Spring, the teenagers adorned their school walls with a message directed at Bashar Assad—the ophthalmologist turned dictator. The violence unleashed in response to these words laid bare the inherent insecurity of the Syrian regime, revealing a ruler so threatened by the mere whisper of dissent that he would drown his country in blood to silence it.

After news spread of the teenagers' arrest, repeated demands for their release were ignored. Then, on 15 March, locals gathered in protest at the Omari mosque in central Daraa in what would come to be known as the Day of Rage. It was then that the regime's security forces responded with deadly force, killing four people. The subsequent funerals became rallies of resistance, as the crowds of mourners swelled into the thousands, publicly condemning the government and targeting symbols of its authority, such as the Ba'ath Party's offices and enterprises owned by Assad's cousin, Rami Makhlouf. Despite the authorities' attempts to quell the uprising with increased brutality and by cutting off essential services to Daraa, the news of their actions spread rapidly on social media. By

18 March, peaceful protests had spread to Homs, Banias, and parts of Damascus, and by 8 April, the wave of discontent had reached Latakia, Tartus, Idlib, Deir ez-Zor, Raqqa, and Hama.

When security forces opened fire on the demonstrators, more took to the streets. The unrest triggered nationwide protests demanding Assad's resignation. The government's use of force to crush the dissent merely hardened the protesters' resolve. The regime's response to the protests would set the stage for one of the most devastating conflicts in recent history, the Syrian Civil War—a war marked by heinous acts of violence, reports of severe torture, the use of starvation tactics, indiscriminate bombings, and chemical warfare.

* * *

The Syrian uprisings were a response to the greater regional dynamics of the Arab Spring, which diffused across the Middle East.[1] Civilian protests in Syria became a precursor for violence as the Assad regime resorted to military force and repression, which further galvanized mass opposition to his presidency.[2] By the summer of 2011, hundreds of thousands were taking to the streets across the country. Opposition supporters eventually began to take up arms, first to defend themselves and later to expel security forces from their local areas. Violence escalated as rebel brigades were formed to battle government forces. With the establishment of the Free Syrian Army, an umbrella opposition force, in July 2011 and the increase in calls from the international community for Assad's resignation, both Russia and Iran sought to strengthen the Syrian regime against the prospects of regime change.

Russia and Iran were not the sole external actors with stakes in Syria's future. By late 2011, Syria's descent into civil war was accelerating, and the conflict was becoming increasingly internationalized as regional and global powers became more involved. Each had their own agendas and interests in shaping Syria's fate.[3] Turkey, initially hopeful for regime change, supported opposition groups and allowed them to operate from its territory with the aim of weakening Assad's grip on power. The United States, concerned about the humanitarian crisis and the rise of extremist groups, provided support to select rebel factions and Kurdish forces. The Gulf states of Qatar, Saudi Arabia, and the United Arab Emirates (UAE) also played a role in supporting rebel groups. Meanwhile, the emergence of the Islamic State as a formidable force further complicated the conflict as it seized territory in Syria and Iraq.

When Putin reclaimed the presidency in 2012, Russia's ties with Iran regained momentum after the restrained pragmatism of the Medvedev years. The descent of Syria into civil war then turned parallel interests into an active partnership. Between 2011 and 2014, Moscow and Tehran became increasingly enmeshed in the struggle to keep Bashar Assad in power, pursuing the same goal by different paths. Throughout the chapter, the shift in Russian foreign policy towards Iran is juxtaposed with the two states' shared concerns about a Western-led military intervention in Syria. Threat perceptions were fluid, and thus, with the rise of the Islamic State, both Russia and Iran feared that Assad would be overthrown and replaced by radical Islamists. As the chapter progresses, it also sheds light on the nascent attempts to foster overt cooperation between Russia and Iran in Syria, situating Russia's policy within the context of its strained relations with the West after the illegal annexation of Crimea in 2014.

Convergence without Coordination

From 2011 to 2014, Russia and Iran, two of the most influential supporters of the Assad regime, found their interests coalescing in Syria.[4] For Iran, Assad's Syria was a close ally, a conduit for Iran's support to Hezbollah, and a bulwark against Sunni-dominated regimes aligned with the West. For Russia, Assad's Syria was an imperfect partner, a market for arms, and an outpost for influence in the Middle East. Both had their own reasons for alarm.

Russia, in particular, had been critical of the way NATO intervention had led to the ousting of Libyan leader Muammar Gaddafi in 2011. Russian support of the "legitimate" government institutions in Syria was portrayed as an alternative to the destabilization of Libya.[5] The Kremlin viewed the civil war as a struggle between religious extremists and a secular state, similar to Russia's own experiences with Chechen separatism.[6] The rise of the Islamic State intensified fears that Assad's downfall could precipitate an extremist takeover in Syria, with repercussions extending well beyond its borders. Foreign Minister Lavrov articulated this sentiment, stating that if extra-regional states "interfere in Syrian domestic matters, there might be quite considerable consequences for the Middle East," since "destabilizing Syria would have repercussions far beyond its borders."[7]

Tehran drew a sharp distinction between the uprisings in Egypt, Tunisia, and Libya from the unrest in Syria. While Iran initially expressed support for the Arab Spring movements as a popular Islamic Awakening against Western-backed autocrats, it took a markedly different stance on Syria. Iranian officials characterized the Syrian situation not as a genuine popular uprising, but as a foreign conspiracy aimed at destabilizing its key regional ally. They suggested that external forces, particularly the United States, Israel, and some Gulf Arab states, were fomenting unrest to weaken Iranian-aligned partners in the region. In June 2011, just a few months into the uprising, Iran's Supreme Leader Ayatollah Khamenei offered one of the first explicit endorsements of the Syrian government, labeling the unrest a U.S. plot and vowing to back Assad.[8] The Iranian Ambassador to Moscow, Saeed Mahmoud Reza Sajjadi, claimed that the Syrian unrest had been "provoked by Israel and the United States" and warned of the consequences of a NATO operation similar to that in Libya, which was an example of "direct interference in the internal affairs of the country."[9] Similarly, in August 2011, Iranian President Ahmadinejad declared his support for Assad and blamed the unrest on "foreign interference."[10]

The shared antipathy towards Western intervention served as common ground for Russia and Iran. As early as August 2011, the Russian Foreign Ministry stated that "in the Middle East and North Africa region, Russia and Iran have very close approaches."[11] In November 2011, during his tenure as Prime Minister, Putin told Iranian Foreign Minister Salehi that Russia agreed with Iran's criticism of the West's hypocritical treatment of the Arab Spring revolutions, since "those arrogant world powers supported the old regimes in North Africa ... [and then] supported the revolutions that overthrew those regimes."[12]

Despite these converging interests and occasional coordination, there was only limited cooperation between Russia and Iran in Syria in this initial period. Differences in approach and regional ambitions kept full alignment at bay. For instance, Russia, with its United Nations Security Council (UNSC) veto power and international clout, was more successful in leveraging diplomatic channels, whereas Iran largely operated on the ground, through military and paramilitary support. While they were aligned on the need to keep Assad in power, how Russia and Iran pursued this goal differed. Even when Russia and Iran did cooperate during the 2011-14 period, it was far from the coordinated campaign that would emerge with Russia's military intervention in 2015.

Russia and Assad's Syria

On the eve of the civil war, in terms of economic and military cooperation, Russia's relationship with Syria was the closest among Arab states in the Middle East—a legacy of the Cold War. The collapse of the Soviet Union changed Russia's influence in the region. In the words of a former Russian ambassador to the Middle East, "Russia withdrew" from the region. Later, Putin began reevaluating Russia's interests in the Middle East.[13] During this time, Russia's relationship with Syria vacillated in levels of interest. Yet, Syria continued to hold a noteworthy role in Moscow's perception of itself as a great power, as the country hosted one of Russia's only naval facilities outside the former Soviet Union in the coastal city of Tartus.

Russia's initial involvement in the Syrian Civil War can be traced back to October 2011, when, in concert with China, it exercised its veto power in the UNSC to block a resolution condemning the Syrian government's violent suppression of protesters.[14] From then on, Russia blocked subsequent UNSC Resolutions targeting the Syrian government, including measures for sanctions and political transition. In June 2012, Russia helped craft the Geneva Communiqué, which outlined principles to end violence in Syria and establish a transitional government, while carefully ensuring no explicit call for regime change was included. Russia's diplomatic intervention proved crucial later that year when, facing threatened U.S. military action over Syria's alleged chemical weapons use, Moscow brokered an agreement for Syria to surrender its chemical arsenal, effectively preventing American intervention. Again, in 2014, Russia used its diplomatic leverage to block another attempt at the UNSC to refer the Syrian regime to the International Criminal Court.

Alongside this political cover, Russia offered material support to Assad's government. As one of Syria's main arms suppliers, Russia continued to deliver military equipment and ammunition throughout 2012 and 2013. Asserting that its arms sales were to a legitimate government, Russia described the weaponry as "defensive" and claimed to be fulfilling pre-existing contracts with Damascus dating to before the 2011 uprising.[15] Initial support steadily escalated from basic equipment to advanced offensive and defensive systems. These included MiG fighter jets, attack helicopters, armed drones, tanks, short-range missiles, and small arms.[16] The frequent voyages of Tapir-class landing ships from Russia to Syria, dubbed the "Syrian Express" by Russian commentators, highlighted the regularity of military support, with about seven ships making ten trips annually.[17] Despite official denials from the Kremlin, evidence indicated that new military contracts had been signed after the onset of violence, something that was later confirmed by Assad himself in 2015.[18]

Beyond military hardware, Russia provided vital support and personnel. Russia showcased its naval capabilities by deploying its fleet to Tartus on several occasions. However, this was largely symbolic, as Russia had quietly reduced its military presence due to safety concerns by 2013, although Russian personnel continued to operate and maintain Russian military equipment in Syria. Like Iran, Russia aided Syria in navigating sanctions imposed by the international community. In June 2011, the European Union (EU) prohibited an Austrian bank from printing Syrian banknotes, aiming to strangle the Assad regime's access to the international financial system and curtail its capacity to finance its repression. The sanctions quickly achieved their intended effect, triggering a severe shortage of banknotes that threatened to paralyze Syria's financial system and the government's ability to pay salaries. Russia, however, intervened decisively to prop up the Syrian regime, delivering more than 30 tons of newly printed banknotes.[19] Throughout the Assad regime's tenure, the Kremlin's ability to prop up the dictatorship revealed how diplomatic protection and financial lifelines, while crucial in the early years, could not substitute for the decisive military support that ultimately preserved Assad's hold on power through 2024.

Iran and Assad's Syria

Iran's support for Assad stemmed from a deep-seated alliance that predated the Syrian Civil War. Syria was one of the few Arab states that maintained ties with Iran following the Islamic Revolution of 1979, as both opposed Saddam Hussein's Iraq and supported Hezbollah in Lebanon. Over time, Syria emerged as a critical member of the so-called Axis of Resistance—Iran's expansive network of allies and non-state partners that included Hezbollah, various Palestinian factions, Iraqi Shia militias, Yemen's Houthi movement, and other regional non-state actors. In particular, both Iran and Syria were "united by opposition to U.S. hegemonic plans for the reconstruction of the Middle East."[20] As the Syrian Civil War unfolded, Iran emerged as a key lifeline for President Assad's embattled regime.

Economically and politically, the rationale behind Iran's intervention in Syria transcended the exigencies of mere regime fidelity. Despite grappling with domestic economic challenges exacerbated by international sanctions, Iran's leadership perceived the stability of the Assad regime as vital to its long-term regional interests. The economic tribulations of the 2010s did little to deter Tehran's commitment. Through billions in credit facilities, oil supply deals, and logistical support, Iran's extensive financial and military lifeline to Damascus was a deliberate strategy to prevent a power vacuum in Syria that could be exploited by forces hostile to Iran.

Iranian aid was believed to consist of military advisors, financial aid, and weapons. In particular, Major General Qassem Soleimani of the Islamic Revolutionary Guard Corps (IRGC) Quds Force, Iran's elite extraterritorial operations unit, served as the architect of Iran's military and strategic support for Syria.[21] During the uprisings in 2011, the Quds Force provided limited technical and financial support to Assad, which evolved into the deployment of IRGC Ground Forces as the situation deteriorated.[22] In the summer of 2012, the IRGC established the pro-government paramilitary Syrian National Defense Forces from members of the Shabiha, the state-sponsored militia, to support the Syrian Arab Army.[23]

Simultaneously, Iran leveraged its extensive network of partners and non-state allies. Hezbollah bolstered the Assad regime by deploying thousands of its fighters to Syria, particularly in key battles such as the recapture of Qusayr in 2013. Beyond combat operations, Hezbollah provided logistical support and coordination with other pro-Assad militias, acting as a force multiplier for Iran's efforts to secure its ally in Damascus. Iran also established new militias, such as the Fatemiyoun Brigade, composed primarily of Afghan Hazara refugees living in Iran. By exploiting their vulnerable status, the IRGC recruited and deployed thousands of these fighters to Syria, often in exchange for legal residency and other benefits in Iran. Iraqi Shia militias, including elements of the Popular Mobilization Forces (PMF), became a crucial pillar of Iran's network, with a primary focus on operations along the Syrian-Iraqi border. Collectively, these IRGC-affiliated groups not only provided additional manpower but also helped establish a coveted land corridor linking Iran to Syria and Lebanon.

Iran's support of the Assad regime during the conflict did not involve the direct participation of Iranian forces in combat until 2014. However, as the regime faced escalating challenges from the advances of the umbrella Syrian opposition, Iran abandoned its previous approach of indirect military intervention in Syria. Thousands of fighters from the IRGC Quds Force soon arrived in Syria to support Assad.

Between 2011 and 2014, Iran found itself excluded from the efforts by the United Nations (UN) to resolve the Syrian conflict, largely due to objections from states over Iran's unwavering support for the Assad regime. Unlike the criticism over Russian abstention in Libya, Iran consistently praised Russia's use of its veto as "a positive move aimed at blocking the path of the perilous Western countries' plans for intervention in the Middle East."[24] In contrast to the position of the U.S. and the Gulf monarchies, Russia vocally advocated for Iranian involvement in peace talks. The Russian government's position was that any comprehensive and long-lasting solution to the Syrian crisis could not be achieved without the involvement of all of the key players in the region, including Iran. However, it would not be until Russia's 2015 military intervention, detailed in Chapter 4, that Iran would secure a place at the table.

The Red Line

In August 2012, President Obama articulated the U.S. threshold for military intervention in the Syrian Civil War: "We have been very clear to the Assad regime, but also to other players on the ground, that a red line for us is [when] we start seeing a whole bunch of chemical weapons moving around or being utilized."[25] This declaration established a clear escalatory framework—the use of chemical weapons would cross an unacceptable threshold that violated international law and demanded an American military response. Obama's "red line" represented more than mere rhetoric; it was a public commitment that staked U.S. credibility on preventing the normalization of chemical weapons use in modern warfare. The statement also served as a warning to Russia and Iran, Assad's primary backers, that their client's actions could trigger direct American military intervention.[26]

One year after Obama's "red line," the specter of American military intervention loomed large with the news of a chemical attack in Eastern Ghouta, outside of Damascus. In August 2013, the Assad regime launched a devastating chemical weapons assault on Eastern Ghouta that resulted in around 1,300 civilian fatalities. The Eastern Ghouta chemical attack was not the first time the Assad regime had used chemical weapons. In fact, in March 2013, a previous chemical incident near Aleppo led the UN to initiate an investigative mission. However, it was the Eastern Ghouta atrocity that ignited intense debate within the United States over the necessity of retaliatory military action against Syria, thus lending weight to President Obama's prior declaration of his administration's "red line."

Map 1: Administrative Divisions of Syria (Governorates)

The Russian government attributed the Eastern Ghouta attack to militants and suggested that it was a premeditated provocation.[27] However, behind the scenes, Russia was critical of the Syrian regime. One Russian expert on the Middle East argued that the use of chemical weapons demonstrated to Moscow that "Assad cannot be controlled."[28] A former Russian diplomat suggested that Assad's weakness had led the Syrian government to engage in "irresponsible" actions in an effort for Assad to be seen as a "strong man."[29]

Multiple Russian experts and officials noted that throughout August and September 2013, Russia was "convinced" that the U.S. would strike militarily in response to Assad's horrific use of chemical weapons.[30] Viewed from Moscow, a military strike against Assad or the imposition of a no-fly zone would pave the way for a larger intervention, potentially leading to regime change in Damascus and "unleashing radical elements" in Syria.[31] Given the U.S. subversion of the UNSC in Iraq and NATO's broad interpretation of the Libya UNSC Resolution, former Foreign Minister Igor Ivanov cautioned against "assuming that if Russia and China exercise their veto power on the UNSC," that the U.S. would not pursue an intervention. Ivanov recalled that U.S. actions in Yugoslavia and Iraq "created dangerous precedents for circumventing the UN in violation of principles of international law."[32]

Fearing a repeat of the "Libyan scenario," Russia undertook decisive diplomatic measures to avert a similar outcome in Syria.[33] Foreign Minister Lavrov proposed eliminating Syria's chemical weapons arsenal.[34] Under the agreement, Syria would accede to the Chemical Weapons Convention, declare its chemical weapons stockpile, and submit it to the Organization for the Prohibition of Chemical Weapons (OPCW) for inspection and destruction.[35] The United States, initially skeptical, saw value in the proposition because it offered a means to achieve the goal of eliminating Syria's chemical weapons without resorting to military action.[36] Behind closed doors, Iran allegedly helped persuade Assad to accept the joint Russia-U.S. initiative and to place the country's chemical weapons stockpile under international control.[37]

Russian cooperation with the U.S. served the dual purpose of preventing U.S. military action and cementing its position as an indispensable arbitrator in Middle Eastern diplomacy.[38] A former Russian ambassador to Libya confirmed in a 2017 interview that Russia's cooperation on the Syrian chemical weapons agreement was driven primarily by a desire to prevent a punitive military strike against Syria.[39] The chemical weapons agreement was seen as a "major diplomatic victory for Russia" that enabled "diplomatic solutions to prevail over the logic of pressure and unilateral intervention."[40] For some in Moscow, the success of the chemical weapons agreement demonstrated the weaknesses of U.S. leadership in the Middle East and reinforced the importance of Russia stepping forward to shape regional diplomacy.[41]

Tides of Change in Iran

The chemical weapons agreement coincided with political changes in Iran following Hassan Rouhani's accession to the presidency. Rouhani, a pragmatic cleric who had previously negotiated arms deals with the Russians as Secretary of Iran's Supreme National Security Council (SNSC), was seen as a moderate alternative to Ahmadinejad. Rouhani's victory, predicated on promises of domestic and international reform, signaled a potential shift in Iran's nuclear policy, though its immediate impact on Syria was minimal.[42] Despite the economic stakes involved, the consensus within the Iranian leadership remained firm on supporting Assad militarily and politically.

In September 2013, Rouhani embarked on his first state visit abroad for the Shanghai Cooperation Organization (SCO) summit in Bishkek, where he met with Russian President Putin.[43] During the Putin-Rouhani meeting, the newly elected president expressed Tehran's desire "to expand and develop" bilateral relations, including "active consultations … on regional issues … in the Middle East."[44] Rouhani lauded the Russian proposal for the removal of chemical weapons from Syria and proclaimed that the conflict "can only be solved politically and through dialogue between the Syrian government and the opposition without a foreign military intervention."[45] The meeting between Putin and Rouhani would be the first of many as Russia and Iran intensified their cooperation over Syria. For Russia, it had become apparent "that events in the Middle East will inevitably make Iran's positions stronger," thus reaffirming the importance of having "strong relations with one of the most influential countries in the region."[46]

One of the most significant early developments of Rouhani's presidency was the revival of nuclear negotiations with the P5+1 (the five permanent members of the UNSC plus Germany). The resumption of nuclear talks came at a critical juncture for Iran, as its economy was reeling under the weight of severe international sanctions. These punitive measures, targeting Iran's vital oil exports and restricting its access to global financial systems, had pushed the country to the brink of economic collapse. Recognizing the urgent need for economic relief, Rouhani saw the nuclear talks as a potential pathway to not only resolve the longstanding dispute over Iran's nuclear program but also to secure much-needed sanctions relief. His administration hoped that a diplomatic breakthrough would pave the way for Iran's reintegration into the global economy, allowing the country to revitalize its struggling industries and stabilize its financial markets.

Russia, for its part, welcomed Iran's renewed commitment to diplomacy with cautious optimism. The Kremlin had grown progressively concerned during the Ahmadinejad era when diplomatic efforts had largely stagnated. Of particular concern to Moscow was the possibility that either the U.S. or Israel would undertake military action to impede Iran's nuclear advancements, unleashing a new wave of instability in the region. Furthermore, Russia saw the revival of diplomatic dialogue as strategically beneficial; by positioning itself as a pivotal mediator, Moscow could protect its economic interests and emphasize its indispensability in shaping diplomatic outcomes, particularly regarding Iran's nuclear program.

Under President Hassan Rouhani, diplomatic negotiations between Iran and the P5+1 resumed in earnest in October 2013. These negotiations rapidly advanced in Geneva, resulting in a significant breakthrough with the signing of the Joint Plan of Action (JPOA) in November 2013. This interim agreement required Iran to implement specific constraints on its nuclear program in exchange for limited economic relief. Specifically, Iran committed to halting the enrichment of uranium beyond 5 percent, neutralizing its stockpile of near-20 percent enriched uranium, and agreeing to more rigorous inspections by the International Atomic Energy Agency (IAEA). In return, the P5+1 agreed to provide Iran with limited but reversible sanctions relief. The interim agreement marked a major breakthrough toward a comprehensive settlement of the Iranian nuclear issue that paved the way for the Iran nuclear deal in 2015.

Geneva not only hosted P5+1 negotiations on the Iranian nuclear issue but was also the venue for the next round of negotiations on the Syrian settlement. After the success of the chemical weapons agreement and building on the momentum of the interim nuclear agreement, Moscow seized the opportunity to shape the political settlement in Syria by pushing for Iran's involvement in the upcoming talks on Syria. Highlighting Tehran's pivotal relationship with the Assad regime, Russia argued that excluding Iran would undermine the viability of any political settlement.

Geneva II

The Syrian Civil War saw various international efforts attempting to restore peace, notably the Geneva talks sponsored by the UN. In June 2012, during the first round of Geneva talks, Russia lobbied to ensure the Geneva Communiqué made no mention of regime change in Syria. The communiqué called for a political transition, constitutional reform, and eventual elections in Syria, but, most importantly, it did not explicitly demand Assad's immediate removal from power. Russia's insistence on this point during the negotiations allowed for the possibility of Assad playing a role in the transition process, even if his authority would be diminished. The ambiguity in language paved the way for a broad interpretation that struck a balance between Assad's supporters and those calling for his removal.[47]

By the time of the Geneva II conference in January and February 2014, the debate on regional participation was intensifying. Russia, aware of Iran's sway over the Assad regime, began advocating for its involvement in November 2013.[48] Iran's invitation to the talks was highly controversial. Initially invited by UN Secretary-General Ban Ki-moon, the invitation saw pushback from the U.S. due to Iran's failure to endorse the Geneva I Communiqué and the invitation was withdrawn.[49]

The Russian Foreign Ministry issued a critical statement, stating that Moscow was "disappointed by the decision of the UN Secretary-General to withdraw an invitation to Iran" because "all key states that influence the development of events in Syria should take part in [Geneva II]," including Iran, which could have played "a significant role in advancing the peace process."[50] Deputy Russian Foreign Minister Gennady Gatilov condemned the U.S. insistence on Iran's acceptance of preconditions because Tehran "could play an important, constructive role" and "should take part in the peace conference alongside the other countries of that region."[51] Later, in a meeting with his American counterpart in January 2014, Foreign Minister Lavrov argued that it would be a "mistake" not to include "all regional countries who influence the situation, including Iran."[52] During his visit to Moscow in mid-January, Iranian Foreign Minister Mohammad Javad Zarif stated that "based on the sense of dignity and honor for our country, [Iran] cannot accept any preconditions for its participation [in Geneva II]" since "Iran has an important role in this region and one cannot ignore this role."[53]

In Geneva, the lack of representation by regional stakeholders, combined with the inflexibility of the government and opposition, rendered the talks a failure. The conflict in approaches and between parties meant that the Geneva II conference was "dead on arrival."[54] The inability to reach an agreement in Geneva prompted the resignation of veteran diplomat Lakhdar Brahimi as UN envoy to Syria. After Geneva II, the ensuing diplomatic stalemate would continue until Moscow's entry into the war in late September 2015, which both shifted the balance of power in Assad's favor and provided the impetus for new negotiations.

Little Green Men

As simultaneous diplomatic initiatives were playing out in Geneva on Syria and Iran's nuclear program, a new crisis was emerging between Russia and Ukraine. In November 2013, Ukrainian President Viktor Yanukovych abruptly abandoned a long-negotiated association agreement with the European Union, opting instead for closer ties with Moscow. This reversal, seen by many Ukrainians as a betrayal of the country's European aspirations, ignited the Euromaidan protests in Kyiv. Over the ensuing weeks, the demonstrations grew larger and more fervent, uniting diverse social and political groups under the call for governmental accountability and a decisive break from Russia's influence. By February 2014, the movement's momentum forced Yanukovych to flee the capital and ultimately seek refuge in Russia. Soon, unmarked soldiers in green uniforms—whom Russia euphemistically labeled "little green men"—appeared across the Crimean Peninsula. These "little green men" seized government buildings, airports, and key communication nodes, effectively cutting off Crimea from the rest of Ukraine. While the Kremlin initially sought to conceal its role, it quickly dispensed with plausible deniability once it became clear that Russian forces were directing operations on the ground.

In a matter of days, local pro-Russian factions staged a hastily organized referendum in March 2014. Based on disputed results, Russia declared that Crimea had "voted" to join the Russian Federation, an action widely denounced by Ukraine, Western governments, and numerous international organizations as illegal and illegitimate. Notably, Russia's illegal annexation of Crimea took place almost simultaneously with Geneva II, a conference where Moscow staunchly advocated Syrian sovereignty. Although Russia repeatedly proclaimed its adherence to international law in Syria, it relied on a mix of quasi-legal arguments, historically distorted narratives, and outright falsehoods to legitimize its annexation of Crimea. Rather than an aberration, Russia's presumption of limited sovereignty over Ukraine was an outgrowth of Moscow's arcane conviction in its "right" to a sphere of influence as a great power. Meanwhile, the annexation of Crimea and the separatist conflict in Eastern Ukraine elevated more hardline views associated with the *siloviki* in the Russian foreign policy establishment.

Iran's position on the 2014 annexation of Crimea was tied to ongoing negotiations on its nuclear program. Officials in Tehran were acutely aware of the potential for the Ukraine crisis to divert attention from the P5+1 negotiations and to jeopardize any progress on reaching an agreement. Iran's absence from the March 2014 United Nations General Assembly (UNGA) vote on Ukraine's territorial integrity and its moderate response rather than outright support of Russian action indicated the delicate balance Tehran was attempting to strike. At an official level, Iran called for non-interference by extra-regional powers yet strayed from aligning with either Russia or the "West" on the Crimea issue.[55] An Iranian Foreign Ministry spokeswoman warned that "foreign interference in Ukraine's developments can deepen conflict and worsen the situation," while Ali Larijani, speaker of Iran's parliament, stated that Iran would "remain neutral on the issue."[56] Iran's Ambassador to Moscow, Mehdi Sanaei, stressed that Iran is "against the interference by foreign countries," adding that "issues that arise in a region should be resolved within a region."[57]

Societal and elite-level reactions to Russian action revealed a wider plurality of opinions as well as the lingering mistrust of Russia among the Iranian population. In Iran, responses to the Crimean annexation varied from calls for adopting a policy of "positive neutrality" to censuring Russia as retribution for historical grievances.[58] Reformist voices pointed to the hypocrisy of Moscow's position in Syria and Ukraine, noting that "Russia's passionate defense of Syria's independence and territorial integrity and the condemnation of foreign intervention in [Syria] conflicts with Russia's military invasion into Ukrainian sovereignty."[59] Others sought to portray the events in Ukraine as "interconnected with Syria," since Western interference in Ukraine occurred "several days after the failure of Geneva II's political plot against Syria," which proved that the U.S. was using its leverage in Ukraine to place Russia under pressure.[60]

The annexation of Crimea not only strained Russia's relations with the West but also sparked more enthusiasm in Russia for its relations with Tehran. The speaker of the State Duma, Sergey Naryshkin, described Iran as a "reliable, promising partner," noting that both countries are "equally critical of the toxic actions of Western countries," which pursue "geopolitical interests" without consideration of "the norms of international law" by intervening in the "internal affairs of sovereign states."[61] In an op-ed for *Rossiyskaya Gazeta*, former Foreign Minister Ivanov highlighted "Russia's interest … to maintain current friendly relations with our southern neighbor" and to intensify relations to a "qualitatively new level" as a means of corresponding to the "new realities" of the world.[62] Likewise, the editor-in-chief of *Natsional'naya Oborona* Igor Korotchenko argued that Iran could become a major and "reliable" new partner in military cooperation in the face of the aggravation of relations with the West.[63]

The initial wave of Western sanctions imposed after Crimea's annexation created an unexpected bond between Moscow and Tehran, as both nations found themselves increasingly isolated from Western-dominated financial and technological systems. These restrictions not only drew direct parallels between the Russian and

Iranian predicaments but also demonstrated that both states had chosen to "refuse to play according to the old Western rules."[64] This shared experience of economic punishment became a cornerstone of bilateral cooperation, with Moscow turning to Tehran for expertise in sanctions evasion—a collaboration detailed extensively in Chapters 6 and 9.

While Russia decried Western interference in the Middle East, Moscow's violation of Ukrainian sovereignty followed its imperialistic policies that would lead to its full-scale invasion in Chapter 8. From exerting pressure with coercive diplomacy to direct military interventions, Russia has repeatedly exercised discretion in its approach to the sovereignty of states in the so-called "near abroad." Ukraine was no exception. The discrepancy between Russia's invocation of sovereignty in Syria and its disregard for sovereignty in Ukraine underlined the hypocrisy in Moscow's foreign policy. More broadly, Russia's annexation of Crimea intensified its resolve to oppose Western dominance and challenge the foundations of the liberal international order.[65]

The Rise of the Islamic State

The dramatic rise of the Islamic State in Iraq and its expansion into Syria diverted attention from Russia's encroachment into Ukraine. Emerging from its roots as an al-Qaeda offshoot during the U.S. occupation of Iraq, the group rebranded itself as the Islamic State of Iraq and Syria. Exploiting the power vacuum left by the Syrian Civil War and Iraq's political instability, the Islamic State seized vast territories in both countries, capturing major cities such as Mosul in Iraq before proclaiming a Caliphate. Their swift expansion prompted a noticeable shift in the Russian discourse towards the Syrian Civil War, as Moscow used the threat of terrorism as a pretext for supporting "legitimate" government institutions. Up until late 2013 to early 2014, Russia framed its support of Assad through its adherence to the principle of sovereign inviolability because extra-regional interventions resulted in regional instability. With the growth of the Islamic State, Moscow invoked the spread of terrorism to the countries along Russia's southern tier as a justification for supporting the Syrian government. Officials and elites vacillated between portraying the conflict in Syria as a struggle against international terrorism and as a struggle against externally orchestrated regime change—the former represented a national security threat while the latter reflected a broader precedent.

In September 2014, the threat of the Islamic State also prompted the U.S. and several Arab allies—Bahrain, Jordan, Qatar, the UAE, and Saudi Arabia—to carry out airstrikes against the group within Syrian territory.[66] In response, Russia stated that any airstrikes "should not be carried out without the consent of the Syrian government" or the UNSC, while Iran called the strikes an "illegal" act against a sovereign state.[67] Ivanov questioned whether the U.S. had learned from "the experience of military actions in Iraq, Libya, and Afghanistan" because "without the participation of Syria, Iran, and Russia, the problem of Islamic extremism in the Middle East cannot be solved."[68] More hardline voices in Russia interpreted the U.S. airstrikes in Iraq and Syria as an attempt to invade Syria and overthrow Assad under the pretext of fighting terrorism.[69]

Though overshadowed by the unfolding developments in Syria and Iraq, Putin met with Rouhani during the Caspian Sea summit in the Russian city of Astrakhan on 29 September 2014.[70] One of the key topics of their discussion was strategizing their combined efforts to counter the growth of militant extremist factions like the Islamic State.[71] The meeting was, in many ways, emblematic of the deepening relationship between Russia and Iran and their unified approach toward the crisis in Syria.[72] In his meeting with Putin, Rouhani stated that Iran shared the Russian position that the most effective response to rampant chaos and terrorism was to strengthen Assad.[73] Both leaders expressed similar concerns about the U.S.-led involvement in fighting the Islamic State in Syria, arguing that it would only make matters worse and trigger the emergence of more terrorist groups. More broadly, the position advanced by Russia and Iran underscored that the U.S.-led campaign against "militants in Syria" had been launched without "the permission of the government in Damascus," which was in "violation of the norms of international law."[74]

In late December 2014, Russia's Supreme Court and Prosecutor General's Office designated the Islamic State and al-Qaeda affiliated Jabhat al-Nusra as terrorist organizations, officially banning them from Russia.[75] As the problem with terrorism intensified, Russia repeatedly called for the creation of a coalition under the auspices of the UNSC to cooperate with the Syrian authorities in the fight against terrorism. At the same time, Russian officials underscored their view that Damascus's forces represented the only credible defense against the Islamic State and other terrorist organizations.[76] Meanwhile, concerns mounted over recruits flocking to the Islamic State from Russia and nearby states. One expert opined that "apart from 2,400 militants from Russia, the Islamic State has recruited around 2,600-4,500 militants from other post-Soviet republics, primarily located in Central Asia, to fight for it in Syria and Iraq," warning of the "growing prospects for the radical external influence of Islam."[77]

From the Kremlin's perspective, Western policies in the Middle East were to blame for the Islamic State's rise. Russian Senator Alexei Pushkov attributed the expansion of the Islamic State to Western interference, arguing that "the 'reset' did not die because of Ukraine, it died because of Syria ... by helping the anti-Assad coalition, America and the West were cultivating a new monster in the Middle East."[78] Yet, the escalating terrorist threat also offered Russia a calculated opportunity to reengage with the West and mitigate the diplomatic isolation that followed its annexation of Crimea. By framing Syria as the frontline in the global fight against international terrorism, Moscow aimed to position itself as a necessary partner in addressing shared security challenges while subtly shifting the narrative away from the contentious issues that had strained relations.

Ultimately, the meteoric rise of the Islamic State reshaped calculations for both Russia and Iran. Alarmed by the potential spillover of extremist ideology, Moscow and Tehran converged on a common conviction that only a reinforced Syrian state could stem the tide of radicalism. Their mutual concerns paved the way for deeper military cooperation in the years that followed, as each pursued more assertive measures to prop up the Assad government and safeguard its own regional interests.

* * *

The period from 2011 to 2014 marked an evolution in the relationship between Russia and Iran, primarily catalyzed by the unfolding crisis in Syria. As the Syrian Civil War escalated from peaceful protests to a full-scale conflict, both Moscow and Tehran found their interests aligned in supporting the Assad regime. This convergence of interests, however, did not immediately translate into coordinated action, as both countries pursued their own strategies and maintained distinct approaches to the conflict. Russia's involvement in Syria during this period was characterized by diplomatic maneuvering and material support. Moscow used its position on the UNSC to shield Assad from international pressure, while simultaneously providing military equipment and economic assistance. Iran, on the other hand, took a more direct approach, offering financial aid, military advisors, and eventually deploying IRGC forces and proxy militias to bolster Assad's forces on the ground. Although their support for the Assad regime was complementary, it lacked significant coordination in these early stages.

The 2014 annexation of Crimea marked a crucial turning point in Russia's international position and, by extension, its relationship with Iran. Facing Western sanctions and diplomatic isolation, Moscow's foreign policy underwent a significant shift, increasingly influenced by hardline elements like the *siloviki*. This development made Russia more receptive to deepening its cooperation with Tehran, as both found themselves as vanguards against Western pressure and efforts to undermine regime stability.

With the rise of the Islamic State, Russia and Iran began to frame their involvement in Syria as part of a broader struggle against terrorism, positioning Assad's government as a bulwark against extremism. As Assad's grip on power weakened and his forces suffered significant territorial losses, the stage was set for an even deeper alignment between Moscow and Tehran. The prospect of regime collapse in Damascus presented both powers with an existential threat to their regional interests, compelling them to consider more direct and coordinated forms of intervention. Looking ahead to Chapter 4, this evolution in Russian-Iranian relations would culminate in their joint military campaign to preserve Assad's rule. This unprecedented level of cooperation would not only prove decisive in altering the course of the Syrian Civil War but would also fundamentally reshape the bilateral relationship between Moscow and Tehran.

4

SAVING ASSAD

RUSSIA AND IRAN'S MILITARY CAMPAIGN

In October 2015, Russia launched a salvo of twenty-six Kalibr cruise missiles from the Caspian Sea, sending them on a 1,500 km journey across Iranian and Iraqi airspace to strike Islamic State and opposition targets in Raqqa, Aleppo, and Idlib.[1] The mission marked the combat debut of the Kalibr missile, showcasing Moscow's newfound long-range precision-strike capabilities—an area where it had once lagged behind the West.[2] Yet the launches also heralded something larger: the start of Russia's military campaign in Syria—the first sustained deployment of Russian forces beyond the post-Soviet space.

As Russia touted its military capabilities, Iran's Islamic Republic News Agency (IRNA) reported that an unknown flying object had crashed in a village in northwest Iran.[3] Shortly thereafter, unnamed officials from the U.S. Department of Defense alleged that four of the launched missiles had crashed in Iran, implying that some of the missiles had failed to reach their intended targets in Syria. Both the Russian and Iranian governments refuted these allegations, firmly denying any incidents of missile crashes.[4] Conservative Iranian media described the reports of missiles landing in Iran as "psychological operations by the U.S. against Moscow."[5] In response,

Russia released video footage purportedly showing all twenty-six Kalibr launches and their impacts, using the visuals to reinforce its narrative of technical precision and success. Yet the footage lacked basic verification markers—such as timestamps or geolocation data—leaving its authenticity impossible to confirm independently.[6]

Before Russia's military intervention, Assad's grip in Syria was weakening. Russian intelligence reports suggested that Damascus maintained control over a mere 10 to 20 percent of the national territory. The Islamic State advanced aggressively through southern and central Syria, pushing steadily toward the north and west. Simultaneously, Jabhat al-Nusra, the al-Qaeda affiliate, expanded its influence across northwestern and southwestern regions. In the north, Kurdish forces were actively consolidating their territorial holdings, particularly through the newly formed Syrian Democratic Forces—a multiethnic coalition established in October 2015 under Kurdish leadership that rapidly secured strategic regions along the Turkish border and established parallel governance structures in territories abandoned by retreating government forces. This three-pronged pressure from opposing forces compelled the Assad regime to abandon peripheral areas and concentrate its dwindling resources on defending major population centers crucial to its survival.

Starting on 30 September 2015, Russia's military intervention heralded a new chapter in the Syrian Civil War. In little over a year, not only did the Assad regime manage to hold its ground but it also launched successful retaliatory strikes and reclaimed territories that had previously been lost. Behind the regime's territorial gains was the military support of its two external patrons: Russia and Iran. This chapter examines Russian and Iranian military cooperation in Syria, including the joint command and control structures, internal deliberations, and campaign strategy to capture the vital city of Aleppo. While the intervention in Syria deepened ties between Russia and Iran, it also revealed the growing pains of a relationship in transition, as the two countries adjusted to the realities of sustained collaboration.

Iran's Overtures

In the months leading up to the Russian intervention in Syria, a series of high-level meetings between Russian and Iranian officials established the basis for a coordinated strategy to support Assad. Throughout late 2014 and into 2015, Tehran sent a stream of envoys to coax Moscow into joining its Syrian campaign. Initially, the Kremlin was wary of becoming mired in an unpredictable and potentially open-ended conflict in the Middle East. The financial and military costs of a full-scale intervention were not negligible, especially as the Russian economy was already reeling from low oil prices and Western sanctions imposed after the annexation of Crimea. Moreover, the potential for success had to be weighed against the risk of becoming bogged down in a prolonged conflict with no clear exit strategy.

Sergey Shoigu's visit to Iran in January 2015 marked an important milestone, being the first visit by a Russian Minister of Defense to Tehran in over fifteen years.[7] The high-level engagement culminated in signing an intergovernmental agreement on bilateral military-technical cooperation and the establishment of a Joint Russia-Iran Commission among their General Staffs, which Shoigu hailed as "a significant step in strengthening relations" between Russia and Iran.[8] According to a Russian defense expert, the comprehensive agreement laid the groundwork for enhancing military collaboration and mending the bilateral arms relationship after the controversy over the cancellation of the S-300 air defense system.[9] The terms of the agreement included arrangements for shared training exercises and military drills designed to enhance military-to-military channels between Russia and Iran, including arrangements for port visits and joint naval maneuvers. It also included provisions for cooperation in the fight against terrorism, such as intelligence sharing. The agreement specifically addressed military-to-military logistics—a stipulation that was put into full use with Iran's assistance for Russia's efforts in transferring equipment to Syria.

Shortly after Shoigu's visit, Ali Akbar Velayati—foreign policy advisor to Supreme Leader Ayatollah Khamenei—arrived in Moscow to meet with President Putin and Shoigu.[10] Velayati's mission was to deliver a personal letter from Khamenei exploring the possibility of Russian military intervention in Syria and to advocate for a face-to-face meeting between Russian military officials and Quds Force commander Qassem Soleimani. In January and February 2015, Soleimani had unsuccessfully requested such meetings in Moscow to stress the deteriorating situation in Syria; rebuffed at first, he settled for discussions with Foreign Minister Sergey Lavrov during his March 2015 visit to Tehran.[11] At the time, Moscow remained circumspect; however, the loss of Syrian territory, along with a series of Islamic State victories, triggered a reassessment in Moscow.

Russia's receptiveness to Iran's outreach occurred against the backdrop of a rebel resurgence in northwest and southern Syria, combined with an Islamic State offensive in the northeast.[12] These military campaigns led to the rapid reduction of the territory controlled by the Syrian government throughout the spring of 2015. Following the Islamic State's advance into Palmyra, "the threat that the regime in Damascus may fall and the country may break up [became] increasingly more real."[13] By July 2015, the regime's tenuous hold on power compelled Assad to publicly announce that the Syrian Arab Army lacked the necessary resources to contain the rebel advance and would thus focus on defending the most critical areas.[14]

From 24 to 26 July, Soleimani covertly met with Putin and Shoigu in Moscow to coordinate the military operation in Syria.[15] Soleimani's visit was shrouded in controversy, not only because of the international sanctions—including travel restrictions and asset freezes—imposed on him by the United Nations Security Council (UNSC) but also due to the timing of his visit, which occurred in the immediate aftermath of the landmark agreement on Iran's nuclear program between Iran and the P5+1. As discussed in Chapter 6, Russia was a major contributor to the agreement, resolving contentious issues and offering technical expertise. The controversial timing of Soleimani's Moscow trip was pointedly criticized by Iran's Foreign Minister Zarif, who saw it as undermining the integrity of the nuclear accord. Zarif's comments underscored a clear divide within Iran's political elite: on one side, those like Zarif who advocated for improved relations with the West and a focus on diplomacy, and on the other, factions such as the military and the Islamic Revolutionary Guard Corps (IRGC), which prioritized closer ties with Russia and a security-focused approach to the nation's priorities.[16]

By the time General Soleimani arrived in Moscow in July 2015, Russia had already committed to direct military intervention in Syria.[17] This commitment was solidified after President Assad formally requested Russian involvement on behalf of the Syrian government.[18] During Soleimani's visit, discussions centered on developing a joint strategy to reclaim territory, combining Russian aerial capabilities with ground operations led by Syrian forces, Iranian-backed militias, and IRGC units. The talks also addressed how Russian support would bolster Iran's existing efforts in Syria by supplying additional military hardware and deploying advisors. Their immediate aim was to reclaim territory from various rebel factions and terrorist groups, including the Islamic State, thereby shifting momentum decisively in Assad's favor. Accordingly, both sides agreed on intelligence sharing, logistical support, and the delineation of operational zones.

Shortly after Soleimani's trip to Moscow, Russia began to send Russian-operated warplanes, T-90 tanks, and artillery, as well as combat troops, to an airbase near the port city of Latakia in Syria.[19] During this period, a series of media reports indicated a growing presence of Russian military hardware and personnel on the ground in Syria, which the Russian Foreign Ministry dismissed as "supplying military equipment to official Syrian authorities to fight terrorists."[20] On 26 August, as Russia transported military equipment into Syria, Russia and Syria signed a secret basing agreement for the Khmeimim airbase in northern Syria.[21] By late September, Khmeimim hosted a mixed aviation regiment primarily comprising tactical bombers, attack aircraft, and multirole fighters, numbering approximately 30 to 40 fixed-wing aircraft. These included modernized Su-24M tactical bombers, Su-25SM ground-attack aircraft, and advanced multirole fighters such as the Su-30SM and Su-35S, providing air cover, precision strike capability, and close air support for coalition ground forces. To safeguard these air operations, Russia also deployed sophisticated air defense assets, notably the long-range S-400 surface-to-air missile system, complemented by shorter-range systems like

Pantsir-S1 to establish a layered air defense shield protecting the Russian military presence and operations at Khmeimim.[22]

Around this time, hundreds of Iranian reinforcements were deployed to join Syrian government forces alongside their Lebanese Hezbollah allies in a major ground offensive in anticipation of Russia's intervention. By mid-September 2015, new detachments from the IRGC were reported to have arrived in Tartus and Latakia, western Syria.[23] In late September, Moscow announced the establishment of the Baghdad Information Center—a joint intelligence-sharing center in Baghdad between Russia, Iran, Iraq, and Syria with the primary function of coordinating intelligence on operations against the Islamic State and around the Syrian-Iraqi border. To smooth the coalition dynamics, Russia dispatched military liaison teams led by senior generals to Tehran and Baghdad.[24] Stationed within the Russian embassies in these cities, these teams were instrumental in coordinating overflight rights with the Iraqi and Iranian governments to establish uninterrupted aerial supply lines.

The foundations for military intervention were laid out, marking an unprecedented level of logistical coordination and planning between Russia and Iran. In his memoirs, Hossein Amir-Abdollahian reflected on the formative period of coordination between Iran and Russia in Syria. Serving at the time as the principal liaison in the Iranian Ministry of Foreign Affairs for Syria, Amir Abdollahian recounted that the initial "negotiations on Syria acted as a catalyst in bilateral relations and caused the Russians to revisit relations with Iran and open a new chapter for bilateral cooperation."[25] This "new chapter" in Russia-Iran relations would reshape the contours of their engagement for years to come.

Russia's Choice

Russia's intervention in Syria was driven by concerns far beyond the Assad government's loss of territory or the convincing arguments of their Iranian counterparts. Central to Russia's military engagement in Syria were its multiple underpinnings. Fears of Western-led regime change and countering the tide of extremism were colored by ambitions to reassert its influence in the Middle

East. Thus, numerous factors and opportunities propelled Russia's foray into Syria.

While the immediate objective was to bolster the Assad regime militarily, the intervention was also deeply rooted in a desire to counter Western-led initiatives for regime change, a sentiment echoed in previous discussions in Chapter 3. Russia's opposition to perceived Western efforts to overthrow unfriendly governments intensified after North Atlantic Treaty Organization (NATO) intervened in Libya. The use of United Nations Security Council (UNSC) Resolution 1973 to support the overthrow of Qaddafi led Russia to veto future resolutions that would authorize international action in Syria. One seasoned Russian expert on the Middle East echoed this, arguing that the "Russian attitude towards the Arab world drastically changed after Libya ... were it not for Libya there would have been no Syria."[26] Likewise, another informed observer close to the Russian Foreign Ministry maintained that the results of the NATO intervention in Libya had a greater impact on Russian foreign policy in Syria than any other development.[27] Moreover, in the months preceding its military intervention, Moscow grew increasingly alarmed by Western discussions about establishing a no-fly zone over Syria—a measure reminiscent of the prelude to regime change in Libya, which intensified Russian fears that a similar scenario could unfold in Syria.

Meanwhile, the loss of Assad's territory to the Islamic State raised the possibility that radical Islamists would be installed in Syria. The Kremlin viewed the Syrian conflict as a struggle between religious extremists and a secular state, similar to Russia's own experiences with Chechen separatism and the Soviet-Afghan War. The Islamic State's aim of establishing a caliphate resonated with some segments of Russia's Muslim population and those in neighboring states.[28] For example, Vitaly Naumkin, a Russian scholar of the Arab world and advisor to the United Nations (UN) Special Envoy for Syria, argued that the "moderate Islamic organizations" assisted by the United States are no better than the "Islamic State radicals," and that distinguishing between "good" and "bad" "bandits" is "extremely dangerous."[29] Moreover, the recruitment of Russian-speaking fighters by the Islamic State led to fears of their potential to inspire domestic extremism or integrate Russian extremists into global terrorist networks.[30]

Though greatly exaggerated, Russian statements reflected a long-held concern about the implications of destabilization in the Middle East for its own security.[31] The movement of foreign fighters from the region contributed to the Russian narrative about a new "arc of instability" from Afghanistan to Syria.[32] Russian intelligence estimates indicated that around 4,000 citizens had traveled from Russia and Central Asia to join the Islamic State; often, official statements would exaggerate the number.[33] For example, one former Russian diplomat remarked that

> there were 10,000 to 20,000 foreign fighters coming from Central Asia and even more from our borders including Chechnya ... Western governments who aid terrorist forces like the White Helmets ... the very same governments who seek to open the doors of chaos on our neighbors, the ones who use human rights as a smokescreen to interfere and bring instability to Russia ... look at the map, now [in Moscow] we are closer to the Middle East than Vladivostok.[34]

In reality, the number was much lower, and there were reports that Russia was handing out passports to these fighters. Russia nevertheless viewed the Middle East as closely connected to its own security. Head of the Russian General Staff Valery Gerasimov expressed concerns that the Islamic State's momentum in Syria could spread to neighboring countries and potentially affect Russia directly, especially in regions such as the Caucasus, Central Asia, and the Volga.[35] This was not a new policy for Russia—in nearly every conflict in the Middle East, Russia has highlighted how destabilization in the Middle East could spread to its borders.

Beyond its immediate military objectives, Russia's intervention in Syria was also shaped by a desire to re-engage diplomatically with the United States following the fallout from the Ukraine crisis. Some Russian experts envisioned the formation of an anti-terrorism coalition as a stepping stone toward renewed dialogue with Washington.[36] In 2017, a long-time observer of Russia and the Middle East argued that military involvement in Syria "started with a wish to improve relations with the West," since the fight against terrorism presented a clear common enemy.[37] Another analyst echoed this view, asserting that the offensive began with the intention of establishing "a basis for Russia-U.S. dialogue."[38] This interpretation is further supported by Russia's initial preference for operations in Deir ez-Zor, an area close to U.S.-led coalition operations, which indicated that Moscow hoped to use the Syrian campaign to reopen channels of communication with Washington.

At the same time, Russia's intervention offered an opportunity to challenge U.S. influence in the Middle East. By positioning itself as a central power broker in Syria, Moscow sought not only to recalibrate its strained relations with Washington but also to assert its standing as a counterweight to American dominance in the region.[39] The representative of the Iraqi Kurdish regional government to Moscow believed that Russia intervened in Syria because it was the country's "last chance" to regain its influence in the Middle East.[40] Yet, Moscow's self-proclaimed "return to the Middle East" hinged on building diverse partnerships and distinguishing its approach from that of the United States.[41] A Russian presidential advisor underscored these aims by remarking that:

> with Syria, Russia returned to the Middle East as a great power. Unlike the U.S., we seek to resolve instability. Unlike the U.S., we have mutually beneficial relations with all actors and do not dictate internal paths to development. We believe that great powers should work with all regional actors for regional security.[42]

A variety of motivations were behind Russia's decision to intervene. Yet, it was the shared goal of combating terrorism that emerged as the most compelling and broadly acceptable rationale for Russia's involvement. Emphasizing the fight against terrorism allowed Russia to frame its intervention in a way that was both domestically and internationally palatable, lending greater legitimacy to its actions.

The Diplomatic Offensive

Ahead of the intervention, the Russian Foreign Ministry was tasked with coordinating a diplomatic campaign to correspond with its military goals. While its influence waned as operations unfolded, the Ministry played a crucial preparatory role by framing the legal and political rationale for action. It emphasized that Russia's intervention was undertaken at Syria's formal request and held numerous consultations with legal advisors to reinforce this justification.[43]

Russia held the presidency of the UNSC in September, meaning that it could set that month's agenda.[44] On 1 September, Russia's UN Ambassador Vitaly Churkin circulated a concept note to schedule a ministerial-level debate for 30 September while also proposing an "antiterrorism coalition" to combat the growth of the Islamic State.[45] According to a Russian diplomat, part of the diplomatic campaign involved using the UNSC debate, scheduled for 30 September, to announce Russia's involvement in Syria to an international audience.[46]

President Putin's speech at the United Nations General Assembly (UNGA) on 28 September, before the scheduled debate, referred to the 1 September concept note and called on the West and regional countries to join a broad international coalition to defeat the Islamic State and settle the Syrian crisis.[47] Consistent with Russia's political justifications, Putin condemned "aggressive foreign interference" in the Middle East for creating a "power vacuum" that was being filled by "extremists and terrorists."[48] Like Putin, President Rouhani's address at the UNGA also focused on the creation of a broad coalition to combat terrorism while maintaining that "the roots of today's wars, destruction and terror can be found in yesterday's occupations, invasions and military interventions."[49]

The start of Moscow's aerial assault on 30 September thus coincided with the ministerial-level UNSC meeting that had been convened at Russia's behest to discuss the proposal of forming an international coalition against terrorism. As Russian fighter jets targeted rebel-held territory around Homs and Hama, Lavrov stated that "following a request from the Syrian leadership," the Russian Federation Council, the upper legislative assembly, had approved the deployment of Russian Armed Forces to "exclusively" target the Islamic State in Syria.[50] Lavrov affirmed that it was "fundamentally important" to approach the aforementioned issues "based on international law, including respect for sovereignty and equality of States and non-interference in internal affairs."[51] Chief of Staff of the

Russian Presidential Administration Sergey Ivanov explained that Assad "turned to [Russia's] leadership, requesting military assistance," which illustrates "a principal difference" in Russia's approach from Western states, who "do not comply with international law."[52]

Iran reacted positively to Russia's intervention, with Foreign Minister Zarif "welcoming Russia's efforts" against "terrorists" in Syria; unlike the U.S.-led airstrikes against the Islamic State, Russia had "embarked on attacks based on the request of the government of Syria."[53] Similarly, Velayati celebrated the Russian military campaign as tilting "the balance of power ... in favor of the Axis of Resistance."[54] An op-ed in the conservative paper *Quds* mirrored this view, arguing that, unlike the United States, which "continues their destructive activities in Syria without permission, the Russian government has acted within the framework of international law."[55] In the reformist paper *Et'emad*, an op-ed portrayed the Russian intervention as not only "legitimate" and in line with "international principles and law" but as an attempt to strengthen the Axis of Resistance in the Middle East.[56]

The narrative within Russia, however, was more nuanced. Commentator Georgiy Bovt remarked that while Russia's military actions in Syria had managed to divert Western focus from Ukraine, "there was no reincarnation of post-9/11 friendship ... Syria has only given new reasons for mutual mistrust, irritation, and confrontation."[57] In contrast, Russian academic Alexei Arbatov argued that "cooperation in Syria may indirectly contribute to the regulation of the Ukrainian problem, relieving of tension between Russia and the West, lifting of economic sanctions, [and] resuming arms control."[58] Whereas the intervention would result in intermittent engagement with Washington, its main impact was to thrust Russia into the center of Middle Eastern affairs.

The Humanitarian Cost

The most tragic outcome of the Syrian Civil War was the staggering number of civilian casualties. Since 2011, humanitarian organizations and monitoring groups have documented between 170,000 and 300,000 civilian deaths directly attributable to the

Syrian regime coalition, many of which were the result of Russian aerial bombardments and Iranian-backed ground assaults.[59] The Syrian regime coalition's relentless assaults on opposition-held territories not only decimated entire communities but also pushed the displaced into dire living conditions, either within Syria's borders in overcrowded and under-resourced internally displaced persons camps or as refugees facing uncertainty abroad. European countries—many of which opened their arms to Ukrainian refugees in 2022—closed their doors to Syrians, limiting their response to the crisis to hollow statements following each chemical weapons allegation.

Both Russian airstrikes and Iranian-backed ground operations indiscriminately targeted residential areas. Iranian-backed forces, supported by Russia's aerial enforcement, employed siege warfare with considerable vigor in Aleppo and Eastern Ghouta, where communities were cut off from food, medicine, and fuel. Intended to force surrender through starvation and deprivation, the sieges were part of a brutal strategy that aimed to punish entire populations. The image of emaciated bodies in besieged towns has been a horrifying testament to the cruelty of such tactics.

By targeting roads and infrastructure, as well as implementing a de facto no-fly zone over parts of Syria, the Syrian regime coalition complicated efforts to deliver food, medical supplies, and other forms of civilian aid. The human cost of Russia's and Iran's military operations in Syria, under the banner of supporting the Assad regime, was unfathomable suffering. Characterized by egregious breaches of international law, these campaigns employed indiscriminate violence, demonstrating flagrant neglect for the sanctity of human life.

* * *

With Moscow's entry into the Syrian conflict on 30 September 2015, Russia and Iran transitioned from parallel backers of Damascus to a fully embedded coalition, operating alongside the Syrian Arab Army and a constellation of Iranian-backed militias. For the first time since the Soviet Union's dissolution, Russia projected power well beyond its "near abroad," committing combat aircraft, naval assets, and special operations teams to the theater of operations. Rather than reestablishing large ground formations, Moscow opted to fuse its aerial and naval firepower with the IRGC's Quds Force, Hezbollah fighters, and local paramilitaries on the ground.

Unlike NATO and other longstanding military alliances, the coalition supporting the Syrian regime lacked experience and established protocols for interoperability—the ability of different forces to effectively operate together by harmonizing command structures, communication systems, and operational procedures. Interoperability involves more than just simultaneous actions; it encompasses the integration of diverse units, logistical support, shared intelligence, and standardized communication methods that allow forces from different countries and services to function cohesively in complex combat environments. Consequently, establishing and sustaining effective interoperability became the Assad regime coalition's first major operational challenge and strategic priority.

The Anatomy of Intervention

From the start of Russia's intervention to the spring of 2016, the focus was on consolidating the Assad regime's control in central and western Syria to establish stability and secure transport links, which were vital for the movement of troops and supplies.[60] Russian air support enabled the IRGC Quds Force, the Syrian Arab Army, and militias to make advances in four key contested operational theaters: northern Latakia, the M5 Highway in Homs and Hama Provinces, Aleppo Province, and Greater Damascus. From the spring of 2016 to the spring of 2017, offensive operations were carried out in the western part of the country to retake Aleppo and its surroundings, including Palmyra, which had been seized by the Islamic State.

In the following phases, discussed in Chapter 5, from the spring of 2017 to the spring of 2018, efforts shifted towards combating the Islamic State in central and eastern Syria. This entailed the consolidation of central regions in Syria and the second battle for Palmyra in 2017, which was part of the operational objective was a push eastward to seize Deir ez-Zor from the Islamic State. Concurrent with a drive toward the Syrian-Iraqi border, the Syrian

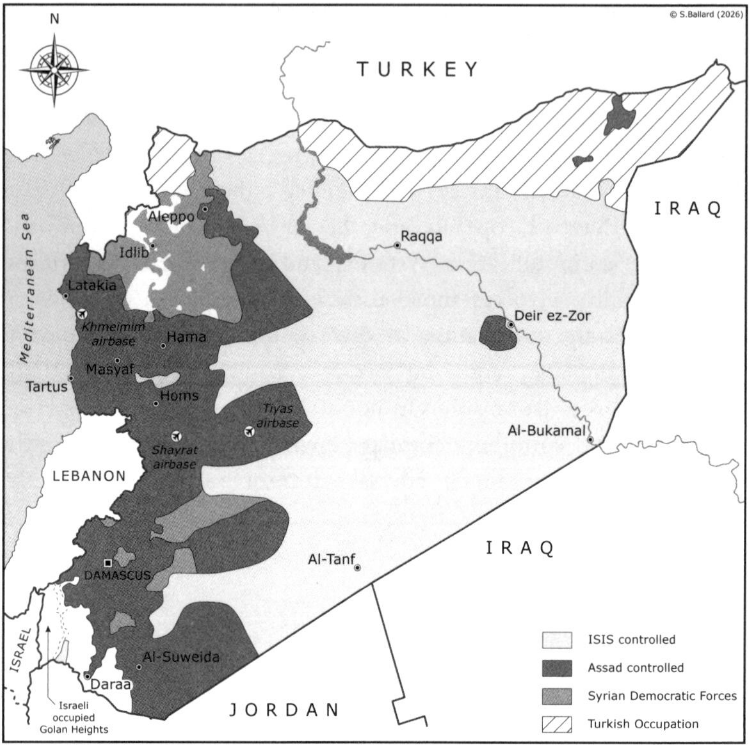

Map 2: Territorial Control in Syria during the Civil War, 2015

regime coalition embarked on a campaign to consolidate regime territorial control in the south towards its borders with Israel and Jordan.[61]

Moscow kept its footprint light. Its 'strategy of limited actions' (*strategiya ogranichennykh deysvtiy*) sought to keep Assad afloat without deep expenditure of Russian manpower. At any given time, Russia had around 2,000 to 4,000 military personnel stationed in Syria, reflecting a restrained ground presence. This strategy encompassed the deployment of Russian air and naval capabilities combined with a modest contingent of ground forces that enmeshed Russian Special Operations Forces with IRGC and Iranian backed non state actors like Hezbollah. This approach enabled Moscow to achieve its immediate aim: Assad's regime was preserved, and the Islamic State was defeated with minimal Russian troop casualties.

A few thousand Russian military personnel—pilots, naval staff, special operatives, and military advisors—were present in Syria at various stages of the intervention, tilting the war's momentum in favor of the Assad regime. The Russian Aerospace Forces, known as VKS (*Vozdushno-Kosmicheskie Sily Rossii*), spearheaded the effort with extensive aerial campaigns against rebel groups, the Islamic State units, and other jihadist entities.[62] Alongside air operations, Russia fortified its position at the Khmeimim airbase and bolstered its naval footprint at the port of Tartus.[63] Russian Special Operations Forces and military advisors were deployed to collaborate with Syrian and Iranian-backed ground forces. The Russian Navy also played a role, launching cruise missiles from its surface vessels and submarines stationed in the Mediterranean and Caspian Seas.[64] The sea route was critical for the so-called "Syrian Express," the maritime resupply route established between Russian ports and the Syrian coast, facilitating the transfer of military equipment, ammunition, and troops.[65] Starting around 2017, the Russian Army's Military Police were central in post-conflict stabilization efforts. They were deployed in various "de-escalation" zones throughout Syria, especially in regions recaptured by the Syrian government, to oversee local ceasefire agreements.

Russia's military presence in Syria was complemented by the Wagner Group, a Private Military Company (PMC) that first appeared in the conflict in late 2015.[66] Despite PMCs being illegal in Russia, Wagner operated under the unofficial supervision of Russian military intelligence and later the security services, with its personnel being transported to Syria via Russian military aircraft and the Syrian Express maritime route.[67] The Wagner Group played central roles in both Palmyra offensives in 2016 and 2017, serving as frontline advisors and forward air controllers while operating with heavy equipment, including T-72 tanks and artillery systems. By mid-2017, their numbers had swelled to approximately 5,000 personnel. After major combat operations, Wagner forces were essential in holding captured territory, allowing Russia to maintain control over strategic areas without committing regular military forces.[68]

Syria was also a testing ground for Russian weaponry. The Kremlin deployed advanced military assets, including the Pantsyr short-range air defense system and the S-400 high-altitude surface-to-air missile system at Khmeimim airbase and subsequently the S-300 in the northwestern city of Masyaf.[69] In addition to these advanced defense systems, Russia positioned the KRET Krasukha-S4 ground-based electronic warfare system, the K-300P Bastion P coastal missile defense system, and the Iskander ballistic missile system in Syria.[70] Ahead of the Battle of Aleppo, Russia further reinforced its aerial capabilities with the deployment of Su-35S fighter jets equipped with electronic countermeasures systems at the Khmeimim airbase.[71]

In contrast to Russia's restrained footprint, Iran's involvement in Syria was expansive, characterized by a deployment of both regular and irregular forces. The IRGC, especially the elite Quds Force under the leadership of General Soleimani until his assassination in 2020, directed and coordinated the majority of coalition operations. Alongside the IRGC, Iran mobilized a vast network of Shia militias, such as Hezbollah from Lebanon, the Fatemiyoun Brigade comprising Afghan Shia fighters, and the Zainabiyoun Brigade with Pakistani Shia fighters. By September 2017, a well-informed Syria expert estimated that around 51,000 Iranian-backed ground forces had been deployed to stabilize Assad's regime.[72]

Before Russia's September 2015 intervention, Iran had provided an extensive array of armaments to sustain Damascus' war effort. Tehran provided Syria with assault rifles such as the AK-47 and AK-74, machine guns, and RPG-7 rocket-propelled grenade launchers. Iran also supplied an assortment of ammunition, ranging from small arms rounds to artillery shells, as well as materials for constructing improvised explosive devices. The heavy armament transfers included Soviet-era T-72 tanks and anti-aircraft systems. As the conflict progressed, Iran enhanced its military assistance by introducing advanced systems like the Fateh-110 ballistic missile platform. Additionally, Iran established and operated drone bases in Syria, deploying drones like the Shahed-129 and Mohajer-6 for both reconnaissance and combat missions.

To transport this military equipment to Syria, Iran used a combination of air, land, and sea routes. Air transport played a primary role, with cargo flights operated by national airlines like Mahan Air, which often involved routing through Iraqi airspace. In some instances, Iran used sea transport to ship large consignments of military hardware, which were then offloaded at ports in Lebanon or Syria and subsequently transported inland by road. Iran's ability to transfer weapons to the Syrian Arab Army was initially restricted by the Islamic State's control of territory along the Syrian-Iraqi borders. However, in Chapter 5, the Syrian regime coalition's eventual recapture of the Syrian-Iraqi border enabled Iran to increase its material support to its allies in Syria. Eventually, overland routes connecting Iran to Syria via Iraq would serve as arteries for the supply of equipment and personnel.

Command and Control

In the run-up to the Russian intervention, Iranian planners had already laid much of the groundwork for military operations in Syria. The IRGC's Quds Force had embedded small advisory teams with the Syrian Arab Army, while Hezbollah and Iraqi, Afghan, and Pakistani Shia brigades were steadily growing in numbers around Homs and Damascus. However, these disparate formations remained separate silos—each with its own chain of command, communications infrastructure, and support systems.

When Russian bombers began attacking rebel supply lines and Islamic State positions in northern Latakia, around Aleppo, and on the approaches to Damascus, Iranian-backed forces immediately pressed forward but often without synchronized air-ground integration. A telling example occurred in early October 2015, when an IRGC-led push toward Khanasir stalled due to fragmented coordination. Iranian-backed militias had advanced expecting Russian close air support that had not been properly scheduled through the Khmeimim deconfliction channel.

To address these issues, Russia and Iran developed an "integrated grouping"—an umbrella structure that combined Iran's network of non-state actors and militias with Russian-trained Syrian Arab Army formations under a single, Russian-led operational command. This integration operated across three levels: strategic, operational, and tactical. Each level featured specific mechanisms for coordination that evolved throughout the Syrian campaign.

At the strategic level, all campaign planning and force-generation decisions were elevated to the highest echelons of both capitals. In Moscow, the General Staff's Main Operational Directorate worked in tandem with a newly created Group of Combat Management inside the National Defense Management Center. In Tehran, the Supreme National Security Council (SNSC) and the General Staff of the Armed Forces appointed dedicated liaison officers to feed into a Joint Planning Cell.[73] Meanwhile, Shoigu's January 2015 visit to Tehran gave birth to the Russia-Iran Joint Military Commission, which continued to meet annually to refine long-term roadmaps, create specialized working groups, and negotiate defenseindustry contracts.[74] For diplomatic and military communication with Moscow, Iran appointed former Defense Minister and Secretary of the SNSC Ali Shamkhani to a newly created position specifically to coordinate policy with Russia on the Syrian military campaign. Operating under the Supreme Leader's authority, the SNSC served as the epicenter of decision-making, orchestrating policies that deeply involved the IRGC and General Staff in both planning and execution phases.

At the operational level, Russia established a command post at Khmeimim airbase to orchestrate combined operations.[75] There, officers from the VKS, the Navy's coastal-strike arm, and Special Operations Forces worked side by side with IRGC Quds Force commanders, Hezbollah advisors, and Syrian Arab Army staff. As Colonel General Aleksandr Dvornikov later recounted, the Syrian General Staff "could not provide the operational planning the situation required," so Russian planners assumed primary responsibility for campaign design and execution under the overall supervision of their General Staff.[76] Consequently, target development, strike-package design, and the sequencing of ground assaults were handed over to Russian officers drawn from the VKS, Special Operations Forces, and the Navy's coastal-strike component.[77]

At the tactical level, Russian, Iranian, and Syrian forces coordinated their ground operations through a network of joint operation centers. Each major battlefront—Damascus, Aleppo, Latakia, and Hama—hosted dedicated command cells where Russian military advisors, IRGC field commanders, and Syrian Arab Army officers planned and executed combined operations. These centers managed battlefield intelligence collection, coordinated artillery strikes, and directed ground force movements.[78] From the outset of Russia's intervention in Syria, the IRGC quickly emerged as Moscow's chief point of contact on the ground, handling most coordination at both the operational and tactical levels. While Russia maintained a formal military-to-military dialogue with Iran's General Staff, it was the IRGC—particularly the Quds Force—that shaped frontline strategy.[79] Eventually, Iran would utilize bases like the Tiyas airbase near Palmyra and the Imam Ali base near the Syrian-Iraqi border to facilitate coordination for weapons transfers. These bases served as nodes for embedding IRGC advisors with local units. They also enabled real-time collaboration through joint operations centers, where Iranian commanders worked alongside Syrian officers and militia leaders.

Iran's unique military organization shaped its Syrian operations in distinctive ways. Unlike Russia's conventionally structured, top-down military, Iran operates a hybrid defense apparatus split between the elite IRGC and the regular military (Artesh). Iran deployed the Artesh's elite 65th Airborne Special Forces Brigade to operate under IRGC command in key areas around Aleppo and Damascus, embedding Artesh officer cadres within the broader IRGC command structure. Simultaneously, the IRGC Aerospace Force (IRGC-AF), under Amir Ali Hajizadeh's leadership, expanded its role significantly after 2016, spearheading Iran's growing drone warfare capabilities and conducting direct ballistic missile strikes from Iranian territory.

On the logistical side, Iran and Russia operated through distinct but complementary supply systems. Iran's Ministry of Defense and Armed Forces Logistics (MODAFL)—which oversees Iran's defense industries and military procurement—managed supply chain operations and coordinated military equipment deliveries to sustain battlefield operations. MODAFL's research institutes and manufacturing facilities produced hardware ranging from unmanned aerial vehicles to missiles while maintaining supply lines to Iranian forces and allied militias in Syria. Russia's logistical structure operated through the Southern Military District, which controlled force flow and coordinated long-range strikes from the

Russian mainland. Coordination between the Russian contingent in Syria and command in Moscow appeared to occur at the level of a Deputy Military District Commander—an unusual arrangement that elevated an operational force to a de facto strategic command.[80]

The integration of these separate logistical systems was managed through the Russia-Iran Joint Military Commission, which established specialized working groups focused on logistics coordination. These working groups standardized supply procedures and managed the complex flow of equipment between Russian bases, Iranian supply networks, and Syrian Arab Army formations. Over the course of the war, MODAFL increasingly adapted their production lines to meet specifications compatible with Russian equipment standards, facilitating interoperability between Iranian-supplied militias and Russian-trained Syrian units.[81]

As examined in Chapter 8, the operational networks and relationships forged between the Russian military and Iran's IRGC and MODAFL during Syria laid the groundwork for Iran's military exports to Russia in 2022. The same MODAFL production sites and IRGC logistics networks that had sustained Iranian operations in Syria were later repurposed to channel military hardware across the Caspian corridor to Russian forces.

Politics by Military Means

Russia's military campaign in Syria was accompanied by a laborious diplomatic offensive. Since the start of the intervention, Russian diplomatic efforts were often calibrated to augment the military campaign to stabilize the Assad regime. Specifically, ceasefires and humanitarian aid deliveries often covered its military activities. At the same time, Russian military diplomacy in Syria also focused on building and strengthening partnerships with key regional powers, including the U.S., Turkey, Jordan, and Israel.

Russia's military intervention in Syria was principally framed as a campaign against the Islamic State and other terrorist factions, a stance that superficially paralleled the objectives of the U.S.-led coalition against terrorism.[82] Although Russia's aspiration of enticing the U.S. into joining its international coalition against terrorism did not come to fruition, the United States and Russia agreed to establish a deconfliction hotline in the wake of a meeting between Presidents Putin and Obama at the UNGA in late September 2015. From the outset of the Russian campaign, there was a high risk of accidental encounters or misinterpretations of military maneuvers with U.S. forces conducting aerial operations. The hotline served as a real-time communication channel, allowing both parties to inform each other of planned operations, flight paths, and troop movements.[83] Despite the hotline's intended purpose of fostering transparency and reducing the risk of miscalculation, its implementation was not devoid of challenges. The dynamics of Syria, coupled with the fluctuating political relations between the U.S. and Russia, often tested the efficacy of this mechanism.[84]

Israeli Prime Minister Benjamin Netanyahu also engaged in extensive discussions with President Putin to champion Israel's security imperatives, which included limiting the influence of Iran. In September 2015, an agreement was brokered between Russia and Israel to establish a high-level General Staff deconfliction channel.[85] The collaboration extended to regular communications between the two defense ministries. Israel's defense ministers, most notably Avigdor Lieberman, a native Russian speaker, held weekly conversations with their Russian counterpart, Defense Minister Sergey Shoigu, often conducted in Russian. As detailed in Chapter 5, Russia found itself in a challenging position, navigating between Israeli concerns and its commitments to Iran. Over the course of the campaign, Israel managed to carry out numerous operations targeting Iranian and Hezbollah positions within Syria. Russia typically refrained from public criticism of these operations, effectively allowing Israel to address perceived security threats while maintaining an appearance of neutrality.

Russia's military intervention in Syria clashed with Turkey's policy in Syria, which centered on opposing the Assad regime, supporting opposition groups such as the Free Syrian Army, and preventing the establishment of an autonomous Kurdish entity near its border.[86] The tension between Russia and Turkey escalated dramatically after Turkish forces shot down a Russian Su-24 jet near the Syrian border in November 2015. Ankara defended its actions by claiming that the jet had violated Turkish airspace, a charge Moscow vehemently denied.[87] The incident triggered a rapid deterioration in bilateral relations. Russia imposed a series of punitive economic sanctions on Turkey, including restrictions on Turkish exports, a ban on charter flights between the two countries, and a prohibition on Russian citizens purchasing tour packages for Turkey.[88] However, the relationship between Russia and Turkey began to show signs of improvement by mid-2016. In June, President Erdoğan publicly expressed regret over the downing of the Russian jet, referring to the incident as a "mistake." Erdoğan's expression of contrition facilitated a dialogue that paved the way for a gradual normalization of diplomatic and economic relations. An additional factor in this thawing of relations occurred in July 2016, when Russia, according to claims by an employee of the Russian Ministry of Defense, allegedly provided Erdoğan with intelligence about an impending coup attempt against his government.[89]

Russia's relations with Saudi Arabia and the United Arab Emirates (UAE) were strained due to their financial and logistical support for opposition groups like the Free Syrian Army and various Islamist factions fighting against the Assad government. After Russia's intervention, Moscow worked to mend tensions with the Gulf monarchies despite their opposition to Assad. Moscow also sought to balance its relations with the Gulf Cooperation Council (GCC) and Iran in the aftermath of the severing of diplomatic ties between Riyadh and Tehran as a result of Saudi Arabia's execution of a prominent Shia cleric, Sheikh Nimr al-Nimr, in January 2016.[90] As examined in Chapter 5, Russia's recognition of the necessity to engage with the GCC would be central to its diplomatic and economic plans for a post-war Syria.[91] However, this would frequently come at the cost of Iranian influence.

Russia and Iran: Strengthening of Ties

President Putin's visit to Iran in November 2015, his first in eight years, heralded a new era of highly visible exchanges between the two nations. The visit took place within the context of a broader multilateral effort, specifically during the Gas Exporting Countries

Forum. Subsequently, the Astana Process became the primary platform for regular and substantive discussions.

During discussions with President Rouhani, Putin highlighted the critical role of Iran's cooperation in the successful anti-terrorist campaign in Syria.[92] Meanwhile, Rouhani underscored the mutual agreement to bolster "cooperation on regional issues, especially in combating terrorism."[93] In Putin's two-hour meeting with Khamenei, the Russian president explained that Moscow considers Tehran a "reliable ally in the region and the world ... unlike certain parties, we are committed to never stabbing our partners in the back," adding that Russia would not "take any behind-the-stage move against our friends" and would instead seek "to resolve any differences that may arise through dialogue."[94] Putin's assurances of loyalty and transparency stood in stark contrast to Russia's actions just five years earlier when his predecessor cancelled the sale of S-300 air defense system.

The prelude to Putin's visit saw Russian efforts to mend these past betrayals. In early November 2015, Sergey Chemezov, head of the state corporation Rostec, announced a deal to supply Iran with the S-300 air defense system, lifting a previous ban from 2010.[95] The decision, made in April before the agreement on the JCPOA, was part of an effort to strengthen defense ties between Russia and Iran. The delivery involved upgrading the originally planned S-300 to the more advanced S-300PMU-2 model, a necessity due to the outdated nature of the initially agreed-upon version. Shoigu's unexpected visit to Tehran in early 2016, followed by the delivery of the S-300PMU-2 to Iran in April that year, underscored Moscow's efforts to overcome the lingering mistrust caused by its 2010 decision.[96]

Amid these developments, key figures within Russian and Iranian foreign policy circles expressed strong support for the partnership. Russian Deputy Prime Minister Dmitry Rogozin hailed the "unprecedentedly good" relations between the two nations, which he attributed to "the restoration of security and peace in Syria."[97] Velayati echoed this sentiment, celebrating the "unprecedented cooperation" against terrorism in the Middle East.[98] Yet even as military and defense collaboration deepened, the relationship remained vulnerable to mistrust and periodic friction. Before the S-300 delivery, rumors circulated in Moscow that the transfer might again be postponed because Iran had allegedly supplied Russian weapons to Hezbollah.[99] Nevertheless, by December 2016 Russia completed the delivery of an S-300 battalion to Iran.

Developments in Syria also spurred debate within Iran over the risks of deepening reliance on Moscow. Foreign policy observer Kayhan Barzegar viewed Russia's involvement in Syria with a mix of skepticism and optimism, recognizing its potential to either bolster Iran's regional influence or undermine its regional autonomy.[100] Similarly, Hassan Beheshtipour, an Iranian expert on Russia, assessed Russia's military presence as beneficial for reshaping regional negotiations in Iran's favor, though he also warned of its potential risks, such as diminishing Iran's status in Syria or compelling it to make unfavorable agreements with Western powers.[101] Notably, suspicions cut both ways, as Russian analysts worried about Iran possibly pivoting closer to the West in light of the July 2015 nuclear deal.[102] As detailed in Chapter 6, Iran's anticipated economic growth in the wake of the nuclear deal fell short. Moreover, subsequent U.S. policy shifts with the election of Donald Trump, diminished any prospects of Iran's realignment towards the West.[103]

Assad Will Stay?

Shortly after Moscow initiated its military intervention in Syria in September 2015, a peace initiative was launched in Vienna. From late October to mid-November, representatives from seventeen countries of the "International Syria Support Group" (ISSG), including the United States, Russia, Iran, Turkey, and Saudi Arabia, met in Vienna to discuss a political solution to the Syrian crisis.[104] While diplomatic talks aimed at establishing peace and ceasefires were ongoing, the reality on the ground reflected a different picture as the Syrian government coalition capitalized on ceasefires for battlefield gains.

Emboldened by its military campaign, Russia was able to successfully push for Iran's involvement in diplomatic talks over Syria. Unlike the Geneva II talks that were discussed in Chapter 3, Iran was no longer sidelined from international diplomacy. From

Russia's perspective, Iran's participation in the Vienna talks was "a major success of Russian diplomacy."[105] Iranian officials expressed a similar sentiment. Foreign Minister Zarif gloated that the international community had recognized that "without Iran being present, there is no way to reach a reasonable solution to the crisis," while Shamkhani attributed Iran's inclusion in the Geneva talks to Russia's military intervention in Syria, adding that it was because of Russia that "supporters of terrorists were forced to ask Iran to join the Syrian talks."[106]

In Vienna, Russia and Iran managed to induce a broader international acceptance of Assad's prolonged stay in the transition process, as the final statement omitted any mention of the Syrian president's removal from office.[107] Rather, the participants produced a nine-point statement that affirmed the "imperative to accelerate all diplomatic efforts to end the war" by implementing a UN-supervised ceasefire. The document also ensured Assad's participation in the transitional government and subsequent elections—a stipulation that essentially enabled Assad to lead the government and manipulate elections to secure his continued rule. Later, in December 2015, the UNSC unanimously approved Resolution 2254, which endorsed the ISSG statements from the Vienna talks and enshrined the sequence of events designed to resolve the Syrian Civil War.[108]

The Vienna talks reinvigorated the flawed peace process in Syria; however, the escalation of attacks by the regime's coalition on opposition-held territory in northwest Syria prompted the suspension of the third Geneva talks in January 2016.[109] The failure of the Geneva Process to de-escalate the conflict and to broker a diplomatic solution between the warring parties resulted in a series of U.S.-Russia-led negotiations on Syria. In February, the ISSG agreed to a temporary "cessation of hostilities" with both Russia and the United States emerging as the primary negotiators and guarantors of the agreement.[110] The temporary ceasefire, which entered into force on 27 February, ordered a halt to the fighting and attempts to capture territory, with the exception of areas held by the Islamic State and Jabhat al-Nusra.[111] During negotiations, Lavrov's responsibility entailed framing any ceasefire agreements in a manner that would not hinder ongoing operations against factions labeled as "terrorists" by the Russians—however, Russia and Iran diverged over what constituted a terrorist. Iran had adopted a much wider view of terrorist groups, encompassing opposition forces, whereas Russia distinguished between moderate opposition groups and extremist groups like the Islamic State.

Iran opposed the U.S.-Russia-brokered ceasefire, viewing it as a way to provide respite to rebel groups opposed to Assad.[112] Several days before the ceasefire was due to be implemented, Rouhani relayed Iran's concern about its terms to Putin, stating that "terrorists should not be given time to reorganize and remobilize resources and arms during the ceasefire" and that "humanitarian aid should respect the territorial integrity and sovereignty of the Syrian government."[113] Iran was concerned that any Russia-U.S. collaboration would sideline Tehran and its position in the subsequent political arrangements or negotiations.[114] Although Rouhani dismissed any "trust" issues between Iran and Russia in Syria, he also stressed this did not mean that Tehran would "condone" all of Moscow's actions.[115]

Shortly after the February 2016 ceasefire, Putin declared that Russia would start withdrawing the "main part" of its military forces from Syria but would not exit the theater entirely.[116] Many Western observers mistook this for a full withdrawal, but in reality, it was aimed at refocusing the forces for the coming Battle of Aleppo.[117] On the ground, in defiance of the ceasefire, the Syrian regime forces advanced towards Palmyra, successfully seizing the city from the Islamic State.[118] Next, the coalition advanced towards Aleppo, initiating a campaign to sever the supply routes to opposition-held territories in the north of the city.

As fighting between the regime and the opposition intensified in Aleppo Province in the spring of 2016, the temporary ceasefire agreement came close to the point of collapse.[119] The U.S. and Russia struggled to salvage the diplomatic process though managed to extend the temporary ceasefire to Aleppo city in early May. Attempting to safeguard opposition-held eastern Aleppo, U.S. diplomats proposed collaborating militarily with Russia against the Islamic State and al-Nusra Front in exchange for a ceasefire and a halt to assaults on Aleppo. Capitalizing on U.S. hesitancy to abandon a potential ceasefire, Russia prolonged negotiations while its military aided pro-regime forces in securing key battlegrounds.[120]

The breakdown in U.S.-Russia mediation efforts over Syria became evident in September 2016 when a new U.S.-Russia-brokered ceasefire agreement collapsed after less than a week. The final straw was a deadly attack on a UN humanitarian aid convoy near Aleppo, which led to the suspension of all aid deliveries in Syria. The U.S. blamed Russia for the attack, an accusation Russia vehemently denied, insisting that rebel forces were responsible. By the winter of 2016, a coalition of Hezbollah, Iranian-backed militias, and Syrian forces—coordinated by the IRGC and reinforced by Russian airstrikes—was edging closer to regaining control of Aleppo.

* * *

The battle for Aleppo in 2016 marked a watershed in the Syrian Civil War. What began as a desperate bid to reclaim Syria's largest city evolved into a demonstration of how external intervention could alter the war's trajectory. Years of division had left Aleppo a microcosm of the conflict itself—rebels entrenched in the east, regime forces confined to the west. By late 2015, Assad's position was precarious, sustained only through growing Russian and Iranian support. The subsequent campaign transformed Aleppo into both a proving ground for Moscow's new expeditionary capabilities and a test of Iran's commitment to preserving its most important regional ally.

The Aleppo campaign represented a change in the extent of direct Russian military assistance on the ground in Syria.[121] While avoiding direct ground combat, Moscow deployed Special Operations Forces, artillery units, and military advisors who proved instrumental in planning, coordination, and fire support.[122] This approach allowed the coalition to attack rebel positions without incurring high-profile Russian losses—an obvious political advantage for the Kremlin, keen to prove its global reach while limiting its domestic casualty figures.[123] Simultaneously, Iranian-led forces operated southwest of the city to prevent opposition fighters in the countryside from breaking the siege, with the IRGC-AF launching precision strikes using Shahed-129 suicide drones from bases in the governorates of Hama and Homs.

The Aleppo offensive unfolded in several phases.[124] The initial stage, from July to August 2016, saw the encirclement of rebel-held areas, effectively cutting off supply lines and isolating opposition forces. A brief rebel counteroffensive in August momentarily threatened pro-regime gains, but from September through December, a relentless air and ground campaign systematically dismantled the rebel stronghold. This phase was marked by a surge in Russian air support. As pro-regime forces tightened their control over East Aleppo, they cut off access to food, water, medical supplies, and other essential resources, triggering a severe humanitarian crisis. The final phase in December 2016 saw the evacuation of the remaining opposition fighters and civilians, effectively consolidating pro-regime control over the city. This evacuation, brokered primarily by Russia and Turkey, led to the mass exodus of tens of thousands of people, many of whom were transported to rebel-held areas in Idlib province. With the departure of opposition forces, Assad's forces—backed by their Russian and Iranian allies—moved to establish control over Aleppo, securing a major victory that would alter the course of the Syrian Civil War until the dramatic events in late 2024.

While the Aleppo campaign initially proved successful for the Syrian regime coalition, it would also reveal the challenges in coordinating the efforts of its principal backers, Russia and Iran. Despite the extraordinary level of cooperation achieved through joint operations, the campaign would expose friction points between Moscow's reliance on air power and Tehran's reliance on ground forces. The Russian focus on minimizing its own casualties while maximizing the impact of air support would sometimes leave Iranian-led ground forces feeling vulnerable and under-supported. Coordination difficulties, though not insurmountable, would foreshadow the deeper divergences between Russia and Iran that would emerge in Syria following Aleppo.

Challenges of Coordination

For the Russia-Iran relationship, the Aleppo campaign illustrated the coordination challenges between Russia's airpower and Iranian ground elements. During the campaign's initial stages, the lack of Russian air support for Iranian forces highlighted the challenges of integrating and coordinating between Iranian-backed ground forces and the Russian VKS.

In May 2016, shortly after Russia agreed to implement a ceasefire with the United States in Aleppo Province, the IRGC suffered one of its biggest military setbacks of the conflict during an al-Nusra siege of Khan Touman.[125] The siege of Khan Touman—a city southwest of Aleppo—led to around 80 to 100 casualties of IRGC and Iranian proxy forces, one of Iran's largest military losses in the Syrian Civil War.[126] Several senior Iranian military officials drew attention to the dearth of air support in Khan Touman as a veiled criticism of Russia's fixation on bilateral diplomacy with the U.S. and the military's public relations spectacle in Palmyra, which included a symphony by Russia's Mariinsky Theater.[127] *Tabnak*, a paper owned by a senior IRGC officer, outwardly attacked Russia's "indifference" towards Iranian losses in Khan Touman and argued that Russia "should play a greater role in sharing military tasks with Syria and its allies" instead of holding a "leisurely" symphony in the ruins of Palmyra.[128] Statements from Iranian officials have periodically surfaced ridiculing Russia's widely publicized public relations campaign celebrating its military operations, reflecting a general sentiment in Tehran that Moscow's interest in Syria has more to do with projecting its status as a great power than achieving military objectives.[129]

Despite the public outcry, the leaderships in Iran and Russia sought to quell concerns about any divisions between the two states.[130] In June 2016, a tripartite summit of Iranian, Russian, and Syrian defense ministers in Tehran focused on the ongoing military campaign in Aleppo—the success of which would bolster Assad's leverage over a future political settlement.[131] The ministers secretly discussed deploying Russian aircraft to Shahid Nojeh airbase near Hamadan in western Iran, which would allow Russia to save fuel and reduce flight time.[132]

The plan to use Iran's airbase materialized in August 2016, as Russian aircraft flew from Shahid Nojeh to strike the Islamic State and Jabhat al-Nusra targets around Aleppo, Deir ez-Zor, and Idlib.[133] On 16 August, the Russian Ministry of Defense announced that its long-range Tu-22M3 bombers and Su-34 front-line bombers, launched from Hamadan's Shahid Nojeh airbase in Iran, had executed a coordinated airstrike on targets associated with the Islamic State and Jabhat al-Nusra in the provinces of Aleppo, Deir ez-Zor, and Idlib.[134] While Russia was keen to showcase its expanding influence in the Middle East, the public disclosure that it was using the Shahid Nojeh airbase ignited a firestorm of anger among officials in Tehran.[135] Significantly, Russia's operation from Shahid Nojeh airbase represented the first time a major power had undertaken military actions from Iranian territory since the 1979 Revolution.

The widely publicized nature of these aviation operations provoked a backlash in Tehran and led to the withdrawal of Russian forces within a week.[136] Iran's historical aversion to the presence of any kind of foreign military base on its territory, codified in Article 146 of the Iranian Constitution, was apparent as over twenty parliamentarians called for a review of the legal basis of Russia's military presence.[137] While dismissing the parliamentarians' accusations over the legality of the Russian presence, Iranian Defense Minister Hossein Dehghan nevertheless criticized Russia's announcement of its use of Shahid Nojeh airbase as an act of "grandstanding and incivility" that was merely designed "to prove that [Russia] is a superpower and can influence all regional and global affairs."[138] The mounting domestic pressure in Iran compelled both the Russian and Iranian Foreign Ministries to announce the withdrawal of the Russian contingent from Iranian territory on 22 August.[139]

Although Iran's Foreign Ministry spokesperson said that Russia's use of the airbase had ended, Ali Larijani, the speaker of Iran's Parliament, indicated that Russian jets continued to use the airbase.[140] Moreover, information began to leak about Russia's continued use of the airbase following a secret meeting between Alexander Lavrentiev, Russia's special presidential envoy for Syria, and Shamkhani in which Iran apparently agreed to allow Russian long-range bombers overflight rights and permission to land at Shahid Nojeh airbase for refueling.

Operation Euphrates Shield: Turkey Enters the Fray

Within days of the Russian departure from Shahid Nojeh, Turkey launched a military operation in northern Syria known as Operation Euphrates Shield.[141] Turkey's military campaign sought to drive back the Islamic State and Kurdish forces from the border region while establishing a safe zone for displaced Syrians. Ankara's concerns also extended to the Assad regime, which Turkey had long opposed.

Before Turkey's military campaign, President Erdoğan's visit to St. Petersburg in early August 2016 set off the Russia-Turkey rapprochement.[142] With Turkey's intervention, some suggested the existence of a "tacit understanding" between Moscow, Tehran, and Ankara on the division of Syria.[143] The editor of the popular journal *Russia in Global Affairs*, Fyodor Lukyanov, postulated a new form of great power diplomacy akin to "the secret agreements of the great powers on the division of the Middle East" as "the region returns to a new version of behind-the-scenes transaction" with Russia, Iran, and Turkey at the helm.[144] The reactions of Russia and Iran to Turkey's military intervention in northern Syria marked a departure from their previous diplomatic stance, contrasting sharply with their vehement opposition to the 2014 U.S.-led campaign against the Islamic State. Moscow and Tehran's measured response seemed to be calculated to achieve two key objectives. By refraining from harsh criticism, Russia and Iran sought to prevent Turkey from impeding their operations in Aleppo while simultaneously encouraging a softening of Turkey's position on Assad's removal from power.

Turkey's intervention in Syria added a new dynamic to the campaign for Aleppo. Russia recognized that the success of the Russia-Iran-Syria military coalition required Ankara's assistance in extricating opposition fighters from eastern Aleppo and brokering a ceasefire agreement.[145] Occasionally, Iran expressed concerns over Russia's interactions with Turkey on the basis that they diminished Tehran's influence. However, clear divergences between Turkey on the one hand and Russia and Iran on the other shaped the trilateral dynamics more so than Iranian marginalization.

Assad's Recapture of Aleppo

The continued Russian aerial bombardment and Iranian-led ground offensives enabled pro-Assad forces to make consistent progress throughout November and, eventually, to stabilize control of Aleppo by the end of 2016. By December, regime forces had successfully achieved their objective of dividing rebel-held Aleppo into smaller pockets, effectively isolating them from external support and supply lines. Gradually, the government forces regained control over key districts, weakening the rebels' hold on eastern Aleppo. As pro-Assad forces, backed by Russian airpower, neared victory in the city, Moscow sought to bring Ankara on board, recognizing that Turkey's influence over various rebel factions was necessary for any lasting settlement.

By mid-December, the Russia-Iran-Syria coalition had recaptured eastern Aleppo from opposition forces, leading to a fragile nationwide ceasefire agreement brokered by Russia and Turkey.[146] Pursuant to the Russia-Turkey ceasefire, buses and ambulances were organized to evacuate thousands of trapped civilians and rebels, transporting them to rebel-held areas in the northwestern province of Idlib. Iran objected to the agreement, as neither Tehran nor Damascus had been consulted on the issue. Moreover, General Soleimani refused to evacuate these forces.[147] In response, Moscow proposed a trilateral meeting of Russia, Iran, and Turkey to assuage concerns in Tehran. Iran eventually relented to the evacuation of forces, but its ability to complicate Russia's lofty great power diplomatic goals would become a reoccurring trend each time Moscow neglected to involve it in the diplomacy surrounding the conflict.

Shortly after the December 2016 Russia-Turkey-brokered ceasefire and evacuation deal, the foreign ministers of Russia, Iran, and Turkey met in Moscow to discuss the future of Syria and establish a framework for peace talks. After the meeting, the foreign ministers issued the Moscow Declaration, which affirmed the "sovereignty, independence, unity, and territorial integrity" of Syria while expressing their "readiness to facilitate and become the guarantors of the prospective agreement, being negotiated, between the Syrian Government and the opposition."[148] The Moscow Declaration would pave the way for the creation of the Astana Process, which operated as a parallel track to the Geneva Process, where Russia, Iran, and Turkey would serve as guarantors.

Following Aleppo, statements from Iranian and Russian officials hailed the accomplishments of the Syrian government coalition. According to Mehdi Sanaei, the Iranian ambassador to Russia, the coalition had helped "to protect peace and stability" and to weaken "the role of terrorists and strengthened the positions of the legitimate government."[149] A Russian presidential advisor for the Middle East noted Russia and Iran were "united by the proximity of approaches to many global and regional problems" that "would be impossible to solve" without their collaboration.[150] Rear Admiral Ali Shamkhani, secretary of Iran's SNSC, stated that cooperation between Russia and Iran in Syria began "within the framework of Russia's determination to support the legitimate government of Syria in the war against terrorism and to secure common strategic interests in this field [with Iran]."[151] The optimistic outlook expressed by Russian and Iranian officials obscured the growing division over Moscow's and Tehran's vision for a post-war Syria.

* * *

Assad's recapture of Aleppo in December 2016 stood as a defining moment for the regime and its backers. Militarily, it freed up regime and allied forces to push eastward against the Islamic State, hastening the eventual offensives around Palmyra and Deir ez-Zor. Morale soared among loyalist ranks, and Russia publicized the victory as proof that its aerial-centric model could reshape conflicts well beyond its immediate neighborhood. Iran, in turn, celebrated the outcome as vindication of its years-long commitment of IRGC troops and proxy militias, reinforcing its claim to a deep strategic presence in Syria.

Beneath these displays of unity, however, the campaign revealed serious coordination strains between Moscow and Tehran. The Russian emphasis on large-scale bombing often left Iranian-led ground forces feeling exposed, particularly during high-casualty events like the Khan Touman debacle in May 2016, when IRGC leaders criticized Russia's perceived lack of timely air support. Iranian officials grew frustrated whenever Russia seemed more focused on diplomatic overtures with Washington or regional posturing than achieving battlefield synergy. Conversely, Russia disliked being tethered to Iran's regional ambitions and objected when Iranian hardliners advocated for an indefinite foreign presence on the ground, which Moscow viewed as diplomatically risky.

Aleppo's recapture definitively shifted the conflict's center of gravity. With the rebels' main northern stronghold broken, the regime and its allies could concentrate resources on the Islamic State-held deserts and the remnants of opposition enclaves elsewhere. Moreover, the siege's success underscored that even if their interests did not align perfectly, Russia and Iran could still mount powerful, coordinated offensives. In the longer term, however, the campaign foreshadowed emerging frictions as each patron sought to assert its blueprint for post-war Syria. Russia planned for a diplomatic settlement to solidify its global legitimacy; Iran aimed to institutionalize its military presence on the ground for strategic depth. These divergent visions would simmer beneath the surface as the war moved into eastern Syria, and as the powers that conquered Aleppo grappled with the far more complex task of managing Syria's eventual stabilization and reconstruction.

Meanwhile, Russian, Iranian, and Turkish representatives convened in Moscow, eventually issuing the Moscow Declaration and setting the stage for the Astana Process. The Astana Process—led by Russia, Iran, and Turkey—became a showcase for Moscow and Tehran's capacity to navigate their divergent ambitions while coordinating strategies with regional stakeholders. Yet this new phase posed fresh dilemmas. U.S. support for Syrian Kurdish forces, an ongoing American military footprint in Syria, and Israel's stepped-up strikes against Iranian assets complicated both Russia's balancing act and Iran's entrenchment plans. Though the partnership proved adept at achieving tactical victories, deeper differences in each country's long-term vision for Syria signaled looming tensions that would reverberate throughout the post-conflict landscape.

5

THE BATTLEFIELD AND BEYOND

RUSSIAN AND IRANIAN EFFORTS TO RESHAPE SYRIA

On the evening of 19 December, Russia's ambassador to Turkey, Andrei Karlov, attended the opening of an art exhibition in Ankara. During the ambassador's speech to the attendees, a solitary assailant brandished a pistol and proclaimed in Turkish: "Don't forget Aleppo. Don't forget Syria. Unless our towns are secure, you won't enjoy security. Only death can take me from here. Everyone who is involved in this suffering will pay a price."[1] The attacker aimed his gun at Ambassador Karlov and discharged a single bullet, killing him on the spot. The assailant who targeted Karlov was motivated by the unfolding tragedy in Aleppo. He vented his rage and despair on a representative of a nation he deemed complicit in the suffering.

Vladimir Putin heard the news of Ambassador Karlov's assassination while heading to watch Alexander Griboyedov's comedy *Woe from Wit* in Moscow. The irony of his planned cultural engagement could not have been starker. Alexander Griboyedov, much more than a celebrated playwright, served as a Russian diplomat and, like Karlov, met a tragic end while on duty. Griboyedov was serving as the Russian envoy to Persia when he was killed in 1829. His role in negotiating the 1828 Treaty of Turkmenchay marked a momentous diplomatic victory for imperial Russia that inflicted deep wounds on Persia. Ceding substantial Persian territories to Russia, the treaty has remained a symbol of betrayal and Russian duplicity in the Iranian historical narrative, stirring resentment that has lingered into the contemporary period. The circumstances leading to Griboyedov's death were fueled by intense local hostility and a tragic misunderstanding. A mob, incensed by unfounded rumors that a Christian convert had been granted asylum within the Russian embassy, launched a violent attack on the Russian compound. Griboyedov and several members of his diplomatic mission were brutally murdered in the ensuing tumult.

The echoes of history colored the present as the Russian press drew parallels between Karlov and Griboyedov.[2] Yet, the legacy of Griboyedov's death, set against the backdrop of nineteenth-century Russian-Persian rivalry, contrasted sharply with Russia and Iran's contemporary partnership in Syria. The assassination occurred a day before scheduled negotiations in Moscow among the foreign and defense ministers of Russia, Iran, and Turkey over the situation in Syria. Once opposing parties in centuries past, Moscow and Tehran were now entrenched in a strange coalition in support of Assad.

Aleppo marked a decisive turning point in the Syrian conflict. Following this victory, Russia and Iran spearheaded massive territorial gains across northwestern and southern Syria, wresting control from umbrella opposition groups and the Islamic State. These successful campaigns enabled the Assad regime coalition to reclaim extensive stretches of the Syrian-Iraqi and Syrian-Jordanian borders. As this chapter explores, Russia and Iran would subsequently face a series of challenges in negotiating Syria's political settlement while navigating the evolving dynamics of their own bilateral partnership.

From Aleppo to Astana

As discussed in Chapter 4, one of the main results of the coalition victory in Aleppo was the inauguration of the Astana Process, led by Russia, Turkey, and Iran, to determine a political solution for Syria. The first round of discussions in January 2017 centered on ensuring the longevity of a fragile ceasefire agreed upon in December 2016.

Key issues included establishing the parameters of the ceasefire, ensuring humanitarian access to affected areas, and coordinating a united front against extremist groups. The first round of talks revealed tensions between the parties and obstacles in the political process, as little was accomplished beyond the creation of a trilateral mechanism to monitor the ceasefire led by Russia, Iran, and Turkey.[3]

A political settlement of the Syrian conflict was not anticipated before the Astana talks due to "a split in the Syrian opposition and disagreements between the initiators of the meeting."[4] Moscow's willingness to include a U.S. delegation in the talks, a proposal Iran staunchly opposed, undermined Putin's earlier efforts to assuage Iranian reservations about the Kremlin's approach to the conflict. Russian Middle East expert Alexei Malashenko told *Kommersant* that Russia had received an "ironic reminder of what constitutes real multipolarity in the world and the Middle East" from Iran, a country that views itself as "an independent center of power" and "claims leadership in a strategically important region."[5] As Russia pursued diplomacy to reaffirm its status as a great power, the country simultaneously engaged with a wide range of regional and international actors to "find a subtle balance between the interests" of the participants.[6]

The Astana talks would continue providing a platform for direct dialogue between the government and parts of the opposition while facilitating the establishment and demarcation of four "de-escalation zones" across key conflict areas in Syria—namely in Idlib Province, northern Homs Province, Eastern Ghouta, and parts of southern Syria.[7] In theory, the de-escalation zones were intended to facilitate the delivery of humanitarian aid to beleaguered population for a critically needed, though temporary, reprieve from the violence that had engulfed the country. However, the ambiguities in implementation, the competing agendas of the guarantor states, and the fragmented approach to engaging with Syrian opposition groups hindered their efficacy. This was later compromised by the continued hostilities within the de-escalation zones, sometimes at the behest of their guarantor states, who used the continued fighting to pursue territorial gains.

As the Syrian Civil War transitioned to a new phase, the differences between the regime's primary international backers, Russia and Iran, became more pronounced. Through the Astana Process, both sought to transform their military successes into political leverage over Syria's future. Despite having jointly intervened on behalf of the Assad regime, Russia and Iran harbored distinct visions for Syria's postwar order. Russian strategists favored a diplomatic approach that could potentially accommodate various actors, including certain segments of the opposition, in hopes of stabilizing the country and preserving Russia's long-term interests. By contrast, Iran—deeply invested in shoring up its position with Assad and Hezbollah—remained wary of any power-sharing arrangements that might dilute its influence or threaten Assad's grip on power. Furthermore, Russia's developing ties with other regional players, such as Saudi Arabia and Israel, often alarmed Iranian officials, who feared that Moscow's desire for a balanced foreign policy might undercut Tehran's regional objectives.

Russia's Fraught Balancing Act

The Syrian Civil War heralded Russia's "return" to the Middle East, a pronounced shift from the years of relative disengagement following the Soviet Union's dissolution. As the war progressed, Russia utilized the Syrian conflict to bolster its regional stature, combining military intervention with diplomacy to establish itself as a major force in the Middle East. This resurgence saw Russian delegations become commonplace in Middle Eastern capitals. In Moscow, orchestrating a political resolution in Syria would be "an important victory [for Russia], proving its ability to resolve international crises far from its own borders."[8] Moreover, the success of the Russia-Iran-Syria entente in Aleppo served as a precursor to realizing Moscow's diplomatic aspirations of becoming an "indispensable power broker" in the Middle East.[9] However, Russia's enhanced profile also introduced diplomatic challenges, most notably in managing relations with Iran while maintaining ties with Israel, the Gulf Cooperation Council (GCC), and the United States.

The inauguration of Donald Trump as U.S. president on 20 January 2017 elicited mixed reactions from Moscow and Tehran. The Kremlin hoped the Trump administration would seek to improve U.S. relations with Russia, potentially aligning closer to Russia's stance in Syria. Iran viewed Trump's ascendancy with caution, fearing that a U.S.-Russia detente might culminate in compromises detrimental to its influence in the region.[10] As explored in Chapter 6, Moscow's initial enthusiasm at Trump's election soon gave way to a more sober assessment when accusations of Russian interference in the U.S. presidential elections began to dominate the political discourse in Washington.

Although the Trump administration initially departed from its predecessor's focus on regime change in Syria, not prioritizing Assad's removal, it nevertheless increased the number of U.S. airstrikes against regime assets. For example, the Assad regime's chemical attack on Khan Sheikhoun in April 2017 led to U.S.-ordered missile strikes on a Syrian airbase—the first time the U.S. had targeted Syrian forces. Starting in 2016, the U.S. established a presence in southeastern Syria at the al-Tanf garrison to train anti-Islamic State fighters. Positioned astride key cross-border supply routes, al-Tanf quickly became a flashpoint: Iranian Revolutionary Guard Corps (IRGC) units and affiliated militias, intent on securing land corridors from Tehran through Baghdad to Damascus and Beirut, repeatedly probed the garrison's defenses and exchanged fire with U.S. forces. Moscow's repeated deconfliction offers—beginning with the 2015 Russian-U.S. aerial deconfliction hotline and reinforced by bilateral military talks in Damascus and Sochi—proved insufficient to restrain Iran's ground assets. The result was a triangular standoff in which U.S., Russian, and Iranian forces each pursued divergent aims, revealing the Kremlin's limited sway over Tehran's expeditionary network and the broader complexity of great power escalation in Syria.

Russia did attempt to engage with the U.S., especially in 2017. After two months of secret negotiations in Amman, U.S. and Russian officials agreed upon a de-escalation zone in and around Daraa, in southwest Syria bordering Jordan. The U.S.-Jordan-Russia arrangement in southern Syria without Iranian input signaled

Moscow's willingness to sideline Tehran's interests when expedient. In response, Iranian Foreign Minister Javad Zarif forcefully asserted Iran's autonomy in Syria, declaring that neither Washington nor Moscow could dictate the terms of Tehran's military presence.[11] American policy on Syria underwent several shifts in 2018-2019. Despite initially maintaining troops in 2018, President Trump's unexpected withdrawal announcement in 2019 enabled a Turkish assault on Kurdish allies—key partners in the fight against the Islamic State. Facing widespread criticism domestically and internationally, the U.S. partially reversed course and redeployed some forces to the region.

Israel's involvement in Syria intensified in late 2017, prompted by the growing threat from Hezbollah and other Iran-backed militias. From September onwards, Israel conducted numerous strikes against pro-regime targets in Syria, including weapons caches and military facilities. These operations relied on a fragile understanding with Russia, which was supplying the Syrian regime with advanced anti-aircraft systems that could pose a threat to Israeli jets.[12] Prime Minister Netanyahu reportedly reached an agreement with President Putin to keep Iranian and Iran-backed forces away from the Israel-Syria border in exchange for Israel's tacit acceptance of the Assad regime's consolidation of power.[13] However, Russia's balancing act between Iran and Israel came under strain as IRGC and Hezbollah forces moved closer to the Golan Heights in southern Syria, establishing weapons depots, intelligence-gathering operations, and training camps for Shia militia fighters. In response, Israel intensified its airstrikes, focusing on disrupting Iranian weapons transfers to Hezbollah and dismantling newly established positions near the Israeli border, further complicating Moscow's balance.[14]

Turkey remained central to the Russia-Iran dynamic in Syria, both diplomatically and militarily. While they cooperated in peace talks and de-escalation initiatives, divergences—such as Turkey's opposition to Syrian Kurdish groups with which Iran and Russia were willing to accommodate—often tested the cohesion of the Astana Process. Less than a year after the conclusion of Turkey's Operation Euphrates Shield, Turkey initiated Operation Olive Branch in early 2018 against the Kurdish People's Defense Units in Afrin, deploying numerous Turkish-backed Free Syrian Army fighters to curb the territorial gains of Kurdish forces in northern Syria. While Moscow and Tehran marshaled their resources to reinforce Assad's grip on power, Ankara's offensive against Kurdish forces and backing of opposition fighters in Idlib threatened to upend their efforts. As pro-Assad forces, buoyed by Russian airpower, prepared to retake Idlib in mid-to-late 2018, Turkey took steps to shore up its own influence, including the establishment of observation posts designed under the Astana and de-escalation agreements. The September 2018 Sochi Agreement between Turkey and Russia aimed to avert a full-scale assault on Idlib by creating a demilitarized zone; however, periodic violations on all sides revealed the tenuous nature of their compromise. Though not a primary actor in Idlib, Iran tacitly supported the regime's goal of reclaiming the province while focusing much of its own effort on consolidating control along the corridors near the Iraqi border and in southern Syria.[15]

After 2017, Russia elevated its diplomacy with the Arab monarchies of Bahrain, the United Arab Emirates (UAE), Saudi Arabia, Oman, and Qatar. This diplomatic push was aimed at enhancing Moscow's stature in the Middle East, diversifying partnerships, and securing regional backing for its operation in Syria. For instance, King Salman of Saudi Arabia's historic visit to Moscow from 4 to 7 October 2017—the first time a reigning Saudi monarch had visited Russia—highlighted a mutual intent to deepen ties beyond energy, discussing Syria's stabilization and economic cooperation despite varying views on Assad's regime. Similarly, Putin's UAE visit on 15 October 2019 underscored shared security interests and economic partnerships, with the UAE accommodating Assad's continued rule. Russia's efforts to normalize Assad within the Arab world would culminate in Syria's readmission to the Arab League in May 2023, having previously been expelled at the start of the civil war in 2011—a major development for Assad's regional standing.[16]

The unfolding situation in Syria served as both a testing ground and a showcase for Russia's diplomatic acumen by forcing it to engage with multiple regional actors. The balancing act, however, was fraught with challenges. Russia continued to support the

Assad regime's consolidation of power but with a keen awareness of the need to manage Turkish concerns and counterbalance Iranian ambitions. Meanwhile, the U.S. and Israel added strain to the equation and demonstrated the limits of Russia's so-called "return" to the Middle East. Russia's aspiration of striking a balance among its various interests in Syria often irked Iran, which viewed Moscow's maneuverings as diversions from the overall goal of bolstering Assad.

Visits in Moscow and Tehran

In the spring of 2017, as the Syrian Civil War entered its seventh year, President Rouhani of Iran embarked on a two-day visit to Moscow from 27 to 28 March for a meeting with his Russian counterpart. Rouhani's meeting, set against a backdrop of growing disagreements between Russia and Iran over how to resolve the Syrian conflict, coincided with the global political changes following Trump's inauguration as U.S. president. Though the two leaders had previously met face-to-face at international summits on eight other occasions, Rouhani's inaugural visit to Russia was the first bilateral summit.[17]

The meeting itself was far from an isolated diplomatic encounter. It formed part of a sequence of high-profile visits to Moscow by prominent regional leaders, including Israeli Prime Minister Benjamin Netanyahu and Turkish President Recep Tayyip Erdoğan. Each of these leaders arrived in the Russian capital with distinct aims: Israel sought assurances regarding Iran's presence in Syria; Turkey wanted to safeguard its interests in northern Syria and manage concerns over Kurdish forces; and Iran focused on bolstering the Assad government while expanding its own regional influence. All three governments looked to Moscow to gain support or, at the very least, neutrality for their respective goals. For its part, Russia was intent on maintaining a balanced rapport with Iran, Israel, and Turkey alike. Yet, in practice, Russia's strategy faced strains.

The anticipation surrounding Rouhani's visit stemmed from its potential to redefine Russia and Iran's collective strategy in Syria at a time when reports of friction between the two allies were increasingly frequent. Another dimension shaping the talks was "Washington's desire to drive a wedge between Russia and Iran," a challenge amplified by the new U.S. administration's more confrontational posture.[18] In this context, Russian experts observed that Rouhani's arrival aimed "to show that differences can be moderated and to mollify Moscow with cooperation."[19] Indeed, once face-to-face, Rouhani and Putin presented a unified stance by reaffirming their support for Assad, underscoring the common ground they continued to share in Syria.[20]

Although Syria was a central topic, the Putin-Rouhani summit also served as a platform to deepen and diversify bilateral relations beyond the war-torn country.[21] Rouhani declared that the two nations were "moving towards establishing strategic ties" and had embarked on "a new phase" marked by a "sustainable and long-term" partnership.[22] Echoing these sentiments, Putin praised Iran as "a good neighbor and a reliable and stable partner," expressing his desire to elevate cooperation "to the next level of strategic partnership."[23] While he did not explicitly label the relationship as strategic, Putin's remarks indicated a clear willingness to strengthen Russia's ties to Iran, even amid the numerous geopolitical headwinds facing both countries.

Within days of Rouhani's visit, the Trump administration's emerging Middle East policy took a dramatic turn. On 4 April 2017, the Syrian regime allegedly deployed sarin gas in the rebel-held town of Khan Sheikhoun, near Idlib, triggering swift international condemnation. In response, the United States launched Tomahawk missiles on 7 April at Syria's Shayrat airbase—southeast of Homs—marking a sharp break from the Obama administration's reluctance to target the Assad government directly. This sudden display of American military force not only signaled a more assertive U.S. stance in Syria but also served as a pointed warning to Russia and Iran about Washington's role in the conflict.[24]

Both Russia and Iran quickly and forcefully criticized the U.S. strikes, arguing they violated Syria's sovereignty, destabilized the region, and risked fueling a resurgence of terrorism. The day after the missile strike, Iran's Chief of Staff Mohammad Bagheri contacted his Russian counterpart, Valery Gerasimov, to coordinate their response. The two military leaders jointly condemned the attack as "definite and obvious aggression against an independent country" and characterized it as a deliberate attempt to "slow the Syrian Army and its allies' victories, while boosting the morale of terrorists and their supporters."[25] On the same day, the Secretary of Iran's Supreme National Security Council (SNSC), Ali Shamkhani, spoke with Russian Security Council Secretary Nikolai Patrushev, and President Rouhani followed suit with a call to President Putin. Both leaders denounced what they described as a "unilateral decision" by Washington to strike the Shayrat airbase.[26]

Yet, even as Moscow condemned the U.S. assault in strong terms, observers in Iran noted Russia's relatively muted criticism of Israeli airstrikes on facilities housing IRGC and Hezbollah assets.[27] This discrepancy highlighted broader tensions in Russian-Iranian relations: while both powers were unified in opposing direct Western interference in Syria, Moscow's attempts to maintain flexibility in its dealings with various Middle Eastern actors sometimes collided with Tehran's more uncompromising stance. Consequently, the U.S. missile strike served as both a rallying point for joint Russian-Iranian condemnation and a reminder of the underlying complexities that continued to test their partnership.

Throughout 2017, diplomatic engagement between Russia and Iran strengthened in parallel with shared battlefield successes. In November, Putin made his third visit to Iran for a trilateral summit focusing on improving transportation links between Russia, Iran, and Azerbaijan. During his one-day working visit, Putin met with both Supreme Leader Ayatollah Ali Khamenei and President Rouhani.[28] An article in the reformist newspaper *Shargh* drew attention to the frequency of the summits, noting that "not long ago the Tehran-Moscow relationship was not very good; meanwhile, under the presidency of Hassan Rouhani, the two presidents have met each other nine times."[29] Putin and Khamenei's meeting lasted approximately 75 minutes, with Khamenei's office releasing a statement quoting Putin's commitment to Iran as a "strategic partner and great neighbor."[30] Notably, however, there was no mention of a strategic partnership in the Russian press release of the meeting.[31]

Following Putin's visit, Iranian concerns surfaced regarding a possible reduction of Russian military assets in Syria, highlighting deeper anxieties about Moscow's intentions and the potential impact on Tehran's regional interests. One month after the meeting, these trepidations initially appeared to be vindicated when Putin made a surprise visit to the Khmeimim airbase. Welcomed enthusiastically by Syrian President Assad, Russian generals, and troops, Putin used the occasion to address the assembled military personnel. In his speech, which made headlines around the world, Putin announced a partial withdrawal of Russian forces from Syria.[32] Like Russia's previous withdrawal announcement in Chapter 4, the statement was widely interpreted as signaling a major shift in Russia's military involvement in the war-torn country. However, the essence of Putin's announcement did not signify the comprehensive cessation of Russian military activities in Syria. With the recapture of key areas previously held by opposition forces and the Islamic State, Russia's military objectives were poised to center more specifically on the remaining conflict zones, notably around Idlib and in certain pockets where the Islamic State still maintained a presence.

* * *

After the victory in Aleppo, the Syrian regime coalition shifted its focus to consolidating control over central regions and advancing toward the Syrian-Iraqi border in the east, then held by the Islamic State. In March 2017, the recapture of Palmyra from the Islamic State marked a critical victory for the coalition, paving the way for the more ambitious goal of liberating Deir ez-Zor.[33] Palmyra, situated in the heart of Syria, was a key gateway to the eastern and northern regions where the Islamic State had entrenched its power. Although the regime's initial campaign had successfully liberated Palmyra in March 2016, the Islamic State managed to reclaim it in December 2016 by exploiting the coalition's diversion towards Aleppo.

Following the successful recapture of Palmyra, pro-Assad forces turned their attention eastward to Deir ez-Zor, a strategic city along the Euphrates River that served as a major Islamic State stronghold and a key gateway to Syria's oil-rich eastern regions.[34] The campaign, which intensified in mid-2017, blended the strengths of multiple factions: Russia provided close air support and targeted airstrikes, while the IRGC directed on-the-ground operations, working alongside Syrian Arab Army units—particularly the elite 25th Special Mission Forces Division—and various pro-government militias, including groups backed or trained by Iran such as Liwa Fatemiyoun.[35] Coordinated offensives from the west, combined with precision Russian airstrikes, broke through the Islamic State's defenses in the countryside, ultimately relieving the long-besieged Syrian garrison in Deir ez-Zor city. By September 2017, the regime coalition had consolidated control over much of the area, though competition with the U.S.-backed Syrian Democratic Forces to secure oil fields north of the river introduced a new layer of tension with U.S.-Iran rivalry spilling into an open conflict in eastern Syria.[36]

Following their victory in Deir ez-Zor in late 2017, pro-Assad forces turned southward toward the provinces of Daraa and Quneitra, areas that had remained under rebel control since the early days of the uprising. By mid-2018, the Syrian Army—augmented by Iranian-backed militias and supported by Russian airpower—launched a sweeping campaign to wrest these territories from opposition hands. In Daraa, the operation targeted entrenched rebel pockets near the Jordanian border, prompting concerns about another potential refugee surge into Jordan. In Quneitra, the focus shifted to eliminating factions operating within striking distance of the Golan Heights—an area keenly watched by Israel, which feared Iranian-sponsored forces might establish a permanent foothold nearby. Leveraging its growing regional clout, Russia engaged in back-channel talks that produced a series of negotiated surrenders. These deals allowed opposition fighters to reconcile with Damascus or relocate to Idlib, ensuring a swift, relatively bloodless conclusion to the southern front.

Unlike earlier offensives, where Moscow and Tehran grappled with command-and-control frictions, the primary hurdle in the campaigns after Aleppo was the two powers' contest for long-term influence. Multiple external actors—including Turkey, the United States, and Israel—also weighed in, each pursuing different objectives ranging from border security to counterbalancing Iranian expansion. The situation was complicated by intermittent skirmishes between factions supported by Russia and those backed by Iran. These skirmishes, though rarely escalating into open conflict, exposed the growing rivalry between Moscow and Tehran as each sought to cement its long-term influence within Syria's military and economic spheres. To contain growing friction between their forces, Moscow and Tehran established a high-level military hotline that elevated battlefield disputes directly to their General Staff. This rapid response mechanism helped prevent tactical clashes from escalating into rifts that could add greater strain to their relationship.[37]

The Campaigns for Central and Eastern Syria

The Syrian government coalition concentrated on regaining territory from the Islamic State in central Syria around Damascus and in northeast Syria on the border with Iraq. Russian and Iranian coordination on the Deir ez-Zor campaign entailed a multi-pronged assault on important territories in the east including the Baghdad-Damascus highway and oil fields located on the eastern bank of the Euphrates River. A joint campaign operating room, established by General Soleimani and led by Iran and Hezbollah, ran part of the operation in Deir ez-Zor with the support of the Russian and Syrian Armed Forces.[38]

Iran deployed significant military assets during this campaign, particularly drones and ballistic missiles. Following the Islamic State's attacks on Iran's parliament and Khomeini's mausoleum in June 2017, the Islamic Revolutionary Guard Corps Aerospace Force (IRGC-AF) retaliated by launching six Zolfaghar mid-range ballistic missiles from bases in Kermanshah and Kurdistan Provinces. These advanced versions of the Fateh-110, capable of carrying cluster munitions, marked Iran's first operational deployment of mid-range projectiles since the Iran-Iraq War.

By early September 2017, the coalition achieved a crucial breakthrough. Syrian troops, reinforced by Iranian-backed Shia brigades and protected by Russian air sorties, broke through the Islamic State's siege of Deir ez-Zor city, establishing a tenuous corridor along the western bank of the Euphrates. The Syrian 17th Division, supported by Hezbollah's elite Radwan Force and Iraqi Popular Mobilization Forces (PMF) units, advanced from the west while pro-Damascus tribal auxiliaries under Iranian guidance pressed northward from the south. Russian Su-34 and Su-35 aircraft provided close air support and severed Islamic State supply routes from Iraq. This breakthrough relieved the besieged 104th Airborne Brigade and positioned forces for deeper advances toward al-Bukamal, the last major border crossing under Islamic State control.[39] After weeks of attritional fighting, a synchronized assault reclaimed al-Bukamal in November 2017. Iranian-backed Iraqi PMF forces, fresh from their liberation of al-Qa'im on the Iraqi side of the frontier, linked with Syrian units advancing from al-Mayadin.[40] The operation effectively severed the Islamic State's western extension into Iraq, collapsing its remaining lines of communication.[41]

Beginning in 2018, Iran spearheaded the initiative to augment the Baghdad Information Center's profile in the joint operations on the Syrian-Iraqi border.[42] Iranian Minister of Defense Amir Khatami's visit to Baghdad in April 2018 coincided with the Iraqi airstrikes in Deir ez-Zor, announced during a meeting at the center with Iraqi, Syrian, Russian, and Iranian representatives.[43] In October 2018, the military forces of Iran, Syria, and Russia held joint drills in the Deir ez-Zor Province along the western bank of the Euphrates River.[44] This occurred only one month after Russia had blamed Israel for tampering with Syrian missile defense systems, which resulted in the accidental downing of the Russian Il-20M reconnaissance aircraft by Syrian forces over Latakia.

With the Islamic State's territorial defeat in Deir ez-Zor by late 2018, Tehran shifted to a consolidation strategy. The IRGC and allied militias established permanent infrastructure across the province: a major depot near al-Assad Military Hospital in Deir ez-Zor city, forward operating bases in al-Mayadin and al-Bukamal, and smaller outposts in the desert triangle between al-Shaddadi and the T2 pumping station.[45] These installations served as transit points for Iranian-supplied Hezbollah-manufactured rockets, long-range drones, and ammunition moving from al-Qa'im border crossings into Syria's interior. Iran also cultivated local proxy forces, organizing sympathetic tribal fighters into units such as Jaish al-Qura, which numbered over 2,500 by early 2019. IRGC officers trained, funded, and indoctrinated these auxiliaries. Simultaneously, Iranian-backed Iraqi groups including Kata'ib Hezbollah, the PMF's

Badr Brigades, and Harakat Hezbollah al-Nujaba strengthened Iranian influence along the Syrian-Iraqi border.[46] Positioned between U.S.-allied territories in al-Tanf and the eastern Euphrates, Deir ez-Zor provided Iran a strategic foothold to threaten American military presence in Syria through equipment transfers to Hezbollah and potential strikes on al-Tanf.[47]

By late 2018, Russian priorities evolved. With the Syrian Arab Army overstretched and heavily dependent on Iranian proxies for territorial control, Russian planners recognized the need to rebalance the coalition toward centralized Syrian state authority. Russian military advisors and their private contractors—most notably the Wagner Group—began to play a more assertive role outside their traditional strongholds near Palmyra. Wagner operatives, estimated at 1,500 to 2,000 personnel by mid-2019, deployed to secure oil and gas fields along the Euphrates and to guard critical infrastructure against the Islamic State resurgence. Operating under tacit Kremlin approval and benefiting from Russian air cover from Khmeimim airbase, these units marked a significant expansion of Russia's ground presence, sometimes in direct competition with Iranian-backed forces.

The Wagner Group's relationship with the IRGC and Iran-backed forces evolved into cautious coexistence marked by cooperation and friction. While Wagner personnel coordinated with Iranian-backed militias during operations like retaking the Conoco gas plant in late 2018, conflicts emerged when priorities diverged. At the same time, in early 2020, a skirmish near the Thayyem oil fields erupted between Wagner guards and Iraqi PMF fighters over oil revenue-sharing, requiring Russian military police intervention. Aware of the latent rivalry on the ground, the Assad regime began to shuffle its regular forces in Deir ez-Zor to rebalance influence. In mid-2020, Damascus redeployed the Iran-linked 4th Division from al-Mayadin northward toward Raqqa, replacing it with units from the Russian-advised 5th Corps. These realignments reshaped rather than eliminated Iranian influence: Iran's allied militias retained responsibility for rural and desert sectors while the 5th Corps manned urban checkpoints and key supply routes.

The resurgence of Islamic State attacks in late 2020 prompted the first significant Russian military deployment to al-Bukamal since its liberation from the Islamic State in 2017.[48] The expanding Russian presence in Deir ez-Zor prompted tactical disagreements between Russian and Iranian-backed ground forces.[49] During the campaign against Islamic State sleeper cells, Iran-backed militias provided direct military support to the Syrian 4th Armored Division—a division of the Syrian Armed Forces that was closely aligned with Iran.[50] However, Iranian desires to assume the command of military operations were a source of tension until the spring of 2021, when this appeared to have been taken up at the ministerial level.[51] Eventually, Iranian-backed militias controlling al-Bukamal provided auxiliary support to Russian military police in the establishment of several checkpoints in the city, while the Russian-backed 5th Assault Corps, deployed near al-Bukamal, took over several posts previously held by Iran-backed al-Nujaba and Iraqi Hezbollah forces.[52]

Russia viewed Iran's deepening control over Deir ez-Zor with mounting concern, seeing Tehran's regional dominance as potentially counterproductive to Moscow's post-war Syrian vision. Iranian influence threatened to alienate Gulf states and other potential reconstruction donors while drawing intensifying Israeli airstrikes against weapons shipments and militia positions. Moscow grew increasingly uneasy as Iran began integrating its militias with Russian-backed formations in Syria and Iraq to shield them from Israeli and U.S. strikes. In response, up until 2022, Russia often tolerated Israeli air operations against Iranian assets elsewhere in Syria, seeing them as a way to limit Tehran's expanding regional footprint while preserving the coalition framework essential to consolidating Assad's control.[53]

The Campaign for Southern Syria

In the early years of the civil war, southern Syria, particularly the provinces of Daraa and Quneitra, became strongholds for opposition groups fighting against the Syrian government. These opposition factions were a mix of moderate rebels, such as the Free Syrian Army, and various Islamist groups, each controlling pockets of territory. The importance of southern Syria, due to its proximity to the Jordanian border and the Israeli-occupied Golan Heights, made it a focal point for external support, with countries like the U.S., Jordan, and the Gulf monarchies providing aid to select opposition groups.[54] Israel's security policy in southern Syria has centered on thwarting Iran and Iranian-backed militias, most notably Hezbollah, from entrenching themselves near the Israeli-occupied Golan Heights. This effort has involved periodic airstrikes, targeted operations against arms shipments, and other measures designed to prevent Tehran's encroachment.

In July 2017, during the G20 summit in Hamburg, Presidents Trump and Putin reached an agreement that would provide reprieve to Israeli security concerns. The agreement was the culmination of months of diplomacy involving the U.S., Russia, Jordan, and Israel to establish de-escalation zones in the key southern Syrian provinces of Daraa, Quneitra, and Suweida. The agreement marked a rare instance of direct cooperation between the United States and Russia in the Syrian crisis. After July 2017, the Syrian regime coalition had largely observed the U.S.-, Russia-, and Jordan-brokered de-escalation zones in the southwestern provinces of Daraa, Quneitra, and Suweida.[55] However, in less than a year, southern Syria would become embroiled in the broader regional conflict between the United States, Russia, Israel, and Iran.

Throughout the spring and summer of 2018, the Syrian regime's offensive in Daraa signaled a breakdown of the de-escalation zone in southern Syria. Backed by Russian airpower, Syrian forces intensified their operations against opposition strongholds in Daraa province and directly infringed upon the southwest de-escalation zone agreed upon by Presidents Trump and Putin in Hamburg. This was followed by the first Russian airstrikes in the region in over a year as the Syrian Army and Iranian ground forces such as the IRGC, the Afghan Fatemiyoun, Imam Hussein Brigade, and the Lebanese Hezbollah captured the cities of Busr al-Harir and Mlehat al-Atash, splitting the remaining rebel-held territory in Daraa Province.

The Syrian regime's advances in Daraa unfolded against a backdrop of escalating regional tensions marked by ongoing Israeli airstrikes targeted at disrupting the consolidation of Iranian military infrastructure and Hezbollah forces in southern Syria. Striving to maintain a balance between Israel and Iran, Russia embarked on diplomatic negotiations with Israel.[56] These talks culminated in an understanding aimed at resolving some of Israel's security concerns—specifically, an agreement was reached to limit the operations of Iranian proxy forces to a distance no closer than 83 km from the Israeli border.[57] Additionally, as reassurance to Israel and to exert some level of control, Russia committed to deploying its military police in the Golan Heights.[58]

Russia sought to curtail Iran's military influence in Syria by professionalizing the Syrian Army and integrating pro-regime militias into its regular ranks.[59] In summer 2018, Moscow reached an agreement in Amman with U.S., Jordanian, and Israeli diplomats that granted special status to opposition fighters in southwest Syria, allowing them to remain as a buffer along the Israeli and Jordanian borders. This arrangement enabled Russia to exert control over the region while sidelining both Damascus and Tehran.[60] Despite Assad's objections, Moscow maintained the deal and prevented pro-Iranian groups from taking over. Under Russian military and police supervision, the 8th Brigade of the 5th Assault Corps—composed of reconciled rebels aligned with Russia—was deployed to enforce order. In early 2021, Russia sought to extend its influence further by offering financial incentives to local Iranian-backed militias, aiming to integrate them into regular army divisions loyal to Russian command structures.[61]

Russia and Iran's protracted struggle to mold Syria's security architecture produced a patchwork force riven by overlapping loyalties. Once the war in Ukraine demanded Moscow's focus and resources, the Kremlin found itself increasingly dependent on Tehran's ground forces and relinquished several key bases to Iranian-backed militias. As explored in Chapter 10, the lack of substantive military reform left Assad's government dangerously reliant on these external patrons. This dependence not only undermined the Syrian Arab Army's cohesion but also set the stage for the regime's ultimate collapse.

Idlib's Rebel Stronghold

The year 2018 witnessed a shift in territorial control throughout Syria as the Assad regime captured the rebel bastions of control.[62] By the close of the summer of 2018, Syrian government forces, aided by Russia and Iran, had taken command of three out of the four de-escalation zones set up in 2017: in Syria's southwest along the Golan Heights, encompassing parts of Quneitra, Suweida, and Daraa Provinces; around the Damascus suburbs, including Eastern Ghouta; and along the Homs-Hama provincial border. In essence, the Syrian government reclaimed most of the territory except for the areas overseen by Turkey in the Idlib de-escalation zone in the northwest and those under Kurdish influence in the northeast.

The Idlib campaign began to take shape in earnest in late 2017 and early 2018, as the Syrian government coalition, supported by Russia and Iran, turned its attention to the last significant opposition stronghold in the country. Following the regime's successful campaigns to retake Aleppo in 2016 and Eastern Ghouta in 2018, Idlib emerged as the final refuge for a complex mix of rebel factions, including groups backed by Turkey and extremist organizations like Hayat Tahrir al-Sham (HTS), a successor to al-Nusra Front.[63]

In September 2018, as the Assad regime began massing troops around Idlib and intensifying airstrikes, fears of an all-out assault escalated. This led to the Sochi Agreement between Russia and Turkey in October 2018, establishing a de-escalation zone and introducing joint Russian-Turkish patrols along Idlib's critical M4 highway to attempt regional stabilization. The agreement established a 15-20 km-wide demilitarized zone where heavy weapons and extremist factions were to be removed. However, true to form, the regime repeatedly violated the ceasefire, while extremist groups operating in Idlib resisted any attempt to disarm them. The Russia-Turkey agreement faltered especially due to resistance from HTS. These operations frequently resulted in significant civilian casualties, displacement, and destruction.

By late 2019 and early 2020, the Assad regime escalated its campaign against Idlib. The offensive, characterized by intensive airstrikes and ground operations, led to the displacement of nearly one million civilians, one of the largest displacements in the Syrian conflict. Turkey responded by reinforcing its military presence in Idlib and launching Operation Spring Shield in February 2020 after dozens of Turkish soldiers were killed in Syrian airstrikes. The subsequent ceasefire brokered by Russia and Turkey in March 2020 temporarily halted the regime's advance and reintroduced joint patrols along the M4 highway. Throughout this period, Iran's role in Idlib remained less direct and overt compared to its involvement in other parts of Syria. While Turkey maintained a military presence and Russia continued to launch airstrikes in Idlib, Iran focused primarily on the south and the areas along the Syrian-Iraqi border.

Up until late 2024, Idlib appeared to be a frozen conflict defined by recurring violence and short-lived ceasefires that failed to resolve core grievances. For the Assad regime, regaining Idlib was the final step in reasserting nationwide control, while Turkey refused to accept a large-scale offensive that would provoke yet another massive refugee influx across its border. This standstill became a linchpin of the Astana Process, laying bare the competing goals of regional powers: Russia and Iran both championed Damascus's sovereign claim to all Syrian territory, whereas Turkey sought to secure its interests in northern Syria and curb Kurdish autonomy. Meanwhile, HTS steadily evolved from a loose militant coalition into a more structured force, boasting dedicated combat units, centralized leadership, and an expanding governance apparatus. As analyzed in Chapter 10, these simmering tensions in Idlib would eventually erupt in late 2024, triggering a decisive cascade that would topple Assad's reign of brutality.

* * *

As the Syrian regime regained most of its territory, the Astana troika continued to pursue a settlement of the Syrian Civil War. In early April 2018, trilateral talks in Ankara sought to demonstrate the continued importance of the Astana Process despite the growing concerns about the Turkish desire to carve out its own sphere of influence.[64] Several days after the meeting, Syria's alleged chemical weapons attack at Douma in Eastern Ghouta spurred the U.S., France, and the UK to retaliate. The ensuing U.S.-UK-French airstrikes deployed over 100 missiles targeting locations linked to chemical weapons production and storage, including a research center and storage site near Damascus and another facility in Homs.[65] Like the attack on Shayrat almost a year earlier, the airstrikes were unequivocally condemned by Russia and Iran.[66]

In the wake of escalating tensions, the issue of foreign forces in Syria became a central point of contention in discussions about the country's future. The presence of numerous foreign actors—including the United States, Turkey, Iran, Russia, and various non-state militias—complicated efforts to negotiate a political resolution to the war. Russia, while deeply intertwined with the Assad regime, advocated for the eventual withdrawal of all foreign forces and militias as a prerequisite for achieving a durable political settlement. Iran, predictably, opposed this position. Tehran viewed any push to expel its forces as a threat to its long-term interests, creating friction with Russia, despite their shared support for Assad.

The Removal of Iran?

Shortly after Russia and Iran's unified front against the U.S.-UK-French strikes, a series of Russian statements appeared to indicate a simmering conflict between Iran and Russia in Syria. In May 2018, during a joint press conference with Syrian President Assad, Putin called for the withdrawal of foreign troops from Syria "in connection with the significant victories and success of the Syrian Army in the fight against terrorism, ... with the beginning of the political process in its more active phase." Many considered this as implicitly referring to Iran. The next day, Russia's special envoy to Syria confirmed that the call for withdrawal encompassed forces from Turkey, the U.S., Iran, and non-state actors like Hezbollah.[67]

Russia would subsequently backtrack on these statements, even defending the lawful nature of Iran's presence in Syria. Russia's ambassador to the United Nations, Vasily Nebenzya, called Iran's presence in Syria "legitimate and undeniable," stressing: "Nobody can deny the issue, whether they like it or not."[68] Four days later, Russian Deputy Foreign Minister Mikhail Bogdanov said that Iran's presence in Syria was advisory in nature and fundamentally aimed at fighting terrorism.[69] Likewise, Russian Foreign Minister Lavrov called the U.S. and Israeli demands for Iran's full withdrawal from Syria "absolutely unrealistic."[70] Despite these statements, the July 2018 Putin-Trump Helsinki summit intensified Iranian anxieties about Russia's evolving position in Syria. Tehran grew increasingly wary of Moscow's accommodating stance toward Israeli security interests and the possibility that Moscow might compromise Iran's regional gains in pursuit of a broader understanding with Washington.

Prior to the summit, U.S. National Security Advisor John Bolton stated that an important part of the agenda of the upcoming summit would be for the United States to ask for Russia's help to oust Iran from Syria.[71] According to Bolton, Trump was reportedly ready to withdraw from Syria and help the Syrian military regain full control over the southern region along the border with Jordan in exchange for Putin's assistance in expelling Iran from Syria.[72] Despite Trump's December 2018 announcement of U.S. withdrawal from Syria, the summit failed to achieve its key objective: securing Iran's removal from the country. This outcome was largely unsurprising, given that Russia likely lacked both the leverage and the genuine desire to compel Iranian forces to leave.

Russia appeared to be mindful of Iranian concerns, organizing meetings with Iranians both before and after meetings with the U.S. and Israel. The Supreme Leader's foreign policy envoy, Ali Velayati, traveled to Moscow two days ahead of the summit to meet with Russian presidential special envoy Alexander Lavrentiev.[73] After the meeting, Velayati stated that there might be "issues" in Russia-Iran relations but that if the United States and Russia have a relationship, "it has no relation to us."[74] In the immediate aftermath of the Helsinki summit, Lavrentiev traveled to Iran, where he apparently spent two hours with Saeed Iravani, the deputy responsible for foreign policy and international security at Iran's Supreme National Security Council (SNSC). Lavrentiev stated that Putin, in his talks with Trump, had denounced Washington's "unilateralism" with the move to re-impose sanctions on Tehran.[75] Iravani, for his part, expressed his gratitude for the Russian president's move to promptly dispatch his special envoy to Iran after the summit and described it as a clear sign of the two countries' commitment to cooperation.

The Helsinki Summit would result in neither the ousting of Iran nor a U.S.-Russia rapprochement. Rather, in the aftermath of Helsinki, relations between Russia and the United States were increasingly confrontational in Syria. On multiple occasions, Moscow accused the U.S. of harboring militants near the al-Tanf garrison and conducted campaigns alarmingly close to U.S.-backed forces. And though President Trump announced in December 2018 that the Islamic State had been defeated in Syria and that U.S. troops would be withdrawn from the country, U.S. forces would nevertheless remain at al-Tanf—an enduring target for Iranian retaliation.

The appearance of tensions between Russia and Iran amplified the challenges of managing a coalition with divergent interests in Syria. According to a former Russian ambassador, it was "natural" that Russia and Iran had differences, but these differences would not "break" the partnership—something that both Russia and Iran seemed to recognize.[76] The deepening of the Russia–Iran relationship did not erase mistrust but institutionalized it, turning coordination into a continuous process of negotiation and adjustment, where each side sought to contain disputes without jeopardizing broader strategic alignment.

Iran and Israel's Shadow War

The evolving military landscape increased Israeli concerns over Iranian-backed forces near its borders and its ability to launch precision airstrikes. Navigating the interests of both Iran and Israel in Syria proved challenging for Russia as it endeavored to maintain productive relationships with these diametrically opposed actors.[77] Russia's balance between Israel and Iran in Syria illustrated the challenges of managing deepened bilateral ties between the two adversaries.[78]

For Russia, in particular, Israeli strikes highlighted concerns about how the proximity of Iranian-backed groups to its own military installations could lead Russian assets to become collateral damage.[79] Russian forces and air defense systems were stationed near Syrian airfields and military bases that were used for Iranian weapons transfers—essentially roving targets for Israeli strikes. The risk of accidental clashes between Israeli and Russian troops was compounded by the possibility of encountering Russian air defense systems like the S-300.

In June 2018, a meeting between Israeli Defense Minister Avigdor Lieberman and Russian Defense Minister Shoigu underscored Moscow's attention to the Israeli role in the region. The discussions, centered on Israel's concerns over Iran's military entrenchment in Syria, coincided with widespread speculation about an undeclared Russian-Israeli arrangement aimed at curtailing the influence of pro-Iranian militias in southern Syria. Iran was unsurprisingly critical of the rumored agreement, raising objections at the ministerial level.[80]

Relations between Russia and Israel deteriorated in September 2018 after Russia's Il-20 aircraft, en route back to the Khmeimim airbase, was mistakenly shot down by Syrian air defenses over the Mediterranean Sea. The incident resulted in the loss of all 15 servicemen aboard. Russia's military leadership attributed the downing of the aircraft to a missile from Syria's S-200 system, which was targeting four Israeli F-16 fighter jets conducting an assault on facilities in Latakia. According to Major General Igor Konashenkov, a spokesperson for the Russian Defense Ministry, the responsibility for the crash lay squarely with the Israeli Air Force and the decision-makers who exploited the Il-20 aircraft as a shield.[81] In response, the Russian government took decisive action by delivering S-300 air defense systems to Syria in October 2018 to thwart further strikes.[82]

The downing of the Russian Il-20 over Latakia appeared to incite greater criticism of Israeli policy among pro-Iranian factions in the Russian elite. In response to Israeli and U.S. criticism of Russian support for Iran, the head of Russia's National Security Council, Nikolai Patrushev, later condemned attempts to "represent Tehran as the main threat to regional security" and emphasized that "Iran was and remains an ally and partner."[83] Moreover, for all the discussion about Russia's permissive attitude to Israeli airstrikes on Iranian assets, Russia often informed Iran about Israeli strikes—either directly or indirectly. In areas where both Russian and Iranian forces were operating, Iran specifically had a member of the Quds Force assigned to monitor deployments of Russian forces and would evacuate whenever Russians evacuated.[84]

However, by early 2019, the relationship between Russia and Israel had begun to thaw. The catalyst for this change was Netanyahu's visit to Moscow in February 2019, marking a step towards diplomatic reconciliation following the September 2018 incident with the Russian Il-20 military plane. Putin had enjoyed a good personal rapport with Netanyahu—a stark contrast to the skepticism among elements within the Russian security services and the Ministry of Defense about the benefits of closer relations with Israel. However, after the September 2018 incident, Moscow's tolerance level for Israeli airstrikes within Syria, which had previously been conducted with a certain degree of Russian acquiescence, began to diminish.

As detailed in Chapter 10, Israel initially attempted a delicate balancing act following Russia's full-scale invasion of Ukraine in February 2022. On one hand, it faced strong U.S. pressure and broader Western condemnation of Russian aggression; on the other, it sought to maintain its historically pragmatic ties with Moscow, especially the deconfliction mechanism in Syria that allowed Israel to strike Iranian-linked targets without risking direct confrontation with Russian forces. However, after the Hamas attacks on 7 October 2023, Israel's relationship with Russia deteriorated sharply when Moscow hosted delegations from Hamas in the immediate aftermath. This move, coupled with Russia's ongoing cooperation with Iran in Ukraine, caused a major rupture in what was already becoming a fragile relationship.

From a Military to a Diplomatic Solution

The Syrian regime's victories in the civil war after 2018 shifted the focus towards a political settlement. Beginning in 2017, Astana hosted Russia, Iran, and Turkey, as well as parts of the Syrian opposition, in a series of talks on resolving the conflict. The Astana talks initially focused on establishing de-escalation zones in Syria to reduce violence and promote stability. Subsequent rounds of negotiations were held in Astana throughout 2017, where the three guarantor countries discussed the implementation and monitoring of the ceasefire and de-escalation zones. The leaders of the guarantor countries of the Astana Process then met in November 2017 in Sochi,

April 2018 in Ankara, and September 2018 in Tehran.[85] During this time, the Astana talks evolved to encompass broader issues related to the political process in Syria, such as the creation of a constitutional committee and the situation in Idlib, the last major stronghold of rebel and jihadist groups opposed to the Syrian government.

Russia's efforts to position itself as the main actor in shaping the future of Syria by coordinating with Iran and Turkey through the Astana Process expanded as Russia proposed a new platform: the Sochi Process.[86] The Sochi Process aimed to gather a broader range of Syrian opposition groups and stakeholders to engage in dialogue and work toward a political settlement.[87] However, as with the 2016 ceasefire, Iran objected to Russia's definition of legitimate opposition forces—many of which Iran considered terrorist groups.

The Astana talks continued alongside the Sochi Process. The negotiations focused on the ceasefire, humanitarian issues, the release of detainees, and the formation of a constitutional committee. Following the National Dialogue Congress—a Russian-led initiative in January 2018 that brought together various Syrian stakeholders to discuss the country's political future—several rounds of talks were held under the Sochi Process. In July 2018, a constitutional committee was formed consisting of representatives from the Syrian government, opposition groups, and civil society. This committee held its first meeting in Geneva on 30 October 2019, with the aim of drafting a new constitution for Syria. However, the committee faced challenges, including disagreements over its composition, and limited progress was made in the drafting process.

Moscow also sought to bridge the gap between the UN-led Geneva and Astana tracks. However, Tehran viewed Moscow's desire to consider the Geneva track as an integral part of the political process as a challenge to its long-term interests in Syria.[88] From an Iranian perspective, the Geneva process was primarily designed to marginalize Iran—a view that was shaped by its exclusion, discussed in Chapter 2. Specifically, Iran remained wary of Russia's intentions, especially around its engagement with other actors in the Syrian crisis, such as Saudi Arabia and Israel.[89] Turkish actions in northern Syria encouraged Russia and Iran to resolve their disagreements over the structure of government institutions, as Russia became willing to compromise over its endorsement of a secular federal structure with ethno-religious autonomy in favor of Tehran's position for a unitary Arab state. Additionally, Turkey's expanded military involvement and its counter-offensive in Idlib triggered alarm in Russia and Iran. Both attempted to delegitimize Turkey's conduct by alleging that Ankara's failure to curb the activities of radical groups in the region served the interests of terrorist organizations.

The post-2019 period was marked by minimal diplomatic progress, while continued attacks on de-escalation zones, particularly in Idlib, revealed that the Astana Process' primary role was reconciling the divergent goals of Russia, Iran, and Turkey in the war. Endorsed by the UN, the Astana Process was perceived as a pathway towards peace. However, the reality diverged from these goals, with the process instead serving to provide a veneer of legitimacy for Russia, Iran, and Turkey's efforts to segment Syria into four designated "de-escalation zones" to manage and contain the conflict while they negotiated their own interests.

Despite their differences, Moscow, Ankara, and Tehran recognized the Astana format's significance, seeing it as a mechanism enabling each state to advance individual agendas and synchronize efforts in shaping Syria's trajectory. Deputy Foreign Minister Sergey Ryabkov remarked that for Russia, the Astana talks were a "success" since they promoted a measured response to hostilities by establishing de-escalation zones and coordinating with a wide range of political actors.[90] For the Astana trio, the process remained essential to their interests in Syria, largely because it offered a platform for managing their influence and coordination in the absence of a more viable alternative.

* * *

The Syrian Civil War drew in various international actors, with Russia and Iran emerging as key supporters of the Assad regime. While both shared the common goal of strengthening Assad's position, their visions for Syria's future diverged in crucial areas, particularly regarding military reform and economic investment.

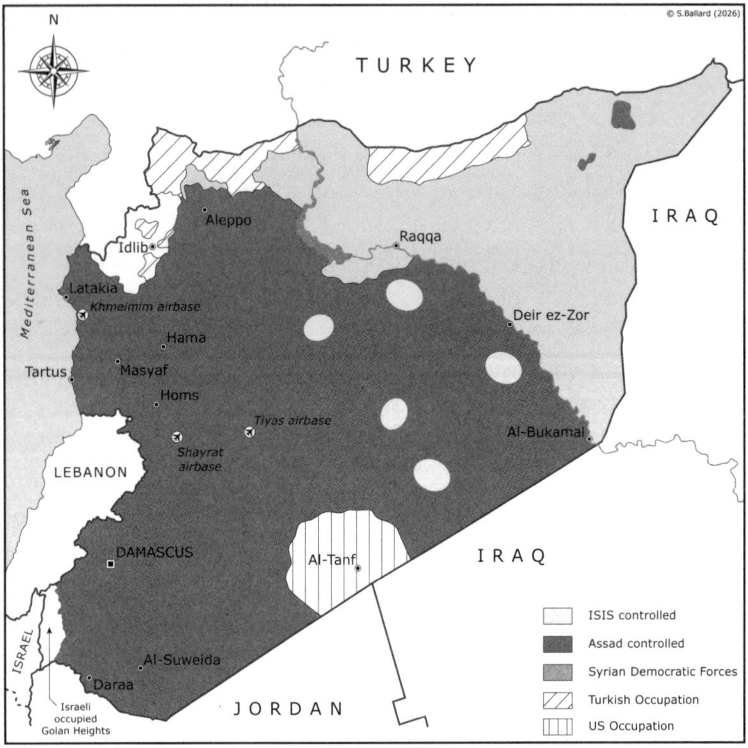

Map 3: Territorial Control and Foreign Military Presence in Syria, 2023

Economic Reconstruction

Aiming to recover costs incurred through their extensive military support for the Assad regime, both Russia and Iran quickly moved to secure lucrative economic ventures in Syria. Moscow prioritized energy and infrastructure concessions—obtaining rights to explore and develop offshore gas fields, operating key ports like Tartus, and overseeing major reconstruction projects in areas retaken by Syrian government forces. Meanwhile, Iran channeled resources into building industrial zones, revitalizing agricultural holdings, and establishing transportation corridors that linked Iranian trade routes to Mediterranean markets. Yet, as each country carved out discrete spheres of influence—backing preferred local militias, securing exclusive contracts, and forging patronage networks—Syria's internal divisions hardened rather than healed.

In 2015, *RBC* estimated that the Russian Ministry of Defense was spending around $620 million USD annually in Syria, which could be attributed to Russia's comparatively modest operational costs due to factors such as streamlined maritime supply routes, reduced salaries for military personnel, and decreased expenses for troop provisions.[91] Former Russian Finance Minister Alexei Kudrin highlighted Russia's minimal costs, stating that "in the medium term, Syria is not a strong burden."[92] In comparison, Iran has incurred substantial costs for its engagement in Syria. The UN estimated that Iran spent around $6 billion annually. Between 2011 and 2020, Iran spent around $30 billion USD in addition to multiple lines of credit of around $3 billion USD per year.[93] Burdened with this financial commitment, both Russia and Iran sought to lock in economic benefits, competing for contracts in oil, gas, phosphates, agriculture, ports, and real estate.

Russia and Iran formed economic councils to manage relations with Syrian partners and secure investment opportunities. Russia's council proved more expansive—reportedly hosting over 100 members, including state-backed enterprises and private firms—while Iran's equivalent featured fewer than a dozen members.[94] Moreover, Russia leveraged Syria's security apparatus to embed itself within the upper echelons of the Syrian state, whereas Iran tapped into grassroots networks of tribal leaders, religious communities, and local businesses, especially in areas like Hasakah, Homs, and Aleppo, where central government attention had waned.[95] These divergent approaches ultimately underlined a shared goal: extracting maximum economic advantage while simultaneously reinforcing sectarian or regional fault lines.

In practice, Russian and Iranian deals often bypassed or co-opted state institutions, strengthening fragmented governance structures in which loyalist strongmen, private security firms, and semi-autonomous militias became de facto gatekeepers of economic development. Rather than fostering a cohesive post-war recovery effort, these arrangements undercut attempts at centralized reconstruction. Critical public services—like health care, education, and infrastructure rehabilitation—were either unevenly distributed or overshadowed by specialized, profit-driven projects aimed at advancing the geostrategic or commercial interests of external sponsors.

A prime example of the competition between Russia and Iran materialized with the phosphate-rich Sharqiyah field near Palmyra. In early 2017, Damascus and Tehran inked a contract granting Iran rights to mine this critical resource. Yet, a mere six months later, Syrian authorities signed a fifty-year deal with Russia's Stroytransgaz to mine and market the same fields, guaranteeing a cut of the proceeds to the Syrian government but sidelining Iran.[96] This reversal epitomized a broader phenomenon: while Iran often secured initial agreements, many of them failed to transform into enduring partnerships, owing partly to Damascus's tactic of playing Moscow against Tehran to obtain more favorable terms. Sanctions also compounded Iran's difficulties; with its economy under strain, Tehran lacked the financial flexibility of its Russian rival, making it easier for Damascus to pivot toward Moscow when more advantageous offers arose.

The competitive dynamics for economic contracts occurred alongside cooperation on broader sanctions evasion schemes for Syria. Promsyrioimport, a subsidiary of Russia's Ministry of Energy, was engaged in a multifaceted scheme designed to evade sanctions between Russia, Iran, and Syria, especially in the energy sector. Promsyrioimport facilitated oil transfers from Iran to Syria, thus providing monetary sustenance to Assad's regime. The Syrian government, in return, sent payments to the sanctioned Russian bank Evrofinance Mosnarbank, which was then redistributed to support various Russian and Iranian initiatives, successfully sidestepping international restrictions.

While Damascus had effectively granted Moscow and Tehran special privileges, the estimated cost of Syria's reconstruction—ranging from $400 billion to $1 trillion—loomed too large for either power to handle alone. The European Union's refusal to finance rebuilding so long as Assad retained power further restricted potential funding sources. In response, Moscow launched a diplomatic campaign to draw in other stakeholders, particularly wealthy Gulf states. The United Arab Emirates reversed its anti-Assad stance in late 2018 by reopening its embassy in Damascus—a move widely attributed to Russian mediation—and later engaged in high-profile diplomatic exchanges, like Foreign Minister Abdullah bin Zayed al-Nahyan's visit to Syria in 2021.[97] Russia encouraged other countries (Algeria, Bahrain, Egypt, Oman, and Jordan) to adopt a similar approach, thereby aiming to dilute Iran's grip and share the financial burden of rebuilding Syria's battered economy.

Events such as the Damascus International Fair and the Rebuild Syria Expo—both heavily sponsored by Russia—evolved into showcases for investment opportunities in infrastructure, energy, and real estate.[98] Gulf countries, previously committed to Assad's downfall, began exploring these venues for potential reconstruction projects.[99] In doing so, Russia sought to serve as a broker and guarantor, reinforcing its indispensable role in Syria's economic future. Rather than focusing on sustainable reconstruction that could survive political changes, Russia and Iran created parallel networks of economic exploitation dependent on Assad's regime protection.

Russia's orchestrated efforts to attract Gulf investment and Iran's web of local business partnerships were built on the assumption of Assad's continued rule. Without him, the entire edifice of exploitative contracts, preferential deals, and sanctions evasion schemes began to unravel.

Reforming Syria's Military

Even though Iranian forces were central to Russia's military strategy, Moscow remained wary about the excessive sway of Iranian-backed militias and non-state actors in post-war Syria. Unlike Tehran's strategy of entrenching pro-Iranian local groups and militias, Moscow's plans for Syrian military reforms broadly focused on building a unified, professional Syrian Army.[100] Iran, on the other hand, placed a greater emphasis on empowering allied militias and cultivating ties with local communities to solidify its influence in Syria.

From the onset of its military campaign, Russia recognized that the Syrian Arab Army was unable to effectively bring stability to the conflict and preserve Syria's sovereignty.[101] Moscow focused on restoring the combat capability of the Syrian Army by training a unified and professionalized force akin to Syria's 25th Special Mission Forces Division while providing the Syrian Arab Army with weaponry, including T-90 tanks, modern armored personnel carriers, and unmanned aerial vehicles.[102] At the end of 2016, Russia announced the creation of the 5th Corps, which consisted of former defectors from the Syrian Army. Unlike the Iranian-aligned 4th Division, which had a limited area of action in Latakia, the 5th Corps was conceived to play a nationwide role.[103] Russia relied on General Suheil al-Hassan's 25th Special Mission Forces Division—formerly known as the Tiger Forces—and Zayd Salih's 5th Volunteer Assault Corps to reinforce its leverage in Syria. In July 2019, Russia also instigated a reshuffling of Syria's security apparatus, which saw new leadership appointed to the National Security Bureau and all four of Syria's intelligence directorates. Those promoted to these influential positions, namely Mohammed Deeb Zeitoun, Generals Ghasan Ismail, Hossam Louka, Nasser Deeb, and Nasser al-Ali, were known for their close ties with Russia's military.[104] Crucially, none of them had any public association with Iran or its interests.

For Moscow, supporting a centralized security apparatus was the most efficient way to ensure stability with minimal effort and risk. Such a strategy involved consolidating control over all armed entities, either by assimilating them into the Syrian military or neutralizing them, and re-establishing government control over public services and the economy. But ultimately, Russia turned a blind eye to the endemic corruption and weakness of the Syrian state. In contrast, Iran pursued a grassroots strategy to embed local Syrian partners within key state institutions, particularly in the security, governance, and economic sectors, while competing with the Arab Gulf states and Turkey for influence beyond traditional governmental structures. While Iran wielded influence over Assad's regime, the sustainability and extent of this influence remained contingent on Assad's continued rule and personal agenda. To hedge against this dependency, Tehran focused on entrenching allegiances with local actors in key provinces such as Aleppo, Homs, Deir ez-Zor, and the Lebanese borderlands.[105]

Russia and Iran's divergent strategies for building influence in Syria created a fundamental contradiction that ultimately undermined the Syrian state they claimed to be supporting. Rather than complementing each other, these parallel approaches created competing chains of command and divided loyalties within Syria's security apparatus. Russia's focus on elite units while neglecting broader structural reforms failed to address the underlying issues of corruption, poor morale, and weak command structures that had plagued the Syrian military since before the civil war. Their competing interventions had produced a hollow structure that required constant external support to maintain even basic functionality. When that support wavered in late 2024—with Russia distracted by Ukraine and Iran weakened by Israeli strikes—the entire edifice crumbled with surprising speed, exposing the fundamental flaw in trying to build state institutions through competing external patronage.

* * *

As discussed in Chapter 10, below, within a matter of days, the decade-long investments of Russia and Iran in propping up Assad's regime came crashing down. Yet, paradoxically, the collapse of their flagship joint venture in Syria did not diminish the broader partnership these two powers had forged. Throughout the war, Moscow and Tehran had developed extensive frameworks for military coordination, intelligence sharing, sanctions evasion, and geopolitical maneuvering—methods that could be repurposed far beyond Syria's borders.

Years before the fall of Assad, the election of Donald Trump in 2016 introduced a new variable that would profoundly reshape Russian-Iranian calculations. Trump's unpredictable foreign policy approach, his administration's "maximum pressure" campaign against Iran, and the broader atmosphere of sanctions and international isolation created external pressures that compelled Moscow and Tehran to deepen their partnership beyond the Syrian theater. Faced with an increasingly hostile and erratic American stance, both powers recognized that their bilateral cooperation offered strategic advantages that transcended their tactical disagreements in Syria.

Despite tensions over territorial control, reconstruction priorities, and regional influence, Russia and Iran had learned to compartmentalize their differences while expanding collaboration in other domains. As detailed in Chapter 6, the uncertainties and challenges posed by Trump's presidency would provide additional impetus for Moscow and Tehran to bridge their differences and expand their partnership into cyber warfare, energy cooperation, and third-country interventions, demonstrating how external pressures could strengthen bilateral ties even as core disagreements over Syria's future persisted.

6

MAXIMUM PRESSURE

In the summer of 2018, U.S. President Donald Trump took to Twitter. His message read: "To Iranian President Rouhani: NEVER, EVER THREATEN THE UNITED STATES AGAIN OR YOU WILL SUFFER CONSEQUENCES THE LIKES OF WHICH FEW THROUGHOUT HISTORY HAVE EVER SUFFERED BEFORE. WE ARE NO LONGER A COUNTRY THAT WILL STAND FOR YOUR DEMENTED WORDS OF VIOLENCE & DEATH. BE CAUTIOUS!"[1] It was this sentiment, this "maximum pressure" ethos, that came to typify the Trump administration's more aggressive U.S. policy stance towards Iran, encapsulated by its unilateral withdrawal from the Joint Comprehensive Plan of Action (JCPOA) and the implementation of stringent economic sanctions. Ostensibly designed to curb Iran's nuclear ambitions and diminish its regional clout, these policies inadvertently drove Iran into closer collaboration with Russia.

When Trump assumed office, the dynamics of the Russia-Iran relationship were changing. The Syrian Civil War had deepened the ties between Russia and Iran. Even though their divergent interests in the Syrian theater presented potential points of friction, these were eventually overshadowed by a sense of dissatisfaction engendered by U.S. policies under Trump. Historically, shared opposition to

U.S. strategies served as a unifying factor, even during periods of tension in their bilateral relationship. Seldom did Russia and Iran act on these convergences. However, their increasing ties in Syria led to the institutionalization of this partnership and a greater ability to compartmentalize relations, building and acting upon areas of convergence while temporarily overlooking divergences.

The Trump administration's policies further accelerated the convergence between Moscow and Tehran. By imposing sweeping sanctions on both states and branding them as threats to U.S. security, Washington inadvertently reinforced their shared sense of isolation and grievance. As this chapter shows, Trump's approach catalyzed a new phase of political alignment: both countries increasingly voiced solidarity and coordinated opposition to U.S. policy. The U.S. withdrawal from the JCPOA and the subsequent "maximum pressure" campaign against Iran elevated Russia's importance in Iranian foreign policy. Simultaneously, the deterioration of U.S.-Russia relations and the imposition of additional sanctions on Russia created fertile ground for Moscow and Tehran to unite in opposition to Washington's unilateralism.

Domestic challenges in both countries reinforced this trend. Although driven by different internal issues, protests in Russia and Iran became catalysts for mutual understanding and solidarity. Facing widespread international condemnation, both nations drew closer together as they mounted a shared defense against what they viewed as foreign meddling in their affairs. Unlike previous decades, Russia-Iran relations progressively strengthened as both countries transformed their mutual grievances into a source of bonding.

Fire and Fury

Michael Wolff's *Fire and Fury: Inside the Trump White House* (2018) offers a controversial and candid account of President Trump's first year in office. Packed with revelations and anecdotes depicting a chaotic White House, the book immediately caught the attention of readers across the globe. In Russia and Iran, the book was swiftly translated and illegally published online. Moreover, numerous references to the book by Russian and Iranian politicians suggested that its content was not just of public interest. For Iran and Russia, *Fire and Fury* was more than just a sensational exposé; it was a window into the chaos and power struggles within an administration that had significant implications for their own security.

The arc of Trump's relationship with Russia was complex, laden with intrigue and accusations of electoral interference. At the beginning, Trump professed a desire to cultivate warmer relations with Russia, a sentiment underscored by his congenial rhetoric about Russian President Putin. Yet, Trump's personal affinity for Putin often seemed to clash with his administration's policy actions. As investigations into Russian interference in the 2016 U.S. presidential election gained momentum, the administration's posture towards Russia grew increasingly guarded and reactive.

In parallel, Trump's hostility towards Iran was evident even during his presidential campaign, when he lambasted the Iran nuclear deal as a "disaster" and pledged to extricate the United States from its commitments. In office, he made good on this promise in May 2018. An advocate for his negotiating prowess, Trump was convinced he could broker a superior deal, one that would address Iran's regional activities and ballistic missile program more effectively. As a way to pressure Iran to the negotiating table after the U.S. withdrawal from the JCPOA, the Trump administration embarked on a "maximum pressure" campaign against Iran involving stringent economic sanctions.

As discussed in the previous chapter, during the early days of the Trump administration, Iran feared that it could become a sacrificial pawn in a "grand bargain" between the U.S. and Russia. Iranian unease stemmed from the possibility that Moscow, hoping to appease Washington, might negotiate a way to restrain Iranian influence in Syria. However, Tehran's concerns gradually abated as the U.S.-Russia dynamic turned frosty, primarily due to allegations of Russian interference in the 2016 U.S. elections.[2] The domestic pushback against Trump effectively stalled potential cooperation between Washington and Moscow, allaying Iran's fears of being leveraged as a bargaining chip by Russia. Moreover, sanctions imposed on Russia and Iran, combined with domestic protests in both countries, provided a further impetus for closer ties.

Sanctioning America's Adversaries

Sanctions became a hallmark of Trump's foreign policy, applied with notable rigor against Iran and, to a lesser degree, Russia. An unintended consequence of these sanctions was the strengthening of cooperation between Russia and Iran, creating an environment in which they united to resist American pressure. Sanctions cemented a partnership of defiance between Moscow and Tehran as Moscow leveraged lessons from Iran's experience to navigate these restrictive measures, a topic thoroughly examined in Chapters 7 and 9.

The Trump administration's sanctions on Iran were part of a wider effort to strangle Iran economically, which later became known as "maximum pressure." In February 2017, the U.S. imposed new sanctions targeting individuals and entities involved in Iran's missile program, including companies associated with the IRGC's procurement of technology and materials. Some of these individuals and companies would eventually play a crucial role in supporting Russia's war in Ukraine through the provision of armaments and drone technology.[3] One month after sanctions had been placed on Iran, Russian defense and intelligence firms were accused of breaching U.S. nonproliferation laws relating to Iran, North Korea, and Syria, resulting in a two-year ban preventing American entities from engaging with the sanctioned firms.[4] Viewed from Russia, these sanctions were seen as an attempt to categorize Russia and Iran as similar adversaries, a perception that intensified with new sanctions in the summer of 2017.[5] This deliberate grouping challenged a fundamental dynamic in Russian-Iranian relations: despite their cooperation, Moscow had consistently positioned itself as the superior partner, cultivating a hierarchical relationship where Russia maintained greater international standing and diplomatic leverage.

The introduction of the Countering America's Adversaries Through Sanctions Act (CAATSA) in August 2017 compounded the challenges in U.S.-Russia relations. Initially conceived as legislation focused on Iran, CAATSA evolved into an amalgamation of several proposed sanctions on Russia, Iran, and North Korea.[6] As CAATSA progressed through Congress, the spotlight increasingly shifted towards Russia due to its alleged election interference, annexation of Crimea, and support for Eastern Ukrainian separatists.[7] With Iran, CAATSA primarily strengthened existing legislation targeting its missile program, support for terrorism, and war-sustaining economic sectors.[8]

The implications of the CAATSA sanctions on Russia were more noteworthy than those imposed on Iran. CAATSA marked the first instance of the United States imposing secondary sanctions on Russia.[9] Unlike primary sanctions directly targeting a country's trade and economic activities, secondary sanctions are designed to dissuade other countries or entities from engaging in specified commercial or trade activities with the targeted country. In the case of CAATSA, the sanctions particularly targeted arms deals and economic activities associated with Russia's military-industrial complex. This not only restricted Russia's access to certain markets but also affected countries that purchased arms from Russia.

Various studies in Russia, some funded by the Russian government, attempted to forecast the impact of CAATSA on the economy. For example, a Russian Academy of Sciences report underscored the impact of secondary sanctions, calling for Russia to adopt import substitution measures similar to those adopted by Iran and China.[10] Russian economic experts emphasized this, highlighting that secondary sanctions were previously more characteristic of programs directed at Iran or North Korea, thus marking a shift in the application and target of these measures and calling for an innovative response.[11] Russian state television covered the sanctions in an episode of *Evening with Vladimir Solovyov*, where the eponymous host pointed out that the sanctions placed Russia "in the same league with Iran and North Korea."[12] Solovyov's guest on the program, military analyst Mikhail Khodarenok, posited that the United States had delineated two overarching objectives with the imposition of the sanctions: first, to ensnare Russia in an economically draining arms race, and second, to curtail Russia's revenue streams. Khodarenok conjectured that the sanctions aimed "to kick Russia out of global arms markets," particularly since they exert pressure on entities that potentially engage with Russia's military-industrial complex.[13]

Many within Russia also emphasized how the sanctions would limit the prospects for constructive engagement between Washington and Moscow. Former Foreign Minister Igor Ivanov underscored that aside from divergent views on cardinal issues in international relations, a "major obstacle to the normalization of bilateral ties is the package of sanctions adopted by Washington with respect to Russia."[14] Secondary sanctions on Russia, along with the focus on Russian interference in the 2016 election, led to a somber assessment of U.S.-Russia relations in Moscow. Russian commentator Dmitry Trenin remarked that August 2017 was a watershed moment in U.S.-Russia relations. The dynamic changed, with congressional leaders taking the reins of America's Russia policy, wresting control from the executive branch. For the first time, there was a bipartisan consensus in Congress against Russia, with Democrats viewing sanctions as a safeguard against any potential compromise of America's interests.[15] A Russian foreign policy expert lamented in 2017 that the allegations of election interference and the difficulty in removing secondary sanctions "will soil U.S.-Russia relations for the next three decades."[16] Although Russia continued to engage with the United States, Moscow recognized the limitations of its ties with Washington.

The simultaneous application of sanctions on Russia and Iran under CAATSA engendered a sense of shared hostility towards the Trump administration. With the United States as the common antagonist, observers opined that Moscow and Tehran should pursue collaborative measures to mitigate the impact of these economic constraints.[17] An analytical report on Gazeta.ru suggested that this confluence of interests under economic duress might prompt the Russian leadership to capitalize on the strained relations between Washington and Tehran, potentially drawing the U.S. into an international quagmire "to exacerbate Washington's relations with Tehran and Pyongyang and draw the [U.S.] into an international conflict which will stretch American resources for years."[18] Some analysts contended that the new circumstances created by the simultaneous imposition of U.S. sanctions on Russia and Iran could lead to a strengthening of military technical collaboration between the two countries, as a means of countering American pressure and mitigating the impact of the economic constraints.[19] The sense of common fates was expressed by Deputy Foreign Minister Sergey

Ryabkov, who noted that Russia and Iran "find [themselves] in a similar situation. Newer and newer sanctions are always being implemented against us. We are confident that the commonality of the line on defending sovereignty and carrying out an independent foreign policy between Russia and Iran will only become stronger."[20]

Iran Looks to Russia

The ripples of CAATSA colored Russian and Iranian interactions, sparking a greater interest in economic projects that had largely been neglected. They also deepened a sense of political affinity, as both governments increasingly emphasized partnership and mutual backing in international forums to project unity against external pressure. During President Vladimir Putin's notable visit to Tehran in November 2017, both countries explicitly voiced their joint opposition to U.S. economic dominance.[21] In Putin's meeting with Khamenei, the Supreme Leader proposed "countering U.S. sanctions and isolating America by refusing to use the dollar and instead using our national currencies in bilateral and multilateral financial operations."[22] Iran found its international stance progressively intertwined with Russia, as exemplified by Deputy Foreign Minister for Asia-Pacific Affairs Ebrahim Rahimpour's characterization of Putin's Tehran visit as a message to U.S. President Trump about Russia's determination to strengthen their relationship despite U.S. opposition. Rahimpour claimed that "this summit is more than just a simple meeting … it sends the message to the Americans that in spite of the statements and positions of the White House officials, countries are seeking to develop their relationships" with Iran.[23]

The uptick in the frequency and scope of Russia-Iran meetings coincided with a "hardening" towards the West in their respective domestic establishments. Russia and Iran also exhibited a newfound willingness to support one another in international settings, teaming up on initiatives that had previously elicited little attention. U.S. policies under Trump thus emerged as a significant driver of Russian-Iranian solidarity. Key American doctrinal documents explicitly identified Russia and Iran alongside China and North Korea as major global threats, fostering a perception of victimization in Moscow and

Tehran. The Trump administration's abandonment of longstanding treaties and promotion of military buildups exacerbated this sentiment.

As the Trump administration sought to redefine American priorities and strategies on the global stage, several documents articulating the contours of his America First strategy were released within the first year of his presidency. The National Security Strategy (NSS) adopted in December 2017 highlighted a return to great power competition, focusing specifically on Russia as a threat.[24] The Russian Foreign Ministry condemned the "anti-Russian passages" of the NSS, reflecting the U.S. aversion to "the strengthening of the economic and military power of Russia" since Washington seeks to retain its position as a leader in "a unipolar world order that focuses exclusively on American interests and needs."[25] Dmitry Peskov echoed this, noting that the document had an "imperial nature" and demonstrated a reluctance to abandon the idea of a "unipolar world."[26] Likewise, the Russian Ministry of Defense stated in U.S. doctrinal documents "the United States openly names Russia and China as its geopolitical rivals because [the U.S.] does not hesitate to declare that trends in international activity and the global economy that do not satisfy the United States can be corrected through reliance on increased military power."[27] Similarly, Iranian analyses concluded that Trump's policy reflected the desire to restore America to greatness by undermining the main countries that oppose U.S. global dominance—Iran, Russia, and China.[28]

Again, in February 2018, Russia's disdain was palpably directed at the "anti-Russian" sentiment in the U.S. Nuclear Posture Review, articulating a "deep disappointment" at the "confrontational charge" of the United States' stance towards Moscow.[29] President Rouhani, who interpreted the U.S. Nuclear Posture Review as a direct threat to Russia, echoed this sentiment of dissatisfaction on 4 February, stating that "today, America threatens Russia with new nuclear weapons, while it believes that the use of this weapon is against international regulations, and no country has the right to use it, but it [the U.S.] is talking about a new weapon—for use or threat."[30]

This solidarity extended to unprecedented mutual diplomatic support. In February 2018, Russia vetoed a United Nations Security

Council (UNSC) resolution backed by the United States that would have imposed additional measures against Iran for allegedly violating an arms embargo on Houthi rebels in Yemen.[31] Ali Akbar Velayati, a senior advisor to Iran's Supreme Leader, celebrated this action as an "indication of the two sides' growing and strategic ties."[32] Likewise, Iranian media highlighted its historical significance as Russia's first veto against an anti-Iranian resolution since the Soviet Union's stance during the 1980 hostage crisis.[33] Iran reciprocated by increasingly supporting Russia's position on Ukraine. Initially cautious about directly undermining Ukraine's territorial integrity, Tehran's stance evolved significantly by mid-2018 following the U.S. withdrawal from the JCPOA and implementation of "maximum pressure" sanctions.[34] Iran subsequently proposed amendments to United Nations General Assembly (UNGA) resolutions favoring Russia's position on contentious issues like the 2018 Kerch Strait incident and joined countries like Bolivia and Syria in opposing resolutions condemning Russian aggression and misconduct in Ukraine.[35]

In the past, Russia's and Iran's discontent with broader international issues was often articulated but seldom translated into action. However, the increase in contacts in Syria and their shared discontent strengthened the basis for cooperation. The Trump administration's aggressive policies—from sanctions to military threats—only accelerated this partnership, pushing Moscow and Tehran to discover new areas of alignment beyond Syria.

United in Repression

As Russia and Iran both faced a hostile external environment, simultaneous domestic threats to regime stability continued to foster a sense of mutual understanding and cooperation. Just like external threats, shared internal threat perceptions can serve as a powerful motivator for states to collaborate and work together by sharing resources, intelligence, and tactics. Russia and Iran harbored deep concerns about Western interference, especially after the Color Revolutions and the 2009 Green Movement. These internal threat perceptions were particularly evident during anti-corruption protests in Russia in 2017 and protests in Iran in 2017-18. As in the past, instances of internal unrest and threats to regime stability have served to strengthen the bonds between Russia and Iran.

In March 2017, widespread anti-corruption protests erupted across Russia, sparked by the release of the investigative film *He Is Not Dimon to You* by Alexei Navalny's Anti-Corruption Foundation.[36] The film exposed the corrupt activities of Prime Minister Dmitry Medvedev, including his expensive footwear collection, gifts of estates by oligarchs, secret villas, and ventures into viticulture and offshore yachts. In response, protests erupted across Russia as hundreds of protestors were detained, and eventually, Navalny was arrested. During the protests, Iranian officials were quick to rush to Moscow's support and accuse the U.S. of direct involvement.[37] Moreover, since the 2011-12 Duma protests, the Kremlin's repertoire of repression had grown, with the deployment of riot police and heightened surveillance. Iran, observing these developments closely, was keen to draw lessons from Russia's expanding toolkit of domestic control, particularly its use of surveillance and policing to preempt organized dissent.

Iran faced its own wave of protests in late December 2017. What began as localized demonstrations against economic hardship in Mashhad quickly engulfed the nation, fueled by youth frustration over unemployment, inflation, and inequality. The Iranian government, adhering to a familiar narrative, accused foreign powers—namely the United States and Israel—of fomenting the unrest. Russian officials echoed Iran's claims of external interference, criticizing the U.S. and its allies for allegedly fueling the protests.[38] This show of solidarity culminated in a January 2018 UNSC meeting, where Russia openly rebuked the U.S. for condemning Iran's suppression of the protests. Moscow's stance was unequivocal: it denounced any foreign attempts to exploit the situation as a means to destabilize Iran or to meddle in "Iran's internal affairs."[39] Russia's Deputy Foreign Minister Ryabkov issued a stern warning to the United States, cautioning "against attempts to interfere in the internal affairs of the Islamic Republic of Iran."[40]

Russia's state-funded broadcasters, *RT* and *Sputnik*, advanced a narrative suggesting that the British secret services may have had a hand in fomenting anti-government demonstrations in Iran.[41]

Both referred to comments made by a convicted hacker residing in the UK who accused GCHQ, the UK organization in charge of signals intelligence, of conducting disinformation operations by infiltrating activist circles to "neutralize" their adversaries.[42] The narrative promoted by Russian state media aligned with Moscow's and Tehran's tendencies of casting doubt on the legitimacy of domestic protests.[43] Such a tactic aligns with efforts to discredit and delegitimize dissenting voices, with their respective state-led media outlets portraying the protests as orchestrated by Western powers.[44]

The partnership between Russia and Iran extended beyond rhetoric, encompassing practical intelligence-sharing and coordinated strategies against domestic unrest. This cooperation was institutionalized through agreements signed by their respective Interior Ministries following previous mass protests, including those in 2009 and 2011-12. These agreements broadly defined cooperation in maintaining public order, deliberately leaving terms like "unrest" ambiguous to justify extensive suppressive measures. Provisions covered exchanging expertise, techniques, and specialized equipment designed to quell demonstrations and manage emergencies like riots or natural disasters.[45] In practice, this cooperation proved effective, as demonstrated in 2019 when Iranian Major General Mostafa Izadi revealed that Russian intelligence had provided advance warnings of impending protests.[46]

Building upon this foundation of coordinated internal security measures, Russia and Iran entered into a bilateral agreement on information security in late 2020. While ostensibly aimed at fostering bilateral cooperation in the cyber domain, the Russia-Iran agreement on information security effectively serves as a conduit for sharing and legitimizing repressive practices.[47] Under its provisions, the two states broadly categorized information security threats as "acts aimed at violating the sovereignty, security, and territorial integrity of states," including actions aimed at the "disruption of public order," "destabilizing the internal political and socio-economic situation," and "interfering in state governance."[48] This expansive interpretation provided a legal rationale for censorship and suppression of dissent, allowing Russia and Iran to exchange information and methodologies designed to neutralize perceived threats under the banner of national security.

The information security pact marked the culmination of Russia and Iran's efforts to manage internal unrest while countering external pressure. Building on earlier interior ministry agreements that enabled intelligence-sharing and protest control, the pact extended this cooperation into the cyber and information spheres, converting episodic coordination into a formalized framework. It reflected a shared calculation that regime stability required linking domestic security with foreign policy. In practice, this collaboration strengthened both governments' capacity to manage dissent and reinforced the political foundations of their rule at home.

* * *

General Soleimani's visit to Moscow in July 2015, detailed in Chapter 4, played a major role in shaping the joint Russia-Iran military campaign in Syria. Soleimani's visit coincided with the signing of the Iran nuclear deal, the JCPOA. Since 2013, Iran and the P5+1, comprising the five permanent members of the UNSC plus Germany, had engaged in negotiations over Iran's nuclear program.[49] During these negotiations, Russian diplomats played a constructive role, especially on technical issues such as creating a 300-kilogram threshold for stockpiled low-enriched uranium. Russia also offered crucial interventions on procedural matters such as the agreement's innovative sanctions snapback mechanism, which allowed any participant in the agreement to trigger the reintroduction (or "snapback") of UNSC sanctions on Iran if they believe Iran has violated the terms of the agreement.[50] Remarkably, despite broader tensions arising from Russia's 2014 annexation of Crimea, Moscow effectively compartmentalized these differences, maintaining pragmatic cooperation with Washington and other negotiating partners to achieve a diplomatic resolution to Iran's nuclear program.[51]

The JCPOA aimed to balance international concerns about Iran's nuclear capabilities with Iran's demand for sanctions relief. The negotiations, characterized by complex technical and diplomatic trade-offs, eventually produced an agreement praised by many as a significant diplomatic success. Under the terms of the agreement, Iran agreed to limit its nuclear program and subject it to enhanced

IAEA inspections in exchange for relief from economic sanctions, which had severely affected its economy.

Russia officially reacted positively to the JCPOA, with President Putin praising the agreement on 14 July 2015 and emphasizing the vital contributions made by the Russian negotiating team.[52] However, some in Russia were apprehensive about the agreement's potential implications. Russian analysts voiced concerns about the potential broader geopolitical shifts that the JCPOA could usher in, particularly the prospect of a détente between the U.S. and Iran, which could undercut Russia's influence.[53] Russian policymakers recognized that lifting sanctions on Iran could disrupt global energy markets and dilute Moscow's influence as a major exporter. The anticipated surge of Iranian oil and gas threatened to depress prices and heighten competition in sectors central to Russia's economy. Yet the Kremlin ultimately judged that supporting the JCPOA served its broader strategic interests. The agreement's framework offered enough protection for Russian energy ventures, while most analysts in Moscow doubted it would trigger a lasting rapprochement between Tehran and Washington—limiting the potential for any geopolitical fallout at Russia's expense.

Withdrawing from the "Worst Deal Ever"

For Donald Trump, the Iran nuclear deal was a "disaster" and the "worst deal ever." During his presidential campaign and while in office, Trump continued to threaten a U.S. withdrawal from the deal. Months of diplomacy, led by Europe, Russia, and China, to convince the Trump administration to remain in the deal were futile. A little more than a year after assuming office, in May 2018, Trump announced the United States' withdrawal from the JCPOA. During his speech announcing the withdrawal, Trump declared that "America will not be held hostage to nuclear blackmail" and would reinstate both primary and secondary sanctions against Iran that had been lifted under the JCPOA.[54]

Predictably, Iran issued a forceful rebuke of the Trump administration's withdrawal, which President Rouhani described as a form of "psychological warfare and economic pressure."[55] Rouhani declared that "Iran is a country that adheres to its commitments," drawing a sharp contrast with the United States, which, in his view, "has never adhered to its commitments."[56] Russia joined Iran in unequivocally condemning Trump's decision and accused the U.S. of pursuing "its own narrow and opportunistic interests," claiming that "the U.S. objections to Iran's absolutely legal nuclear activity are nothing but a smokescreen for settling political scores with Iran."[57]

After the Trump administration's withdrawal from the JCPOA, Russia continued to denounce "the illegitimate unilateral sanctions and the wider U.S.-led anti-Iran campaign" while pressuring Tehran to abide by its obligations under the accord.[58] When the U.S. moved to re-impose JCPOA-related sanctions on Iran through the snapback mechanism, a member of the Russian Foreign Ministry's international law committee indicated that Moscow had preparations in place to oppose Washington's actions.[59] To this end, Russia and China constructed a sophisticated rejoinder to the Trump administration's moves to trigger the snapback provision, eventually blocking U.S. efforts to reimpose sanctions on Iran.

The U.S. exit from the JCPOA marked a turning point, intensifying the perception that Washington was stepping back from its international commitments. For Iran, the withdrawal not only represented a betrayal but was also seen as an existential threat due to the reinstated sanctions. Russia saw it as further evidence of U.S. indifference to international treaties, echoing its own grievances related to Washington's abrogation of agreements.[60] In the aftermath of the JCPOA withdrawal, the Trump administration intensified its assertive stance towards arms control, turning its scrutiny toward the Intermediate-Range Nuclear Forces (INF) Treaty. The INF Treaty prohibited the possession, production, and flight-testing of ground-launched ballistic and cruise missiles with ranges of 500 to 5,500 km, effectively removing a whole category of nuclear weapons from Europe. In October 2018, citing alleged Russian noncompliance as the rationale, President Trump announced that the U.S. intended to withdraw from the treaty. Russia reacted with vehement protest, viewing the withdrawal as a unilateral American action that disregarded its interests and potentially opened the door for unchecked U.S. missile deployments near Russian borders.

With its repeated withdrawals from key international agreements—most notably the JCPOA and the INF Treaty—the Trump administration reinforced perceptions in Moscow and Tehran of U.S. unilateralism and disregard for established norms. For Iran, the U.S. abandonment of the nuclear deal represented both a betrayal and a direct existential threat due to renewed sanctions, while Russia viewed Washington's actions as confirmation of American unwillingness to honor international commitments when inconvenient. As explored in Chapter 7, these developments allowed Russia to position Iran at the center of a broader diplomatic effort aimed at harnessing global discontent against U.S. policies, particularly by challenging Washington's use of sanctions, its selective approach to human rights, and its erosion of state sovereignty as justifications for interference in the internal affairs of other countries.

Unleashing Maximum Pressure

Following its exit from the JCPOA, Washington embarked on its "maximum pressure" campaign. The campaign saw the imposition of stringent economic sanctions against Iran, focusing on critical sectors such as oil, banking, and metals, with the aim of crippling its economy and forcing Tehran back to the negotiating table for a more favorable deal.[61] The rationale was that by maximally exploiting its economic levers, the U.S. could secure concessions from Iran regarding not only its nuclear program but also some of its regional activities that Washington and its allies viewed as a source of instability. Moreover, secondary sanctions imposed by the Trump administration forced entities worldwide to choose between trading with Iran or maintaining access to the U.S. market.[62] Affecting sectors like energy, shipping, and finance, these sanctions targeted foreign financial institutions dealing with Iran's Central Bank and Iranian banks' access to SWIFT, a global financial messaging system that facilitates cross-border payments. By the close of 2018, the U.S. had enacted an additional twenty rounds of sanctions against Iran.

The initial Iranian reaction was one of restraint. Tehran sought to work closely with the remaining signatories of the agreement, particularly the E3 (France, the UK, and Germany), Russia, and China, in an attempt to circumvent U.S. sanctions and preserve the economic benefits promised under the accord. Despite these efforts, the crippling impact of reimposed U.S. sanctions began to take a toll on the Iranian economy, leading to widespread societal discontent and pressuring the regime to reconsider its stance on the nuclear deal.

On 8 May 2019, exactly one year after the U.S. withdrawal from the JCPOA, President Rouhani announced in a televised address that Iran would suspend commitments it had voluntarily made under the JCPOA.[63] Every ninety days, Iran would initiate a step-by-step withdrawal from its obligations under the JCPOA, aiming to pressure the European Union and other signatories to mitigate the effects of American sanctions. These measures included increasing its uranium stockpile and enrichment levels beyond the thresholds in the agreement and hindering the access of IAEA inspectors to nuclear sites.[64]

Iran's announcement coincided with Foreign Minister Zarif's visit to Moscow to meet with his Russian counterpart Sergey Lavrov. After the meeting, Lavrov stated that Russia acknowledged that the U.S. administration's revocation of sanctions waivers for nuclear cooperation with Iran had made it difficult for Tehran to fulfill its obligations.[65] Behind closed doors, Lavrov and Zarif were reported to have been "screaming" at each other, which was overheard by journalists awaiting the subsequent press conference.[66] Despite public statements in support of Iran's actions, Russia opposed Iran's decision to resume and expand its enrichment activities. From the Kremlin's perspective, Iran's decision would inadvertently play into the narratives of hardline voices in the U.S. and Israel, providing them with a stronger rationale for military action against Tehran. Reflecting on this concern, a former Russian diplomat remarked that "Iran was doing exactly what the U.S. wanted it to do" to justify a military escalation.[67]

The belief in Russian diplomatic circles was that Iran's actions, whether intended or not, provided the very pretext the U.S.

might have been seeking for broader escalation.[68] Russia's stance extended beyond mere support for the JCPOA. It included a word of caution to Iran against unintentionally setting the stage for a war with Washington. In the summer of 2019, a Russian foreign policy observer encapsulated Moscow's position, stating "Russia's position is clear. Moscow rejects the United States' actions against Iran, including unilateral sanctions that forced Iran to freeze some of the terms of the nuclear deal … but who wants another war in the Middle East?"[69]

* * *

"Maximum pressure" reverberated to the Persian Gulf.[70] Throughout 2019, a series of incidents and escalations brought the U.S. and Iran to the brink of direct military conflict. Russia, sensing both opportunity and danger in this escalation, positioned itself as Iran's diplomatic shield while working to de-escalate tensions and establish itself as an indispensable power broker in the region.[71] The United States' unprecedented decision to designate the IRGC Quds Force as a foreign terrorist organization—marking the first time such a label had been applied to another nation's military apparatus—proved to be the catalyst for an escalatory spiral.[72] Iran's swift retaliation, labeling the U.S. as a "state sponsor of terrorism" and demanding American military withdrawal from the Middle East, signaled its willingness to match Washington's aggressive posture. Meanwhile, Russia, through Foreign Ministry spokeswoman Maria Zakharova, seized this moment to chastise U.S. policy as part of a broader "demonizing" strategy against Iran.[73]

The crisis intensified when the U.S. moved to strangle Iran's economic lifeline by ending oil purchase waivers for eight countries, effectively isolating Tehran from its primary source of foreign revenue.[74] Then, National Security Advisor John Bolton announced the deployment of an aircraft carrier strike group to the Middle East to respond to any kind of attack from Iran or its proxies.[75] The crisis took a turn for the worse when Iran initiated a series of aggressive actions targeting oil tankers in the Persian Gulf, followed by attacks on crucial infrastructure. In retaliation, the U.S. ramped up its military presence in the area and advocated for the formation of a coalition akin to an "Arab NATO" against Iran to safeguard vital maritime trade routes.

Tankers, Troops, and Drones

On 12 May 2019, four oil tankers—two Saudi, one Norwegian, and one Emirati—were targeted near the port of Fujairah in the UAE. Initial suspicions gravitated towards Iran, with such speculation gaining substantial ground in July when the U.S. furnished evidence implicating the IRGC. According to the U.S., a total of almost twenty IRGC swift inshore attack boats were launched from Iran's territorial sea in the Strait of Hormuz just prior to the sabotage. In response, the U.S. bolstered its verbal threats to Iran with the deployment of an additional 1,500 troops to the Middle East, a move President Trump said was aimed at countering Iran more effectively.[76] Russian Foreign Minister Lavrov criticized additional U.S. troop deployments, warning that "risks always grow during a military buildup."[77]

Concerned by the mounting conflict, President Putin convened a meeting of the Russian Security Council to deliberate on the situation in Iran and the escalating tension in the region.[78] The Russian Security Council meeting was indicative of the concern among Russian officials that a direct U.S.-Iran military confrontation would trigger a perilous escalation and adversely impact Russia's interests.[79] A former Russian diplomat rebuked the U.S. for its policies, noting that "while the U.S. proclaims its intention to change the approach of the Iranian government, Russia perceives these efforts as a disguised plan to topple the existing regime, and [Russia] is prepared to oppose it."[80] Similarly, Russian Senator Alexei Pushkov believed that the United States was preparing for an invasion of Iran akin to "the Iraqi scenario." According to Pushkov:

> In 2003, U.S. Vice President Cheney said: It's time to take Iraq. But they took it so much that they didn't know how to quit later. Now Bolton is playing the role of Cheney, calling for a strike on Iran. The Pentagon is ready to send 120,000 soldiers to the Middle East ... A war is being prepared.[81]

Russia's concerns about a looming war were not without foundation, as both the U.S. and Iran appeared to be heading toward direct military confrontation. Still, Russian officials dismissed the accusations leveled against Iran, insinuating an orchestrated campaign of provocations designed to escalate regional tensions.[82] The dismissive stance was reiterated in the Russian press over allegations about Iran's involvement in the sabotage of the tankers. An article in *Moskovskiy Komsomolets* claimed that:

> the direct involvement of Iran in the attack remains questionable ... the assault on tankers might have been a calculated provocation executed by a particular entity targeting Iran, especially given that the Middle East is a hotbed of Tehran's adversaries, from Israel to Saudi Arabia, all desiring the demise of the Iranian regime.[83]

Similarly, Vladimir Fitin, a Russia-based specialist on Iran, claimed that the attacks may have been orchestrated by the Gulf monarchies, who were keen on fueling tensions between Washington and Tehran, or by Israeli intelligence agencies.[84]

Russia defended Iran on the international stage, especially during a U.S.-organized UNSC meeting where Washington presented evidence of Iran's involvement in the Fujairah attacks. During the UNSC meeting, the Russian representative criticized the United States' claims of Iran's involvement in earlier attacks, likening the situation to the pretext for the 2003 Iraq invasion. Dismissing U.S. allegations, Russia declared "that the situation in the Persian Gulf is being artificially ramped up and is jeopardizing peace and security in the region," adding that Russia is "not convinced by the so-called proof" of Iran's culpability and describing the situation as "increasingly reminiscent of the events of March 2003, when arguments were fabricated to justify an invasion of Iraq."[85] While Russia was outwardly supportive of Iran, several Russian experts doubted Tehran's innocence, with some implying that Russia may be intentionally overlooking Iran's culpability to portray the U.S. as a bad-faith actor.[86]

Exactly one month after the attacks in Fujairah, the path of confrontation between Washington and Tehran continued unabated.

In June, two more tankers—the Norwegian-owned *Front Altair* and the Japanese-owned *Kokuka Courageous*—were attacked in the Gulf of Oman. The U.S. accused Iran of being responsible, citing video evidence allegedly showing IRGC personnel removing an unexploded mine from one of the vessels.[87] The second attack on tankers in the Persian Gulf coincided with the Shanghai Cooperation Organization (SCO) summit in Bishkek, where both Putin and Rouhani were in attendance.[88] With Iran under increasing pressure from the United States, Putin emphasized Russia's support for Iran and rebuked the United States for "destabilizing the region."[89]

The tensions reached a flashpoint on 20 June 2019 when Iran's Islamic Revolutionary Guard Corps Aerospace Force (IRGC-AF) downed a U.S. RQ-4A Global Hawk spy drone.[90] IRGC Commander, Hossein Salami, alleged the drone had violated Iranian airspace, with Iran's response sending a "clear message" to the United States.[91] U.S. Central Command contended that the downing was an "unprovoked attack," insisting the drone was over international waters in the Strait of Hormuz.[92] The U.S. claim was later disputed by the Secretary of the Russian National Security Council, Nikolai Patrushev, during a meeting between U.S. National Security Adviser John Bolton and Israel's National Security Adviser Meir Ben-Shabbat. During the trilateral meeting with his Israeli and U.S. counterparts, Patrushev presented military intelligence indicating that the U.S. drone was indeed within Iranian airspace when it was shot down, defying Washington's account of the incident.[93]

Russia again supported Iran in early July 2019 when Gibraltar, with the help of the Royal Navy, impounded *Grace I*, a tanker suspected of carrying Iranian oil to Syria in violation of EU sanctions.[94] Khamenei called the seizure of the oil tanker an act of "piracy" and vowed to retaliate, while Zarif scolded the UK for "helping the United States to impose its illegal oil sanctions against Iran."[95] In apparent retaliation, Iranian forces seized the British-flag tanker *Stena Impero* while transiting through the Strait of Hormuz on 19 July 2019.[96] Russia attributed the UK's measures to influence from the United States, suggesting a coordinated effort between London and Washington. Russian analysis indicated that the UK's involvement "was likely to have been carefully prepared not only in

London but also in Washington."[97] In light of these events, Russian diplomats issued a series of warnings against "anti-Iranian" initiatives by Western powers, cautioning that such moves could lead to a military conflict in the Gulf.[98]

In perhaps the most noteworthy indication of Iran's military advances, two of Saudi Arabia's primary oil facilities, Abqaiq and Khurais, were targeted in a coordinated attack in September 2019. Though the attack was initially claimed by the Houthis in Yemen, subsequent investigations led primarily by the U.S. placed the responsibility on Iran. The investigations unveiled evidence indicating that the drones and missiles used in the attack bore technological characteristics consistent with Iranian design and production capabilities.[99] The trajectory analysis contradicted the Houthi rebels' initial claims by revealing that the launch site was located north of the targeted facilities, suggesting the attack originated from Iran's territory rather than Yemen.

According to a Russian defense expert, the Iranian drone and missile attack on Saudi Arabia impressed Russia, leading it to realize "how far Iran's [missile and drone] program" had progressed.[100] The individuals behind this demonstration of Iran's military prowess, particularly IRGC-AF Commander Brigadier General Amir Ali Hajizadeh and Brigadier General Saeed Aghajani, would later become pivotal figures in facilitating Iranian drone transfers and knowledge-sharing with Russia during the war in Ukraine.[101] Yet, despite Russia's acknowledgment of Iran's enhanced military capabilities, Moscow simultaneously worked to de-escalate tensions, aiming to leverage regional instability to position itself as a diplomatic broker and stabilizing influence in the Persian Gulf.

A Peace Plan for the Persian Gulf

Amid rising tensions between Iran and the U.S. in the Persian Gulf, the Russian Foreign Ministry announced its "Collective Security Concept for the Persian Gulf," which was followed by Iran's parallel intra-regional proposal Hormuz Peace Endeavor (HOPE).[102] On 23 July 2019, Special Presidential Representative for the Middle East and Africa and Deputy Foreign Minister Mikhail Bogdanov presented

Russia's Collective Security Concept for the Persian Gulf at a meeting with GCC, Iraq, Iran, Turkey, the five permanent members of the UNSC, the European Union, and the Arab League.[103]

Moscow and Tehran have historically advocated for a collective security framework in the Persian Gulf, an approach first proposed during the Brezhnev era in diplomatic outreach to the Shah of Iran and periodically revived during periods of regional tension.[104] In early 2016, Russian officials and policy experts revisited and expanded this idea, proposing an inclusive Middle East security structure that would not only encompass Arab states but also integrate Iran, Turkey, and even Israel.[105] At its core, this vision was driven by a recognition among regional and external powers of the need to collectively address instability, prevent conflict escalation, and manage crises in a region fraught with persistent tensions and rivalries.[106]

Following Russia's rapprochement with Turkey in the latter half of 2016, policymakers in Moscow saw an opportunity to solidify Russia's image as an influential and impartial power broker, one capable of diplomatic outreach to all regional actors regardless of competing interests or historical antagonisms. The deteriorating regional security environment—exacerbated by the confrontational posture of the Trump administration toward Iran, and subsequent military escalations in the Persian Gulf—offered Moscow precisely the opening it sought.[107] In promoting a collective security concept, Russia aimed not only to stabilize the region and reduce the risk of direct U.S.-Iranian confrontation but also to strategically position itself as a diplomatic counterweight to Washington.[108]

Shortly after Russia put forward its proposed Persian Gulf Security Concept, Iran unveiled its invitation for all Persian Gulf littoral states—Bahrain, Iraq, Saudi Arabia, Oman, and the UAE—to join HOPE, which elucidated a series of objectives and principles as well as a roadmap for Tehran's "subject-oriented and inclusive plan" for security in the region. Iran has advocated for a collective security system in the Persian Gulf without the involvement of non regional powers, often invoking UNSC Resolution 598, which called for a ceasefire and laid the groundwork for ending the Iran-Iraq War, as the legal basis for such an initiative. Beyond establishing a ceasefire between Iran and Iraq, Resolution 598 called upon the

UN Secretary-General to explore "measures to enhance the security and stability of the region" through consultations with Iran, Iraq, and neighboring states.[109]

Russia's and Iran's proposals for collective Persian Gulf security, though framed as measures for regional stability, encountered significant resistance and skepticism. Central to both plans was the contentious demand for the withdrawal of foreign, primarily U.S. military forces from the region, a stance that immediately alienated key Gulf states reliant on longstanding American security guarantees. This rejection underscored not only the enduring distrust of Iranian intentions and suspicion regarding Russia's strategic ambitions but also highlighted the complex security dilemmas faced by Arab states caught between regional rivalries and their established defense partnerships with Western powers.

Given these entrenched divisions, the envisioned collective security initiatives struggled to gain meaningful support. Rather than serving as platforms for regional cooperation, the proposals inadvertently reinforced existing fault lines, further illustrating the difficulty of bridging competing national interests and security perceptions. Ultimately, this diplomatic impasse left the region vulnerable to instability, as diplomatic channels failed to defuse escalating tensions. These unresolved tensions soon manifested vividly in a series of dangerous military incidents in early 2020 during a series of heightened confrontations between Iranian and American forces.

* * *

In December 2019, the naval forces of Russia, Iran, and China conducted their first-ever trilateral naval exercise in the Gulf of Oman. This trilateral exercise was more than a mere demonstration of naval interoperability among these nations; it was a coordinated move, signaling a united front against what was perceived as the Trump administration's unchecked unilateralism.[110]

The naval exercises took place against the backdrop of a surge in tensions over an attack on the K1 military base, hosting both American and Iraqi forces in Kirkuk. On 27 December, the base was hit by over thirty missiles, claiming the life of a U.S. civilian contractor and wounding several American and Iraqi personnel. The U.S. swiftly attributed the attack to the Iranian-supported militia Kata'ib Hezbollah and launched strikes targeting the group's strongholds in Iraq and Syria.[111] By 31 December, the U.S. embassy in Baghdad had been besieged by crowds of protesters, many identified as members of militia groups, who set parts of the embassy ablaze and engaged in extensive vandalism. The situation necessitated the evacuation of embassy staff, and non-emergency personnel were urged to leave Iraq posthaste. The events of December 2019 served as a precursor to the even more tumultuous events that would unfold in the early days of 2020.

In the early hours of 3 January 2020, Major General Qassem Soleimani, the commander of Iran's elite IRGC Quds Force, arrived in Baghdad on a covert mission to meet with Iraqi militia leaders. Despite his attempts to maintain secrecy, U.S. intelligence had been tracking his movements closely. Upon landing at Baghdad International Airport, Soleimani was greeted by Abu Mahdi al-Muhandis, a key Iraqi militia leader and deputy commander of the Iran-backed Popular Mobilization Forces (PMF). As Soleimani's motorcade exited the airport perimeter, an MQ-9 Reaper drone, loitering on station, released a Hellfire missile with surgical precision.[112] The strike killed Soleimani, al-Muhandis, and seven of their entourage in under a minute. The United States' assassination of Major General Soleimani triggered a maelstrom enveloping the Islamic Republic of Iran and its neighbors.

In Tehran, mourners thronged the hospitals and streets, beating their chests and chanting "We will avenge you, General"—a ritual of collective grief and defiance.[113] The Iranian parliament convened an emergency session, unanimously condemning the assassination and designating all U.S. forces in the region as "terrorists." Supreme Leader Ayatollah Khamenei, visibly enraged, vowed "severe revenge" and declared three days of national mourning.

Iran's retaliatory response, codenamed "Operation Martyr Soleimani," unfolded just five days later. In the early morning of 8 January, the IRGC launched a salvo of more than a dozen medium-range ballistic missiles—primarily Fateh110 and Qiam1 variants—at two Iraqi bases hosting American troops: the sprawling Ain al-Asad airbase in Anbar province and the Erbil garrison in Iraqi Kurdistan.[114] In a rare demonstration of direct Iranian firepower against U.S. forces, Tehran issued warnings that were transmitted through Iraqi channels and even a late-night tweet to allow personnel to seek shelter.[115] At approximately 6:30 a.m., the first missiles struck runway aprons, munitions depots, and command centers, leaving craters in hardened pads and damaging several aircraft hangars. No U.S. service members were killed, though dozens would later be diagnosed with concussive injuries.

The assassinations and counterstrikes reverberated in Syria, where Russia's so-called "return" to the Middle East through its intervention was predicated on the use of Iranian-backed ground forces under Soleimani's command. Soleimani's role in strengthening Russian and Iranian military cooperation was clear in the Russian Ministry of Defense's statement describing the Quds commander as "a competent military leader, [with] well-deserved authority and significant influence in the entire Middle East."[116] This sentiment was echoed by Velayati, who attributed Soleimani to the formation of the Russia-Iran partnership and the development of a close relationship with Russian President Putin.[117] Yet when Soleimani was killed, Moscow's response was deliberately measured: a strongly worded denunciation of U.S. actions, coupled with quiet diplomatic overtures aimed at de-escalation. Russia recognized that a broader U.S.-Iran conflagration would threaten its foothold in Syria and risk unraveling the delicate web of partnerships it had spent years weaving.

The Past, Present, and Future of Russia-Iran Relations

In the pre-dawn stillness of 8 January 2020—just hours after Iran's "Operation Martyr Soleimani" began—Ukraine International Airlines Flight PS752 lifted off from Tehran's Imam Khomeini International Airport bound for Kyiv. As one of the few regular carriers connecting Iran to Europe and North America, PS752 was crowded with students, professionals, and families returning home or traveling abroad.[118] At 6:16 a.m., less than three minutes after departure, a pilot on Baseman Airlines Flight 3768 radioed Tehran's approach controller: "We're seeing a series of flares—like a missile launch."[119] The controller, unaware of any such activity, replied, "No information on that here." Four minutes later, the Baseman pilot's tone had turned urgent: "It was an explosion, sir—we're seeing a huge flash."[120] The devastating realization would soon dawn: the explosion was Flight PS752, and all 176 passengers and crew on board had perished.

In the immediate aftermath of the crash, the cause of the tragedy surrounding Flight PS752 was shrouded in mystery. The wreckage suggested a mid-air explosion. Iranian officials denied any foul play, but the context surrounding Flight PS752 played into the idea that it could have been shot down by a missile. The flight's crash occurred several hours after Iran retaliated for Soleimani's killing on 3 January. With the air defense systems in Iran on high alert and operators likely on edge, there were concerns that Flight PS752 could have been mistaken for a hostile target.

Iran initially denied allegations that the aircraft had been shot down by its military, suggesting that a technical malfunction had caused the crash. However, as evidence pointing to a missile strike—including videos and satellite data—started to emerge, Iran's stance changed. On 11 January, three days after Operation Martyr Soleimani, Iran admitted that its military had unintentionally shot down the aircraft due to "human error." Brigadier General Amir Ali Hajizadeh, the commander of the IRGC-AF, took responsibility for the downing of the aircraft. In a press conference, Hajizadeh explained that the missile operator mistook the airplane for a cruise missile and only had ten seconds to decide whether to shoot it down. The operator reportedly tried to contact his commanders for guidance with little success and opted to act on his own. Hajizadeh stated that once he realized the magnitude of the error, he wished he had died rather than witnessing such an event.[121] Despite this, neither Hajizadeh nor any of the top leadership in the IRGC were demoted.

Russia was merely an observer in the series of escalations that culminated in the loss of Flight PS752. However, the individuals at the center of the tragedy—Soleimani, who served as the catalyst, and Hajizadeh, who admitted Iranian responsibility—and the weapon itself, the Russia-made Tor-M1, each played a distinctive role in the contours of Russia's relationship with Iran. In essence, the Tor-M1 shed light on the past, Soleimani shaped the present, and Hajizadeh foreshadowed the future of Russia-Iran relations.

As detailed in Chapter 2, the Tor-M1 acquisition exemplifies the longstanding military cooperation between Moscow and Tehran. Following the devastating Iran-Iraq War, Iran sought sophisticated defense systems from the Soviet Union, initiating agreements that stalled under Yeltsin's presidency but were revitalized by Vladimir Putin in the early 2000s. Following Russian Defense Minister Igor Sergeyev's visit to Tehran in 2000, Iran specifically pursued the Tor-M1 missile defense system, drawing considerable opposition from Washington, which feared Tehran might deploy such systems to protect its nuclear program. Nevertheless, amid Russia's growing frustration with U.S. missile defense initiatives in Europe and Western support for "Color Revolutions," Moscow approved the sale of the Tor-M1 system in 2005. The transaction served both economic and geopolitical purposes, signaling Russia's readiness to defy U.S. objections.

As discussed in Chapter 4, with the Syrian Civil War, the relationship transformed into a more robust partnership when Soleimani himself traveled to Moscow in the summer of 2015 to lay the foundation for the Syrian military campaign. Iran was already involved in the Syrian Civil War when the Quds Force General flew to meet with Defense Minister Shoigu and President Putin. Following Soleimani's outreach, Russia and Iran established a joint military campaign to support Assad. General Soleimani played a pivotal role, acting as the main liaison between the Iranian and Russian military forces. The ties between Russia and Iran deepened during the Syrian Civil War, extending beyond personal relationships and into the realm of institutional cooperation.

At the time of the downing of PS752, Brigadier General Hajizadeh's role in Russia-Iran cooperation was less well known. As the commander of the IRGC-AF, Hajizadeh was instrumental in advancing Iran's missile and drone programs. As discussed in Chapter 8, following Russia's invasion of Ukraine in February 2022, Moscow sought military reinforcements, turning to Tehran for support. The drones, which were a product of Hajizadeh's leadership in technological innovation and armaments, found their way to the

Ukrainian frontlines. Hajizadeh's role transcended mere material provision: he marshaled IRGC-AF specialists to Crimea, ensuring knowledge transfer to Russian drone contingents. Russia, once the bedrock of Iran's defense procurements, had metamorphosed into a consumer of Iranian arms.

* * *

The political landscapes within Russia and Iran during the Trump presidency witnessed the rise and consolidation of hardline factions. Vladimir Putin's return to the Russian presidency in 2012 ushered in a notably assertive foreign policy stance. Concurrently, within Iran, the Trump administration's withdrawal from the JCPOA unintentionally empowered domestic hardliners at the expense of moderates who supported diplomatic engagement with the West. The collapse of the nuclear deal reinforced skepticism toward Western intentions among Iran's conservative factions and accelerated Tehran's geopolitical pivot towards Russia and China. Thus, Trump's aggressive foreign policy, whether deliberate or accidental, significantly deepened the strategic alignment between Moscow and Tehran by reinforcing their opposition to American unilateralism.

Increasingly, both Russia and Iran portrayed themselves as leaders advocating for a multipolar world order, positioning Eastern powers as counterbalances to U.S. global hegemony. For Iran, closer alignment with Russia offered an opportunity to circumvent Western-imposed isolation. Meanwhile, Russia viewed strengthened relations with Iran as vital to demonstrating the viability of alternative global power centers capable of resisting Western pressures, thereby reinforcing Moscow's vision of a more balanced international order.

7

FORWARD TO EURASIA AND THE SEARCH FOR MULTIPOLARITY

Amid record-low voter turnout and an acute internal economic crisis, Ebrahim Raisi, a staunch conservative with a prior tenure as chief of the judiciary, became the uncontested leader in Iran's presidential election of June 2021. The electoral process, marred by the disqualification of numerous candidates, left Raisi virtually unopposed. Notably, the first international leader to extend congratulations to the president-elect Raisi was Russian President Vladimir Putin.[1] In a statement issued before the election results had even been formalized—an implicit acknowledgment of the election's foregone conclusion—Putin expressed his hope that "relations between the two countries would keep progressing towards mutual constructive cooperation."[2] The Iranian media extensively circulated Putin's message, signaling the symbolic weight of Russia's prompt recognition of Raisi's presidency. The timing of Putin's congratulatory note was heralded by many, including the Iranian ambassador to Moscow, Kazem Jalali, who described it as a testament to the close ties between Russia and Iran.[3]

This exchange of diplomatic pleasantries set the tone for a tenure that would deepen Iran-Russia relations as both were experiencing internal shifts that intensified the trajectory of their foreign policies away from the West. Russia was actively pursuing closer economic, political, and military cooperation with countries in the East, particularly China, to diversify its economic partnerships, access new markets, and counterbalance Western dominance.[4] The transition from Rouhani's presidency, which had been marked by attempts at engaging with the West through the Joint Comprehensive Plan of Action (JCPOA), to Raisi's tenure also signified a transformation in Iran's foreign policy orientation. Whereas, under Rouhani, the foundations of the Russia-Iran relationship were laid through the Syrian Civil War, the Raisi presidency heralded an intensified focus on the East, particularly in fortifying connections with Russia.

Shared frustrations with the liberal international order crystallized in both Moscow's and Tehran's foreign policy strategies. As an alternative to U.S. hegemony, Russia introduced its official concept of multipolarity (*mnogopolyarnost*) in the 1990s. Increasingly vocal about the emerging multipolar world, Russia sought partners disillusioned with U.S. dominance of the international system. The concept of multipolarity became intertwined with Russia's "Turn to the East" (*Povorot na Vostok*) policy, a shift that gained traction with Putin's return to the presidency in 2012.[5]

Iran's alignment with Russia's push for multipolarity was indicative of its broader foreign policy orientation during the Trump administration, which saw Tehran increasingly look to the East, forging closer ties not only with Russia but also with China and engaging in non-Western multilateral initiatives such as the Belt and Road Initiative (BRI), the Eurasian Economic Union (EAEU), and the Shanghai Cooperation Organization (SCO). Raisi's election solidified this direction, heralding a rise in ultra-conservative and nationalist sentiments within Iran, which mirrored the worldview of the *siloviki* in Russia.

Set against the backdrop of the gravitation towards multipolarity and a pivot towards the East, this chapter elucidates the underlying synergies in the Russia-Iran relationship. Russia and Iran's partnership of defiance, born out of shared grievances with the liberal international order, evolved through the institutionalization of their partnership in Syria. At the heart of this exploration is an understanding of how multipolarity and the Eastern orientation serve as cornerstones for Russia and Iran's joint efforts to challenge Western global predominance.

* * *

Russia and Iran have emerged as prominent challengers of the liberal international order, both through individual actions and, increasingly, through coordinated efforts.[6] The liberal international order encompasses a set of interrelated principles and institutions. These include democracy, human rights, free trade, multilateralism, and the rule of law. Proponents argue that this system has fostered unprecedented global stability and prosperity with the promise of progress. However, Russia and Iran view these principles not as universal values, but as instruments of Western, particularly American, hegemony.

The foundational ethos of Russia and Iran's alignment lies in a deep-seated frustration with the perceived inequities and sense of marginalization in the liberal international order. These shared grievances have found expression in the notion of "multipolarity"—a vision of an international order that selectively prioritizes state sovereignty to insulate states like Russia and Iran from critiques over human rights abuses while also fostering a global environment more conducive to the pursuit of their own interests.

In international relations theory, the term "multipolarity" refers to the distribution of power among multiple actors in a system. It usually denotes a fortuitous balance based on objective indicators like economic and military power. For Russia and Iran, however, the term is prescriptive; it challenges Western primacy and rallies collaboration among the order's discontents. Their multipolar world is less concerned with equity or democracy than with advancing narrow interests and defended spheres of influence. While Russia and Iran champion the principles of sovereignty and non-interference, they have not hesitated to intervene in the affairs of other states when it suits their interests, as demonstrated by Russia's actions in Ukraine and Iran's support for the Axis of Resistance across the Middle East.

The idea of multipolarity has been a unifying thread for Russia and Iran, even during the contentious periods in their relations. It offered a common language through which Russia and Iran could articulate their grievances. Moreover, multipolarity evolved into a practical framework that enabled cooperation among diverse states united primarily by their opposition to the West. In essence, multipolarity allowed Russia and Iran to position themselves as leaders of an alternative global order—one that fundamentally questions and challenges the legitimacy of Western-centric norms, values, and institutions.

Russia's Quest for Multipolarity

The Russian concept of multipolarity emerged in the post-Cold War era as a response to Moscow's weakened global position.[7] Rooted in a quest to reclaim its status as a major power and reassert its centrality in global affairs, the concept of multipolarity arose from debates among Russian scholars and policymakers about the nature of the international system and Russia's role within it.[8] The integration of multipolarity as a foreign policy strategy was championed by figures like Primakov who called for counterbalancing Western authority by promoting countervailing centers of power.[9] During the 1990s, Russian policymakers argued that multipolarity would "democratize" international relations, using the term to mean diversification of global power centers rather than the spread of democratic governance.[10] For example, Yevgeny Bazhanov, former Rector of Russia's Diplomatic Academy, advocated for Russia to "balance flexibly between the West, the East, and the South" to amplify its global influence.[11]

The invocation of multipolarity, while ostensibly about flexible balancing and creating a network of partnerships to counterweight Western power structures, also served broader Russian aspirations. It became a rhetorical tool to justify Russia's self-perceived great power status and claim certain special responsibilities in global affairs. For Russia, multipolarity has signified a world where its interests are recognized and respected and where it can exercise influence commensurate with its self-perceived status as a great power.[12] This self-image is inextricably linked to Russia's dualistic approach to state sovereignty and non-interference, wielding sovereignty as both a shield and a sword. It fiercely defends its own sovereignty against perceived Western encroachment, particularly regarding democracy promotion or humanitarian intervention, framing this as resistance to Western hegemony. However, Russia has also demonstrated a willingness to violate these very principles within what it considers its "sphere of influence," as evidenced by its incursions into Georgia and Ukraine. Multipolarity became not just a foreign policy strategy, but a cornerstone of Russia's narrative about its privileges as a great power.

What began as a balancing strategy has morphed into a frontal challenge to Western predominance. Russia has courted states dissatisfied with the U.S.-dominated order, notably through the India-Russia-China strategic triangle and the creation of non-Western organizations.[13] Iran's value as a counterweight figured prominently in Russian calculations: alignment with power centers opposed to U.S. primacy would hasten the West's decline.[14] Consequently, the doctrine of multipolarity expresses Russia's understanding of its global position and rationalizes its partnerships with Iran, China, and India—states that espouse a similar vision of world order.

Since the 2000s, Russia has embraced the narrative that the end of the Cold War led the "West" to assume that the international order would be increasingly receptive to "Western" values. Russian observers suggest that U.S. foreign policy has been guided by a messianic identity, portraying itself as the defender of liberal values against undemocratic regimes and believing in the universality of American society.[15] To this end, Russia has countered liberal values by invoking the imperative to preserve "the diversity of culture and civilizations" and to foster "a dialogue of civilizations."[16] This civilizational discourse serves a dual purpose: it legitimizes Russia's alternative vision for global order while implicitly challenging the claim that Western liberal norms represent universal human aspirations. By positioning itself as a defender of civilizational plurality, Russia crafts intellectual space for its authoritarian governance model while appealing to non-Western powers skeptical of liberal internationalism.

Today, multipolarity has matured from a diplomatic doctrine into a comprehensive worldview. It challenges Western claims to universal legitimacy and offers an alternative intellectual architecture—one that serves Russian interests while resonating with states skeptical of the liberal order. At its core, it provides the conceptual foundation for Russia's great-power resurgence, allowing Moscow to assert regional dominance and cast itself as the vanguard of a broader counter-hegemonic movement.

Iran and Multipolarity

For Iran, the appeal of multipolarity has been deeply rooted in its revolutionary ideology and its opposition to U.S. primacy. . Iran's vision of international order is shaped by its commitment to the principles of independence (*esteqlal*) and the right of sovereignty (*hoq hakemiyat*), free from the domination of any single power.[17] At times, this worldview has led Iran to be critical of great powers, including Russia and China, in perpetuating what it sees as the inequalities and imperialism inherent in the current international system. For instance, Tehran has publicly criticized both Moscow and Beijing for supporting UN Security Council sanctions against Iran, even while simultaneously cultivating these relationships as strategic counterweights to Western pressure. However, Iran's profound antagonism toward Washington has consistently overshadowed these critiques of other great powers, creating a dissonance that has seen Tehran overlook Russia's imperialist actions in its immediate neighborhood when convenient for broader anti-Western objectives.

The concept of multipolarity gained sharper focus for Tehran in the 2000s, when Iranian officials began presenting it as an explicit alternative to U.S. efforts "to impose a unipolar world."[18] Ali Akbar Velayati argued that both Iran and Russia are bound to assume pivotal responsibilities in a future world order defined by multiple poles of power. Velayati claimed that by strengthening Russia's ability to counter Western-led blocs, Iran's relationship with Russia will facilitate an inevitable transition to an international system that elevates the status of Russia, China, and the Muslim world.[19] Iranian policymakers have likewise highlighted the propensity for non-Western organizations and countries such as Iran, India, Brazil, China, and Russia to dilute Western power.[20] From a conceptual standpoint, a multipolar system is seen as offering Iran greater opportunities to assert its influence at both the regional and international levels. In a world where power is distributed among multiple regional centers, rather than concentrated in the hands of a single dominant state, Iran believes it will be better positioned to pursue its interests and resist external pressures.[21]

Like Russia, Iran expressed a clear antipathy to American democracy promotion, human rights, North Atlantic Treaty Organization (NATO) expansion to the East, and U.S. unilateralism in the Middle East, Southeast Asia, and Central Asia.[22] For Jahangir Karami, an Iranian expert on Russia, in the period from 1990 to 2000 the international system fluctuated between a unipolar and a multipolar system, during which the U.S. imposed its leadership and gradually increased its hegemony over other countries. Karami concludes that the rise of countries like China and Russia, coupled with the relative decline of American power in the aftermath of the global financial crisis of 2008, has made it difficult for the United States to shape the international order unilaterally.[23]

Like Russia, Iran's vision of a multipolar world order is also closely tied to its emphasis on civilizational and cultural diversity.[24] Iran's promotion of a "dialogue of civilizations" under former President Khatami, for example, echoed Russia's own efforts to assert its distinct civilizational identity and challenge the universality of Western values.[25] For both Iran and Russia, the invocation of cultural diversity and respect for civilizational differences has served as an instrumental tool in their broader critique of the liberal international order. By framing values such as human rights and democracy as foreign impositions that are incompatible with local contexts and traditions, Tehran and Moscow seek to undermine the normative foundations of the U.S.-led system and legitimize their own repression domestically.

Russia's proclivity to promote ideas about world order that challenge the basis of unipolarity has persisted as a source of intrigue for Tehran, even during periods of constructive engagement with Western powers.[26] Viewed from Tehran, Russia's resistance to unipolarity helps guarantee Iran's national security by facilitating the emergence of a system where Iran wields far greater authority. Through collaboration with Russia and other like-minded states,

Iran hopes to accelerate the transition towards a multipolar world order, one in which the United States is no longer able to dictate the terms of international politics.

* * *

Over the years, multipolarity became intertwined with Russian and Iranian ambitions to enhance the global weight of the East—a geopolitical and ideological construct rather than a strictly geographical one, which has encompassed countries resistant to or critical of Western dominance. Moscow and Tehran have consistently highlighted various developments they believe signal the ascendance of the so-called East. These include the economic rise of China and India; the emergence of multilateral initiatives like the SCO, EAEU, and BRI; and a perceived erosion of Western soft power and moral authority.

The notion of a rising East is predicated on the conviction that non-Western powers will increasingly shape the future of global influence and authority. Russia and Iran, in particular, have positioned themselves as vanguards of this emerging bloc. Diplomatically, both have intensified their engagement with countries in Asia, the Middle East, Africa, and Latin America as well as in non-Western multilateral organizations. Economically, they've pursued diversification strategies, developing alternative financial systems and promoting trade in national currencies to reduce dependence on Western markets.

However, Russia's and Iran's narratives of an "East" rising against a declining "West" present a reductionist binary that fails to capture the complexities of international relations. This Manichean worldview, reminiscent of Samuel Huntington's "Clash of Civilizations" thesis, ignores the diversity within these purported blocs and the increasing interconnectedness of the global political economy. Regardless of the oversimplification inherent in this narrative, it has been the crux of Russian and Iranian efforts to mobilize states dissatisfied within global order while legitimizing their own worldviews.

Russia's Pivot to the East: The Bridge of Greater Eurasia

Russia's concept of multipolarity has undergone a significant transformation since Vladimir Putin's return to the presidency in

2012, shifting toward an "Eastern pivot" that positions Russia as a crucial Eurasian bridge connecting East and West. This strategy serves multiple objectives for Moscow. First, it reduces Russia's dependence on Western markets and institutions, providing economic alternatives amid deteriorating relations with Europe and the United States. Second, it allows Russia to leverage its vast geographic expanse—stretching from Europe to the Pacific—as a unique connector between different civilizations and economic zones. Third, by promoting these macro-regional initiatives, Russia positions itself not merely as a regional power but as an architect of alternative global governance structures that could eventually rival Western-led institutions like NATO and the G7.

Russian leaders have interpreted various global events as indicators of the West's decline, presenting Russia's pivot to the East as a strategic choice rather than a necessity. A key turning point in this narrative was the 2008 global financial crisis, which revealed vulnerabilities in the Western-led economic order and accelerated the shift towards multipolarity. In the wake of the crisis, Russian political commentators such as Vyacheslav Nikonov were quick to declare the end of Western dominance, arguing that the growth of independent power centers in Asia, Africa, and Latin America were bound to fundamentally reshape the global balance of power.[27] This sentiment was echoed in official Russian foreign policy statements and strategic documents, which emphasized the need for Russia to adapt to a changing global landscape.[28] For example, the 2013 Russian Foreign Policy Concept highlighted the growth of new centers of influence, which will "change the usual balance of power and, on this basis, objectively claim a role commensurate to the weight of traditional world centers, previously represented by the countries of the West."[29]

As Russia's relations with the West deteriorated in the aftermath of the Ukraine crisis and the annexation of Crimea in 2014, Moscow's pivot towards the East took on an even greater urgency.[30] Russian leaders began to speak of a "Turn to the East" as an imperative, driven by the need to diversify Russia's economic partnerships.[31] It was seen as part of a broader process of global reconfiguration, in which Russia would shape the contours of a new, post-Western world order.[32] This reorientation manifested in Moscow's efforts to reintegrate the post-Soviet space through the EAEU and focus on regional organizations like the BRICS and the SCO.[33]

Russia's Turn to the East evolved into an even more ambitious concept: "Greater Eurasia." This expansive vision, championed by Russian intellectuals and policymakers, went beyond simply reorienting Russia's foreign policy towards the East. Instead, it aimed to reshape the entire Eurasian supercontinent into a new geopolitical and economic reality, with Russia serving as a bridge between Europe and Asia. Russia's vision of Greater Eurasia was also pragmatic. It sought to capitalize on the massive infrastructure investments and the economic potential of China's BRI while allowing Russia to maintain influence in Central Asia and benefit from increased Eurasian connectivity. Notably, a boost to Greater Eurasia occurred in May 2015 with an agreement between Presidents Putin and Xi to connect the EAEU with the BRI.

Around 2016, Iran started to be cited as a critical junction in Moscow's vision for Eurasian integration and a like-minded partner in the transition to the East. At the St. Petersburg International Economic Forum in June 2016, Putin articulated Moscow's intention to initiate the "Great Eurasian partnership"—a framework for macro-regional political, security, and economic integration encompassing the states of the EAEU and the CIS, as well as China, India, Pakistan, and Iran.[34] One of the leading architects of Greater Eurasia, Sergey Karaganov, argues that "Iran is almost destined to become a dynamic center of the new supercontinent, unless it falls victim to new aggression … Iran can connect the Persian Gulf and India with the north of the continent."[35] For Russia, the notion of Greater Eurasia is consistent with its promotion of multipolarity and the transition towards an international order revolving around non-Western regional security and economic institutions such as the SCO and the EAEU.[36]

The international fallout from the war in Ukraine heightened the urgency of developing Russia's vision for Greater Eurasia. With Western sanctions severing many of Russia's traditional economic ties, Moscow has been forced to look to new markets and partnerships across Asia, the Middle East, and even Africa. As detailed in Chapter

9, this reorientation has not been without its challenges. While Russia has made inroads with countries that either sympathize with its anti-Western stance or are neutral in the conflict, these relationships often come with conditions and do not compensate for the loss of access to Western markets, capital, and technology.

Iran's Policy of Looking to the East

Iran's emphasis on the East predates Russia's Pivot to the East. For years, various Iranian presidents have proposed cooperating with the East as a counterweight to the continuous pressure from the West. Historically, the Iranian policy of "neither East nor West," rooted in the period following the 1979 Revolution, emphasized non-alignment, steering clear of reliance on either the Eastern or Western blocs during the Cold War. However, this policy evolved in the post-Soviet period as Iran navigated the constraints imposed by U.S. primacy and international isolation. Tehran began to explore partnerships with states outside the Western alliance system, laying the groundwork for what would later become a more pronounced "Look East" policy.[37]

Under Ahmadinejad, the "Look East" (*Negah beh Sharq*) policy was introduced to offset Washington's pressure over its nuclear program by building relations with "Eastern" countries such as Russia, China, India, the Central Asian states, and the "anti-imperialist global south."[38] The Look East policy sought to create a coalition of states with a shared sense of hostility towards the West as a means of defying Iran's international isolation, though, under Ahmadinejad, Tehran often struggled to translate its Eastern vector into policy.[39]

While the Look East policy under Ahmadinejad laid the groundwork for this approach, proponents of Iran's Eastern pivot argued for a more comprehensive and deeply integrated strategy. Many saw the potential for Iran to shape a new global order alongside other major non-Western powers, moving beyond the initial goal of merely offsetting Western pressure to actively participating in the creation of new power structures and international norms.[40]

Like Russia, Iran has envisaged a world order where regional power centers in the East dilute the centralization of power in the

West and limit America's ability to restrain Iran.[41] Consequently, Tehran's bilateral and multilateral engagement with Russia has aimed to promote an alternative set of norms and values to challenge the basis of the Western-led international order.[42] Tehran has framed its potential contribution to Russia's multipolar vision based on the country's status as an "independent regional power" to counter U.S. hegemony, thus creating a "Eurasian alliance against American unilateralism."[43]

The presidency of Ebrahim Raisi marked a resurgence of Iran's Look East policy, elevating it to a central pillar of the country's foreign policy strategy. This renewed emphasis on eastern orientation was, in large part, a response to the heightened tensions and increased pressure from the West, particularly during the Trump administration's "maximum pressure" campaign against Iran.[44] Similar to the Ahmadinejad era, the revival of Iran's Look East policy emerged as both a response to immediate pressures and a long-term vision for Iran's place in a changing global order. Under Raisi, the policy aimed to mitigate Iran's economic vulnerability to Western sanctions through its ties to Russia, China, and the global south as well as engagement with the SCO, EAEU, and BRICS. Yet, like Russia, Iran has struggled to fully recoup gains from its eastward pivot. Iran's economic challenges are compounded by ongoing sanctions, which have crippled key sectors and deterred foreign investment, even from Eastern partners. Thus, for both Russia and Iran, their grand visions of Eastern partnerships as a panacea for Western isolation have encountered hurdles in transforming these aspirations into tangible policy successes.

* * *

Russia's and Iran's invocation of multipolarity and the ascendance to the East have obscured the limited progress both countries have made in translating these orientations into policy gains. Russia has spearheaded the creation of various blocs and organizations with the ostensible purpose of realizing the Eastern vector of its foreign policy. Iran has been an eager participant in these endeavors. However, it was not until Russia had exhausted its options and attempts to integrate with the West, albeit on its own terms, that Russia truly pursued such projects with particular vigor. Chapter 9 explores how some of these projects, like alternative trade routes, were revitalized after the 2022 war in Ukraine.

Attempts to build durable and expansive economic ties with non-Western partners have been hampered by endemic challenges such as weak financial connectivity, infrastructural limitations, and the enduring dominance of the U.S. dollar. Similarly, initiatives aimed at institutionalizing non-Western political and security cooperation have struggled to match their rhetoric with achievements. Despite these obstacles, Russia and Iran remain committed to their long-term project of challenging Western dominance and empowering the East.

The Eurasian Economic Union

The EAEU grew out of efforts to maintain regional economic connectivity following the collapse of the Soviet Union. In the 1990s, various initiatives were floated about creating a comprehensive economic bloc to integrate the Soviet successor states. But it was not until 2000 that these initiatives bore fruit when Russia, along with Belarus, Kazakhstan, Kyrgyzstan, and Tajikistan, formed the Eurasian Economic Community, the precursor to the EAEU. The five countries later signed an agreement in 2010 to create a customs union, which eventually expanded to include Armenia. In 2011, during his tenure as prime minister, Vladimir Putin proposed the formation of the EAEU with the aim of fostering closer economic ties among post-Soviet states. The treaty establishing the EAEU was signed in May 2014 and came into effect on 1 January 2015. Modeled after the European Union, the EAEU creates a single market for goods, services, capital, and labor. It implements a common customs tariff and a common customs code to facilitate the free movement of goods within the union. Such measures were designed to pool the economic strengths of the member countries and reassert Russia's influence in the region.

The EAEU has faced considerable criticism for falling short of its ambitious goals, which has been marked by inefficacies and numerous impediments. It has struggled with implementing meaningful economic integration, where despite promises, non-tariff barriers persist that undermine the premise of a unified market. Moreover, barriers have impeded free trade and the movement of goods, services, capital, and labor across member countries and expose the superficial level of integration achieved thus far. Beyond its economic shortcomings, Russia has sought to leverage the bloc to solidify its grip across the former Soviet space—sometimes at the expense of genuine economic collaboration. Moscow's dominance has not only stirred unease among some member states that fear over-reliance on Russia but has also discouraged them from making commitments due to a fear that their sovereignty will be eroded. Even with all the EAEU's shortcomings, Iran saw it as an opportunity to break into new markets.

Iran's interest in the EAEU and its predecessor, the Customs Union, dates to as early as 2013, well before the escalation of tensions following the U.S. withdrawal from the JCPOA. Within Iran, the EAEU was hailed as "the greatest case of regionalism and convergence in the new era."[45] Iranian officials actively promoted their country's strategic potential to Russian counterparts, emphasizing Iran's capacity to serve as a crucial geographic bridge connecting the EAEU to Persian Gulf and South Asian markets.[46] Russia gradually responded to Iranian diplomatic initiatives by incorporating Iranian representatives into various Eurasian integration conferences and programs.[47] In 2014, Iran's Moscow embassy initiated a series of business networking events, facilitating meetings between Iranian merchants and Russian business leaders.[48] Shortly thereafter, the Trade Promotion Organization of Iran engaged in multiple discussions with the EAEU trade minister to explore potential areas of cooperation.[49]

Although Iran's interest predated the Trump administration, the JCPOA withdrawal and the reimposition of sanctions led Iran to place a greater emphasis on the EAEU as part of its renewed "Look East" policy. Mehdi Sanaei, the Iranian Ambassador to Russia, stated:

> The sanctions [against Iran] show that we must try to find ways to carry out financial transactions and trade outside the West's system. Now that Russia is facing a wave of sanctions by

> the West, the need for cooperation between Iran and Russia is more necessary. Indeed, we must develop joint anti-sanction mechanisms to thwart them or minimize their impact.[50]

Likewise, Iran's Chamber of Commerce suggested that the EAEU "can open a new door for Iran's economy, allowing it to easily establish and expand economic relations" as well as "compensate for some of the effects of sanctions."[51]

In May 2018, mere days after the U.S. withdrawal from the Iran nuclear deal, Iran and the EAEU signed an interim preferential trade agreement.[52] The agreement, which entered into force in October 2019, marked Iran's first regional economic agreement of this nature, as the country's World Trade Organization (WTO) membership application had been pending since 1996. Iran's interim agreement with the EAEU introduced preferential tariffs for 862 agricultural and industrial product categories, with 502 of these being Iranian. Although the tariffs varied and were eliminated in some cases, Iran generally imposed higher duties on incoming EAEU goods compared to the tariffs EAEU members levied on Iranian products.[53]

Despite covering approximately 50 percent of bilateral trade, the economic incompatibilities between Iran and the EAEU member states limited the preferential trade agreement's potential. Iran maintained a 4 percent across-the-board minimum import tariff designed to protect domestic production, while varying regulatory standards and customs procedures created non-tariff barriers that complicated implementation. Moreover, energy exports—theoretically a major Iranian comparative advantage—remained minimal to most EAEU countries due to Russia's dominance in regional energy markets and existing supply arrangements.

The interim trade agreement between Iran and the EAEU produced measurable, if uneven, results. According to 2019 data from the Eurasian Economic Commission, Russia was the destination for nearly half of Iran's $823 million USD of exports to the EAEU, while Armenia received 40 percent and Kazakhstan 10 percent.[54] These exports included fruits, vegetables, nuts, cement, various metal products, and petroleum products, such as crude and liquefied natural gas (LNG). Russia accounted for nearly three-quarters of

Iran's $1.6 billion USD in EAEU imports, with Kazakhstan and Armenia contributing under 20 percent and 5 percent, respectively.[55] Merely three commodities—sunflower oil, barley, and chicken feed—made up 69 percent of Iran's imports from the EAEU.

Despite modest volumes, the agreement's symbolic and political importance far exceeded its economic scale. It marked Iran's first major regional trade accord since the 1979 Revolution and demonstrated the country's capacity to pursue alternative economic partnerships despite international sanctions.[56] For Iranian President Hassan Rouhani, who attended the October 2019 EAEU summit in Yerevan, the agreement represented validation of Iran's eastward pivot. During his meeting with Putin, both leaders spoke optimistically about future cooperation, with Putin noting that Russia and Iran were "working together on Iran's accession to the EAEU" and Rouhani observing that "during the 500 years of our relations, we have reached unprecedented sincerity."[57]

Even with its limited reach, the preferential trade accord created the momentum necessary to move toward a more institutionalized, long-term arrangement.[58] Between 2019 and 2023, Iranian and EAEU officials held roughly sixty rounds of talks, but progress was repeatedly stalled by technical, political, and economic hurdles.[59] Iran's historically high tariffs and extensive subsidies created domestic constituencies opposed to liberalization, while EAEU members worried about exposing their agricultural and manufacturing sectors to Iranian competition. The negotiation of rules of origin proved particularly complex, as both sides needed to ensure that preferential treatment applied only to genuinely domestic products rather than third-country goods transshipped through member territories. However, after the 2022 war in Ukraine, Russia's strong incentive to cement alternative trade partnerships, combined with Iran's proven track record under the interim arrangement, helped overcome technical obstacles and domestic resistance.

In late December 2023, during a meeting of the Supreme Eurasian Economic Council—the highest governing body of the EAEU—in St. Petersburg, the EAEU signed a new free trade agreement (FTA) with Iran.[60] Building on the interim accord, the 2023 Free Trade Agreement (FTA) substantially broadened the scope of tariff liberalization. It abolishes import duties on roughly 90 percent of agricultural and industrial goods, covering more than 95 percent of the existing trade volume between Iran and the EAEU. Under the new framework, Iran's average tariff on EAEU products drops from about 20 percent to 5 percent, while EAEU members reduce their duties on Iranian exports from 8–10 percent to nearly zero for most categories. The remaining 13 percent of goods fall under a special regime designed to protect sensitive sectors during the transition.

Beyond tariff reductions, the FTA establishes a more institutionalized framework for trade governance. It introduces chapters on customs cooperation, sanitary and phytosanitary standards, technical regulations, and trade remedies, aiming over time to create a "barrier-free trade space." A key innovation is the Joint Committee of Iran and all EAEU member states, tasked with overseeing implementation, resolving disputes, and coordinating compliance. The committee also serves as a platform to deepen sectoral cooperation—for instance, in logistics, digital trade facilitation, and standards harmonization—ensuring that the agreement functions not only as a tariff-cutting instrument but as a living mechanism for economic integration.

The projections about the future of Iranian trade with the EAEU tend to overlook the challenges the FTA faces. Bureaucratic challenges are at the forefront, with varying regulatory standards and customs procedures likely to obstruct the seamless exchange of goods and services across member states. The full realization of free trade benefits is unlikely given that 13 percent of commodities remain tariff-bound, curtailing the economic integration the agreement aims to achieve. Iran's trade with the EAEU is disproportionately dominated by Russia and Armenia, with Tehran unable to break into the markets of Kazakhstan, Belarus, and Kyrgyzstan. As discussed below, Iran's ties to the EAEU have been further affected by the logistical and territorial challenges arising from the 2020 Nagorno-Karabakh War.

Despite its problems, the EAEU offers some benefits to Iran. It has bolstered the country's non-oil economy and supported Tehran's objectives of increasing exports, diversifying markets, and promoting import substitution. Furthermore, Iran's location along key transportation routes could position it to play a vital role within the EAEU, potentially mitigating some of the economic disparities between Iran and member states and addressing the limited scope of trade liberalization in their agreements.

The Shanghai Cooperation Organization

The creation of the SCO in 2001 resulted from a series of confidence-building measures on border security between China and four of its former Soviet neighbors—Russia, Kazakhstan, Kyrgyzstan, and Tajikistan. With the inclusion of Uzbekistan at its formal establishment in 2001, the SCO grew to address the threats posed by what the organization termed the "three evils," that is, religious extremism, ethnic separatism, and regional terrorism.[61]

Differences between individual member states have constrained the bloc's policy coordination and regional integration. This is partly due to institutional design—the SCO is governed by consensus, which limits the extent of substantive cooperation, while its two permanent bodies—the Secretariat in Beijing and the Regional Anti-Terrorist Structure in Tashkent—lack the legal capacity to enforce decisions. Consequently, the SCO functions more as a forum for discussion and engagement than a formal regional alliance akin to the EU or NATO. Despite the issues with the SCO, Iran has viewed the organization as a vehicle to promote the expansion of its bilateral relations with Russia, China, and the Central Asian states, as well as an important forum for intra-regional cooperation on security issues.[62]

The formation of the SCO occurred against the backdrop of the Iranian leadership's ongoing efforts to end its international isolation by expanding bilateral and multilateral ties with neighboring states.[63] Iran was granted observer status in the SCO at the July 2005 summit in Astana, having submitted its application in the previous year.[64] Tehran applied for full membership in 2008, but China, Uzbekistan, and Kazakhstan were apprehensive about going that far at the time, in part because of the regime's continued intransigence over its nuclear program and the resultant international pressure. Later, at the 2010 Tashkent summit, the SCO adopted new criteria stipulating that an aspiring member state "should have no sanctions imposed on it by the United Nations Security Council"—a move explicitly directed at Iran.[65]

The lack of progress on accession did not impede substantive interactions: Iranian personnel frequently participated in SCO summits, ministerial meetings, conferences, and counterterrorism exercises. As early as 2007, the SCO started allowing observer states to participate more regularly and deeply in ministerial meetings, working groups, and the Regional Anti-Terrorist Structure, a shift that gave Iran access to limited information sharing on terrorism, extremism, and drug trafficking. Moreover, the SCO's aversion to democracy promotion and external interference has long resonated with the Iranian regime, often influencing its methods of holding onto power at home. Iranian legislation on information security began to emulate the language used in Russian, Chinese, and SCO documents, particularly in linking state sovereignty to control over the internet and restrictions on NGOs.

Once UNSC sanctions were removed in the wake of the 2015 JCPOA, substantive discussions began to be held about admitting Iran as a full member. Yet this was delayed due to several factors, including the accession of India and Pakistan, the downturn in Iran's relations with Tajikistan, and Beijing's continued hesitance about Iran exploiting the SCO to promote anti-American policies. However, at the September 2021 summit in Dushanbe, the SCO announced its approval of Iran's bid for membership, representing a major diplomatic victory for Raisi and his Eastern-oriented foreign policy.

In July 2023, Iran officially became the ninth member of the SCO, during the 23rd SCO summit, nearly two decades after Iran first applied for membership in 2005. This milestone followed Iran's signing of a memorandum of obligations at the 2022 Samarkand summit, initiating the formal accession process. In practical terms, Iran's SCO membership held modest but notable implications. As a full member, Tehran possesses the ability to participate in SCO decision-making processes, including the preparation and signing of documents. It can also invite SCO election monitors for domestic elections, potentially lending a veneer of legitimacy to its elections. Additionally, Iran can formally designate certain groups "terrorist, extremist, or separatist" organizations on the classified list maintained by the Regional Anti-Terrorist Structure—a practice that several SCO states use to marginalize domestic opposition.

The prestige that Iran accrued from membership is more significant. Joining the organization fulfilled one of Tehran's longstanding objectives, representing an extension of its efforts to enhance international legitimacy and deepen ties with Eastern powers. Iranian officials have framed the SCO as emblematic of shifting global power dynamics, emphasizing the organization as a counterweight to U.S. influence and a marker of the rise of collective non-Western cooperation. However, the limitations of the SCO's capacity as a security organization were starkly highlighted by the 2024 Iran-Pakistan border skirmishes, during which the two member states exchanged rounds of missile strikes. In this context, the SCO has proved more valuable to Iran for the status it confers than for its practical ability to resolve regional disputes or deescalate tensions. Its primary utility lies in the symbolic affirmation of Iran's place within an emerging non-Western bloc, rather than in the organization's capacity to deliver concrete outcomes.

International North-South Transit Corridor

Russia and Iran have actively promoted the realization of the International North-South Transit Corridor (INSTC)—a multi-modal network of railways, roads, and shipping routes that seeks to connect Eurasia to the Persian Gulf and South Asia.[66] Russia, India, and Iran formalized an agreement on the INSTC in 2002. The intention was to create a corridor that connected all three countries through a series of maritime and land routes. Despite the formalization of the INSTC in 2002, the development of the corridor faced substantial setbacks in its first decade owing to domestic economic weaknesses, lack of political will, and international constraints. The INSTC's subsequent expansion to countries beyond Russia, Iran, and India, combined with the growth of investment and diplomatic ties between its participants, has allowed the INSTC to progress at a modest rate.

Iran's port infrastructure and inland road and rail networks form a crucial node in the overall scheme of the INSTC by connecting

South Asia to Europe via rail and maritime trade.[67] For Moscow, Iran's geographical location offers a direct and shorter route to connect Russia with markets in the Middle East, South Asia, and even farther towards Southeast Asia. This reduces both the travel time and the costs associated with longer alternative routes, such as those via the Suez Canal. Under such a scheme, goods originating in Mumbai, India, could be shipped by sea to the Iranian port of Bandar Abbas in the Strait of Hormuz. From there, these goods could be transported by road or rail north to Bandar Anzali on Iran's Caspian Sea coast. Goods could then be shipped across the Caspian Sea to the Russian city of Astrakhan, from where they can be transported farther into Russia or Europe.

Rail infrastructure is critical to the realization of the INSTC. In 2005, Russia, Iran, and Azerbaijan pledged to establish a railway network linking Iran to Azerbaijan. Initially, it was anticipated that the project would be completed within a span of two years because it only required the construction of an additional 350 km of track to integrate Iran with the pre-existing routes between Azerbaijan and Russia.[68] However, the start of construction work on Iran's segment of the railway was delayed by nearly a decade.

Given its strained financial resources, Iran sought foreign investment for the project. In 2017, Azerbaijan stepped forward, pledging a loan for nearly half of the projected construction cost. With a $500 million USD loan from Baku, the goal has been to expand the railroad line to connect Rasht to the Caspian port city of Bandar Anzali and to Astara on the Iran-Azerbaijan border.[69] Consequently, the inauguration of the Qazvin-Rasht section of the Qazvin-Rasht-Astara railway in March 2019 was a noteworthy development in the plans to connect Iran to Russia through Azerbaijan. However, the remainder of the route, extending from Rasht to Astara, has been delayed by unexpected technological hurdles that will require further financing to overcome.

The INSTC has the potential to enhance Iran's centrality in the emerging geopolitical and geoeconomic processes shaping Eurasia. However, the imperative to modernize and expand infrastructure has been stalled by a lack of financing and international sanctions on Iran and Russia. Chapter 9 explores how the geopolitical shifts brought about by the war in Ukraine gave a new impetus to the INSTC, as both Russia and Iran have sought to accelerate their pivot towards the East and reduce their dependence on Western markets.

The Armenian and Azerbaijan Factor

The Second Nagorno-Karabakh War erupted in September 2020, lasting forty-four days and fundamentally altering the regional balance of power. Azerbaijan, backed by Turkish military advisors and advanced drone technology, systematically dismantled Armenian defensive positions that had held for over two decades. The conflict shattered the frozen status quo that had benefited both Russia and Iran since 1994, when the first war ended with Armenian control over Nagorno-Karabakh and seven surrounding districts.[70] Russia's mediation of the November 2020 ceasefire and deployment of roughly 2,000 peacekeepers reinforced its image as a regional arbiter, yet also exposed the limits of its security guarantees to Armenia. For Iran, the war posed an unprecedented threat to its northwestern frontier, strengthening Azerbaijan's alignment with Turkey and Israel and raising fears that new territorial corridors could sever Iran's vital land link to Armenia.

Before 2020, both Moscow and Tehran had quietly profited from the frozen conflict. Russia maintained influence through the unresolved conflict, keeping former Soviet republics within its orbit while selling arms to both Armenia and Azerbaijan despite being Armenia's treaty ally via the Collective Security Treaty Organization (CSTO)— a Russia-led military alliance consisting of Armenia, Belarus, Kazakhstan, Kyrgyzstan, Russia, and Tajikistan. Iran, for its part, cultivated close ties with Yerevan, viewing Armenian control of Nagorno-Karabakh as essential for maintaining overland access to the Black Sea and European markets. Tehran also served as the only land bridge between mainland Azerbaijan and its Nakhchivan exclave, a position that conferred strategic leverage. Given Azerbaijan's partnership with Israel, Iran viewed reduced border contact with Azerbaijan as limiting Israeli influence and access to Iranian territory.[71]

In November 2020, as Azerbaijani forces advanced toward Stepanakert, President Putin personally negotiated the ceasefire that halted Azerbaijan's momentum just short of total victory. The ceasefire placed 1,960 Russian peacekeepers along the Lachin Corridor—the vital 5-km link between Armenia and Nagorno-Karabakh. While Russia and Turkey jointly undertook this initiative, Iran was conspicuously excluded from the peacekeeping operation. Moscow later attempted to mitigate any perceived snub by endorsing Iran's proposal for a 3+3 cooperation format encompassing Russia, Iran, Turkey, Armenia, Azerbaijan, and Georgia.[72]

The ceasefire did not restore stability. Azerbaijan's renewed incursions into Armenian territory in September 2022 revealed glaring weaknesses in the CSTO's security architecture; Armenia's appeals for assistance went unanswered. These clashes brought Azerbaijani forces perilously close to Iran's border, heightening Tehran's anxiety about losing access to Armenia and the wider Caucasus. Russia's muted reaction, a symptom of the war in Ukraine, deepened Iranian mistrust.

In September 2023, Azerbaijan launched a swift military operation that resulted in the full recapture of Nagorno-Karabakh. This victory strengthened Baku's territorial ambitions, especially its push to establish the Zangezur Corridor—a transport route through Armenia's Syunik Province that would connect Azerbaijan proper to its Nakhichevan exclave. Although Baku invoked the 2020 ceasefire's clause on reopening regional transport links, the plan alarmed Tehran.[73]

For years, Iran had invested in Syunik as a strategic trade gateway, developing the Meghri Free Trade Zone to channel exports into the EAEU under Armenia's preferential terms and thereby circumvent Western sanctions.[74] The proposed Zangezur Corridor threatened to upend this arrangement entirely.[75] It threatened to establish a direct land bridge between Azerbaijan and Turkey that would both bypass Iran's north–south trade routes and undermine its role as a regional transit hub.[76]

Moscow's reaction was notably ambivalent. Although the Zangezur Corridor undercuts Iran's position, Russia has refrained from open opposition, signaling flexibility as long as its logistical and

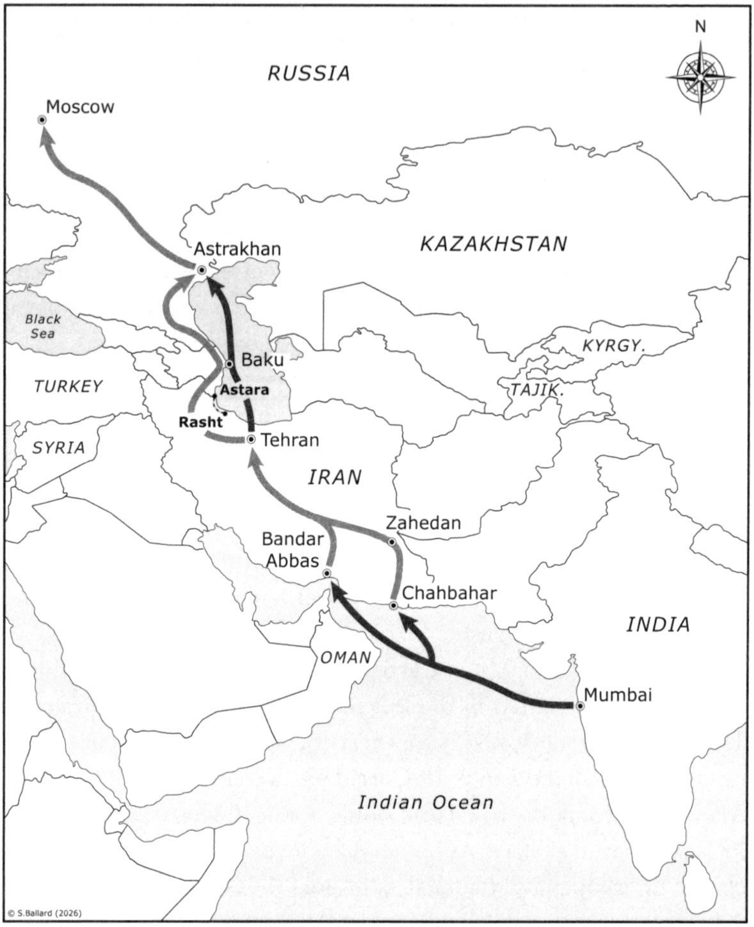

Map 4: The International North–South Transport Corridor (INSTC)

political interests are preserved.[77] One Iranian observer expressed ire over Russia's openness to the corridor; however, within days, that same observer said that Russia had assured Iran it would not obstruct Iran's trade connections.[78] Still, the INSTC's reliance on Azerbaijan for equipment transit faces uncertainties due to strained Tehran-Baku relations and Azerbaijan's exploration of alternative routes that potentially bypass Iran.[79]

Territorial disputes in the South Caucasus are only one of many factors complicating the realization of Russia's and Iran's eastward ambitions. Both states advocate a multipolar order in which regional powers assert greater autonomy from the West, yet the results have been uneven. Flagship projects such as the INSTC and the EAEU demonstrate both the potential and fragility of this vision. The Armenia–Azerbaijan conflict underscored how regional instability can derail integration efforts, while enduring sanctions, capital shortages, and logistical bottlenecks continue to constrain implementation.

The Elusive Power of the East

The emphasis on multipolarity and the transformative power of the East has been a defining feature of Russia-Iran relations, born out of necessity and shared grievances against Western dominance. The Russia-Iran relationship exemplifies a broader phenomenon where states united by shared grievances against the prevailing international order and perceptions of exclusion from global power structures forge alternative power blocs. Together, Russia and Iran have used their partnership to project their vision of the international order, one where power is more dispersed and less reliant on Western hegemony. Yet, translating this vision into meaningful policy has been fraught with challenges. While initiatives such as the EAEU, INSTC, and SCO have provided platforms for cooperation, they have struggled to deliver the economic and political benefits initially envisioned, hindered by sanctions, regional politics, and divergent national interests.

Despite these setbacks, Russia and Iran have persisted in their efforts to deepen bilateral ties and promote alternative power structures on the global stage. Their shared antipathy towards Western influence and desire for greater autonomy in international affairs has continued to drive cooperation, even in the face of practical obstacles. For many in Moscow, Iran's resistance to the liberal world order has long been admired as an example of defiance against a system perceived to be unjust and coercive. As articulated by Timofey Bordachev, one of the proponents of Greater Eurasia, Iran "embarked on the path of struggle against the liberal world order at a time when the prospect of the collapse of this international system was not even visible."[80] Russia's admiration for Iran's steadfast opposition to Western hegemony became a key factor in Russia's growing alignment with Tehran, particularly as Moscow's own relations with the West deteriorated.

As Russia and Iran faced increasing Western sanctions and isolation, this relationship, though initially slow to develop into substantive cooperation, began to crystallize. In 2022, Russia's full-fledged invasion of Ukraine intensified its need for partners willing to support its efforts against the West, while Tehran embraced the war as a harbinger of an emerging multipolar order. The war in Ukraine has served as a catalyst, dramatically accelerating the deepening of ties between Iran and Russia. What began as a partnership of defiance, rooted in their shared experiences in Syria and mutual antipathy towards the West, evolved into a relationship of mutual reliance.

8

ARMS FROM THE AYATOLLAHS

In his nightly address on 24 May 2023, President Volodymyr Zelensky posed a question to Iran: "Why are you complicit in Russian terror? Why are you on the side of an evil state? The world sees what is happening, and all of you in Iran witness it. Support for evil cannot be denied." Referring to Iran's provision of Shahed drones to Russia, Zelensky proclaimed that "your Shaheds, which terrorize Ukraine every night, signify that the people of Iran are being inexorably drawn deeper into the shadowy annals of history."[1] Merely a few hours after his address, Ukrainian civilians and their infrastructure fell prey to attacks from Iranian-manufactured drones under the command of Russian forces.

The provision of Iranian drones, also known as unmanned aerial vehicles (UAVs), to Russia for its campaign in Ukraine marked an evolution in the Russia-Iran relationship. For the first time in their history, Moscow found itself dependent on Tehran for critical military support, dramatically reversing the traditional dynamics where Russia had been Iran's primary supplier of military equipment. This chapter examines how Russia's 2022 invasion of Ukraine transformed its relationship with Iran, particularly through Iran's provision of military drones to Russia. What began as ideological alignment against Western influence evolved into deep cooperation:

Iran supplied Russia with essential military hardware and expertise while gaining battlefield insights and advanced technology in return.

* * *

On 24 February 2022, Russian President Vladimir Putin released a prerecorded statement that aired in Moscow at 5:30 a.m. In his speech, Putin announced the start of a "special military operation" for the "demilitarization and denazification" of Ukraine.[2] Over the previous year, Russia had conducted a series of military exercises along the border with Ukraine and had progressively amassed over 100,000 Russian troops along the Ukrainian border at the end of 2021. Three days before Putin's morning announcement about the "demilitarization and denazification" of Ukraine, Russia formally recognized the independence of the Donetsk and Luhansk People's Republics—both of which have been under Russian occupation since 2014.

Almost immediately after Putin's speech, Russia launched missile strikes on key Ukrainian cities, including Kyiv, Kharkiv, Odesa, and Donetsk. Russia anticipated a swift and decisive victory that would result in the ousting of Ukrainian President Volodymyr Zelensky and the subsequent installation of a regime favorable to the Kremlin. However, this expectation was derailed by several unexpected factors: the Ukrainian military's robust and determined resistance, a constant supply of both Soviet-era and North Atlantic Treaty Organization (NATO)-standard arms to Ukraine, and an array of logistical and strategic errors on Russia's part.[3] A year into the invasion, Russia's military gains were limited to specific regions such as Luhansk, Mariupol, and portions of Kherson and Zaporizhzhia. Most tellingly, the grand plan to instigate regime change in Kyiv was resoundingly rebuffed, leaving Russia's more ambitious objectives unfulfilled.

Within the context of Russia's need for military supplies, Moscow looked to Tehran for weapons and was met with open arms. By April 2022, Russia's attempt to take Kyiv had failed. Around this time, the *Guardian* reported that Iran was smuggling weapons from Iraq to Russia.[4] When Russia's cache of drones was dwindling in early July, U.S. intelligence sources disclosed an Iranian plan to replenish

Russia's stock.[5] Russia and Iran vehemently refuted claims about the transfer of Iranian drones to Russia; however, the events that unfolded validated U.S. intelligence.

In September 2022, Ukraine intercepted a Russian drone that bore the inscription "Geran-2" prominently on its wing. "Geran" is the Russian word for geranium. The drone's distinctive silhouette—a sleek, wing-shaped body with a pointed nose and dual vertical tails—revealed its true identity. This was no Russian design, but the unmistakable profile of an Iranian Shahed-136. The "Geran" label was a thin veil, poorly concealing a contentious truth: Iran had entered the fray, not with boots on the ground, but with drones in the air. The drone's rightful designation was "Shahed," meaning witness—consistent with Iran's tradition of assigning names with Islamic or revolutionary connotations to its military equipment. Adding credence to U.S. intelligence, within a month following the Geran-2 incident, advisors from the Islamic Revolutionary Guard Corps Aerospace Force (IRGC-AF) were present in Crimea to train Russian personnel in operating these Iranian drones.[6]

The appearance of Iranian drones on the Ukrainian battlefield was not an isolated incident but the culmination of a series of events that predate Russia's war in Ukraine. The foundation for this partnership was laid by a convergence of mutual external threats and internal insecurities, which fostered a shared objective between Russia and Iran to challenge the Western-centric international order and advocate for a multipolar world. However, these ambitions largely remained ideational, with both countries making minimal progress in realizing these goals. As discussed in Chapter 7, Russia's and Iran's rhetoric often outpaced their actions. What propelled Russia and Iran into a concrete partnership was mobilizing the networks forged during the Syrian Civil War. These networks proved crucial for the physical manifestation of their partnership, turning rhetoric into tangible military cooperation.

Raisi Visits Russia

One month before Russia's invasion, Iranian President Ebrahim Raisi embarked on an official state visit to Moscow. Ahead of his departure at Tehran's Mehrabad Airport, Raisi stated that his visit to Russia was a "turning point for elevating" Iran's relations with Russia, describing both as "independent and powerful" countries whose cooperation can ensure "security in the region and will counter unilateralism in the world."[7] Iran was hoping to upgrade its ties with Russia by revising their 2001 Treaty on Mutual Relations, signed during Khatami's visit to Moscow. Though Iran did not achieve this goal, the war in Ukraine would soon transform their relationship beyond what either side had envisioned.

As more than 100,000 Russian troops amassed at Ukraine's borders, Putin and Raisi held a three-hour meeting where they discussed ways to expand the relationship. On Iranian social media, the meeting was seemingly upstaged by the peculiar arrangement of furniture within the room, specifically Putin's infamous long table. The expanse between them conveyed a visually striking image of distance, which reformists decried as a form of disrespect.[8] With a twenty-foot table separating the two leaders, President Raisi stated that "we in Iran have no limits for expanding ties with Russia." Raisi communicated Tehran's disapproval of any further Western military deployment in the region, cautioning that the encroachment of NATO forces, under any pretext, "will threaten the common interests of independent countries."[9]

At the conclusion of their meeting, President Raisi rearticulated Iran's position that relations with Russia would be "strong and comprehensive…not short-term or positional, but permanent and strategic."[10] While President Raisi emphasized a vision for "permanent and strategic" cooperation, the rhetoric from the Russian side was more restrained.[11] Putin conspicuously refrained from employing the term "strategic" to describe their bilateral relations. Instead, he merely stated Russia's desire to "create a long-term foundation for cooperation" with Iran.[12] Yet, Russia's hesitancy to describe relations as strategic did not dissuade Iran from capitalizing on the growing chasm between Russia and NATO.

During Raisi's visit to Moscow, the Iranian president spoke at a plenary meeting of the State Duma, where Iran readily aligned itself with Moscow's narrative about NATO encroachment in Ukraine.[13] Raisi proclaimed that "NATO is engaged in penetrating the geographical spaces of different countries under various pretexts and covers" as a way to spread the Western political model.[14] Iran's readiness to project and support the Russian narrative about NATO was, of course, instrumental—it was an attempt to curry favor with their Russian hosts while simultaneously playing into Iranian domestic narratives about the West. While the tangible outcomes of the Putin-Raisi summit initially appeared limited, the tremors set in motion by Russia's invasion of Ukraine would soon redefine the nature of cooperation between the two states. In the coming months, Russia's longstanding hesitancy to describe ties with Iran as "strategic" would undergo a noteworthy shift.

Iran's Embrace

When Russia launched its full-scale invasion of Ukraine on 24 February, Putin called his Iranian counterpart, Raisi, to outline the details of Russia's so-called "special military operation."[15] During the call, Raisi expressed Iran's understanding of Russia's security concerns and asserted that "NATO expansion is a serious threat to the security and stability of independent nations."[16] Rather than expressing alarm, Iranian officials appeared to endorse Russia's revisionist perspective on Ukraine while portraying the invasion as a precursor to Western decline.[17] The official Iranian stance leaned sympathetically towards Russia, starkly contrasting with Iran's initial impartiality in the wake of Russia's 2014 annexation of Crimea.[18]

A statement from Iran's government spokesman on 25 February asserted that "security concerns over the intensifying and provocative expansion of NATO to the east is understandable to all independent nations that are opposed to U.S. hegemony."[19] Iranian state-led media mirrored this stance, with outlets like the IRGC-linked *Fars News Agency* adopting terminology consistent with Russian descriptions of the conflict, framing Putin's actions as a response to Ukrainian aggression and referring to the invasion as a "special military operation."[20] Hardline publications such as *Hamshahri* and *Kayhan* viewed the war as emblematic of Western decline while scrutinizing Ukraine's dependence on Western support and suggesting that President Zelensky's reliance on Western promises had compromised

Ukraine's sovereignty.[21] Some outlets highlighted the war's potential advantages for Iran, with *Et'emad* suggesting potential concessions for Iran from the West over its nuclear program and benefits from rising oil prices.[22]

The official and state-led narrative diverged from responses among segments of the Iranian public and reformist politicians who expressed sympathy for Ukraine and drew parallels between Putin and the Tsars, invoking Iran's historical experience with Russian imperialism.[23] After the onset of Russia's military campaign, protests erupted in Tehran, with demonstrators gathering in front of the Ukrainian embassy, voicing anti-Putin slogans and chanting "Death to Putin."[24] The outpouring of public and reformist sentiment in favor of Ukraine highlighted the duality within Iran, with a populace sensitive to Russia's imperial history and a state machinery focused on strategic gains.

During his annual televised address on 1 March, marking the religious feast of Mab'ath, Khamenei addressed the war in Ukraine without mentioning Russia's involvement or its responsibility for initiating the war. Khamenei described Ukraine as "a victim of the crises concocted by the United States" to benefit its arms industry, which shows that "states that depend on the support of the U.S. and Western powers need to know they cannot trust such countries." Khamenei also claimed that "America brought Ukraine to this point" by instigating protests and Color Revolutions.[25] In the leadership's portrayal of the crisis, Ukraine was a casualty of U.S. machinations and not the victim of Russia's imperialistic war of aggression.

The Iranian establishment welcomed Russia's war in Ukraine as a "divine gift" for Iran, with multiple opportunities to reap benefits from the turmoil.[26] For example, one report from Iran's parliamentary research recommended leveraging the conflict for financial, military, and scientific gains.[27] That same report, however, also warned that Russia's diverted attention could create a power vacuum in places like Syria—potentially allowing regional actors such as Turkey to strengthen their foothold.[28] Another assessment suggested the war might compel Ukrainian nuclear scientists and experts from various fields to seek lucrative opportunities in Iran, offering what the report described as an "opportunity to benefit from the power of these scientists in advancing [Iran's] nuclear program," as well as in the development of rockets, space technology, aviation, radar systems, and shipbuilding.[29]

The political leadership in Tehran interpreted the Ukraine crisis as additional validation for the anti-Western stance that has characterized its foreign policy since the 1979 Islamic Revolution. From this perspective, Russia's military activities were not aggressive or expansionist in nature; instead, they were a response to persistent Western encroachments that have undermined Russia's regional security. More broadly, for Iran, Russia's war in Ukraine symbolized a perceived waning of Western dominance and a shift towards a multipolar world order.

The Iran Nuclear Deal Becomes Another Casualty in Russia's War

Russia's invasion of Ukraine cast a dark shadow over ongoing talks in Vienna to restore the 2015 Iran nuclear deal, officially known as the Joint Comprehensive Plan of Action (JCPOA). A little more than a year before Russia's invasion, the inauguration of Joseph Biden as President of the United States in January 2021 signaled a departure from Donald Trump's maximum pressure campaign. A critic of the Trump administration's withdrawal from the accord, Biden sought to re-engage with Iran and revive the agreement. Consequently, in April 2021, Biden's diplomatic efforts led to the commencement of indirect talks between Iran and the U.S. in Vienna, aimed at resurrecting the JCPOA. Mediated by the remaining parties to the agreement, these discussions made steady headway, with Russia playing an influential role—at times urging Iran to restore monitoring cameras at nuclear facilities and facilitating International Atomic Energy Agency (IAEA) visits to Tehran. In fact, in the days leading up to the Russian invasion, officials in Vienna expressed optimism that an agreement to reinstate the JCPOA was imminent.

Everything changed once Russian troops crossed into Ukrainian territory. Moscow's assault on Ukraine immediately overshadowed the progress in Vienna and introduced a wave of uncertainty. With its attention now diverted by the unfolding crisis—and facing new Western sanctions—Russia emerged as a disruptive force, putting forward additional demands related to its own economic and strategic interests. On 5 March, Russian Foreign Minister Lavrov demanded "written guarantees" that Western sanctions over Ukraine "will by no means affect our right to free and full-fledged trading, economic, investment, military and technical cooperation with Iran."[30] Russia's demand served as the first indication of Moscow's departure from its once-constructive engagement on the Iranian nuclear program.

Iranian reactions to Lavrov's comments indicated that Tehran had neither been consulted nor even informed beforehand by their Russian counterparts. On 7 March, Ali Shamkhani, the Secretary of Iran's Supreme National Security Council (SNSC), who was officially in charge of coordinating Iran's position in the nuclear talks, wrote on Twitter that Tehran is "assessing new elements that bear on the negotiations." Shamkhani stressed that "Vienna participants act & react based on interests and it's understandable," implicitly alluding to Russia.[31] Hours later, Iranian Foreign Ministry spokesman Saeed Khatibzadeh said Iran was awaiting "clarification" about Moscow's position, adding that Russia's approach to the Vienna talks had been "constructive" up until Lavrov's comments.

Interestingly, Russian diplomats in Vienna and Tehran appeared to possess little knowledge about the reasoning behind their foreign minister's comment. Mikhail Ulyanov, Russia's permanent representative to the IAEA and chief negotiator in Vienna, presented a document detailing guarantees for Russian civilian nuclear cooperation with Iran under the JCPOA.[32] The document did not extend to sanction exemptions for Russia's economic, investment, or military-technical cooperation with Iran. Similarly, Russia's ambassador to Iran, Levan Dzhagaryan, described reports about Russia's demand as a "misunderstanding."[33] But Lavrov's phone conversation with his Iranian counterpart, Hossein Amir-Abdollahian, that same evening left no doubt that Moscow was seeking concessions from the West beyond the original JCPOA.[34] According to Lavrov: "The revival of the JCPOA must provide for all participants to have equal rights in relation to the unhindered development of cooperation in all areas without any discrimination."[35]

Russia's underlying strategy appeared to be driven by an attempt to circumvent Western sanctions imposed following its invasion of Ukraine. By adopting this approach, Russia seemed to be contemplating the use of Iran as a conduit to bypass Western sanctions.[36] These demands might have incorporated legal loopholes that would enable the pursuit of transactions with Iran no longer constrained by sanctions. Such aspirations did not escape the notice of the Western parties involved in the deal, which consequently rejected the request for guarantees outright.

Ten days after Lavrov's demand, all indications of disagreement or annoyance had appeared to subside when the Russian and Iranian foreign ministers held a joint press conference in Moscow.[37] Lavrov retracted Russia's previous demands, as he clarified that his country had already been provided with "written guarantees … included in the text of the agreement itself on the resumption of the JCPOA."[38] Although the immediate dispute over written guarantees appeared resolved, the damage to the negotiating process had already been done. Western capitals concluded that Russia was no longer committed to shielding the nuclear talks from its broader disputes with the West—a suspicion that only grew over the course of the war.

After February 2022, Russia allocated less diplomatic capital to the nuclear deal than it had before the invasion. When Russia did engage, it was to defend Iran's progressive expansion of its nuclear activities from scrutiny. In June 2022, for instance, Russia opposed an IAEA Board of Governors' resolution calling on Iran to cooperate with inspections at three undeclared nuclear sites.[39] After the vote, Iran disconnected IAEA cameras at nuclear facilities and faced neither protest nor concern from Russia, which instead blamed the board's resolution for provoking Tehran. Subsequently, following the expiration of United Nations Security Council (UNSC) sanctions on Iran's missile imports and exports in October 2023, Russia offered unequivocal support to Iran and condemned the decision by the E3 (France, the UK, and Germany) to extend ballistic missile sanctions on Iran.

The JCPOA steadily unraveled, its fate increasingly intertwined with mounting concerns over Iran's human rights violations and its provision of drones to Russia. Unlike 2014, when Russia compartmentalized the Iranian nuclear file from its broader relations with the West, the 2022 war in Ukraine proved to be a game-changer in Russia's policy towards the nuclear program. Moscow's new approach appeared to reflect a dual assessment: first, that reducing Western anxieties about an "Iranian nuclear threat" would redirect international attention toward Russia's actions; and second, that an Iran isolated by Western sanctions would prove a more reliable partner in Russia's broader competition with the West, particularly concerning Ukraine.

Strategic in Nature

In June 2022, Putin embarked on his first international trip since the start of Russia's "special military operation" to attend the sixth summit of Caspian littoral states in Ashgabat, Turkmenistan. While there, he met with Iranian President Ebrahim Raisi. Historically, Iranian press releases surrounding such meetings tended to highlight the warmth of bilateral ties, occasionally embellishing Putin's remarks to emphasize solidarity. Yet, during the Ashgabat summit, it was the Russian side that appeared more eager to underscore the closeness of their relationship.

During his meeting with Raisi, Putin declared that Russia-Iran relations "are of a deep strategic nature" and that Russia and Iran are "in constant interaction" in the political, security, and economic spheres.[40] This explicit use of the word "strategic" marked a shift in Russia's rhetoric. Merely a few months earlier, during a meeting between Raisi and Putin, Moscow had been more circumspect in characterizing bilateral ties, in large part to avoid provoking Iran's adversaries in the Persian Gulf and Israel.[41] However, the war in Ukraine prompted an overall reassessment of Iran's value to Russia.

After February 2022, the number of meetings between high-level Russian and Iranian officials grew exponentially. According to a Russian expert on Iran, the changing perception of Tehran was not confined to "Russian officials, specifically those who have so far dealt with Iran in the past," but extended across "the entire Russian government and beyond," including "business entities, state-led enterprises, and non-affiliated [with the government] who are developing a genuine interest in Iran."[42] These developments underscored a broader consensus in Moscow that Iran could serve as a valuable partner for Russia—economically, militarily, and diplomatically—at a moment when many of Russia's traditional avenues of cooperation with the West had been severed or heavily constrained.

One month after the Ashgabat summit, Tehran was the destination for Putin's second trip abroad since the invasion of Ukraine. It was also the Russian president's first visit to Iran during Raisi's tenure as president. Like Putin's previous visits, the meeting was organized as part of the Syrian Civil War's Astana Process. Despite Syria being the official agenda, the gathering was inevitably overshadowed by the ongoing conflict in Ukraine and Russia's growing need for international legitimacy and practical support.

While in Tehran, Putin received a level of political endorsement from Iranian Supreme Leader Ali Khamenei that even some of Russia's closest partners were hesitant to provide. In his meeting with Putin, Iran's Supreme Leader described NATO as a "dangerous creature" that opposes a strong and independent Russia, suggesting that, had Moscow refrained from action, NATO would have launched a war "under the pretext of Crimea."[43] The significance of this endorsement was not lost on Russian observers—the editor-in-chief of *Russia in Global Affairs*, Fyodor Lukyanov, hailed the summit as a testament to Russia's defiance of Western efforts to "isolate" Moscow, highlighting how Tehran's unwavering support served to counter the narrative of international isolation that Western sanctions were designed to create.[44]

Putin was not the only high-ranking Russian official visiting Iran that summer. In July 2022, U.S. intelligence reports revealed that Russia was seeking Iranian combat drones for use in Ukraine.[45] Although Iran officially denied these claims, unconfirmed reports in the Ukrainian media suggested that drones had already been transferred from Iran via the Caspian Sea. Iranian Foreign Minister Hossein Amir-Abdollahian dismissed the U.S. allegations on July 15, attributing them to "certain political goals."[46] His remarks were seemingly contradicted by the Commander of the Iranian Army's Ground Forces, Kioumars Heydari, who praised Iran's drone technology and stated that the country was "ready to export arms and military equipment to friendly countries."[47] Over the following weeks and months, mounting evidence confirmed the transfer of Iranian drones to Russia, facilitated by the military logistics networks both countries had developed during their cooperation in the Syrian Civil War.

* * *

Gleb Pivkin and Yevgeniy Glukhov were products of starkly different worlds. Born in Turkmenistan in 1995, Gleb Pivkin enjoyed playing his guitar and practicing parkour during his teenage years. His family eventually moved from Turkmenistan to Russia, where he obtained citizenship in 2009, and later immersed himself in studying agriculture at the Agrotechnological University in Ryazan. Yevgeniy Glukhov's life took a more regimented path. Born in Volgograd in 1997, fate led him into the stern arms of his uncle, a lieutenant in Russia's internal security services in 2011. With a legacy of discipline and duty guiding him, Yevgeniy commenced his military education early and joined the Cadet Boarding School in the ninth grade. This foundation, with its emphasis on initial flight training, paved the way for his eventual enrollment in the prestigious Air Force Academy in Voronezh. Gleb's and Yevgeniy's paths would converge in Kolomna, Russia, where both men were stationed as servicemen at the Russian Ministry of Defense's 924th State Center for Unmanned Aviation—the main training center for drone operators in Russia.

In August 2022, Gleb and Yevgeniy traveled to Iran to participate in the International Army Games alongside their colleagues from the 924th State Center for Unmanned Aviation.[48] The aerospace division of Iran's IRGC hosted a "Falcon Hunting" competition, involving UAVs, as part of the seventh iteration of wider annual military games launched by Russia in 2015.[49] The competition provided a cover for Iran to train Russian UAV operators who would eventually operate these drones in Ukraine.[50] Each night, drone operators like Gleb and Yevgeniy would unleash unfathomable terror on innocent Ukrainians as flurries of Iranian-made drones targeted civilian infrastructure.

The history of the Iranian drone program began long before August 2022.[51] During the Iran-Iraq War, Iran faced severe military disadvantages, including international arms embargoes and limited access to advanced weaponry, making the development of indigenous military capabilities not just strategic but existential. Led by Hassan Tehrani Moghaddam, the father of Iran's ballistic missile program, Iran began to invest in research and development to build its own drone capabilities.[52] In subsequent years, major strides in developing indigenous drone technology and operational use of these drones occurred under the leadership of Brigadier General Hajizadeh, the commander of the IRGC-AF.[53] Hajizadeh transformed experimental projects into operational military assets by developing increasingly sophisticated unmanned systems, progressing from rudimentary surveillance drones to advanced attack platforms capable of long-range precision strikes, including reverse-engineering captured foreign drones such as the U.S. RQ-170 Sentinel seized in 2011.

Iran's emphasis on drone technology has been fundamentally driven by the chronic weakness of its conventional air force, which remains heavily dependent on aging pre-revolutionary U.S. aircraft—primarily F-4 Phantoms and F-14 Tomcats—that have become increasingly difficult to maintain due to decades of international sanctions restricting spare parts and technical support. Recognizing this vulnerability, Iranian military planners embraced drones and missiles as cost-effective alternatives that could deliver significant operational impact without requiring the massive financial investments and international cooperation necessary for modern fighter aircraft. These platforms have become central pillars of Iran's "forward defense" doctrine, which aims to project power beyond Iran's borders to neutralize threats before they can reach Iranian territory, enabling Tehran to gather intelligence, conduct surveillance, and execute precision strikes across the Middle East while maintaining plausible deniability through its Axis of Resistance.[54]

Russia, both directly and indirectly, took note of Iran's expanding capabilities.[55] Iran actively deployed its drones in conflict zones across the Middle East, using them in operations and providing them to the Axis of Resistance.[56] One prominent example was the battle for Aleppo in 2016, where Iranian-supplied UAVs such as the Shahed-129 and the Ababil furnished real-time intelligence to Syrian and Russian troops. Over the course of the war, these drones collected crucial data on rebel positions and carried out strikes. [57] As detailed in Chapter 6, Iran's attacks on Saudi infrastructure in late 2019 further showcased the precision and combat potential of its drone fleet.[58] Those attacks, which likely employed swarming tactics involving drones and possibly cruise missiles, overwhelmed Saudi air defenses—a strategy Russia would later adopt with Iranian drones in Ukraine. By launching multiple low-flying drones simultaneously from multiple directions, Iran exposed the weaknesses of traditional air defense systems designed for high-altitude threats like missiles and fighter jets.

Iran's drone advancements have not gone unnoticed at defense exhibitions in Russia. In 2016, during a Russian arms expo, Major General Mohammad Bagheri, the head of the Iranian General Staff, disclosed that Russia had expressed interest in acquiring Iranian technology to build long-range drones capable of precision targeting within a one-square-meter radius.[59] That following year, at the 2017 Russia Air Industries Exhibition, Iran showcased its drones' surveillance, advanced guidance, and long-range capabilities with the display of drones like the Mohajer, Karrar, and Yasir. During the exhibition, the managing director of the IRGC-affiliated Iran Aviation Industries Organization stated that Iran "has initiated joint work with the Russians, which includes collaboration in designing and exporting certain drones that we can send to Russia" and claimed that "Russia has a great willingness to cooperate in this area, which will be reciprocal, and we will also use some of their technologies."[60]

Russia's growing interest in Iranian drones was also evident in its military literature. In November and December 2021, as Russia prepared to invade Ukraine, the Russian Ministry of Defense's journal *Armeiskiy Sbornik* published several articles examining Iran's drone capabilities—particularly those demonstrated during the Syrian campaigns in Eastern Ghouta and Aleppo.[61] One article emphasized that "Syria has become a testing ground for Iranian UAVs. This allowed Iranian designers, engineers, and military personnel to significantly increase their combat effectiveness."[62] Another article suggested that "Iran, like Russia, is under discriminatory international financial, economic, and trade sanctions. Therefore, Iran's experience in developing scientific, technological, and production potential to provide its armed forces with modern weapons and military equipment may be of interest to Russia."[63] Other articles underscored the benefits low-cost drones offered beyond direct engagement, particularly their ability to compromise the efficacy of enemy air defenses by compelling the adversary to deplete precious resources, such as anti-aircraft missiles, on seemingly lesser threats.[64]

As Russia's military campaign in Ukraine faltered, Iranian drones emerged as an appealing solution to reinforce Moscow's depleted arsenal.[65] Facing a pressing need to sustain its operations, Russia leveraged its 2015 military-technical cooperation agreement with Iran, initiating discussions with Iranian authorities on procuring drones to bolster its dwindling stockpiles.[66] Within this framework, the Russian Ministry of Defense coordinated with their Iranian counterparts on production timelines and technical support, including training and the deployment of Iranian drone operators to Ukraine. On the Iranian side, Brigadier General Hajizadeh stood out as the driving force behind these drone transfers. He not only championed the export of UAVs to Russia but also orchestrated the involvement of key Iranian military entities—including the IRGC-AF, the Ministry of Defense and Armed Forces Logistics (MODAFL), and various subsidiary organizations tasked with drone production.

The diplomatic groundwork for these transfers crystallized in March 2022, when Russian Deputy Minister of Defense for Military-Technical Cooperation Alexander Fomin met with General Sayed Hojatollah Qureishi, the head of MODAFL's Supply, Research, and Industrial Affairs Division, to discuss expanded military cooperation possibilities.[67] Fomin brought considerable relevant experience to these negotiations, having overseen international military cooperation with Iran since January 2017 and gained significant firsthand operational knowledge working alongside Iranian forces during their joint intervention in Syria.[68] Meanwhile, Qureishi's extensive remit encompassed all critical aspects of supporting and equipping Iran's armed forces, from initial research and development through production, procurement, and personnel allocation, making him the ideal counterpart to finalize the complex agreement to supply Iran's advanced drones to Russia.

The Shahid Karimi UAV base at Kashan airfield, located 190 km south of Tehran and operated by the IRGC-AF, became the focal point of Moscow's search for drones to sustain its faltering offensive in Ukraine. Throughout June and July 2022, a series of high-level Russian military delegations traveled to the facility to assess Iran's capabilities.[69] During the initial visit in June, Russian officials inspected the Shahed-129 and Shahed-191 models, evaluating their operational performance and potential battlefield applications. A second delegation returned in July for more detailed technical assessments of Iran's drone inventory. The urgency and frequency of these visits did not escape Western intelligence: shortly after the second Russian delegation departed, White House National Security Advisor Jake Sullivan publicly disclosed that Iran was preparing to provide Russia with "up to several hundred" drones for deployment in Ukraine.[70]

In August 2022, when Russian UAV operators like Gleb and Yevgeniy participated in military games in Iran, a series of intelligence disclosures warned about the transfer of Iranian drones to Russia. Oleksiy Arestovych, a Ukrainian presidential advisor, claimed that Iran had sent 46 UAVs to Russia for potential use against Ukraine.[71] The transfer was confirmed by the State Department, which claimed that Russian officials had recently received training on drone technology in Iran. On 19 August, the *Washington Post* reported that Russian cargo planes had departed from Tehran carrying at least three types of Iranian drones capable of reconnaissance and attack missions.[72] The next day, Russian military aircraft arrived in Tehran, carrying a substantial amount of cash, a British NLAW anti-tank missile, a U.S. Javelin anti-tank missile, and a U.S. Stinger anti-aircraft missile. Sky News reported that these munitions were originally intended for Ukraine but were intercepted by Russia. In exchange for the intercepted munitions, Iran provided Russia with 160 UAVs, including 100 Shahed-136 suicide drones, a type of UAV designed to crash into a target and detonate an explosive payload, destroying both the drone and the target.[73]

Russian and Iranian officials resolutely denied the allegations of cooperation. Dmitry Peskov, the Kremlin spokesman, accused the *Washington Post* of publishing fake news, commenting that "the

Washington Post, unfortunately, has been publishing a lot of false information lately."[74] Iranian authorities similarly rejected the accusations and challenged Ukraine to provide concrete evidence of any transfers. This blanket denial, however, proved difficult to sustain: in November 2022, Iranian officials quietly acknowledged that a limited supply of drones had been delivered to Russia, though they claimed the transfers occurred before the February 2022 invasion.[75]

The physical confirmation of Iranian drones in Ukraine came on 13 September, when Ukraine shot down an Iranian-made Shahed-136 drone in the Kupyansk region. Two days later, the Directorate for Strategic Communication of the Armed Forces of Ukraine posted a Telegram message: "We have documented a second deployment of Iranian UAVs by the Russian army. The remains of a Shahed-136 UAV (Russian marking Geran-2) were found in Nikopol, Dnipropetrovsk Region. The UAV can be identified by the Iranian engine Mado M550 which usually remains intact after an explosion."[76] A senior U.S. defense official confirmed that the Shahed drones were identified by their distinctive honeycomb lining, the same feature observed in Iranian drones in the Middle East, and the Mado engine.[77]

The Legacy of Syria

The appearance of Iranian drones in Ukraine was far from coincidental. The Syrian Civil War reinforced military channels and enhanced the military interoperability for logistical coordination between Russia and Iran. Key individuals and entities instrumental in the Syrian Civil War transitioned into roles facilitating the coordination and shipment of Iranian military technology to Russia.

Russian and Iranian military officials have used covert channels and sophisticated shipping strategies, originally developed by Iran for dispatching supplies to Syria and its proxies across the Middle East, to facilitate these transactions. Through its expansive network of conglomerates and subordinates, MODAFL supervised the development and production of drones that were delivered by Iranian airlines to Syria.[78] Together, MODAFL and IRGC-AF ensured the secure and discreet transportation of drones to designated locations, mitigating the risks associated with interception or compromise during transit.

The strategy underpinning Iran's delivery of drones to Russia borrowed heavily from tactics previously employed in Syria. Russia and Iran established both a maritime and an aerial corridor to facilitate the transfer of military equipment and advisors specializing in drone operations. Initially, the aerial route was pivotal in delivering the first consignments of drones, a choice dictated by Iran's propensity for leveraging both civilian and state-operated airlines to transport military assets. Many of the former carriers that delivered weapons to Syria, like Iran Air, Mahan Air, Qeshm Fars Air, and Saha Airlines, maintained a steady flight schedule to Russia.[79] These carriers operated approximately twice-weekly flights into Russia after the start of the war in Ukraine, with Iranian passenger aircraft frequently observed in Russian civilian and military airports.[80] As Iran began to deliver larger drones and components, most of the armaments were shipped via the Caspian Sea.[81]

The Caspian Sea emerged as the primary logistical corridor for Iranian-Russian military transfers. The supply chain began at manufacturing facilities near Tehran, where Iranian drones were produced and then transported to two Caspian ports: Amirabad and Anzali. From these northern Iranian ports, the military cargo crossed the Caspian Sea to Makhachkala, the capital of Russia's Republic of Dagestan. Upon reaching Russian territory, the drones were distributed to two key operational airbases: the Seshcha airfield in Bryansk region, positioned close to the Ukrainian border, and the Primorsko-Akhtarsk facility in Krasnodar region, which provided access to southern Ukraine.

Both Russian- and Iranian-flagged vessels have been known to obscure their movements by disabling tracking systems or manipulating their locations, particularly around the Sea of Azov, via the Volga and Don Rivers, en route to the Caspian Sea. Between May and June 2023, maritime tracking data revealed significant surveillance gaps in the Caspian Sea region. The Automatic Identification System (AIS), a mandatory maritime safety protocol that broadcasts vessels' locations and movements in real time, registered numerous disruptions. Approximately 150 Russianflagged ships showed 630 tracking interruptions, while fifty Iranian vessels averaged 200 gaps per month.[82] Analysis from Lloyd's List identified a pattern of vessels systematically "going dark" by disabling their AIS transponders at Iran's Amirabad and Russia's Astrakhan—a pattern that suggested these ports served as key transfer points in the clandestine movement of military cargo across the Caspian Sea.[83] Beyond its military function, the Caspian Sea corridor also facilitated efforts to deepen Russia and Iran's economic ties. As discussed in Chapter 9, Moscow and Tehran strategically blended these military shipments with legitimate economic activities.

Iranian Drones and Russian Battlefield Aims

The primary drones deployed in Russia's war against Ukraine were the Shahed-136 (Geran-2), its smaller version, the Shahed-131 (Geran-1), and the Mohajer-6. All of the drones are operated by IRGC-AF and constructed by affiliated subsidiaries of MODAFL, including the Shahed Aviation Industries and Quds Aviation Industries. Russian forces concentrated most of these systems at the Seshcha airfield in Bryansk Oblast and the Primorsko-Akhtarsk facility in Krasnodar Oblast, where they were launched into Ukraine.[84]

Personnel from Iran's IRGC-AF operated in Russian-occupied areas of Crimea and Kherson, where they trained Russian military personnel on the deployment of Iranian-made loitering munitions. In October 2022, Ukrainian forces attacked these operations, resulting in the deaths of at least ten Iranian personnel in Kherson and Crimea. Additionally, in the same month, IRGC operators were observed in Mykulichi, Belarus, preparing to launch Shahed-136 suicide drones targeting infrastructure in Kyiv and other locations in Ukraine.[85]

The Shahed-136, along with its more compact variant, the Shahed-131, are suicide drones designed to execute strikes on designated targets.[86] With a flight range of 2,000 kilometers, these drones are particularly adept at neutralizing stationary targets within Ukrainian territory at a low cost.[87] While Russia initially focused on acquiring the larger Shahed-136, Iran expanded the deal to include the smaller Shahed-131. Yet leaked documents exposed quality issues in the arrangement: approximately 25 percent of the delivered drones arrived damaged or entirely inoperable.[88]

The Mohajer-6 has mostly been deployed to gather intelligence on enemy movements and positions, whereas the Shahed drones have been part of Russian combat operations. The Mohajer-6 is designed for intelligence, surveillance, and reconnaissance, but it is also capable of carrying out strikes with air-to-surface missiles.[89] The Mohajer-6 drone offers longer flight times compared to other drones, making it a valuable asset for military or intelligence operations that require extended aerial coverage, such as persistent surveillance or long-distance reconnaissance missions.[90]

Russia chose Iranian drones for their cost-effectiveness and ease of production. In Ukraine, Russia has deployed these drones primarily as decoys to saturate and confuse Ukrainian air defenses. According to a Russian Ministry of Defense journal, Iranian drones have been "effective in the targeted destruction of the infrastructure of the control system, artillery and tanks in firing positions, air defense facilities, rear areas and communications of the enemy."[91] This has enabled the subsequent disruption, assault, and suppression of Ukraine's defense apparatuses, setting the stage for an ensuing barrage of cruise missile strikes. Shaheds have often been dispatched in multiple waves, each tasked with reconnaissance, identification of air defense systems, jamming operations, decoy formation, and ultimately, target engagement and destruction. The strategy, known as a "swarm" attack, has been designed to overwhelm and incapacitate even robust air defenses that lack specific countermeasures against drones.

The financial calculus initially favored Russia: each drone costs around $50,000 USD to manufacture, while Ukrainian forces expended interceptors costing several hundred thousand dollars. Russia has tolerated high loss rates—often losing more than 75 percent of its drones—in an effort to gradually overwhelm Ukrainian air defenses.[92] However, throughout the war, Ukraine adapted by developing innovative countermeasures, including new interceptor systems costing around $5,000 USD that can effectively neutralize Shahed drones and electronic warfare tactics that cause approximately two out of every five Shahed drones to fail to reach their targets through spoofing and interference.

* * *

The first concrete evidence of Iranian drones in Ukraine coincided with a wave of intense domestic unrest in Iran. In September 2022, Mahsa Amini, a 22-year-old Kurdish woman, was arrested by Iran's notorious "morality police" for the alleged crime of improperly wearing her hijab. What followed was a brutal demonstration of the regime's ruthlessness. Eyewitnesses reported that Amini was savagely beaten inside the police van. She arrived at the detention center bloodied and barely conscious. Despite her dire condition, authorities delayed medical attention, treating her with callous indifference. When Amini finally was admitted to the hospital, she was in a coma, her body bearing the unmistakable marks of extreme physical trauma. Leaked medical records revealed the horrifying extent of her injuries: severe brain hemorrhage, skull fractures, and internal organ damage consistent with blunt force trauma. The regime's attempts to cover up the true cause of her injuries by claiming a pre-existing condition crumbled in the face of overwhelming evidence.

Amini's death on 16 September ignited long-suppressed rage. Across Iran, people poured into the streets. Women publicly cut their hair and burned their hijabs, acts of disobedience that carried severe penalties. The regime's response was swift and merciless. Security forces unleashed a campaign of terror against protesters. Heavily armed riot police fired live ammunition into crowds of unarmed demonstrators. Snipers positioned on rooftops picked off protesters, including children. The Iranian regime, drawing on its experience from previous upheavals like the 2009 Green Movement, deployed a sophisticated array of riot control tactics and digital suppression techniques to quell the Mahsa Amini protests.

As the protests related to Amini's death intensified, there were mounting concerns about Russia's possible role in aiding the Iranian government's efforts to control and suppress them. The White House hinted at Moscow potentially providing Tehran with guidance on managing dissent. Unconfirmed reports even suggested Iran had

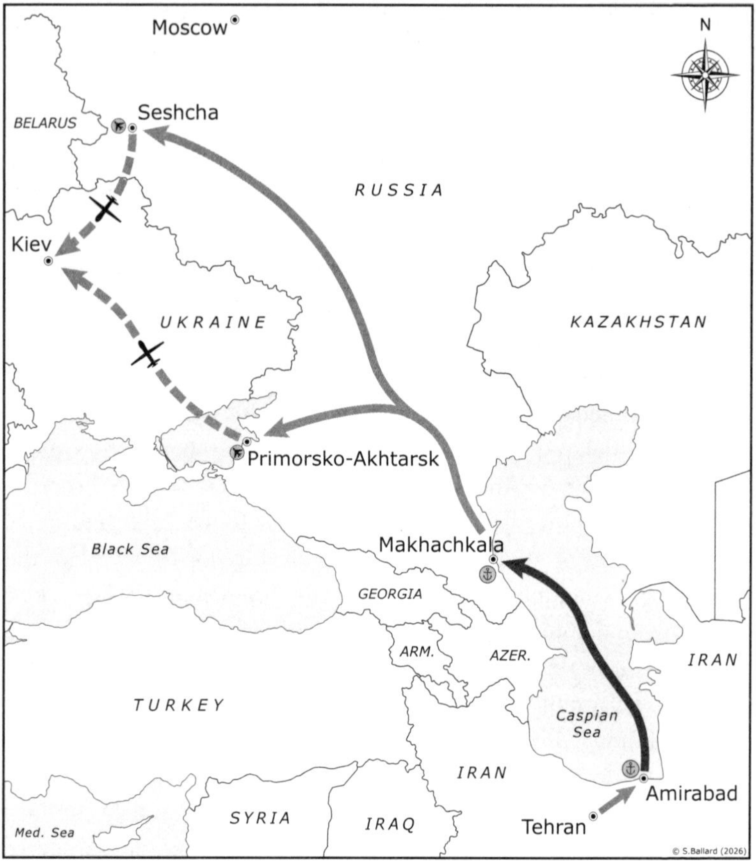

Map 5: Iranian Drone Transfers to Russia via the Caspian Sea

attempted to procure Russian anti-riot equipment and training.[93] More alarmingly, the digital dimension of Iran's crackdown showcased a level of sophistication that strongly suggested Russian involvement. The regime's ability to selectively disrupt internet services while maintaining its own communications infrastructure mirrored techniques used by Russian authorities during protests in Moscow. Advanced deep packet inspection technology, allowing for granular monitoring and filtering of internet traffic, bore the hallmarks of systems developed by Russian tech firms with close ties to the Kremlin. As detailed in Chapter 9, Russia supplied Iran with cutting-edge cyber weapons and surveillance software that enabled

Tehran to more effectively monitor, infiltrate, and disrupt opposition networks.

The allegations of Russia's support for the Iranian regime's repertoire of repression coincided with an international effort to implicate Iran in Russia's war. In October 2022, Kyiv invited UN experts to inspect downed drones of alleged Iranian origin used by Russian forces, a move intended to provide concrete evidence of Iran's involvement and preemptively counter potential denials with physical proof.[94] Up until this point, Iranian officials had steadfastly rejected accusations of drone transfers to Russia. With international pressure on Iran mounting, Russian newspaper *Nezavisimaya Gazeta* published a front-page article titled "Iran to Pay with Internal Stability for Drones" on 19 October.[95] The article explicitly connected Iran's alleged military support for Russia to the regime's growing vulnerability at home, forecasting that the combination of brutal protest suppression and defiant military cooperation with Moscow would further cloud Iran's economic recovery prospects and nuclear diplomacy.

The issue of Iranian drones in Ukraine soon catapulted to the forefront of international diplomacy, culminating in a high-level UNSC meeting.[96] During the UNSC meeting, Ukraine, backed by the United States and European Union, presented a compelling case. They argued that the drone transfers constituted a clear violation of UNSC Resolution 2231, which endorsed the JCPOA. Specifically, Kyiv pointed to the resolution's prohibition on the transfer of ballistic-related technology from Iran until October 2023. This legal argument transformed the drone issue from a mere policy dispute into a potential breach of Iran's obligations under the JCPOA.

The meeting was characterized by tense diplomatic exchanges with Russia and Iran adopting a unified front. Russia's representative, Vasily Nebenzya cautioned the UN Secretariat against conducting what he derided as a "pseudo-investigation at the behest of Western capitals" into Russia's alleged use of Iranian drones in Ukraine. Nebenzya warned that any investigation would be in violation of the UN Charter and would compel Russia "to reassess our entire relationship with the UN Secretariat, because in this case, we will no longer be able to proceed from the impartiality of the UN

Secretariat." Iran's UN envoy, Saeed Iravani, mirrored Russia's defiance. He vehemently denied the "unfounded and unsubstantiated claims" on the drone transfers. Iravani said Ukraine's invitation "lacks any legal foundation" and called on the UN Secretary-General "to prevent any misuse" of UN officials on issues related to the war in Ukraine.[97]

As Iran confronted escalating international criticism over its drone exports and widespread domestic unrest, Nikolai Patrushev, Secretary of Russia's Security Council and a close Putin confidant, embarked on a timely visit to Tehran in November 2022.[98] As in the past, Patrushev chose a crucial moment of domestic tension in Iran for his high-level diplomatic engagements in Tehran—a far from subtle signal of Moscow's support. In substantive talks with Iranian President Raisi and his counterpart Ali Shamkhani, Secretary of Iran's SNSC, Patrushev advanced discussions on Ukraine while developing joint strategies against what both sides termed "Western interference."[99] Their bilateral consultations specifically focused on "cooperation in the field of law enforcement, including public security and the fight against terrorism and extremism," terms often used by Russian and Iranian authorities to encompass tools of domestic repression.[100]

Patrushev's visit was not an isolated event. It was preceded by a Russian interdepartmental delegation led by Patrushev's deputy, Oleg Khramov, which focused on cooperation in information security and digital technologies.[101] The sequence and nature of these visits suggested a combined effort to enhance both nations' capabilities in suppressing internal dissent and managing information flows, assets that had been prominently displayed during Iran's crackdown on the Mahsa Amini protests.

When the Wagner Group, a Russian mercenary organization, staged a brief coup attempt against the Russian government in June 2023, Iran swiftly expressed unequivocal support for Moscow. Iran's official reaction underscored a commitment to Russia's internal stability and sovereignty.[102] In the wake of the Wagner rebellion, Iran firmly reaffirmed its partnership with President Putin and endorsed the "rule of law" in Russia. Nasser Kanaani, spokesperson for the Iranian Foreign Ministry, characterized the events explicitly as an "internal affair" while expressing support for the rule of law in the Russian Federation.[103] This position was reiterated by Foreign Minister Hossein Amir-Abdollahian during a phone call with his Russian counterpart, Sergey Lavrov, where he conveyed confidence in Russia's ability to overcome the situation.[104] Subsequently, on 26 June 2023, President Raisi voiced Iran's unanimous support for the Russian government—an assurance that was directly relayed to President Putin.[105]

Iranian outlets aligned with government perspectives consistently portrayed the events as minor and under control, directly countering Western narratives of chaos and instability.[106] State-affiliated Iranian media, including Nour News, downplayed the significance of the Wagner rebellion, framing it as insufficiently organized to pose any substantial threat to Russian authority.[107] Moreover, Iranian conservative analysts and commentators quickly interpreted the rebellion as a Western-orchestrated destabilization attempt. They argued that NATO and various Western intelligence agencies sought to weaken Russia from within, with some commentators even alleging involvement by foreign entities such as Israel's Mossad.[108]

Russia and Iran subsequently widened their cooperation on internal unrest with several key agreements to facilitate knowledge sharing between their domestic security agencies.[109] For example, in 2023, Iran's Chief of Police Ahmad-Reza Radan had a meeting with the head of Russia's National Guard (*Rosgvardiya*), Viktor Zolotov, where they signed a cooperation agreement aimed at enhancing security and law enforcement collaboration between Tehran and Moscow. Building on Patrushev's meeting with Shamkhani, the document included measures to strengthen bilateral cooperation in law enforcement, protection of vital governmental facilities, combating terrorism and destabilizing actions, and providing joint supportive measures to combat crime.[110] Amid recurring waves of protest and mounting external scrutiny, both governments now cast domestic security cooperation as an existential imperative rather than mere expediency.[111]

Project Boat

Alabuga is a district in Tatarstan, an autonomous republic in Russia. Known for its Soviet-era tractor and automobile factories, Alabuga became an industrial hub for foreign investment in the 2000s. Like other regions in Russia seeking to attract capital and reduce unemployment, Alabuga became a Special Economic Zone (SEZ) in 2006 with attractive tax breaks and incentives for investment.[112] With the onset of Russia's war in Ukraine, the Alabuga SEZ would pivot from civilian heavy industry to become a key hub for Russia's war machine.

Following Russia's invasion of Ukraine, the Alabuga SEZ became home to a joint Russia-Iran initiative: the domestic production of Iranian drones on Russian territory. Designated "Project Boat" in an apparent attempt to mask its military purpose, the joint venture revealed Russia's substantial reliance on Iranian technical expertise and technological know-how to establish indigenous drone manufacturing capabilities. The localization effort—transitioning from imports to domestic production—elevated the extent of direct Russia-Iran collaboration. The details of the contracts were revealed by an investigation by the independent online newspaper Protokol and the YouTube channel Razvorot, which acquired numerous documents relating to the project, including the contract for drone production personally signed by Sergey Shoigu.[113] Subsequent reporting by the *Washington Post* and documents released by Prana, a hacking group, painted a fuller picture of the extent of Russian and Iranian military cooperation.[114]

The Alabuga drone project's internal documents reveal multiple layers of attempted secrecy. Throughout the documents, in a seemingly deliberate obfuscation, the term "Shaheds" was changed to "Boats." Likewise, in what appears to be an additional effort to hide Iran's involvement, official documents referred to Iran as either "Belarus" or "Ireland"—even though accompanying maps clearly depicted Iranian territory. Despite the intention to keep the project's specifics confidential, the leaked planning documents included detailed technical drawings and diagrams that clearly showed the design and components of a Shahed-136 drone.[115] The leaked documents also included detailed PowerPoints with Shahed assembly instructions for factory workers, many of whom were recruited from Africa and Central Asia under false promises of educational opportunities.

Beyond failed attempts at secrecy, the scope of Russian-Iranian collaboration proved far more extensive than simple licensed production. One of the key components of this initiative was the two-way transfer of expertise. Iran committed to providing 600,000 hours of specialized training—half conducted in Iran and half at Russia's Alabuga facility—to establish a foundation in drone manufacturing expertise. While absorbing this knowledge, Russian engineers actively identified opportunities for modernization, particularly in what they considered "outdated manufacturing techniques" in the Iranian production process.[116] These improvements included equipping the Shahed drones with thermobaric warheads for enhanced destructive power against fortified targets, adding radar absorbing carbon fiber coatings to reduce detectability, and integrating Russian Kometa navigation units and Chinese control boards to improve guidance accuracy. This created a mutually beneficial arrangement: Russia gained immediate access to battle-proven drone designs, while Iran stood to benefit from observing these designs enhanced with Russian modifications.

When U.S. intelligence began warning about the Iranian transfer of drones to Russia, Moscow and Tehran were already engaged in discussions about the joint production of Shaheds on Russian territory. The Alabuga Joint Stock Company (JSC)—the company managing the Alabuga SEZ—was awarded the contract for assembling Geran-2 drones in partnership with a local UAV producer, Albatross, to construct drone factories. In November 2022, specialists from the Alabuga JSC visited Tehran to acquire drone manufacturing technology for local production in Russia, with a target of manufacturing 6,000 drones domestically by 2025. The delegation from Alabuga visited Iranian factories for avionics, engines, gliders, and assembly production.[117]

The visit of the Alabuga delegation to Iran was followed by Deputy Defense Minister Fomin's trip to Tehran, where he met with senior Iranian defense officials, including those affiliated with MODAFL. Then, in early January 2023, a high-level Iranian delegation traveled to the Alabuga SEZ to survey potential facilities. The Iranian delegation was led by sanctioned Brigadier General Abdollah Mehrabi, head of the IRGC Research and Self-Sufficiency Jihad Organization, which specializes in military technology development and indigenous weapons production, and Ghassem Damavandian, the chief executive of Iran's Quds Aviation Industry, a MODAFL subsidiary focused on manufacturing military aircraft and UAVs; both Mehrabi and Damavandian managed parts of UAV and military aircraft production, procurement, and maintenance in Iran and were planning to bring such capabilities to Russia

Russia and Iran also held bilateral meetings to discuss the adaptation of parts that could be sourced from the Russian side to expedite project implementation.[118] In March 2023, an Iranian delegation visited the subsidiaries of JSC Technodinamika, a Rostec holding company of numerous aviation-related enterprises, to determine the sourcing of potential parts. Meanwhile, Russian-sanctioned entities were tasked with importing components, parts, and materials from Iran and other countries. Various visits to Iran by delegations from Alabuga secured technological documents for producing fuselages, engines, and printed circuit boards, as well as source codes for the flight controller, jamming-resistant GPS signal receiver, and air data system.[119]

The costs associated with Russia's localization of the Shahed drones exceeded the initial estimates. According to the leaked information from the Prana project, Iran initially set the price for each drone unit at 23 million rubles, which was equivalent to about $375,000 USD at the time of the negotiations. Russian negotiators managed to obtain a discount for bulk purchasing the drones, where 2,000 Shaheds would be priced at $290,000 USD per unit, whereas a larger order of 6,000 units saw the price drop to $193,000 each. The overall agreement, encapsulating technology transfer, equipment, 6,000 drones, and software, reached a value of 108.5 billion rubles (around $1.7 billion USD). The high figure likely includes the expedited timeline for technology and equipment transfers, accounting not just for the cost of the drones but also for sustaining Iran's domestic production during the transition.[120]

The contract's implementation hit an unexpected roadblock when Iran rejected payment in rubles—a striking paradox given both nations' vocal support for de-dollarization and their public commitment to trading in national currencies. Instead, Iran demanded to be paid in gold. However, once the gold had been loaded onto a plane for transport to Iran as part of the payment agreement, the Iranian side unexpectedly changed its stance and insisted on being paid in U.S. dollars instead. While no official explanation was provided for this abrupt change, the decision likely stemmed from the dollar's unrivaled position as a stable and liquid currency in global markets. Ultimately, this episode highlighted a crucial reality: regardless of political rhetoric about monetary independence, when faced with actual transaction decisions, neither Russian rubles nor Iranian rials proved sufficiently attractive for major bilateral trade deals.

To fulfill the contract, the head of VTB Bank, Andrei Kostin, eventually managed to transfer the money to Iran. VTB's role in the deal was no coincidence. As Russia's second-largest bank with a newly established representative office in Iran, VTB was positioned to strengthen bilateral banking relationships and facilitate military-technical transactions.[121] In addition to VTB's fulfilment of the contract, Iran received additional payments in gold, facilitated by Alabuga Machinery, a subsidiary handling the Alabuga SEZ's financial dealings with the Iranian government. Through this mechanism, Russia compensated Iran by transferring 2,067,795 grams of gold bullion to Sahara Thunder, an IRGC front company.

The financial arrangements for Project Boat revealed an extensive transfer of Iranian expertise in sanctions evasion and clandestine manufacturing to Russia. Moreover, the project's structure and execution mirror Iran's refined methods of circumventing international restrictions, developed over decades of operating under sanctions. Russia has rapidly adopted these Iranian tactics, creating elaborate networks of front companies and procurement channels to acquire critical technology, components, and expertise for its military production. This adoption is exemplified by Drake LLC, a Russian-based company established for drone components and related technology on behalf of the Russian government. Operating as a third-party intermediary, Drake LLC employed a network of front companies and brokers, including entities in Kazakhstan, to obscure the origins of its purchases and evade export restrictions from suppliers in China and the United States—directly replicating Iran's well-established procurement methods.

What makes Project Boat particularly significant is how it transcends simple technology transfer to become a blueprint for industrial autarky, showing how sanctioned states can develop parallel manufacturing and financial ecosystems outside Western control. More than just a drone factory, Project Boat represented a new phase in Russian-Iranian relations where mutual technological development and sanctions resistance could create the foundation for deeper military cooperation.

* * *

When Russia launched its full-scale invasion of Ukraine in February 2022, Russia and Iran had already formed a partnership from their experience in Syria. The war in Ukraine acted as a catalyst, accelerating the trend for deepening ties between Iran and Russia. Despite forging closer ties with Tehran since the Syrian Civil War, Moscow has carefully navigated its relationship to avoid alienating the West and Israel. However, the war in Ukraine and the resulting severance of ties between Russia and the West have positioned Iran as one of Moscow's most reliable partners.

Iranian drone technology has played a pivotal role in the battlegrounds in Ukraine. The unfolding military dynamics between the two nations represented their mutual reliance on each other for mitigating outside threats and ensuring regime endurance. Beyond the provision of hardware and repressive technologies, Iran is also gaining battlefield knowledge from Russia's war in Ukraine. As one expert put it, Russia can provide Iran with sensitive information on Ukrainian air defense systems and the effectiveness of Western military equipment.[122] Furthermore, as discussed in Chapter 9, Iran's supply of drones to Russia has also led to a greater Russian willingness to supply Iran with more advanced technologies.

Russia and Iran's partnership of defiance has extended to the realm of economics, where both have jointly worked on creating financial mechanisms and trade practices that bypass Western-controlled systems. Facing isolation from Western markets, Russia and Iran have increasingly turned towards one another to fulfill their economic and technological needs. In Chapter 9, Russia's and Iran's creation of alternative trade routes, barter trade systems, and local currency settlements would showcase a shared determination to operate outside the purview of Western economic influence—one that arose due to necessity.

9

RESISTANCE BY NECESSITY

In a display of diplomatic grandstanding, December 2023 saw Russia and Iran release the "Declaration by the Russian Federation and the Islamic Republic of Iran on the Ways and Means to Counter, Mitigate, and Redress the Adverse Impacts of Unilateral Coercive Measures."[1] The declaration, with an exhaustive title that could serve as a thesis statement, articulated a litany of grievances about sanctions, inconspicuously directed at the West. These so-called unilateral coercive measures encompass any violation of "non-interference in internal affairs of States," including "pressure in any form ... to compel a change in the policy of another State by causing costs and damage to that State and those who support its political course." The declaration categorically deems such "pressure"—whether political, judicial, financial, or economic—as "illegal," urging states to neither recognize nor implement these measures. In essence, the document provides a legal framework for sanctions evasion, declaring that states and private companies possess "immunity" from asset confiscation when violating "unilateral coercive measures" while holding sanctioning states liable for any resulting economic damage.

It is no surprise that Russia and Iran would seek to legalize sanctions evasion, given that both countries have actively engaged in such activities. In fact, Russia and Iran's collaboration against "unilateral coercive measures" flourished in the wake of the 2022 invasion of Ukraine. Moscow quickly surpassed Iran to become the world's most-sanctioned country, a notable feat given Iran's decades-long experience with international restrictions due to its nuclear program and regional proxy activities. Tehran's expertise in circumventing sanctions through shell companies, intermediaries, and black-market operations made it an invaluable partner for Russia as Moscow sought to mitigate its growing economic isolation.

These circumstances revived dormant initiatives and opened new avenues of collaboration under a shared narrative of resistance. This chapter highlights the strategies and narratives the two countries have used to counter economic isolation and how this has led to cooperation due to the lack of alternatives.

Resistance Economics

As Russian forces waged war on Ukraine, the West embarked on an "economic war" with Russia through the use of sanctions and financial measures.[2] Two days after Russia's invasion, the U.S. and Europe imposed economic sanctions on the Central Bank of Russia. As a result, at least $300 billion USD of approximately $476 billion USD in foreign-currency reserves was frozen, limiting Moscow's access to dollar-denominated foreign reserves. By March 2022, seven of Russia's largest banks had been cut off from the Society for Worldwide Interbank Financial Telecommunication (SWIFT) interbank payment system. Combined with the sanctions on the central bank, this effectively blocked Russia's access to a portion of the international financial system. Efforts to diminish Russia's revenue streams included sanctions on its oil industry, limits on the sale price of Russian oil, and bans on imports into the European Union (EU).[3] Aware of the potential economic onslaught, Russian officials looked to Iran as a model for economic resilience under heavy sanctions.

In the years preceding the Ukraine War, particularly after 2014 sanctions over Crimea in Chapter 3 and the Countering America's Adversaries Through Sanctions Act (CAATSA) sanctions in

Chapter 6, the Russian policy elite began to study Iran's "resistance economy" (*eghtesad e-moghavemati*) with growing interest.[4] Launched in the 2010s amid intensifying international sanctions, Iran's "resistance economy" was devised to bolster its economic resilience against external economic shocks and stressors by reducing import dependence, favoring domestic goods, fortifying knowledge-based industries, and reducing reliance on oil revenues. The Supreme Leader described the concept of a "resistance economy" as a form of self-reliant entrepreneurship, attributing its genesis to two key factors—"economic pressure from adversaries" and "the country's preparedness for self-dependency."[5] An outgrowth of Iran's broader foreign policy, the resistance economy has been framed as a nationalistic duty drenched in a moral obligation to support Iranian independence amid Western strangulation.

Russia's pivot toward a similar model accelerated after the 2014 Ukraine crisis when the first wave of Western sanctions hit Moscow. It was during this period that Vladimir Putin first articulated Russia's position on self-sufficiency (*samodostatochnost'*), declaring that "Russia is not going to get all worked up, get offended or come begging at anyone's door. Russia is a self-sufficient country."[6] Iranian strategies for navigating sanctions offered a valuable blueprint, prompting Russian researchers to study and adapt these lessons to Russia's more industrialized economy.[7] After 2014, Russian policymakers launched a program for economic self-reliance: promote domestic production, reduce import dependence, and fix structural weaknesses. Their goal was twofold: to develop an indigenous model of economic resistance while simultaneously addressing long-standing structural vulnerabilities in the Russian economy.[8] Sanctions imposed in 2022 further necessitated adaptation and innovation, leading Russia to draw from Iran's experience in seeking alternative trading partners and exploiting legislative loopholes to maintain economic stability and advance political objectives despite external constraints.[9]

Alone in Good Company

The bilateral trade relationship between Russia and Iran, historically the weakest link in their partnership, gained new significance after the full-scale war in Ukraine.[10] A Russian foreign policy expert argued that since February 2022, there has been "a lot of serious work" between Russian and Iranian officials to improve their economic ties, which was "always a weak point" in the relationship.[11] Attention to boosting trade ties with Iran, according to a Russian expert, has been "one area where there is a transformation" in Russian thinking.[12] Russian officials have argued that Iran can replace the loss of markets in areas such as industrial services, trade, and export routes.[13] However, the implementation and realization of such efforts have faced numerous hurdles ranging from the state of the Russian and Iranian economies to challenges with customs and logistics.[14]

Officials on both sides have been notably enthusiastic, treating shared sanctions exposure as a foundation for deeper economic collaboration. This sense of solidarity has been repeatedly emphasized in official statements, with leaders from both sides framing their partnership as a defiant response to external pressures and a commitment to economic sovereignty. During a visit to Iran in May 2022, Deputy Prime Minister Alexander Novak declared that Russia was "one of the few countries in the world that sincerely supported the Iranian people during the period of sanctions and now, having come under unprecedented sanctions pressure, is ready to study the experience of Iran and jointly develop important trade and economic projects."[15] In June 2022, during a meeting with Raisi, Lavrov declared that "all countries experiencing the negative impact of the selfish line of the U.S. and its satellites have an objective need to reconfigure their economic ties in such a way as not to depend on the whims of our Western partners."[16] Similarly, in October 2022, Russian Prime Minister Mikhail Mishustin noted that Russia and Iran intended to strengthen their cooperation in all areas due to the "illegitimate economic sanctions that unfriendly states imposed on both Russia and Iran."[17]

A redirected focus on alternative export destinations and import sources beyond the West has highlighted the potential for enhanced Russia-Iran bilateral trade relations, but a substantial gap remains between official rhetoric and the practical realities of implementation.[18] In 2022, the trade dynamic between Russia and

Iran demonstrated a promising upward trend, with bilateral trade turnover witnessing an increase of 20 percent, reaching $4.9 billion USD. However, the trend reversed in the following year: by the end of 2023, the trade volume between the two nations had dipped by 17 percent, falling to $4 billion USD. Iranian exports to Russia experienced an uptick, growing by 15.8 percent to $1.29 billion USD. The overall decrease in trade volumes can primarily be attributed to a substantial drop in Russian exports to Iran, which plummeted by 27.1 percent to $2.7 billion USD.[19] Although considerable, the potential opportunities for Russia within Iran are counterbalanced by the inherent challenges that both Russian private enterprises and governmental structures must navigate.

The chief challenge lies in the similarity between Iran's and Russia's economies, which do not naturally foster a thriving trade relationship. There is a significant overlap between the two economies, with nine out of their top fifteen exported goods categories being identical; moreover, ten out of their fifteen most imported goods match as well. Only two out of Russia's fifteen most sought-after goods are among Iran's top exports.[20] Even where there are apparent gaps in Iran's demands that could potentially be filled by Russia, in the automobiles, electronics, and machinery sectors, for example, Russia's production capacity poses a constraint.[21]

Notwithstanding structural economic incompatibilities, the absence of reliable banking channels has limited trade between Russia and Iran for decades, and little progress has been made on mitigation measures. Due to U.S. sanctions and the difficulty of conducting trade in dollars, Iran and Russia have been forced to trade in rubles and rials in bilateral trade and to integrate their financial messaging services to handle two-way banking transactions.[22] Yet, converting currencies and settling payments between Russia and Iran has proven cumbersome. For instance, one conduit has been Iran's Mir Business Bank in Moscow (a subsidiary of Bank Melli Iran), which uses Iran's fixed official exchange rate for the rial. This means Russian exporters incur losses of 20-25 percent on each transaction due to the gap between Iran's overvalued official rate and the real market rate. In practice, Russian traders found it cheaper to literally carry cash in so-called "suitcase schemes" than to wire money through an official channel.

Softer barriers also impede commerce. Iranian analysts point to a litany of issues: misaligned customs regulations, complex import rules, lack of mutually recognized standards, and inadequate marketing. Multiple Iranian government assessments stress the difficulty of making the trade between Russia and Iran "operational and accessible."[23] Iranian exporters often lack familiarity with Russian demand and regulation; Russian firms, for their part, struggle with Iranian bureaucracy.

Despite these hurdles, the war transformed Russian interest in the economic relationship. Iran had always expressed an interest in Russia as a potential trade partner; however, Russia previously had other options. During Raisi's visit to Russia in January 2022, Nikolai Kozhanov, former Russian diplomat in Iran and expert on Russia-Iran relations, observed that Iran wanted to move beyond "situational interaction on certain political issues," since the relationship would "be unstable without an economic basis."[24] With the imposition of sanctions on Russia in 2022, the prospects for moving beyond situational interaction would manifest out of expediency.

Replacing Western Markets

Since February 2022, Russian authorities have been aiming for economic self-reliance by fostering local industries through import substitution, echoing Iran's attempt to establish a "resistance economy" to reduce dependency on foreign suppliers. At the 2023 meeting of the Valdai Club, Putin stated that "the greatness of Russia today lies in strengthening its sovereignty … based on self-sufficiency in technology, finance, [and] the economy as a whole, in the field of defense and security."[25] The journey for Russia and Iran towards economic self-reliance and import substitution has included the use of parallel imports, barter deals, and alternative financial mechanisms to offer some respite from economic sanctions.[26] The inherent irony in Russia's efforts at self-sufficiency, however, is the overwhelming reliance on other countries to achieve this goal.

To maintain access to essential foreign goods, Moscow authorized parallel imports, which entail "the purchase of goods and technology without the approval of its license holder—effectively authorizing piracy."[27] Russia's use of parallel imports, long employed by Iran to circumvent official channels and the trademark owner's consent, has enabled Russia to secure various sanctioned goods, particularly auto parts and household appliances, often re-exported through countries like Kazakhstan.[28] Like Iran, Russia has leveraged third parties in Turkey, the United Arab Emirates (UAE), Hong Kong, and Malaysia to facilitate the import of sanctioned materials.

Numerous agreements have been signed between Russia and Iran to foster mutually beneficial alternatives to the now-curtailed Western imports. Highlighting this potential, Vladimir Obydenov, chairman of the Russian-Iranian Business Council, remarked that Iran could "replace a number of Western goods in [Russian] markets" and serve as "an alternative to certain Western products."[29] Among these sectors, automotive and heavy machinery have drawn particular interest.

Iran provided critical vehicle components otherwise inaccessible to Russian manufacturers under sanctions. A significant milestone occurred in August 2022 at the MIMS Automobility Moscow exhibition, where Iranian Industries Minister Reza Fatemi-Amin secured memoranda worth $700 million USD for joint production and parts supply.[30] Between March 2022 and March 2023, Iran's auto-part exports to Russia surged from $13 million USD to over $66 million USD, while overall industrial exports grew by nearly one-third. Building on this momentum, gas-turbine technology has emerged as another promising avenue: Iranian manufacturers now position themselves as drop-in replacements for Western suppliers such as Siemens. To this end, in late 2022, Russian Energy Minister Nikolai Shulginov announced an agreement with Iran's MAPNA Group to supply 40 large-scale turbines.[31] While logistical and financial constraints remain, gas turbines constitute a promising area of cooperation where Iran's expertise aligns well with Russian needs.

Collaborative ventures have not advanced uniformly. The civil aviation sector presents particular difficulties, with both Russia and Iran facing sanctions-driven shortages. Russia, cut off from official

Boeing and Airbus supply chains, has sought alternative methods to sustain its commercial fleet. Iran, constrained by longstanding U.S. sanctions, similarly struggles to maintain modern aircraft and parts inventories.[32] Although Moscow and Tehran have agreed in principle on joint aircraft production and maintenance projects, their mutual dependence on foreign-made, high-tech components limits immediate progress. Effective cooperation in civil aviation will likely rely heavily on parallel imports, with Russia already importing more than $180 million in original Boeing and Airbus parts, primarily from countries such as the UAE, China, and Turkey.[33]

Barter has also emerged as a practical means of keeping commerce flowing between Tehran and Moscow without relying on Western financial networks. Building on a 2015 oil swap model, barter arrangements have allowed Iran to transfer oil to Russia in exchange for wheat, sunflower oil, and other essential imports.[34] By circumventing global oversight, these swaps provide "off-the-books" mechanisms for liquidity that sidestep the obstacles posed by restricted banking channels. Although barter alleviates some immediate financial bottlenecks, it also highlights the precarious nature of the relationship: neither country can fully realize its ambitions for economic self-sufficiency without paradoxically relying on foreign partners, covert supply chains, and non-transparent trade practices that only partly substitute for stable trade.

Empty Promises

Memoranda of Understanding (MoUs) became a hallmark of Iran's economic policy under President Raisi, particularly in the context of the country's deepening ties with Russia. These non-binding agreements, which outline broad areas of cooperation and mutual intentions, have been touted by both Russian and Iranian officials as evidence of the two countries' growing partnership. However, a closer examination reveals that the MoUs have often failed to translate into concrete policy actions or tangible economic outcomes.

The disconnect between the rhetoric surrounding Russia-Iran MoUs and the reality of their implementation is perhaps best exemplified by the $40 billion USD energy cooperation agreement signed between the National Iranian Oil Company (NIOC) and Russia's Gazprom during Putin's visit to Iran in 2022.[35] The MoU, which was widely publicized as a milestone in bilateral relations, included ambitious plans for the joint development of gas fields in the Persian Gulf, collaboration on Liquified Natural Gas (LNG) projects, and the construction of gas export pipelines.[36] On paper, the NIOC-Gazprom MoU appeared to be a logical fit, given Russia's expertise in secondary gas production technology and Iran's need for investment in its sanctions-hit energy sector.[37]

The likelihood of the agreement materializing into actual investments and projects remains highly uncertain, due in large part to the sanctions and restrictions faced by both countries.[38] One Iranian economic expert recalled that in 2017, Gazprom expressed an intention to invest in Iran's Bushehr LNG plant; however, this project has not progressed due to various factors, including the impact of U.S. secondary sanctions.[39] Moreover, economic authorities within Iran are skeptical about Gazprom's capability and willingness to ultimately make these investments. Compounding the dim prospects of the NIOC-Gazprom MoU is a subsequent $20 billion USD agreement between Iran and four local companies in the South Pars field. This new agreement overlaps with the 2022 MoU between Iran and Gazprom, as it assigns these local companies' contracts for the same fields that were previously covered under the Gazprom agreement.[40]

The gap between the promises of Russia-Iran MoUs and their actual implementation has not gone unnoticed within Iran. Economic initiatives with Russia have faced criticism from various quarters, with detractors labeling them as ineffective and misguided in the face of the country's persistent economic woes, including high inflation and unemployment. Accordingly, within Iran, Raisi's initiatives with Russia were labeled as "incompetent" and inept.[41] The most prominent criticism of Raisi's policies was made by the Supreme Leader in his 2024 Nowruz speech, when he criticized the numerous MoUs as "ineffective." Khamenei further stated that these MoUs "should transform into national, legally binding, and executive contracts that are applicable so that their results are clear and tangible in practice."[42]

However, the limitations of the MoU-driven approach to economic cooperation have led to a growing recognition that the true nature of the Russia-Iran economic partnership may lie outside the realm of formal agreements and official channels. Given the sanctions and restrictions faced by both countries, it is likely that their economic collaboration will increasingly pivot towards mutual support for sanctions evasion strategies and enhanced cooperation within the informal and clandestine economic sectors.

Shadow Networks

Russia has increasingly drawn from Iran's established playbook for sanctions evasion, adopting sophisticated strategies including shadow banking networks, front companies, and illicit shipping methods. In the past, Russia capitalized on Iran's covert procurement networks to streamline oil transfers to Syria, where Russian enterprises noted how Iranian investments skillfully used intermediary firms to dodge sanctions.[43] While traditional spheres of trade and investment between the two countries remain limited, Iran's expertise in circumventing international restrictions has proved particularly valuable to Russia. International sanctions have inadvertently thrust Russia and Iran into direct competition within the shadowy world of illicit oil trade. As legitimate export channels narrow because of sanctions, both countries have been forced to rely increasingly on clandestine markets to sell their oil.[44]

Recognizing the value of Iran's expertise, Russia has studied and replicated its use of shadow banking networks to facilitate sanctioned international trade.[45] Iran's modus operandi involves clearinghouses overseeing networks of overseas front companies, primarily registered in jurisdictions with lenient regulations such as China, the UAE, and Turkey.[46] When Iranian entities need to conduct restricted transactions, they work through local banks that coordinate with these exchange houses. Payments are then channeled through multiple shell companies, effectively masking their origin.[47] Russia has adopted similar tactics, with the U.S. government warning about Russia's "use of third-party intermediaries or transshipment points" to disguise sanctioned entities.[48] For example, Konstantin Malofeyev, a Russian businessman and financier of Russia's war in Ukraine, was involved in creating a global network to circumvent sanctions that mirrored Iran.[49]

In maritime logistics, Russia has explicitly integrated Iranian strategies to sustain its petroleum exports amid intensifying international restrictions. A hallmark Iranian practice involves disabling vessels' Automatic Identification Systems (AIS), effectively making tankers invisible to maritime monitoring systems.[50] Additionally, Tehran routinely conducts ship-to-ship oil transfers in international waters, far from the oversight of port authorities, coupled with intricate financial operations involving subsidiaries and shell corporations. Post-February 2022, Russia rapidly adopted similar tactics, exemplified by the decision of Russia's state-owned shipping firm Sovcomflot to withhold destination information for approximately one-third of its tanker fleet starting in April 2022.[51] Russian tankers have increasingly reflagged from Russia to jurisdictions with minimal oversight, such as the Marshall Islands and Saint Kitts and Nevis. Russia has also employed Venezuelan-style oil blending and rebranding practices to obscure the origin of its crude.

Sanctions led Moscow to export oil on the same black markets as Iran, with both countries competing to secure a greater market share.[52] Competition has primarily occurred in markets east of Suez, specifically China and India, where both countries have vied for customers through an overlapping network of illicit tankers.[53] Data from Vortexa has illustrated this overlap: between February and June 2023, 135 unique tankers that previously transported Iranian and Venezuelan crude were tracked carrying Russian oil.[54] An Iranian government research report has acknowledged the challenge for Iran, noting that Russia's aggressive price discounts are successfully attracting Iran's traditional customers.[55] The common pressures of international sanctions have created a paradoxical relationship between Russia and Iran, simultaneously driving them toward cooperation while forcing them into competition. As both navigate restricted access to global markets, they find themselves not only sharing expertise and networks but also competing for the same limited pool of willing trade partners, shipping capacity, and financial channels.

Although sanctions have spurred competition in the black-market oil trade, Iran has assisted Russia's shipment of stolen grains from occupied territories in Ukraine. Traditionally, grains have constituted a large part of the bilateral trade relationship, with Iran importing Russian cereals and grains.[56] Iran continued to be one of the main buyers of Russian wheat following the invasion of Ukraine, when global wheat prices peaked and Russian exports faced uncertainties due to sanctions.[57] One of the major developments to emerge from the war has been Iran's new role as both a re-export destination for Russian grains and a purchaser of grain from occupied Ukrainian territories.[58] Iran offered Moscow assistance in exporting Russian grain to third countries, facilitating payment through barter or non-dollar currencies. As Iranian Deputy Minister of Economy and Finance for Economic Policy Seyyed Ali Rouhani emphasized, "the Russian side can count on Iran as a reliable and long-term partner ... the conflict in Ukraine and the subsequent Western sanctions against the Russian Federation have practically made the Iranian route a safe and alternative route for the export of Russian grain."[59]

The scale and sophistication of Iran's involvement in shipping Ukrainian grain from occupied territories became apparent through a series of revelations beginning in 2022. The first public indication came in June 2022, when the *Moscow Times* reported a vessel carrying 7,000 tons of cereal departing from the occupied Ukrainian port of Berdyansk, establishing a new maritime route for exporting Ukrainian wheat to third countries. By 2023, satellite imagery revealed that this initial operation had expanded into a comprehensive smuggling network, with Russian grain exports flowing from multiple occupied territories, including Sevastopol, Feodosia, Mariupol, Berdyansk, and Kerch.[60] These smuggling operations adopted methods used in illicit oil trading to mask their activities: ships disabled their AIS signals to conceal their movements, and operators began using ship-to-ship transfers to further obscure the grain's origin.[61]

In early 2023, vessels previously known to transport grain to Syria and Turkey began appearing in Iranian ports. The investigative journalism group Bellingcat documented this change, tracking vessels like the *Mikhail Nenashev* and *Matros Shevchenko* making direct voyages from Sevastopol to Iran's southern ports.[62] These ports, such as Bandar Khomeini and Bandar Abbas, have a superior cargo handling capacity compared to Caspian ports like Amirabad and Anzali. This advantage made them ideal discreet gateways for Russia's grain exports from occupied territories. Meanwhile, Russian companies have also shown an increased interest in Iran's southern ports, with various delegations traveling to Iran to establish contracts with IRGC-affiliated economic charities known as *bonyads*. The logistics of these operations are multi-layered, involving the physical movement of grain as well as a sophisticated web of ownership transfers and financial transactions designed to obscure the beneficiaries of these shipments.

The black market represents a fundamentally inadequate foundation for sustainable Russia-Iran cooperation, characterized by inherent instability, vulnerability to sudden disruption, and the absence of institutional frameworks necessary for long-term economic planning. Illicit trade networks operate under constant threat of exposure and enforcement action, while lacking the transparency, legal protections, and scalability required for sophisticated economic partnerships. However, the progressive tightening of Western sanctions has systematically eliminated many of the legitimate channels for bilateral commerce, creating a paradoxical situation where both nations recognize their dependence on suboptimal shadow networks yet possess few viable alternatives. This regulatory stranglehold has trapped Russia and Iran in a cycle where immediate economic necessities override long-term strategic considerations, suggesting that while their partnership may deepen in scope, it will simultaneously become more fragile and less capable of generating the sustainable growth both countries ultimately need to offset the costs of international isolation.

De-Dollarization

U.S. and EU sanctions have severely restricted the ability of Iran and Russia to access global financial and banking platforms. Russian and Iranian officials openly acknowledge that this has undermined their ability to boost trade and investment globally and bilaterally.[63] Following the surge of sanctions in response to Russia's invasion of Ukraine, Russia intensified its existing efforts to circumvent these limitations.[64] One strategy involved bolstering collaboration with Iran to fortify alternative banking channels and advocate for the de-dollarization of international trade.[65] While the concept of de-dollarization predates the Ukraine crisis, it has gained prominence in recent years as Russia and Iran became among the leading states advocating for greater financial independence from the U.S. dollar, championing de-dollarization as the economic aim of multipolarity.[66]

In 2023, marking a historic first, the head of Russia's Central Bank, Elvira Nabiullina, visited Iran. The visit followed a series of interactions between Russian and Iranian financial and business authorities throughout 2022 and 2023.[67] Central to these discussions was the promotion of national currencies—the Russian ruble and the Iranian rial—in bilateral trade and investment, alongside efforts to enhance banking cooperation through integrated financial messaging services that bypass Western-dominated platforms like SWIFT.[68]

The journey towards financial independence began years earlier for both Russia and Iran. After the 2014 Ukraine crisis, the Central Bank of Russia launched its financial message transmission system, *Sistema Peredachi Finansovykh Soobscheniy* (SPFS), to effectively neutralize the threat of disconnecting Russia from the SWIFT system.[69] This domestic solution enabled Russian banks, corporations, and government entities to securely communicate financial information independently of Western systems.[70] Similarly, Iran had pursued financial autonomy even earlier, initiating its *Samaneh-ye Peygam-Resani-ye Elektroniki-ye Melli* (SEPAM) in 2011, which became operational by 2013.[71] At the height of sanctions on the country, SEPAM provided a critical safeguard that allowed Iranian banks to remain operational despite isolation due to Western sanctions.[72]

Efforts to connect these two domestic messaging systems culminated in January 2023, marking a significant turning point in their bilateral financial cooperation.[73] The agreement signed between the Central Bank of Iran and the Bank of Russia effectively created a secure, closed-channel platform allowing transactions in their respective national currencies without interference or oversight by Western financial institutions. By February 2023, major Russian banks such as Sberbank and VTB had integrated into this new joint system, enabling practical financial exchanges including letters of credit, guarantees, and fund transfers, free from U.S. interference. Yet, the SPFS-SEPAM connection has faced technical and operational limitations. SPFS, for instance, remains significantly smaller than SWIFT, boasting only about 584 participating institutions by the end of 2024, of which only a few hundred are foreign entities. This pales in comparison to SWIFT's global network of over 11,000 institutions. Moreover, SPFS has encountered practical challenges, such as restricted operating hours, limited message sizes, and integration difficulties with non-Russian banks.[74]

Consistent with their efforts to integrate SPFS and SEPAM, Iran and Russia have rapidly expanded local-currency trade as a cornerstone of their broader de-dollarization strategy. Vyacheslav Volodin, speaker of Russia's State Duma, emphasized that expanding local-currency usage was "extremely important under sanctions pressure" facing both countries.[75] According to the Kremlin, bilateral transactions settled in rubles or rials surged to 96 percent by the end of 2024, representing a dramatic increase from approximately 60 percent just one year earlier.[76]

However, the full realization of local-currency trade continues to face notable practical challenges, with currency instability being the primary obstacle. Both the Iranian rial and the Russian ruble have been prone to sharp fluctuations and significant devaluations, creating considerable unpredictability for businesses. Consequently, many companies still rely on the U.S. dollar for pricing and negotiating contracts to ensure stability and predictability, even if final settlements are ultimately converted to local currencies.[77] Iran's complex dual-rate exchange system further exacerbates these difficulties, consisting of an official subsidized exchange rate and a separate floating market rate. Throughout 2023, for example, the official rate was about 430,000 rials per USD, whereas the market rate reached around 520,000 rials per USD. This disparity often resulted in substantial financial losses for Iranian exporters converting ruble earnings through official channels rather than the open market. In an attempt to mitigate these issues, Russia and Iran formalized a monetary agreement in late 2024, mandating settlements at mutually determined market rates. Subsequently, Iran introduced a specialized ruble trading platform in early 2025, designed to transparently determine exchange values based on market dynamics, aiming to facilitate smoother transactions between Iranian and Russian businesses.

To support their financial partnership, Tehran and Moscow have moved to integrate key banking services and institutions. In May 2023, VTB opened a representative office in Tehran—marking the first presence of a major Russian bank on Iranian soil.[78] According to Iranian officials, by 2025, "no limitations" existed for Russian banks in Iran, with Sberbank receiving explicit invitations alongside VTB's planned upgrade to full branch status. Reciprocally, Iran expanded beyond Bank Melli's existing Moscow subsidiary with two additional Iranian banks preparing Russian offices by mid-2023. Parallel to deepening institutional ties, Iran and Russia have moved to integrate their domestic retail payment infrastructures, expanding cooperation to the consumer and commercial sectors. Following a 2023 agreement, Russia's Mir payment system—a national electronic payment network developed after Western sanctions cut off Visa and MasterCard services in 2014—was formally linked with Iran's Shetab banking network, which handles interbank transactions and domestic card clearing. This integration allows Russian and Iranian citizens to conduct cross-border purchases and ATM withdrawals more easily, circumventing U.S.-led financial restrictions and reinforcing both countries' broader effort to establish alternatives to the Western-dominated financial system.

The efforts of both parties have largely been impeded by the limited liquidity of the Russian ruble and Iranian rial in their respective foreign exchange markets. Russian and Iranian banks can handle investments in smaller ports and railways.[79] For more substantial investments, the involvement of banks from countries like China and the UAE is crucial. However, these financial institutions remain hesitant due to concerns over U.S. sanctions and the potential risk to their access to U.S. financing.

Overcoming the challenge of creating an independent and robust financial system capable of handling large transaction volumes while ensuring stability and reliability is no easy task. Shifting away from the dominance of the U.S. dollar and towards local currencies or alternative systems necessitates a substantial level of trust and willingness from other countries. Moreover, the adoption of alternative currencies or systems for international trade depends on several factors, including the stability of those currencies and the associated benefits and risks of embracing such alternatives. While Russia and Iran face challenges in finding stable alternatives to the U.S. dollar and euro, the majority of countries still have access to these major currencies for international trade and finance.

North-South Transport

The development of the International North-South Transit Corridor (INSTC), discussed in Chapter 7, has attracted considerable interest since Russia invaded Ukraine.[80] Sanctions have considerably curtailed Russian access to European markets, prompting a pivot towards Asian markets and the diversification of trade routes.[81] To bypass Western-dominated trade routes, Russia has sought to reinvigorate the INSTC to augment Russian exports of agricultural and petrochemical products, machinery, and fertilizers into Asian markets.[82]

Conceived as an integrated transport link connecting India and Russia via Iran, the INSTC promises to substantially reduce transit times and costs compared to traditional routes. As noted in Chapter 7, the INSTC failed to progress due to a lack of investment and international sanctions against Iran. As one Russian economic expert notes, "Russia did not adopt a strategic outlook when dealing with Iran … over two decades of discussions without commitments. [Russia] could have funded the corridor and it would have yielded rewards but Russia was not committed until it became a necessity."[83] Russia's appetite for investment in the INSTC changed following the Ukraine war. During Putin's 2023 speech to the Russian Federal Assembly, he highlighted Russia's "special attention to the International North-South Transport Corridor … to open new routes for business cooperation with India, Iran, Pakistan and the

Middle East."[84] The INSTC's revival is now seen as critical, not only to address logistical challenges posed by sanctions but also to adapt to shifting global markets, where economic activity is increasingly concentrated in China, Southeast Asia, and the Persian Gulf.[85]

Iranian authorities recognize the window of opportunity the Ukraine war presents. The consensus within Iran's scientific and policy circles is to leverage Russia's newfound interest in developing transit routes by attracting investments in transportation and logistics to align with China's BRI and the INSTC. Iran's Parliamentary Research Center has suggested that the INSTC can "increase Iran's foreign exchange earnings and facilitate trade" and "strengthen Iran's strategic and geopolitical position in the region."[86] Another report claims that Iran must "remove political obstacles in the transit routes of Iran and Russia" to reap the full benefits of the INSTC."[87]

As part of INSTC and bilateral trade flows, Russia and Iran have sought to improve the infrastructure in the Caspian Sea.[88] In order to improve the ports, a contract was signed for the construction of a cargo ship for operations at the Caspian Sea's Solyanka Port in Astrakhan, under Russian oversight.[89] Iran acquired a 53 percent stake in the port and invested $10 million USD, partly supported by Russian banks, to purchase a 270-container capacity vessel. The sanctioned Islamic Republic of Iran Shipping Lines (IRISL) also invested $10 million USD in Russia's Astrakhan port for development and vessel acquisition.[90] In 2022, Iran committed to eleven infrastructure projects worth nearly $13 billion USD, with Russia pledging a slightly higher amount towards these ventures. At the twenty-fifth St. Petersburg International Economic Forum in 2022, Russia and Iran reached a preliminary agreement for a joint shipbuilding venture, a proposal backed by the head of the Astrakhan region, Igor Babushkin.[91] Part of this is consistent with Russia's desire to expand Iran's ability to transport agricultural products between the two countries.[92] It also reflects the extensive use of the Caspian for the shipment of artillery shells, spare parts, and components for Russia's war.

As discussed in Chapter 7, a major factor in the realization of the INSTC is the development of the Rasht-Astara railway. In May 2023, Putin and Raisi oversaw the signing of an agreement to finance the design, construction, and supply of goods and services for the realization of the Rasht-Astara railway in Iran. Putin extolled the corridor's "competitive advantages," including the "delivery of goods from St. Petersburg to Mumbai" in "about ten days," which will enable "Russian and Iranian goods to receive more convenient and geographically diverse access to foreign markets."[93] According to a Russian expert, "Moscow is interested in entering the railroad system of Iran, but not for the sake of the railroads of Iran per se, but ... to redirect the flow of goods towards Asia."[94]

Challenges over investment and competing economic corridors remain impediments to the realization of the INSTC. Despite Russia's earmarking of a $5 billion USD loan to Iran specifically for infrastructure improvements, investors remain hesitant about the project's profitability.[95] Within Russia, apprehensions persist over the financial viability of the Rasht-Astara segment, especially when compared to the cost-effective road transport in Iran.[96] Moreover, the Russian-backed Eurasian Development Bank estimates that over $26 billion USD of investment is needed in both Russia and Iran to fully realize the INSTC.[97] The apparent reluctance among private investors will likely necessitate substantial financial backing from governments. Yet, it remains unclear if Russia, Azerbaijan, China, or India can commit to footing this bill.

* * *

Russia's and Iran's strategies of resistance manifest beyond the economic realm, permeating the domains of defense, cybersecurity, and space technology to counteract Western sanctions and pressures. As Russia's military-industrial complex faced shrinking global market shares due to sanctions, Iran emerged as a prime candidate for enhanced cooperation. Since the war, Moscow has shown increased willingness to provide Tehran with more sophisticated technology, ranging from advanced aircraft to assistance in space launches. The trajectory of their cooperation illustrates how sanctions have accelerated a convergence between Moscow and Tehran, turning parallel forms of resistance into a coordinated project of technological self-sufficiency.

Military and Resistance Economics

Prior to Russia's invasion of Ukraine, the military-security relationship between Moscow and Tehran was primarily characterized by a patron-client dynamic, with Russia providing Iran with weapons and military equipment. The war in Ukraine changed the nature of military-technical cooperation between Russia and Iran. The evolution of this partnership was marked by Sergey Shoigu's first and last visits to Tehran in his capacity as Defense Minister. His first visit in January 2015 came at a time when Iranian officials were still primarily seeking to procure Russian weaponry, months before the two powers would launch their joint intervention in Syria. In September 2023, during his final visit to Tehran as Defense Minister, the roles had dramatically reversed. Iran was now showcasing its own advanced military capabilities to Russia, including the Fateh family of short-range ballistic missiles and new Shahed-136 drone launchers, positioning itself as a critical supplier for Moscow's war effort in Ukraine.[98]

As discussed in Chapter 8, Iran's support for Russia's war effort has been multifaceted and substantial. It has supplied a diverse array of UAVs, including the Mohajer-6, Shahed-131, and Shahed-136, which have enhanced Russia's ability to suppress Ukrainian air defenses and conduct long-range strikes. Beyond direct transfers, Iran has assisted Russia in establishing domestic production lines for these drones, a joint effort known as Project Boat. Drawing from its extensive experience in circumventing international restrictions, Iran has shared strategies to help Russia's defense industry mitigate the impact of Western sanctions and export controls. This expertise, combined with Iran's success in achieving defense production self-sufficiency through domestication (*bumi-sazi*) of weapon systems, has proven invaluable to Russia's efforts to maintain its military capabilities under sanctions.[99]

Perhaps most significantly, in September 2024, U.S. and European officials confirmed Iran's transfer of hundreds of short-range ballistic missiles to Russia, including systems from the Fateh missile family.[100] The Fath-360, a compact variant of the Fateh-110 missile, became the cornerstone of these transfers. With a range of 80 to 100 km and satellite navigation capabilities, possibly leveraging Russia's GLONASS network, these missiles offer Russia increased tactical flexibility on the battlefield. While not introducing entirely new capabilities, these Iranian systems would allow Russia to conserve its more advanced missiles for high-value targets deeper within Ukraine, while maintaining a steady supply of precision munitions for ongoing operations. In return, Russia bolstered Iran's military capabilities through various agreements and technology transfers.

As discussed in Chapter 6, CAATSA affected Russia's arms exports, leading to a decrease in its global market share from 22 percent in 2013-17 to 16 percent in 2018-22.[101] Notably, some contracts, such as a Su-35 agreement with Egypt, were nullified due to U.S. pressure following the enactment of CAATSA.[102] Before Egypt canceled the Su-35 deal, Russia allegedly denied Iran's request for either Su-35 or Su-30SM fighters and instead offered the older generation Su-27SM3 fighters due to Moscow's concerns about sharing sensitive technologies with Tehran.[103] Arms sales to Iran had clear implications for Russia's foreign policy in the Middle East, which has been contingent on maintaining close relations with Iran while concomitantly expanding its ties with Iran's adversaries, including Israel, the UAE, and Saudi Arabia.[104] A Russian defense expert suggested that there was "an obvious tension between Moscow being interested in supplying Iran with defense equipment and Tehran's wish to purchase offensive arms," which would provoke staunch opposition among the UAE, Saudi Arabia, and Israel.[105] At the time, some experts speculated that arms sales would be limited to defensive weapons like air defense systems that Iran had previously purchased from Russia.[106]

However, Russia's stance shifted markedly following Egypt's withdrawal from its Su-35 contract under American pressure. With approximately fifteen to sixteen Su-35 aircraft already in advanced production stages for Egypt, Rosoboronexport—the Russian state arms exporter—urgently sought alternative buyers. Initial hopes to redirect at least eleven of these jets to Indonesia, a long-time operator of Sukhoi combat aircraft, were dashed when Washington successfully pressured Jakarta into rejecting the deal.[107] Russia's hesitation towards supplying Iran with advanced fighters notably diminished between 2018 and 2019, catalyzed by dialogues initiated during high-level Iranian visits to Moscow in October 2018 and the Moscow Defense Exposition in 2019.[108] Despite these promising discussions, early collaboration attempts faltered due to Iran's inability to finance arms purchases competitively and Moscow's reluctance to engage in barter transactions.[109]

As international sanctions isolated Moscow from traditional arms markets and forced Russia to rely increasingly on Iranian drone and missile support, the Kremlin became willing to offer Tehran military technologies previously deemed too sensitive to share. This shift resulted in Russia proposing an unprecedented weapons package that included advanced electronics, air defense systems, attack helicopters, sophisticated radar systems, Yak-130 combat trainer aircraft, and most significantly, the coveted Su-35 fighter jets.[110] The Su-35 represented the solution to Iran's decades-old vulnerability stemming from the 1979 Islamic Revolution, after which Iran's Air Force remained technologically stagnant, still relying on aging American-made F-14 Tomcats and F-4 Phantoms acquired before the revolution. While cutting-edge in the 1970s, these aircraft were hopelessly outmatched by contemporary standards and could not compete with the advanced fourth and fifth-generation fighters operated by regional rivals such as Israel. The Su-35 procurement would provide Tehran with modern radar systems, long-range air-to-air missiles, and electronic warfare capabilities necessary to defend Iranian airspace effectively.

The deal's public disclosure emerged through a series of official confirmations that began in late 2022 and continued through early 2023. Brigadier General Hamid Vahedi, commander of the Iranian Air Force, provided the first official acknowledgment in September 2022, publicly confirming that acquiring Su-35 fighters from Russia was definitively on the Air Force's strategic agenda. Then, in January 2023, parliamentarian Shahriar Heidar explicitly announced the anticipated delivery of twenty-four Su-35s by mid-2023. Highlighting the significance of this procurement, Heidar stated, "The Su-35 fighter jets ordered from Russia will enter Iran in early next year," a statement that indicated Tehran's expectation of swift fulfillment.[111]

Iranian sources revealed that the initial order comprised 24 Su-35 fighters, precisely enough to equip two complete Iranian Air Force squadrons. [112] The agreement extended beyond aircraft procurement to include Russian life-extension and overhaul services for Iran's existing fleet of 23 MiG-29 fighters and 25 Su-24MK strike aircraft.[113] While some sources speculated that Tehran allocated approximately $3 billion worth of crude oil for the Su-35Es as part of a broader $10 billion arms agreement, Iranian officials familiar with the arrangement indicated that the payment structure primarily involved credit arrangements with deferred payment schedules rather than direct barter transactions.[114] Despite speculation that the Su-35 procurement could serve as partial compensation for Iranian drone and missile supplies to Russia, Iranian officials consistently maintained these were separate transactions, not a *quid pro quo* arrangement.

The Su-35 deliveries to Iran have experienced significant delays extending well beyond initial projections. Iranian military and government representatives have systematically addressed these setbacks through public statements designed to manage expectations while maintaining confidence in the agreement's eventual fulfillment. For example, in June 2023, Brigadier General Vahedi acknowledged the uncertainty surrounding delivery timelines, stating, "We need the Sukhoi [Su-35], but we don't know when it will join our squadron."[115] One month later, the situation appeared to deteriorate further when Defense Minister Mohammad-Reza Ashtiani suggested that the deal had possibly collapsed, emphasizing Iran's own capacity to meet its defense needs domestically.[116] Another Iranian defense official echoed this sentiment shortly thereafter, downplaying Iran's reliance on the Russian jets.[117] However, by November 2023, Deputy Defense Minister Brigadier General Seyed Mehdi Farahi offered renewed optimism, telling Iranian media that the acquisition of Su-35 fighters, along with Yak-130 trainer aircraft and Mi-28 attack helicopters, "has been finalized and the process is underway."[118]

Within Iran, commentators opined that either disagreements over contractual terms or technical and production constraints within Russia's defense industry were causing these delays.[119] Yet, Russian defense experts consistently maintained the strategic importance of the deal for both countries, as one expert underscored:

> there's a price to pay for everything ... At a certain stage, Russia needed to show it was a loyal partner. The Su-35 was a red line for the Iranians. The delivery of the Su-35 was a real signal that Russia wanted to deepen relations and was serious about cooperation with Iran.[120]

Late 2023 brought a positive development when Iran's Air Force acquired Russian-made Yak-130 combat trainer aircraft. This delivery was widely interpreted as a precursor to the Su-35 deal, as the Yak-130 would provide essential training for Iranian pilots transitioning to frontline fighter aircraft.[121] Around this time, a defense reporter with connections to the Iranian military confirmed that pilots had already been selected for training in Russia, reinforcing expectations that the full delivery of the 24 Su-35 fighters was imminent.[122] Adding to the noise around the agreement, Iranian media outlets with connections to the Revolutionary Guard Corps repeatedly published reports claiming Su-35s would arrive "in the coming days," only to later retract these stories after consultations with the Defense Ministry. These premature announcements became so frequent that Iranian officials eventually issued formal denials, with the Defense Ministry explicitly stating that while Iran had received Yak-130 trainers and Mi-28 helicopters from Russia, the much-discussed Su-35s had not yet been delivered.[123]

Two years after the announcement of the deal, optimism about the delivery of the Su-35 waned when Algeria, another prospective buyer, received its aircraft ahead of Tehran. In March 2025, satellite imagery confirmed the presence of Su-35 fighters at Algeria's Ain Beida Air Base. These aircraft bore Algerian roundels but retained the Egyptian camouflage scheme, indicating they were originally produced for Egypt before its cancellation of the order under U.S. pressure.[124] Persian news analysis captured the disappointment, noting that the "Su-35 fighters, which were thought to be headed to Iran, suddenly were seen in Algeria." Iranian defense circles proposed that Tehran may have rejected the Egyptian jets to pursue a customized Su-35 variant—possibly a "special model" with local licensed production or a twin-seat version—rather than accepting the original Egyptian units.[125]

A consistent message from Iranian officials maintains that Russia is not reneging on the deal, but rather that the process is proceeding more slowly than anticipated.[126] Hassan Qashqavi, a member of Parliament's National Security and Foreign Policy Commission, recently emphasized that, according to confidential information provided to Iranian lawmakers, "Russia has not broken its promise in delivering the Su-35 fighter jets to Iran."[127]

Iran's objectives extend beyond merely acquiring the Su-35 fighters; they encompass gaining the capability for domestic production and significant technology transfer. Consequently, cooperation with Russia may expand beyond hardware transfers to include substantial technical guidance and support aimed at improving Iran's existing defense systems, strengthening local production capacity, and enhancing the capabilities of domestically manufactured weapon systems. If technical and logistical obstacles persist, Russia might instead facilitate Iranian domestic production through licensing arrangements for components or entire aircraft, aligning with Iran's long-term goal of military self-sufficiency. [128]

Cooperation in the Cosmos

The Russia-Iran space partnership, dating back to the early 2000s, has evolved from tentative commercial arrangements into a comprehensive strategic alliance with significant military implications. While this collaboration began modestly with Russia's launch of Iran's first satellite in 2005, it has accelerated dramatically since 2022. This deepening partnership now encompasses satellite development, intelligence sharing, and technology transfer with dual-use implications that could enhance Iran's civilian and military aerospace capabilities.

Iran's space ambitions emerged in the post-Soviet era when Tehran sought Russian expertise to develop its nascent program. The relationship's first tangible achievement came in October 2005 when Russia's Plesetsk Cosmodrome launched Sina-1, Iran's first artificial satellite. This 170-kg imaging and store-and-forward communications satellite, produced by Russia's Polyot, represented a modest beginning to what would become an increasingly significant partnership.[129] During this early period, Iran pursued other collaborative satellite projects, including the Mesbah-1 microsatellite (co-developed with Italy's Carlo Gavazzi Space) and plans for Zohreh telecommunications satellites with Russia's ISS Reshetnev.

However, this early collaboration faced significant obstacles. Under U.S. and UN pressure concerning Iran's nuclear and missile activities, Russia scaled back space cooperation with Iran in the late 2000s. Many projects stalled, with plans for Russian-built Zohreh satellites shelved. Iranian officials later described these joint ventures as a "bitter experience" (*tajrobeh-ye talkh*), having invested years of effort with little to show.

The tide began to turn after the 2015 Iran nuclear deal, when Tehran and Moscow signed a new defense cooperation agreement and formed a High Commission on Technology Cooperation that included dedicated committees on space and aviation. Iran subsequently secured deals with Russian firms like NPK BARL and VNIIEM to develop remote-sensing satellites as well as Russia's Reshetnev for a geostationary satellite project.

This pre-2022 cooperation extended to military domains as well. In 2015, facing the Islamic State, Russia and Iran established a Baghdad coordination center (with Syria and Iraq) to share reconnaissance data, likely including satellite imagery. During Iran's January 2020 ballistic missile strike on U.S. bases in Iraq, Iranian forces allegedly utilized Russian GLONASS positioning data to improve targeting accuracy.

Post-Ukraine invasion dynamics significantly intensified this partnership, with Russia expanding cooperation both with the civilian Iranian Space Agency (ISA) and its military counterpart, the IRGC Aerospace Force (IRGC-AF).[130] Western sanctions have severed Russia from many of its lucrative international space contracts, pushing Moscow to seek new partners. For Iran, this isolation has created an opportunity; collaboration with Russia offers access to advanced launch technology and engineering expertise vital to its ten-year space program.[131] Russian technological support is particularly critical given Iran's numerous setbacks, such as the

Simorgh rocket's repeated orbital failures and the 2019 Nahid-1 satellite launchpad explosion.

In December 2022, the leaders of the Iranian and Russian space agencies, ISA and Roscosmos, solidified their commitment to bolster space cooperation through an agreement covering satellite development, launch-facility construction, and prospective Iranian astronaut missions to Russia's space station.[132] Speaking at the signing ceremony, ISA chief Hassan Salariyeh hailed the accord for its propensity to accelerate Tehran's space ambitions. Head of Roscosmos Yuriy Borisov proclaimed that "we are all witnessing the historic bonding of our two countries, Russia and Iran, on the global arena ... Our country has ample experience in this domain, we are the pioneers of space exploration, and we are ready to share our accomplishments with the Iranian people."[133] One month later, Russia's Roscosmos expanded this partnership by signing launch service agreements with two Iranian entities, SAHAB and SpaceOmid. Despite their formally private status, these companies are effectively state-operated due to the Iranian government's exclusive oversight of its military and space sectors.

A few months prior to the accord, the partnership had already reached a milestone with the launch of the Khayyam satellite aboard a Soyuz-2 rocket from Baikonur Cosmodrome. Named after the renowned eleventh-century Persian poet, mathematician, and astronomer Omar Khayyam, this sophisticated Earth observation satellite represented a leap in Iran's remote sensing capabilities.[134] Developed through close collaboration between Roscosmos, the Iranian Space Agency, and Iran's Bonyan Danesh Shargh technology firm, the Khayyam satellite was manufactured by Russia's NPK VNIIEM to Iranian design requirements. The project combined Russian engineering and launch infrastructure with Iranian mission planning and payload specifications, establishing a division of labor that balanced Iran's limited technical base with Russia's surplus capacity under sanctions.

The partnership has continued to expand with multiple successful satellite launches in the years following Khayyam. In February 2024, Russia's Vostochny Cosmodrome hosted the launch of Pars-1, a more sophisticated 130-kg Iranian-made imaging satellite carrying multispectral cameras designed to map Iranian terrain from a 500 km orbit.[135] Later that year, two additional Iranian satellites were deployed as secondary payloads on another Russian Soyuz-2 launch from Vostochny.[136] Iranian space officials candidly acknowledged the necessity of Russian launch services, noting that Iran's indigenous Safir and Simorgh rockets lack the capability to reach the sun-synchronous orbits required for optimal Earth observation missions.

While officially described as civilian systems for environmental monitoring, telecommunications, and scientific research, these satellites, particularly Khayyam and Pars-1, provide Iran with unprecedented intelligence, surveillance, and reconnaissance capabilities. Though publicly characterized as a non-military initiative, Khayyam's capabilities have sparked serious concern among Western powers and Israel regarding its potential for gathering detailed intelligence on sensitive military installations, critical infrastructure, and troop movements throughout the Middle East. Moreover, advanced satellite imagery directly improves Iran's own missile accuracy by providing precise target coordinates, terrain data, and post-strike battle damage assessment capabilities.

Perhaps the most significant—and concerning—aspect of Russia-Iran space cooperation involves its explicit military dimensions and the close relationship between civilian space technology and missile development capabilities. This connection was inadvertently revealed in "Parchamdar" (*Flagbearer*), an Iranian documentary about the country's drone program. During a filmed meeting between Iranian officials and a Russian military delegation, IRGC-AF Commander Amir Ali Hajizadeh explicitly proposed a straightforward exchange: "You will help create a space command; we will help you develop a drone command."[137] This candid statement unveiled the quid pro quo nature of the partnership—Russian expertise would enhance Iran's military space capabilities while Iran would provide Russia with combat drone technology desperately needed for its war in Ukraine.

The most consequential dimension involves cooperation on space launch vehicles (SLVs) and their relationship to intercontinental ballistic missile (ICBM) technology. Every satellite launch vehicle inherently contains technologies directly applicable to long-range missiles—the primary difference being the payload (peaceful satellites versus warheads) and trajectory (orbital versus suborbital). In July 2022, CIA Director William Burns explicitly warned about this connection, stating that "the defense partnership between Russia and Iran right now is a useful two-way street... Russian technicians [are] working on the space launch vehicle program in Iran and other aspects of their missile programs."[138] Evidence suggests such technical assistance is indeed occurring. In 2023, Russian technicians were reportedly observed at Iran's Semnan space center working on rocket engines and telemetry systems.[139]

Iran's indigenous SLV program has historically struggled with three critical technical challenges that Russian expertise can directly address. First, Iran has faced difficulties developing sophisticated multi-stage rockets capable of reaching higher orbits, with its Simorgh launcher experiencing multiple high-profile failures. Russian expertise in stage separation mechanics and propellant management could help overcome these obstacles, simultaneously enhancing Iran's ability to deliver heavier payloads to orbit or potentially warheads at intercontinental ranges. Second, Iranian engineers have struggled with advanced propulsion systems, particularly in achieving stable thrust and optimal fuel efficiency. Russian rocket engine technology, among the world's most sophisticated, could significantly improve Iran's liquid and solid-fuel systems. Third, and perhaps most critically, precise guidance and control mechanisms have eluded Iranian developers. Russian navigation systems and flight control algorithms could provide the accuracy needed for precise orbital insertions—or, in military applications, accurate long-range strikes.

Space cooperation represents a natural extension of existing military collaboration, building upon established links between Iran's IRGC-AF and Russia in drone technology. Given the constraints of Russia's defense industrial base, space cooperation could serve as a mechanism for Russia to support Iran's missile programs through knowledge transfer rather than direct technology provision. Such technical assistance enables Iran to enhance its missile capabilities while maintaining plausible deniability about direct military assistance. Iranian observers have notably characterized this intensified space cooperation as sending "a political message that

Russia wanted to convey to Western countries... to demonstrate that their alliance with Iran has become stronger."[140]

Cyberwarfare and National Internets

Over the past decade, Iran has made strides in bolstering its information security and cyber infrastructure, driven by a combination of defensive necessities and offensive ambitions. Initially, Iran's focus was primarily on controlling its domestic internet landscape. However, in response to sophisticated cyberwarfare tactics employed by adversaries such as the United States and Israel, Iran has sought out partnerships that could accelerate its offensive cyber capabilities, with Russia emerging as a key ally in this endeavor.

Chapter 6 detailed the signing of the information security agreement between Russia and Iran, which outlined various stipulations for the exchange of information and formalized cooperation in areas such as cyber defense, information sharing, and joint strategies to counter external threats. Since then, as explored in Chapter 8, Russia-Iran cyber cooperation has deepened. Russia has provided Iran with sophisticated communication-surveillance technologies, enhancing Tehran's ability to monitor domestic and international networks. These technologies include advanced interception systems and software for tracking encrypted communications, tools critical for both state security and the suppression of dissent.

During nationwide protests in Iran, the *Wall Street Journal* reported that Russia was directly helping Iran via the provision of surveillance tools, hacking software, and know-how about exploitation methods for a range of common consumer products. One transfer came from the Russian company PROTEI, which has provided Iranian authorities with censorship software including for Iranian mobile service providers like Ariantel. Known for its communications monitoring technologies and its ties to the Russian Defense Ministry, PROTEI is believed to have assisted Iran's ability to intercept the digital footprint of dissidents.[141] According to the University of Toronto's Citizen Lab, the tools developed by PROTEI would "enable state authorities to directly monitor, intercept, redirect, degrade, or deny all Iranians' mobile communications, including those who are presently challenging the regime."[142]

Driven by a shared determination to inoculate themselves against foreign influence and domestic dissent, Moscow and Tehran have each constructed a "sovereign internet": a national segment that can be disconnected from the global network by administrative command. Russia's Runet, the first full-scale implementation, has become Tehran's reference model; Iranian engineers have systematically mapped its topology of choke-point switches, deep-packet inspection gateways, and domestic DNS hierarchies to build the National Information Network. Yet Iran still relies on scattered, foreign-built hardware and uneven domestic traffic routing; Moscow could close those gaps by supplying standardized data-center racks, pre-configured filtering software, and surplus Russian fiber routes that let Tehran complete the off-switch without Western components.

Russia also boasts the potential to transfer knowledge and technology for Iran's offensive cyberwarfare capabilities. In 2022, Iran launched a cyber assault on Albania that employed tactics strikingly similar to those used by Russian state-sponsored hackers. While Iran's primary motivation stemmed from Albania's hosting of the Mujahedeen-e-Khalq, an Iranian opposition group, the attack's execution revealed a level of technical sophistication that suggested possible Russian influence or assistance. It featured a combination of ransomware and data-wiping malware, the latter being a hallmark of Russian cyber operations, particularly those targeting Ukraine.

With both countries harboring concerns about domestic instability, collaboration in cyberspace is likely to continue. For Russia and Iran, cyber and informational security are representative of a shared mutual interest in countering Western influence and bolstering authoritarian governance.

* * *

The concept of resistance economics emerged as a solution for Iran to combat its deepening isolation due to international sanctions. At its core, resistance economics aimed at bolstering domestic production, reducing reliance on imports, and promoting self-reliance. Iran has been an archetype of this model, employing it as a defense mechanism against international sanctions. Russia, finding itself increasingly under the weight of sanctions after its 2022 invasion of Ukraine, sought inspiration from Iran's response to economic sanctions. Faced with similar challenges from Western sanctions, Russia and Iran have embarked on a path of mutual learning and cooperation to mitigate the impacts of economic isolation. This has also led to parallel narratives about resistance against sanctions. For years, Iran had been eager to solidify and enhance its economic ties with Russia, seeing an advantage in a strengthened bilateral relationship, but faced minimal receptivity from Russia.

The war in Ukraine became the unexpected catalyst that expedited the realization of this vision. Russia and Iran began actively rejuvenating earlier collaborative projects, such as the INSTC, which had been languishing due to a lack of interest and capital. One major objective in this rejuvenated partnership was de-dollarization. The aim was to reduce their reliance on the dollar and, by extension, U.S. financial influence. By promoting the use of their own currencies, Russia and Iran hoped to realize their vision of a multipolar world and shift their economic focus towards the East. However, the constraints placed on both nations by the international community have led them into a forced economic marriage, even if it appears more of an arrangement of necessity than a natural partnership.

Russian and Iranian efforts to circumvent sanctions have involved multiple realms of economic activity. Russia and Iran have forged a network of shadow banking, front companies, and covert shipping practices, designed not just to sustain but also to expand their economies. Russia has directly benefited from Iran's skills in covert logistics, including disabling tracking systems on ships and managing clandestine ship-to-ship transfers. Moreover, with the potential market share shrinking for Russia's military-industrial complex, Iran has emerged as a prime candidate for deepened military collaboration.

Resistance economics and drives for self-sufficiency are not a panacea. The grievances both nations vocalize, often echoing a resistance to Western economic policies, underscore how their economic interactions are still significantly influenced, if not constrained, by the very external pressures they seek to defy. Their economic relationship is fundamentally reactive, fueled more by a consensus on what both nations oppose rather than a shared commitment to an overall economic vision.

10

THE WAR CAME FULL CIRCLE

FROM SYRIA TO UKRAINE AND BACK AGAIN

On 19 May 2024, at 10 p.m. Moscow time, Russian President Vladimir Putin convened an emergency meeting with Iran's Ambassador to Russia, Kazem Jalali.[1] The urgency of this unusual late-night diplomatic engagement stemmed from a grave crisis: Iran's President Ebrahim Raisi and Foreign Minister Hossein Amir-Abdollahian had gone missing. Earlier in the day, the helicopter carrying the two high-ranking Iranian officials had vanished when returning from the inauguration of a remote dam in Azerbaijan. The search and rescue efforts were marred by poor weather and little visibility.

The gathering at the Kremlin in the dim hours of the night took on additional significance, not solely because of the circumstances. Vladimir Putin had convened some of the most influential figures in Russia's corridors of power: newly appointed Russian Defense Minister Andrei Belousov, Security Council Head Sergey Shoigu, and Chief of the General Staff Valery Gerasimov. The meeting's nominal purpose was to offer Moscow's support for Iran's ongoing efforts to locate the helicopter carrying President Raisi and his foreign minister. The underlying message of the high-level gathering was clear: Russia's commitment to Iran would not be tied to a single president.

Within hours of the meeting's conclusion, two Russian planes and about fifty special rescue forces from Russia's Ministry of Emergency Situations were dispatched from Moscow to the Iranian city of Tabriz, where Raisi's helicopter had last been spotted. However, by the time the Russian planes landed, Iran had already officially announced the deaths of both Raisi and Amir-Abdollahian.[2]

The Kremlin's outreach in the initial stages of the search and rescue operations reflected the importance Russia placed on its ties to Iran since the onset of its 2022 war in Ukraine. Moscow has relied on Iranian drones and munitions to support its war machine. Facing Western sanctions, Russia has looked to Iran for tactics and access to black market networks to weather the economic storm. Aside from the immediate exigencies of the war in Ukraine, Russia and Iran have found common ground in their efforts to repress internal dissent—a hallmark of Raisi's tenure as president. The sharing of best practices in this regard has further cemented the relationship between the two countries, as they both have worked to maintain their grip on power and quell domestic opposition.

The improvement in Russia-Iran ties under Raisi's tenure was memorialized in the letter Putin sent to Iranian Supreme Leader Ali Khamenei after the crash. Putin described Raisi as "a true friend to Russia who made an invaluable personal contribution to the establishing of neighborly relations" alongside "great efforts to elevate them to the level of strategic partnership." Putin concluded by declaring he "will forever remember [Raisi] as the most wonderful person."[3] However, for many Iranians, Raisi was anything but a "wonderful person." His reputation as a hardline conservative and his role in the 1988 mass executions of political prisoners, known as the "death commissions," earned him the moniker "the butcher" among opposition groups and human rights activists.[4] As president, Raisi oversaw a brutal crackdown on protests and dissent, most notably sparked by the 2022 death of Mahsa Amini in police custody.[5] The stark contrast between Putin's glowing tribute and the perception of Raisi among many in Iranian society highlighted the divergent priorities that underpin the Russia-Iran relationship. For

Moscow, Raisi's hardline stance and predilection for Russia were assets. Collaboration with a like-minded authoritarian with a bent on confronting the West proved particularly valuable after Russia's full-scale invasion of Ukraine.

Raisi was not unique in his views. He was a reflection of a system that afforded his ascendance to power. Throughout his career, Raisi enjoyed Khamenei's tutelage, which enabled a swift rise through the ranks of Iran's judiciary, where he gained a reputation for his loyalty to the Islamic Republic's core principles. Raisi's alignment with Khamenei's vision was pivotal to his 2021 presidential election victory, which positioned him as a key player in Iran's conservative establishment and a potential contender for Supreme Leader. As detailed in Chapter 7, Raisi's victory was symptomatic of a larger shift internally away from the previous Rouhani administration's failed outreach toward the international community through the Joint Comprehensive Plan of Action (JCPOA). Raisi oversaw a greater emphasis on Iran's ties to China and Russia, though this development was not solely a result of his leadership. In Iran's political system, foreign policy is largely shaped by the Supreme Leader with input from a cadre of advisers such as members of the Supreme National Security Council (SNSC), the General Staff, and the Islamic Revolutionary Guard Corps (IRGC). These entities wield considerable influence over Iran's international relations, often overshadowing the role of the president. In many ways, Raisi served as a willing vestibule to implement the policy choices of an establishment that increasingly saw Russia as a favorable alternative to offset Western pressure.

The death of Raisi, a proponent of Russia-Iran relations, came amid changes in the Russian government. Following his fifth presidential reelection in May 2024, Vladimir Putin initiated a major reshuffling of the country's leadership. Sergey Shoigu, the long-standing Minister of Defense, was reassigned to head the Security Council and replaced Nikolai Patrushev who was assigned to a new role as a special presidential aide. Andrei Belousov, an economic planner, replaced Shoigu as Defense Minister. His appointment suggested a shift in emphasis toward managing the complexities of the war economy more effectively, especially as Western sanctions continued to exert pressure on Russia's defense sector. Despite these major changes in the Russian leadership, Moscow's swift and coordinated response to the disappearance of Raisi underscored its determination to maintain the momentum of Russia-Iran relations.

The ripples of Raisi's death brought changes to Iran. In June 2024, Masoud Pezeshkian, a moderate, was elected as president following a run-off election against the hardline candidate Saeed Jalili. Pezeshkian's campaign focused on rebuilding trust between the government and the Iranian people, advocating for economic liberalization, reducing political repression, and opening the prospects of a revived nuclear deal. The election of Pezeshkian initially posed questions about the future trajectory of Russia-Iran relations, given the new Iranian president's ostensible inclination toward an improved relationship with Europe. Yet, under Pezeshkian, Russia would remain high on Iran's agenda—a reflection of the deeper institutional ties that had developed between Moscow and Tehran. In an op-ed written ahead of his presidency, Pezeshkian emphasized the importance of maintaining strong ties with Russia, noting that "Russia consistently stood by us during challenging times" and affirming that "Russia is a valued strategic ally and neighbor to Iran, and my administration will remain committed to expanding and enhancing our cooperation."[6]

* * *

The dramatic circumstances of Raisi's death would soon become a mere footnote, overshadowed by the seismic events that reshaped the Middle East. This chapter examines how interconnected wars across Syria, Ukraine, and the broader Middle East triggered the stunning collapse of Bashar al-Assad's regime in late 2024—a downfall that began not in Damascus, but in the chaos unleashed by Hamas's devastating assault on Israel. The convergence of conflicts proved decisive: Russia's invasion of Ukraine had forced a gradual reduction of its forces in Syria, while the 7 October 2023 Hamas attack on Israel triggered an aggressive Israeli campaign against Hezbollah and IRGC commanders across Syria and Lebanon. These interlocking crises revealed how thoroughly Syria's fate had become bound up not just in the Russia-Iran relationship, but in their expanding involvement across multiple theaters from Ukraine to Lebanon, Gaza to the Red Sea.

In late November 2024, nearly a decade after forging their unlikely partnership in Syria, Russia and Iran watched their carefully constructed influence unravel in a matter of days during a stunning opposition offensive. The campaign began when Hay'at Tahrir al-Sham (HTS) and allied opposition groups launched a lightning offensive from Idlib that culminated in the capture of Aleppo in just three days. After securing Aleppo by 29 November, opposition forces swept south, capturing Hama and Homs in rapid succession. By 8 December, Damascus had fallen without resistance, as government forces—demoralized, poorly organized, and lacking effective command—simply melted away. Russia, consumed by its grinding war in Ukraine, and Iran, staggered by Israeli strikes that had decimated its Axis of Resistance, found themselves powerless to prevent their Syrian project from unraveling.

The Ripples of Ukraine into Syria

The Syrian Civil War and Russia's full-scale invasion of Ukraine represented not separate conflicts but interconnected chapters in the Russia-Iran relationship. Syria, where Russian airpower was combined with Iranian ground forces to devastating effect, created the institutional frameworks and operational patterns that would later prove crucial in Ukraine. The same Iranian drones that Russia first encountered supporting Assad's forces in Syria were later modified and mass-produced for use against Ukrainian cities.

The exigencies of Russia's full-scale invasion of Ukraine reverberated across Syria's fractured landscape, forcing Moscow to recalibrate its military presence. Russian forces evacuated from some of their bases in the central and eastern parts of Syria, ostensibly to redeploy troops to the Ukrainian front and optimize military expenditure. Moscow redeployed some aircraft and an S-300 air defense system to Ukraine, but Khmeimim airbase remained highly functional.

Russia never had a substantial ground presence in Syria. When Russian forces intervened in Syria in September 2015, they did so with a surprisingly light footprint. Rather than deploying massive ground forces, Moscow opted for what it called a "strategy of limited actions." With just 2,500-4,500 personnel at any given time, Russia focused on air power and special forces. Operating from Khmeimim airbase, Russian tactical aviation supported ground operations. Long-range bombers operating from Russia, along with cruise missiles from Russian warships in the Mediterranean, targeted positions deep inside Syria. Russia did deploy select ground forces—primarily special operations units, military police, advisors, and artillery teams for key operations. However, by 2018, the Wagner Group had become the cornerstone of Russia's military footprint, leading combat operations against the Islamic State and opposition forces while securing Syria's oil and gas infrastructure in the east.

The Kremlin reduced its already limited ground presence and reorganized command structures to ensure continued influence over key areas. The June 2023 Wagner Group rebellion, discussed in Chapter 9, hastened this process. Following Wagner's aborted march on Moscow, Russian military police, in coordination with allied militias, moved swiftly to dismantle the group's operations in Syria, focusing on its entrenched bases in Homs and Deir ez-Zor. In the ensuing reshuffle, Moscow coordinated closely with Iranian-backed units that had long operated alongside Russian forces, transferring portions of Wagner's equipment and logistical assets to them.[7] Iran then launched a targeted recruitment effort aimed at former Wagner-affiliated Syrian fighters, particularly in Homs Province, seeking to integrate their combat experience into Iranian militia operations in Deir ez-Zor and Hasakah.

As Russia increasingly focused its military resources on the escalating conflict in Ukraine, it found itself compelled to deepen its reliance on Iranian-backed forces to secure and manage substantial territories under Bashar Assad's control in Syria.[8] Simultaneously, Russia intensified its collaboration with Iran to exert heightened military and political pressure on U.S. forces stationed in Syria. This cooperation represented a clear example of Russia's broader strategy of horizontal escalation: deliberately fostering secondary theaters of tension to stretch American military capabilities and distract Washington from fully committing its resources and attention to supporting Ukraine. For example, in March 2023, the U.S. expressed concern that Russian jets were no longer adhering to agreed deconfliction measures. Later, reports indicated that Russian military intelligence actively assisted Iranian-aligned militias in launching targeted missile attacks against U.S. bases, most notably the critical al-Tanf facility in eastern Syria.

The most striking manifestation of the Syria-Ukraine interdependence has been the reciprocal development of drone warfare capabilities. The Shayrat Airbase, long subjected to punitive strikes by Western coalitions, was where the IRGC and Hezbollah instructors delivered advanced Shahed-series operational training to Russian drone operators destined for the Ukrainian theater.[9] Meanwhile, Ukraine established its presence in northwestern Syria, sending approximately 20 experienced operators and 150 first-person-view drones to support opposition forces in Idlib.[10] This circular flow of expertise, personnel, and military hardware between the two theaters exemplified how Russia and Iran had evolved into a partnership that bound their fates together across multiple fronts.

Russia calculated it could preserve its interests in Syria through minimal military adjustments, urging regional and international acceptance of Assad while hoping to negotiate limited concessions with Turkish President Recep Tayyip Erdoğan. Yet genuine progress toward a political settlement stalled entirely: Russia repeatedly blocked efforts to convene Syria's constitutional committee, and Assad flatly refused to accommodate Erdoğan's demands on Kurdish-held areas. In the interim, Russia's limited presence inadvertently entrenched Iran's military footprint, as the IRGC and allied militias faced little opposition from Moscow when filling the vacuum. This precarious balance would ultimately shatter in the wake of October 2023.

* * *

The 7 October 2023 Hamas attack on Israel set in motion a cascade of events that would culminate in the collapse of Bashar Assad's regime. On the morning of 7 October, Hamas launched an unprecedented and coordinated assault involving over 4,300 rockets fired into Israel and ground incursions breaching the Gaza-Israel barrier. The attack resulted in devastating losses—approximately 1,139 people were killed, including around 695 Israeli civilians, and about 250 individuals were taken hostage, representing the most significant invasion of Israeli territory since the state's founding in 1948.

Israel's military response was swift and severe, initiating one of the most devastating campaigns in recent history. The operation began with extensive aerial bombardments, targeting Hamas infrastructure and leadership, and escalated into a large-scale ground invasion on 27 October with the dual objectives of dismantling Hamas and rescuing hostages.[11] The military offensive inflicted catastrophic damage on Gaza, exacerbating an already dire humanitarian crisis. Hundreds of thousands of Palestinians were killed, many of them civilians, and countless others were injured or displaced. Essential infrastructure such as hospitals, schools, and residential areas was reduced to rubble, deepening human suffering amid dwindling supplies of food, water, medicine, and electricity.

In response to the intense devastation in Gaza and the plight of Palestinian civilians, Iran's Axis of Resistance swiftly mobilized throughout the region. Beginning in early October 2023, Hezbollah initiated near-daily barrages of rockets and short-range missiles into northern Israel. Simultaneously, Yemen's Houthi movement launched multiple waves of armed drones and ballistic missiles at Red Sea shipping lanes and select Israeli targets. In Iraq, a collection of predominantly Shia militias, some formally linked to the IRGC Quds Force, claimed responsibility for coordinated drone strikes on installations inside Israel. Throughout these operations, Tehran itself maintained a studied restraint: public statements expressed solidarity with Palestinians and decried Israel's actions in Gaza, but the Islamic Republic initially refrained from deploying its own forces directly into the fray.[12]

Moscow, for its part, interpreted the regional conflagration through the lens of its own strategic imperatives in Ukraine. Kremlin strategists calculated that Western capitals, distracted by Gaza's unfolding crisis, might divert political capital, military support, and media attention away from its war of aggression against Kyiv. Yet, despite the sudden eruption of hostilities on 7 October, Russia remained conspicuously silent for two full days. When it finally broke its silence, the Foreign Ministry released a terse statement observing only that "the number of victims on both sides has already exceeded 1,400 people, including civilians," carefully omitting any reference to Hamas's initial assault. Equally striking was Moscow's blanket defense of Tehran: Foreign Minister Sergey Lavrov dismissed any suggestion of Iranian complicity in the escalation as "quite provocative," thereby shielding Iran from international censure even as the region spiraled toward wider conflagration.[13]

Russia had occupied an uneasy midpoint between tacitly permitting Israeli strikes on Iranian positions in Syria and sustaining the Assad regime through cooperation with IRGC-backed forces, as detailed in Chapter 5. Even before October 2023, Moscow's deployment of Shahed-series drones to Ukraine had alarmed Israeli planners, who feared Iran was sharpening its unmanned-aviation capabilities under real combat conditions. It was, however, Russia's response to the Gaza war—granting diplomatic cover to Hamas and deepening ties with Iran's proxy network—that finally fractured its relationship with Israel. By February 2024, Tel Aviv had severed critical deconfliction links with Moscow and even made the decision to provide Ukraine with early warning systems to counter Russian and Iranian drones.[14]

As its ties with Israel deteriorated, Russia's integration with Iran's regional network accelerated across multiple fronts. IRGC operatives assumed formal liaison roles, connecting Russian forces with militias from Yemen to Iraq. This cooperation manifested in Yemen, where Moscow provided satellite data through IRGC operatives to enhance Houthi targeting capabilities against shipping vessels in the Red Sea. The partnership deepened further with reports of a potential $10 million USD weapons deal negotiated by Russian arms dealer Viktor Bout with the Houthis, allegedly disguised as humanitarian aid.[15] In Lebanon, Russia reportedly facilitated the transfer of sophisticated weaponry to Hezbollah, including advanced anti-tank guided missiles that were later used in strikes against an Israeli military base.

On the diplomatic stage, Russia's public endorsement of Iran and its allies grew increasingly explicit. The Kremlin hosted multiple Hamas delegations in Moscow, while at the United Nations (UN) it framed itself as a staunch defender of Palestinian rights—often drawing parallels between Israel's tactics in Gaza and Nazi Germany's actions during World War II.[16] UN Ambassador Vasily Nebenzya went so far as to accuse Israel of seeking to "mop up" Gaza, commit war crimes, and "bomb [it] into the Stone Age."[17] Equally striking was Russia's consistent support for Houthi attacks on Red Sea shipping, reflecting a broader strategy of opening new fronts to challenge the United States and divert Western resources away from Ukraine.

The outbreak of the Israel-Gaza War initially appeared advantageous for Moscow, as it temporarily shifted Western focus and political bandwidth away from Ukraine toward the rapidly unfolding crisis in the Middle East. However, that advantage proved surprisingly short-lived as Israel, determined to neutralize Iranian influence in Syria, swiftly escalated its air campaign. Israeli operations evolved from sporadic strikes on weapons depots to systematic targeting of senior IRGC and Hezbollah commanders across Syrian territory. Russia, having come to rely heavily on Iran's ground forces to secure key terrain in Assad-controlled areas, suddenly found these surrogate forces under relentless pressure; each Israeli strike that degraded Iranian militias' command posts and logistics hubs in Syria simultaneously weakened the backbone that sustained Moscow's reduced presence in the country.

By late 2023, an effective land and air blockade prevented Iran from channeling reinforcements to its affiliates, including Hezbollah, through Syrian territory. Russia, once able to position itself as a neutral arbiter between competing regional powers, found that its deepening dependence on Iran's ground forces rendered diplomatic neutrality unsustainable. Moscow began openly condemning Israeli strikes, prompting Israel to terminate its long-standing practice of providing advance warning to Russia about impending operations in Syrian airspace.[18] Increasingly frustrated with Israel's intensifying air campaign in Syria, Russia escalated electronic warfare operations that caused significant disruptions to Israeli commercial aviation and complicated Israel's military operations throughout the region. The precarious equilibrium Moscow had engineered gradually eroded as the conflict between Israel and Iran intensified. By the end of 2024, Russia would eventually find itself inadvertently bearing the brunt of the very regional instability it had initially sought to exploit for its advantage in Ukraine.

Out of the Shadows

The latter half of 2023 and much of 2024 marked a dramatic turning point in the long-simmering conflict between Israel and Iran, as tensions escalated into direct military confrontation. What began with Israel's intensified campaign against Iranian assets in Syria—targeting weapons shipments, infrastructure, and ground forces—culminated in unprecedented direct strikes between the two adversaries. This period also witnessed a deepening of Iran's relationship with Russia, as Tehran sought to leverage Moscow's support in its escalating conflict with Israel. However, as the Israeli-Gaza war expanded to engulf Iran's broader Axis of Resistance, Russia's ambitions to act as a decisive power broker in the Middle East were sharply curtailed. Instead of shaping outcomes, Moscow found itself largely sidelined, reduced to the role of a spectator as Israel systematically dismantled the regional network that Russia had come to rely upon for influence.

The immediate path to this dangerous escalation was paved by Israel's campaign against Iran's command and control in Syria. In December 2023, Israeli airstrikes claimed their first major casualty with the killing of Seyyed Razi Mousavi, a senior IRGC adviser who coordinated Iranian interests in Syria. The following month, an Israeli airstrike in Damascus claimed the lives of Brigadier General Sadegh Omidzadeh, an intelligence officer with the IRGC Quds Force, along with four other IRGC officers. In January 2024, Iran launched ballistic missiles at what it claimed was a "Mossad espionage base" in Iraqi Kurdistan as retribution for the series of Israeli assassinations.[19] However, Iran failed to deter further Israeli actions, setting the stage for even more escalations to come.[20]

The critical turning point came on 1 April 2024, when Israeli F-35 fighter jets conducted a precision strike on the consular section of the Iranian Embassy in Damascus. This attack, which involved six missiles, killed General Mohammad Zahedi, the former head of the IRGC Ground Forces.[21] It was no ordinary attack. By targeting a diplomatic compound—protected under international law and considered sovereign Iranian territory—Israel crossed a red line, escalating beyond its usual strikes on military sites and weapons factories. Israel was no longer holding back.

For nearly two weeks, Iran released a series of statements about its impending response to Israel. In his Eid al-Fitr speech, Supreme Leader Ali Khamenei stated that Israel had "committed another mistake" and that "when they attack our consulate, it means they have attacked our soil."[22] Hardline factions within the country had grumbled about Tehran's tepid responses to Israeli aggression, claiming that inaction would only embolden Israel further at a time when strength was demanded.[23] Behind the scenes, Iran communicated through various channels to emphasize its stance and intentions. Utilizing the Swiss Embassy, Tehran issued a warning to Washington that U.S. military bases in the region could become targets if the United States supported an Israeli counterstrike.

A little after midnight on 14 April, the sky over Iran lit up with more than 170 drones, over 30 cruise missiles, and roughly 120 ballistic missiles—an unprecedented barrage that marked *Operation True Promise*. Under the command of Brigadier General Amir Ali Hajizadeh, head of the IRGC Aerospace Force (IRGC-AF)—the same figure responsible for the contentious supply of Iranian drones to Russia—the operation represented the largest single military action undertaken by Iran since the Iran-Iraq War of the 1980s.[24] More significantly, Operation True Promise was Tehran's first direct strike on Israel from its own territory, signaling a new and more overt phase in the protracted shadow confrontation between the two adversaries.[25]

Despite the massive scale of the operation, Iran's advanced warning inadvertently compromised the effectiveness of the strike, enabling a robust multinational defensive response. A U.S.-led coalition swiftly mobilized warplanes and naval assets to intercept many of the projectiles over international airspace and waters. Those missiles and drones that penetrated closer to Israeli territory faced Israel's sophisticated air defense systems, including the Arrow and David's Sling. Assisted by the defense capabilities and intelligence support from the U.S., U.K., France, and Jordan, these integrated defenses intercepted most of the munitions. Although the physical impact of the attack was largely mitigated and the damage minimal, Iran aimed primarily to establish a new strategic equation with Israel.

In the immediate aftermath of its April 2024 attack, Iran sought to craft the narrative that Russia was firmly in its camp. IRGC-affiliated Iranian social media channels circulated a message claiming that Russian President Vladimir Putin declared Russia would support Iran if the United States or Israel attacked Iranian soil.[26] This message went viral and eventually made its way into English-language social media accounts. Yet, no such statement could be found in Russian media or the Kremlin's press releases. In fact, Putin's only public comments came two days later, urging "sensible restraint" in a call with his Iranian counterpart, Ebrahim Raisi.[27] The Iranian version of the readout, however, differed, claiming Putin characterized the strike as the best way to punish Israel.[28]

The spread of fabricated statements suggesting Russia's support for Iran in a direct military confrontation with Israel represented more than mere disinformation. It signified the value more hardline elements, particularly those within the IRGC, placed on Russia within Iran's political system. Iran's ties with Russia were being exploited both as a virtual deterrent against retaliation and a morale boost domestically. Yet, the reality was far less dramatic. While Russia's Foreign Ministry did justify Iran's actions as legitimate self-defense under the UN Charter, Moscow stopped short of offering any concrete military support.[29] At the United Nations Security Council (UNSC), Russia's Ambassador Vasily Nebenzya took a firmer stance, arguing that Iran's response was provoked by the international community's failure to condemn Israel's strike on its consulate in Damascus.30 Even so, the gap between Iran's inflated claims and Russia's measured rhetoric underscored the limits of their partnerships—and the lengths to which Tehran was willing to go to bolster its position.

Just days after the Iranian barrage, Israel launched its own retaliatory operation on 19 April, targeting Iran's S-300 PMU-2 air defense system positioned near Natanz. The choice of target was symbolically potent. For years, the S-300 had been the centerpiece of Iran's defensive modernization and a recurring flashpoint in Russian-

Iranian relations, its delayed delivery emblematic of Moscow's ambivalent support. The battery, touted by Tehran as a deterrent shield protecting critical nuclear infrastructure, had become a showcase of Iran's military self-reliance. Israeli F-16I fighters, exploiting regional air corridors and electronic warfare cover, struck the site with precision-guided munitions during the night. Iranian authorities immediately claimed that their defenses had intercepted all incoming missiles, attributing local explosions to interceptor debris. Yet high-resolution satellite imagery released by independent analysts showed otherwise: both the radar array and several launchers were heavily damaged. Iranian efforts to downplay the damage suggested a desire to avoid further escalation as government officials explicitly stated they had no plans for retaliation.

Iran's April 2024 attacks were intended to establish a new equation in its longstanding conflict with Israel, one in which Israeli actions against Iranian interests would be met with direct military responses.[30] Yet, Israeli strikes on Iranian interests in Syria and Hezbollah in Lebanon continued in the following months. On 31 July, Israel conducted an airstrike in Beirut's southern suburbs, targeting senior Hezbollah official Fouad Shukr.[31] Later that same day, Hamas leader Ismail Haniyeh was assassinated in a compound on the outskirts of Tehran, just hours after attending the inauguration of Iran's new president, Masoud Pezeshkian. While Israel did not claim responsibility, all evidence pointed to its involvement.

Like the earlier attack on its consulate in Damascus, Iranian officials vowed retribution for the assassination of Haniyeh.[32] However, Iran, along with Hezbollah, refrained from a response, partly to allow the ongoing ceasefire talks over Gaza to proceed. By doing so, they aimed to achieve through diplomatic means, and at a lower cost, what they could not accomplish through military action: halting Israel's offensive against the Axis of Resistance. Behind the scenes, Iranian officials appeared to be looking for further reinforcements to bolster its defenses.

Five days after Ismail Haniyeh's assassination, former Russian Defense Minister Sergey Shoigu—who had recently transitioned to Secretary of Russia's National Security Council—arrived in Tehran on what Iranian officials described as an "unexpected working visit."

Given the ongoing tensions and Iran's focus on strengthening its defenses against Israeli airstrikes, the timing and seniority of this visit raised immediate speculation about deeper strategic aims. Shoigu's presence in Tehran brought him face-to-face with several pillars of Iran's security apparatus: Secretary of Iran's SNC chief Ali Akbar Ahmadian, Armed Forces Chief of General Staff Mohammad Bagheri, and President Masoud Pezeshkian. While initial briefings portrayed the talks as routine consultations, The *New York Times* later confirmed that their agenda included the transfer of advanced Russian radar systems—technology intended to enhance Iran's detection capabilities against high-speed and low-signature threats.[33] The partnership quickly revealed itself to be reciprocal rather than one-sided. Barely a month after Shoigu's trip, U.S. Secretary of State Antony Blinken disclosed in a press briefing that Iran had supplied Russia with short-range ballistic missiles.[34]

By late August, Iran's strategy of restraint had unraveled. In response to mounting Israeli pressure and domestic criticism of inaction, Hezbollah launched a salvo of more than 300 rockets into northern Israel. The escalation shattered the fragile truce. Israel's retaliation was swift and devastating. On 27 September, Israeli F-15I fighters conducted a precision strike on an underground headquarters in Beirut's Dahieh suburb, killing both Hezbollah Secretary-General Hassan Nasrallah and IRGC Deputy Commander of Operations Abbas Nilforoushan. These strikes not only eliminated Hezbollah's most influential leader but also demonstrated Iran's inability to protect its key allies and senior military leadership.

The assassinations became a tipping point. In the early hours of 1 October, Israel launched a large-scale ground incursion into southern Lebanon, citing an urgent need to dismantle Hezbollah strongholds that threatened Israeli border communities.[35] Only fifteen hours later, Tehran initiated its second direct attack on Israel.

Iran's October strikes on Israel, unlike the mixed systems used in April—ballistic missiles, drones, and cruise missiles—Iran's offensive relied solely on ballistic missiles in an apparent bid to shorten detection times and overwhelm Israeli air defenses. While the barrage momentarily saturated Israel's intercept systems, it caused relatively minor damage on the ground. Iran framed the strikes as "self-defense," expressly referencing the assassinations of Haniyeh, Nasrallah, and Nilforoushan. Yet Israeli Prime Minister Benjamin Netanyahu vowed immediate and decisive retaliation, warning, "Iran made a big mistake…and it will pay for it."[36]

Russia seized the opportunity to criticize the United States. Maria Zakharova, Russia's Foreign Ministry spokesperson, framed the attack as a "complete failure of the Biden administration in the Middle East." In a sharply worded statement, she described the situation as "a bloody drama that is only gaining momentum," accusing the White House of "incoherent statements" and "complete helplessness in resolving crises." At the UNSC, Russia's ambassador, Vasily Nebenzya, defended Iran, asserting, "It is becoming increasingly clear that the Israeli leadership is looking to trigger a direct conflict between its main regional adversary, Iran, and the United States—and it will spare no effort to do that."[37] Moreover, Kremlin spokesperson Dmitry Peskov confirmed that Russian President Vladimir Putin had no plans to hold a phone conversation with Israeli Prime Minister Benjamin Netanyahu following Iran's attack.[38] Behind these public statements, however, quiet coordination between Moscow and Tehran appeared to intensify.

A week after Iran's ballistic missile attack on Israel, Russian media revealed that Putin and Pezeshkian would meet for the first time since the Iranian president took office in July. The setting was unconventional: a celebration of the 300th birthday of Magtymguly Pyragy, an 18th-century Turkmen philosopher, during the Interrelation of Times and Civilizations forum in Ashgabat, Turkmenistan. The choice of venue was not only an unlikely backdrop for such a high-level meeting, but it also contradicted earlier reports that the leaders planned to hold their first meeting in Kazan merely a few weeks later. Adding to the intrigue, the announcement came just three days before the event, and Turkmen media had not even reported on the forum beforehand.[39]

In what appeared to be a hastily organized event, the Ashgabat bilateral meeting held on 11 October focused little on the commemoration of the philosophy of Magtymguly Pyragy but squarely on showcasing the Russia-Iran relationship amid the impending Israeli reprisal for Iran's ballistic missile attack. During his press conference with Pezeshkian, Putin hailed Russia's relations with Iran as "sincere and strategic," emphasizing that "relations with Iran are a priority for us."[40] Pezeshkian echoed these sentiments, describing Iran-Russia ties as "friendly and strategic." According to a report published on the Iranian president's website, Pezeshkian urged Russia to take stronger action against "the crimes of Israel in Gaza and Lebanon." While the public symbolism of Russian support was unmistakable—two leaders meeting under extraordinary circumstances to demonstrate unity—the reality behind closed doors was more complex. Despite the theatrical displays of solidarity, Russia remained deeply reluctant to become a direct participant in the military escalation, preferring instead to offer political cover while avoiding the risks of deeper involvement in a potential regional war.

Putin and Pezeshkian would meet again with their scheduled meeting at the BRICS summit in Kazan on 22 October. If the Ashgabat meeting was meant to demonstrate Russian solidarity with Iran in the Middle East, then the meeting in Kazan was aimed at elevating their vision for a multipolar order. Kazan held particular significance as it marked the first summit since Iran, Egypt, and the United Arab Emirates (UAE) had joined BRICS as full members, part of a broader initiative to reduce dependence on Western-dominated financial institutions like the IMF and World Bank.[41] During their bilateral meeting, Putin emphasized the alignment between Russia and Iran, stating, "The approaches of Russia and Iran to the global agenda are close or completely coincide." He added that both nations were united by "the desire to form a fair multipolar world order." Pezeshkian, speaking with a sharper tone, called for a disruption of Western dominance. "We have to disrupt the global domination that is [the West's] intention and be able to cooperate with each other in economy, politics, culture, science, and technical spheres," he said.[42]

Only three days after the BRICS summit concluded, Israel responded decisively to Iran's earlier missile attack by initiating a massive retaliatory campaign aimed at severely weakening Iran's military infrastructure.[43] The Israeli offensive specifically targeted Iran's remaining S-300 air defense batteries, its early-warning radar installations, and crucial missile manufacturing facilities.[44] In a series of coordinated nighttime air raids, Israeli aircraft systematically disabled Iran's Ghadir radar network—an advanced domestic system built on the framework of Russian Rezonans-NE technology—crippling Tehran's capability to track stealth or low-altitude incursions. Subsequent strikes inflicted severe damage on critical choke points in Iran's missile production supply chain, destroying specialized components necessary for the fabrication of Iran's sophisticated ballistic missile systems. The campaign culminated in a symbolic yet impactful strike on a building within the historically significant Parchin complex, which has long been associated with Iran's nuclear research and development. Again, while Iranian state media downplayed the extent of the damage, independent satellite imagery indicated substantial losses to both radar and missile-related infrastructure that effectively rendered large swaths of Iran's air defense grid obsolete.

Russia, publicly cautious yet sympathetic toward Tehran, could offer little tangible support beyond diplomatic gestures. Moscow called for steps to prevent a "catastrophic scenario" while placing responsibility on Israeli and U.S. actions. Foreign Ministry spokeswoman Maria Zakharova described the situation as an "ongoing explosive escalation" and cautioned, "We must stop provoking Iran to respond and get out of the spiral of uncontrolled escalation."[45] Meanwhile, at the UN, Nebenzya noted Iran had shown "exceptional" patience until that point.[46] The reality was that Iran was backed into a corner, in desperate need of Russian reinforcements for its air defenses and radars. However, Moscow's inability to swiftly replace or upgrade Iran's air defenses, hampered by its military-industrial constraints amid the war in Ukraine, highlighted the practical boundaries of Russian support. While Iran continued to supply Russia with drones, missiles, and ammunition for its war effort, it found itself unable to secure reciprocal defensive support from Moscow at a critical juncture.

Within less than a year, Tehran faced cascading setbacks across the Middle East: its assets in Gaza and Lebanon had been decimated, its command-and-control structures in Syria severely undermined, and its homeland defenses shattered. Moscow's reliance on Iranian-backed militias to secure territory in Syria had already proven problematic due to Israel's intensified strikes, but now, as Tehran desperately sought Russian assistance, the interdependency between conflicts in Ukraine and the Middle East became starkly apparent. Yet, as Tehran braced for yet another impending crisis, it would no longer endure the consequences alone.

* * *

In the months before his fall, Bashar Assad's position within the Iran-led Axis of Resistance had grown increasingly precarious. When Hezbollah almost immediately opened a support front against Israel following the eruption of the Israel-Gaza war, Syria remained conspicuously silent. When Israel mounted aggressive strikes against Iranian assets in Syria, including the elimination of key Quds Force commanders and the destruction of an Iranian diplomatic compound in Damascus, Assad's response was similarly muted. Even the Israeli assassination of Hezbollah Secretary-General Hassan Nasrallah—the very leader who kept the regime afloat—in Beirut drew only a tepid statement from Damascus. Assad's drift from the Axis of Resistance accelerated as he pursued rapprochement with Saudi Arabia, even closing the Houthi's diplomatic mission in Damascus. Moreover, the continued strikes against Iranian assets in Syria heightened suspicions in Tehran that Damascus was leaking intelligence about Iranian movements to Israel.

Iran found its once-considerable influence over Damascus waning. The Quds Force, which had previously operated with relative freedom throughout Syria, now faced increasing constraints from Syrian authorities. Assad refused to allow the use of the Golan Heights as a potential front against Israel and had begun limiting Shiite religious activities throughout Syria. Prior to 7 October, Assad met Hezbollah leader Hassan Nasrallah and IRGC Commander Mohammad Reza Zahedi to discuss the redeployment of forces in Syria—both of whom would succumb to their deaths due to Israeli strikes.[47] Assad, displaying increasing independence from his patrons, demanded the withdrawal of Iranian and Hezbollah forces from key governorates including Aleppo, Hama, and Homs. Yet, Assad confidently asserted that Syrian and Russian forces could maintain security without reinforcements from Iran or Hezbollah despite Moscow's reduced presence. This miscalculation would prove devastating when the

Israeli incursion into Lebanon later forced Iran to concentrate on preserving supply lines rather than defending Syrian territory.

Russia, Assad's most powerful ally, had grown increasingly disillusioned with the Syrian president's refusal to cooperate on any meaningful reforms. Though entrenched in its war of aggression in Ukraine, Moscow was particularly incensed by Assad's repeated violations of the Idlib de-escalation agreement and his stubborn resistance to any form of negotiated settlement with Turkey. These frustrations were compounded by the failed attempts at restructuring the Syrian Arab Army, an endeavor Moscow had backed in hopes of creating a more disciplined force. Instead, the Syrian Arab Army remained riddled with corruption and factionalism, causing persistent operational gaps that Russia, despite its potent airpower, struggled to address.

Turkey's already contentious relationship with Assad had similarly reached a breaking point. After years of hosting over 3.5 million Syrian refugees, Ankara had attempted to negotiate their return through diplomatic normalization with the government in Damascus. These efforts included multiple rounds of discussions between Turkish and Syrian officials throughout 2023 and early 2024, with Russia attempting to mediate. However, Assad consistently stonewalled these initiatives, refusing to provide meaningful guarantees for refugee returns or implement the political reforms that Turkey demanded. The situation deteriorated further when Assad rebuffed a series of Turkish proposals in mid-2024 that would have established a framework for refugee repatriation and political reconciliation. Instead, he continued to insist on unconditional Turkish withdrawal from northern Syria and the handover of opposition-held territories.

The three guarantor states of the Astana process—Iran, Russia, and Turkey—continued to pursue their own goals in Syria with varying levels of success. While Russia and Iran primarily competed in terms of military reform and economic contracts in government-held territory, Turkey focused on Idlib. Since the March 2020 Idlib ceasefire, Ankara's support to opposition forces like HTS and the Syrian National Army took both direct and indirect forms. Turkey's persistent military presence effectively shielded HTS from regime offensives, allowing the group to reorganize from a loose coalition of armed factions into a more structured, conventional force. Meanwhile, Turkey's management of international aid and cross-border trade not only bolstered Idlib's local economy but also conferred a degree of legitimacy on HTS.

The Astana troika's regular meetings, once focused predominantly on de-escalation zones and constitutional reforms in Syria, began taking on a broader regional scope following the Israeli-Gaza and Israeli-Lebanon wars. When Iran, Russia, and Turkey convened for the 22nd session of the Astana Process in early November, their joint statement went far beyond standard pronouncements on Syria. It explicitly condemned what they termed the "aggressive actions of the Zionist regime throughout the region," accusing Israel of "violations of international law" in Gaza, Lebanon, and the West Bank. They further decried the "genocide" in Gaza, called for an immediate ceasefire, and denounced repeated Israeli airstrikes on Syrian territory.[48] Barely a month later, the troika would meet again—this time in Doha—under circumstances that could hardly have been more dramatic. By the night of the meeting, the Assad regime was collapsing, the Syrian capital lay vulnerable to rebel forces, and Damascus had effectively lost the war it had waged for over a decade. As the 23rd round of Astana talks commenced, the rapid unraveling of Assad's final strongholds heralded a new era—one without the patronage of either Russia or Iran.

The Anatomy of Assad's Fall

Bashar Assad's refusal to negotiate with Turkish President Recep Tayyip Erdoğan proved to be a critical strategic error. By repeatedly spurning Ankara's overtures for a political settlement, Assad all but invited Erdoğan to adopt a military solution. In late November 2024, the battle-hardened forces of HTS and elements of the Syrian National Army launched a stunning offensive from Idlib. Their sudden advance caught the regime and its allies entirely off guard. Within days, by 27 November, rebel forces had already surged toward Aleppo, marking the first time in years that Assad-controlled territory faced such a rapid and cohesive assault from the opposition.

The HTS-led offensive soon threatened the heart of what Russia and Iran once considered their defining achievement in Syria: the 2016 recapture of Aleppo. This time, however, the situation was starkly different. Unlike their earlier successes, neither could effectively counter the assault. Iranian-backed forces, weakened by continuous Israeli strikes and constrained by an Israeli-enforced air blockade, struggled to mobilize reinforcements. Meanwhile, Russia, unable to provide sufficient air support against the large-scale offensive, faced limitations exacerbated when Iraq refused Iranian-backed militia passage into Syria, a decision Iran surprisingly accepted without resistance.[49] As regime defenses deteriorated, Assad urgently traveled to Moscow on 28 November in hopes of military aid. His appeal failed disastrously. While he was abroad, Aleppo fell to opposition forces. Returning to Syria empty-handed, Assad resorted to deception, falsely promising imminent Russian reinforcements to his commanders.

The loss of Aleppo triggered a cascade of withdrawals. Russian forces abandoned their positions in the northern cities of Ain al-Arab and Manbij, consolidating toward Qamishli in the northeast. Iranian-backed forces similarly retreated around the Aleppo countryside, leaving behind arsenals of equipment in their haste.[50] The once-formidable Axis of Resistance, which had propped up Assad for over a decade, was now in disarray. In a desperate bid to stabilize the situation, Russian Defense Minister Andrei Belousov convened an emergency call with Iranian Chief of General Staff Mohammad Bagheri, Iraqi Army Chief of Staff General Abdel Emir Yarallah, and Syrian Army Chief of Staff General Abdul Karim. According to Tasnim News Agency, the military leaders pledged to "resolutely support the legitimate government of Syria" and promised "necessary measures to support the Syrian army."[51] Yet, this public pledge of support did little to stabilize the situation.

The crisis deepened on 2 December when Iranian Foreign Minister Abbas Araghchi arrived in Damascus for urgent consultations.[52] During these meetings, regime officials acknowledged a harsh reality: the Syrian Armed Forces could not effectively counter the rebel offensive. In public statements, Araghchi maintained a diplomatic facade, describing the meetings as "helpful, clear, and friendly" while characterizing the rebel offensive as a "conspiracy" by "enemies of regional security and stability." He specifically framed the opposition's advance as evidence of U.S. and Israeli coordination, claiming it was meant to offset the "Zionist failure" against Iran's Axis of Resistance.[53] The entire performance was a farce. In reality, Assad had already rejected Iranian offers of military reinforcements, too terrified of provoking Israeli retaliation to accept help from his supposed ally.

With the Iranian Foreign Minister in Damascus, Iranian President Masoud Pezeshkian initiated a call with Russian President Vladimir Putin. According to the Kremlin press service, both leaders characterized the opposition offensive as "large-scale aggression by terrorist groups and gangs" aimed at undermining Syria's "sovereignty, political and socio-economic stability."[54] They expressed "unconditional support" for Assad's efforts to restore "constitutional order and territorial integrity," while emphasizing the importance of coordination through the Astana format with Turkey.[55] Yet beyond the rhetoric, neither Moscow nor Tehran could meaningfully alter the course of events. The Russian-Iranian partnership in Syria, which had sustained Assad for over a decade, was now unraveling under the weight of its own contradictions.[56]

The opposition's momentum showed no sign of abating after the fall of Aleppo, pushing southeast toward Hama, a critical junction linking Syria's northern, southern, eastern, and coastal regions. By 4 December, rebel forces advanced from three directions, with Russia mounting its coordinated defense: warplanes conducted strikes supporting pro-Iranian militias around key roundabouts while Russian warships fired rockets at rebel positions in the overlooking hills. Despite the combined firepower, the regime's 25th Special Mission Forces Division was unable to hold its ground. By 5 December, opposition forces breached Hama's northeastern sector, capturing the 66th Brigade. In their haste to withdraw, regime and allied formations abandoned a significant array of equipment, including T-72 tanks, infantry fighting vehicles, and stockpiles of anti-tank guided missiles.[57]

Following their takeover of Hama, HTS led its offensive on Homs, the last major stronghold shielding Damascus. Russian and Iranian commanders, grasping the high stakes, scrambled to consolidate a defensive line across central Syria. From Tiyas Airbase, Russian jets staged intense air operations, launching at least ten targeted strikes in an attempt—ultimately unsuccessful—to destroy the strategic bridge linking Hama and Homs.[58] Throughout the region, IRGC-backed militias and Hezbollah fighters rushed to fortify their stronghold around Al-Qusayr, near the Lebanese border, hoping to block opposition advances along key supply corridors. Their efforts, however, were systematically undercut by Israel, whose forces aggressively targeted Hezbollah's logistics networks and infrastructure along the Syrian-Lebanese frontier.[59] Isolated from fresh armaments and manpower, the Iranian-aligned units soon found themselves overextended and vulnerable, allowing the rebel factions to maintain their momentum toward the gateway of Damascus.

Simultaneously, a major offensive towards Damascus erupted in southern Syria. A coalition of Syrian rebel groups, composed of various opposition factions that had previously operated in the southern provinces of Daraa, Suweida, and Quneitra, launched a coordinated assault. These forces advanced rapidly, coming within 20 km of Damascus. As opposition forces approached, the entire government apparatus crumbled. The governor, police chief, prison authorities, and local Baath Party leadership all abandoned their posts. Soon, local fighters had taken control of key checkpoints throughout the province, while the Syrian Arab Army retreated toward Damascus in a desperate attempt to establish a "defensive and security belt" around the capital.[60]

The opposition's multi-front offensive had brought them to the gates of Damascus. The facade of military strength crumbled as the Syrian Arab Army—the same force that had mercilessly barrel-bombed civilian populations and deployed sarin gas against children—abandoned their posts, leaving behind arsenals of equipment in a retreat that exposed the regime's hollow foundation.[61] As his forces dissolved around him, Assad watched helplessly as his longtime patrons, Russia and Iran, orchestrated their own withdrawals.

Before the fall of Damascus, Iran began withdrawing its personnel from Syria in the early hours of 6 December, evacuating top IRGC Quds Force commanders and ordering the evacuation of its embassy in Damascus and military bases across the country.[62] In a stunning development, Iranian-backed forces abandoned their most strategic asset—control of the Syrian-Iraqi border crossing—without any resistance, leading to the swift capture of the crucial Qa'im-Bukamal border crossing by the Syrian Democratic Forces. Hezbollah, too, withdrew hundreds of fighters from Al-Qusayr and surrounding villages toward Lebanon. Having exhausted its options and unwilling to commit more resources to a losing battle, Russia evacuated its forces to coastal strongholds in Latakia and Tartus.[63] The Russian embassy in Damascus went into lockdown as rebels approached the city, and Moscow issued urgent orders for all Russian citizens to evacuate the country immediately.

With Assad's forces now confined to Damascus and the coastal enclaves of Latakia and Tartous, the three powers convened what was widely viewed as the final round of the Astana talks—its 23rd session—on 7 December in Doha.[64] Representatives from Ankara, Tehran, and Moscow met alongside key regional players, including Qatar, Saudi Arabia, the UAE, Jordan, and Iraq, ostensibly to negotiate an end to the conflict. The talks yielded little substance on the ground; rebel forces continued their southward surge while what remained of the regime's loyalist units clung to shrinking pockets around the capital and the coastline. Many delegates in Doha privately acknowledged that the regime's collapse seemed inevitable and that the meeting served more to manage the fallout than to salvage Assad's rule.

That same night, under the cover of darkness, Bashar Assad executed a final act of deception that epitomized his regime. While the palace staff in the hilltop Presidential Palace prepared for what they believed would be a televised address—allegedly announcing a power-sharing agreement with the opposition—Assad quietly slipped out of the capital. Camera crews had already set up equipment, and aides stood by with talking points for an impending announcement. Yet the speech was nothing more than a ruse. After dusk, Assad flew first to a Russian military base in northern Syria before boarding a Russian jet to Moscow.

Assad's flight marked a stunning end to his family's fifty-year grip on Syria, leaving even his most devoted supporters feeling betrayed. The facade of normalcy he had maintained until the very end—working from his office and betraying no sense of alarm to his staff—crumbled into chaos after midnight when word of his escape finally reached the palace. His abandoned aides fled in panic, leaving the palace gates wide open for advancing rebels. The dramatic collapse revealed the hollowness at the core of Assad's power: in his final days, Putin had stopped taking his calls, Iran had concluded he could not survive and began quietly withdrawing its assets, and Iraq refused his requests for support. The ophthalmologist-turned-dictator who had overseen incomprehensible brutality against his own people ended his reign by fleeing in the night while leaving others to face the consequences of his crimes.

On 8 December 2024, the Kremlin announced that it had granted Bashar Assad asylum in Russia for "humanitarian purposes," emphasizing that the deposed dictator would no longer be active in politics.[65] In the weeks that followed Assad's unceremonious arrival, a stream of increasingly surreal rumors began circulating about the fallen strongman's future plans. Russian media outlets, apparently eager to normalize his presence, floated stories claiming that Assad intended to return to his roots as an ophthalmologist. Reports suggested he was considering opening a private eye clinic in Moscow, a career change from a dictator who had overseen the deaths of hundreds of thousands of Syrians into an eye doctor serving Russian patients. The almost absurd banality of these reports underscored just how dramatically Assad's world had collapsed in a matter of days.

Yet while Assad retreated into obscurity and rumors of medical practice, the earthquake he left behind sent shockwaves through the regional order that Russia and Iran had spent over a decade constructing. Russia moved swiftly to secure agreements with the interim government, hoping to preserve access to its naval facility in Tartous and its airbase in Latakia. Russia pressed for agreements with the interim government—led by Ahmed al-Sharaa—to retain vital access to naval and air facilities in Tartous and Latakia, arguing that a continued Russian presence would bolster "regional stability." Iran, on the other hand, faced a far more uncertain future in post-Assad Syria. Having spent years and vast resources propping up the old regime, Tehran sought to preserve economic agreements and political influence but now faced a government far less willing to accommodate its ambitions.[66] Behind closed doors, Russian and Iranian envoys coordinated messaging in an effort to safeguard at least some of their overlapping stakes in the country—yet the power vacuum left by Assad's plight was more conducive to other actors

.

* * *

The inglorious fall of Bashar Assad's regime in December 2024 resulted from a confluence of these factors that gradually eroded the pillars supporting his rule. After surviving the initial uprising in 2011 and subsequent civil war through brutal repression and crucial backing from Russia and Iran, Assad's position appeared relatively secure after major campaigns in the south, central, and northeast parts of the country. The March 2020 Idlib ceasefire agreement, as discussed in Chapter 5, seemed to cement his control over most of Syria's major population centers, while diplomatic initiatives by several Arab states to normalize relations with Damascus suggested growing regional acceptance of his continued rule.

Beneath this veneer of stability, the foundations of Assad's power were steadily weakening. His regime had become increasingly dependent on a complex network of corruption and drug trafficking, particularly the production and distribution of Captagon. This criminal enterprise, while providing crucial revenue, also contributed to the regime's moral and institutional decay, with military commanders and local warlords growing more focused on protecting their illegal enterprises than maintaining effective security forces. Russia's assumptions about its progress in Syrian military reform proved misguided. Endemic corruption marred any meaningful advancement, while Iran's efforts to create factions within the Syrian Arab Army only contributed to institutional fragmentation. Neither Moscow nor Tehran foresaw how their competing efforts to carve out influence would undermine the Assad regime's already fragile foundation.

The most decisive factor in Assad's eventual downfall was the weakening of his two main international backers. Iran's regional setbacks, particularly Israel's systematic campaign against Hezbollah and the weakening of its own homeland defenses, helped create conditions favorable to the Aleppo offensive. Meanwhile, Turkey, Russia's partner in the Astana process, sensed an opening to settle unfinished business in Syria. The confluence of these factors —a weakened Iran, a disengaged Russia, a decimation of Hezbollah's fighting capacity, and Turkey's opportunistic moves—ultimately contributed to the fracturing of the uneasy power-sharing arrangement that once bound Moscow and Tehran in Syria.

When Assad's regime crumbled in late 2024, the vast networks of economic exploitation Russia and Iran had built in Syria—from phosphate mining contracts to energy deals to sanctions evasion schemes—disintegrated with startling speed. Yet paradoxically, the fall of their first major joint venture did little to weaken the broader strategic partnership they had forged in the process. Syria had served as their laboratory for developing frameworks for military coordination, intelligence sharing, and knowledge transfer.

* * *

Formed as a desperate effort to bolster Bashar Assad, the Russia and Iran partnership evolved into a framework of defense coordination and strategic planning that outlived the very regime it was originally meant to safeguard. Paradoxically, the downfall of their Syrian project only underscored how completely Moscow and Tehran's interests had converged beyond Assad's survival. The organizational mechanisms they developed there—joint command centers, logistical pathways, and intelligence-sharing protocols—quickly found new life in Russia's war in Ukraine, where Iranian drones now darken the skies over Kyiv.

What began as a partnership to save Assad had evolved into a complex web of military cooperation that, when stressed on multiple fronts, ultimately failed to preserve the regime it was created to protect. Yet, paradoxically, the loss of Syria—where their partnership was first forged in 2015—demonstrated how thoroughly their relationship had evolved beyond its original purpose. The institutional mechanisms developed to coordinate operations in Syria had already been repurposed for Russia's war in Ukraine, where Iranian drones now darkened the skies over Kyiv. The partnership that began with a desperate attempt to save Assad had become something far more consequential: a strategic partnership that would endeavor to reshape the international order even as their first joint venture crumbled into dust.

The Russia-Iran relationship was not born from a deliberate policy or a comprehensive strategy to strengthen bilateral ties. Rather, it arose out of mutual necessity. Haunted by the prospect of Western-backed regime change and wary of their own internal vulnerabilities, both viewed Syria as a critical proving ground for resisting the liberal international order. Shared opposition to these policies served as the bedrock for what can be described as a partnership of defiance. Fundamentally, Russia and Iran found themselves bound by a common cause: opposition to Western policies and liberal norms that both countries deeply opposed and sought to defy. Domestically, the leaderships in Moscow and Tehran harbored an acute sense of vulnerability stemming from fears of external interference and potential regime change. Over time, this oppositional stance became a cornerstone of their foreign policy postures, transforming what began as a narrowly focused tactical arrangement into a deep and enduring alliance. Even Assad's downfall could not unmake it; in fact, the collapse of their Syrian adventure only highlighted that what Russia and Iran truly secured in their years of intervention was each other.

CONCLUSION

One month after Bashar Assad's inglorious fall, an audio recording attributed to Brigadier General Behrouz Esbati, a senior commander in Iran's Armed Forces, surfaced in Iranian media. The recording, reportedly made during a speech at a mosque in Tehran, offered a rare glimpse into the internal frustrations and recriminations surrounding the collapse of Assad's regime. Esbati blamed the downfall on a combination of "Russian betrayal" and the regime's internal corruption, accusing Moscow of misleading Tehran by claiming its jets were targeting Syrian rebels when, in reality, they were allegedly dropping bombs on empty fields.[1] The speech, delivered in part to boost morale and pacify hardline conservatives demanding a more forceful Iranian response, revealed the cracks in the Russia-Iran partnership.

A blame game between Moscow and Tehran seemed inevitable in the wake of Assad's fall. After all, it was the Syrian dictator's precarious grip on power that had thrust the two countries together in the first place, transforming their historically fraught relationship into a strategic partnership. Yet, the recriminations over Syria's collapse revealed the enduring tensions that have long characterized the Russia-Iran relationship—tensions that persist even as the two countries have moved toward deeper strategic alignment. Despite years of battlefield cooperation and shared opposition to Western pressure, the fundamental asymmetries, mutual suspicions, and competing interests that have historically defined their ties remained beneath the surface. Assad's fall had not created new fractures between Moscow and Tehran; it had simply exposed the existing faultlines in a partnership built more on necessity than natural affinity.

Yet, the reality was that their ties had grown far beyond Syria. The shared experiences of coordinating military operations, evading Western sanctions, and confronting common adversaries had created a foundation for deeper collaboration that transcended any single conflict or client state. Soon after Assad's fall, this evolving partnership would be formalized through a comprehensive strategic partnership agreement, setting the stage for even broader agenda cooperation. The accord cemented an even greater level of institutionalized cooperation between Russia and Iran, formalizing through treaty provisions what had previously existed as ad hoc coordination. Yet it was shadowed by unresolved tensions and a legacy of mistrust—carrying forward the same contradictions that had shaped their relationship for decades: a shared commitment to regime preservation and defiance of Western hegemony, coupled with persistent wariness about each other's reliability and intentions.

Tensions Persist

Russia and Iran are inextricably linked by geography, frequently divided by history, and currently united in defiance. This relationship, spanning centuries, has been marked by territorial disputes, imperial ambitions, and mutual suspicion. While the war in Ukraine has brought Russia and Iran closer, it has not erased the deep-seated frictions that have long riddled the countries' ties. Moscow's historical tendency to use Iran as a bargaining chip in its dealings with Western powers has left an indelible mark on Iranian collective memory. Within Iran's political establishment, conservative factions, particularly the Islamic Revolutionary Guard Corps (IRGC), advocate for stronger ties with Russia as a counterweight to Western pressure. However, this position has encountered resistance from Iran's reformist camp and civil society, who remain skeptical of Russian intentions based on historical precedent. Even among proponents of Russian cooperation, there exists an underlying wariness of Moscow's reliability as a partner, stemming from instances where Russia has prioritized its interests at Iran's expense—such as voting for UN sanctions against Iran's nuclear program or repeatedly delaying the completion of the Bushehr nuclear power plant.

Russia, at times, does not seem to be attuned to the sensitivities within Iran. As discussed in Chapter 4, Russia's publicity campaign around its use of the Hamedan airbase sparked harsh criticism in Iran, where the presence of foreign military forces remains a deeply sensitive issue. More recently, in July 2023, Russia released a joint statement with the Gulf Cooperation Council (GCC) that questioned Iran's sovereignty over three disputed islands in the Persian Gulf. This prompted a vehement response from Tehran, including the formal summoning of the Russian ambassador. Similarly, in December 2023, Russian Foreign Minister Sergey Lavrov's call for Iran to engage in mediation over the islands drew sharp criticism, even from staunch advocates of closer Russia-Iran ties like Ali Akbar Velayati.[2] While some of this backlash is performative and directed at domestic audiences, it nevertheless reflects a deep-seated perception in Iran that Russia continues to loom over the relationship, often prioritizing its own interests at Iran's expense.

Tensions have also flared over Russia's growing ties to Azerbaijan, particularly regarding the proposed Zangezur Corridor. Russia's public support for Azerbaijan's call for an east-west land corridor through Armenia provoked a sharp response from Tehran, which views the project as a potential threat to its regional influence and access to Europe. Iran's late Foreign Minister Hossein Amir-Abdollahian took the unusual step of publicly rebuking Russia, stating that any threat to territorial integrity or changes to regional boundaries would be a "red line" for Iran.[3] This criticism came alongside the formal summoning of the Russian Ambassador to Tehran to express Iran's displeasure, mirroring previous diplomatic incidents. Even figures like Mohsen Rezaei, a former IRGC commander and advocate of closer ties with Moscow, condemned Russia's actions, stating, "The behavior of Russian statesmen was not acceptable and in clear contradiction with their declaration of friendship with Iran. These ambiguities must be resolved."[4]

Areas of cooperation, like international sanctions, have inadvertently thrust Russia and Iran into direct competition, particularly within the shadowy world of illicit oil trade. As legitimate export channels narrow because of sanctions, both countries have been forced to rely increasingly on clandestine markets to sell their oil. Historically, Iran has been a dominant player in markets east of Suez, particularly in China and India. However, Russia's entry into these clandestine markets, particularly those where it has offered steep discounts to attract buyers, has directly encroached on Iran's position. Moscow's aggressive pricing has eroded Tehran's traditional customer base, undermining Iran's ability to sustain its share in lucrative sanctions-evading trade networks.

Indeed, the Russia-Iran partnership has been tested. Yet, the Russia-Iran relationship has endured, sustained by pragmatism and a shared recognition of their overlapping interests. The leaders in Russia and Iran recognize the value of working together and bolstering each other to safeguard their regimes in the face of Western pressure. As long as they continue to face isolation, the relationship will endure even amid persistent tensions and occasional divergences.

* * *

The 2001 Treaty on Mutual Relations between the Russian Federation and the Islamic Republic of Iran, discussed in Chapter 1, was the culmination of nearly a decade of Iranian diplomatic efforts to formalize and strengthen its relationship with Russia. Beginning in September 1992, Iran pursued negotiations to establish a strategic partnership with Russia, seeing Moscow as a potential counterweight to Western influence. The Iranians achieved an initial milestone in March 1993 when Russian Foreign Minister Kozyrev and Iranian Foreign Minister Velayati met in Tehran to initial a draft agreement, which was intended to pave the way for a summit between Presidents Yeltsin and Rafsanjani. However, this high-level meeting never materialized during the 1990s due to a lack of interest on the Russian side.

Iran's aspirations for the treaty were finally addressed in March 2001, when Russian President Vladimir Putin and Iranian President Mohammad Khatami met in Moscow to sign the agreement. At that time, Putin was early into his presidency, and Russia was still grappling with the consequences of NATO's airstrikes on Serbia—an event that left Moscow embittered and wary of American unilateralism. Against this backdrop, Russia viewed Iran as a valuable partner through which it could express discontent with Western policies and position itself as a counterbalance to U.S. dominance.

However, the final agreement revealed significant limitations in Russia's commitment. Although Moscow was prepared to collaborate with Tehran in challenging Western hegemony, it refrained from providing the substantial, unconditional support Iran had envisioned. This was particularly evident in the military aspects of the treaty. Instead of committing to mutual military support in the event of an attack, the treaty only stipulated that neither side would assist any aggressor. Consequently, the treaty established only a broad and non-binding framework for cooperation, falling short of the strategic partnership that Tehran had hoped would anchor their bilateral relations.

The treaty was set to last for an initial term of ten years, automatically renewable in five-year increments. Yet, over the years, it became clear that the treaty did not reflect the evolving nature of the Russia-Iran relationship, which had grown in the face of shared international challenges and mutual adversities. In 2019, during Foreign Minister Mohammad Javad Zarif's visit to Moscow, Russia and Iran first signaled their intent to update their 2001 Treaty on Mutual Relations. The initiative gained momentum from 2021 onward, with the proposed treaty update becoming a recurring agenda item in virtually every high-level meeting between Russian and Iranian officials. When Raisi made his first official visit to Moscow in January 2022, discussed in Chapter 8, he presented a draft of a 20-year cooperation agreement, declaring Iran had "no limits for expanding ties with Russia." Yet Putin's response remained measured, avoiding the term "strategic" and speaking only of creating a "long-term foundation for cooperation."[5]

Russia's calculus shifted dramatically after its full-scale invasion of Ukraine in February 2022. By June of that year, at the Caspian Summit in Ashgabat, Putin described Russia-Iran relations as having "a deep strategic nature." Facing military challenges in Ukraine and growing isolation from Western sanctions, Moscow increasingly relied on Tehran for military equipment, particularly drones. Emboldened by Russia's dependence, Iran leveraged this position to extract more favorable terms in the treaty negotiations. However, progress stalled under Raisi, who used Iran's newfound leverage to push for better conditions. Raisi's unexpected death in May 2024 further complicated negotiations, prompting Iran to pause discussions until after snap presidential elections in June, allowing the new leadership to reassess the terms.

In the summer of 2024, the pause in negotiations sparked a public back-and-forth between the two countries, often played out in statements to state-led media. In June 2024, the head of the Russian Foreign Ministry's Second Asia Department Zamir Kabulov stated that the agreement had temporarily stalled due to challenges by their Iranian counterparts while expressing confidence in its eventual completion.[6] Kabulov's comments elicited a swift response from Iran's ambassador to Russia, Kazem Jalali, who denied any suspension of the process, accusing Iranian media of mistranslating Russian reports. Adding to the multitude of narratives, Russian Foreign Minister Sergey Lavrov stated that, while a comprehensive agreement between Russia and Iran cannot yet be signed due to "procedural legislative actions," its text had been fully coordinated.[7]

By September 2024, the lingering tensions between Russia and Iran appeared to subside. A clear indication came when the Kremlin published a brief yet significant presidential decree titled "The Order on Signing the Comprehensive Strategic Partnership Treaty Between Russia and Iran."[8] This concise, one-page directive formally approved the treaty text and authorized negotiators to make only non-substantive amendments during the final stages of the talks. Initially, both governments had planned to finalize the treaty at the October BRICS summit in Kazan, a timeline confirmed by President Pezeshkian soon after his election. However, following his first bilateral meeting with Putin in Ashgabat, the approach shifted. Iran's Ambassador to Russia announced that the two leaders had agreed to conclude the treaty during dedicated bilateral visits instead, with President Putin extending an invitation for Pezeshkian to travel to Moscow.

On 17 January 2025, Russian President Vladimir Putin and Iranian President Masoud Pezeshkian met in Moscow to sign the long-anticipated Comprehensive Strategic Partnership Treaty. During the signing ceremony, Putin praised the relationship as "large-scale and mutually beneficial," while Pezeshkian emphasized that the treaty would "prepare the necessary channel for further cooperation."[9] The timing was laden with symbolism: the ceremony occurred just days before Donald Trump's return to the U.S. presidency and a month after the collapse of the Syrian regime. If Assad's fall underscored the fragility of their earlier alignment, the treaty signaled an ambition to anchor cooperation in future collaboration.

A Partnership of Defiance, Not an Alliance

Few developments so vividly capture the evolution, strengths, and inherent constraints of the Russia-Iran relationship as the 2025 Comprehensive Strategic Partnership Treaty. Signed two decades after Khatami visited Moscow, the 2025 Comprehensive Strategic Partnership Treaty officially supersedes the 2001 Treaty on Mutual Relations.[10] Viewed side by side, these two texts—separated by years of collaboration—exemplify how Russia and Iran have evolved. The 2001 accord was deliberately cautious, sidestepping mutual defense obligations and reflecting Moscow's post-Yeltsin strategy of keeping its options open vis-à-vis the West. In contrast, the 2025 treaty reflects an evolved relationship: one shaped by battlefield cooperation in Syria, mutual isolation in the wake of the Ukraine war, and the intensification of shared threats to regime survival.

Like the Russia-Iran relationship itself, the treaty does not promise an unshakeable alliance; it does not stipulate binding mutual defense or unconditional commitments to intervene in each other's wars. In this sense, it does not create a formal alliance but qualitative transformation—officially designating the relationship as "strategic." Still, the treaty codifies a framework of unified necessity that cements overlapping interests in security, economic resilience, and a joint rejection of what they see as Western unilateralism. Its forty-seven articles cover military-technical cooperation, economic coordination, intelligence sharing, cultural diplomacy, and cyberspace governance. At its core, the treaty reflects what has driven Russia-Iran cooperation: a reactive posture to Western pressure, solidified through necessity more than design.

The treaty's ideological foundation centers on what both regimes have increasingly positioned as their central foreign policy doctrine: the emergence of multipolarity as an alternative to Western hegemony. The preamble explicitly calls for "a new fair and sustainable multipolar world order," while Article 2 frames this aspiration in explicitly oppositional terms through "rejection of unipolarity and hegemony in world affairs" and opposition to "interference by third parties in the internal and external affairs" of either signatory. As discussed in Chapter 7, multipolarity has long featured in rhetoric and policy documents, specific treaty provisions highlight how Russia's "Turn to the East" and Iran's "Look to the East" policies became practical necessities under sustained Western sanctions. Consequently, both increasingly engaged with non-Western networks like the Shanghai Cooperation Organization (SCO) and the Eurasian Economic Union (EAEU), with Article 14 explicitly promoting deeper regional collaboration.

Transforming multipolar rhetoric into economic reality has proven substantially more difficult than diplomatic positioning for Russia and Iran. While the treaty's economic provisions express ambitious goals to challenge U.S.-led financial systems and create alternative frameworks, they reveal a fundamental disconnect between stated objectives and practical capabilities. Article 19 exemplifies this tension by designating unilateral coercive measures as "internationally unlawful and unfriendly acts" while simultaneously legitimizing the very gray-market activities these sanctions target, including Iran's oil smuggling networks and Russia's shadow tanker operations. Rather than fostering genuine economic integration, it constructs a framework oriented primarily toward circumventing existing constraints.

Subsequent provisions address practical measures to minimize reliance on dollar transactions and develop alternative trade routes, like the International North-South Transport Corridor (INSTC), intended to enhance self-sufficiency and market diversification under international isolation. However, the treaty also highlights significant limitations: both countries remain dependent on foreign intermediaries and global reserve currencies, complicating the ambition outlined in Article 20 for independent payment infrastructures. Structural barriers—such as competitive hydrocarbon exports, overlapping market targets, and limited financial mechanisms—further constrain practical cooperation. Articles 21 and 22 promote collaborative infrastructure development and industrial cooperation, yet also underscore the inherent incompatibility of their economies, marked by similar export profiles and internal inefficiencies.

While these initiatives evoke a spirit of mutual resilience and Eastern-oriented integration, they also underscore a precarious reality: the two economies, despite rhetorical unity, are not naturally complementary. The repeated drive to diversify trade routes, for instance, echoes the difficulties of reconciling parallel export structures, whether in oil, natural gas, or manufactured goods. In essence, the economic chapters of the treaty reveal how far the partnership has come in articulating a joint strategy to counter Western financial dominance, yet also how vulnerable it remains to global market forces and internal inefficiencies. Neither state can entirely escape reliance on foreign currencies or competition in sectors like energy; both still rely on international channels that they cannot wholly control.

The treaty's real backbone lies in mutual regime preservation. At its core, the 2025 Treaty on Comprehensive Strategic Partnership is a pact between two deeply insecure regimes determined to shield themselves from internal and external threats. Russian and Iranian leaders have long shared a deep-seated fear of Color Revolutions and Western-backed regime change. The leadership in both countries has consistently interpreted domestic uprisings as evidence of foreign interference aimed at undermining their rule. Russia and Iran's parallel experiences of domestic instability have spurred close cooperation among their security services, from sharing surveillance tactics to coordinating cyber strategies aimed at preventing potential revolts. Part of this was formalized in 2014 when their Ministries of Interior signed an agreement that created a framework for sharing tactics to quell dissent. Article 4 of their current agreement represents the culmination and expansion of this intelligence relationship to cover both internal and external threats, explicitly establishing formal cooperation between their security services and mandating that they "exchange information and experience and increase the level of their cooperation" to strengthen "national security and counter common threats."

Closely linked to regime preservation is the treaty's explicit linkage between information security and national sovereignty. Article 33 commits both parties to jointly combat "disinformation and negative propaganda," curbing the spread of "unreliable socially significant information" deemed threatening to their national interests. Article 11 similarly underscores the importance of reinforcing national sovereignty in cyberspace. These provisions align with the broader framework of their information security agreement, mandating "cooperation in countering the use of information and communication technologies for criminal purposes" and advocating the "internationalization of Internet governance." Collectively, these provisions create a legal framework to systematize and expand their ad hoc arrangements, enabling more structured sharing of technical intelligence, counterintelligence, and operational expertise.

A substantial portion of the treaty—nearly one-third—addresses military-technical cooperation, reflecting the dramatic expansion in this domain since Russia's involvement in Syria. The agreement establishes extensive collaboration through military delegation exchanges, reciprocal naval port visits, personnel training programs, and joint exercises designed to counter shared threats. Moscow and Tehran explicitly commit to "strengthening peace and security" across strategic regions, including the Caspian, Central Asia, Transcaucasia, and the Middle East—a formulation that implicitly targets U.S. influence by opposing external interference and destabilizing third-party presence.

Crucially, the Russia-Iran treaty diverges from Russia's 2024 agreement with North Korea by avoiding binding mutual defense obligations. Instead, it maintains the narrower commitment established in their 2001 agreement: if either party faces aggression, the other must refrain from assisting the aggressor. This circumscribed commitment reflects realities on the ground. Tehran explicitly sought to avoid becoming directly entangled, notably refraining from sending troops or engaging militarily in support of Moscow, a sharp contrast to North Korea's direct military involvement. Concurrently, Russia's restrained response during Iran's heightened tensions and escalations with Israel underscored clear limits in its willingness to commit explicitly to Iranian defense needs.[11] As a result, both sides deliberately avoided explicit commitments that could compel them to intervene in each other's military conflicts.

Even without binding defense commitments, the treaty creates new avenues for deepening security cooperation by delineating specific roles for each side. It permits joint exercises "on the territory of both Contracting Parties and beyond," potentially enabling Iran to expand its presence in regions where Russia operates. While this does not obligate Iran to support Russian military campaigns like Ukraine, it establishes structured mechanisms for coordination and interoperability that could be activated if strategic conditions shift. Article 6 further institutionalizes annual meetings between defense industry bodies, under the auspices of the Joint Russia-Iran Military-Technical Commission, laying the groundwork for long-term cooperation in weapons development, knowledge-sharing, and technology transfer.

Beyond conventional military collaboration, Article 30 broadens the scope through "joint scientific and technical projects," including academic exchanges between research institutions. Although framed as civilian, these initiatives facilitate the transfer of dual-use technologies applicable to both commercial and defense sectors. The provision for exchanging scientific and technical information formalizes a channel for collaboration that might otherwise be subject to international restrictions. For Iran, these provisions are not only a means of accessing Russian expertise but also a pathway toward defense-industrial self-sufficiency, particularly through licensing arrangements, localized production, or the institutional diffusion of technical know-how.

Although Russia is unlikely to intervene directly in a military conflict involving Iran, cooperation may unfold in less visible but no less consequential forms. Technical support to Iran's integrated air defense systems, intelligence sharing, and logistical facilitation are all plausible vectors of assistance that avoid the political costs of overt arms transfers or direct military assistance. Russia's own military-industrial constraints, compounded by the war in Ukraine, reinforce Iran's longstanding pursuit of self-sufficiency. In a crisis that threatens the survival of the Iranian regime, Russian support would likely remain limited to deniable and indirect forms—such as the provision of matériel, battlefield intelligence, or enabling technologies—rather than overt military intervention.

The 2025 Comprehensive Strategic Partnership Treaty captures a defining pattern in Russia-Iran relations: a partnership of defiance, grounded in shared grievances and regime security concerns, yet constrained by divergent interests and persistent economic limitations. Over years of occasionally uneasy cooperation, Moscow and Tehran have cultivated a distinctive form of defiance to what they view as an overly interventionist, U.S.-dominated international order. In this sense, the partnership is less the product of natural affinity than of mutual vulnerability. The treaty marks both the culmination of these shared anxieties and a formal effort to translate reactive alignment into sustained policy coordination. It reflects a partnership rooted in joint opposition to liberal internationalism and a common preoccupation with regime preservation—yet one deliberately structured to preserve the strategic ambiguity and flexibility that both states rely on to navigate external pressure.

* * *

A strategic partnership between Russia and Iran was far from inevitable. Long-lasting mistrust, unmet expectations, and weak economic ties have historically marred the Russia-Iran relationship. For decades, Moscow and Tehran collided over unresolved territorial disputes, canceled arms contracts, and delays in constructing the Bushehr Nuclear Power Plant.[12] Less than a decade before Iranian drones appeared in Ukraine, the Russia-Iran relationship was characterized by tension and discord, as detailed in Chapter 2. Yet this changed when Moscow and Tehran were thrust into a joint military campaign to support Assad in Syria. Despite their cooperation, the partnership was not without its challenges, ranging from tensions on the battlefield to the complexities introduced by the involvement of other countries like the United States and Israel.

For decades, Moscow and Tehran cultivated parallel grievances against a Western-dominated international order that both perceived as fundamentally hostile to their legitimate aspirations for regional influence and global recognition. The post-Cold War unipolar system relegated Russia from its former superpower status while systematically isolating Iran as a pariah state, creating shared resentments about their marginalization within liberal international institutions. Both nations interpreted Western policies—ranging from NATO expansion and democracy promotion to comprehensive sanctions regimes—as coordinated efforts to constrain their emergence as autonomous centers of power capable of challenging American hegemony. Yet despite this ideological convergence and their mutual opposition to Western dominance, Moscow and Tehran consistently failed to transform their parallel worldviews into substantive cooperation, as historical mistrust, competing regional interests, and Russia's intermittent pursuit of rapprochement with the West repeatedly undermined the realization of a strategic partnership.

The question of regime security provided an even more compelling basis for alignment, as both authoritarian systems confronted similar existential concerns about Western efforts to orchestrate internal political transformation. Putin's Russia and the Islamic Republic alike viewed democracy promotion, civil society assistance, and human rights advocacy as sophisticated instruments of regime change, interpreting the Color Revolutions and subsequent regional upheavals as evidence of systematic Western campaigns to eliminate non-compliant governments. This shared vulnerability to external interference fostered profound psychological connections between Russian and Iranian elites, who developed comparable strategies for suppressing domestic opposition, controlling information environments, and characterizing internal dissent as foreign-sponsored subversion.

When the Syrian Civil War erupted in 2011, it presented both Moscow and Tehran with precisely the kind of existential challenge that their shared worldview had long anticipated—a Western-backed popular uprising threatening to topple a key regional ally and potentially inspiring similar movements closer to home. Unlike previous crises where their interests had diverged or where one party could afford to remain on the sidelines, Syria demanded action from both countries.

The Syrian Civil War began with popular demands for dignity and freedom from the grip of a brutal autocracy. In response, the Assad regime unleashed indiscriminate violence, used chemical weapons against civilians, and invited foreign military support to maintain its hold on power. Russia and Iran intervened decisively to sustain Assad's rule—militarily, economically, and diplomatically—until his eventual fall in late 2024. Yet far more consequential than Assad's temporary survival was what Syria became for Moscow and Tehran: a proving ground for institutionalized cooperation. Through joint military commissions, coordinated air-ground operations, and diplomatic deconfliction, Russia and Iran developed the mechanisms of wartime collaboration that would later define their relationship.

When Russia launched its full-scale invasion of Ukraine in 2022, the frameworks first forged in Syria enabled an unprecedented deepening of bilateral ties. What began as coordination on the Syrian battlefield evolved into sustained military-industrial cooperation—from drone transfers and joint weapons production to intelligence sharing and sanctions evasion. Economic ties also expanded through barter mechanisms, energy exchanges, and financial coordination, as both regimes adapted to long-term confrontation with the West. Syria had not just aligned their interests—it had created the habits of collaboration, trust, and institutional linkages that would prove critical in the face of future challenges.

What emerged from their intervention in Syria ultimately outlasted the war—and even the regime it was intended to protect. The collapse of Assad's government did not undermine the Russia–Iran partnership. Perhaps most paradoxically, the collapse of Assad's government in late 2024 only underscored the extent to which the Russia–Iran partnership had matured into a self-sustaining partnership—no longer tethered to Assad's survival. In the process, Russia and Iran gained something more enduring than a client state: they gained each other.

Still, the relationship remains bounded by significant constraints. Asymmetries in power, resources, and global reach continue to structure the partnership unequally in Russia's favor. Iran's distrust of great power manipulation lingers beneath the surface, while Russia remains cautious of entanglements that could jeopardize its relations with other regional actors. Economic cooperation has been constrained by structural capacity gaps and the weight of international sanctions. In addition, divergent long-term interests in regions such as the South Caucasus, Central Asia, and global energy markets have periodically resurfaced, generating moments of tension. For all its institutional depth, the partnership is not without friction, nor is it immune to recalibration.

Russia and Iran's partnership of defiance emerged not from deliberate design but from circumstance—a reactive alignment forged in response to perceived encirclement, domestic vulnerability, and marginalization within a U.S.-led international order. It was shaped through necessity, not strategy. Repeated crises, overlapping threat perceptions, and the shared experience of isolation gradually fostered habits of coordination and a deeper recognition of their intertwined political fates. Over time, the reactive logic that once defined the relationship gave way to a more durable foundation. In the end, the Russia–Iran relationship is best understood not as a fixed axis, but as a dynamic and adaptive compact—tempered by constraints, hardened through conflict, and unexpectedly fortified by the very instability it was built to resist.

NOTES

INTRODUCTION

1. "Tehran Declaration, 'Historic Opportunity' for Obama: Ahmadinejad," ISNA, 26 May 2010, https://en.isna.ir/news/8903-03745/Tran-declaration-historic-opportunity-for-Obama-Ahmadinejad.
2. Robert Axelrod and Robert O. Keohane, "Achieving Cooperation under Anarchy: Strategies and Institutions," *World Politics* 38, no. 1 (1985): 226-54, https://doi.org/10.2307/2010357, and Kenneth A. Oye, "Explaining Cooperation under Anarchy: Hypotheses and Strategies," *World Politics* 38, no. 1 (1985): 1-24, https://doi.org/10.2307/2010349.
3. This view is typically associated with scholars who emphasize the self-help nature of international politics. According to this logic, states exist in an anarchic system, meaning that there is no central authority or world government to regulate their behavior. Stephen M. Walt, "Alliances in a Unipolar World," *World Politics* 61, no. 1 (2009): 86-120; Kenneth N. Waltz, "Structural Realism after the Cold War," *International Security* 25, no. 1 (2000): 5-41; John J. Mearsheimer, *The Tragedy of Great Power Politics* (New York: W.W. Norton, 2001).
4. Michael C. Williams and Iver B. Neumann, "From Alliance to Security Community: NATO, Russia, and the Power of Identity," *Millennium* 29, no. 2 (1 June 2000): 357-87, https://doi.org/10.1177/03058298000290020801; Amitav Acharya, *Constructing a Security Community in Southeast Asia: ASEAN and the Problem of Regional Order*, Politics in Asia Series (London: Routledge, 2001).
5. With all due respect to political scientists, there is no hypothesis-testing in this book. It is written for a wider audience.
6. Shared threat perceptions explain why states form alignments. See Robert Jervis, *Perception and Misperception in International Politics*, new edn with a new preface by the author (Princeton: Princeton University Press, 2017). According to this perspective, states are more likely to align with one another when they perceive a common threat, as such threats can create a sense of urgency and promote cooperation. Shared threat perceptions highlight the importance of understanding how states perceive threats, and how these perceptions can shape their alignment behavior in the international system. For example, during the Cold War, the United States and its allies formed

NATO in response to the perceived threat posed by the Soviet Union and its allies in the Warsaw Pact. Stephen Walt suggests that states balance against threats determined by three key factors related to military power: the capabilities of the potential threat, its offensive intentions, and the degree of security that cooperation with other states can provide. Stephen M. Walt, *The Origins of Alliances*, Cornell Studies in Security Affairs (Ithaca, NY: Cornell University Press, 1987). However, shared threat perceptions can arise from various factors not limited to military threats, including ideology, domestic security, and prestige. While the balance of threat theory is traditionally focused on the material capabilities of states and the threat they pose, it can also be argued that shared norms and values can be incorporated into this framework. States with shared norms and values are likely to see each other as natural partners, and they may be more willing to align themselves to counter the perceived threat from a common enemy. These shared values and norms can create a sense of trust and cooperation among states and provide a basis for promoting mutual interests and objectives. This is consistent with the literature on democracies, which argues that alignments and alliances form due to shared values and norms.

7. My understanding of international order and the formation of ties between states is implicitly informed by the view that international order is generative—it generates social, material, and economic hierarchies and institutionalizes patterns of exclusion and inclusion. Christian Reus-Smit, *On Cultural Diversity: International Theory in a World of Difference* (Cambridge: Cambridge University Press, 2018); Andrew Hurrell, *On Global Order: Power, Values, and the Constitution of International Society* (Oxford: Oxford University Press, 2007). Power inequalities combined with the unequal distribution of legitimacy and authority in international order fuel struggles for recognition and provide the conditions for contestation over the prevailing rights, rules, and norms. Axel Honneth, *The I in We: Studies in the Theory of Recognition* (Cambridge: Polity, 2012); Nancy Fraser and Axel Honneth, *Redistribution or Recognition? A Political-Philosophical Exchange* (London: Verso, 2003); Axel Honneth, *The Struggle for Recognition: The Moral Grammar of Social Conflicts* (Cambridge, MA: MIT Press, 1996).
8. Similarly, it is often the case that Western analyses portray the relationship as simply an anti-Western coalition bound by a common identity. Moreover, treating anti-Westernism as an identity is superficial. The problem with the anti-Westernism approach is that it reduces Russia-Iran relations simply to a response to the West, rather than uncovering the deeper basis of these ideas. Academic literature on ontological security places too great an influence on given identities, including referential predispositions towards the West as the Other. This framework, especially when analyses eschew engagement with foreign-language sources, often overemphasizes civilizational factors without critically analyzing the instrumental use of narratives.
9. Gilford John Ikenberry, *Liberal Leviathan: The Origins, Crisis, and Transformation of the American World Order*, Princeton Studies in International History and Politics (Princeton: Princeton University Press, 2011), 2.
10. In Russian, the word *derzhava* implies "a holder of the international equilibrium of power" that possesses the necessary capabilities for "defending itself by relying on its own individual strength" through its chief goal of "the preservation of [great power] status"; Andrei Tsygankov, *Russia's Foreign Policy: Change and Continuity in National Identity*, 4th edn (Lanham: Rowman & Littlefield, 2016), 99.
11. Interview with a former deputy foreign minister (Moscow), 2019; interview with a former Russian ambassador to Europe (Moscow), 2019.

12. Andrei P. Tsygankov, *Mezhdunarodnye Otnosheniya: Traditsii Russkoi Politicheskoi Mysli* [International Relations: Traditions of Russian Political Thought] (Moscow: Al'fa-M, 2013).
13. Russian preference for the UNSC as an expression of sovereign equality among great powers directly collided with Iran's anti-hegemonic discourse about the tyranny of great powers, which rose commensurate with the scrutiny over Iran's nuclear program. Iran's critique of hegemony, though often directed towards the West, also encompassed Russia, as Ahmadinejad would frequently condemn Russian support for various sanctions resolutions in the UNSC. See Muḥammad Javād Lārījānī, *Kāvishhā-Yi Naẓarī Dar Siyāsat-i Khārij* [Theoretical Studies in Foreign Policy] (Tehran: Shirkat-i Intishārāt-i ʻIlmī va Farhangī, , 1996), 178.
14. The modern structure of Russian foreign policymaking decisions bears the impact of the institutional experience of the Soviet Union. The creation of the Inter-Agency Foreign Policy Commission of the Security Council in December 1992 and the Presidential Council in February of 1993 contributed to the progressive centralization of foreign policy in Russia. Viktor Averkov, "Prinyatie Vneshnepoliticheskikh Reshenii v Rossii [The Adoption of Foreign Policy Decisions in Russia],"" *Mezhdunarodnye Protsessy* 10, no. 2 (29) (2012): 110-23.
15. For example, central figures representative of the *siloviki*, like Nikolai Patrushev, have also played an essential role in forging ties between the Russian and Iranian elite Nikolai Patrushev, "Interv'"yu Sekretarya Soveta Bezopasnosti Rossiiskoi Federatsii N.P. Patrusheva [Interview with Secretary of the Security Council of the Russian Federation N.P. Patrushev],"" *Kommersant*, 12 January 2012; "Glava Sovbeza Patrushev Rasskazal Iranskomu Kollege Ob Organizatorah Himataki v Sirii [Security Council Chief Patrushev Told His Iranian Counterpart about the Organizers of the Chemical Attack in Syria],"" *Parlamentskaya Gazeta*, 8 April 2017.
16. Abdolrasool Divsallar, "The Foreign Policy Establishment in Iran," in *The Sacred Republic: Power and Institutions in Iran*, ed. Mehran Kamrava (London: Hurst, 2023), 221-57.
17. I would like to thank Abdolrasool Divsallar for allowing me to cite his working paper on this and for his feedback.
18. Andrew Hurrell, "Can the Study of Global Governance Be Decentred?," in *Global Governance from Regional Perspectives: A Critical View*, ed. Anna Triandafyllidou (Oxford: Oxford University Press, 2017), 25-44.
19. Vladislav Surkov "Nasha Rossiyskaya Model' Demokratii Nazyvaetsya '"Suverennoy Demokratiey'" [Our Russian Model of Democracy Is Called '"Sovereign Democracy'"],"" Edinaya Rossiya (ofitsial'nyy sayt partii), 28 June 2006, Integrum Digital Archive.
20. Abbas Firuzi, *Mabānī-i jang-i narm va rīshah'yābī-i ān dar tahājum-i farhangī* [Foundations of Soft War and Its Roots in Cultural Invasion] (Qom: Shikūfah-i Yās, 2010).
21. Gregorio Bettiza and David Lewis, "Authoritarian Powers and Norm Contestation in the Liberal International Order: Theorizing the Power Politics of Ideas and Identity," *Journal of Global Security Studies* 5, no. 4 (7 October 2020): 559-77, https://doi.org/10.1093/jogss/ogz075.
22. In addition to interstate positional anxiety, the denial of recognition or equality creates a disparity between a claimed self-image and the image held by others, which therefore generates the desire to pursue relations with states that recognize these

valued attributes. Honneth's work demonstrates that the struggles for "legal respect and social recognition for their collective identity" among marginalized social groups and minorities have been grounded in "shared experiences of exclusion, indignity or disrespect, which motivates the members of such a group to band together and fight in solidarity for legal or cultural recognition." Honneth, *Struggle for Recognition*, 139.

23. For background on interoperability, see Patricia A. Weitsman, *Waging War: Alliances, Coalitions, and Institutions of Interstate Violence* (Stanford: Stanford University Press, 2013).
24. The primary method for collecting sources was through various databases. For Russian sources, I used Eastview and Integrum. For Persian sources, I used Magiran and Sid.ir.
25. Ariane Tabatabai and Dina Esfandiary's *Triple-Axis* attempts to study the trilateral interactions between Russia, Iran, and China. A major shortcoming of the book is its lack of grounding, empirically and contextually, in the Russian perspective. See Ariane Tabatabai and Dina Esfandiary, *Triple-Axis: Iran's Relations with Russia and China* (London: Bloomsbury, 2018). Conversely, John Parker's *Persian Dreams* offers an excellent study of the Russia-Iran relationship up to the Ahmadinejad era but primarily relies on Russian sources for the study. See John W. Parker, *Persian Dreams: Moscow and Tehran since the Fall of the Shah*, 1st edn (Washington, DC : Potomac, 2009).
26. For the participants' safety, interviews with individuals currently residing in Russia or Iran are anonymized.
27. Yevgeny Primakov, "Blizhnevostochnyi Kurs Rossii: Istoricheskie Etapy [Middle Eastern Course of Russia: Historical Stages]," and Vitaly Naumkin, "Vmesto Predisloviia: Krugovorot Arabskogo Probuzhdeniia [The Cycle of the Arab Awakening]," in *Blizhnii Vostok, Arabskoe Probuzhdenie i Rossiia: Chto Dal'she? Sbornik Statei* [The Middle East, the Arab Awakening, and Russia: What's Next? Collection of Articles], ed. Vasiliy Kuznetsov, Vitaly Naumkin, and Veniamin Poppov (Moscow: Institut Vostokovedeniia RAN, 2012), 21-30 and 3-20.
28. Hassan Rouhani, "Duktar Rūḥānī Dar Ijlās-i Sarān-i ʻuẓv-i Sāzmān-i Hamkārī-i Shānghāy [Doctor Rouhani at the Shanghai Cooperation Organisation's Conference of the Head of States]," Riyāsat-i Jumhūrī-i Islāmī-i Īrān, 10 June 2018; "Āyatollāh Ra'īsī dar Bist-o-Dovvomīn Ajlās-i Sarān-i Sāzmān-i Hamkārī-i Shānghāy [Ayatollah Raisi at the Twenty-Second Summit of the Shanghai Cooperation Organisation Leaders]," Pāyegāh-i Etlā" Rassānī-i Sayyid Ibrāhīm Ra'īsī,, 16 September 2022.
29. With the inception of China's Belt and Road Initiative (BRI) in 2013, Russia sought to determine ways to manage China's growing influence in the region that encompasses the CIS and to capitalize on its relations with Beijing for economic benefits. In May 2015, Russian President Putin and Chinese President Xi Jinping signed an agreement to connect the Eurasian Economic Union (EAEU) with the BRI. One year later, at the St Petersburg International Economic Forum in June 2016, Putin articulated Moscow's intention to initiate the "Great Eurasian partnership"—a framework for macro-regional political, security, and economic integration encompassing the states of the EAEU and CIS as well as China, India, Pakistan, and Iran. The Russian discourse on Greater Eurasia stresses Iran's potential to assume a pivotal role as a regional center of power and geographic bridge connecting Eurasia to the Middle East and South Asia.

1. THE WEIGHT OF HISTORY

1. "International Contest on Imam Khomeini's Historic Letter to Gorbachev Extended until 3rd of March," http://en.imam-khomeini.ir/en/n29683/Book-reading-contest-features-Imam-Khomeini-s-letter-to-Gorbachev.
2. The letter was delivered by Javadi Amoli, the Supreme Leader's envoy. During Amoli's meeting with Gorbachev to deliver Khomeini's letter, the imam's envoy noted that the Soviet Union's appreciation for "the diversity of views and beliefs" and "non-interference in the internal affairs of other countries" creates "the basis for an in-depth discussion of the fundamental issues of life." Responding to Amoli, in a statement characteristic of Moscow's view of Tehran, Gorbachev professed: "Our relationship goes back centuries. We have traditions and share a vast border. We are 'doomed' to maintain good relations, to cooperate. Though we profess different worldviews and adhere to different philosophies, this should not prevent the development of Soviet-Iranian relations in the spirit of good traditions and give them a new quality today." See "Iz Besedy s Lichnym Predstavitelem Imama Khomeini Ayatolloi Dzhavadi-Amoli Moskva [From a Conversation with the Personal Representative of Imam Khomeini Ayatollah Javadi Amoli]," AGF Fond 1, Opis 1, 4 January 1989.
3. ʻAbd Allāh Javādī Āmulī, *Āvā-yi tawḥīd: nāmah-ʼi Imām Khumaynī salām Allāh ʻalayhi bih Gūrbāchuf va sharḥ-i nāmah* [Monotheism: Imam Khomeini's, May Peace Be upon Him, Letter to Gorbachev and Commentary] (Tehran: Mu'assasah-i Tanẓīm va Nashr-i Ās̱ār-i Imām Khumaynī, 1995).
4. "Matn-i Kāmil-Nāmih-yi Tārikhi Imam Khomayni (RAH) va Pāsukh Gorbāchav [The Complete Historical Letter of Imam Khomeini (RAH) and Gorbachev's Response]," *Kayhan*, 20 December 2006, https://www.magiran.com/article/1316192.
5. Elena Dunaeva and Lyudmila Kulagina, *Rossiya i Iran: Istoriya Formirovaniya Granits* [Russia and Iran: The History of the Formation of Borders], 2nd edn (Moscow: Institut Vostokovedeniya RAN, 2007), 7.
6. Russia's relations with Iran date to the Safavid dynasty, where economic ties and diplomatic exchanges began. The primary trade route used the Caspian Sea and the Volga River. Although Mongol invasions in the thirteenth and fourteenth centuries disrupted these connections, by the mid-fifteenth century commerce and political ties rebounded, with Russian merchants often conducting diplomacy alongside trade. The liberation of Kazan and Astrakhan in the mid-1500s further strengthened the trade route, leading to exchanges of Iranian silk and Russian furs. The relationship between Safavid Iran and Muscovy initially focused on opposing the Ottomans but faced strain due to changes in alliances and conflicts over the Caucasus.
7. Jahangir Karami, *Ravābiṭ-i Jumhūrī-i Islāmī-i Īrān va Fidirāsyūn-i Rūsīyah: ʻaṣr-i Nuvīn-i Hamakārī'hā* [Relations between the Islamic Republic of Iran and Russia: New Era of Cooperation] (Tehran: Daftar-i Muṭālaʻāt-i Siyāsī va Bayn al-Milalī, 2009), 228.
8. Mandana Tishehyar, "O Razvitii Irano-Rossiiskogo Sotrudnichestva [On the Development of Iranian and Russian Cooperation]," in *Rossiisko-Iranskie Otnosheniya: Problemy i Perspektivy*, ed. Vladimir Sazhin and Elena Dunaeva (Moscow: Institut vostokovedeniya RAN, 2015), 20.
9. For background on the historical evolution of Russia-Iran relations, see Cronin, *Iranian-Russian Encounters*.
10. Mohammad Mahdian, *Istoriya Mezhgosudarstvennykh Otnosheniy Irana i Rossii* [History

of Interstate Relations between Iran and Russia] (Moscow: Institut Vostokovedeniya RAN, 2014).

11. Maziar Behrooz, "Revisiting the Second Russo-Iranian War (1826-28): Causes and Perceptions," *Iranian Studies* 46, no. 3 (2013): 359-81.
12. For the history of Griboyedov in Iran, see Ol'ga Ivanovna Popova, *A.S. Griboyedov v Persii: 1818-1923 gg.; Po Novym Dokumentam* [A.S. Griboyedov in Persia: 1818-1923; Based on New Documents], Biblioteka dokumentov, zapisok i vospominaniy 25 (Moscow: Kooperativnoe izd-vo "Zhizn' i Znanie," 1929).
13. Mark Katz, "Russian-Iranian Relations in the Ahmadinejad Era," *Middle East Journal* 62, no. 2 (2008): 202-16.
14. Abbas Amanat, "'Russian Intrusion into the Guarded Domain': Reflections of a Qajar Statesman on European Expansion," *Journal of the American Oriental Society* 113, no. 1 (1993): 35-56, https://doi.org/10.2307/604195.
15. The Russians were also involved in Iran's constitutional revolution and eventually deployed Russian troops to Iran; for background, see James D. Clark, "Constitutionalists and Cossacks: The Constitutional Movement and Russian Intervention in Tabriz, 1907-1911," in Cronin, *Iranian-Russian Encounters*, 231-58.
16. In 1920, the Soviet Union supported the establishment of the Persian Socialist Soviet Republic in Gilan, Iran, as part of its international efforts to spread socialism and counteract British influence in the region. This backing included military and political support but was short-lived, ending in 1921.
17. Oliver Bast, "Duping the British and Outwitting the Russians? Iran's Foreign Policy, the 'Bolshevik Threat,' and the Genesis of the Soviet-Iranian Treaty of 1921," in Cronin, *Iranian-Russian Encounters*, 261-97, https://research.manchester.ac.uk/en/publications/duping-the-british-and-outwitting-the-russians-irans-foreign-poli.
18. F. Eshraghi, "Anglo-Soviet Occupation of Iran in August 1941," *Middle Eastern Studies* 20, no. 1 (1984): 27-52.
19. Jamil Hasanli, *SSSR-IRAN: Azerbaydzhanskiy Krizis i Nachalo Kholodnoy Voyny (1941-1946 gg).* [USSR-IRAN: Azerbaijani Crisis and the Beginning of the Cold War (1941-6)] (Moscow: Geroi Otechestva, 2006).
20. Louise L'Estrange Fawcett, *Iran and the Cold War: The Azerbaijan Crisis of 1946* (Cambridge: Cambridge University Press, 2009).
21. Yuriy Lamin and Ruslan Pukhov, *Persidskiy Bastion* [Persian Bastion] (Moscow: Tsentr analiza strategiy I tekhnologiy, 2019), 282.
22. Elena Doroshenko, *Shiitskoe Dukhovenstvo v Sovremennom Irane* [Shiite Clergy in Modern Iran] (Moscow: Nauka, 1975).
23. For an excellent overview of the Islamic Revolution, see Fred Halliday, "The Genesis of the Iranian Revolution," *Third World Quarterly* 1, no. 4 (1979): 1-16.
24. Boris Ponomarev, "Sovmestnaya Bor'ba Rabochego i Natsional'no-Osvoboditel'nogo Dvizhenii Protiv Imperializma za Sotsial'nyi Progress [The Joint Struggle of the Workers and the National Liberation Movements against Imperialism for Social Progress]," *Kommunist*, no. 16 (1980): 30-44; Salech Aliev, "Antimonarkhicheskaya i Antiimperialisticheskaya Revolyutsiya v Irane [Anti-Monarchist and Anti-Imperial Revolution in Iran]," *Narody Azii i Afriki*, no. 3 (1979): 45-47; Rostislav Ul'ianovskii, "Iranskaya Revolyutsiya i Ee Osobennosti [Iranian Revolution and Its Peculiarities]," *Kommunist*, no. 10 (1982): 101-12.
25. Leonid Shebarshin, *Ruka Moskvy: Zapiski Nachal'nika Sovetskoi Razvedki* [Hand of Moscow: Notes by the Head of Soviet Intelligence] (Moscow: Tsentr-100, 1992).

26. Jahangir Karami, *Shūravī va jang-i Īrān va 'Irāq* [The Soviet Union and the Iran-Iraq War] (Tehran: Intishārāt-i Ṣafḥāh-i Jadīd, 2012).
27. At a July 1982 UNSC meeting following the Iranian advance into Iraq and refusal to accept a ceasefire, the Soviet representative proclaimed that Moscow is "interested in the removal of the sources of considerable tension in areas in the immediate vicinity of its own borders as well as in all other parts of the world." UNSC, "Official Records, 37th Year, 2383rd Meeting: The Situation between Iran and Iraq" (New York: United Nations, 12 July 1982), 3.
28. The first Soviet delegation to visit Tehran since the 1979 Revolution was led by Foreign Minister Eduard Shevardnadze. According to Shevardnadze's memoirs, during the visit Ali Akbar Velayati stated "do you know how important [your visit] is for us? It is a sign of great respect." Eduard Shevardnadze, *Kogda Rukhnul Zheleznyi Zanaves: Vstrechi i Vospominaniya* [When the Iron Curtain Crashed: Meetings and Memories] (Moscow: Evropa, 2009), 102-8.
29. During the summit, the Soviet leader and future president of Iran signed the Declaration on Principles of Relations between the USSR and Iran. The declaration stated that bilateral relations "will be built invariably on the basis of the aims and principles of the UN Charter ... mutual respect for national sovereignty and territorial integrity, non-aggression, non-interference in each other's internal affairs." "Deklaratsiya Printsipov Otnosheniy Druzhhestvennogo Sotrudnichestva mezhdu Soyuzom Sovetskikh Sotsialisticheskikh Respublik i Islamskoy Respublikoy Iran [Declaration of the Principles of Relations and Friendly Cooperation between the Union of Soviet Socialist Republics and the Islamic Republic of Iran]," *Pravda*, 22 June 1989. Eastview Digital Library.
30. Andrei Kozyrev, *Preobrazhenie* [Transfiguration] (Moscow: Mezhdunarodnye Otnosheniya, 1995).
31. The 1993 Russian constitutional crisis was a political standoff between President Boris Yeltsin and the Russian parliament, which culminated in a military siege of the parliament building and the forceful dissolution of the legislature. The crisis was fueled by deep divisions within the Russian political establishment, with conservative factions in parliament opposing Yeltsin's liberal economic reforms and pushing for a more assertive foreign policy that would restore Russia's great power status. Alexei Pushkov, "Mezhdu Velichiem i Bessiliem [Between Greatness and Powerlessness]," *Nezavisimaya Gazeta*, 23 December 1998, Integrum Digital Archive; Sergey Proskurin, "Sila i Bessilie Velikikh Derzhav [The Strength and Impotence of Great Powers]," *Nezavisimaya Gazeta*, 12 March 1997, Integrum Digital Archive; Stanislav Kondrashov, "Pritvoryat'sya Velikoy Derzhavoy ili Byt' Eyu [To Pretend to Be a Great Power or to Actually Be One?]," *Izvestiya*, 5 December 1995, Integrum Digital Archive; Vsevolod Rybakov, "Stanet Li Rossiya Velikoy Derzhavoy? [Will Russia Become a Great Power?]," *Nezavisimaya Gazeta*, 20 June 1992, Integrum Digital Archive.
32. Neil Malcolm et al., eds, *Internal Factors in Russian Foreign Policy* (New York: Oxford University Press, 1996).
33. Starting in 1994, the Office of Presidential Cooperation actively attracted scientists and engineers from post-Soviet nations to share sensitive technologies with Iran, facilitated by the Ministry of Intelligence and the Ministry of Defense. Russia has played a crucial role in training Iranian experts in high-tech fields since the early 1990s.
34. Vladimir Sazhin and Bondar' Yuriy, *Voennaya Moshch' Islamskoi Respubliki Iran* [The

Military Power of the Islamic Republic of Iran] (Moscow: Izdatel'stvo Moskovskogo universiteta, 2014), 95-118.

35. Pavel Felgenhauer, "Stoiat Li Rossiyskie Postavki Oruzhiya Iranu Ssory s Amerikoy [Are Russian Arms Deliveries to Iran a Quarrel with America?]," *Moskovskiye Novosti*, 28 November 2000, Integrum Digital Archive.

36. Gregoriy Strel'tsov, "Rossiiskii Eksport Vooruzhenii [Russian Arms Exports]," *Kommersant*, 3 February 1992; Anastasiya Romashkevich, "Rossiya Osvaivaet Aziatskie Rynki Oruzhiya [Russia Masters Asian Arms Markets]," *Kommersant*, 16 April 1993, Integrum Digital Archive; Vladimir Mikheev, "Iran Obzavelsya Raketnym Oruzhiem [Iran Has Acquired Missile Weapons," *Izvestiya*, 25 July 1998, Integrum Digital Archive.

37. Dmitry Gornostaev and Igor Korotchenko, "Sdelka Gor-Chernomyrdin: Ushcherb Rossii; Chetyre Milliarda? [Gore-Chernomyrdin Deal: Russia's Damage; Four Billion?]," *Nezavisimaya Gazeta*, 19 October 2000, Integrum Digital Archive; Dmitry Gornostaev and Igor Korotchenko, "Kreml" Otkazalsia Prodolzheniya El'tsinskoi Vneshnei Politiki [The Kremlin Refused to Continue the Yeltsin Foreign Policy]," *Nezavisimaya Gazeta*, 24 November 2000, Integrum Digital Archive.

38. Ivan Safronov, "Yadernye i Raketnye Programmy Irana i Bezopasnost' Rossii: Ramki Rossiysko-Iranskogo Sotrudnichestva [Iran's Nuclear and Missile Programs and Russia's Security: A Framework for Russian-Iranian Cooperation]," *Nauchnye Zapiski*, no. 8 (PIR Center, 1998), https://www.files.ethz.ch/isn/55031/nz8.pdf.

39. Interview with a former Minatom Official (Moscow), 2019.

40. Vladimir Nadein, "Andrey Kozyrev Zhaluetsya na Dvoynye Standarty Oon [Andrei Kozyrev Complains about the UN's Double Standards]," *Izvestiya*, 28 August 1995, Integrum Digital Archive; Vladimir Orlov, "'Yadernyy Predel': Vzglyad Rossiyskogo Razvedchika ['Nuclear Limit': The View of a Russian Intelligence Officer]," *Moskovskie Novosti*, 12 January 1994, Integrum Digital Archive; Vladimir Novikov, "Raketno-Yadernoe Nerasprostranenie: Vopros Irana [Nuclear Missile Nonproliferation: The Iran Question]," *Yadernyy Kontrol'*, 2002, 50-4.

41. Russia's commitment to building Bushehr "was reinforced by the political backlash in Russia to Yeltsin's agreement, in July 1993 after more than a year of stonewalling, to abandon a Soviet-era contract to sell 140 million worth of missile parts, production equipment, and technology to India." Parker, *Persian Dreams*, 104. The significance of light-water reactors in the context of nuclear nonproliferation is that they are considered less prone to being used for the production of weapons-grade nuclear materials compared to other types of reactors. In the context of Russia's nuclear cooperation with Iran, Moscow's insistence on constructing a light-water reactor at the Bushehr Nuclear Power Plant, while forgoing other projects that could have dual-use applications for nuclear weapons technology, was likely an attempt to balance its commercial interests with international concerns about Iran's nuclear ambitions. By focusing on light-water technology, Russia could argue that it was supporting Iran's peaceful nuclear energy program while minimizing the risk of contributing to any potential weapons program.

42. Vladimir Frolov and Yurii Melinikov, "Vokrug 'Yadernoy Sdelki' Rossii i Irana [Around the Russia-Iran Nuclear Deal]," *Kommersant*, 22 April 1995, Integrum Digital Archive.

43. In the case of Iran and India, the West's opposition to the implementation of these contracts was "an attempt to block a competitor"; although "on a global scale, the counterbalance to the West created by such agreements is very modest ... it

undermines the monopoly of world economic leaders in the field of high technologies, forcing them to reckon more with the interests of other states. This is an additional important factor of mutual interest of Russia and the most advanced countries of the South in the development of broad international cooperation." Rachik Avakov and Nodari Simoniya, eds, *Rossiya i Yug: Vozmozhnosti i Predely Vzaimodeistviya* [Russia and the South: Opportunities and Limits of Interaction] (Moscow: Finstatinform, 1996), 177.

44. "Iran: Arms and Weapons of Mass Destruction Suppliers," Everycrsreport.com (Congressional Research Service, 26 January 2001), https://www.everycrsreport.com/reports/RL30551.html#_1_6.
45. For example, the 1993 Russian Foreign Policy Concept explicitly mentions Iran as "a source of dangerous unpredictability and instability in the region, rendering vague the prospects of its general political development … Having ceased to be a U.S. partner, yet coming no closer to us, Iran represents a tangible factor of uncertainty in regional international affairs. The region in question is directly linked with some internal conflicts in the CIS, which is clearly visible in the way Tajikistan is being directly influenced by Iran and Afghanistan."
46. Alexei Bogaturov, Mikhail Kozhokin, and Konstantin Pleshakov, "Mezhdu Vostokom i Zapadom Kontseptsiya Vneshnei Politiki Rsfsr v Perekhodnyi Period [Between East and West: Foreign Policy Concept of the Russian Federation in Transitional Period]," *Nezavisimaya Gazeta*, 25 August 1991.
47. "Kontseptsiya Vneshnei Politiki Rossiiskoi Federatsii [Foreign Policy Concept of the Russian Federation]," *Diplomaticheskii Vestnik*, 1993, Eastview Digital Library.
48. Aziz Niyazi, "Tajikistan: Islam i Obshchestvo [Tajikistan: Islam and Society]," *Aziya i Afrika Segodnya*, no. 7 (1996): 26-31; Alexander Kuzmin, "Tajikistan: Prichiny i Uroki Grazhdanskoy Voyny [Tajikistan: Causes and Lessons of the Civil War]," in *Postsovetskaya Tsentral'naya Aziya: Poteri i Obreteniya* (Moscow: Vostochnaya literatura RAN, 1998), 220-39; Seyyed Rasoul Mousavi, "Naqsh-i Jomhūrī-i Islāmī-i Īrān Dar Pīshbar-i Moẓākerāt-i Ṣolḥ-ye=e Tājīkestān [The Role of the Islamic Republic of Iran in the Tajik Peace Mediation]," *Faslnāmah-i Motāla'āt-i Āsīyā-yi Markazī va Qafqāz*, no. 39 (2004): 7-27; Rakhimbek Bobokhonov, "Grazhdanskaya Voina v Tadzhikistane (1992-1997 Gody): Prichiny, Khod, Posledstviya i Uroki [The Civil War in Tajikistan (1992-7): Causes, Course, Consequences, and Lessons]," *Obshchestvennye Nauki i Sovremennost'*, no. 4 (2011): 74-83.
49. Mahmoud Vaezi, *Mīyānī'garī Dar Āsīyā-Yi Markazī va Qafqāz: Tajribah-i Jumhūrī-i Islāmī-i Īrān* [Mediation in Central Asia and the Caucasus: The Experience of the Islamic Republic of Iran] (Tehran: Daftar-i Muṭāla'āt-i Siyāsī va Bayn al-Milalī, 2010). Moreover, early skepticism of Iranian proselytization in the Muslim republics of the former Soviet Union was also tied to the civil war in Afghanistan and Moscow's fear of the ensuing instability emanating from Islamic extremism. Although Russia and Iran supported the Northern Alliance—a loose coalition of Afghan militias that formed in 1996 to resist the Taliban's rule in Afghanistan—there were genuine fears in Moscow that Iranian influence in Tajikistan would create a protracted conflict akin to the ongoing Afghan Civil War, which would necessitate Russia's involvement.
50. Interview with a former Russian diplomat (Moscow), 2019.
51. Vladimir Petrovich Kazimirchuk and Institut gosudarstva i prava (Rossiiskaya akademiya nauk), *Konstitutsiya i Zakon: Stabil'nost' i Dinamizm* [Constitution and Law: Stability and Dynamism], Konflikt Zakona i Obshchestva (Moscow: Yurid. kniga,

1998), https://catalog.hathitrust.org/Record/004015108; Vladimir Pryakhin, *Regional'nye Konflikty na Postsovetskom Prostranstve: (Abkhaziya, Yuzhnaya Osetiya, Nagornyi Karabakh, Pridnestrov'e, Tadzhikistan)* [Regional Conflicts in the Post-Soviet Space: (Abkhazia, South Ossetia, Nagorno-Karabakh, Transnistria, Tajikistan)] (Moscow: OOO "Izdatel'stvo GNOM i D," 2000).

52. Iranian and Russian interviewees who were involved in their governments in some capacity in the 1990s suggested that the IRGC actually helped train Russian special forces against the Chechen insurgency.

53. In December 1999, a delegation headed by Iranian Foreign Minister Kamal Kharrazi visited Moscow, as well as Dagestan, North Ossetia, and Ingushetia, which was followed one month later by another delegation of representatives of the foreign ministries of the OIC countries, headed by Deputy Iranian Foreign Minister Zarif. Konstantin Kazeev, "Poslanie Ministra Inostrannyh del Rossii po Situatsii na Severnom Kavkaze Peredano Rukovoditeliu MID Irana [Message from the Minister for Foreign Affairs of Russia on the Situation in the North Caucasus Handed Over to Iranian Foreign Minister]," ITAR-TASS, 10 December 1999, Arkhivy federal'nykh SMI, ITAR-TASS Novosti 1999-2002: ZAO; Kazeev, "Iran Prizyvaet k Mirnomu Uregulirovaniyu Chechenskogo Krizisa [Iran Calls for a Peaceful Settlement of the Chechen Crisis]," ITAR-TASS, 7 November 1999; "Sostoialsia Telefonnyi Razgovor Ministra Inostrannykh del Rossiiskoi Federatsii I.S. Ivanova s Ministrom Inostrannykh del Islamskoi Respubliki Iran K. Kharrazi [Telephone Conversation between the Minister of Foreign Affairs of the Russian Federation I. Ivanov and the Minister of Foreign Affairs of the Islamic Republic of Iran K. Kharrazi Took Place]," Press-Tsentr MID RF, 30 March 1999.

54. "Iran Kategoricheski protiv Vmeshatel'stva NATO i SShA v Uregulirovanie Situatsii na Severnom Kavkaze [Iran Is Categorically against NATO and U.S. Intervention in the Settlement of the Situation in the North Caucasus]," RIA Novosti, 2 February 2000.

55. Aleksei Gromyko, "Rossiya i Iran: Novaya Real'nost' [Russia and Iran: New Reality]," *Nezavisimaya Gazeta*, 26 June 1998.

56. Mehdi Sanaei, *Ravābiṭ-i Īrān va Āsiyā-yi Markazī: ravand'hā va chashm'andāz'hā* [Relations between Iran and Central Asia: Trends and Perspectives] (Tehran: Daftar-i Muṭāla'āt-i Siyāsī va Bayn al-Milalī, 2011).

57. Ghulam Riza Hashimi, *Pīshīnah-i Muẕākarāt va Asnād-i Panj Jānibah-i Daryā-Yi Khazar* [The History of Caspian Sea Negotiations and Documents from the Five Sides] (Tehran: Idārah-i Chāp va Intishārāt-i Vizārat-i Umūr-i Khārijah, 2020); Stanislav Pritchin, "Sotrudnichestvo Rossii i Irana v Regione Kaspiiskogo Moria: Novye Tendentsii i Perspektivy [Russia and Iran in the Caspian Region: Trends and Prospects]," in Sazhin and Dunaeva, *Rossiisko-Iranskie Otnosheniya Problemy i Perspektivy*, 75-82; Abd al-Karim Shahaydar, *Ḥall-i Ikhtilāfāt-i Rizhīm-i Ḥuqūqī-i Daryā-Yi Khazar* [Resolving Disputes of Legal Regime of Caspian Sea] (Tehran: Intishārāt-i Dādgustar, 2012).

58. Elena Dunaeva, "IRI i Kaspiiskaya Problema [Iran and the Caspian Problem]," in *Rol' i Mesto Irana v Regione*, ed. Nina Mamedova and Mahdi Imanipur (Moscow: Institut Vostokovedeniya RAN, 2007), 89-98; Dina Malysheva, "Geopoliticheskie Manevry na Kaspii [Geopolitical Maneuvers on Caspian]," *Mirovaya Ekonomika i Mezhdunarodnye Otnosheniya*, no. 5 (2006); Vitaly Naumkin, "The Security of the Caspian Sea Region," in *The Security of the Caspian Sea Region*, ed. Gennady Chufrin, 17.

59. Andranik Migranyan, "Rossiya-Iran: Popytka Torpedirovat' Neftyanoi Konsortsium

po Kaspiyu [Russia-Iran: Attempt to Torpedo Caspian Oil Consortium]," *Moskovskaya Pravda*, 9 November 1995, Integrum Digital Archive.

60. "Putin i Akhmadinezhad Vystupili za Sozdanie na Kaspii Voenno-Morskoi Gruppy Operativnogo Vzaimodeistviya 'Kasfor' [Putin and Ahmadinejad Advocated for the Creation of the Caspian Sea Naval Cooperation Task Group 'Casfor']," ITAR-TASS, 16 October 2007.
61. KASFOR is a coalition of the Caspian Sea littoral states—Russia, Kazakhstan, Azerbaijan, Turkmenistan, and Iran—aimed at enhancing regional maritime security. It focuses on joint naval operations, counter-terrorism, and information sharing to protect the Caspian Sea from threats like piracy and smuggling. "Iran Privetstvuet Predlozhenie Rossii po Sozdaniyu Sil Bystrogo Reagirovaniya na Kaspii [Iran Welcomes Russia's Proposal to Create a Rapid Reaction Force in the Caspian]," RIA Novosti, 6 November 2005; Igor Pugatarev, "Moskva Skolachivaet Voennyi Blok v Protivoves Vashingtonu [Moscow Knocks Together a Military Bloc in Opposition of Washington]," *Nezavisimaya Gazeta*, 25 January 2006.
62. Georgii Shakhnazarov, *Natsional'nye Interesy i Problemy Bezopasnosti Rossii: Doklad po Itogam Issledovaniya, Provedennogo Tsentrom Global'nykh Programm, Gorbachev-Fonda, v 1995-1997 gg* [National Interests and Security Problems of Russia: Report on the Results of a Study Conducted by the Center for Global Programs, Gorbachev Foundation, in 1995-7] (Moscow: Gorbachev-Fond, 1997); Sergey Kortunov, "Potentsial'nye Soyuzniki Rossii [Potential Allies of Russia]," *Nezavisimaya Gazeta*, 1 March 1996, Integrum Digital Archive.
63. The overwhelming success of the Communists in the December 1995 elections, like 1993, had an impact on Yeltsin's decision to replace Kozyrev with Yevgeny Primakov as foreign minister. Primakov's tenure as foreign minister was marked by greater attention to Moscow's interests in the CIS and an impetus to diversify foreign policy.
64. Viktor Kremenyuk, "Teryaet Li Zapad Rossiyu? [Is the West Losing Russia]," *Nezavisimaya Gazeta*, 1 December 1995, Integrum Digital Archive.
65. Pavel Felgenhauer, "Rossiiskoe Obshchestvo Prikhodit k Konsensusu po Voprosu o Natsional'nykh Interesakh [Russian Society Comes to a Consensus on the Issue of National Interests]," *Segodnya*, 26 May 1995, Integrum Digital Archive.
66. In October 1997, Khamenei stated that "the only ringing voice that declares its stance in the world in the face of arrogant policies without any consideration and is standing up to the order which the Americans wish to present as a unipolar order in the world is the Islamic Republic of Iran." At a meeting in Moscow with an Iranian parliamentary delegation led by Majlis Speaker Ali Akbar Nateq-Nuri in April 1997, Duma Chairman Gennadiy Seleznyov declared that "Iran like Russia does not see the need for NATO enlargement, is opposed to a unipolar world subordinate to U.S. interests." Vasily Pakin, "Iranskiy Vizit [Iranian Visit]," *Kommersant*, 12 April 1997, Integrum Digital Archive.
67. Mikhail Karpov and Dmitry Gornostayev, "Rossiya i SShA Soglasilis', Chto Ne Soglasny Drug s Drugom na Rasshirenie Severoatlanticheskogo Soyuza Moskva Otvetit Svoim Prodvizheniem na Vostok [Moscow and the USA Agreed to Disagree on the Enlargement of the North Atlantic Alliance, Moscow Will Respond with Its Advance to the East]," *Nezavisimaya Gazeta*, 22 March 1997.
68. The statement added that the goals of such cooperation are "to consolidate peace and regional security, strengthening the nonproliferation regime, establishing equal interaction between our states, creating favorable conditions for their economic

growth based on respect for sovereignty and avoidance of hegemonism and any form diktat on the world stage, the eradication of all forms of international terrorism." "Postanovlenie Gosudarstvennoi Dumy Federal'nogo Sobraniya Rossiiskoi Federatsii: O Zayavlenii Gosudarstvennoi Dumy Federal'nogo Sobraniya Rossiiskoi Federatsii 'O Rasshirenii Sotrudnichestva Mezhdu Rossiiskoi Federatsiei i Islamskoi Respublikoi Iran' [On the Statement of the State Duma of the Federal Assembly of the Russian Federation 'On Expanding Cooperation between the Russian Federation and the Islamic Republic of Iran']," *Gosudarstvennaya Duma*, 21 October 1998, https://base.garant.ru/6259155

69. Interview with a deputy foreign minister (Moscow), 2019.
70. Oleg Zhirnov and T. Ivleva, *Kosovskiy Krizis i Yego Posledstviya dlya Mirovogo Soobshchestva* [The Kosovo Crisis and Its Consequences for the World Community] (Moscow: Rossiyskaya akademiya nauk, 2002).
71. With the outbreak of the Bosnian Civil War, Russia joined the implementation of UNSC Resolution 757 and froze political, economic, scientific, and cultural ties with Serbia. Russia's support of economic sanctions on Serbia unleashed a slew of criticism from the Russian elite, eventually resulting in the December 1992 Supreme Soviet Resolution calling for sanctions on all parties and demanding Russia wield its veto in the case of a military intervention. Until 1994, Russian diplomacy, due to certain internal and external circumstances, failed to develop an independent foreign policy position in the Balkans conflict. The overall shift in foreign policy after the events in the autumn and winter of 1993 resulted in Russia's greater willingness to diverge from U.S. interests, though Moscow's limited capability to do so was clear in its role in the Dayton Accords. During the Bosnian Civil War, Iran's criticism of the UNSC and the arms embargo combined with its covert weapons supplies to Bosnian Muslims through Croatia inflamed Russian concerns about the Islamic factor in the conflict. See Boris Shmelev, "Yugoslavskiy Krizis i Rossiya [Yugoslavian Crisis and Russia]," in *Balkany mezhdu Proshlym i Budushchim* [The Balkans between Past and Future] (Moscow: Izd-vo "Aprel' 85," 1995), 79-91; Konstantin Voronov, "Evropa i Rossiya posle Balkanskoy Voyny 1999 G.: Dramatichnye Uroki [Europe and Russia after the Balkan War of 1999: Dramatic Lessons]," *Mirovaya Ekonomika i Mezhdunarodnye Otnosheniya*, no. 4 (2000): 27-35; Viktor Kremenyuk, "Rossiya-SShA: Pervye Uroki Balkanskogo Krizisa 1999 G. [Russia-USA: The First Lessons of the 1999 Balkan Crisis]," *SShA-Kanada: Ekonomika, Politika, Kul'tura*, no. 1 (2001): 5-15. Iran capitalized on the situation in the Balkans to demonstrate its role as a champion of oppressed Muslim populations, which was at odds with Russia's increasingly pro-Serbian policy after 1994. Russia engaged with Iran, which served as a member of the Islamic contact group during the Bosnian Civil War and, later, as the chairman of the contact group during the Kosovo crisis. See Hashemi Rafsanjani, See Hashemi Rafsanjani, *Sardār-i sāzandagī: kārnāmah va khāṭirāt-i Hāshimī Rafsanjānī sāl-i 1375* [Sardar Sazandegi: Biography and Memoirs of Hashemi Rafsanjani in 1996] (Tehran: Daftar-i Nashr-i Ma'ārif-i Inqilāb, 2019); Aḥmad Ja'farī and Ḥabīb Allāh Valī Allāhī Malikshāh, *Rīshah'hā-yi buḥrān-i Kūzuvū va dakhālat-i niẓāmī-i Nātū* [Roots of Kosovo's Crisis and the Military Intervention of NATO] (Tehran: Daftar-i Muṭāla'āt-i Siyāsī va Bayn al-Milalī, 2001). Sergei Guly, "U Nato v Kosovo Svoia Gruppirovka, i u Rossii Budet Svoia [Nato Has Its Group in Kosovo and Russia Will Have Its Own]," [Sardar Sazandegi: Biography and Memoirs of Hashemi Rafsanjani in 1996] (Tehran: Daftar-i Nashr-i Ma'ārif-i Inqilāb, 2019); Aḥmad Ja'farī and Ḥabīb Allāh Valī Allāhī Malikshāh,

Rīshah'hā-yi buḥrān-i Kūzuvū va dakhālat-i niẓāmī-i Nātū [Roots of Kosovo's Crisis and the Military Intervention of NATO] (Tehran: Daftar-i Muṭāla'āt-i Siyāsī va Bayn al-Milalī, , 2001). Sergey Guly, "U Nato v Kosovo Svoia Gruppirovka, i u Rossii Budet Svoia [Nato Has Its Group in Kosovo and Russia Will Have Its Own]," *Novye Izvestia*, 2 July 1999; Marat Razhbadinov, "Udary po Iugoslavii Razdelili Islamskii Mir [Impact of the Yugoslavian Conflict on the Muslim World]," *Nezavisimaya Gazeta*, 13 April 1999.

72. Rosemary Foot, "Introduction," in *Order and Justice in International Relations*, ed. Rosemary Foot, John Lewis Gaddis, and Andrew Hurrell (Oxford: Oxford University Press, 2003), 17.
73. Anatolii Torkunov, "Mezhdunarodnye Otnosheniya posle Kosovskogo Krizisa [International Relations after the Kosovo Crisis]," *Mezhdunarodnaya Zhizn* 12, no. 1 (1999): 45.
74. In Tehran, President Mohammad Khatami described military action as illegal, arguing that "the steps taken against Yugoslavia would not benefit the oppressed Muslims of Kosovo but would only serve the interests of major powers seeking to impose their domination over the Balkans." "Iran Report: Khatami's French Trip Canceled," RFE/RL, 5 April 1999.
75. William Samii, "Iran: Tehran Looks to Moscow in Kosovo Crisis," RFE/RFL, 9 April 1999.
76. Peter Vlasov and Pavel Bykov, "Kosovskaya Reviziya [Kosovo Revision]," *Ekspert*, 26 April 1999.
77. Yuri Tavrovsky, "Tri Kruga Novoi Ideologii [Three Circles of New Ideology]," *Nezavisimaya Gazeta*, 8 August 1999; Rajab Safarov, "Iranskaya Al'ternativa [Iranian Alternative]," *Oborona I Bezopasnost"(Vps)*, 17 May 1999.
78. Alexander Lukin, "Nato i Rossiya posle Kosovo [NATO and Russia after Kosovo]," *Nezavisimaya Gazeta*, 9 June 1999.
79. "Ministry Inostrannykh del Rossii i Irana Vystupili s Sovmestnym Zayavleniem po Pravam Cheloveka [The Foreign Ministers of Russia and Iran Issued a Joint Statement on Human Rights]," RIA Novosti, 28 November 1999, Integrum Digital Archive.
80. In an interview with *Rabochaya Tribuna*, Iran's Foreign Minister Kharrazi expressed Iran's desire to be a part of Primakov's proposed "strategic triangle" between Russia, China, and India as a "union of four civilizations … different races, nations, and religions." The Iranian foreign minister stressed that if such a union came to fruition, "the political map of the world will change and together we will be a real force. The world will cease to be unipolar and, therefore, can develop harmoniously." Kirill Voronin, "Soyuz Chetyrekh: Iran Khochet Prisoedinit'sya k Soyuzu Rossii, Kitaya i Indii [Union of Four: Iran Wants to Join the Union of Russia, China, and India]," *Rabochaya Tribuna*, 4 November 1999, Integrum Digital Archive.
81. Anatoly Torkunov and Artem Mal'gin, *Sovremennye Mezhdunarodnye Otnosheniya* [Modern International Relations] (Moscow: Aspekt Press, 2012).
82. It also underscored the primacy Russia placed on the UN, stipulating that Moscow rejects "all attempts to introduce into international language such concepts as 'humanitarian intervention' and 'limited sovereignty' in order to justify unilateral force that bypasses the UNSC"; "Kontseptsiya Vneshnei Politiki Rossiiskoi Federatsii [Foreign Policy Concept of the Russian Federation]," *Diplomaticheskii Vestnik* 8 (2000): 3-11.
83. Khatami's visit to Moscow was preceded by a surge of U.S. accusations about the dangers of military-technical and civilian nuclear energy cooperation between Russia

and Iran. Alexander Shumilin, "Putin i Hatami Vspomnili o Vesne [Putin and Khatami Remembered the Spring]," *Izvestiya*, 13 March 2001. Vladimir Sazhin noted that the convergences in Russian and Iranian interests in the Middle East and the Near Abroad provided the basis for a new alignment directed at the emergence and intensification of various threats. Vladimir Sazhin, "Kakovy Ramki Rossiiski-Iranskogo Partnerstva?" [What Are the Frameworks of the Russian-Iranian Partnership?]," *Nezavisimaya Gazeta*, 1 March 2001.

84. In October 2000, Sergey Ivanov, the head of the Russian Security Council and an influential voice who advocated for closer relations with Iran, met with Khatami and the Iranian leadership in Tehran. In Iran, Ivanov conveyed a personal message from Putin, which stated that "one of Russia's long-term foreign policy priorities" was "the development of good-unneighborly relations" with Iran. "Prezident Rossiiskoi Federatsii V.V. Putin Napravil Poslanie Prezidentu Islamskoi Respubliki Iran Seiedu Mohammadu Hatami [President of the Russian Federation Vladimir Putin Sent a Message to the President of the Islamic Republic of Iran Seyyed Mohammad Khatami]," Press-Sluzhba Prezidenta RF, 16 October 2000.

85. The Color Revolutions were sparked by disputed elections and fueled by popular discontent with corruption, economic stagnation, and political repression. These movements often adopted distinctive colors or symbols, such as the Rose Revolution in Georgia (2003), the Orange Revolution in Ukraine (2004), and the Tulip Revolution in Kyrgyzstan (2005). The Color Revolutions were widely perceived as a threat by Russia, which viewed them as Western-backed attempts to undermine its influence in the post-Soviet space and promote regime change in countries closely aligned with Moscow.

86. The implications of Putin's stance became evident in December 2000 when Defense Minister Igor Sergeyev's visit to Iran set the stage for deeper military engagement between the two countries. Sergeyev's trip culminated in a series of high-level discussions in Moscow with his Iranian counterpart, Defense Minister Ali Shamkhani, that paved the way for the negotiation of fresh arms contracts, signaling a revitalized partnership between Russia and Iran that was no longer constrained by the terms of the prior agreement with the United States. Later, the agreement for the Tor-M1 occurred during then-Secretary of Iran's SNSC Hassan Rouhani's meeting with President Putin in 2004.

87. "Voenno-Tekhnicheskoe Sotrudnichestvo Irana i Rossii [Military-Technical Cooperation between Iran and Russia]," TASS, 15 January 2015, Integrum Digital Archive.

88. Vadim Kozyulin, "Voenno-Tekhnicheskoe Sotrudnichestvo Rossii s Problemnymi Stranami [Russia's Military-Technological Cooperation with Problematic Countries]," *Voprosy Bezopasnosti: PIR-Tsentr* 5, no. 19 (109) (October 2001).

89. For more on the S-300 and the connection to the Iranian nuclear program, see John W. Parker, "Russia and the Iranian Nuclear Program: Replay or Breakthrough?," Institute for National Strategic Studies Strategic Perspectives (Washington, DC, March 2012).

90. Signed in 1972, the Anti-Ballistic Missile (ABM) Treaty between the United States and the Soviet Union limited the development and deployment of nationwide missile defense systems. By restricting such defenses, the treaty sought to preserve strategic stability by maintaining mutual vulnerability to nuclear retaliation.

91. Anatoli Diakov, "The Nuclear Fuel Cycle," in *At the Nuclear Threshold: The Lessons of*

North Korea and Iran for the Nuclear Non-Proliferation Regime, ed. Alexei Arbatov (Moscow: Carnegie Endowment for International Peace, 2007), 127-41.

92. Despite ongoing criticisms in Tehran, Russian and Iranian representatives met to discuss the Russian proposal in January 2006. While Russian negotiators advised Iran not to abandon its enrichment moratorium, Iran defied the moratorium by ordering IAEA inspectors to remove their seals from the Natanz facility and resuming enrichment activities. Despite expressing concern, President Putin instructed Foreign Minister Lavrov to continue seeking a diplomatic solution while safeguarding Russia's economic interests. After Iran resumed conversion at Esfahan in August 2005 and enrichment at Natanz in January 2006, Russia ultimately backed the IAEA Board of Governors' decision in March 2006 to transfer the discussion of the Iranian nuclear issue to the UNSC.
93. To protect business interests, Moscow pressured Tehran to return spent fuel to Russia to quell U.S. concerns over Iran's ability to convert spent fuel from Bushehr into weapons-grade plutonium. Throughout the P5+1 meetings, Russia generally advocated for softer approaches, even proposing a plan in 2005 for Iran to shift its enrichment program to Russia, which was rejected by Iran. Anton Khlopkov and Anna Lutkova, "Pochemu tak Dolgo Stroilas' Busherskaya AES? [Why Did the Bushehr Nuclear Power Plant Take So Long to Build?]," Tsentr energetiki i bezopasnosti, 8 September 2011, 14. Aleksandr Kalyadin, "Yadernyi Vyzov Irana v Rakurse Soveta Bezopasnosti OON [Iran Nuclear Challenge from the Perspective of the UN Security Council]," *Mirovaya Ekonomika i Mezhdunarodnye Otnosheniya*, no. 12 (2008), https://elibrary.ru/item.asp?id=11634252&. Aleksei Georgievich Arbatov, "Iranskii Yadernyi Uzel [Iran's Nuclear Knot]," *Aziya i Afrika Segodnya*, no. 2 (631) (2010), https://elibrary.ru/item.asp?id=16901349.
94. Russian arms sales to Iran faced increasing scrutiny following the December 2006 UN arms embargo on Tehran and a series of U.S. sanctions in 2006, 2007, and 2008 on Rosoboroneksport, Russia's state-owned arms exporter. Although Russia voted in favor of UNSC Resolution 1737, which prohibited the supply of technology related to nuclear weapons, the imposition of U.S. sanctions on Rosoboroneksport inflamed anti-American sentiment among members of the political establishment, who viewed it as an affront to Moscow's independence.
95. Arbatov, "Iranskii Yadernyi Uzel [Iran's Nuclear Knot]."
96. Kalyadin, "Yadernyi Vyzov Irana v Rakurse Soveta Bezopasnosti OON [Iran Nuclear Challenge from the Perspective of the UN Security Council]."
97. Alexei Bogaturov, "Tri Pokoleniya Vneshnepoliticheskikh Doktrin Rossii [Three Generations of Russian Foreign Doctrines]," *Mezhdunarodnye Protsessy* 5, no. 1 (13) (2007): 54-69; Anatolii Torkunov, "Slovo i Delo v Otnosheniyakh SShA s Rossiei," *Izvestiya*, 31 March 2009.
98. In particular, by offering a pretext to securitize issues of domestic state order, the War on Terror emboldened the discursive legitimacy of the Russian narrative on the "arc of crisis" from Afghanistan to Chechnya.
99. Elena Dunaeva, "Regionalizm vo Vneshnei Politike Islamskoi Respubliki Iran (k Voprosu o Vstuplenii IRI v ShOS) [Regionalism in the Foreign Policy of the Islamic Republic of Iran (on the Issue of Iran's Membership in the SCO)]," in *Aktual'nye Problemy Rasshireniya Shankhaiskoi Organizatsii Sotrudnichestva: Materialy Mezhdunarodnoi Konferentsii (Foruma); "Na Vtorom Treke. Rol' Grazhdanskogo Obshchestva i Obshchestvennoi Diplomatii v Dal'neishem Razvitii i Rasshirenii Shankhaiskoi Organizatsii Sotrudnichestva"*

[Current Issues of the Expansion of the Shanghai Cooperation Organisation: Materials of the International Conference (Forum): "On the Second Track: The Role of Civil Society and Public Diplomacy in the Further Development and Expansion of the Shanghai Cooperation Organisation] (Moscow: Institut Stran SNG, 2016), 85-90.

100. Enayatollah Yazdani, Najmah Massoudi, and Hosein Dalvand, "Bar'rasī-i Rūykard-i Amnīyatī-i Jumhūrī-i Islāmī-i Īrān Bih Āsiyā-Yi Markazī [Survey of the Islamic Republic of Iran's Security Approach to Central Asia]," *Faslnāmah-i Mutāla'āt-i Āsiyā-Yi Markazī va Qafqāz* 18, no. 79 (1 November 2014): 139-66.

101. Parker, *Persian Dreams*, 219.

102. In January 2003, Russian Deputy Foreign Minister Vyacheslav Trubnikov met with Iranian Deputy Foreign Minister Mohsen Aminzadeh in Moscow to signal the two countries' shared commitment to UNSC Resolution 1441 and a political and diplomatic settlement of the Iraqi problem "under the aegis of the United Nations and on the basis of international law." "O Vizite v Rossiiu Zamestitelya Ministra Inostrannyh del Irana M. Aminzade [On the Visit to Russia of the Deputy Minister of Foreign Affairs of Iran M. Aminzade]," Press-Tsentr MID RF, 15 January 2003. Two weeks later, Deputy Foreign Minister Yuri Fedotov traveled to Tehran for consultations with Kharrazi on the Iraq issue, during which both countries stressed there was a need for "strengthening the central role of the UN" and vowed to continue "close consultations" on developments. "O Vstreche Zamestitelya Ministra Inostrannyh del Rossii Iu. V. Fedotova s Ministrom Inostrannyh del Irana K. Harrazi [Russian Deputy Minister of Foreign Affairs Yuri Fedotov Meets with Iranian Minister of Foreign Affairs Kamal Harrazi]," Press-Tsentr MID RF, 3 February 2003. During Fedotov's trip, Kharrazi reiterated Iran's support for the continuation of UN inspections in Iraq, while President Khatami lauded Russian, French, and German efforts to reach a political-diplomatic solution. Nikolai Terekhov, "Rossiya i Iran za Tsentral'nuiu Rol' OON [Russia and Iran for the Central Role of the UN]," RIA Novosti, 3 February 2003.

103. "Stenogramma Vystupleniya Ministra Inostrannykh del Rossiiskoi Federatsii I.S. Ivanova na Press-Konferentsii po Itogam Peregovorov s Ministrom Inostrannykh del Islamskoi Respubliki Iran K. Kharrazi, Tegeran, 11 Marta 2003 Goda [Transcript of Remarks by Russian Minister of Foreign Affairs I.S. Ivanov at Press Conference following Talks with Iranian Foreign Minister K. Kharrazi, Tehran, 11 March 2003]," Press-Tsentr MID RF, 11 March 2003; "O Rossiisko-Iranskih Konsul'tatsiyah [On Russian-Iranian Consulations]," Press-Tsentr MID RF, 4 February 2003.

104. Ebrahim Mottaghi, Khoram Baghayee, and Maysam Rahimi, "Bar'rasī-i Siyāsat-i Khārijī-i Āmrīkā Dar Khāvar-i Miyānah Pas Az 11 Siptāmbar [A Study of American Foreign Policy in the Middle East after September 11]," *Faṣlnāmah-i 'Ilmī Taḥqīqāt-i Siyāsī va Bayn al-Milalī-i* 1, no. 4 (1 December 2009): 1-26; Mandana Tishyar, *Barrasi-Yi Naqsh-i Jughrafiya-Yi Siyasī-Yi* [Foreign Policy of Iraq: The Role of Iraq's Geopolitics in Its Relations with Neighbors] (Tihrān: Muallifin, 2005); Elaheh Koolaee, Mandana Tishehyar, and Mahmud Muhammadi, *Sāzmān-i Paymān-i Ātlāntīk-i Shimālī (Nātū): digargūnī dar ma'mūrīyat'hā va kārkard'hā* [North Atlantic Treaty Organization: Changes in Missions and Functions] (Tehran: Mu'assasah-i Chāp va Intishārāt-i Dānishgāh-i Tihrān, 2007).

105. Vladimir Sazhin, "Problemy Regional'noi Bezopasnosti i Iran [Problems of Regional Security and Iran]," in *Politika RF I IRI v Regional'nom Kontekste: TsA, Kavkaz, Blizhnii Vostok* [The Policies of the Russian Federation and Iran in the Regional Context:

Central Asia, the Caucasus, and the Middle East], ed. Elena Dunaeva and Nina Mamedova (Moscow: Institut Vostokovedeniya RAN, 2011), 149.

106. Vitaly Naumkin, "Tegeran Mog by Prinyat' k Svedeniyu [Tehran Might Take Note]," *Vremya Novostei*, 11 October 2007.

107. Farhad Dimashqee, "Nigāh-i Takāpū-Yi Dushmanān Barā-Yi Ījād-i Inqilāb-i Makhmalīn Dar Īrān [Enemies Trying to Look for a Velvet Revolution in Iran]," *Rūznāmih-i Īrān*, 2 July 2009.

108. Ḥujjat Ilāh Murādī, 'Alī Muḥammad Nā'īnī, and Amīr Hūshang Ṭahmāsbī'pūr, *Qudrat va jang-i narm: az naẓarīyah tā 'amal* [Power and Soft War: From Theory to Practice] (Tehran: Nashr-i Sāqī, 2009); Amīr Hūshang Ṭahmāsbī'pūr and Humāyūn Ārāmish, *Abzārhā-yi jang-i narm 'alayh-i Jumhūrī-i Islāmī-i Īrān* [Soft War Tools against the Islamic Republic of Iran] (Tehran: Nashr-i Sāqī, 2011); Abbas Firuzi, *Mabānī-i jang-i narm va rīshah'yābī-i ān dar tahājum-i farhangī* [Foundations of Soft War and Its Roots in Cultural Invasion] (Qom: Shikūfah-i Yās, 2010).

109. Mohiaddin Mesbahi, "Eurasia between Russia, Turkey, and Iran," in *Key Players and Regional Dynamics in Eurasia: The Return of the "Great Game"*, ed. Maria Raquel Freire and Roger E. Kanet (London: Palgrave Macmillan, 2010), 167.

110. Andrei Baklanov, "Bol'shoi Blizhnii Vostok i Bol'shaya Politiki: Blizhnevostochnyi Mirnyi Protsess: Kak Vosstanovit" Dinamiku? [Greater Middle East and Greater Politics: The Middle East Peace Process; How to Restore Momentum?]," *Aziya i Afrika Segodnya*, no. 6 (2006): 32-42.

111. Interview with a former Russian ambassador to Libya (Moscow), 2019,

112. Bogaturov, "Tri Pokoleniya Vneshnepoliticheskikh Doktrin Rossii [Three Generations of Russian Foreign Doctrines]."

113. "Vystuplenie i Diskussiya na Myunkhenskoy Konferentsii po Voprosam Politiki Bezopasnosti [Speech and Discussion at the Munich Conference on Security Policy]," Press-Sluzhba Prezidenta RF, 10 February 2007,http://kremlin.ru/events/president/transcripts/24034.

114. Two months after assuming office, in July 2008, Medvedev approved a new version of the Russian Foreign Policy Concept that set out the following principles of Russian foreign policy: the rejection of unipolarity and the formation of a polycentric world order and the vigorous protection of Russia's interests in the "near abroad." "Kontseptsiya Vneshney Politiki Rossiyskoy Federatsii [The Concept of Foreign Policy of the Russian Federation]," Press-Sluzhba Prezidenta RF, 15 July 2008, http://kremlin.ru/acts/news/785.

115. Roy Allison, "Russia Resurgent? Moscow's Campaign to 'Coerce Georgia to Peace,'" *International Affairs (Royal Institute of International Affairs 1944-)* 84, no. 6 (2008): 1145-71.

116. Ronald Asmus, *A Little War That Shook the World: Georgia, Russia, and the Future of the West* (New York: St. Martin's Publishing Group, 2010).

117. "Pāsukh-i Īrān Bih 5+1: Nātū, 'āmil-i Buḥrān Dar Qafqāz [Iran's Response to the 5+1: NATO, the Crisis Factor in the Caucasus]," *Resalat*, 23 April 2009, 21.

118. Niloofar Mansourian, "Bāzi-ye Irān va Rusiyah Ejlās-e Shānghāy [Iran and Russia's Game at the Shanghai Summit," *E'temād*, 30 August 2008, 1.

2. RETRENCHING AFTER THE RESET

1. Robert Tait, "From Russia, without Much Love," RFE/RL, 15 November 2010, https://www.rferl.org/a/From_Russia_Without_Much_Love_/2220933.html.

2. For an overview of U.S.-Russia relations, see Angela E. Stent, *The Limits of Partnership: U.S.-Russian Relations in the Twenty-First Century; Updated Edition* (Princeton: Princeton University Press, 2015).
3. Roy Allison, *Russia, the West, and Military Intervention* (Oxford: Oxford University Press, 2013).
4. Eduard Solov'ev, "Rossiya Vo Vneshnepoliticheskoi Strategii B. Obamy: Preemstvennost" i Obnovlenie [Russia in Barack Obama's Foreign Policy Strategy: Continuity and Renewal]," *Mirovaya Ekonomika I Mezhdunarodnye Otnosheniya*, no. 8 (2010).
5. Alexei Arbatov, "Iranskii Yadernyi Uzel [Iranian Nuclear Knot]," *Sovremennaya Evropa*, no. 1 (29) (2007): 24-36.
6. "Avalīn Nīshānahā-Yi Sūstī-i Qat'nāmah 1696 Āshkār Shud [The First Signs of Weakness in Resolution 1696 Revealed]," *Keyhan*, 6 August 2006, 2.
7. "Nīgarānī Shadīd-i Rījīm-i Ṣahyūnīstī Az Furūsh-i Sīstam-i Mūshakī - as 300-i Rūsīyah Bih Īrān [Severe Concern of the Zionist Regime over Russia's Sale of the S-300 Missile System to Iran]," *Keyhan*, 23 December 2008; "Rūsīyah va Amrīkā Bāyad Hamkārī Nazdīkī Dāshteh Bāshand [Russia and America Must Have Close Cooperation]," *E'temad*, 7 March 2009. This hesitancy was underscored when the last sanctions resolution before Obama took office, UNSCR 1803, was adopted on 3 March 2008. The resolution was a response to Iran's persistent defiance of previous UN resolutions and the IAEA's demands that Tehran halt its uranium enrichment and reprocessing activities.
8. William Joseph Burns, *The Back Channel: A Memoir of American Diplomacy and the Case for Its Renewal* (London: Hurst, 2019).
9. "Avalīn Nīshānahā-Yi Sūstī-i Qat'nāmah 1696 Āshkār Shud [The First Signs of Weakness in Resolution 1696 Revealed]," 2.
10. Andrei Baklanov, "Rossiiskoe Posrednichestvo na Peregovorakh Vokrug Yadernoi Programmy Irana [Russian Mediation in the Negotiations on Iran's Nuclear Program]," *Etnosotsium i Mezhnatsional'naya Kul'tura*, no. 9 (41) (2011), https://elibrary.ru/item.asp?id=18813647.
11. Michael McFaul, *From Cold War to Hot Peace: An American Ambassador in Putin's Russia* (New York: HarperCollins, 2018).
12. Some in Russia were skeptical about the prospects of the reset, such as Sergey Karaganov, who wrote that there was a need for a fundamental "reconfiguration" rather than just a "reset" in U.S.-Russia relations, which would not address Russia's primary interests. Sergey Karaganov, "Perenastroyka, a Ne 'Perezagruzka' [Reconfiguration, Not 'Reset']," *Rossiya v Global'noi Politike*, 31 August 2009, 60-72.
13. Anonymized interview with a Russian diplomat (Moscow), 2019.
14. Vasily Krivokhizha, "Problemy i Nekotorye Rezul'taty Kursa 'Perezagruzki' v Rossiisko-Amerikanskikh Otnosheniyakh [Problems and Some Results of the 'Reset' Course in Russian-American Relations]," *SShA-Kanada: Ekonomika, Politika, Kul'tura*, no. 4 (520) (2013): 3-24.
15. Arslan Morshifi, "Taqābal Baḥāyi Ta'āmul [Confrontation Instead of Interaction]," *Jam i Jam*, 20 June 2010, 10.
16. "Medvedev Dar Dīdār Bā Clinton: Taḥrīm'hā-Yi Jadīd 'alīh-i Īrān Ẓarūrī Khāhad Būd Agar ... [Medvedev in Meeting with Clinton: New Sanctions against Iran Will Be Necessary If ...]," *Rūznāmah-i Āftāb Yazd*, 14 October 2009, 11.

17. "Neudavshayasya Oranzhevaya Revolyutsiya [Failed Orange Revolution]," *Politicheskii Klass*, 15 August 2009, Integrum Digital Archive.
18. "Ra'īs-i Jumhūr bāzgasht bih Tihrān: Naqsh-i Īrān dar ijlās-i Shānghāy muhimm va ta'<u>s</u>īr'guzār ast [President Returns to Tehran: Iran's Role in the Shanghai Summit Is Important and Influential]," *Kayhan*, 18 June 2009, 3; "6 Pīshnihād-i Ra'īs-i Jumhūr bih Ijlās-i Shānghāy [The President's Six Proposals to the Shanghai Summit]," *Jam-i Jam*, 17 June 2009, 2.
19. "Glavy Gosudarstv: Uchastnikov ShOS Pozdravili Prezidenta Irana s Pobedoy na Vyborakh [Heads of the SCO Member States Congratulated the Iranian President on the Election Victory]," RIA Novosti, 16 June 2009, Integrum Digital Archive.
20. "Barrasī-i muhimtarīn vīzhagī hā-yi Inqilāb-i makhmalīn [The Study of the Most Important Features of a Velvet Revolution]," Fars News, 7 July 2009.
21. Farhad Dimashqee, "Nigāh-i Takāpū-Yi Dushmanān Barā-Yi Ījād-i Inqilāb-i Makhmalīn Dar Īrān [Enemies Trying to Look for a Velvet Revolution in Iran]," *Rūznāmih-i Īrān*, 2 July 2009.
22. "Qānūn-i mu'āhadahnāmah-'i hamkārī bayn-i Vazārat-i Kishvar-i Jumhūrī-i Islāmī-i Īrān va Vazārat-i Kishvar-i Fidirāsiyūn-i Rūsīyah [Law of the Cooperation Agreement between the Ministry of Interior of the Islamic Republic of Iran and the Ministry of Interior of the Russian Federation]," Majlis-i Shūrā-yi Islāmī 53160/266 (12 December 2013), https://rc.majlis.ir/fa/law/show/867603.
23. Interview with a former Rosatom deputy director (Moscow), 2019.
24. Interview with a former diplomat in Russia's arms control department (Moscow), 2019.
25. Hanna Notte, "UN Security Council Resolution 1929 on Iran: US-Russian Cooperation and the Quest for Diffuse Reciprocity," in *The United States, Russia, and Nuclear Nonproliferation*, ed. Sarah Bidgood and William C. Potter (Basingstoke: Palgrave, 2020), 37-86.
26. For background, see Notte, "UN Security Council Resolution 1929 on Iran."
27. Prior to Fordow and the TRR, Russia was reluctant to endorse additional sanctions on Iran. According to a Russian nonproliferation expert, the Russians already considered sanctions unproductive and not conducive to the resolution of the crises. However, Russian thinking on Iran was shifting. In Moscow, there was a view that the Obama administration would offer an opportunity for change.
28. "Iran Snova Prigrozil Nachat' Obogashchenie Urana [Iran Threatens to Resume Uranium Enrichment]," Pravda.ru, 24 January 2010.
29. "Gosudarstvennyi Komitet Rossiiskoi Federatsii po Rybolovstvu Informatsionno-Analiticheskii Tsentr [Information-Analytical Center of the State Committee of the Russian Federation for Fisheries]," IA Integrum Media: Novosti Kompanii, 6 December 2001.
30. In November 2009, reports indicated that Iran was "mortally offended" by Russia's support for the latest IAEA resolution on the Iranian nuclear program. Iranian newspapers and political commentators described Russia's stance as a betrayal, arguing that it violated existing agreements between the two countries. Some blamed the Green Movement on the Russian and Chinese vote too. "Ra'y-i Chīn va Rūsīyah 'alayhah-'i Īrān natījah-'i shi'ārhā-yi iṣlāḥ'ṭalabān ast! [The Vote of China and Russia against Iran Is the Result of the Slogans of the Reformists!]," *Aftab-e Yazd*, 30 November 2009, 3, https://www-magiran-com.ezp-prod1.hul.harvard.edu/article/1995236.

31. Specifically, in reference to Iran's ballistic missile program, Russia wanted to ensure that the language would not support U.S. claims about Iran's ballistic missile threat as a pretext to deploy more missile defense systems in Europe.
32. "Iran Snova Prigrozil Nachat' Obogashchenie Urana [Iran Threatens to Resume Uranium Enrichment]," Pravda.ru, 24 January 2010, Integrum Digital Archive
33. "Ahmadinejad: Fursathā-yi ziādi bih Obama dādim [Ahmadinejad: We Gave Many Opportunities to Obama]," ISNA, 4 May 2010.
34. Arslan Morshidi, "Pāyān-i māh-i ʻasal-i Īrān va Rūsīyah [The End of the Honeymoon Month for Iran and Russia]," *Jam-i Jam*, 10 May 2010. At the Conference on Interaction and Confidence-Building Measures in Asia, Ahmadinejad declared that "Russian leaders should not create a situation that makes [the] Iranian people place Russia in the ranks of their historic enemies. Today, it has become difficult for us to explain Medvedev's behavior to the Iranian nation. The [Iranian] people don't know whether [the Russians] are our friends or are after something else." "Russian President Medvedev Warns Iran to Heed Voice of International Community," Voice of America, 5 June 2010, https://www.voanews.com/a/medvedev-deal-exists-for-iran-nuclear-sanctions-95681929/118868.html.
35. Hossamuddin Brouman, "Gham′nāmah-ī bih nām-i qaṭʻ′nāmah [A Lament Named Resolution]," *Keyhan*, 13 June 2010, 2, https://www-magiran-com / article/2104634.
36. Arslan Morshidi, "Taqābal Baḥāyi Taʻāmul [Confrontation Instead of Interaction]," *Jam-i Jam*, 20 June 2010, 10; "Iran Says Resolution 1929 Is Illegal, Threatens Retaliation," Mehr News Agency, 18 June 2010, https://en.mehrnews.com/news/40393/Iran-says-Resolution-1929-is-illegal-threatens-retaliation; "Īqdam-i Ẓidd-i Īrānī-i Medvedev Dar Ij'rā-yi Qatʻnāmah 1929 [Medvedev's Anti-Iranian Action in Implementing Resolution 1929]," *Keyhan*, 3 October 2010, 2.
37. "Taḥrīmhā-yi jadīd ʻalayhi-i Īrān irtibāṭī bā nīrūgāh-i Būshihr va furūsh-i S-300 nadārad [The New Sanctions against Iran Have Nothing to Do with the Bushehr Power Plant and the Sale of the S-300]," Fars News, 10 June 2010, https://tinyurl.com/ytfem642; "Ta'khīr dar rāh-andāzī nīrūgāh-I Būshihr bih Dalāyil-i Sīyāsī [The Delay in the Launch of the Bushehr Power Plant Is Due to Political Reasons]," *Hamshahri*, 5 July 2010, hamshahrionline.ir/xXfx
38. Mark N. Katz, "Russia and Iran," *Middle East Policy* 19, no. 3 (1 September 2012): 54-64, https://doi.org/10.1111/j.1475-4967.2012.00547.x.
39. According to Ahmadinejad: "Some people are influenced by Satan. They thought the Iranian nation will be harmed if they unilaterally and illegally stop or cancel defense contracts they signed with us." "Iran: Russia Gives in to 'Satan' with Missile Ban," Associated Press, 3 November 2010.
40. Aleksandr Gabuev, Ivan Safronov, and Elena Chernenko, "Isk Za S-300 Razvorachivayut protiv Irana [S-300 Lawsuit Deployed against Iran]," *Kommersant*, 10 August 2012, https://www.kommersant.ru/doc/1998722.
41. Elaheh Koolaee and Afifeh Abedi, "Farāz va Furūd-i Ravābiṭ-i Īrān va Rūsiyah [Ups and Downs of Iran-Russia Relations, 1992-2016]," *Muṭālaʿāt-i Ravābiṭ-i Bayn al-Milal* 10, no. 40 (20 February 2018): 135-64.
42. Elena Chernenko, "Rossiya Izluchaet Yadernoe Uregulirovanie [Russia Radiates Nuclear Settlement]," *Kommersant*, 17 August 2011, Integrum Digital Archive.
43. Marina Sapronova, "Rossiisko-Arabskoe Sotrudnichestvo do i posle 'Arabskoi Vesny'

[Russian-Arab Cooperation before and after the 'Arab Spring']," *Vestnik MGIMO-Universiteta* 36, no. 3 (2014): 34.

44. Sergey Lavrov, "Interv'iu Ministra Inostrannyh del Rossii S.V. Lavrova Rukovoditeliu Avtorskoi Programmy 'Aktual'nyi Razgovor' Telekompanii '3 Kanal' V. Solov'evu [Interview of Russian Minister of Foreign Affairs Sergey Lavrov to V. Soloviev, Head of the Author's Program 'Actual Conversation' of the '3 Channel' TV Company]," Press-Tsentr MID RF, 13 March 2011.
45. Vladimir Kreslavskii, "Net u Revoliutsii Kontsa [The Revolution Has No End]," *Moskovskaya Pravda*, 1 March 2011; Artur Blinov, "Obama Menyaet Doktrinu [Obama Changes the Doctrine]," *Nezavisimaya Gazeta*, 24 May 2010.
46. Allah Khor Moshtaghi and Bahram Akhavan Kazemi, "Bīdārī Īslāmī va ā'll Ān Bā Takīd Bar Nizirāt Miqām m'azim Rahburī [Islamic Awakening and Its Causes, with Emphasis on the Views of the Supreme Leader]," *Siasayi-Jahan Islam* 1, no. 1 (2013): 31-60.
47. In mid-February 2011, amid Gaddafi's mass crackdown on civilian protestors, the Russian Ministry of Foreign Affairs reaffirmed "the inadmissibility of any external interference in the internal political processes in the countries of the region," stating that "external pressure could only worsen the atmosphere." Alexander Lukashevich, "Otvet Ofitsial'nogo Predstavitelia MID Rossii A.K.Lukashevicha na Vopros SMI o Situatsii v Riade Gosudarstv Blizhnego Vostoka [Russian MFA Spokesman Alexander Lukashevich Response to a Media Question regarding the Situation in Some Countries of the Middle East]," Press-Tsentr MID RF, 18 February 2011, Integrum Digital Archive.
48. In an attempt to illustrate Moscow's political commitment to the "reset," Russia supported UNSC Resolution 1970, which placed an arms embargo on Libya. Vladislav Vorobyev, "Rossiya Podklyuchilas' k Sanktsiyam protiv Livii [Russia Joined with Sanctions against Libya]," *Rossiyskaya Gazeta*, 11 March 2011, Integrum Digital Archive.
49. "Rossiya Vystupaet Protiv Voennoi Interventsii v Liviiu [Russia Opposes Military Intervention in Libya]," *Kommersant*, 8 March 2011.
50. Adopted on 17 March, UNSC Resolution 1973 authorized member states to "take all necessary measures … to protect civilians and civilian populated areas" in addition to establishing a no-fly zone and to enforcing an arms embargo on Gaddafi's regime. S/PV.6498, "United Nations Official Document 1973," 17 March 2011, https://www.securitycouncilreport.org/atf/cf/%7B65BFCF9B-6D27-4E9C-8CD3-CF6E4FF96FF9%7D/Libya%20S%20PV%206498.pdf.
51. Moshtaghi and Kazemi, "Bīdārī Īslāmī va ā'll Ān Bā Takīd Bar Nizirāt Miqām m'azim Rahburī [Islamic Awakening and Its Causes, with Emphasis on the Views of the Supreme Leader]," 40.
52. Marziyeh Sakhavati, "Muskū Chi Khūāhad Kard? [What Will Moscow Do?]," *Siyasat-i Rūz*, 6 March 2011.
53. Boris Dolgov, "Siriyskiy Konflikt [The Syrian Conflict]," in *Konflikty i Voyny XXI Veka: Blizhniy Vostok i Severnaya Afrika* [Conflicts and Wars of the Twenty-First Century: The Middle East and North Africa], ed. Vitaly Naumkin and Dina Malysheva (Moscow: Institut Vostokovedeniya RAN, 2015), 401-22.
54. Dmitry Ermolaev, "Dmitry Medvedev i Tselostnost" Rossiiskoi Pozitsii po Livii [Dmitry Medvedev and the Integrity of Russia's Position on Libya]," IA Regnum, 22 March 2011.

55. Vladimir Chamov, "Liviyskaya Drama: Videnie Rossiyskogo Diplomata [Libyan Drama: Vision of the Russian Diplomat]," in *Blizhniy Vostok, Arabskoye Probuzhdenie i Rossiya: Chto Dal'she? Sbornik Statey*, ed. Vasiliy Kuznetsov, Vitaly Naumkin, and Veniamin Popov (Moscow: Institut vostokovedeniya RAN, 2012), 574.
56. Interview with a former foreign intelligence officer stationed in the Middle East (Moscow), 2017.
57. "Zasedaniya Gosudarstvennoy Dumy: O Situatsii v Livii [Meeting of the State Duma: On the Situation in Libya]" (Moscow: Gosudarstvennaya Duma Federal'nogo Sobraniya Rossiyskoy Federatsii, 23 March 2011).
58. See, for example, Yevgeny Grigoryev, "Liviya: Dalee Vezde? [Libya: Will It Spread Everywhere?]," *Nezavisimaya Gazeta*, 21 March 2011; Vladimir Karyakin, "Voennye Uroki Liviyskoy Operatsii NATO [Military Lessons of NATO Operation in Libya]," *Strategicheskaya Stabil'nost'* 61, no. 4 (2012): 36-41; Anatoly Tsyganok, *Voina v Livii: 2011 i Ee Posledstviya dlya Blizhnego Vostoka i Kavkaza* [The War in Libya: 2011 and Its Consequences for the Middle East and Caucasus] (Moscow: AIRO-XXI Institut stran SNG, 2012).
59. Aidan Hehir, "The Permanence of Inconsistency: Libya, the Security Council, and the Responsibility to Protect," *International Security* 38, no. 1 (July 2013): 137-59; Anatoly Tsyganok, *Interventsiya SShA i NATO v Livii i Ee Posledstviya dlya Sirii, Irana, Kavkaza: Russkiy Vzglyad* [U.S. and NATO Intervention in Libya and Its Consequences for Syria, Iran, and the Caucasus: The Russian View] (Moscow: AIRO-XXI Institut stran SNG, 2012).
60. Primakov, "Blizhnevostochnyi Kurs Rossii: Istoricheskie Etapy [Middle Eastern Course of Russia: Historical Stages]."
61. Maria Khodynskaya-Golenishcheva, *Liviyskiy Urok: Tsel' Opravdyvaet Sredstva?* [The Libyan Lesson: The Ends Justify the Means?] (Moscow: OLMA Media Grupp, 2013), 250.
62. Vitaly Naumkin, "Vmesto Predisloviya: Krugovorot Arabskogo Probuzhdeniya [Instead of a Preface: The Cycle of the Arab Awakening]," in Kuznetsov, Naumkin, and Popov, *Blizhniy Vostok, Arabskoye Probuzhdenie i Rossiya*, 8.
63. Jahangir Karami and Ali Reza Nouri, "Rūsiyah Bahār-i "Arabī va 'chālish Sīstamī' Dar Khāvarmaynah [Russia, the Arab Spring and the 'System Challenge' in the Middle East]," *Faslnāmah-i Mutāla'āt-i Āsiyā-Yi Markazī va Qafqāz*, no. 78 (2012): 167-92; Baranov Aleksei Vladimirovich, "'Islamskoe Probuzhdenie' i 'Arabskaya Vesna': Vneshnepoliticheskaya Doktrina Islamskoi Respubliki Iran [Islamic Awakening and Arab Spring: Foreign Policy Doctrine of the Islamic Republic of Iran]," *Izvestiya Saratovskogo Universiteta: Novaya Seriya; Seriya Istoriya; Mezhdunarodnye Otnosheniya* 13, no. 3 (2013), https://cyberleninka.ru/article/n/islamskoe-probuzhdenie-i-arabskaya-vesna-vneshnepoliticheskaya-doktrina-islamskoy-respubliki-iran
64. Habibollah Abolhassan Shirazi, "Ta'sīrāt-i Bahār-i 'Arabī va Inqilābha-Yi Rangi Dar Āsiyā-Yi Markazī va Qafqāz [Influences of Arabic Spring and Color Revolutions in Central Asia and the Caucasus]," *Muṭāla'āt Ravābiṭ-i Bayn al-Milal* 5, no. 19 (2012): 9-36.
65. Fatimah Sulaymani Purlak and Pizhuhishkadah-i Mutala'at-i Rahburdi, *Qudrat-i narm dar istirātizhī-i Khāvar-i Miyānah'ī-i Āmrīkā* [Soft Power in U.S. Middle East Strategy] (Tehran: Pizhūhishkadah-'i Muṭāla'āt-i Rāhburdī, 1390, 2011). Shirazi, "Ta'sīrāt-i Bahār-i 'Arabī va Inqilābha-Yi Rangi Dar Āsiyā-Yi Markazī va Qafqāz [Influences of Arabic Spring and Color Revolutions in Central Asia and the Caucasus]." Karami and

Nouri, "Rūsiyah Bahār-i "arabī va 'chālish Sīstamī' Dar Khāvarmaynah [Russia, the Arab Spring, and the 'System Challenge' in the Middle East]," 167-92; Vladimirovich, "'Islamskoe Probuzhdenie' i 'Arabskaya Vesna': Vneshnepoliticheskaya Doktrina Islamskoi Respubliki Iran [Islamic Awakening and Arab Spring: Foreign Policy Doctrine of the Islamic Republic of Iran]."

66. Sovereign democracy posits that Russia's democratic processes and governance structures are unique and must be insulated from external influences, which are often couched in the rhetoric of human rights and liberal democracy but are perceived as veiled attempts at undermining national sovereignty.
67. S. Neil MacFarlane, "Russian Perspectives on Order and Justice," in Foot, Gaddis, and Hurrell, *Order and Justice in International Relations*, 180.
68. Interview with professor at the Department of Oriental Studies, Moscow State Institute of International Relations (Moscow), 2017; interview with a former foreign intelligence officer stationed in the Middle East (Moscow), 2017.
69. Vladimir Putin, "Rossiya i Menyayushchiisya Mir [Russia and the Changing World]," *Moskovskie Novosti*, 27 February 2012.
70. Putin, "Rossiya i Menyayushchiisya Mir [Russia and the Changing World]."
71. Ibid.
72. Ibid.
73. Putin expressed profound disgust over the death of Gaddafi, stating that "the entire family of M. Gaddafi was almost entirely killed, his corpse was shown on all world channels—it is impossible to watch without disgust. A person covered in blood, wounded, still alive, is being finished off, and all of this is 'rolled out' on screens." "Putin: Nevozmozhno bez Otvrashcheniya Smotret' na Kadry Ubiystva Kaddafi [Putin: It's Impossible to Look at Footage of Gaddafi's Murder without Disgust]," RIA Novosti, 26 October 2011, Integrum Digital Archive.
74. Interview with a former foreign intelligence officer stationed in the Middle East (Moscow), 2017.

3. SYRIA DEVOLVES INTO CIVIL WAR

1. Jason Brownlee, *The Arab Spring: Pathways of Repression and Reform* (Oxford: Oxford University Press, 2015).
2. Marc Lynch, *The New Arab Wars: Uprisings and Anarchy in the Middle East* (New York: PublicAffairs, 2016).
3. Christopher Phillips, *The Battle for Syria: International Rivalry in the New Middle East* (New Haven: Yale University Press, 2016), 84.
4. "Īrān va Rūsīyah Bar Ḥal-i Sīyāsī-i Buḥrān-i Sūrīyah Tākīd Kardand Kardand [Iran and Russia Emphasized the Political Resolution of the Syrian Crisis]," *Keyhan*, 19 December 2012.
5. Roland Dannreuther, "Russia and the Arab Spring: Supporting the Counter-Revolution," *Journal of European Integration* 37, no. 1 (2 January 2015): 77-94, https://doi.org/10.1080/07036337.2014.975990.
6. Vladimir Skosyrev, "Rossiya Prizvala Provesti Konferentsiyu po Sirii [Russia Called for Holding a Conference on Syria]," *Nezavisimaya Gazeta*, 16 June 2013, Integrum Digital Archive; Vladimir Akhmedov, "Siriya [Syria]," in Kuznetsov, Naumkin, and

Popov, *Blizhniy Vostok, Arabskoe Probuzhdenie i Rossiya*, 305-20; Georgiy Mirsky, "What Are West's Next Moves in Middle East?," *Nezavisimaya Gazeta*, 17 February 2012.

7. Sergey Lavrov, "Foreign Minister Sergey Lavrov Makes Remarks and Answers Questions at Joint Press Conference following Talks with Iranian Foreign Minister Ali Akbar Salehi, Moscow, August 17, 2011," Press Center of the Russian Ministry of Foreign Affairs of the Russian Federation, 17 August 2011.
8. "Kudām bakhsh az sukhanān-i rahbarī tītr-i rasānahā-yi manṭaqah shud [Which Part of the Leader's Speech Became Regional Media Headlines?]," Khamenei.ir, 5 June 2011.
9. Maria Petrova, "Syrians Held Conference in Iran," Vestnik Kavkaza, 22 November 2012.
10. "Pīshnihād-i Aḥmadī'nizhād bih Urdūghān barā-yi Sūrīyah [Ahmadinejad's Proposal to Erdoğan for Syria]," Irdiplomacy.ir, 28 August 2011.
11. Lavrov, "Foreign Minister Sergey Lavrov Makes Remarks and Answers Questions at Joint Press Conference following Talks with Iranian Foreign Minister Ali Akbar Salehi, Moscow, August 17, 2011."
12. "Pūtīn: Īrān Rāst Mī'gūyad, Gharb Ḥāmī Dīktātūr'hā-Yi Minṭaqah Būd [Putin: Iran Speaks Truthfully, the West Was a Supporter of Regional Dictators]," *Kayhan*, 9 November 2011.
13. Boris Dolgov, "Siriyskiy Konflikt [The Syrian Conflict]," 401-22.
14. One month after the outbreak of protests in Daraa, the UNSC held an open debate about the violence in Syria. Russia opposed raising the issue in the Security Council, arguing that that the protests and internal unrest in Syria do "not present a threat to international peace and security"; instead, "a real threat to regional security ... could arise from outside interference in Syria's domestic situation," which would descend into civil war and unrest throughout the Middle East S/PV.6524, "United Nations Security Council Meeting Record: The Situation in the Middle East," UNSC, 27 April 2011.
15. "Russia Supplying Arms to Syria under Old Contracts: Lavrov," Reuters, 5 November 2012, https://www.reuters.com/article/idUSBRE8A40DS.
16. Christopher Phillips, *The Battle for Syria: International Rivalry in the New Middle East* (New Haven: Yale University Press, 2016).
17. Yu. Shepovalenko, ed., *Siriyskiy Rubezh* [Syrian Frontier] (Moscow: Tsentr analiza strategiy i tekhnologiy, 2016)
18. Phillips, *Battle for Syria*.
19. Shaun Walker, "Plane Loads of Cash: Flight Records Reveal Russia Flew 30 Tonnes of Bank Notes to Syrian Regime," *The Independent*, 26 November 2012, https://www.independent.co.uk/news/world/europe/plane-loads-of-cash-flight-records-reveal-russia-flew-30-tonnes-of-bank-notes-to-syrian-regime-8352790.html.
20. Liudmila Kulagina and Vladimir Akhmedov, "Iran i Revoliutsionnye Dvizheniya na Arabskom Vostoke [Iran and the Revolutionary Movements in the Arab East]," in *Politika RF I IRI v Regional'nom Kontekste: TsA, Kavkaz, Blizhnii Vostok*, ed. Elena Dunaeva and Nina Mamedova (Moscow: Institut Vostokovedeniya RAN, 2011), 180.
21. Soleimani's operations against the U.S. in Iraq post-2003 earned him a formidable reputation, contributing significantly to making the U.S. occupation untenable and transforming Iraq into a solid ally of Iran. His influence extended to facilitating the return to power of Iraqi Premier Nouri al-Maliki in 2010. Syria, however, presented different challenges from those in Iraq. In Iraq, he had supported irregular forces

against a regular military in a collapsed state, whereas in Syria he faced a robust regime fighting an insurgency without the same societal ties Iran had in Iraq.

22. IRGC personnel were actively involved in Syria between 2012 and 2013, offering intelligence, paramilitary training, and high-level advisory support to the Assad regime. S/2012/395, "Final Report of the Panel of Experts Established Pursuant to Resolution 1929 (2010)," 4 June 2012; interview with the director of the Institute of CIS Countries (Moscow), 2017.
23. For background on Iran's strategy in Syria and the role of non-state actors, see Pierre Boussel, "The Quds Force in Syria: Combatants, Units, and Actions," Combating Terrorism Center, West Point, 23 June 2023; Hamidreza Azizi, "Integration of Iran-Backed Armed Groups into the Iraqi and Syrian Armed Forces: Implications for Stability in Iraq and Syria," *Small Wars & Insurgencies* 33, no. 3 (3 April 2022): 499-527, https://doi.org/10.1080/09592318.2021.2025284; Abdolrasool Divsallar and Hamidreza Azizi, "Towards a Non-Western Model of Security Assistance: How Iran Assists Militaries," *Mediterranean Politics* 0, no. 0 (26 February 2023): 1-23, https://doi.org/10.1080/13629395.2023.2183661; Hamidreza Azizi and Amir Hossein Vazirian, "The Role of Armed Non-State Actors in Iran's Syria Strategy: A Case Study of Fatemiyoun and Zainabiyoun Brigades," *Journal of Balkan and Near Eastern Studies* 25, no. 3 (4 May 2023): 540-57, https://doi.org/10.1080/19448953.2022.2143864.
24. "Tegeran Privetstvuet Blokirovanie Rossiey Rezolyutsii Zapada v SB OON po Sirii [Tehran Welcomes Russia's Blocking of the Resolution of the West in the UN Security Council on Syria]," ITAR-TASS, 10 October 2011.
25. Barrack Obama, "Remarks by the President to the White House Press Corps," White House Office of the Press Secretary, 20 August 2012.
26. Sergey Rogov, "Doktrina Obamy: Vlastelin Dvukh Kolets [Obama Doctrine: Lord of the Two Rings]," *Rossiyskaya Gazeta*, 17 April 2013.
27. "Vlasti Sirii Oprovergli Soobshcheniya o Primenenii Khimoruzhiya v Damaske [Syrian Authorities Have Denied Reports of the Use of Chemical Weapons in Damascus]," RIA Novosti, 21 August 2013, https://ria.ru/20130821/957634346.html; "MID Rossii: Primenennyy Pod Aleppo Boepripas Byl Izgotovlen Kustarno [Russian Foreign Ministry: The Ammunition Used Near Aleppo Was Homemade]," RIA Novosti, 4 September 2013, https://ria.ru/20130904/960816266.html.
28. Interview with a senior researcher at the Institute of Oriental Studies (Moscow), 2017.
29. Interview with a former Russian diplomat in the Middle East (Moscow), 2019.
30. Interview with a former Russian ambassador to Libya (Moscow), 2019; interview with a senior researcher at the Institute of Oriental Studies (Moscow), 2017.
31. Eduard Gushchin et al., "Kto Vystupayet za Politicheskoye Resheniye Siriyskogo Konflikta [Who Advocates for a Political Solution to the Syrian Conflict]," *Rossiyskaya Gazeta*, 9 September 2013; Andranik Migranyan, "Gumanitarnyye Interventsii Zakanchivayutsya Gumanitarnoy Katastrofoy [Humanitarian Interventions End in a Humanitarian Catastrophe]," *Izvestiya*, 9 September 2013; Farida Rustamova and Mariya Makutina, "Zavversheniye Raboty Vmesto Perezagruzki [Shutting Down Instead of Rebooting]," Gazeta.ru, 7 August 2013, https://www.gazeta.ru/politics/2013/08/07_a_5545601.shtml.
32. Igor' Ivanov, "Predotvratit' Inostrannuyu Agressiyu v Sirii Eshche Mozhno [It Is Still

Possible to Prevent Foreign Aggression in Syria]," *Rossiyskaya Gazeta*, 1 September 2013, https://rg.ru/2013/09/01/agressia-poln.html.

33. Interview with a senior researcher of the Iranian Studies Department of the Institute of Oriental Studies (Moscow), 2019.
34. Pavel Felgenhauer, "Segodnya v Sirii a Zavtra? [Today in Syria but Tomorrow?]," *Novaya Gazeta*, 28 August 2013.
35. Later, Lavrov revealed that Iran introduced the provision that called for the ratification of the OPCW by all UN member states; see Sergey Lavrov, "Interv'yu s Sergeyem Lavrovym: Ugrozy Primenit' Silu protiv Sirii Ostro Stavyat Vopros o Normakh Mezhdunarodnogo Prava [Interview with Lavrov: Threats to Use Force against Syria Sharply Raise the Question of the Norms of International Law]," *Rossiyskaya Gazeta*, 10 October 2013.
36. Pavel Felgenhauer, "Beshoznoe Siriiskoe Himoruzhie [Unattended Syrian Chemical Weapons]," *Novaya Gazeta*, 1 October 2013, https://www.novayagazeta.ru/articles/2013/10/01/56588-beshoznoe-siriyskoe-himoruzhie.
37. Maryan Soltanipour, "Piyām Jahān-ī Dikhālat Larzān-i Āmrīkā Dar Sūriyah [World's Message to America's Indecisive Intervention in Syria]," *Javan*, 19 December 2013, https://www.javanonline.ir/002d1R.
38. At the UNSC, Lavrov clarified that the agreement "does not allow for any automatic use of coercive measures of enforcement" since it does not fall under Chapter VII of the UN Charter, which permits the use of force. S/PV.7038, "United Nations Security Council Record: The Situation in the Middle East," UNSC, 27 September 2013.
39. Interview with a former Russian ambassador to Libya (Moscow), 2017.
40. Maria Khodynskaya-Golenishcheva, *Na Pravil'noy Storone Istorii: Siriyskiy Krizis v Kontekste Stanovleniya Mnogopolyarnogo Mirovoustroystva* [On the Right Side of History: The Syrian Crisis in the Context of the Formation of a Multipolar World Order] (Moscow: OLMA Media Grupp, 2015), 326. Gennady Gatilov, "Formula Uregulirovaniya v Sirii: Mezhsiriyskiy Dialog, Pomnozhennyy na Effektivnuyu Rol' Vneshnikh Igrakov [Formula for Settlement in Syria: Inter-Syrian Dialogue Coupled with the Effective Role of External Players]," *Mezhdunarodnaya Zhizn'*, November 2013.
41. Interview with an expert on U.S., Russia, and the Middle East (Moscow), 2017; interview with a former Russian ambassador to a GCC state (Moscow), 2019.
42. Hassan Beheshtipour, "Siyāsat-i Muvāzanah-i Muṣībat Rūḥānī [Rouhani's Policy of Positive Balancing]," *Rūznāmih-i Īrān*, 11 September 2014, www.magiran.com/n2897644.
43. Elena Chernenko and Ivan Safronov, "Rossiya i Iran Nashli Oruzhiye Sblizhayushchego Deystviya [Russia and Iran Found a Weapon of Rapprochement]," *Kommersant*, 11 September 2013; "Glavy MID RF i Irana Obsuzhdayut Regional'nuyu Problematiku i Razvitiye Torgovo-Ekonomicheskogo Sotrudnichestva [Russian and Iranian Foreign Ministers Discuss Regional Issues and Development Trade and Economic Cooperation]," ITAR-TASS, 11 December 2013.
44. "Vstrecha s Prezidentom Irana Khasanom Rukhani [Meeting with Iranian President Hassan Rouhani]," Press-Sluzhba Prezidenta RF, 13 September 2013.
45. Hassan Rouhani, "Matn-i Kāmil-i Suḥanrānī-i Ra'īs-i Jumhūrī-i Islāmī-i Īrān Dar Nishast-i Sarān-i Sāzmān-i Hamkārī-i Shānghāy [Full Text of the Speech of the President of the Islamic Republic of Iran at the Shanghai Cooperation Organisation

Summit]," Riyāsat-i Jumhūrī-i Islāmī-i Īrān, 13 September 2013, http://president.ir/fa/71098/printable.

46. Fedor Lukyanov, "Igra s Otkrytym Finalom [A Game with an Open Ending]," *Rossiyskaya Gazeta*, 22 January 2014.
47. Dmitry Kosyrev, "Fantom Zhenevskoi Konferentsii i Al'ians SShA s Asadom [A Geneva Phantom and the U.S.-Assad Alliance]," RIA Novosti, 8 November 2013.
48. Andrei Yashlavsky, "Priglashenie Iranu na Konferentsiyu 'Zheneva-2' Otozvali Menee Chem za Sutki do Nachala [The Invitation to Iran to the 'Geneva-2' Conference Was Recalled Less than a Day before the Start]," *Moskovskiy Komsomolets*, 22 January 2014, Integrum Digital Archive.
49. Sabah Zanganeh, "Naqsh-i Irān Dar Tūāfiq-i Zihinv [Iran's Role in the Geneva Agreement]," *E'temad*, 2 January 2014.
50. "A.K. Lukashevicha v Svyazi s Resheniem Gensekretarya OON Otozvat' Priglashenie Iranu na Mezhdunarodnuyu Konferentsiyu po Sirii ('Zheneva-2') [Russian MFA Spokesman A. Lukashevich's Commentary regarding the Decision of the UN Secretary-General to Withhold the Invitation to Iran for the International Conference on Syria (Geneva-2)]," Press-Tsentr MID RF, 21 January 2014, Integrum Digital Archive.
51. Gennady Gatilov, "Interview with Russian Deputy Foreign Minister Gennady Gatilov (In Russian)," *Rossiyskaya Gazeta*, 8 November 2013.
52. "Iran Dolzhen Prinyat' Uchastie v Mezhdunarodnoy Konferentsii po Sirii—Lavrov [Iran Should Take Part in the International Conference on Syria—Lavrov]," ITAR-TASS, 13 January 2014.
53. "Iran Ne Priemlet Predvaritel'nykh Usloviy dlya Uchastiya v 'Zheneve-2' [Iran Does Not Accept the Preconditions for Participation in the 'Geneva-2']," IA Regnum, 16 January 2014.
54. Phillips, *Battle for Syria*, 193.
55. It should be noted that Iran's response to Crimea resembled the country's concern about a U.S.-Russia conflict emerging from instability in South Ossetia during the 2008 Russian-Georgian War.
56. "lārījānī gft darbārih āūkrāīn [Larijani Spoke about Ukraine]," *Khabar*, 4 April 2014.
57. Elena Porotikova, "Iran Sledit za Sobytiyami na Ukraine i Schitaet Vvedenie Mezhdunarodnykh Sanktsii Neproduktivnym Putem Resheniya Voprosov—Posol Irana v RF [Iran Follows Developments in Ukraine and Considers the Introduction of International Sanctions Unproductive Way to Resolve Issues—Iran's Ambassador to Russia]," ITAR-TASS, 17 March 2014.
58. Hassan Beheshtipour, "Rūsīh āz āūkrāīn nimīgizard [Russia Does Not Pass on Ukraine]," Tabnak, 4 March 2014; "Zamistān-i Rūsīyah dar khānah-i Urūpā'īhā [Russia's Winter in Europe's Home]," *Donya-e Eqtesad*, 10 March 2014; Mohammad Safari, "Āmrīkā Pūtīn Ra Tarhīk Mīkund [The U.S. Is Provoking Putin]," *Siyāsat-i Rūz*, 10 March 2014.
59. Yosef Mowla'i, "Aūkrāyn-i Baḥrān Zamīngir-i Hughhūgh Bāyn Āl-Milalī [Ukraine's Crisis Crippling International Law]," *Shargh*, 12 March 2014.
60. Sa'dollah Zar'ei, "Āūkrāīn Dar Marz-i Sharq va Gharb [Ukraine on East-West Border]," *Kayhan*, 11 March 2014, http://kayhan.ir/fa/news/7225.
61. Alexander Levchenko and Alexei Tsypin, "RF Vidit v Irane Nadezhnogo, Perspektivnogo Partnera [Russia Sees a Reliable, Promising Partner in Iran]," ITAR-TASS, 18 November 2014.

62. Igor Ivanov, "Vozvrashchenie Irana [Return of Iran]," *Rossiyskaya Gazeta*, 17 July 2014, Integrum Digital Archive.
63. "Ėkspert: Rossiya i Iran Dolzhny Nachat' Voenno-Tehnicheskoe Sotrudnichestvo [Expert: Russia and Iran Should Start Military-Technical Cooperation]," RIA Novosti, 4 April 2014.
64. Karaganov, "Mir Stanovitsya Vse Menee Prozapadnym [The World Is Becoming Less pro-Western]," *Rossiyskaya Gazeta*, 24 April 2014.
65. For debates in Iran on Russia's annexation of Crimea, see Amir Ahmadi-Arian, "Eḥtemāl-i Jang-i Dākhlī Dar Ūkrāyn [The Possibility of a Civil War in Ukraine]," *Shargh*, 20 February 2014; Kabari Akish, "Amrīkā va Gharb Bāzandegān-i Tawāfoq-i Chahārjahāneh-i Ūkrāyn [The U.S. and the West Are the Losers of the Quadrilateral Agreement on Ukraine]," *Rūznāmah-i Īrān*, 21 April 2014; Jahangir Karami, "Rūsīyah, Ūkrāyn Rā Federalī Mī Khāhad [Russia Wants Ukraine as Federal]," *Rūznāmah-i Īrān*, 10 May 2014; Seyyed Hossein Mousavi, "Būḥrān-i Ūkrāyn; Kātalīzūr-i Ravābiṭ-i Rūsīyah–Īrān–Chīn [Ukraine Crisis: Catalyst for Russia-Iran-China Relations]," *Donyā-Yi Eqteṣād*, 19 March 2014.
66. Andrei Kazantsev et al., "Islamskoe Gosudarstvo: Fenomen, Evolyutsiya, Perspektivy [Islamic State: Phenomenon, Evolution, Perspectives]," in *Analiticheskie Doklady, Yavlyayetsya Prilozheniem k Periodicheskomu Izdaniyu "Ezhegodnik IMI"* (Moscow: Institut mezhdunarodnykh issledovaniy MGIMO MID Rossii, 2016).
67. "Telefonnyy Razgovor s General'nym Sekretarem OON Pan Gi Munom [Telephone Conversation with UN Secretary-General Ban Ki-moon]," Press-Sluzhba Prezidenta RF, 23 September 2014, Integrum Digital Archive; Olga Kuznetsova, "Na Siriyskom Fronte Proizoshli Peremeny [The Syrian Front Has Undergone Changes]," *Kommersant*, 24 August 2014, Integrum Digital Archive.
68. Igor Ivanov, "Zamenyat Li Bomby Diplomatiyu? [Will Bombs Be Replaced by Diplomacy?]," *Rossiyskaya Gazeta*, 3 October 2014, Integrum Digital Archive.
69. "MNENIE: SShA Pytaiutsia Svergnut' Prezidenta Sirii Pod Predlogom Bor'by s Terrorizmom [Opinion: The U.S. Is Trying to Overthrow the Syrian President under the Pretext of Fighting Terrorism]," RIA Novosti, 20 September 2014, Integrum Digital Archive.
70. "Zayavleniya Glav Gosudarstv: Uchastnikov IV Kaspiyskogo Sammita dlya Pressy [Statements by the Heads of State of the Fourth Caspian Press Summit]," Press-Sluzhba Prezidenta RF, 29 September 2014, Integrum Digital Archive.
71. "'Kaspiyskaya Pyaterka': O Chem Dogovorilis' Uchastniki Sammita v Astrakhani ['Caspian Five': What the Participants of the Summit in Astrakhan Agreed On]," *RBK*, 29 September 2014, Integrum Digital Archive.
72. Maxim Suchkov, "Looking behind the Russia-Iran Relationship," Al-Monitor, 9 October 2014, https://www.al-monitor.com/originals/2014/10/russia-iran-sanctions-summit.html
73. "Prezident Irana: V Sluchae Kraha Pravitel'stva Siriya Stanet Pribezhishchem dlya Terroristov [President of Iran: In Case of Government Failure, Syria Will Become a Refuge for Terrorists]," *Moskovskiy Komsomolets*, 28 September 2015; "Rouhani: Esli My Hotim Pobedit' Terrorizm, Pravitel'stvo v Damaske Nel'zia Oslabliat' [Rouhani: If We Want to Defeat Terrorism, the Government in Damascus Must Not Be Weakened]," ITAR-TASS, 28 September 2015.
74. Irina Fedorova, "Nekotorye Politicheskie Aspekty Sotrudnichestva Rossiiskoi

Federatsii i Islamskoi Respubliki Iran na Srednem Vostoke [Some Aspects of Russia-Iranian Cooperation in the Middle East]," in Sazhin and Dunaeva, *Rossiisko-Iranskie Otnosheniya Problemy I Perspektivy*, 87.

75. Founded in 2012, Jabhat al-Nusr was an al-Qaeda-affiliated jihadist group that initially focused on fighting against the Syrian government and later became one of the most powerful rebel factions in the conflict. In 2016, Jabhat al-Nusra formally severed its ties with al-Qaeda and rebranded itself as Jabhat Fatah al-Sham, and later as Hayat Tahrir al-Sham, although its ideology and goals remained largely unchanged. Natsional'nyy antiterroristicheskiy komitet, "Reshenie Verkhovnogo Suda RF Priznat' Mezhdunarodnye Organizatsii 'Islamskoe Gosudarstvo' i Dzhebhat an-Nusra (Front Pobedy) Terroristicheskimi i Zapretit' Ikh Deyatel'nost' na Territorii Rossiyskoy Federatsii [Decision of the Supreme Court of the Russian Federation to Recognize the International Organizations 'Islamic State' and Jabhat al-Nusra (Victory Front) as Terrorist and to Prohibit Their Activities on the Territory of the Russian Federation]," Pub. L. No. AKPI14-1424S (2014).
76. Alexander Valerianov, "IGIL Mozhet Nanesti Udar po Rossii [ISIL Can Strike Russia]," *Tribuna*, 9 July 2015, Integrum Digital Archive; Anna Glazova, ed., "Politika Regional'nykh Stran v Otnoshenii IGIL [The Policy of Regional Countries in Relation to ISIL]," in *IGIL Kak Ugroza Mezhdunarodnoy Bezopasnosti* [ISIL as a Threat to International Security] (Moscow: Rossiyskiy institut strategicheskikh issledovaniy, 2015), 81-102.
77. Irina Zvyagelskaya, *Blizhnevostochnyy Klinch: Konflikty na Blizhnem Vostoke i Politika Rossii* [Middle Eastern Clinch: Conflicts in the Middle East and Russia's Politics] (Moscow: Aspekt Press, 2014), 196.
78. Alexei Pushkov, "'Strannaya Izolyatsiya' Provalilas' ['Phony Isolation' Has Failed]," *Rossiyskaya Gazeta*, 8 July 2015, Integrum Digital Archive.

4. SAVING ASSAD

1. "Kaspiiskii Flot RF Porazil 11 Tselei 'Islamskogo Gosudarstva' v Sirii [The Russian Caspian Fleet Hit Eleven Islamic State Targets in Syria]," Interfax, 7 October 2015, https://www.interfax.ru/world/471814.
2. "Pervoe Boevoe Primenenie Noveyshikh Krylatykh Raket Mozhno Nazvat' Istoricheskim [The First Combat Use of the Latest Cruise Missiles Can Be Called Historic]," Vzglyad, 7 October 2015, https://vz.ru/society/2015/10/7/771068.html.
3. "Voqū' Chand Ḥādeseh Dar Masīr-e 'ubūr Mūshakhāy-e Rūsī Bar Farāz-e Īrānn [Several Incidents Occurred on the Path of Russian Missiles Crossing over Iran]," Radio Farda, 8 October 2015, https://www.radiofarda.com/a/f7-some-accidents-in-the-path-of-russian-missiles-to-syria-on-iran/27295897.html.
4. "Āyā mūshak'hā-yi Rūsī dar Īrān suqūṭ kardah'and? [Have Russian Missiles Crashed in Iran?]," Mashregh News, 10 October 2015, https://www.mshrgh.ir/479409
5. "Syria Crisis: Russian Caspian Missiles 'Fell in Iran,'" BBC News, 8 October 2015, sec. Europe, https://www.bbc.com/news/world-europe-34479873.
6. "Massirovannyy Udar Vysokotochnym Oruzhiem po Ob'ektam IGIL v Sirii iz Akvatorii Kaspiyskogo Morya [Massive Strike with Precision Weapons on ISIS Targets in Syria from the Caspian Sea]," *Minoborony Rossii*, 7 October 2015,

https://www.youtube.com/watch?v=iMasnaAf_H4&ab_channel=%D0%9C%D0%B8%D0%BD%D0%BE%D0%B1%D0%BE%D1%80%D0%BE%D0%BD%D1%8B%D0%A0%D0%BE%D1%81%D1%81%D0%B8%D0%B8.

7. Yurii Tsarik, "Rossiya-Iran: Novye Vozmozhnosti i Bremia Otvetstvennosti [Russia-Iran: New Opportunities and Burden of Responsibility]," *Izvestiya*, 23 January 2015.
8. Ivan Safronov, "Gruz-300: Voennoe Sotrudnichestvo Rossii s Iranom Rasshiritsia [The Cargo Is 300 Tons: Russia's Military Cooperation with Iran Will Expand]," *Kommersant*, 21 January 2015.
9. Interview with a Russia-based defense expert (Moscow), 2017.
10. "Vstrecha so Spetspredstavitelem Prezidenta Irana, Sovetnikom po Mezhdunarodnym Delam Ali Akbarom Velayati [Meeting with the Special Representative of the President of Iran, Foreign Affairs Advisor Ali Akbar Velayati]," Press-Sluzhba Prezidenta RF, 28 January 2015, Informatsiya ofitsial'nyh uchrezhdenii: Press-Sluzhba Prezidenta RF (2000-18).
11. "Ẓarīf dar fāyl-i ṣavtī-yi janjalī darbārah-i Rūsīyah chih guft? [What Did Zarif Say about Russia in the Controversial Audio File?]," Ensaf News, 8 January 2022, https://tinyurl.com/mprryute.
12. Phillips, *Battle for Syria*; Anna Polyakova, "Kak Razviazat' Siriiyskii Uzel [How to Untie a Syrian Knot]," *Krasnaya Zvezda*, 15 May 2015.
13. Strokan and Maxim Yusin, "Ni Mira, Ni Pal'miry [Neither Peace, Nor Palmyra]," *Kommersant*, 22 May 2015.
14. "Asad: Armiya Sirii Ne Mozhet Uderzhat' Vsiu Stranu [Assad: Syrian Army Cannot Protect the Whole Country],"Vzglyad, 27 July 2015.
15. Elena Chernenko, Ivan Safronov, and Olga Kuznetsova, "Iranskiy Deyatel' Okazalsya Slishkom Vidnym [The Iranian Figure Turned Out to Be Too Prominent]," *Kommersant*, 15 August 2015, https://www.kommersant.ru/doc/2787855. Russia denied accusations of Soleimani's visit, see "MID RF: Rossiya Soobshchila SShA, Chto Iranskii General Suleimani v Moskve Ne Nahodilsia [Russian Foreign Ministry: Russia Informed the U.S. that Iran's General Soleimani Was Not in Moscow]," ITAR, 14 August 2015; Olga Kuznetsova, "Iranskii General Poteryalsya mezhdu Tegeranom i Moskvoi [Iranian General Lost between Tehran and Moscow]," *Kommersant*, 14 August 2015.
16. "Ẓarīf dar fāyl-i ṣavtī-yi janjalī darbārah-i Rūsīyah chih guft? [What Did Zarif Say about Russia in the Controversial Audio File?]."
17. "How Iranian General Plotted Out Syrian Assault in Moscow," Reuters, 6 October 2015, https://www.reuters.com/article/us-mideast-crisis-syria-soleimani-insigh/how-iranian-general-plotted-out-syrian-assault-in-moscow-idUSKCN0S02BV20151006.
18. Interview with a current Russian diplomat (Moscow), 2019.
19. "Kak v SMI Narastalo Prisutstvie Rossiiskih Voennyh v Sirii [In the Media, How the Presence of Russian Military in Syria Increased]," *Kommersant*, 8 September 2015.
20. Markendov, "Rossiya i Siriya: Pochemu, Zashchishchaya Asada, My na Samom dele Zashchishchaem Sebia [Russia and Syria: Why, through Defending Assad, We Are in Fact Defending Ourselves]," RIA Novosti, 11 September 2015, https://ria.ru/analytics/20150911/1244293347.html; Ivan Rodin and Vladimir Mukhin, "Rossiya Nachala Svoiu Blizhnevostochnuiu Voinu [Russia Began Its Middle East War]," *Nezavisimaya Gazeta*, 1 September 2015.
21. Rossiyskaya Federatsiya and Siriyskaya Arabskaya Respublika, "Soglashenie mezhdu

Rossiyskoy Federatsiey i Siriyskoy Arabskoy Respublikoy o Razmeshchenii Aviatsionnoy Gruppy Vooruzhennykh Sil Rossiyskoy Federatsii na Territorii Siriyskoy Arabskoy Respubliki [Agreement between the Russian Federation and the Syrian Arab Republic on the Deployment of an Aviation Group of the Russian Armed Forces on the Territory of the Syrian Arab Republic]," 2015; Michael Birnbaum, "The Secret Pact between Russia and Syria That Gives Moscow Carte Blanche," *Washington Post*, 16 December 2021, https://www.washingtonpost.com/news/worldviews/wp/2016/01/15/the-secret-pact-between-russia-and-syria-that-gives-moscow-carte-blanche.

22. Yu. Shepovalenko, *Siriyskiy Rubezh* [Syrian Frontier].
23. Sara Ma'sumi, "Rūsiah va Irān، ā'rāb Rā Shūkih Kardand [Russia and Iran Shocked the Arabs]," *E'temad*, 4 October 2015. With many Syrian Arab Army and National Defense Forces units reassigned to more tumultuous fronts, Russia and the IRGC bolstered their positions by establishing military checkpoints with the Latakia Governorate and Masyaf in the East Tartus Governorate.
24. Interview with a Russian defense expert (Moscow), 2019.
25. Hossein Amir Abdollahian, *Ṣubḥ Shām: Riwāyatī az Buḥrān-i Sūrīyah, Khāṭirāt-i Duktur Ḥusayn Amīr ʻAbdallāhyān* [Levant's Morning: A Narrative of the Syrian Crisis, Memoirs of Dr Hossein Amir-Abdollahian] (Tehran: Shirkat-i Intishārāt-i Sūrah-i Mihr, 2019).
26. Interview with a Russia-based expert on the Middle East (Moscow), 2017
27. Interview with a Russia-based expert on the Levant (Moscow), 2017.
28. Vitaly Naumkin, "Islamskiy Radikalizm i Vneshnee Vmeshatel'stvo v Gluboko Razdelennykh Obshchestvakh Blizhnego Vostoka [Islamic Radicalism and External Intervention in the Deeply Divided Societies of the Middle East]," in Naumkin and Malysheva, *Konflikty i Voyny XXI Veka*, 25-52.
29. Irina Komissina, "Ugroza Destabilizatsii Tsentral'noy Azii i Zakavkaz'ya [The Threat of Destabilization in Central Asia and Transcaucasia]," in *IGIL Kak Ugroza Mezhdunarodnoy Bezopasnosti* [ISIL as a Threat to International Security], ed. Anna Glazova (Moscow: Rossiyskiy institut strategicheskikh issledovaniy, 2015), 150-62.
30. Gennady Gatilov, "Formula Uregulirovaniya v Sirii: Mezhsiriyskiy Dialog, Pomnozhennyy na Effektivnuyu Rol' Vneshnikh Igrokov [Formula for Settlement in Syria: Inter-Syrian Dialogue Coupled with the Effective Role of External Players]," *Mezhdunarodnaya Zhizn'*, November 2013.
31. Alexander Valerianov, "IGIL Mozhet Nanesti Udar po Rossii [ISIL Can Strike Russia]," *Tribuna*, 9 July 2015; Glazova, *IGIL Kak Ugroza Mezhdunarodnoi Bezopasnosti* [ISIL as a Threat to International Security].
32. S. Ivanov, "Radikal'nyy Islam Kak Ugroza Mezhdunarodnoy Bezopasnosti [Radical Islam as a Threat to International Security]," *Zarubezhnoe Voennoe Obozrenie*, 31 January 2015, https://on-demand.eastview.com/browse/doc/43086711; Andrei Kazantsev et al., "Islamskoe Gosudarstvo: Fenomen, Evolyutsiya, Perspektivy [Islamic State: Phenomenon, Evolution, Perspectives]," in *Analiticheskie Doklady*.
33. S.M. Samuilov and M.M. Panyuzheva, "Bor'ba Ssha S Igil i Otvet Rossii [U.S. Struggle against ISIS and Russia's Response]," *SShA-Kanada: Ekonomika*, no. 1 (January 2016): 3-21.
34. Interview with a former Russian diplomat in the Middle East (Moscow), 2019.
35. Viktor Baranets, "Nachal'nik Genshtaba Vooruzhennykh Sil Rossii General Armii Valery Gerasimov: 'My perelomili khrebet udarnym silam terrorizma' [Chief of the General Staff of the Russian Armed Forces, Army General Valery Gerasimov: 'We

broke the back of the terrorist strike forces'],” Kp.ru, 27 December 2017, https://www.kp.ru/daily/26775/3808693.

36. Round Table, “Blizhniy Vostok: Okno Vozmozhnostey ili Zapadnya dlya Atlantistov? [Middle East: Window of Opportunity or Trap for Atlanticists?],” *Mirovaya Ekonomika i Mezhdunarodnye Otnosheniya* 63, no. 7 (2019): 111-20, https://doi.org/10.20542/0131-2227-2019-63-7-111-120.
37. Interview with a researcher at the Institute of Oriental Studies (Moscow), 2017.
38. Interview with a Russia-based Middle East expert (Moscow), 2017.
39. Aleksandr Khrmchikhin, “Za Rodinu, za Asada [For the Motherland, for Assad],” *VPK: Voenno-Promyshlennyi Kur'er*, 11 November 2015, https://dlib-eastview-com/browse/doc/45682106; Evgeniy Satanovskiy, “Stavka Bol'she, Chem Asad [The Bet Is Bigger than Assad],” *Voenno-Promyshlennyy Kur'er*, 28 September 2015, Integrum Digital Archive.
40. Interview with a Russian specialist on counter-terrorism strategies in the Middle East (Moscow), 2017.
41. Conversation with a Russian diplomat on Moscow's mediation efforts between conflicting Middle Eastern parties (Moscow), 2018.
42. Interview with a Russian presidential advisor for Middle Eastern affairs (Moscow), 2017.
43. Interview with a member of the Russian Foreign Ministry Committee on International Law (Moscow), 2019.
44. Mikhail Zygar', Konstantin Lantratov, and Ivan Safronov, “Rossiya Gotovitsya k Evakuatsii [Russia Is Preparing to Evacuate],” *Kommersant*, 13 January 2016, https://www.kommersant.ru/doc/640497.
45. The concept note encouraged the UNSC to “play a key role in harmonizing collective approaches” to terrorism in the Middle East and underscored the “need to focus on aiding the legitimate national Governments that are fighting terrorism on their territory… on the basis of rejection of double standards and respect for the principle of national sovereignty” (S./2015/678 2015).
46. Interview with a Russian political analyst on Russia-Middle East relations (Moscow), 2019.
47. “Terroristy Zaniali 60% Sirii, Ėto Protivorechit Zayavleniyam o Bor'be Asada s Narodom—Putin [Terrorists Occupied 60 percent of Syria, This Contradicts the Statements about Assad's Struggle with the People—Putin],” RIA Novosti, 28 September 2015.
48. Alexei Arbatov, “Blizhnevostochnyi Gambit Putina [Middle Eastern Gambit of Putin],” *Nezavisimaya Gazeta*, 6 November 2015.
49. A/70/PV.13, “United Nations General Assembly Record: General Debate,” UNGA, 28 September 2015.
50. “Soveshchanie s Chlenami Pravitel'stva [Meeting with Members of the Government],” Press-Sluzhba Prezidenta RF, 30 September 2015, Informatsiya ofitsial'nyh uchrezhdenii: Press-Sluzhba Prezidenta RF (2000-18); “Rossiya Nachala Nanosit' Aviaudary v Sirii [Russia Started Airstrikes in Syria],” *Kommersant*, 30 September 2015.
51. S/PV.7527, “United Nations Security Council Meeting Record: Maintenance of International Peace and Security,” 30 September 2015, sec. Settlement of Conflicts in the Middle East and North Africa and Countering the Terrorist Threat in the Region.
52. Markendov, “Rossiya i Siriya: Pochemu, Zashchishchaya Asada, My na Samom Dele

Zashchishchaem Sebya [Russia and Syria: Why, through Defending Assad, We Are in Fact Defending Ourselves].

53. "Ṭūfān-i havāyī-i Rūsīyah 'alayhī-i mawāẕi'-i Dā'ish dar Sūrīyah [Russian Airstrikes against ISIS in Syria],"Tasnim, 10 October 2015.

54. Amir-Hossein Yazdanpanah, "Āīyā Ravābiṭ-i Īrān va Rūsīyah Rāhburdī Mī Shūd? [Will Iran-Russia Relations Be Strategic?]," *Khorasan*, 24 November 2015.

55. Hassan Hanizadah, "Rūsiyah va taghyīr-i muvāzanah-'i qudrat dar Sūrīyah [Russia and the Change in the Balance of Power in Syria]," *Quds*, 3 October 2015.

56. Ma'sumi, "Rūsiah va Irān، ā'rāb Rā Shūkih Kardand [Russia and Iran Shocked the Arabs]."

57. Georgy Bovt, "Bitva za Siriyskuyu Pustynyu [Battle for the Syrian Desert]," Gazeta.ru, 19 October 2015, Integrum Digital Archive.

58. Arbatov, "Blizhnevostochnyy Gambit Putina [Middle Eastern Gambit of Putin]."

59 "Behind the Data: Recording Civilian Casualties in Syria," OHCHR, 2023, https://www.ohchr.org/en/stories/2023/05/behind-data-recording-civilian-casualties-syria#:~:text=Related&text=Over%20the%20past%20ten%20years,conflict%20began%20in%20the%20country; user8, "Syrian Revolution 13 Years On: Nearly 618,000 Persons Killed since the Onset of the Revolution in March 2011," Syrian Observatory For Human Rights, 15 March 2024, https://www.syriahr.com/en/328044.

60. Victor Litovkin, "Voennaya Operatsiya v Sirii: Itogi i Prognozy [Military Operation in Syria: Results and Forecasts]," *Izvestiya*, 16 March 2016.

61. Michael Kofman, "Syria and the Russian Armed Forces: An Evaluation of Moscow's Military Strategy and Operational Performance," Foreign Policy Research Institute, September 2020; Michael Kofman and Matthew Rojansky, "What Kind of Victory for Russia in Syria?," *Military Review* 24, no. 2 (2018): 6-23; Dmitry (Dima) Adamsky, "Russian Campaign in Syria: Change and Continuity in Strategic Culture," *Journal of Strategic Studies* 43, no. 1 (2 January 2020): 104-25.

62. A.D. Tsyganok, "Gruppirovka Rossiyskikh Voysk v Sirii v Bor'be s IGIL (Strategiya i Stsenarii) [Grouping of Russian Troops in Syria in the Fight against ISIL (Strategy and Scenarios)]," *Vestnik Akademii Voennykh Nauk*, 31 March 2016, 10-20.

63. Pryganov, "Ugostili Shpiona 'Krasukhoy' [They Treated the Spy with 'Krasukha']," *Voennyi Vestnik Iuga Rossii*, 30 November 2020, Eastview Digital Library.

64. Shepovalenko, *Siriyskiy Rubezh* [Syrian Frontier].

65. Andrey Riskin, "'Siriyskiy Ekspress' Zhivet Lish' za Schet Staren'kikh Desantnykh Korabley [The Syrian Express Survives Only on Old Landing Ships]," *Nezavisimaya Gazeta*, 17 January 2018, Integrum Digital Archive.

66. John W. Parker, "Putin's Syrian Gambit: Sharper Elbows, Bigger Footprint, Stickier Wicket," *Institute for National Strategic Studies Strategic Perspectives* 25, National Defense University Press, 2017.

67. Kimberly Marten, "Informal Political Networks and Putin's Foreign Policy: The Examples of Iran and Syria," *Problems of Post-Communism* 62, no. 2, 4 March 2015.

68. For an overview of the Wagner Group and PMCs, see, John Lechner, Death Is Our Business: Russian Mercenaries and the New Era of Private Warfare (Bloomsbury Publishing, 2025).

69. "Minoborony Soobshchilo, Chto Rossiyskie PVO Sbili Rakety Izrailya v Sirii [The Ministry of Defense Reported that Russian Air Defenses Shot Down

Israeli Missiles in Syria]," RBK, 26 August 2022, https://www.rbc.ru/rbcfreenews/6309205e9a794721cd469186.

70. Vladimir Mukhin, "Doletet' Do Tseley 'Tomagavkam' Pomeshali "Krasukhi [The 'Krasukha' Systems Prevented the 'Tomahawks' from Reaching Their Targets]," *Nezavisimaya Gazeta*, 18 April 2018, Eastview Digital Library; "Ispytano Siriey, Zavereno 'Patriotom' [Tested by Syria, Certified by Patriot]," *Voenno-Promyshlennyy Kur'er*, 5 September 2017, Integrum Digital Archive; "Minoborony RF Usilivaet Gruppirovku Sredstv REB v Sirii [The Russian Ministry of Defense Strengthens the Grouping of Electronic Warfare Equipment in Syria]," *Voenno-Promyshlennyy Kur'er*, 25 September 2018, Integrum Digital Archive; "Pentagonu Ne Daet Usnut' Rossiyskaya REB 'Krasukha' [The Pentagon Can't Sleep Because of the Russian EW 'Krasukha']," *Voenno-Promyshlennyy Kur'er*, 20 August 2018, Integrum Digital Archive.
71. The variety and sophistication of deployed military technologies suggested that Russia's objectives extended beyond merely combating IS. This notion is underpinned by the fact that ISIS neither possessed nor planned to develop an air force, yet the Kremlin deployed advanced anti-air systems. See Anatoliy Sokolov, "Zontik nad Siriey [Umbrella Over Syria]," *VPK: Voenno-Promyshlennyi Kuryer*, 25 May 2016, Integrum Digital Archive; Vladimir Il'in, "Voennye-Vozdushnye Sily Sirii [Syrian Air Forces]," *Aviatsiya i Kosmonavtika*, 31 January 2016, Integrum Digital Archive.
72. One former Russian military official estimated in 2017 that the Iranian-backed forces consist of Iranian ground forces and pro-Iranian militias (11,000); Hezbollah (15,000); Afghan Hazaras (15,000); and Iraqi Shiites (10,000).
73. Adamsky, "Russian Campaign in Syria," 104-25.
74. Beyond direct coordination in Syria, the establishment of the Russia-Iran Joint Military Commission during Shoigu's visit to Tehran in January 2015 facilitated an even more routine mechanism for high-level contact between Russian and Iranian defense officials. Meeting annually in Tehran or Moscow, this commission helped shape the trajectory of bilateral defense cooperation. While the Syrian Civil War remained a key focus, the commission's scope extended beyond it to negotiate long-term roadmaps, establish specialized working groups, and conclude contracts for joint projects. Collectively, these linkages enabled the Russia-Iran military partnership to deepen and diversify, adapting to evolving dynamics within and beyond Syria.
75. For background on Russian operations see, Kofman, "Syria and the Russian Armed Forces," 9-11.
76. Aleksandr Dvornikov, "Formy Boevogo Primeneniya i Organizatsiya Upravleniya Integrirovannymi Gruppirovkami Vooruzhennykh Sil na Teatre Voennykh Deistvii [Forms of Combat Use and the Organization of the Management of Integrated Groups of the Armed Forces at the Theater of Military Operations]," *Vestnik AVN* 63, no. 2 (2018): 37-41.
77. Ibid.
78. Interview with a Moscow-based expert on Syria (Moscow), 2017.
79. Interview with a Moscow-based expert on the Russian military (Moscow), 2017.
80. Kofman, "Syria and the Russian Armed Forces," 9
81. Interview with a Moscow-based expert on the Russian military (Moscow), 2017
82. However, the reality of Russia's involvement was more nuanced, focusing primarily on supporting the Assad regime against a broad array of opposition forces, not all of which were linked to the Islamic State.

83. Andrei Bezrukov et al., "Strasti po Perimetru [Passion along the Perimeter]," *Kommersant*, 18 January 2016.
84. At the strategic level, Chief of the Russian General Staff Valery Gerasimov and U.S. Chairman of the Joint Chiefs of Staff General Joseph Dunford maintained a channel for senior engagement. They used this channel during times of tension when battlefield campaigns converged, such as in Aleppo in 2016 and Deir ez-Zor in 2017 and 2018. At the campaign level, the Russian commander in Syria and the three-star U.S. general commanding Combined Joint Task Force: Operation Inherent Resolve established a channel for operational battlefield deconfliction. At the tactical level, a twenty-four-hour "hotline" was created between Russian military headquarters at Khmeimim airbase in Syria and U.S. personnel at the Combined Air Operations Center in Qatar, serving as the primary day-to-day line of communication between the two sides. Andrew S. Weiss and Nicole Ng, "Collision Avoidance: The Lessons of U.S. and Russian Operations in Syria," Carnegie Endowment for International Peace, 20 March 2019, https://carnegieendowment.org/2019/03/20/collision-avoidance-lessons-of-u.s.-and-russian-operations-in-syria-pub-78571.
85. John W. Parker, "Putin's Syrian Gambit."
86. Interview with a former Russian diplomat in the Middle East (Moscow), 2017.
87. Dmitry Sergeev, "Chem Grozit Turtsii Napadenie na Siriyu [What Threatens Turkey with the Attack on Syria]," *Boevaya Vakhta*, 12 February 2016, Eastview Digital Library.
88. Interview with a professor at the Russian Diplomatic Academy (Moscow), 2017.
89. Discussion with a Russian Ministry of Defense employee (Moscow), 2019.
90. Nikolai Kozhanov, "Chem Grozit Rossii Uchastie v Irano-Saudovskoi Konfrontatsii [What Threatens Russia's Participation in the Iran-Saudi Confrontation]," *RBK*, 15 January 2016.
91. Strokan and Maxim Yusin, "Podkhody Moskvy i Tegerana k Siriyskoy Probleme Razlichayutsya [The Approaches of Moscow and Tehran to the Syrian Problem Differ]," *Kommersant*, 21 April 2016.
92. Andrei Kolesnikov, "Tegeran Rabotal do Poslednego Posetitelya [Tehran Worked until the Last Visitor]," *Kommersant*, 24 November 2015.
93. "Gustarish-i hamkārīhā-yi difāʿī va fannī-i Īrān va Rūsīyah lāzimah-'i s̲abāt va amnīyat-i manṭaqah'ī ast [The Expansion of Defense and Technical Cooperation between Iran and Russia Is Essential for Regional Stability and Security]," *Quds*, 23 August 2015.
94. "Siriyskaya Tema na Peregovorakh V. Putina s A. Khamenei [Syrian Issue at the Talks of V. Putin with A. Khamenei]," Institut Blizhnego Vostoka, 24 November 2015.
95. "RF i Iran Podpisali Novyi Kontrakt Po S-300 [Russia and Iran Sign New Contract on the S-300]," IA Regnum, 9 November 2015.
96. "Ministr Oborony Rossii General Armii Shoygu Vstretilsya s Iranskim Kollegoy [Russian Defense Minister Army General Shoigu Meets with His Iranian Counterpart]," Ministerstvo Oborony RF, 16 February 2016.
97. Oleg Odnokolenko, "Moskva i Tegeran Otkryvaiut Novuiu Stranitsu Voenno-Tehnicheskogo Sotrudnichestva na Fone Boevyh Deystviy v Sirii [Moscow and Tehran Open a New Page of Military-Technical Cooperation on the Background of Military Action in Syria]," *Nezavisimaya Gazeta*, 17 February 2016.
98. "Deystviya VKS RF v Sirii Imeli Pozitivnye Posledstviya—Ministr Oborony Irana [Russia's Military Operations in Syria Had Positive Consequences—Iran's Defense Minister]," RIA Novosti, 16 February 2016; Ivan Safronov and Elena Chernenko,

"Iran Pritsenivaetsya k Rossiiskomu Voenpromu [Iran Is Checking Out the Russian Defense Industry]," *Kommersant*, 15 February 2016.

99. Interview with Russia-based Middle East specialist (Moscow), 2017.

100. Kayhan Barzegar, ""Amā va Agarhā-Yi Ḥuẓūr-i Rūsīyah Dar Sūrīyah Barāy Īrān [The Pros and Cons of Russia's Presence in Syria for Iran]," *E'temad*, 17 November 2015. Kayhan Barzegar, one of Iran's most prominent foreign policy commentators, suggested that Russia's involvement in Syria should be viewed through varying lenses of skepticism and strategic optimism. Russia's presence is viewed as an aggressive assertion of geopolitical ambitions, aiming to secure its strategic military bases and expand its global influence, with motivations tied to President Putin's vision of restoring Russia as a global power. Conversely, the optimistic view argues that Russia's intervention is primarily driven by national security concerns, aiming to combat terrorism directly in Syria to avoid fighting on its own borders and to uphold global security by addressing terrorism as an international challenge. Barzegar explores how Russia's military presence impacts Iran's national security and interests, with pessimistic views fearing it could undermine Iran's regional position, while the optimistic stance sees it as strengthening Iran's role in promoting a political solution to the Syrian crisis and enhancing its strategic value on the international stage.

101. Hassan Beheshtipour, "Īrān Nabāyad Nīrū-Yi Dar Sāyah-i Rūsīyah Talqī Shavad [Iran Should Not Be Considered as a Force in the Shadow of Russia]," *E'temad*, 17 November 2015. Hassan Behstepur took a different stance: the military presence of Russia has coerced Saudi Arabia and Turkey into negotiations, potentially favoring Iran's strategic interests in the region. Russia's involvement facilitated Iran's participation in international summits on Syria, highlighting Iran's significant role in resolving the crisis. There is a risk that Iran's pivotal role in Syria could be overshadowed by Russia's military actions, potentially diminishing Iran's influence and contributions. The possibility of Russia negotiating deals with the West that could be detrimental to Iran's interests is also considered a significant threat.

102. Interview with a Russian foreign policy specialist (Moscow), 2017.

103. Safronov and Chernenko, "Iran Pritsenivaetsya k Rossiiskomu Voenpromu [Iran Is Checking out the Russian Defence Industry]"; "Dey'stviya VKS RF v Sirii Imeli Pozitivnye Posledstviya—Ministr Oborony Irana [Russia's Military Operations in Syria Had Positive Consequences—Iran's Defense Minister]," RIA Novosti, 16 February 2016.

104. Ekaterina Zabrodina, "Na Venskikh Podmostkakh Rozhdaetsya Mir [Peace Being Born on Viennese Stage]," *Rossiyskaya Gazeta*, 30 October 2015.

105. Khodynskaya-Golenishcheva, *Liviyskiy Urok: Tsel' Opravdyvaet Sredstva?* [The Libyan Lesson: The Ends Justify the Means?].

106. Qassim Ghafuri, "Vin Rā Durust Bashināsim [Vienna We Should Understand Correctly]," *Siyāsat-i Rūz*, 29 October 2015; Javid Qorbanoghli, "Īrān va Pāzil Sūrīyah Dar Ājlās Vīn [Iran and Syrian Puzzle in the Vienna Talks]," *Shargh*, 29 October 2015.

107. Amid Moscow's ongoing military operations in Syria in November 2015, the Kremlin reportedly proposed a six-point plan to resolve the Syrian conflict ahead of an impending Vienna meeting on Syria. Reports indicated that this plan allowed for Assad's participation in a transitional process and suggested labeling all insurgent groups as terrorists, which posed challenges for Western officials. However, the West, appearing hesitant, did not take immediate action, while Moscow had already used military force to underscore its stance.

108. S/PV.7588, "United Nations Security Council Meeting Record: The Situation in the Middle East," UNSC, 18 December 2015.
109. Regime forces, backed by an intense campaign of Russian airstrikes and with the support of Russian military advisors on the ground, secured control of all the major towns and cities in Northern Latakia Province. Igor Subbotin and Renat Abdullin, "Rossiya Predlagaet Plan po Sirii na Fone Nastupleniya v Aleppo [Russia Offers a Plan for Syria against the Background of the Offensive in Aleppo]," *Moskovskiy Komsomolets*, 12 February 2016.
110. "ANONS: V Sirii Vstupaet v Silu Rezhim Prekrashcheniya Boevyh Deystviy [Announcement: In Syria the Regime of Cessation of Hostilities Comes into Effect]," ITAR-TASS, 27 February 2016, Integrum Digital Archive.
111. "Miunhenskiy Dogovor: Chego Zhdat' ot Siriyskogo Peremiriya [The Munich Treaty: What to Expect from the Syrian Armistice]," RBK, 12 February 2016, Integrum Digital Archive.
112. Yegor Sozaev-Guryev, "Kreml' Dobivaetsyya Peremiriya v Sirii [The Kremlin Is Seeking an Armistice in Syria]," *Izvestiya*, 25 February 2016, Integrum Digital Archive; Leonid Ivashov, "Blizhnevostochny Gambit [Middle East Gambit]," *Komsomolskaya Pravda*, 2 March 2016, Integrum Digital Archive.
113. "Rūsihāyi Dar Sūrīyah Chigūnih Mī Jangand [How Do the Russians Fight in Syria]," Mehr, 19 October 2015.
114. Russia seemed to be aware of this and would frequently follow up with discussions with the Iranians. "Glavy MID Rossii i Irana Obsudili Vypolnenie Rezhima Prekrashcheniya Ognia v Sirii—MID RF [Russian and Iranian Foreign Ministers Discussed the Implementation of the Ceasefire in Syria—RF MFA]," ITAR-TASS, 18 March 2016, Integrum Digital Archive.
115. "Horoshie Otnosheniya s RF Ne Oznachaiut Odobreniya Irana Kazhdogo Ee Shaga po Sirii—Rouhani [Good Relations with Russia Do Not Mean Iran's Approval of Each Step in Syria—Rouhani]," RIA Novosti, 6 March 2016.
116. "Putin: Rossiya Vypolnila Zadachi v Sirii [Putin: Russia Fulfilled the Tasks in Syria]," RIA Novosti, 14 March 2016; "Putin Prikazal Nachat' Vyvod Osnovnyh Sil RF iz Sirii s 15 Marta [Putin Ordered the Withdrawal of the Main Russian Forces from Syria to Begin on 15 March],"TASS, 14 March 2016.
117. "Iran i RF Prodolzhat Missiiu Voennyh Sovetnikov v Sirii dlia Bor'by s Terrorizmom—Shamhani [Iran and Russia Will Continue the Mission of Military Advisors in Syria to Combat Terrorism—Shamkhani]," ITAR-TASS, 16 March 2016; "Vyvod Chasti VKS RF Ne Povliyaet na Sotrudnichestvo s Soiuznikami v SAR—Sovetnik Lidera IRI [The Withdrawal of a Part of the Russian Air Force Will Not Affect the Cooperation with the Allies in the UAR—an Advisor to the Leader of the IRI]," ITAR-TASS, 16 March 2016.
118. Yevgeny Medvedev, "Siriyskaya Mnogokhodovka Grozit Ssoroy s Iranom [The Syrian Multimove Threatens a Quarrel with Iran]," *Nezavisimaya Gazeta*, 17 March 2016.
119. Ahmad Vakhshiteh, "Āz a'shq-i Rūs'hā Nabāīd Tarsīd [We Should Not Be Scared of Russia's Love]," Ensafnews, 5 April 2016.
120. Interview with a Russia-based military expert and commentator (Moscow, Russia), 2017.
121. Sa'dollah Zar'ei, "Rūsīyah Dar Sūrīyah [Russia in Syria]," *Kayhan*, 22 April 2016.
122. One key hub was located at Al Safira, around 30 km southeast of Aleppo. Here, Syrian commanders, Russian advisors, IRGC officers, and Hezbollah field leaders

gathered to map out target priorities, synchronize artillery schedules, and plan the overarching siege strategy. From Al Safira, senior officers rapidly relayed updates to various localized command posts scattered around Aleppo's perimeter.

123. Kofman, "Syria and the Russian Armed Forces."
124. In the first phase, from May to September 2016, the objective was to complete the encirclement of East Aleppo. Russian air forces conducted intensive airstrikes on the Castello Road, the main supply route for the rebels, and pro-regime troops made advances to cut off the road. By late July, the road was under full control of pro-regime forces, and East Aleppo was encircled again. The second phase, from September to October 2016, focused on intensifying the siege of the rebel enclave. Russian air and artillery strikes supported pro-regime forces as they pressed the offensive on the northern edge of East Aleppo. However, the opposition forces, well entrenched in urban terrain, were able to withstand the attacks, and minimal gains were made across the city's other siege lines. In the third phase, from November to December 2016, the objective was to clear and capture East Aleppo. Pro-regime forces, with increased Russian special operations and reconnaissance presence on the ground, launched swift ground assaults and negotiated evacuations of opposition fighters and civilians. With heavy Russian air and artillery support, pro-regime forces were able to seize key districts and weaken the opposition. By late December, the regime had regained control of most of Aleppo. See Seth Jones, ed., *Moscow's War in Syria* (n.p.: Center for Strategic & International Studies, 2020).
125. The umbrella group was called Jaysh al-Fatah. It was coalition of Islamist rebel groups formed in March 2015 to coordinate opposition efforts against the Syrian government in the Idlib and Hama Provinces.
126. Khan Touman, located in the southern countryside of Aleppo, served as a critical link between Aleppo and the city of Hama. It was strategically important for both the Syrian government forces and the opposition groups in terms of securing supply routes and gaining a tactical advantage in the larger Battle of Aleppo. The Battle of Khan Touman was part of the government's wider offensive strategy to encircle and isolate rebel-held areas in Aleppo. By capturing Khan Touman, the government forces aimed to cut off supply lines and reinforcement routes for the opposition fighters in Eastern Aleppo. It also served as a launching point for subsequent offensives on other rebel-held areas.
127. "Dar 'khān ṭūmān' chih ītifāqī ūfatād [In Khan Touman What Happened]," *Dunyā-yi Iqtiṣād*, 17 May 2016; "Taḥlīl-i sīyāsī-i haftih [Political Analysis of the Week]," *Jumhūrī-i Islāmī*, 6 May 2016.
128. "Dar 'Ḥalab' Sūrīyah chih khabar ast? Guzārishhā-yi ẓidd va naqīẓ az 'Khān'Ṭūmān' dar miyānah-'i bī'tavajjuhī-i Rūsīyah [What's the News in Aleppo, Syria? Reports of Contradictions regarding 'Khan Touman' amid Russian Indifference]," Tabnak, 7 May 2016.
129. "Vākunish'hā bih īistifādih-i Rūsīyah āz Pāygāh-i Nūzhah [Reactions to Russia's Use of Nojeh Base]," *Dunyā-yi Iqtiṣād*, 20 August 2016, https://www.donya-e-eqtesad.com/fa/tiny/news-1065040.
130. Neknam Ershidinia, "Zanjīrih-i Nishasthāyī-i Nākām Dar Buḥrān-i Sūrīyah [Chain of Failed Talks in Syrian Crisis]," *Rūznāmih-i Īrān*, 23 May 2016; "Tauṣī'ah Rūḥānī Bih Kārshanāsān Ravābiṭ Īrān va Rūsīyih: Bīshtar Bih Ayandeh Negāh Kunīd [Rouhani's Advice to Iran-Russia Relations Experts: Pay More Attention to the Future]," *Aftab*, 19 May 2016.

131. Ivan Safronov, "Respubliku Zashchishchayut Silami Trekh Ministrov [The Republic is Protected by the Forces of Three Ministers]," *Kommersant*, 9 June 2016; "Ministr Oborony Rossii General Armii Shoigu Vyletel s Rabochim Vizitom v Iran [Russian Defense Minister Army General Shoigu Flew to Iran on a Working Visit]," Ministerstvo Oborony RF, 9 June 2016.
132. "Samolety VKS RF Tu-22M3 i Su-34, Vzletev s Aėrodroma Hamadan v Irane, Nanesli Aviaudar po Ob#ektam Terroristov v Sirii [Tu-22M3 and Su-34 Aircraft, Taking Off from the Airfield Hamadan in Iran, Inflicted an Airstrike on the Objects of Terrorists in Syria]," Ministerstvo Oborony RF, 16 August 2016; Vladimir Mukhin, "V Bor'bu s Terroristami Vstupila Novaya Rossiyskaya Aviabaza v Irane [New Russian Airbase in Iran Joins in the Fight against Terrorists]," *Nezavisimaya Gazeta*, 16 August 2016.
133. Ivan Petrov, "Bomby na Podlete [Bombs on Approach]," *Rossiyskaya Gazeta*, 16 August 2016; Alexei Nikolsky, "Rossiyskie Bombardirovshchiki Budut Letat' v Siriyu iz Irana [Russian Bombers Will Fly to Syria from Iran]," *Vedomosti*, 16 August 2016; "Sotrudnichestvo Moskvy i Tegerana v Sirii Stanovitsia Bolee Znachimym—Sovetnik Glavy Irana [Cooperation between Moscow and Tehran in Syria Becomes More Significant—Advisor to the Head of Iran]," *RIA Novosti*, 4 February 2016; Vladimir Mukhin, "V Bor'bu s Terroristami Vstupila Novaya Rossiiskaya Aviabaza v Irane [New Russian Airbase in Iran Joins in the Fight against Terrorists]," *Nezavisimaya Gazeta*, 16 August 2016; Mohammad Safari, "Āghāz Dardsarhāy-ī Buzurg Barāyi Ḥāmīān Tirūrīsm [Beginning of Major Headaches for Terrorism Supporters]," *Siyāsat-i Rūz*, 17 August 2016.
134. "Samolety VKS RF Tu-22M3 i Su-34, Vzletev s Aėrodroma Hamadan v Irane, Nanesli Aviaudar po Ob#ektam Terroristov v Sirii [Tu-22M3 and Su-34 Aircraft, Taking off from the Airfield Hamadan in Iran, Inflicted an Airstrike on the Objects of Terrorists in Syria]"; "Rossiiskie Bombardirovshchiki Su-34 s Aerodroma Khamadan v Irane Nanesli Aviaudar po Ob'ektam Gruppirovki 'Islamskoe Gosudarstvo' v Provintsii Deir-Ez-Zor [Russian Su-34 Bombers Launched an Airstrike on 'Islamic State' Facilities in the Deir ez-Zor Province from Hamadan Airfield in Iran]," Ministerstvo Oborony Rossiiskoi Federatsii, 18 August 2016, https://function.mil.ru/news_page/country/more.htm?id=12093053@egNews.
135. "Pāyīān Ḥiẓūr-I Rūsīyah Dar Nūzhih [The End of Russia in Nojeh]," *Mehr*, 22 August 2016.
136. "Tājir-i Aslaḥah Dar Khāvar-i Miyānah [Arms Dealer in the Middle East]," *El'timād*, 30 May 2016.
137. Interestingly, the legal basis of the prohibition of foreign military bases on Iranian territory was pursued by the Soviet Union in 1962 with the shah and later became enshrined in the Iranian constitution. "Nāmhāyī bih rīaīs-i majils [Letter to the Head of the Majilis]," *Entekhab*, 18 August 2016, http://www.entekhab.ir/fa/news/286996.
138. "Vākunish'hā bih ıistifadih-i Rūsīyah āz Pāygāh-i Nūzhah [Reactions to Russia's use of Nojeh Base]," *Dunyā-yi Iqtiṣād*, 20 August 2016, https://www.donya-e-eqtesad.com/fa/tiny/news-1065040.
139. "Pochemu Rossiyskie Samolety Pokinuli Aviabazu Hamadan [Why Did Russian Aircraft Leave the Hamadan Airbase?]," *RBK*, 22 August 2016.
140. "Vākunish'hā bih īistifādih-i Rūsīyah āz Pāygāh-i Nūzhah [Reactions to Russia's Use of Nojeh Base]."
141. Evgeniy Satanovskiy, "Kurdskaya Ruletka [Kurdish Roulette]," *VPK: Voenno-*

Promyshlennyi Kur'er, 31 August 2016, https://on-demand.eastview.com/browse/doc/47089608.

142. Georgiy Stepanov, "Sposobny Li Podruzhit'sia i Sblizit'sia Rossiya, Turtsiya i Iran [Are Russia, Turkey, and Iran Able to Stay Friends and Get Closer?]," *Kommersant*, 15 August 2016.
143. Strokan and Maxim Yusin, "Turtsiya Probuetsia na Novuiu Rol' v Sirii [Turkey Is Being Tested for a New Role in Syria]," *Kommersant*, 29 August 2016.
144. Fyodor Lukyanov, "Na Blizhnem Vostoke Vozmozhno Vse i Srazu [In the Middle East, Everything Is Possible at Once]," Gazeta.ru, 25 August 2016.
145. Yevgeny Medvedev, "Siriiskaya Mnogohodovka Grozit Ssoroi s Iranom [Multinational Syria Threatens Quarrel with Iran]," *Nezavisimaya Gazeta*, 17 March 2016.
146. Seyyed Hossein Mousavi, "Jang-i Īstrātzhīk Ḥaleb [Aleppo's Strategic War]," *Rūznāmih-i Īrān*, 6 August 2016.
147. In his telephone conversation with Rouhani, Putin sought to quell Tehran's concerns, affirming that "Iran and Russia have been and will be each other's partners in resolving regional crises, and this cooperation and consultation will particularly continue in Syria"; "Duktar Rūḥānī Dar Guft va Gū Tilifunī Bā Rīa'īs Jumhūrī Rūsīyah [Dr Rouhani in a Telephone Conversation with the Russian President]," *Riyāsat-i Īrān*, 24 December 2016, http://president.ir/fa/96581.
148. "Sovmestnoe Zayavlenie Ministrov Inostrannykh del Islamskoy Respubliki Iran, Rossiyskoy Federatsii, Turetskoy Respubliki po Soglasovannym Meram, Napravlennym na Ozhivlenie Politicheskogo Protsessa s Tselyu Prekrashcheniya Siriyskogo Konflikta, Moskva, 20 Dekabrya 2016 Goda [Joint Statement by the Foreign Ministers of the Islamic Republic of Iran, the Russian Federation, and the Republic of Turkey on Agreed Steps to Revitalize the Political Process to End the Syrian Conflict, Moscow, 20 December 2016]," Press-Tsentr MID RF, 20 December 2016.
149. Remarks by the Iranian ambassador to Russia, Russian Academy of Sciences (Moscow), 2017.
150. Interview with a Russian presidential advisor for the Middle East (Moscow), 2019.
151. Ali Shamkhani, "Musāhabih Bā Alī Shamkhānī [Interview with Ali Shamkhani]," *Mūa'sasah Muṭāl'āt-i Īrān va Āūrāsīā (Īrās)*, 8 June 2017.

5. THE BATTLEFIELD AND BEYOND

1. Kareem Shaheen and Shaun Walker, "Moscow and Ankara Present United Front after Russian Ambassador's Murder," *The Guardian*, 20 December 2016.
2. Arseniy Zamostyanov, "Aleksandr Griboedov: Pogibshiy za Rossiyu [Alexander Griboyedov: Died for Russia]," *Voennoe obozrenie*, 25 December 2016, https://topwar.ru/106212-aleksandr-griboedov-pogibshiy-za-rossiyu.html
3. "Furṣathā va Tahdīdhāyī 'Astānah' [Opportunities and Threats of Astana]," *Khorasan*, 24 January 2017; Sa'dollah Zar'ei, "Astānah Iz'ān Bih Baqā va Iqtidār-i Āssad [Astana, Acknowledging Assad's Continuation and Authority]," *Kayhan*, 24 January 2017.
4. Strokan and Maxim Yusin, "Rossiya i SShA Okazalis' po Raznye Storony Irana [Russia and the U.S. Were on Different Sides of Iran]," *Kommersant*, 9 February 2017.
5. Strokan, "Peregovornyi Protest [Negotiating Protest]," *Kommersant*, 24 January 2017.
6. Marianna Belenkaya, "Iskusstvo Torga [Art of Bargaining]," *Profil'*, 30 January 2017.

7. The initial Astana talks in January and February 2017 centered on a joint surveillance method for the semi-adhered ceasefire, proposed by Russia, Turkey, and Iran. However, when Russia resumed these talks in March and May, the opposition declined to attend due to the regime violating the nationwide and short-lived Eastern Ghouta ceasefire. Regardless of the opposition's absence, the three nations discussed and conceptually approved the idea of "'de-escalation zones"—'areas under opposition dominion where all involved parties would agree to halt conflicts and allow relief for civilians. Subsequent discussions in July about these zones 'failed to yield concrete results.
8. Vladimir Frolov, "Rossiia Dogovorilas' o Peremirii v Sirii: Naskol'ko Ėto Ser'ezno? [Russia Agrees to Ceasefire in Syria: How Serious Is It?]," *Slon*, 30 December 2016, Integrum Digital Archive.
9. Vladimir Frolov, "Igra na Kompleksakh: Kakoy Tsenoy Dalos' Peremirie v Sirii" [Playing on Complexes: The Cost of the Truce in Syria], *Slon*, 22 February 2016, Integrum Digital Archive.
10. Mani Mehrabi, "Rūsīyah Īrān Rā Dūr Nazadh Ast [Russia Has Not Ignored Iran]," *E'temad*, 11 January 2017, 6; Ghasem Ghafouri, "Andīshah'hā-Yi Pūtīn [Putin's Reflections]," *Siyāsat-i Rūz*, 4 January 2017, http://siasatrooz.ir/images/magazine/0003/files/atfl00001559-0008.pdf.
11. For an overview of the tensions, see Parker, "Putin's Syrian Gambit."
12. Vladimir Sazhin, "Iran vs Izrail' [Israel vs Iran]," *Mezhdunarodnaya Zhizn'*, 12 March 2021.
13. Former Russian Defense Minister Shoigu had stated that Israel's request for a 40-km buffer zone was excessive. However, on 23 July Russian Foreign Minister Lavrov and Chief of the Russian General Staff Gerasimov proposed a 100-km strip, while Israel insisted on the total removal of Iranian forces from all of Syria.
14. Elena Vasetsova, "Rossiya i Izrail' v Siriiskom Krizise [Russia and Israel in the Syrian Crisis]," *Vestnik Rossiiskogo Universiteta Druzhby Narodov. Seriya: Politologiya*, no. 2 (2016): 7-14.
15. "Istoriya Voennykh Operatsii Turtsii v Sirii [History of Turkey's Military Operations in Syria]," TASS, 9 October 2019, Integrum Digital Archive.
16. Aidan Lewis and Sarah Safty, "Arab League Readmits Syria as Relations with Assad Normalise," Reuters, 7 May 2023, https://www.reuters.com/world/middle-east/arab-league-set-readmit-syria-relations-with-assad-normalise-2023-05-07.
17. Putin and Rouhani met at a trilateral summit in Baku on 8 August 2016, which featured the participation of Azerbaijani President Ilham Aliyev.
18. Yevgeny Pudovkin, "Vashington Ispytyvaet na Prochnost' Otnosheniia Rossii i Irana [Washington Is Testing the Relations between Russia and Iran]," *Nezavisimaya Gazeta*, 3 February 2017.
19. Nina Ilyina, "Prezident Irana Prodemonstriroval v Kremle Otsutstvie Protivorechii s Rossiei [The President of Iran Demonstrated in the Kremlin the Absence of Contradictions with Russia]," *Vedomosti*, 29 March 2017.
20. "Muẕākirāt-i fishurdah va muhimm-i ru'asā-yi jumhūrī-i Īrān va Rūsīyah dar Kākh-i Krimlīn/Pūtīn: Īrān hamsāyah-'i khūb va sharīk-i muṭma'inn-i Rūsīyah ast [Intensive and Important Negotiations between the Presidents of Iran and Russia at the Kremlin Palace/Putin: Iran Is a Good Neighbor and a Reliable Partner for Russia]," IRNA, 28 March 2017.
21. "Sovmestnoe Zayavlenie Prezidenta Rossiyskoy Federatsii i Prezidenta Islamskoy

Respubliki Iran [Joint Statement by the President of the Russian Federation and the President of the Islamic Republic of Iran]," Press-Sluzhba Prezidenta RF, 28 March 2017, Integrum Digital Archive.

22. "Duktar Rūḥānī Dar Dīdār Ra'īs Jumhūrī Rūsīyah [Dr Rouhani Meets the Russian President]," *Riyāsat-i Īrān*, 29 March 2017.
23. "Vstrecha s Prezidentom Irana Hasanom Ruhani [Meeting with the President of Iran Hassan Rouhani]," Press-Sluzhba Prezidenta RF, 28 March 2017, Integrum Digital Archive.
24. Hamidreza Azizi, "5 Reasons to Watch Rouhani's Visit to Russia," Al-Monitor, 26 March 2017, https://www.al-monitor.com/originals/2017/03/iran-rouhani-russia-official-visit-putin-meeting-elections.html
25. The two sides stressed that the "fight against terrorism will continue unabated."They also stated that "the chemical episode was suspect, and we believe an independent fact-finding committee should look into the issue and provide clear information as to the perpetrators."The two sides promised that "the fight against terrorism will continue, and the operations against terrorists in Syria will be intensified." "Guftūgū-i Tilifunī Bāqirī Bā Ra'īs Sitād Gul Nīrūhāyī Rūsīyah [Bagheri's Telephone Conversation with Chief of Staff of Russian Forces]," *Jahān*, 9 April 2017.
26. "Glava Sovbeza Patrushev Rasskazal Iranskomu Kollege ob Organizatorakh Khimataki v Sirii [Security Council Chief Patrushev Told His Iranian Counterpart about the Organizers of the Chemical Attack in Syria]," *Parlamentskaya Gazeta*, 8 April 2017, Integrum Digital Archive. Rouhani claimed that "reports indicate that terrorists have access to chemical weapons and the U.S. [air]strikes will prompt terrorist groups to use chemical weapons once again." Rouhani reiterated Tehran's readiness to "consult, cooperate, and coordinate with Moscow" in the fight against terrorism. Rouhani also called Syrian President Assad on 9 April. Rouhani stressed that the airstrikes "will not have any effect on the outcomes of combating terrorism and the future of Syria" and expressed hope that the "free countries of the world" will "explicitly condemn such attacks and acts of aggression." Rouhani warned that "such attacks only contribute to encouraging the terrorists who have suffered heavy losses in Syria and Iraq in recent months." "Telefonnyi Razgovor s Prezidentom Irana Khasanom Rukhani [Telephone Conversation with Iranian President Hassan Rouhani]," Press-Sluzhba Prezidenta RF, 9 April 2017, Integrum Digital Archive; "Guftūgū-ī Tilifunī Bā Pūtīn [Telephone Conversation with Putin]," *Riyāsat-i Īrān*, 9 April 2017.
27. "Iddi'ā-yi vazīr-i Ṣahyūnīst: Rūsīyah va Isrā'īl manāfi'-i mushtarakī dar Sūrīyah dārand [Zionist Minister's Claim: Russia and Israel Have Common Interests in Syria],"Tasnim, 26 January 2019; "Luzūm-i hushyārī-i bīshtar-i Īrān dar qabāl-i bāzī-i iḥtimālī-i Rūsīyah va Isrā'īl dar Sūrīyah [The Necessity of Increased Vigilance by Iran regarding the Potential Game between Russia and Israel in Syria]," Irdiplomacy.ir, 22 September 2018, https://tinyurl.com/57s5xs54.
28. Tat'yana Zamakhina, "Rossiya, Iran i Azerbaidzhan Dogovorilis' o Tamozhennom Koridore [Russia, Iran, and Azerbaijan Agree on a Customs Corridor]," *Rossiiskaya Gazeta*, 1 November 2017, https://rg.ru/2017/11/01/rossiia-iran-i-azerbajdzhan-dogovorilis-o-tamozhennom-koridore.html.
29. Leila Ebrahimian, "Paydā va pinhān-i Pūtīn [The Public and Hidden Putin]," *Shargh*, 1 November 2017.
30. Igor Kryuchkov and Valentin Loginov, "Putin v Irane: Izolirovat' Amerikantsev i Podvinut' Kitai [Putin in Iran: Isolate Americans and Push China Forward]," Gazeta.

ru, 2 November 2017, https://www.gazeta.ru/politics/2017/11/02_a_10967756.shtml.
31. "Vstrecha s Ali Khamenei [Meeting with Ali Khamenei]," Press-Sluzhba Prezidenta RF, 1 November 2017, Integrum Digital Archive; "Vstrecha s Prezidentom Irana Khasanom Rukhani [Meeting with Iran's President Hassan Rouhani]," Press-Sluzhba Prezidenta RF, 1 November 2017, Integrum Digital Archive.
32. Anastasiya Agamalova, Aleksey Nikol'skiy, and Nina Il'ina, "Putin Prikazal Vyvesti Voyska iz Sirii [Putin Orders the Withdrawal of Troops from Syria]," *Vedomosti*, 11 December 2017, https://www.vedomosti.ru/politics/articles/2017/12/11/744805-putin-siriyu
33. V.V. Kondrashov, "Grazhdanskaya Voina v Sirii (Fevral' 2017) [Civil War in Syria (February 2017)]," *Voenno-Strategicheskii Analiz*, 31 March 2017, https://dlib-eastview-com/browse/doc/49772803.
34. V.V. Kondrashov, "Grazhdanskaya Voina v Sirii (Mai 2017) [Civil War in Syria (May 2017)]," *Voenno-Strategicheskii Analiz*, 30 June 2017, https://dlib-eastview-com/browse/doc/49773002.
35. Pavel Ivanov, "Deyr-Ez-Zor: Komu Slava, Komu Pozor [Deir ez-Zor: Who Gets Glory, Who Gets Shame]," *Voenno-Promyshlennyy Kur'er*, 3 July 2017, Integrum Digital Archive.
36. "Zarb-i Shast-i Pūtīn [Putin's Countermove]," *Donyā-yi Eqteṣād*, 30 July 2017, magiran.com/n3600722.
37. Interview with a Russia-based expert on the Middle East (Moscow), 2019.
38. Interview with a Russia-based expert with links to the intelligence services (Moscow), 2019.
39. "Khuṭūṭ Dafā'ī Dā'ish Dar Shahr Dīr Al-Zawr Shakasta Shud [The Defense Lines of ISIS Were Broken in the City of Deir ez-Zor]," *Donya-ye-Eqtesad*, 31 August 2017.
40. "Shahr-i Dayr al-Zūr bih ṭūr-i kāmil āzād shud [The City of Deir ez-Zor Has Been Completely Liberated]," Fars News, 3 November 2017.
41. "Sūriyah Bi-Kamk Ḥizb Allāh Wa-Lashkar Fāṭimīyūn Dayr al-Zawr Rā Bi-Ṭūr Kāmil Āzād Kard [Syria, with the Help of Hezbollah and the Fatemiyoun Brigade, Completely Liberated Deir ez-Zor]," *Kayhan*, 4 November 2017, https://www.magiran.com/article/3656452.
42. "Nigāhī bih nishast-i 4 jānibah-'i Īrān, Rūsīyah, Sūrīyah va 'Irāq dar Baghdād; Tihrān va i'tilāfhā-yi muvaffaq-i manṭaqah'ī [A Look at the Four-Way Meeting of Iran, Russia, Syria, and Iraq in Baghdad; Tehran and Successful Regional Coalitions]," Tasnim, 20 April 2018.
43. "Wazīr Al-Difā' Yazūr Markaz al-Ta'āwun al-Amnī al-Rubā'ī [The Minister of Defense Visits the Quadrilateral Security Cooperation Center]," YouTube, https://www.youtube.com/watch?v=jLYqvtnPpXo.
44. "Siriya, Rossiya i Iran Provodyat Sovmestnye Voennye Ucheniya [Syria, Russia, and Iran Conduct Joint Military Exercises]," MigNews, 3 October 2019, https://mignews.com/news/expert/siriia-rossiia-i-iran-provodiat-sovmestnye-voennye-ucheniia.html.
45. "Chigūnah Kurd'hā va Rūsīyah dar Dayr al-Zawr mī'khvāhand kār-i Dā'ish rā yik'surah kunand! [How the Kurds and Russia Intend to Eliminate ISIS in Deir ez-Zor]," *Khabar*, 6 October 2018, khabaronline.ir/x8Tt5.
46. "Ākhirīn nafas'hā-yi Dā'ish [The Last Breaths of ISIS]," Tasnim, 6 August 2016.
47. "¯rān bih dunbāl-i jang-i qudrat bā Rūsīyah dar Sūrīyah nīst/Āmrīkā, Isrā'īl va Su'ūdīhā

bih dunbāl-i tasalluṭ bar Sūrīyah būdand [Iran Is Not Seeking a Power Struggle with Russia in Syria/America, Israel, and the Saudis Were Seeking Dominance over Syria]," Tabnak, 13 May 2020, http://www.tabnak.ir/fa/news/978349.

48. "Rossiiskie Voennye v Sirii Perebrosili Boevuyu Tekhniku Cherez Evfrat [Russian Military in Syria Transferred Military Equipment across the Euphrates]," RIA Novosti, 26 August 2020.
49. Kirill Semenov, "Confrontation between US, pro-Iranian Groups in Syria and Iraq Poses Challenges for Russia," Al Monitor, 12 July 2021, https://www.al-monitor.com/originals/2021/07/confrontation-between-us-pro-iranian-groups-syria-and-iraq-poses-challenges.
50. For background on the 5th Corps, see Gregoriy Lukyanov and Ruslan Mamedov, "Nazad k Poryadku [Back to Order]," RIAC, 13 April 2017, https://russiancouncil.ru/analytics-and-comments/analytics/nazad-k-poryadku.
51. Interview with a Russia-based military expert (Moscow), 2019.
52. This was a broader conflict between Russia and Iran, especially near Russian military installations "Okhrana Aviabazy Khmeimim Glazami Ochevidtsa: 'Dazhe taksistov poprosili perebazirovat'sya' [Security at the Khmeimim Airbase through the Eyes of an Eyewitness: 'Even taxi drivers were asked to relocate']," *Moskovskiy Komsomolets*, 9 January 2018, https://www.mk.ru/politics/2018/01/09/okhrana-aviabazy-khmeymim-glazami-ochevidca-dazhe-taksistov-poprosili-perebazirovatsya.html.
53. "Rūsīyah dar manāṭiq-i taḥt-i nufūẕ-i Āmrīkā dar Sūrīyah pāygāh-i niẓāmī iḥdāṡ kard [Russia Establishes a Military Base in Areas under American Influence in Syria]," *Donyā-ye Eqteṣād*, 27 October 2023.
54. In 2019, the United States became the first country to recognize Israeli sovereignty over the territory in the Golan Heights.
55. "Sharāyiṭ-i vīzhah dar junūb-i gharb-i Sūrīyah Āmrīkā va rizhīm-i Ṣihyūnīstī dast bih dāmān-i Rūsīyah shudand [Special Conditions in Southwest Syria Have Led America and the Zionist Regime to Seek Russia's Assistance]," *Keyhan*, 30 June 2018.
56. "Guftugū-yi vazīr-i jang-i Isrā'īl va hamtā-yi Rūs dar bārah-'i ḥuẕūr-i Īrān dar Sūrīyah [Discussion between the Israeli Minister of Defense and His Russian Counterpart regarding Iran's Presence in Syria]," Mehr News, 1 July 2018.
57. "Jābirī Anṣārī: qadrat va nufūẕ dar manṭaqah hazīnah dārd [Jaberi Ansari: Power and Influence in the Region Are Costly]," Fars News, 6 March 2019.
58. Russia has sought to limit the presence of pro-Iranian groups on Israel's borders by integrating parts of the former opposition into the 5th Corps, yet competition between Hezbollah and Iranian-backed groups continues in Daraa and Quneitra. Hamidreza Azizi, "Why Putin Won't Throw Iran under the Bus in Syria," Al-Monitor, 10 July 2018, https://www.al-monitor.com/originals/2018/07/iran-syria-presence-putin-trump-summit-helsinki-assad.html.
59. Interview with a Russia-based expert on Syria (Moscow), 2019.
60. Interview with a Russia-based expert on militaries in the Middle East (online), 2021.
61. Correspondence with a reporter from a local Syrian outlet; Russia offers monthly salaries of 240,000 SYL to each fighter that splits from Iranian-backed militias and joins the Russian-backed formation, which is double the salary offered by Iran. Moreover, the new recruits of the Russian-backed formations serve in headquarters in Deir ez-Zor on a five-hour-shift each day. Tens of fighters have abandoned serving in Iranian-backed militias and switched to working for the Russians.
62. "Jaysh Sūriyah Ṣaḥrāy Dīr Al-Zawr Rā Bi-Ṭūr Kāmil Āzād Kard [The Syrian Army

Completely Liberated the Desert of Deir ez-Zor]," Fars News, 27 June 2018. Airstrikes and sieges enabled these advances, pressuring rebel factions into surrendering and accepting evacuation terms. Prominent rebel factions faced devastating defeats, and by the year's close, they were primarily located in the northwest, forming alliances in order to survive. Although a demilitarized zone was established in northwestern Syria by the end of 2018, its sustainability was questionable, especially considering the regime's history and indications from its officials suggesting potential future offensives.

63. Previously, in October 2018, Russia and Turkey, despite backing opposing sides in Syria, signed the Sochi Agreement to try to quell the violence in Idlib by forming a demilitarized zone.
64. "Beseda s Prezidentom Irana Khasanom Rukhani [Conversation with Hassan Rouhani]," Press-Sluzbha Prezidenta RF, 4 April 2018.
65. Ibid.
66. "Tib'āt Ḥamilih Mūshikī-i Trāmp Bih Sūrīyah Barāyī Āmrīkā va Rūsīyah [The Consequences of the Trump Missile Strike on Syria for the U.S. and Russia]," Tabnak, 7 April 2018.
67. This was not about a change in Russia's foreign policy priorities, since the Iranian presence, like the Russian one, is based on an invitation from Damascus, but about the priority of restoring Syria's territorial integrity, which is impossible without agreements with the United States.
68. "Nebenzya Napomnil, Chto Iran Nakhoditsya v Sirii na Zakonnykh Osnovaniyakh [Nebenzya Recalled That Iran Is in Syria Legally]," TASS, 28 June 2018, https://tass.ru/politika/5333656.
69. "Iran Has Advisory Role in Anti-Terror Fight in Syria: Russia," *Tehran Times*, 2 July 2018.
70. Zvi Bar'el, "As Syrian Army Heads South, Assad Will Require New Agreements with Israel—Israel News," Haaretz.com, 6 July 2018, https://www.haaretz.com/israel-news/2018-07-06/ty-article/as-assads-forces-head-south-israel-needs-a-solid-buffer-zone/0000017f-e036-d38f-a57f-e6769e970000.
71. Margaret Brennan, "At Trump-Putin Summit, Trump to Enlist Russia's Help to Oust Iran from Syria," CBS News, 2 July 2018.
72. Michelle Kosinski and Zachary Cohen, "Trump Privately Floats Plan for Deal with Putin on Syria," CNN, 28 June 2018.
73 Alluding to Lavrentiev's earlier comments, Velayati stated that Iran's "presence in Syria has no connection to America's demands or other Western countries that follow America's policies ... We are in Syria at the request of the legal government in Damascus." Ali Akbar Velayati, "Bih Moskou i'timād Dārim [We Trust Moscow]," *Shargh*, 18 July 2018.
74. Maxim Suchkov, "Khamenei Adviser Warns Moscow of 'Empty Promises' from US," Al-Monitor, 13 July 2018; "Vstrecha s Sovetnikom Verkhovnogo Rukovoditelya Irana po Mezhdunarodnym Voprosam Ali Akbarom Velayati [Meeting with Advisor to the Supreme Leader of Iran on International Affairs Ali Akbar Velayati]," Prezident Rossii (Kremlin.ru), 12 July 2018, Integrum Digital Archive.
75. "Tegeranu Radovat'sya? [Should Tehran Rejoice?]," *Novaya Gazeta*, 8 August 2018, Integrum Digital Archive; "Du Haftah Pas Az Dafā' Az Ḥuẓūr-i Īrān Dar Sūrīyah Rūsīyah Az Ḥuẓūr-i Ḥizbullāh Dar Sūrīyah Ham Dafā' Kard [Two Weeks after

Defending Iran's Presence in Syria, Russia Also Defended Hezbollah's Presence in Syria]," *Resalat*, 15 July 2018, https://www-magiran-com/article/3771964.

76. Interview with a former Russian ambassador to multiple Middle Eastern countries (Moscow), 2019.
77. Yurii Barmin, "Rossiya i Izrail': Blizhnevostochnoe Izmerenie Otnoshenii [Russia and Israel: The Middle Eastern Dimension of Relations]," Russiancouncil.ru, 24 October 2018.
78. However, it is important to note that Russia's interactions with Israel do not indicate a U-turn in its attitude towards Iran. Russia recognized the role of Iran and Hezbollah in the war. Russia also recognized that it had a limited ability to restrain Iranian-backed forces.
79. In response, Russia's special envoy held talks with the Secretary of Iran's SNSC, Ali Shamkhani, in Tehran. The discussions primarily focused on the Israeli airstrike conducted in Syria and threats by President Trump to attack the country.
80. Illustratively, in June 2019, Shamkhani met with Patrushev in Russia, followed by a U.S.-Russia-Israel trilateral national security advisor meeting in Jerusalem a week later. Subsequently, in July 2019, Putin's special envoy for Syria, Lavrentiev, consulted with Iran's SNSC Secretary Shamkhani in Tehran, briefing Iranian authorities on the outcomes of the trilateral meeting.
81. Marianna Belen'kaya, "Minoborony RF Obvinilo Izrail' v 'Prestupnoy Khalatnosti' i 'Neblagodarnosti' [The Russian Ministry of Defense Accused Israel of 'Criminal Negligence' and 'Ungratefulness']," *Kommersant*, 23 September 2019, https://www.kommersant.ru/doc/3750773.
82. The new S-300 battalion was initially placed in a strategic position in the mountains of Tartus Province along the coast, close to pre-existing Russian S-400 and Syrian S-200 units. Additional battalions were stationed at the T4 (Tiyas) airbase near Damascus and potentially at the Deir ez-Zor military airbase, enhancing the defensive perimeter and potentially impacting U.S. anti-ISIS coalition air operations in eastern Syria. Russia took steps to consolidate control over Syrian air defense forces in 2018, aiming for a unified command system that integrates both Russian and Syrian air defense. "Russia Expands Its Air Defense Network in Syria," Institute for the Study of War, 2018, https://www.iswresearch.org/2018/11/russia-expands-its-air-defense-network.html..
83. Marianna Belen'kaya, "Rossiya Davala Uroki Iranskogo [Russia Was Giving Iranian Lessons]," *Kommersant*, 26 June 2019, https://www.kommersant.ru/doc/4012107.
84. Discussion with an Iran-based security expert (online), 2023.
85. There was also a meeting in November 2018; see "Sovmestnoe Zayavlenie Irana, Rossii i Turtsii po Itogam Mezhdunarodnoi Vstrechi po Sirii v Astane (MBCA-11), 28-29 Noyabrya 2018 Goda [Joint Statement by Iran, Russia, and Turkey following the International Meeting on Syria in Astana (MBCA-11), 28-9 November 2018]," Press-Tsentr MID RF, 29 November 2018.
86. Yurii Barmin, "Siriiskii Kongress v Sochi: Slishkom Rano dlya Uregulirovaniya [Syrian Congress in Sochi: Too Early for Settlement]," Russiancouncil.ru, 5 February 2018.
87. Ardeshir Senai and Abbas Golro, "Siyāsat-i Rūsīyah dar qabāl-i buhrān-i Sūrīyah bā ta'kīd bar muẕākirāt-i Āstānah va Sūchī [Russia's Policy towards the Syrian Crisis with Emphasis on the Astana and Sochi Negotiations]," *Faṣlnāmah-i Muṭāla'āt-i Āsiyā-yi Markazī va Qafqāz* 27, no. 116 (20 February 2022): 121-38.
88. Hamidreza Azizi, "Astaninskii Format i Perspektivy Trekhstoronnego

Vzaimoponimaniya po Sirii [Astana Format and Prospects for Trilateral Mutual Understanding on Syria]," Valdai, 15 July 2019, https://ru.valdaiclub.com/a/highlights/astana-i-perspektivy.

89. Andrei Kortunov, "Iz Astany v Zhenevu s Ostanovkoi v Sochi? [From Astana to Geneva with a Stop in Sochi?]," Russiancouncil.ru, 14 November 2017.
90. Comments by Ryabkov at a closed-door meeting in Moscow, 2019.
91. "Rassledovanie RBK: Skol'ko Tratit Rossiya na Voynu v Sirii [RBC Investigation: How Much Russia Is Spending on the War in Syria]," *RBK*, 28 October 2015, https://www.rbc.ru/investigation/politics/28/10/2015/562f9e119a79471d5d7c64e7
92. Leili Rustamovna Rustamova, "Usiliya Islamskoi Respubliki Iran v Bor'be s Terrorizmom v Sirii i Perspektivy Siriiskogo Uregulirovaniya [The Efforts of the Islamic Republic of Iran in the Fight against Terrorism in Syria and the Prospects for a Syrian Settlement]," *Natsional'naya Bezopasnost' / Nota Bene*, no. 5 (2019).
93. Ahmad Salloum, "How Much Is Iran Spending in Syria?," Iranwire.com, 18 March 2022, https://iranwire.com/en/features/66730.
94. Sinan Hatahet, "Russia and Iran: Economic Influence in Syria," Middle East and North Africa Programme, Chatham House, March 2019, https://www.chathamhouse.org/sites/default/files/publications/research/2019-03-08RussiaAndIranEconomicInfluenceInSyria.pdf.
95. Interview with a Russia-based expert on Syria (Moscow), 2019.
96. Hatahet, "Russia and Iran."
97. "UAE Foreign Minister Meets Assad, Most Senior Emirati Visit to Syria Since War Began," Reuters, 9 November 2021, https://www.reuters.com/world/middle-east/uae-foreign-minister-arrives-damascus-visit-lebanese-media-reports-2021-11-09/.
98. Julien Barnes-Dacey, "The Geopolitics of Reconstruction: Who Will Rebuild Syria?," European Council on Foreign Relations, 16 September 2019, https://ecfr.eu/publication/the_geopolitics_of_reconstruction_who_will_rebuild_syria/.
99. The UAE was at the forefront of this economic engagement. In 2020, the UAE announced plans to construct a 300-megawatt solar power plant near Damascus. Even Saudi Arabia, despite its previous reluctance, began preliminary discussions about potential investments in Syria's agricultural sector under the Assad regime. "Syria Signs Agreement with UAE Firms to Build 300 Megawatt Power Station - State Media," Reuters, 11 November 2021, https://www.reuters.com/article/business/energy/syria-signs-agreement-with-uae-firms-to-build-300-megawatt-power-station-state-idUSC6N2S101M/.
100. S. Ivanov, "Uregulirovanie Siriyskogo Konflikta: Vazhnyy Shag na Puti k Regional'noy Stabil'nosti [Resolving the Syrian Conflict: An Important Step towards Regional Stability]," *Mirovaya Ekonomika i Mezhdunarodnye Otnosheniya*, no. 11 (2020): 53-61.
101. Aleksei Khlebnikov, "Razvitie Siriiskikh Vooruzhennykh Sil: Osnovnye Tendentsii i Problemy [Development of the Syrian Armed Forces: Main Trends and Problems]," Russiancouncil.ru, 6 December 2018.
102. "Ne Tol'ko Tanki: Chto Svyazyvaet Rossiyu i Siriyu [Not Only Tanks: What Connects Russia and Syria]," *RBK*, 24 September 2015, https://www.rbc.ru/business/24/09/2015/560168269a7947597c281379.
103. In addition, the fact that it was supposed to include former defectors, as well as those who tried to avoid conscription, was intended to try to eliminate confessional strife in the army and legally return Sunnis to the armed forces. The Kremlin hoped that by reintegrating rebel forces through initiatives like the 5th Corps and taking a leading

role in post-conflict stabilization and reconstruction efforts, it could help consolidate the Syrian government's control over the country and shape its future in line with Russian interests. 'By fostering the development of a unified and professionalized Syrian military and assisting in the restoration of government control over key sectors, Russia sought to secure its long-term influence in Syria and limit the space for other actors, including Iran, to pursue divergent agendas.

104. Charles Lister, "Russia, Iran, and the Competition to Shape Syria's Future," Middle East Institute, 12 September 2019, https://www.mei.edu/publications/russia-iran-and-competition-shape-syrias-future
105. Hossein Aghaei, "Āyā Īrān qādir bih tadāvum-i ḥuẕūr-i niẓāmī-i khvud dar Sūrīyah khvāhad būd? [Will Iran Be Able to Continue Its Military Presence in Syria?]," Markaz-i Muṭāliʻāt-i Īrānī Ānkārā (Īrām), 16 September 2018, https://iramcenter.org/fa/will-iran-be-able-to-maintain-military-presence-in-syria

6. MAXIMUM PRESSURE

1. Twitter, @realDonaldTrump, 23 July 2018, https://twitter.com/realDonaldTrump/status/1021234525626609666?lang=en.
2. Abdollah Motavalian, "Tahdīd'hā va Furṣat'hā-Yi Intikhāb-i Trāmp Barā-Yi Īrān [Threats and Opportunities of Trump's Election for Iran]," *Javān*, 27 January 2017, https://www.javann.ir/003VFJ
3. The U.S. also imposed sanctions on Russia for allegedly "violating the Iran, North Korea, and Syria Nonproliferation Act, which has no connection to Russia. In effect, this U.S. decision has been precipitated by a trivial desire to get even with Russia over the failed missile attack on Syria, which the United States, Britain and France launched on 14 April in violation of international law." In response, the Russian Foreign Ministry condemned Washington's "desire to maintain its unilateral global domination despite the costs involved" and claimed that this desire "is prompting the United States to take irrational and openly dangerous steps." The statement advised U.S. politicians "that trying to 'punish' everyone who pursues an independent policy is not a good idea." "Kommentarii Departamenta Informatsii i Pechati MID Rossii v Svyazi s Novymi Antirossiiskimi Sanktsiyami SShA [Comment by the Information and Press Department on the New U.S. Sanctions against Russia]," Press-Tsentr MID, 9 May 2018, Integrum Digital Archive.
4. "Pushkov Predlozhil Trampu Trizhdy Podumat' Pered Vvedeniem Sanktsii protiv RF [Pushkov Suggested That Trump Think Three Times before Introducing Sanctions against the Russian Federation]," *Nezavisimaya Gazeta (Ng.ru)*, 10 April 2017, Integrum Digital Archive; Eduard Lozansky, "Zamknutyi Krug Trampa [Trump's Vicious Circle]," *Izvestiya*, 31 March 2017, Integrum Digital Archive.
5. Lyubov Glazunova, "Provalivsheesya Gosudarstvo: Kak Novye Sanktsii SShA Otrazyatsya na Rossii [A Failed State: How New U.S. Sanctions Will Affect Russia]," *Moskovskiy Komsomolets*, 27 July 2017, Integrum Digital Archive.
6. Smirnov, "Tramp Podpisal Zakon o Sanktsiyakh protiv Rossii [Trump Signs Russia Sanctions Bill]," *Vedomosti*, 2 August 2017, https://www.vedomosti.ru/politics/articles/2017/08/02/727721-tramp-sanktsiyah
7. Daniel Fried and Brian O'Toole, "The New Russia Sanctions Law: What It Does and How to Make It Work," Atlantic Council, 29 September 2017, https://

www.atlanticcouncil.org/in-depth-research-reports/issue-brief/the-new-russia-sanctions-law.

8. "Tavāfoq-i Demokrāt'hā va Jomhūrī Khāhān Bar Sar-i Taḥrīm'hā-Yi Īrān va Rūsīyah [Democrats and Republicans Agree on Sanctions against Iran and Russia]," *Donya-ye Eqtesad*, 24 July 2017, 2. Though not the primary focus, the legislation encompasses provisions addressing human rights abuses in Iran and authorizes the imposition of sanctions on those responsible for violations, including censorship and repression.
9. For a critical view of the Russian foreign policy course and its culpability in the sanctions, see Elena Vinogradova, Alexei Nikolsky, and Ekaterina Burlakova, "Pochemu Sanktsii protiv Rossii Vneshne Neeffektivny [Why Sanctions against Russia Are Apparently Ineffective]," *Vedomosti*, 13 August 2017, https://www.vedomosti.ru/economics/articles/2017/08/14/729205-sanktsii-neeffektivni.
10. Aleksandr Salitsky and Vladimir Yuratev, "Sanktsii i Zameshchenie Importa na Primere Opyta Irana i Kitaya [Sanctions and Import Substitution on the Example of the Experience of Iran and China]," *Vestnik Rossiiskoi Akademii Nauk* 87, no. 3 (2017), https://doi.org/10.7868/S0869587317030112.
11. Ivan Tkachev, "Litsenziya na Izolyatsiyu [A License for Isolation]," *RBK*, 2 November 2017, https://www.rbc.ru/newspaper/2017/11/02/59f995d19a79477abe151714
12. "Vecher s Vladimirom Solov'evym [Evening with Vladimir Solovyov]," Pervyy kanal, 2 November 2017, https://smotrim.ru/video/1729571,
13. Ibid.
14. Ivan Timofeev, Yulia Sokol'shchik, and Vyacheslav Morozov, "Sanktsii protiv Irana: Uroki dlya Rossii v Novykh Mezhdunarodnykh Usloviyakh [Sanctions against Iran: Lessons for Russia in the New International Conditions]," *Vestnik Sankt-Peterburgskogo Universiteta: Mezhdunarodnye Otnosheniya* 15, no. 4 (2022): 405-20; Timofeev, "A Pyrrhic Victory: The History of the Sanctions War against Iran," Russian International Affairs Council, 20 April 2018, http://russiancouncil.ru/en/analytics-and-comments/analytics/a-pyrrhic-victory-the-history-of-the-sanctions-war-against-iran.
15. Dmitry Trenin, "The Relationship between the USA and Russia in the Trump Era," Carnegie Endowment for International Peace, 14 May 2019.
16. Interview with a Russian foreign policy specialist and member of the Valdai Discussion Club (Moscow), 2017.
17. Andrei Petrov, "Rossiya i Iran Dadut Torgovyi Otvet na Sanktsii SShA [Russia and Iran Will Provide a Trade Response to U.S. Sanctions]," Rossiiskii Institut Strategicheskikh Issledovanii, 26 November 2018, Integrum Digital Archive.
18. Igor Kryuchkov and Valentin Loginov, "Putin v Irane: Izolirovat' Amerikantsev i Podvinut' Kitai [Putin in Iran: Isolate Americans and Push China Forward]," Gazeta.ru, 2 November 2017, https://www.gazeta.ru/politics/2017/11/02_a_10967756.shtml
19. Evgeniy Pudovkin, "Kongress Idet na Povodu u TsRU [Congress Follows the Lead of the CIA]," *Nezavisimaya Gazeta*, 13 July 2017, Integrum Digital Archive.
20. "Ryabkov Nazval Sanktsii Evrosoyuza protiv Irana Nepriemlemymi [Ryabkov Called EU Sanctions Action against Iran Unacceptable]," RIA Novosti, 11 February 2019, Integrum Digital Archive.
21. Egor Sozaev-Gur'ev, "'My Podoshli k Novomu Etapu' [We Have Reached a New Stage]," *Izvestiya*, 23 November 2017, Integrum Digital Archive.
22. "Putin Poprosil Peredat' Dukhovnomu Lideru Irana 'nailuchshiy Privet' [The Spiritual

Leader of Iran Named a Way to Isolate the United States]," *RBK*, 22 November 2017, Integrum Digital Archive.

23. Ebrahim Rahimpour, "Payām safar Pūtīn bah Īrān barāy Trāmp [The Message of Putin's Trip to Iran for Trump]," *Dīplomāsī īrānī*, 31 October 2017, https://shorturl.at/cOU25
24. The White House, "National Security Strategy of the United States of America," Washington, DC, December 2017, https://trumpwhitehouse.archives.gov/wp-content/uploads/2017/12/NSS-Final-12-18-2017-0905.pdf
25. "Kommentariy Departamenta Informatsii i Pechati MID Rossii v Svyazi s Novoy Strategiey Natsional'noy Bezopasnosti SShA" [Commentary from the Department of Information and Press of the Russian Foreign Ministry in Connection with the New U.S. National Security Strategy], Ministerstvo inostrannykh del Rossiyskoy Federatsii, 19 December 2017, Integrum Digital Archive.
26. "Kremlin Hails US Readiness to Cooperate with Russia," TASS, 10 December 2017, https://tass.com/politics/981802
27. "Na VII Moskovskoy Konferentsii po Mezhdunarodnoy Bezopasnosti Vystupil Zamestitel' Nachal'nika Glavnogo Upravleniya General'nogo Shtaba VS RF Vitse-Admirala Igor' Kostyukov [Deputy Chief of the Main Directorate of the General Staff of the Russian Armed Forces, Vice Admiral Igor Kostyukov, Spoke at the Seventh Moscow Conference on International Security]," Ministerstvo Oborony RF, 5 April 2018, Integrum Digital Archive.
28. "Istrātizhi-i amnīyat-i millī-i Āmrīkā; taqābul bidūn ta'āmul [U.S. National Security Strategy; Confrontation without Engagement]," *Hamshahri*, 23 December 2017, https://tinyurl.com/bddbxy9r
29. "Majmū'ah-yi gozāresh-i rāhbardī, barrasī-yi istrātezhī-yi amnīyat-i millī-yi Iyālat-i Muttaḥidah-yi Āmrīkā [A Collection of Strategic Reports on the Examination of the National Security Strategy of the United States of America and the Website of the Think Tank], *Tabbyin*, January 2018, https://tinyurl.com/5n6rssra
30. "Matn-i kāmil-i guftugū-yi shabakah-i tilivīzyunī-i En.Bi.Si Āmrīkā bā Duktur Rūḥānī [Full Text of the TV Interview on the NBC America Television Network with Dr Rouhani]," Riyāsat-i Jumhūrī-i Islāmī-i Īrān, 25 September 2019, https://www.president.ir/fa/71342
31. "Avvalīn Vītū-Yi Rūsīyah Bih Naf'-i Īrān Dar Shūrā-Yi Amnīyat [Russia's First Veto in Favor of Iran on the Security Council]," *Hamshahri*, 3 March 2018, 12.
32. "Vītū-Yi Rūsīyah Bih Naf'-i Īrān [Russia's Veto in Favor of Iran]," *Donya-ye Eqtesad*, 28 February 2018, https://tinyurl.com/ym576pdk
33. "Vilāyatī; Vītū-yi qaṭ'nāmah-i ẕiddĪrānī-i tavassuṭ-i Rūsīyah Nishānah Rushd-i Istirātizhīk-i Ravābiṭ dar dū kishvar āst [Velayati: Russia's Veto of the Anti-Iranian Resolution Is a Sign of the Growing Strategic Ties between the Two Countries]," Tasnim, 28 February 2018, https://tn.ai/1669017
34. The Kerch Strait incident occurred in November 2018, when Russian coast guard ships fired upon and captured Ukrainian navy vessels attempting to pass through the strait. The Minsk process, on the other hand, refers to a series of agreements signed in 2014 and 2015 to resolve the ongoing conflict in Eastern Ukraine between Russian-backed separatists and Ukrainian government forces. By proposing amendments that soften language critical of Russia's actions or align more closely with its narrative, Iran demonstrated its support for Moscow's position on two salient matters for Russia.

35. Farhad Mamdouhi, "General Assembly Official Records, 73rd Session: 3rd Plenary Meeting," UNGA A/73/PV.3 (21 September 2018), 8; Farhad Mamdouhi, "General Assembly Official Records, 73rd Session: 56th Plenary Meeting," UNGA A/73/PV.56 (17 December 2018),
36. Matti Jan Dollbaum, Morvan Lallouet, and Ben Noble, *Navalny: Putin's Nemesis, Russia's Future?* (London: Hurst, 2021).
37. "I'tirāẓāt-i Rūsīyah dalīlī barā-yi dakhālat-i dūbārah-'i Urūpā dar sarzamīn-i Tazārhā [Russia's Protests Are a Reason for Europe's Renewed Intervention in the Land of the Tsars]," Mehr, 28 July 2019, mehrnews.com/xPMnh.
38. Polina Khimshiashvili, "Persidskii Protest: Kak v Irane Nachalis' Massovye Stolknoveniya [Persian Protest: How Mass Clashes Began in Iran]," *RBK*, 2 January 2018, https://www.rbc.ru/politics/02/01/2018/5a4b5ab09a79475e2b588658; Vladimir Ardaev, "Ruka Vashingtona: Chem Zakanchivaetsya Vmeshatel'stvo SShA v dela Drugikh Stran [Washington's Hand: How Does U.S. Interference in the Affairs of Other Countries End?]," RIA Novosti, 15 April 2018, https://ria.ru/20180415/1518610109.html; Dmitry Egorchenkov and Nikita Danyuk, "Islamskaya Respublika Iran Kak Ob'ekt Realizatsii 'Tsvetnoi Revolyutsii' v Kontekste Geopoliticheskikh Podkhodov SShA [The Islamic Republic of Iran as an Object of the 'Color Revolution' in the Context of U.S. Geopolitical Approaches]," *Gosudarstvennoe Upravlenie*, no. 67 (2018): 314-37.
39. "Rossiya Schitaet Sobytiya v Irane Vnutrennim Delom Strany [Russia Considers Events in Iran an Internal Matter of the Country],"TASS, 1 January 2018, https://tass.ru/politika/4854822
40. "Rossiya Schitaet Sobytiya v Irane Vnutrennim Delom Strany [Russia Considers Events in Iran as an Internal Matter of the Country]."
41. "UK Intelligence Agency Actively Plotted Social Disruption in Iran," Sputnik International, 2 January 2018, https://sputnikglobe.com/20180102/uk-intelligence-agency-plotted-disruption-iran-1060484534.htm; "Could GCHQ Influence Iran Protests?They've Done It Before, Claims Researcher," RT International, 2 January 2018, https://www.rt.com/uk/414831-gchq-influence hack protest
42. Meanwhile, the liberal media in Russia refute the notion that "outside interference" plays a significant role in driving protests, both in Iran and Russia; see "Novogodnie Protesty v Irane: Chto Izvestno na Shestoi Den' Besporyadkov [New Year's Protests in Iran: What Is Known on the Sixth Day of Unrest]," *TV Dozhd*, 2 January 2018, Integrum Digital Archive.
43. Yegeniya Kozlova, "Margarita Simon'yan Zayavila o Rabote Bi-Bi-Si po Metodichke [Margarita Simonyan Spoke about the Work of the BBC according to the Manual]," *Izvestiya*, 16 December 2018, https://iz.ru/824344/2018-12-16/margarita-simonian-zaiavila-o-rabote-bi-bi-si-po-metodichke
44. Again, in 2019, coordination between Russia and Iran was strengthened when both countries faced renewed waves of protests. In Russia, the Moscow City Duma protests erupted in July 2019 with demands for fair elections and political reforms Concurrently, Iran grappled with widespread protests against economic hardship and political repression.

    "'Sobyanin, vykhodi': Sotni Chelovek Vyshli Protestovat' protiv Fal'sifikatsiy na Vyborakh v Mosgordumu ['Sobyanin, come out': Hundreds of People Came Out to Protest against Fraud in the Moscow City Duma Elections]," Forbes.ru, 14 July 2019, https://www.forbes.ru/obshchestvo/380005-sobyanin-vyhodi-sotni-chelovek-vyshli-protestovat-protiv-falsifikaciy-na-vyborah

45. The agreement also included provisions for the exchange of expertise and innovative methods to quell unrest and stifle public dissent, including the transmission of "special means, techniques, and equipment" and "exchange of information on conducting events to ensure public order during emergency situations (quarantines, mass riots, natural disasters)." "Qānūn-i mu'āhadahnāmah-'i hamkārī bayn-i Vazārat-i Kishvar-i Jumhūrī-i Islāmī-i Īrān va Vazārat-i Kishvar-i Fidirāsiyūn-i Rūsīyah [Law of the Cooperation Agreement between the Ministry of Interior of the Islamic Republic of Iran and the Ministry of Interior of the Russian Federation]," Majlis-i Shūrá-yi Islāmī 53160/266 (12 December 2013), https://rc.majlis.ir/fa/law/show/867603

46. "Sardār Sarlashgar Muṣṭafá Īzadī farmāndah qarārgāh-i sāybirī va tahdīdāt-i nuvīn-i qarārgāh-i markazī-i Khātam al-Anbiyā' (ṣ) dar barnāmah-i Dastkhaṭ [Commander Major General Mostafa Izadi, Commander of the Cyber and Modern Threats Headquarters of the Central Headquarters of Khatam al-Anbiya (PBUH), in the Dastkhat Program]," Nour News, 28 February 2020, https://NourNews.ir/n/43905

47. "Qānūn-i īntarnit-i millī-i Rūsīyah [National Internet Law of Russia]," Pazhūhishgāh-i markaz-i millī-i faẓā-yi majāzī, 2020.

48. "O Podpisanii Soglasheniya mezhdu Pravitel'stvom Rossiyskoy Federatsii i Pravitel'stvom Islamskoy Respubliki Iran o Sotrudnichestve v Oblasti Obespecheniya Informatsionnoy Bezopasnosti [On the Signing of an Agreement between the Government of the Russian Federation and the Government of the Islamic Republic of Iran on Cooperation in the Field of Information Security]," Pravo.ru, no. 3005-r (16 November 2020), http://ips.pravo.gov.ru/?doc_itself=&nd=102910776&page=1&rdk=0&link_id=16#I0

49. Vladimir Ivanenko, "Iranskaya Yadernaya Programma i Rossiysko-Iranskie Otnosheniya [Iranian Nuclear Program and Russian-Iranian Relations]," *Mezhdunarodnaya Politika* 34, no. 1 (2016): 109-31.

50. Following Crimea's annexation, Russian officials implied a potential recalibration of their stance on Iran nuclear talks as a response to Western pressure over the Ukraine conflict. Despite a halt in policy coordination with entities like the G8 group and the NATO-Russia Council, Moscow hinted at leveraging the Iran nuclear talks as a potential obstruction tool. This possibility was amplified when Russian Deputy Foreign Minister Ryabkov suggested reassessing Russia's position on the Iranian nuclear issue in light of the sanctions imposed due to Russia's annexation of Crimea. President Putin's October 2014 Valdai speech subtly intimated that Russia's cooperation on the Iranian nuclear issue could be influenced by external factors, suggesting that the talks might be used as leverage against the West. Ryabkov, "Zamglavy MIDa Ryabkov: 'Rossiya protiv "igry na povyshenie stavok" na peregovorakh po Iranu' [Deputy Head of the Russian Ministry of Foreign Affairs, Ryabkov, Said: 'Russia is against "playing for higher stakes" in negotiations on Iran']," Interfax.ru, 20 March 2014, https://www.interfax.ru/interview/366039; "'Valdayskaya' Rech' Putina: Kritika Zapada Kak Put' k Dialogu ['Valdai' Speech by Putin: Criticism of the West as a Path to Dialogue]," RIA Novosti, 24 October 2014, https://ria.ru/20141024/1029977993.html

51. See Toby Dalton et al., "Dimming Prospects for U.S.-Russia Nonproliferation Cooperation," Carnegie Endowment for International Peace, 14 March

2024, https://carnegieendowment.org/2024/03/14/dimming-prospects-for-u.s.-russia-nonproliferation-cooperation-pub-91958

52. "'Mir vzdokhnul s bol'shim oblegcheniem': Mezhdunarodnaya Reaktsiya na Soglashenie s Iranom ['The world breathed a sigh of relief': International Reaction to the Iran Deal]," TASS, 14 July 2015, https://tass.ru/mezhdunarodnaya-panorama/2117750. "Vstrecha s Prezidentom Irana Khasanom Rukhani [Meeting with President of Iran Hassan Rouhani]," Press-Sluzhba Prezidenta RF, 9 July 2015, http://www.kremlin.ru/events/president/transcripts/49897

53. For background on the nuclear issue, see Kayhān Barzgar and 'Alī Isma'īlī Ardakānī, eds, *Majmū'ah-i maqālāt-i hamāyish-i dīplimāsī-i hastah'ī: hashtumīn Hamāyish-i Sālānah-i Anjuman-i 'Ulūm-i Siyāsī-i Īrān* [Proceedings of the Conference on Iran's Nuclear Diplomacy] (Tehran: Intishārāt-i Dānishgāh-i 'Allāmah Ṭabāṭabāyī, 2016); Raḥman Ghahramanpour, *Siyāsat-i Khārijī va Dīplumāsī-i Hastah'ī-i Īrān Az Taqābul Tā I'timād'sāzī* [Foreign Policy and Iranian Nuclear Diplomacy from Confrontation to Confidence Building] (Tehran: Intishārāt-i Tīsā, 2017); Muhammad Javad Zarif et al., *Rāz-i sar bih muhr: Barjām kūshishī siturg barā-yi ḥuqūq, amnīyat va tawsa'ah-i Īrān* [The Nuclear Deal: The Untold Story of JCPOA; Protecting Iran's Security, Rights, and Development] (Tehran: Intishārāt-i Iṭṭilā'āt, 2021).

54. "Full Transcript of Trump's Speech on the Iran Nuclear Deal," *New York Times*, 8 May 2018, https://www.nytimes.com/2018/05/08/us/politics/trump-speech-iran-deal.html

55. "Mardom Hich Negarānī Nadāshte Bāshand; Az Modathā Pish Mīdānestim Trāmp Qābel-e e'temād Nist [People Should Not Worry; We Knew for a Long Time That Trump Is Not Trustworthy]," Riyāsat-i Jumhūrī-i Islāmī-i Īrān, 10 May 2018.

56. Unlike Rouhani, the Supreme Leader expressed skepticism not only towards the U.S. but also towards European powers involved in the JCPOA. He stated: "We do not trust the three European countries, like we don't trust the U.S.; without receiving a strong guarantee from these three European countries, we won't stick to the nuclear agreement [the JCPOA]." Khamenei further stressed that the ongoing nuclear dispute was merely a smokescreen to realize the United States' true intention of dominating Iran. According to him, the real bone of contention for the U.S. was the influence it lost over Iran following the Islamic Revolution: "The real reason behind the opposition of the U.S. towards the Islamic Republic's system is the fact that [before the revolution] the U.S. had complete dominance over our country, eventually, their hands were severed from Iran by the Islamic Revolution."

57. "Zayavlenie MID Rossii po Situatsii Vokrug Sovmestnogo Vseob'emlyushchego Plana Deystviy po Iranskoy Yadernoy Programme [Statement by the Russian Ministry of Foreign Affairs on the Situation around the Joint Comprehensive Plan of Action on the Iranian Nuclear Program]," Ministerstvo inostrannykh del Rossiyskoy Federatsii, 8 May 2018, https://mid.ru/en/foreign_policy/international_safety/1570640/?lang=ru

58. Elena Chernenko and Pavel Tarasenko, "Partneram Irana Dali 180 Dnei na Razmyshlenie [180 Days to Think about It]," *Kommersant*, 10 May 2018, Integrum Digital Archive. "Zayavlenie MID Rossii po Situatsii Vokrug Sovmestnogo Vseob'emlyushchego Plana Deistvii po Iranskoi Yadernoi Programme [Statement by the Russian Ministry of Foreign Affairs on the Situation around the Joint Comprehensive Plan of Action on the Iranian Nuclear Program]," Press-Tsentr MID RF, 8 May 2018; "Kommentariy Departamenta Informatsii i Pechati MID Rossii v Svyazi s Vosstanovleniem

Eksterritorial'nykh Sanktsiy SShA protiv Irana [Commentary from the Department of Information and Press of the Russian Foreign Ministry regarding the Restoration of U.S. Extraterritorial Sanctions against Iran]," Ministerstvo Inostrannykh del Rossiiskoi Federatsii, 7 August 2018, Integrum Digital Archive.

59. Interview with member of the Russian Foreign Ministry International Law Council (Moscow), 2019.
60. "Tramp protiv Vsekh: Glavnoe o Sanktsiyakh SShA v otnoshenii Irana [Trump against Everyone: The Main Thing about U.S. Sanctions against Iran]," *RBK*, 7 August 2018, https://www.rbc.ru/politics/07/08/2018/5b68741e9a794776015a6c62
61. Aleksandr Shumilin, "SShA-IRAN: Mezhdu 'Maksimal'nym Davleniem' i 'Geroicheskoi Gibkost'yu' [USA-IRAN: Between 'Maximum Pressure' and 'Heroic Flexibility']," *Mirovaya Ekonomika i Mezhdunarodnye Otnosheniya* 64, no. 7 (2020), https://doi.org/10.20542/0131-2227-2020-64-7-69-79
62. For the Russian perspective on the impact of sanctions, see Dmitry Butrin, "Antiiranskie Sanktsii SShA Okazalis' Nevygodnymi, no Effektivnymi [U.S. Anti-Iranian Sanctions Turned Out to Be Unprofitable, but Effective]," *Kommersant*, 15 May 2019, Integrum Digital Archive.
63. Marianna Belenkaya and Elizaveta Naumova, "Tegeran Postavil Ul'timatum Evrope [Tehran Delivers Ultimatum to Europe]," *Kommersant*, 8 May 2019, Integrum Digital Archive.
64. As a last-ditch effort, Rouhani's announcement also included a sixty-day ultimatum to the European signatories of the nuclear deal. He called on them to take practical steps towards easing the reinstated U.S. sanctions, particularly in the banking and oil sectors. If Europe failed to provide the economic benefits promised by the accord, Iran would no longer adhere to its obligations under the JCPOA related to its stock of low-enriched uranium and heavy water.
65. "Vstupitel'noe Slovo Ministra Inostrannykh del Rossii S.V. Lavrova v Khode Peregovorov s Ministrom Inostrannykh del Irana M.D. Zarifom [Opening Remarks by Russian Foreign Minister Sergey Lavrov during Negotiations with Iranian Foreign Minister M.D. Zarif, Moscow, 8 May 2019]," Ministerstvo Inostrannykh del Rossiiskoi Federatsii, 8 May 2019, Integrum Digital Archive.
66. Discussion with a Russian journalist in the Foreign Ministry press corps (Moscow), 2019.
67. Interview with a former Russian diplomat to the Middle East (Moscow), 2019.
68. Vladimir Evseev, "SShA Pytayutsya Zadushit' Iran Ekonomicheski [The U.S. Is Trying to Strangle Iran Economically]," Rossiyskiy Institut Strategicheskikh Issledovaniy (Riss.ru), 20 May 2019, Integrum Digital Archive; Vladimir Frolov, "Posrednichestvo, Dorogo: Pomozhet Li Moskva Trampu i Iranu Dogovorit'sya? [Mediation Is Expensive: Will Moscow Help Trump and Iran Reach a Deal?]," Republic, 4 June 2019, https://republic.ru/posts/93851
69. Interview with a senior Russia-based expert on international affairs (Moscow), 2019.
70. "Ādryān: Rahā Dar Daryā [Adrian: Liberated in the Sea]," *Hamshahri*, 17 August 2019, http://newspaper.hamshahrionline.ir/; Sa'idah Sadat Fahri, "Birītāniyā, Dar Sūdāyi Bāzgasht Bih [Britain, Longing to Return to the Persian Gulf]," *Donya-ye Eqtesad*, 7 August 2019.
71. In March, the U.S. State Department and Treasury sanctioned Harakat al Nujaba, an Iranian-backed militia in Iraq, and its leader, Akram Abbas al Kabi. In the same month, the U.S. State Department and Treasury sanctioned thirty-one Iranian entities

and individuals linked to the Organization of Defensive Innovation and Research. Also in March, the U.S. sanctioned a network of front companies that evaded U.S. sanctions to provide support to the IRGC and Iran's MODAFL. In April 2019, under the Trump administration, the United States designated the IRGC a foreign terrorist organization. This was the first time the U.S. had designated part of another country's government as a terrorist organization. In response, Iran declared U.S. forces in the Middle East to be a terrorist organization. The U.S. move was intended to allow it to impose further sanctions, particularly affecting the business sector, given the IRGC's involvement in Iran's economy.

72. Interview with a senior Russia expert on foreign affairs (Moscow), 2019.
73. "Zakharova: Priznav KSIR Terroristicheskoy Organizatsiey, SShA Demoniziruyut Iran [Zakharova: Recognizing the IRGC as a Terrorist Organization, the U.S. Is Demonizing Iran],"TASS, 11 April 2019, https://tass.ru/politika/6324648
74. Tom DiChristopher, "Trump Aims to Drive Iran's Oil Exports to Zero by Ending Sanctions Waivers," CNBC, 22 April 2019, https://www.cnbc.com/2019/04/22/trump-expected-to-end-iran-oil-waivers-try-to-drive-exports-to-zero.html
75. Kate Sullivan, Barbara Starr, and Brad Lendon, "US Deploying Carrier and Bomber Task Force in Response to 'Troubling' Iran Actions," CNN, 6 May 2019, https://www.cnn.com/2019/05/05/politics/iran-carrier-bomber-task-force/index.html
76. A mere two days after the Fujairah episode, Iranian-backed Houthi rebels in Yemen launched drone attacks on Saudi oil pipelines. The Houthi attack on the Saudi oil pipeline occurred while Lavrov met with his American counterpart Mike Pompeo in Sochi. During the talks, Lavrov stated that Russia hopes "to find a political solution to the situation around Iran" and that Russian diplomacy would do everything to help ensure the situation did not lead to a military conflict. "Lavrov Nadeetsya, Chto Slukhi ob Otpravke Voennykh SShA na Blizhnii Vostok Bezosnovatel'ny [Lavrov Hopes That Rumors about Sending the U.S. Military to the Middle East Are Unfounded],"TASS, 14 May 2019. Integrum Digital Archive.
77. "Lavrov: Otpravka 1,5 tys. Voennykh iz SShA na Blizhnii Vostok Povysit Riski v Regione [Lavrov: Sending 1.5 Thousand Troops from the United States to the Middle East Will Increase Risks in the Region],"TASS, 27 May 2019; "Kommentarii Zamestitelya Ministra Inostrannykh del Rossii S.A. Ryabkova o Situatsii s Realizatsiei Sovmestnogo Vseob'emlyushchego Plana Deistvii po Uregulirovaniyu Vokrug Iranskoi Yadernoi Programmy (SVPD) [Commentary by Deputy Minister of Foreign Affairs of Russia S.A. Ryabkov on the Situation with the Implementation of the Joint Comprehensive Plan of Action to Resolve the Iranian Nuclear Program (JCPOA)]," Press-Sluzhba MID RF, 18 June 2019, Integrum Digital Archive.
78. "Soveshchanie s Postoyannymi Chlenami Soveta Bezopasnosti" [Meeting with the Permanent Members of the Security Council]," Press-Sluzhba Prezidenta RF, 24 May 2019, Integrum Digital Archive.
79. Putin told Iran not to overreact, stating that "as soon as Iran undertakes some counter-measures, declares it's going to abandon some parts of the agreement the next day everyone will forget that the U.S. was the first to initiate the collapse of the deal and Iran will take the full burden of guilt for it." "'Rossiya—ne pozharnaya komanda i ne mozhet spasat' vse': Putin o Yadernoi Sdelke s Iranom ['Russia is not a fire brigade and cannot save everything': Putin on the Nuclear Deal with Iran]," Telekanal "Zvezda," 15 May 2019.
80. Interview with a former Russian ambassador to a GCC country (Moscow), 2019.

81. "Nichego Ne Mozhet Byt' Khuzhe: Kto Proigraet bez Sdelki s Iranom [Trump's Bluff: We Will Make Iran Beg for Mercy in Negotiations]," Gazeta.ru, 8 May 2019, Integrum Digital Archive.
82. "SShA i Iran: Peregovory Pod Pritselom Udarnoy Avianosnoy Gruppy [U.S. and Iran: Talks under the Gun of an Aircraft Carrier Strike Group]," Rossiyskiy Institut Strategicheskikh Issledovaniy (Riss.ru), 20 May 2019, Integrum Digital Archive.
83. Andrei Yashlavsky, "Kak Nakanune Vtoroi Mirovoi: V Atake na Tankery Obvinili Iran [Like on the Eve of World War II: Iran Was Blamed for the Attack on Tankers]," *Moskovskiy Komsomolets*, 14 June 2019, Integrum Digital Archive.
84. Vladimir Fitin, "Razzhat' Tiski [Release the Vice]," *Izvestiya*, 20 May 2019, Integrum Digital Archive.
85. For the full transcript, see "Security Council, 74th Year: 8564th Meeting, Wednesday, 26 June 2019, New York," United Nations Digital Library System, 2019, https://digitallibrary.un.org/record/3811281?ln=en
86. Interview with a Russian foreign policy expert (Moscow), 2017.
87. Marianna Belen'kaya and Yuriy Barsukov, "V Omanskom Zalive Razgorayutsya Tankery [Tankers Catch Fire in the Persian Gulf]," *Kommersant*, 13 June 2019, Integrum Digital Archive.
88. Shahab Shahsari, "Rūḥānī Dar Ḥalaqah-i Rufaqā [Rouhani in the Circle of Comrades]," *E'temad*, 15 June 2019, 2.
89. "Na Sammite ShOS Putinu Pozhalovalis' na SShA [At the SCO Summit, Putin Complained about the United States]," *Moskovskiy Komsomolets*, 15 June 2019, Integrum Digital Archive; "Iran Pozhalovalsya Putinu na SShA [Iran Complains to Putin about the U.S.]," *Komsomol'skaya Pravda*, 15 June 2019, Integrum Digital Archive.
90. This was preceded by developments in June when the U.S. intensified its military posture, dispatching a B-52 bomber and an aircraft carrier to conduct exercises in the Persian Gulf, signaling a direct response to perceived threats from Iran. Yahya Rahim Safavi, a senior military aide to Iran's Supreme Leader Ayatollah Khamenei, responded by warning that U.S. military assets in the Gulf were within range of Iranian missiles and that any military clash would not only spike oil prices above $100 USD per barrel but would also be intolerable for the U.S., Europe, and their allies. "Iran Renews Threats against U.S. Bases and Warships in Gulf Region," Radio Free Europe/Radio Liberty, 2 June 2019, https://en.radiofarda.com/a/iran-renews-threats-against-u-s-bases-and-warships-in-gulf-region/29977347.html.
91. "Strait of Hormuz: US Confirms Drone Shot down by Iran," BBC News, 20 June 2019, https://www.bbc.com/news/world-middle-east-48700965.
92. Sara Ma'sumi, "Nah Bih I'tilāf-i ẕiddĪrānī-i Āmrīkā [No to America's Anti-Iranian Coalition]," *E'temad,* 24 July 2019, 5.
93. "Putin Aide: Downed U.S. Drone Was in Iranian Airspace," Reuters, 25 June 2019. The situation in the Persian Gulf was also discussed during Trump and Putin's meeting at the G20 in late June. According to Lavrov, the two leaders shared a mutual understanding that the situation concerning Iran needed to be addressed through political and diplomatic avenues rather than escalating towards a potential military conflict. Lavrov clarified that Putin and Trump discussed Iran "in the context of the current situation around the Joint Comprehensive Action Plan on the Iranian nuclear program and what is happening in the Gulf of Oman. The situation is difficult, but both presidents confirmed that they want to find a diplomatic way out of this

situation." "Lavrov: Putin i Tramp Prizvali Izbegat' Shagov, Kotorye Sprovotsirovali by Gonku Vooruzhenii [Lavrov: Putin and Trump Called for Avoiding Steps That Would Provoke an Arms Race]," TASS, 28 July 2019.

94. Kirill Krivosheev, "Velikobritaniya Obvinila Iran v Popytke Zaderzhat' Ee Tanker [Britain Accused Iran of Trying to Detain Its Tanker]," *Kommersant*, 11 July 2019. Amid the drama of *Grace 1* and *Stena Impero*, Iran's Navy Commander Hossein Khanzadi arrived in St. Petersburg on 27 July for a three-day visit to attend festivities marking Russia's Navy Day and discuss the development of maritime cooperation with Russian partners, which resulted in a memorandum on expanding naval cooperation Iran, including planned military exercises in the Strait of Hormuz. "Iran i Rossiya Podpisali Dokument o Rasshirenii Voennogo Sotrudnichestva [Iran and Russia Signed a Document on Expanding Military Cooperation]," TASS, 29 July 2019, Integrum Digital Archive.

95. Fahri, "Birītāniyā, Dar Sūdāyi Bāzgasht Bih [Britain, Longing to Return to the Persian Gulf]."

96. "Naftkish Ingilīs Cherā Tawqīf Shud? [Why Was the British Tanker Seized?]," *Iran*, 21 July 2019, 2.

97. Vladimir Mukhin, "Rossiyu Vtyagivayut v Tankernuyu Voinu [Russia Is Being Dragged into a Tanker War]," *Nezavisimaya Gazeta*, 31 July 2019. The UK was also accused of becoming "America's colony in foreign policy" and attempting "to hold Tehran responsible for the tensions in the Strait of Hormuz and the Persian Gulf region in order to play a role in the U.S.-intended coalition in this region" by the Iranian press. "Yārkushī Dar Tangah-i Hurmuz [Competitive Games in the Strait of Hormuz]," *I'timād*, 13 July 2019, 2

98. "Rossiya Prizyvaet Otkazat'sya ot Ul'timatumov i Sanktsiy po Persidskomu Zalivu—Nebenzya [Russia Calls for Abandoning Ultimatums and Sanctions on the Persian Gulf—Nebenzya]," RIA Novosti, 23 July 2019, Integrum Digital Archive; "Posol Irana Obsudil s Ryabkovym Voprosy Bezopasnosti v Persidskom Zalive [The Iranian Ambassador Discussed Security Issues in the Persian Gulf with Ryabkov]," RIA Novosti, 31 July 2019, Integrum Digital Archive.

99. Comments by a senior Department of Defense official, Washington, DC, October 2023.

100. Interview with a Russia-based expert with links to the intelligence services (Moscow), 2019.

101. IRGC-AF Brigadier General Saeed Aghajani, who oversees the IRGC ASF UAV Command, directs the planning, equipment, and training for IRGC-AF UAV operations, was allegedly responsible for orchestrating the attack in 2019. He later organized the 29 July 2021 attack on the commercial shipping vessel *Mercer Street* off the coast of Oman, which resulted in the deaths of two crewmen. Ehsan Mehrabi, "MV Mercer Street Attack Puts Spotlight on IRGC's Secretive Drone Unit," Iran Wire, 18 March 2022, https://iranwire.com/en/features/70094.

102. "RF Predlozhila Sozdat' Organizatsiyu po Bezopasnosti v Persidskom Zalive s Uchastiem SShA i KNR [The Russian Federation Proposed Creating a Security Organization in the Persian Gulf with the Participation of the United States and China]," RIA Novosti, 23 July 2019, Integrum Digital Archive; "MID RF Ozvuchil Kontseptsiyu Kollektivnoi Bezopasnosti v Persidskom Zalive [The Russian Foreign Ministry Announced the Concept of Collective Security in the Persian Gulf]," *Krasnaya Zvezda*, 23 July 2019, Integrum Digital Archive.

103. "Rossiiskaya Kontseptsiya Kollektivnoi Bezopasnosti v Zone Persidskogo Zaliva [Russia's Collective Security Concept for the Persian Gulf]," Press-Sluzhba MID RF, 24 August 2019, Integrum Digital Archive.
104. Russia had consistently mentioned the need to "form a genuinely inclusive security architecture" in the Persian Gulf. Russia alluded to Resolution 598, which ended the Iran-Iraq War, as the legal basis for such an initiative. Beyond establishing a ceasefire between Iran and Iraq, Resolution 598 called upon the UN secretary-general to explore "measures to enhance the security and stability of the region" through consultations with Iran, Iraq, and neighboring states.
105. Interview with a senior Russian international security expert (Moscow), 2019; interview with a Russian foreign policy expert (Moscow), 2017; interview with a senior researcher on the Middle East (Moscow), 2017.
106. Interview with a former Russian ambassador to a GCC country (Moscow), 2019.
107. Interview with a former Russian ambassador to a Middle Eastern country (Moscow), 2019.
108. Marianna Belen'kaya, "Rossiya Udarila Kontseptsiei po Koalitsii [Russia Hits the Coalition with the Concept]," *Kommersant*, 25 July 2019, Integrum Digital Archive.
109. As well as establishing a ceasefire between Iran and Iraq, Resolution 598 called upon the UN Secretary-General to explore "measures to enhance the security and stability of the region" through consultations with Iran, Iraq, and neighboring states.
110. *E'temad* published a photo of the start of the drill in Chabahar under the headline "Maritime Security according to the East."The conservative *Siyasat-e Ruz* newspaper wrote of the "naval drill's implied message to America." Similarly, hardline outlet Javan ran the headline "Asian Powers' Drill against the American Coalition" over a picture of senior Iranian and Russian naval officers shaking hands on the Chabahar coast.
111. Russia has described deadly airstrikes by U.S. forces on targets in Iraq and Syria as unacceptable and counterproductive while urging all sides to avoid fueling tensions in the Middle East. Dmitry Peskov said Washington had not given it warning of the strikes against three targets in Iraq and two in Syria. "Peskov: Rossiya Ne Poluchala ot SShA Informatsiyu ob Udarakh v Irake i Sirii [Peskov: Russia Did Not Receive Information from the United States about Strikes in Iraq and Syria]," Interfax, 30 December 2019, Integrum Digital Archive.
112. "Intiqām-i Sakht-i Muqāvimat dar Rāh Ast [Hard Revenge of the Resistance is Coming]," *Mehr News Agency*, 3 January 2020, https://www.mehrnews.com/news/4815311/.
113. "Shahādat-i Sardār Sulaymānī va Jābijāyī-i Khuṭūṭ-i Qirmiz [Martyrdom of General Soleimani and the Shifting of Red Lines]," *Mehr News Agency*, 3 January 2020, https://www.mehrnews.com/news/4815311/.
114. "Intiqām-i Shahādat-i Sardār Sulaymānī Ḥaqq-i Millat Ast [Avenging the Martyrdom of General Soleimani is the Nation's Right]," *Rūznāmah-yi Īrān*, 15 January 2020, https://www.pishkhan.com/news/209187/.
115. "Sardār Ḥājīzādah: Mūshakhā-yi Shilīk Shudih bih Pāygāh-i 'Ayn al-Asad Tanhā Āghāz-i Intiqām-i Sakht Ast [Commander Hajizadeh: Missiles Fired at Ain al-Asad Base Are Only the Beginning of Hard Revenge]," *Tasnim News Agency*, 9 January 2020.
116. "Shoigu Provel Peregovory s Glavoi Genshtaba Irana v Svyazi s Ubiistvom Suleimani [Shoigu Held Talks with the Head of the General Staff of Iran in Connection with

the Assassination of Soleimani]," Interfax, 6 January 2020, https://www.interfax.ru/russia/690327.

117. "Vilāyatī: 'Āmil aṣlī Ittiḥād-i Īrān va Rūsīyah, Sardār Sulaymānī būd [The Main Factor of the Alliance of Iran and Russia was Sardar Soleimani]," ISNA, 5 January 2020, https://www.isna.ir/news/98101511709.
118. For reporting on the PS752, see Anna Raskaya, "Ukraine Says Iran Must First Reveal the Full Truth about Downing of Airliner," RFE/RL, 19 August 2020.
119. "Juz'iyyāt-i tamās-i khalabān-i Bū'īng 737 Uk̲rāyinī bā burj-i Mihrābād tā pīsh az suqūṭ [Details of Ukrainian Boeing 737 Pilot Contact with Mehrabad Tower before Collapse]," Fars News, 8 January 2020.
120. "Barrasī-yi ṣāniḥah, Shirkat-i havāpaymāyī-i Ukrāyn Intarnashunal, Daftar-i barrasī-yi sāvanḥ va ḥavādes-i havāyī PS752 [Accident Investigation Ukraine International Airlines PS752],"Tehran: Jumhūrī-yi Islāmī-yi Īrān, nazdīk-i furūdgāh-i baynalmilalī-yi Imām Khomeynī, 17 March 2021.
121. "Fīlm-i kāmil-i iẓ̲hārāt-i Sardār Ḥājīzādah darbārah-'i suqūṭ-i havāpaymā-yi Ūkrāyinī/ Vaqtī mutma'in shudam ārzū-yi marg kardam [Full Video of Sardar Hajizadeh's Remarks about the Crash of a Ukrainian Plane/When I Was Sure I Wished for Death]," Fars News, 11 January 2020, http://fna.ir/dedmi4.

7. FORWARD TO EURASIA AND THE SEARCH FOR MULTIPOLARITY

1. Hamidreza Azizi, "What Raisi's Presidency Will Mean for Iran-Russia Relations," Amwaj.media, 9 July 2021, https://amwaj.media/article/what-raisi-s-presidency-means-for-iran-russia-relations
2. "Pūtīn pīrūzī-i Ra'īsī dar intikhābāt-i Īrān rā tabrīk guft [Putin Congratulated President Raisi on His Victory in the Iranian Elections]," Tasnim, 19 June 2021, https://tn.ai/2524139.
3. "Raisi otvetil Putinu na pozdravlenie s izbraniem prezidentom Irana [Raisi Responded to Putin's Congratulations on His Election as President of Iran]," RIA Novosti, 6 July 2021, https://ria.ru/20210706/iran-1740131667.html.
4. W Sergey Karaganov, "S Vostoka na Zapad, ili Bol'shaya Evraziya [From East to West, or Greater Eurasia]," *Rossiiskaya Gazeta*, 24 October 2016, https://rg.ru/2016/10/24/politolog-karaganov-povorot-rossii-k-rynkam-azii-uzhe-sostoialsia.html.
5. On the background to the concept, see Alexander Gabuev, "Russia's Policy towards China: Key Players and the Decision-Making Process," Carnegie Endowment for International Peace, 5 March 2015.
6. Nicole Grajewski, "An Illusory Entente: The Myth of a Russia-China-Iran 'Axis,'" *Asian Affairs* 53, no. 1 (3 January 2022): 164-83, https://doi.org/10.1080/03068374.2022.2029076.
7. See for example, the debates about Russia that emerged in the 1990s; Sergey Rogov, "Rossiya i SShA v Mnogopolyiarnom Mire [Russia and the USA in a Multipolar World]," *SShA: Ekonomika, Politika, Ideologiya*, no. 10 (1992): 3-14; Sergey Rogov, "Novaya 'Versal'skaya Sistema'? [New 'Versailles System'?]," *Zhurnal Ogonek*, 6 November 6, 1995, Integrum Digital Aarchive; Anatolii Torkunov, "Mezhdunarodnye Otnosheniya pPosle Kosovskogo Krizisa [International Relations after the Kosovo Crisis]," *Mezhdunarodnaya Zhizn* 12, no. 1 (1999): 45-52; Alexei Bogaturov, "Pliuralisticheskayia Odnopolyiarnost' i Interesy Rossii [Pluralistic Unipolarity and

the Interests of Russia]," *Svobodnaia Mysl'*, no. 2 (1996): 25-36; Vladimir Kulagin, "Mir v XXI Veke: Mnogopolyusnyi Balans Sil iIli Global'nyi Pax Democratica? [Peace in the Twenty-Fir21st Century: A Multipolar Balance of Power or Global Pax Democratica?]," *Polis:. Politicheskie Issledovaniya*, no. 1 (2000): 23-37.

8. Though its intellectual roots have been traced back to Tsarist-era foreign policy and the Concert of Europe, multipolarity was commonly associated with Yevgeny Primakov—Russia's foreign minister from 1996 to 1998—who advocated for the "democratization of international relations" and the diversification of Russian foreign relations with states such as China, India, and Iran. Present-day Russian foreign policy ideas on multipolarity have been argued to derive from an amalgamation of Soviet-era ideas as well as a revisiting of imperial Russian ideas. For a discussion of multipolarity and its historical roots, see Martin A. Smith, "Russia and Multipolarity since the End of the Cold War," *East European Politics* 29, no. 1 (March 2013): 36-51.
9. Yevgeny Primakov, "A Multipolar World and the United Nations," *International Affairs (Moscow)* 43, no. 6 (1997).
10. The language of the diversity of interests and the multipolar or democratic world order has been used in countless foreign policy statements such as the 2000 Russian Foreign Policy Concept, which stated Russia's desire "to achieve a multi-polar system of international relations that really reflects the diversity of the modem world with its great variety of interest" (Diplomaticheskii Vestnik 2000).
11. Yevgeny Bazhanov, *Aktual'nye Problemy Mezhdunarodnykh Otnoshenii: Izbrannye Trudy v Trekh Tomakh* [Actual Problems of International Relations: Selected Works in Three Volumes] (Moscow: Nauchnaya kniga, 2001).
12. Both the 2000 and 2009 National Security Doctrines defined Russia's national interests as "upholding its sovereignty and strengthening its position as a great power and as one of the influential centers of a multipolar world," whereas threats to Russia constituted "attempts by other states to oppose a strengthening of Russia as one of the influential centers of a multipolar world … and to weaken [Russia's] position in Europe, the Middle East, Transcaucasus, Central Asia, and the Asia-Pacific Region."
13. Mikhail Margelov, "Rossiya i Ne-Zapad: Paradoksy Mul'tipolyarnosti [Russia and Non-West: Paradoxes of Multipolarity]," *Rossiiskaya Gazeta*, 25 August 2022; Yevgeny Primakov, "Mezhdunarodnye Otnosheniya Nakanune XXI Veka: Problemy, Perspektivy [International Relations on the Eve of the Twenty-First Century: Problems, Prospects]," in *Vneshniaia Politika i Bezopasnost' Sovremennoĭ Rossii 1991-2002* [Foreign Policy and Security of Modern Russia 1991-2002], ed. Tatiana Shakleina, vol. 1, 4 vols. (Moscow: Moskovskiĭ Gosudarstvennyĭ Institut, 2002), 193-203.
14. Margelov, "Rossiya i Ne-Zapad: Paradoksy Mul'tipolyarnosti [Russia and Non-West: Paradoxes of Multipolarity]"; Boris Martynov, "Mnogopolyarnyi ili Mnogotsivilizatsionnyi Mir? [Multipolar or Multi-Civilization World?]," *Mezhdunarodnye Protsesi* 7, no. 3 (2009): 60-8.
15. Vladislav Leonidovich Inozemtsev, "Starye Protivorechiya 'Novogo' Imperializma [The Old Contradictions of the 'New' Imperialism]," *Polis: Politicheskie Issledovaniya*, no. 3 (2004): 173-7; Aleksandr Terent'ev, "Miroustroistvo Nachala Xxi Veka: Sushchestvuet Li Al'ternativa 'Amerikanskoi Imperii'? [World Order at the Beginning of the Twenty-First Century: Is there an Alternative to the 'American Empire'?]," *Mirovaya Ekonomika i Mezhdunarodnye Otnosheniya*, no. 10 (2004): 35-46.
16. "Sovmestnoe Kommyunike po Itogam Trekhstoronney Vstrechi Ministrov

Inostrannykh del Indii, Rossii i Kitaya [Joint Communiqué on the Tripartite Meeting of the Foreign Ministers of India, Russia, and China]," Press-Tsentr MID RF, 14 February 2002, Integrum Digital Archive.

17. Majid Adibzadeh, *Zabān, guftimān va siyāsat-i khārijī: diyāliktīk-i bāznamāyī az Gharb dar jahān-i namādīn-i Īrānī* [Language, Discourse, and Foreign Policy: Representational Dialectics on the West in the Iranian Symbolic World] (Tehran: Nashr-i Akhtarān, 2008); Jalal Dihghani Firoozabadi, *Siyāsat-i khārijī-i Jumhūrī-i Islāmī-i Īrān* [Foreign Policy of the Islamic Republic of Iran], 3rd edn (Tehran: Sāzmān-i Muṭāla'ah va Tadvīn-i Kutub-i 'Ulūm-i Insānī-i Dānishgāh'hā, 2010).

18. Kamal Kharazi, *Siyāsat-i Khārijī-i Mā: Majmū'ah-i Sukhanrānī'hā-Yi Kamāl Kharrāzī, Vazīr-i Umūr-i Khārijah* [Our Foreign Policy: The Speech Collection of the Islamic Republic of Iran's Foreign Minister, Kamal Kharrazi] (Tehran: Markaz-i Asnād va Tārīkh-i Dīplūmāsī, 2002); Muhammad Khatami, *Guzīdah-'i Sukhanrānīhā-Yi Ra'īs-i Jumhūr Dar'bārah-i Tawsi'ah-i Siyāsī, Tawsi'ah-i Iqtiṣādī va Amnīyat* [President's Speeches on Political Development, Economic Development, and Security] (Tehran: Ṭarḥ-i Naw, 2000).

19. Ali Akbar Velayati, Bih Sū-yi Niẓām-i Chand'quṭbī [Towards a Multipolar System]," *Hamshahri*, 18 September 2006.

20. Hanif Ghafari, "Jahān-i Chand Quṭbī [Multipolar World]," *Resalat*, 2 September 2008; Velayati, "Bih Sū-yi Niẓām-i Chand'quṭbī [Towards a Multipolar System]."

21. Jalāl Dihghan Firoozabadi, *Chārchūbī-i mafhūmī barā-yi arzyābī-i siyāsat-i khārijī-i Jumhūrī-i Islāmī-i Īrān* [Conceptual Framework for Evaluating the Foreign Policy of the Islamic Republic of Iran] (Tehran: Daftar-i Gustarish-i Tawlīd-i 'Ilm (vābastah bah Mu'āvanat-i Pizhūhishī-i Dānishgāh-i Āzād-i Islāmī), 2008), 118.

22. See for example Ḥabīb Allāh Valī Allāhī Malikshāh and Aḥmad Ja'farī, *Rīshah'hā-yi buḥrān-i Kūzuvū va dakhālat-i niẓāmī-i Nātū* [The Roots of the Kosovo Crisis and NATO's Military Intervention] (Tehran: Daftar-i Muṭāla'āt-i Siyāsī va Bayn al-Milalī, 2001); Ghulam Riza Khadimi, *Nātū: Sāzmān-i Paymān-i Ātlāntīk-i Shumālī* [NATO: North Atlantic Treaty Organization] (Tehran: Mu'assasah-i Muṭāla'āt-i Andīshah'sāzān-i Nūr, 2008); Elaheh Koolaee, Mandana Tishehyar, and Mahmud Muhammadi, *Sāzmān-i Paymān-i Ātlāntīk-i Shimālī (Nātū): digargūnī dar ma'mūrīyat'hā va kārkard'hā* [North Atlantic Treaty Organization: Changes in Missions and Functions] (Tehran: Mu'assasah-i Chāp va Intishārāt-i Dānishgāh-i Tihrān, 2007); Sattar Azizi, "Istiqlāl-i Kuzivū: Barrasī-yi Mashrū'iyyat-i Judā'ī-yi Yikjānbih dar Ḥuqūq-i Bayn al-Milal [The Independence of Kosovo: The Legality of Unilateral Secession in International Law]," *Majjalih-i Ḥuqūqī Bayn al-Milalī* 25, no. 38 (1 January 2008): 11-45, https://doi.org/10.22066/cilamag.2016.17396; Babak Pūr'qahramānī et al., eds, *Īrān va chālish'hā-yi ḥuqūqī-i bayn al-milalī* [Iran and the Challenges of International Law], (Tehran: Intishārāt-i Khursandī, 2016); Habibollah Abolhassan Shirazi, "Ta'ṯīrāt-i Bahār-i 'Arabī va Inqilābha-Yi Rangi Dar Āsiyā-Yi Markazī va Qafqāz [Influences of Arabic Spring and Color Revolutions in Central Asia and the Caucasus]," *Muṭāla'āt Ravābiṭ-i Bayn al-Milal* 5, no. 19 (2012): 9-36; Shu'ayb Bahman, *Inqilābha-Yi Rangi va Inqilāb-i Islāmi-Yi Irān* [Color Revolutions and the Islamic Revolution of Iran], Cha¯p-i 3. (Tihrān: Markaz-i Asnād-i Inqilāb-i Islāmī, 2010).

23. Jahangir Karami, *Ravābiṭ-i Jumhūrī-i Islāmī-i Īrān va Fidirāsyūn-i Rūsīyah: 'aṣr-i Nuvīn-i Hamakārī'hā* [Relations between the Islamic Republic of Iran and Russia: New Era of Cooperation] (Tehran: Daftar-i Muṭāla'āt-i Siyāsī va Bayn al-Milalī, 2009)..

24. Hamid Reza Anvari and Morteza Rahmani Muvahhid, *Sāzmān-i Hamkārī-i Shānghāy: chashm'andāzī bih sū-yi jahān-i chand quṭbī* [Shanghai Cooperation Organisation: Outlook to a Multipolar World] (Tehran: Markaz-i Chāp va Intishārāt-i Vizārat-i Umūr-i Khārijah, 2008); Amir Mohammad Haji Yousefi and Marzieh Sadat Alvand, "Sāzmān-i Hamkārī-i Shānghāy va Īrān: Hizhmūnī va Ẕidd-i Hizhmūnī [Iran and Shanghai Cooperation Organisation: Hegemony and Counter-Hegemony]," *Pizhūhish'nāmah-i 'ulūm-i Siyāsī* 2, no. 10 (2010): 163–; Ali Reza Azghandi, *Siyāsat-i Khārijī-i Jumhūrī-i Islāmī-i Īrān* [Foreign Policy of Islamic Republic of Iran] (Tehran: Nashr-i Qūmis, 2002); Hamid Mowlana and Manuchehr Muhammadi, *Siyāsat-i khārijī-i Jumhūrī-i Islāmī-i Īrān dar dawlat-i Aḥmadī'nizhād* [Foreign Policy of the Islamic Republic of Iran under Ahmadinejad] (Tihrān: Nashr-i Dād'gustar, 2008); Hossein Mafi Moghaddam, "Jahān-i Chand Quṭbī va Zāyish-i Buhrān'hā [Multipolar World and the Emergence of Crises]," *Shargh*, 21 September 2017.
25. Ahmad Samii, *Duktrīn-i Khātamī Dar Guftugū-Yi Tamaddun'hā va Farhang'hā* [Khatami's Doctrine in the Dialogue of Civilizations and Cultures] (Tehran: Chakād: Amīr Bahādur, 2001); Eradzh Boev, "Tsivilizatsionnye Tsennosti Kak Faktor Sblizheniya Rossii i Irana [Civilizational Values as a Factor of Convergence of Russia and Iran]," in Sazhin and Dunaeva, *Rossiisko-Iranskie Otnosheniya: Problemy i Perspektivy*, 173-8.
26. Ali Akbar Jafari, Meisam Belbasi, and Shahram Esfandiyar, "Manāfi'-i Millī va 'uẕvīyat-i Īrān Dar Sāzmān-i Hamkārī-i Shānghāy [National Interest and Iran's Membership in the Shanghai Cooperation Organisation]," *Pizhūhishī-i Dānish Siyāsī-i* 13, no. 2 (20 February 2018): 163–200.
27. Viacheslav Nikonov, "Zakat Odnopoliarnoi Epokhi," *Izvestiya*, 15 October 2008.
28. Such a sentiment is reflected in the 2014 Strategy for Russia issued by the influential Council on Foreign and Defense Policy, which characterizes the period from the Iraq War to the Arab Spring as one marked by the erosion of Western influence, coinciding with the rapid rise of China and India, Russia's recovery, and the emergence of non-Western powers with alternative views on the world order. The report notes that "growing dissatisfaction with rising powers" and ongoing "processes of redistribution of power and influence" have "undermined the credibility of the Western model" of international order, necessitating the development of a polycentric system that accounts for the diversity of views. *Strategiya dlya Rossii* [Strategy for Russia] (Moscow: Sovet po Vneshnei i Oboronnoi Politike, 2014).
29. "Kontseptsiya Vneshnei Politiki Rossiyskoy Federatsii [Foreign Policy Conception of the Russian Federation]," 2016; "Novye Tsentry Sily v Azii i Mnogopolyarnyi Mir: Zayavleniya Putina i Drugikh Liderov na SVMDA [New Centers of Power in Asia and a Multipolar World: Statements by Putin and Other Leaders at the CIS Summit]," TASS: Mirovye Novosti, 13 October 2022.
30. Mikhail Titarenko and Vladimir Petrovskii, *Rossiya, Kitai i Novyi Mirovoi Poryadok* [Russia, China, and the New World Order] (Moscow: Ves' Mir, 2016), 9, http://old.ifes-ras.ru/publications/article/1430-titarenko-ml-petrovskij-ve-rossiya-kitaj-i-novyj-mirovoj-poryadok.
31. Fyodor Lukyanov, "Povorot na Vostok [Turn to the East]," Gazeta.ru, 16 February 2010; Maksim Braterskiy, "Kontseptsii Bol'shoi Evrazii Tri Goda [The Concept of Greater Eurasia over Three Years]," *Aktual'nye Problemy Evropy*, no. 1 (109) (2021), https://www.elibrary.ru/item.asp?id=44721591.
32. Alexander Lukin and Tamara Troyakova, "Mnogopolyarnaya Vostochnaya Aziya: Tendentsiya ili Uzhe Real'nost'? [Multipolar East Asia: A Trend or Already a Reality?],"

Problemy Dal'nego Vostoka, 31 December 2010, 168-73; Alexander Lukin, "Rossiya i Kitai v Bol'shoi Evrazii [Russia and China in Greater Eurasia]," *Polis: Politicheskie Issledovaniya*, no. 5 (2020).

33. With the inception of China's BRI in 2013, Russia sought to determine ways to manage China's growing influence in a region that encompasses the CIS and to capitalize on its relations with Beijing for economic benefits. In May 2015, Russian President Putin and Chinese President Xi Jinping signed an agreement to connect the EAEU with the BRI.
34. Vladimir Putin, "Plenary Session of St Petersburg International Economic Forum," President of Russia, 17 June 2016, http://en.kremlin.ru/events/president/news/52178.
35. Sergey Karaganov, "The New Cold War and the Emerging Greater Eurasia," *Journal of Eurasian Studies* 9, no. 2 (1 July 2018): 85-93.
36. Alexander Cooley, "Ordering Eurasia: The Rise and Decline of Liberal Internationalism in the Post-Communist Space," *Security Studies* 28, no. 3 (27 May 2019): 588-613, do i:10.1080/09636412.2019.1604988.
37. ʿAlī Aṣghar Ḥaqdār, *Guftimān-i Farhangī-Siyāsī-i Khātamī* [Cultural-Political Discourse of Khatami] (Tehran: Shafīʿī, 1999); Hashemi Rafsanjani, *Sardār-i sāzandagī: kārnāmah va khāṭirāt-i Hāshimī Rafsanjānī sāl-i 1375* [Sardar Sazandegi: Biography and Memoirs of Hashemi Rafsanjani in 1996] (Tehran: Daftar-i Nashr-i Maʿārif-i Inqilāb, 2019).
38. Nasir Saqafi ʿAmiri and Afsanih Ahmadi, *Īrān va siyāsat-i nigāh bih sharq* [Iran and the Look East Policy] (Tehran: Majmaʿ-i Tashkhīṣ-i Maṣlaḥat-i Niẓām, 2008). Mahmoud Ahmadinejad, *ʿAdl va ṣulḥ: guftār'hā-yi Raʾīs-i Jumhūrī-i Islāmī-i Īrān dar chahārumīn safarkārī bih Amrīkā* [Justice and Peace: Speeches by the President of the Islamic Republic of Iran during His Fourth Visit to the United States], ed. Bihnam Sadri (Tehran: Nashr-i Jumhūr-i Īrān, Markaz-i Pizhūhish va Asnād-i Riyāsat-i Jumhūrī, 2009); Shahrdād Is̱ná ʿAsharī, *Az dawlat-i iṣlāḥī tā dawlat-i Islāmī: taḥlīlī bar āsīb'shināsī-i ʿilal-i guẕār az dawlat-i Khātamī bih dawlat-i Aḥmadī'nizhād* [From the Reform Government to the Islamic State: An Analysis of the Pathology of the Causes of the Transition from Khatami's Government to Ahmadinejad's Government] (Tehran: Intishārāt-i ʿAṭāʾī, 2007); Ghulam Riza Haddad, *Rivāyatī Az Chīstī va Chirāyī-i Siyāsat-i Khārijī-i Dawlat-i Maḥmūd Aḥmadī'nizhād* [Narrative of the Foreign Policy of Mahmoud Ahmadinejad's Government] (Tehran: Intishārāt-i Chāpakhsh, 2021).
39. Aʿẓam Salāmatī, *Siyāsat-i hastah'ī-i dawlat-i Aḥmadī'nizhād va mavāẓiʿ-i shakhṣīyat'hā* [Nuclear Policy of Ahmadinejad's Administration and Positions of Personalities] (Tehran: Markaz-i Asnād-i Inqilāb-i Islāmī, 2014).
40. Sergey Karaganov, "S Vostoka na Zapad, ili Bol'shaya Evraziya [From East to West, or Greater Eurasia]," *Rossiiskaya Gazeta*, 24 October 2016; Andrei Bezrukov et al., "Strasti po Perimetru [Passion along the Perimeter]," *Kommersant*, 18 January 2016; Timofei Bordachev, "Sozdavaya Evraziiu Vmeste [Creating Eurasia Together]," *Izvestiya*, 16 April 2015.
41. Hanif Ghafari, "Jahān-i Chand Quṭbī [Multipolar World]," *Resalat*, 2 September 2008, 21; Banafsheh Gholami, "Jahān-i Chand'quṭbī Dar Nigāh-i Sharq va Gharb [Multipolar World in the Eyes of East and West]," *Rūznāmah-i Īrān,* 28 September 2014, 21; Yousef Molaei, "Shikast-i Hizhmūnī Dar Jahān-i Chand Quṭbī [Failure of Hegemony in a Multipolar World]," *Dunyā-yi Iqtiṣād*, 24 December 2017, 29.

42. Seyyed Rasoul Mousavi, "Nigāh-i mā bih Sharq mubtanī bar manāfi'-i millī ast [Our Approach to the East Is Based on National Interests]," Khamenei.ir, 4 March 2022.
43. Mohammad Sadegh Kushki and Seyyed Mohammad Hosseini, "Furṣat'hā va Chālish'hā-Yi 'uẓvīt Jumhūrī-i Islāmī-i Īrān Dar Sāzmān-i Hamkārī-i Shānghāy [Opportunities and Challenges of the Membership of the Islamic Republic of Iran in the Shanghai Cooperation Organisation]," *Faṣlnāmah-i Siyāsat* 47, no. 3 (September 2017): 747.
44. Mohesen Pak Ayeen, "Ūrāsiyā, Quṭb-i Nū Ẓuhūr I'tilāf'hā-Yi Jahānī [Eurasia, the Emerging Pole of Global Integration]," *Jām-i Jam*, 24 September 2017.
45. Abbas Zarei and Ismail Abbasi, "Ittiḥādīyah-'i iqtiṣādī-i Ūrāsiyā dar chashm'andāz-i Rūsī [The Eurasian Economic Union in Russia's Outlook]," *Faṣlnāmah-i Muṭāla'āt-i Āsiyā-yi Markazī va Qafqāz* 24, no. 104 (21 January 2019): 34
46. Hojjat Mahkavi and Mahnaz Goodarzi, "Ta'sīr-i Ittiḥādīyah-i Iqtiṣādī-i Ūrāsiyā Bar Mawqi'īyat-i Zhi'ūikūnūmīk-i Jumhūrī-i Islāmī-i Īrān [The Impact of the Eurasian Economic Union on the Geoeconomic Position of the Islamic Republic of Iran]," *Muṭāla'āt-i Urāsiyā-i Markazī* 12, no. 2 (23 September 2019): 519-38.
47. Interview with a Russia-based expert on Iran (Moscow), 2017.
48. Iranian foreign policy observers welcomed the "the formation of the Eurasian Economic Union in 2015 as a final step in economic convergence ... with the aim of integrating customs policies and facilitating the flow of goods, services and capital," describing it as a "new phase" in tapping into the region's potential. Seyed Kazem Sajjadpour and Maryam Soleimani, "Kālbud'shikāfī-i hamgarāyī-i Ūrāsiyāyī-i Rūsīyah: chārchūbhā-yi mafhūmī va 'amalīyātī [Anatomy of Russia's Eurasian Convergence: Conceptual and Operational Frameworks]," *Faṣlnāmah-i Muṭāla'āt-i Āsiyā-yi Markazī va Qafqāz* 21, no. 90 (1 October 2016): 106.
49. Interview with an Iranian diplomat at a high-level conference on Russia and Iran (Moscow), 2017.
50. Elena Chernenko, "'Ekonomika Ostaetsya Slabym Mestom Nashikh Dvustoronnikh Otnoshenii' [The Economy Remains a Weak Point in Our Bilateral Relations]," *Kommersant*, 18 December 2019, Integrum Digital Archive.
51. "Ravāyat-i Ikunūmīst az shetāb-i Tehrān va Moskow barāy dawr zadan-i taḥrīm-hā [The Economist's Narrative of Tehran and Moscow's Acceleration to Circumvent Sanctions]," EcoIran, 21 June 2023, https://www.ecoiran.com/fa/tiny/news-34810
52. "Reshenie Kollegii EEK po Stavkam Vvoznykh Tamozhennykh Poshlin, Primenyaemykh v Sootvetstvii s Vremennym Soglasheniem s Iranom [Decision of the EEC Board on the Rates of Import Customs Duties Applied in Accordance with the Temporary Agreement with Iran], Evraziiskoi ekonomicheskoi komissiil, 22 January 2019, https://eec.eaeunion.org/upload/medialibrary/fd8/Reshenie-Kollegii-EEK-_10-na-01.01.2022.pdf.
53. "Barrasī-i ab'ād-i 'uẓvīyat-i Jumhūrī-i Islāmī-i Īrān dar Ittiḥādīyah-'i Iqtiṣādī-i Ūrāsiyā [Examining the Dimensions of the Islamic Republic of Iran's Membership in the Eurasian Economic Union]," Mu'āvanat-i Dīplumāsī-i Iqtiṣādī Vizārat-i Umūr-i Khārijah-'i Jumhūrī-i Islāmī-i Īrān, 27 February 2021.
54. Kevjn Lim, "Iran's Eurasian Wager," Washington Institute, 27 April 2020, https://www.washingtoninstitute.org/policy-analysis/irans-eurasian-wager
55. Najma Bidmal and Muslim Ansari Nasab, "Rāhbard-i Tawse'ah-i Tijārī-i Irān - Ittiḥādīyah-Yi Iqtisādī-Yi Uurāsiyā [The Strategy of Iran–Eurasian Economic Union

Trade Development]," *Faṣlnāmah-i Muṭāla'āt-i Āsiyā-yi Markazī va Qafqāz* 28, no. 118 (23 August 2022): 61–86.

56. Nadezhda Tolstoukhova, "Vostochnyi Bazar [Eastern Bazar]," *Rossiiskaya Gazeta*, 25 April 2019.
57. "Sammit EAES v Erevane Voidet v Istoriyu [The EAEU Summit Will Go Down in History],"TASS, 1 October 2019, Integrum Digital Archive.
58. "Ratifitsirovano Vremennoe Soglashenie o Zone Svobodnoi Torgovli mezhdu EAES i Iranom [A Temporary Agreement on a Free Trade Zone between the EAEU and Iran Has Been Ratified]," Prezident Rossii (Kremlin.ru), 28 November 2018.
59. The EAEU and Iran agreed to extend the existing interim agreement for an additional three years while negotiations continued. Victoria Panfilova, "Iran Idet na Sblizhenie s Evraziiskim Ekonomicheskim Soyuzom [Iran Is Moving towards Rapprochement with the Eurasian Economic Union]," *Nezavisimaya Gazeta*, 1 October 2019.
60. "EAES i Iran Sozdayut Polnoformatnuyu Zonu Svobodnoy Torgovli [The EAEU and Iran Are Creating a Full-Scale Free Trade Zone]," Evraziyskaya ekonomicheskaya komissiya, 24 December 2023, https://eec.eaeunion.org/news/eaes-i-iran-sozdayut-polnoformatnuyu-zonu-svobodnoy-torgovli.
61. The SCO's founding documents and subsequent declarations have advanced the "Shanghai Spirit"—a set of principles emphasizing the autonomy and sovereignty of individual member states. This perspective challenges more liberal approaches that often advocate for universal human rights standards, sometimes clashing with traditional or national characteristics. Consequently, liberal norms are often dismissed by the SCO, which instead favors a relativist perspective that frames human rights as derivative of "historical traditions" and "national features." The SCO is particularly focused on combating what it describes as the "three evils": terrorism, extremism, and separatism. It allows member states to frame their domestic challenges and issues of governance stability as being external threats, which can sometimes justify significant security measures.
62. Mehdi Sanaei, "Evraziya i Mesto Irana v Regional'nom Sotrudnichestve [Eurasia and the Place of Iran in Regional Cooperation]," in Dunaeva and Mamedova, *Politika RF I IRI v Regional'nom Kontekste*, 28-34; Nina Mamedova, "Iran i ShOS [Iran and the SCO]," in *ShOS i Strany Blizhnego i Srednego Vostoka* [The SCO and the Countries of the Near Abroad and Middle East], ed. Marianna Arunova and Bakhtier Khakimov (Moscow: Institut Vostokovedeniya RAN, 2011), 31-46; Elena Dunaeva, "Regionalizm vo Vneshnei Politike Islamskoi Respubliki Iran (k Voprosu o Vstuplenii IRI v ShOS) [Regionalism in the Foreign Policy of the Islamic Republic of Iran (on the Issue of Iran's Membership in the SCO)]," in *Aktual'nye Problemy Rasshireniya Shankhaiskoi Organizatsii Sotrudnichestva: Materialy Mezhdunarodnoi Konferentsii (Foruma): "Na Vtorom Treke. Rol' Grazhdanskogo Obshchestva i Obshchestvennoi Diplomatii v Dal'neishem Razvitii i Rasshirenii Shankhaiskoi Organizatsii Sotrudnichestva"* (Moscow: Institut Stran SNG, 2016), 85-90.
63. Nicole Bayat Grajewski, "Iran and the SCO: The Quest for Legitimacy and Regime Preservation," *Middle East Policy* 30, no. 2 (2023): 38-61, https://doi.org/10.1111/mepo.12684.
64. Iran's admission as an observer at the 2005 Astana summit, which called for a timetable for the withdrawal of foreign forces from the region, contributed to the perception of the SCO's growing anti-Western orientation—a sentiment that only intensified during the presidency of Ahmadinejad.

65. Nicole Bayat Grajewski, "Iran and the SCO: The Quest for Legitimacy and Regime Preservation," *Middle East Policy* 30, no. 2 (2023): 38-61, https://doi.org/10.1111/mepo.12684.
66 Alexandr Polyshchuk, "Rossiisko-Iranskoe Sotrudnichestvo po Realizatsii Mezhdunarodnogo Transportnogo Koridora 'Sever-Yug' [Russian-Iranian Cooperation on the Implementation of the International North-South Transport Corridor]," in *Rol' i Mesto Irana v Regione*, ed. Nina Mamedova and Mahdi Imanipur (Moscow: Institut Vostokovedeniya RAN, 2007), 161-7; Nina Mamedova, "Mezhdunarodnyi Transportnyi Koridor 'Sever-Yug' Kak Sovremennyi Analog Velikogo Volzhskogo Puti [International North-South Transport Corridor as a Modern Analogue of the Great Volga Route]," *Vostochnaya Analitika*, no. 3 (2018): 149-56.
67. Pravitel'stvo Rossiiskoi Federatsii, "Strategiya Razvitiya Rossiiskikh Morskikh Portov v Kaspiiskom Basseine, Zheleznodorozhnykh i Avtomobil'nykh Podkhodov k Nim v Period do 2030 Goda [Strategy for the Development of Sea Ports in the Caspian Sea and Rail and Road Links to Them until 2030]," no. 1365 § (2017), http://static.government.ru/media/files/zACqKSgh6AdU2bWZahEb92qpLifBzJIr.pdf.
68. Interview with a Russia-based expert on Iran (Moscow), 2019.
69. "Mezhdunarodnyi Transportnyi Koridor 'Sever-Yug' [International North-South Transport Corridor]," Ministerstvo inostrannykh del Rossiiskoi Federatsii, 1 November 2016.
70. In September 2020, the Second Nagorno-Karabakh War between Armenia and Azerbaijan over the disputed Nagorno-Karabakh region had direct implications for Iran's and Russia's visions for economic integration and trade. The Second Karabakh War followed a prolonged period of tensions and sporadic skirmishes since the end of the First Nagorno-Karabakh War in 1994, which placed Nagorno-Karabakh under Armenian control. For background on the Caucasus, see Thomas De Waal, *Black Garden: Armenia and Azerbaijan through Peace and War* (New York: NYU Press, 2003).
71. Emil Avdaliani "Azerbaijan and Iran Seek Common Ground amid Regional Tensions," Jamestown, 27 March 2024, https://jamestown.org/program/azerbaijan-and-iran-seek-common-ground-amid-regional-tensions.
72. Aleksandr Anan'ev "'3+3': Vremya Sobirat' Kamni na Yuzhnom Kavkaze ['3+3': Time to Collect Stones in the South Caucasus]," *Mezhdunarodnaya Zhizn'*, 2 November 2023, https://interaffairs.ru/news/show/43031.
73. In September 2023, Azerbaijan initiated a rapid military offensive in Nagorno-Karabakh, effectively ending thirty years of self-declared independence for the enclave. Before this recent conflict, Nagorno-Karabakh had been the focal point of two significant wars. The initial skirmishes escalated into a full-blown conflict following the dissolution of the USSR, culminating in a ceasefire in 1994 that led to the creation of the Nagorno-Karabakh Republic, recognized as independent only in a de facto sense. The second conflict, in 2020, saw Azerbaijan reclaim territories previously held by ethnic Armenians, further cutting off Nagorno-Karabakh. The ceasefire for this war was brokered by Russia, which subsequently deployed peacekeeping forces to oversee the cessation of hostilities in the area.
74 Discussion with an Iran based journalist (online), 2023.
75. Correspondence with an Azerbaijani expert, 2023.
76. Vali Kaleji, "Russia and Iran Diverge in the South Caucasus," Cacianalyst.org, 15 June 2023, https://www.cacianalyst.org/publications/analytical-articles/item/13758-russia-and-iran-diverge-in-the-south-caucasus.html.

77. Artur Avakov, "Strany Yuzhnogo Kavkaza i Ikh Sosedi Dogovorilis' Ne Voevat' Drug s Drugom [The Countries of the South Caucasus and Their Neighbors Have Agreed Not to Wage War against Each Other]," *Nezavisimaya Gazeta*, 24 October 2023, https://www.ng.ru/cis/2023-10-24/5_8860_tehran.html.
78. Correspondence with Iran-based foreign policy expert (online), 2023.
79. Additionally, the minimized border length with Azerbaijan reduced the potential avenues for Israel—a key Azerbaijani ally and notable adversary of Iran—to penetrate Iranian territories. Natalya Skorlygina, "Koleya v Bol'shuyu Igru: Chto Zabotit Partnerov Rossii po Koridoru Sever-Yug [A Rut in the Big Game: What Worries Russia's Partners along the North-South Corridor]," *Kommersant*, 9 June 2023, https://www.kommersant.ru/doc/6030407.
80. Timofei Bordachev, "Pochemu Bessmyslenno Ugrozhat' Iranu [Why it Makes no Sense to Threaten Iran],"Vzglyad, 18 October 2022, Integrum Digital Archive.

8. ARMS FROM THE AYATOLLAHS

1. Volodymyr Zelensky, "Address by the President of Ukraine," Official Website of the President of Ukraine, 24 May 2023, https://www.president.gov.ua/en/news/pershij-zhe-ukrayinskij-f-16-stane-odnim-iz-najsilnishih-sig-83129.
2. "Obrashchenie Prezidenta Rossiiskoi Federatsii [Address by the President of the Russian Federation]," Press-Sluzhba Prezidenta RF, 28 February 2022, http://kremlin.ru/events/president/news/67843.
3. Michael Kofman and Rob Lee, "Not Built for Purpose: The Russian Military's Ill-Fated Force Design," War on the Rocks, 2 June 2022, https://warontherocks.com/2022/06/not-built-for-purpose-the-russian-militarys-ill-fated-force-design.
4. Bethan McKernan, "Russia 'Using Weapons Smuggled by Iran from Iraq against Ukraine,'" *The Guardian*, 12 April 2022, https://www.theguardian.com/world/2022/apr/12/russia-using-weapons-smuggled-by-iran-from-iraq-against-ukraine.
5. "Iran Preparing to Send 'Several Hundred' Drones to Russia, Sullivan Says," Politico, 11 July 2022, https://www.politico.com/news/2022/07/11/iran-uav-drones-russia-00045195.
6. Aamer Madhani and Zeke Miller, "US: Iranian Troops in Crimea Backing Russian Drone Strikes," AP News, 21 October 2022, https://apnews.com/article/government-and-politics-8b085070758120c31d421f68a65e4b14.
7. "Ra'īs-i Jumhūr dar Maskū/Az ta'kīd-i Pūtīn bar tavsi'ah-i ravābiṭ bā Īrān tā tashvīq-i Ra'īsī dar Dūmā-yi Rūsīyah [President in Moscow: From Putin's Emphasis on Developing Relations with Iran to Encouraging Russian Counterpart]," Fars News, 21 January 2022.
8. Ali Mohammad Bidarmaghz, "Sath-i esteghbāl az rūsā-yi jomhūr dar cheh sowrat-i tohin-i talqī mishavad? Dalīl-i shakl-i mīz va fāṣlah-i Pūtīn va Ra'īsī; chera parcham-hā nabūd? [How Is the Reception of Presidents Perceived as Insult? The Reason for the Table Shape and the Distance between Putin and Ra'isi; Why Were There No Flags?]," *Hamshahri*, 23 January 2022.
9. "Prezident Irana Poblagodaril Putina za Sodeistvie Vstupleniyu Tegerana v ShOS [The Iranian President Thanked Putin for Facilitating Tehran's Accession to the SCO]," TASS, 19 January 2022, https://tass.ru/mezhdunarodnaya-panorama/13470215.

10. "Prezident Irana Poblagodaril Putina za Sodeistvie Vstupleniyu Tegerana v ShOS [The Iranian President Thanked Putin for Facilitating Tehran's Accession to the SCO]."
11. Both leaders highlighted the impact of cooperation on Syria in their relations, with Raisi noting the "very good experience of cooperation between Iran and Russia in Syria" as a positive precedent, emphasizing that such successful collaboration "can create prerequisites for its expansion and use in other areas." Dīdār-i Rūsā-yi Jomhūr-i Īrān va Rūsiyah [Meeting of the Presidents of Iran and Russia]," *Riyāsat-i Īrān*, 19 January 2022.
12. "Vstrecha s Prezidentom Irana Seyedom Ebrakhimom Raisi [Meeting with the President of Iran Ebrahim Raisi]," Prezident Rossii, 19 January 2022, http://kremlin.ru/catalog/persons/680/events/67608.
13. "Prezident Irana Vystupil na Plenarnom Zasedanii GD [The President of Iran Spoke at the Plenary Meeting of the State Duma]," Gosudarstvennaya Duma, 20 January 2022, Integrum Digital Archive.
14. "Rossiisko-Iranskie Peregovory [Russian-Iranian Negotiations]," *Ekspert*, 24 January 2022, Integrum Digital Archive.
15. "Telefonnyy Razgovor s Prezidentom Irana Seyedom Ebrakhimom Raisi [Telephone Conversation with Iranian President Ebrahim Raisi]," Prezident Rossii, 24 February 2022, http://kremlin.ru/catalog/persons/680/events/67849.
16. "Goftgū-yi Telefonī Āyatollāh Ra'īsī Bā Ra'īs-i Jomhūr-i Rusīyeh [Ayatollah Raisi's Telephone Conversation with the Russian President]" Raisi.ir, 24 February 2022.
17. "Āmrīkā 'āmel-i aslī-yi moskel-i emruz-i Ūkrāyīn ast/Eropā bāzandeh-yi jang khāhad bū [America Is the Main Cause of Today's Problem in Ukraine/Europe Will Be the Loser of the War]," IRNA, 25 February 2022.
18. "Goftugū-yi telefonī-yi vazīr-i umūr-i khārij-i kishvar-i mān bā vazīr-i umūr-i khārij-i rūsyeh [Telephone Conversation between the Minister of Foreign Affairs of Our Country and the Minister of Foreign Affairs of Russia]," Vizārat-i amūr-i khārejeh-yi jomhūrī-yi eslāmī-yi īrān, 25 February 2022, https://mfa.ir/portal/newsview/671685.
19. Twitter, @alibahaadori, 25 February 2022, https://twitter.com/alibahaadori/status/1497132417441619970.
20. "Lahzeh Be Lahze Ba Tahavolāt-i Ūkrāyn; Kyiv Ravābet Bā Moskov Rā Qat' Kard [Moment by Moment with Ukraine Developments; Kyiv Cut Relations with Moscow]," Fars News, 24 February 2022, http://fna.ir/76a7w.
21. "Gharb-i Ūkrāyin rā tanhā guẕāsht; shart-i Rūsīyah barā-yi muẕākirah | bahā-yi ittikā bih Gharb dar Sharq [The West Has Abandoned Ukraine; Russia's Condition for Negotiation; The Cost of Relying on the West in the East]," *Hamshahri*, 26 February 2022; "Āyā jang-i jahānī āghāz shudah ast? [Has a World War Started?]," *Kayhan*, 28 February 2022.
22. "Īrān va Jang-i Ūkrāīn [Iran and the Ukraine War]," *Et'emad*, 26 February 2022.
23. "Forṣathā-yi eqtesād-i Īrān az jang-i Ūkrāyn va Rūsiyah [Iran's Economic Opportunities from the Ukraine-Russia War]," ISNA, 16 March 2022.
24. Golnaz Esfandiari, "Iran Criticized at Home for Tepid Response to Russia's Invasion of Ukraine," RFE/RFL, 1 March 2022.
25. The Supreme Leader said a solution to any crisis "is only possible by identifying its root cause, and in Ukraine that is American and Western policies," adding that Iran "supports the end of war." The Supreme Leader rearticulated this in his Nowruz speech several weeks later, declaring that "the war in Ukraine was launched by

the U.S. to expand NATO to the east, and now, while the people of Ukraine are trapped and suffering from different problems, the U.S. and its arms industry is profiting the most from the war, and because of this, it is hindering the necessary initiatives to end the war." "Baḥrān-i Ūkrāīn va Mawḥiẓ Thābit-i Īrān [Ukraine Crisis and Iran's Fixed Position]," Khamenei.ir, 1 March 2022, https://farsi.khamenei.ir/others-note?id=49681;"Sukhanrānī-Yi Ṭilvīzyūnī-i Rahbar-i Inqilāb Bih Munāsibat-i 'Īd-i Mub'ath [The Leader of the Revolution's Televised Speech on the Occasion of Eid Mu'baat]," Khamenei.ir, 1 March 2022, https://farsi.khamenei.ir/news-content?id=49673.

26. Ellie Geranmayeh and Nicole Grajewski, "Alone Together: How the War in Ukraine Shapes the Russian-Iranian Relationship," European Council on Foreign Relations, 6 September 2023, https://ecfr.eu/publication/alone-together-how-the-war-in-ukraine-shapes-the-russian-iranian-relationship.
27. This would potentially include activating international monetary exchanges under sanctions and completing infrastructure projects like the North-South Corridor, enhancing Iran's business cycle with Russia.
28. Mohammad Sajjad Najafi, Mohammad Qasemi, and Shima Haji, "Asār va tab'āt-i jang-i Rūsiyah va Ūkrāyn: Forsathā va tahdīdhā [The Effects and Consequences of the Russia-Ukraine War: Opportunities and Threats]," Markaz-i Pazhuhesh-haye Atāq-i Īrān, 2022.
29. "Ehtemāl-i Taghyīr-i Rāhbard-i Īrān Dar Jang-i Ūkrāīn [The Possibility of Changing Iran's Strategy in the Ukraine War]," *Donya-ye Eqtesad*, 2 February 2023, https://www.magiran.com/article/4383457.
30. "Rossiya Prizvala SShA Garantirovat', Chto Sanktsii Ne Pomeshayut Sotrudnichestvu s Iranom [Russia Urges U.S. to Ensure Sanctions Do Not Interfere with Cooperation with Iran]," Interfax, 5 March 2022, https://www.interfax.ru/russia/826559.
31. Twitter, @alishamkhani_ir, 7 March 2022: "Vienna Participants Act & React Based on Interests and It's Understandable. Our Interactions with 4+1 Are Also Solely Driven by Our People's Interests. Thus, We're Assessing New Elements That Bear on the Negotiations and Will Accordingly Seek Creative Ways to Expedite a Solution," https://twitter.com/alishamkhani_ir/status/1500723187319025665.
32. Laurence Norman, "Iran Chief Negotiator Unexpectedly Leaves Vienna as Nuclear Talks Hit Standstill," *Wall Street Journal*, 7 March 2022, https://www.wsj.com/articles/iran-chief-negotiator-unexpectedly-leaves-vienna-as-nuclear-talks-hit-standstill-11646683825.
33. "Vākānish-i rasmi bih sukhanān-i Lavrov [Official Response to Lavrov's Remarks]," *Donya-ye Eqtesad*, 6 March 2022, https://donya-e-eqtesad.com/fa/tiny/news-3848633.
34. "Otmena Sanktsii protiv Irana Ne Dolzhna Zaviset' ot 'Alchnosti' Vashingtona—Glava MID Irana [Cancelation of Sanctions against Iran Should Not Depend on the 'Greed' of Washington—Iranian Foreign Minister]," RIA Novosti, 10 March 2022. "Iran: Atmosfera Sanktsii Ne Dolzhna Vliyat' na Sotrudnichestvo s Rossiei [Iran: The Atmosphere of Sanctions Should Not Affect Cooperation with Russia]," Vzglyad, 8 March 2022. Integrum Digital Archive.
35. "Russia's Lavrov Says Iran Deal Cannot Discriminate," Reuters, 7 March 2022.
36. On legal loopholes, see "Tablūr-i Iqtiṣād-i Muqāwamatī dar Rūsīyah dar Mavājihah bā Taḥrīm-hā-yi Gharb [Tableau of Resistance Economy in Russia in the Face of Western Sanctions]," Fars, 21 March 2022, http://fna.ir/1o505n.

37. "Amīr'Abdallāhīān: Rūsīyah mān'ī barāy-i rasīdan bih tavāfuq nīst [Amir-Abdollahian: Russia Is Not an Obstacle to Reaching an Agreement]," Tabnak, 15 March 2022, https://www.tabnak.ir/004ehk.
38. Barak Ravid, "Lavrov Says Russia Received 'Written Guarantees' over Iran Deal," Axios, 15 March 2022.
39. Hanna Notte, "Russia's Invasion of Ukraine: The Iran Nuclear Price Tag," Friedrich-Ebert-Stiftung, February 2023, https://library.fes.de/pdf-files/international/20083.pdf.
40. "Putin Pobesedoval s Prezidentom Irana [Putin Spoke with the President of Iran]," Vestnik Kavkaza, 29 June 2022.
41. Similarly, in September 2022, Putin noted that Russia and Iran would sign "a new major Russian-Iranian treaty that will elevate our relations to the level of strategic partnership." "Vstrecha s Prezidentom Irana Seyedom Ebrakhimom Raisi [Meeting with President of Iran Ebrahim Raisi]," Prezident Rossii, 15 September 2022, http://kremlin.ru/catalog/persons/680/events/69354.
42. Interview with a Russian expert on Iran (Zoom), May 2023.
43. "Dīdār-i Raisjumhūr-i Rūsiyah bā Rahbar-i Inqilāb [The Meeting of the President of Russia with the Leader of the Revolution]," Khamenei.ir, 19 July 2022, https://farsi.khamenei.ir/news-content?id=50657.
44. Fedor Lukyanov, "Iran i Turtsiya Predstavlyayut Soboy Vazhneyshie Gosudarstva na Krayne Znachimom dlya Rossii Napravleniiyug [Iran and Türkiye Are the Most Important States in a Direction That Is Extremely Important for Russia—the South]," *Rossiyskaya Gazeta*, 20 July 2022, https://rg.ru/2022/07/20/o-polze-izoliacii.html.
45. Eric Schmitt, Thomas Gibbons-Neff, and John Ismay, "As Russia Runs Low on Drones, Iran Plans to Step In, U.S. Officials Say," *New York Times*, 17 July 2022.
46. "Guftugū-yi tilifunī-i vazrā-yi umūr-i khārijah-'i Jumhūrī-i Islāmī-i Īrān va Ūkrāyīn [Telephone Conversation between the Foreign Ministers of the Islamic Republic of Iran and Ukraine],"Vizārat-i umūr-i khārijah-'i Jumhūrī-i Islāmī-i Īrān, 15 July 2022, https://mfa.gov.ir/files/Pdf/0687123-newsExportb3c58c7d69144bde9c6709cdb11e39fa.pdf.
47. "Amīr Ḥaydarī: Pīchīdah'tarīn puhpādhā rā tavlīd kardah'īm/Āmādagī-i ṣādirāt-i tajhīzāt-i niẓāmī rā dārīm [Amir Heydari: We Have Produced the Most Sophisticated Drones/We Are Ready for the Export of Military Equipment],"Tasnim, 19 July 2022, https://tn.ai/2745204.
48. Elizaveta Chip, "Operatori Shahed: Rosiis'ko-irans'ka Kazka pro 'Sokolinnuyu okhotu' [Shahed Operators: Russian-Iranian Tale of 'Falcon Hunt'], NGL.media, 20 November 2022.
49. "The purpose of holding the international military competition in 2022 is to convey the message of peace, friendship and cooperation of the Islamic Republic of Iran with other countries of the world to fight global terrorism and factors that make the world dangerous, as well as to increase the level of readiness, combat power and transfer military experience and achievements in the unmanned field to friendly countries," said General Sardar Ali Bilali, senior advisor to the commander of the Iranian Air and Space Forces, during the opening ceremony of the competition. "Āghāz-i raqbāt-i pahpādī chahār kishvar dar Kāshān [Commencement of Drone Competition among Four Countries in Kashan],"Tasnim, 15 August 2022.
50. The use of military competitions and exercises as covert training was discussed in Iran's military journal, which examined avenues for covert military cooperation. See

Ahmad Vahidi et al., "Ṣūratbandī-i Shenāsā'ī-i Shākhṣihā-Yi Dīplumāsī Panahān Dafā'ī [Framework for Identifying Covert Defensive Diplomatic Indicators]," *Faṣlnāmeh-i ʿilmī-i Maṭāleʿāt-i Bīn-Rashtehā-Yi Dānesh-Rāhbardī* 13, no. 50 (21 April 2023): 31-7.

51. UAV units (squadrons) are based at airfields in the settlements of Konarek, Jask, Qeshm, Chogadak, Hamadan. The testing site is located at the Kashan airport. Operators for drones are trained at the UAV school located at the Kushke Nosrat Air Base (Qom Province).
52. For background on Iran's missile program, see Behnam Ben Taleblu, "Arsenal: Assessing the Islamic Republic of Iran's Ballistic Missile Program," Foundation for the Defense of Democracy, 15 February 2023, https://www.fdd.org/analysis/2023/02/15/arsenal-assessing-the-islamic-republic-of-irans-ballistic-missile-program.
53. The unveiling of the Shahed-129 in 2012 represented a major breakthrough, as it was Iran's first "domestically produced" drone capable of long-range surveillance and combat missions, though the Shahed-129 drone mirrors the design of the Israeli Hermes 450, indicating that Iran possibly acquired Israeli models potentially lost during covert operations and used reverse-engineering technologies. "Iran: Armed Drones in the Middle East," Royal United Services Institute, 2018, https://drones.rusi.org/countries/iran/#:~:text=Iran%20deploys%20UAVs%20mainly%20to,targets%20in%20Syria%20and%20Iraq.
54. Divsallar and Azizi, "Towards a Non-Western Model of Security Assistance."
55. Aleksei Brusilov and Aleksei Moiseev, "Iranskie Udarnye Bespilotniki Prodemonstrirovali Svoyu Moshch' na Video [Iranian Attack Drones Demonstrate Their Power on Video]," *Rossiiskaya Gazeta*, 20 March 2019, https://rg.ru/2019/03/20/iranskie-udarnye-bespilotniki-prodemnstrirovali-svoiu-moshch-na-video.html.
56. "Kudām Pahpādhā-Yi Īrānī Dar Fihrist-i Ṣādirāt Qarār Dārand? [Which Iranian Drones Are on the Export List?]," *Donya-ye Eqtesad*, 29 October 2020, https://donya-e-eqtesad.com/fa/tiny/news-3706042; "Artish bih laḥẓah-'i tiknūlūzhī-i jahānī-i 'puhpādhā-yi intiḥārī dārā-yi hūsh-i maṣnū'ī rasīd/'Yūrish-i fūjī' puhpādhā-yi Īrānī az zamīn bih āsmān raft [The Army Reached the Edge of the Global Technology of 'Suicide Drones with Artificial Intelligence'/'Fuji Attack' of Iranian Drones Went from the Ground to the Sky]," *Mashregh News,* 26 April 2021, mshrgh.ir/1208967.
57. Denis Fedutinov, "Bespilotniki v Siriyskom Konflikte [UAVs in the Syrian Conflict]," Russiancouncil.ru, 27 May 2019, https://russiancouncil.ru/analytics-and-comments/analytics/bespilotniki-v-siriyskom-konflikte.
58. Iranian-backed militias in Syria and Iraq use Iranian-supplied drones to gather intelligence, coordinate attacks, and provide real-time battlefield information in support of their allied forces. See Stanislav Ivanov, "Protivostoyanie Saudovskoy Aravii i Irana kak Faktor Nestabil'nosti v Zone Persidskogo Zaliva [Confrontation between Saudi Arabia and Iran as a Factor of Instability in the Persian Gulf Area]," *Zarubezhnoe Voennoe Obozrenie*, no. 9, 17-20 (2020), https://www.imemo.ru/files/File/ru/articles/2020/zvo-2020-09-Ivanov.pdf.
59. "Iran, Russia Sharing Drone Technology," *Tehran Times*, 23 July 2017, https://www.tehrantimes.com/news/415305/Iran-Russia-sharing-drone-technology.
60. "Amīr Banī Ṭarafī Khabar Dād: Ṣāderāt-i Pahpād'hā-Yi Īrānī Bih Rūsīyah [Amir Bani Tarafi Announced: Export of Iranian Drones to Russia]," *Resalat*, 24 July 2017, 2; "Ṣāderāt-i Pahpādhā-yi Īrānī Be Rūsyah/Tavasohh-i Hamkārī Dar Tarāhhī-i Anvā'eh Pahpād [Exporting Iranian UAVs to Russia/Developing Cooperation in the Design of UAVs]," Mehr News, 23 July 2017, https://www.mehrnews.com/news/4038275.

61. V. Yu. Gumelev et al., "Iranskie Bespilotnye Letatel'nye Apparaty 'Mokhadzher' i 'Ababil'" [Iranian Unmanned Aerial Vehicles 'Mohajer' and 'Ababil'']," *Tekhnika i Vooruzhenie:Vchera, Segodnya, Zavtra*, no. 11 (2021): 2-11.
62. V. Yu. Gumelev et al., "Iranskie Bespilotnye Letatel'nye Apparaty Semeistva 'Saiga' [Iranian Unmanned Aerial Vehicles of the Saiga Family]," *Armeiskii Sbornik*, no. 12 (2021), https://army.ric.mil.ru/Stati/item/370796.
63. V.Yu. Gumelev et al., "Bespilotnaya Komponenta [Unmanned Component]," *Armeiskii Sbornik*, no. 11 (2021), https://army.ric.mil.ru/Stati/item/362113.
64. For a more recent study on it, see V. Litvinenko, "Barrazhiruyushchie Bespilotniki: Boepripasy [Loitering Drones: Ammunition]," *Armeiskii Sbornik* 4 (2023), https://army.ric.mil.ru/Stati/item/481638.
65. Iran's desire to export these technologies was already on display prior to Russia's war when it signed an agreement with Tajikistan to construct Ababil drones.
66. After Russia failed to swiftly capture Kyiv in the early spring of 2022, reports began to appear about Iran's smuggling of weapons from Iraq to Russia. U.S. intelligence disclosed cooperation between Russia and Iran. By the autumn of 2022, it had been confirmed that Iran had supplied drones to Russia. "Mājirā-yi puhpādhā-yi Īrānī va tanāquẕ̤gūyī-i mukarrār-i Āmrīkā'īhā [The Saga of Iranian Drones and the Recurring Denials of Americans]," Nour News, 31 August 2022, https://NourNews.ir/n/104265; "Puhpādhā-yi Īrānī vārid-i jang-i Ūkrāyīn shudah'and [Iranian Drones Have Entered the Ukraine War]," *Khabar*, 14 July 2022, khabaronline.ir/xj3DV.
67. "Zamministra Oborony Rossii General-Polkovnik Aleksandr Fomin Provel Peregovory s Zamestitelem Ministra Oborony i Podderzhki VS Irana Brigadnym Generalom Khodzhatolloi Koreishi [Deputy Minister of Defense of Russia, Colonel General Alexander Fomin, Held Talks with Deputy Minister of Defense and Support of the Iranian Armed Forces, Brigadier General Hojatollah Koreishi]," *Zakon, Poryadok, Gosudarstvo*, 30 March 2022, Integrum Digital Archive.
68. "Moskou: Rusīyih va Īrān irtibātāt dar bakhsh-i difā'ī rā tosi'ih mī-dihand [Moscow: Russia and Iran Are Expanding Communications in the Defense Sector," *Et'emad*, 9 October 2023.
69. At Tiyas Air Base in Syria, Russian planes were stationed alongside Iranian drones such as the Shahed-129, Mohajer, and Saegheh.
70. Matt Berg, "Iran Preparing to Send 'Several Hundred' Drones to Russia, Sullivan Says," Politico, 11 July 2022.
71. "Arestovich Zayavil, Chto Iran Peredal Rossii Bespilotniki i Armiya RF Uzhe Ispol'zuet Ikh v Ukraine [Arestovich Said That Iran Transferred Drones to Russia and the Russian Army Is Already Using Them in Ukraine]," Strana.ua, 5 August 2022.
72. At the time, Russian military analyst Yuri Laimin stated that if true, the choice is very logical, since these are the most battle-tested Iranian attack drones. Telegram, 30 August 2022, https://t.me/ImpNavigator/3807.
73. Deborah Haynes, "Russia Flew €140m in Cash and Captured Western Weapons to Iran in Return for Deadly Drones, Source Claims," Sky News, 9 November 2022.
74. "Peskov Nazval Vbrosom Informatsiyu o Postavkakh Iranskikh Bespilotnikov v Rossiyu [Peskov Called Information about the Supply of Iranian Drones to Russia a Hoax]," TASS, 30 August 2022.
75. "Iran Says It Supplied Drones to Russia before Ukraine War Began," *The Guardian*, 5 November 2022.
76. "Russia Fired at the Nikopol District with Iranian UAVs," Militarnyi, 15 September

2022, https://mil.in.ua/en/news/russia-fired-at-the-nikopol-district-with-iranian-uavs.

77. Discussion with a senior U.S. defense official, 2023.
78. The IRGC-AF significantly influences the design and production phases of the drones, ensuring compliance with precise operational and tactical requisites. See *Barnāmah-i haftum; ab'ād-i niẓāmī va difā'ī* [Seventh Program: Military and Defense Dimensions] (Tehran: Pazhūhishgāh-i markaz-i millī-i faẕā-yi majāzī, 2021).
79. In April 2022, Mahan Air increased its service into Moscow, Russia, by adding two weekly flights to Moscow's Sheremetyevo Airport to its current service into Moscow's Vnukovo Airport. United States Federal Register: Notices, vol. 87, no. 218, 14 November 2022, https://www.govinfo.gov/content/pkg/FR-2022-11-14/pdf/2022-24682.pdf.
80. Many of the planes are owned by companies linked to Iran's IGRC. The U.S. sanctioned a subsidiary of Iran Air, Safiran Airport Services, in September 2022 for coordinating Russian military flights between Iran and Russia, including those associated with transporting Iranian UAVs, personnel, and related equipment from Iran to Russia "Treasury Sanctions Iranian Persons Involved in Production of Unmanned Aerial Vehicles and Weapon Shipment to Russia," U.S. Department of the Treasury, 28 August 2023, https://home.treasury.gov/news/press-releases/jy0940.
81. Comments by a senior U.S. Department of Defense official, Washington, DC, 2023.
82. Elisabeth Braw, "Sanction-Busting Russian Ships Are Going Under the Radar," *Foreign Policy*, 14 December 2022, https://foreignpolicy.com/2022/12/14/sanction-busting-russian-ships-automatic-identification-system-radar.
83. On 1 November, the Ukrainian Defense Ministry's Main Intelligence Directorate announced on Telegram that Iran planned to send about 200 combat drones to Russia, including the Shahed-136, Mohajer-6, and Arash-2. These drones were to be delivered via the Caspian Sea to Astrakhan, assembled in Russia, and repainted with Russian designations, specifically Geran-2 for Shahed-136. Lauren Kent and Salma Abdelaziz, "Iran Has a Direct Route to Send Russia Weapons—and Western Powers Can Do Little to Stop the Shipments," CNN, 26 May 2023.
84. The 960th Guards Assault Aviation Regiment, military unit 75387, which is part of the 1st Guards Mixed Air Division of the 4th Air Force and Air Defense Army, is stationed at the airfield in Primorsko-Akhtarsk. The regiment is armed with Su-25, Su-25UB, and Su-25SM3 attack aircraft. This regiment was used in Russia's wars in Georgia and Syria. Since 2015, part of the flight and flight technical personnel of the regiment has been involved in Russia's military operation in Syria. "Vlasti SShA: Rossiya Sovmestno s Iranom Stroit Zavod Dronov v Tatarstane, on Mozhet Zarabotat' v Sleduyushchem Godu [U.S. Authorities: Russia, together with Iran, Is Building a Drone Factory in Tatarstan; It Could Start Operating Next Year]," Nastoyashchee Vremya, 9 June 2023.
85. "Iranian Drone Instructors Spotted in Belarus - Report," Jerusalem Post, 24 October 2022, https://www.jpost.com/international/article-720425.
86. A report from Ukraine's armed forces details the tactics used by the Russian forces to essentially swarm Ukrainian air defense. "Metodichni Rekomendatsii Zagal'noviis'kovim Pidrozdilam Shchodo Borot'bi z Udarnimi BpLA Irans'kogo Virobnitstva 'Shahed-136' ('Geran'-2') Ta Rf 'Lantset-2' [Methodical Recommendations to the Combined Military Units on Combating the Iranian-Made Shahed-136 (Geran-2) and Russian Lancet-2 Attack UAVs]," Tsentr Operativnikh

Standartiv i Metodiki Pidgotovki Zbroinikh Sil Ukraini Spil'no z Golovnim Upravlinnyam Doktrin ta Pidgotovki General'nogo Shtabu Zbroinikh Sil Ukraini, 2023, http://chtyvo.org.ua/authors/Zbroini_syly_Ukrainy/Metodychni_rekomendatsii_zahalnoviiskovym_pidrozdilam_schodo_borotby_z_udarnymy_BpLA_iranskoho_vyrob.

87. The engine in this UAV is a copy of a successful German model; it is produced in factories in Iran and China.
88. "Alabuga: Iranskie Drony po Franshize [Alabuga: Iranian Drone Franchise]," Protokol, 3 July 2023, https://protokol.band/2023/07/03/alabuga-iranskie-drony.
89. Mikhail Nikol'skiy, "Iranskie Razvedyvatel'nye i Udarnye Bpla Samoletnogo Tipa [Iranian Aerial Intelligence and Strike UAVs]," *Aerokosmicheskoe Obozrenie*, no. 6 (31 December 2022): 26-37.
90. A. Kuleshov et al., "Nuzhen Li Rossii Persidskii 'Luk' [Does Russia Need a Persian 'Luk'?]," *Armeiskii Sbornik*, no. 1 (2022), https://army.ric.mil.ru/Stati/item/446640.
91. Kuleshov et al., "Nuzhen Li Rossii Persidskii 'Luk' [Does Russia Need a Persian 'Luk']"; Litvinenko, "Barrazhiruyushchie Bespilotniki: Boepripasy [Loitering Drones: Ammunition]."
92. V. Yu. Gumelev et al., "Iranskie Bespilotnye Letatel'nye Apparaty 'Mokhadzher' i 'Ababil'' [Iranian Unmanned Aerial Vehicles 'Mohajer' and 'Ababil']," *Tekhnika i Vooruzhenie: Vchera, Segodnya, Zavtra*, no. 11 (2021): 2-11.
93. Dov Lieber, Benoit Faucon, and Michael Amon, "Russia Supplies Iran with Cyber Weapons as Military Cooperation Grows," *Wall Street Journal*, 27 March 2023.
94. "Na Dogovore Shapka Gorit [The Agreement Is on Fire]," *Izvestiya*, 19 October 2022, Integrum Digital Archive.
95. "Iran Rasplatitsya za Drony Vnutrennei Stabil'nost'yu [Iran Will Pay for Drones with Domestic Stability]," *Nezavisimaya Gazeta*, 19 October 2022, Integrum Digital Archive.
96. "Dron, Ty Chei? Sovbez OON Ne Uderzhit Tegeran ot Kontaktov s Moskvoi [Drone, Whose Are You? UN Security Council Won't Keep Tehran from Contacting Moscow]," NEWS.ru, 20 October 2022, Integrum Digital Archive.
97. "Amid New Allegations of Atrocities in Ukraine Regions Returned to Government Control, Political Affairs Chief Tells Security Council Accountability Remains Crucial," Un.org, 21 October 2022, https://press.un.org/en/2022/sc15074.doc.htm.
98. "Iran Napugal Zapad Zayavleniem, Kotoroe Moglo Byt' Mest'yu Rossii [Iran Scared the West with a Statement That Could Have Been Russia's Revenge]," Pravda.ru, 11 November 2022; Evgeniy Shakirov, "V SShA Obespokoilis' Vizitom Patrusheva v Iran [The U.S. Expressed Concern about Patrushev's Visit to Iran]," Gazeta.ru, 11 November 2022, https://www.gazeta.ru/politics/news/2022/11/11/19007203.shtml.
99. "Patrushev Obvinil Spetssluzhby Zapada v Organizatsii Massovykh Besporyadkov v Irane [Patrushev Accuses Western Intelligence Agencies of Organizing Mass Disorder in Iran]," Vzglyad (vz.ru), 9 November 2022. "Patrushev: Rossiya Schitaet Vazhnym dlya Svoei Natsbezopasnosti Vzaimodeistvie s Iranom [Patrushev: Russia Considers Interaction with Iran Important for Its National Security]," VPS-Monitoring "Banki i Birzhi Segodnya," 11 November 2022.
100. "Nīklāy Pātrūshūf dar dīdār bā Shamkhānī: Ḥattá agar buḥrān-i Ūkrāyin nīz shakl nimīgirift taḥrīmhā-yi gharb 'alayhī-i Rūsīyah i'māl mīshud [Nikolai Patrushev in

a Meeting with Shamkhani: Even if the Ukraine Crisis Did Not Occur, Western Sanctions against Russia Would Still Be Imposed]," Nour News, 27 May 2022, https://nournews.ir/n/97382.

101. "V Tegerane Sostoyalis' Rossiysko-Iranskie Konsul'tatsii po Voprosam Bezopasnosti [Russian-Iranian Consultations on Security Issues Took Place in Tehran]," Press-Sluzhba Soveta Bezopasnosti RF, 9 November 2022, Integrum Digital Archive.
102. "Ravāyatī az yak khabar-i akhbār-i sākhtagī-i Gharb barāy-i taẓ'īf-i Karmalīn [Narrative of a Fake Western News Story to Undermine the Kremlin]," IRNA, 25 June 2023, https://irna.ir/xjMMDg.
103. "Kun'ānī: Īrān az ḥākīmīyat-i qānūn dar Rūsīyah ḥimāyat mī-kunad [Kanaani: Iran Supports the Rule of Law in Russia]," Mashregh, 23 June 2023, mshrgh.ir/1502311.
104. "Ed'ā-yi kūdatā dar Rūsyeh; grūh-i Vāgnr chīst va cheh mīkunad?[Alleged Coup in Russia: What Is Wagner Group and What Does It Do?]," IRNA, 23 June 2023.
105. "Sekretar' Soveta Bezopasnosti Rossiyskoy Federatsii Nikolay Patrushev Provel v Moskve Vstrechu s Glavnokomanduyushchim Silami Pravoporyadka Islamskoy Respubliki Iran Akhmadrezoy Radanom [Secretary of the Security Council of the Russian Federation Nikolai Patrushev Held a Meeting in Moscow with the Commander-in-Chief of the Law Enforcement Forces of the Islamic Republic of Iran, Ahmadreza Radan]," Press-Sluzhba Soveta Bezopasnosti RF, 28 June 2023, Integrum Digital Archive.
106. Hamid Reza Azizi, "How the Wagner Rebellion Was Seen in Iran," European Leadership Network, 27 June 2023, https://europeanleadershipnetwork.org/commentary/how-the-wagner-rebellion-was-seen-in-iran/ .
107. "Abʿād-i shūrish-i Vāgnir va jang-i shinākhtī-i gharb ʿalayh-i Rūsīyah [Dimensions of the Wagner Rebellion and the West's Cognitive War Against Russia]," Noor News, 24 June 2023, https://nournews.ir/n/143565.
108. "Guftugū-yi Raʾīsī va Pūtin/Himāyat-i kāmil-i Īrān az Rūsīyah dar pay-i shūrish-i Vāgnir'hā [Raisi-Putin Conversation: Iran's Full Support for Russia Following Wagner Rebellion]," Dunyā-yi Iqtiṣād, 26 June 2023, https://donya-e-eqtesad.com/fa/tiny/news-3979791.
109. "Īrān va Rūsiyah Dar Tāmīn-i Amnīyat Bayn al-Mellalī Hamkārī Mīkonnand [Iran and Russia Cooperate in Ensuring International Security]," IRNA, 14 August 2023, https://irna.ir/xjNbH5.
110. "Mohimtarīn barnāmahā-yi Sardār Rādān dar Rūsīyah chih būd? [What Were the Most Important Programs of Commander Radan in Russia?]," Fars News, 1 July 2023, http://fna.ir/3dikpv.
111. "Muwāfaqatnāmah-i hamkārī-i Īrān bā Rūsīyah dar ḥawzah-i amnīyat-i ittilāʿāt/Matn-i lāyihah [Agreement on Iran's Cooperation with Russia in the Field of Information Security/Text of the Bill]," Didbaniran.ir, 11 July 2022.
112. "Alabuga: Iranskie Drony po Franshize [Alabuga: Iranian Drone Franchise]."
113. Ibid.
114. Twitter/X post, Nicole Grajewski (@nicolegrajewski), 7 February 2024: "Rolling Thread on the Leaked Documents about Russia, Iran, and the Drone Factory in Alabuga," https://twitter.com/NicoleGrajewski/status/1755122140926325045.
115. "Alabuga: Iranskie Drony po Franshize [Alabuga: Iranian Drone Franchise]."
116. Dalton Bennett and Mary Ilyushina, "Inside the Russian Effort to Build 6,000 Attack Drones with Iran's Help," *Washington Post*, 17 August 2023, https://www.

washingtonpost.com/investigations/2023/08/17/russia-iran-drone-shahed-alabuga.

117. Due to the threat of airstrikes, all factories have two backups dispersed throughout Iran; the final assembly is located in a secret tunnel under a mountain near Tehran. Despite the challenges imposed by international sanctions, internal documents from Alabuga SEZ note that Iran has achieved a remarkable feat of 90 percent localization for all components, relying on non-unique, publicly available imported parts to complete their manufacturing processes. The documents also reveal Iran's elaborate schemes for procuring this technology.
118. The documents indicate that the Alabuga SEZ was initially struggling to obtain necessary drone components from foreign sources, as Russia only produces four of the 130 necessary internal components, and recent U.S. blanket sanctions have further hindered Russia's ability to acquire some electrical components.
119. This occurred during the November 2022 and April 2023 visits of the Alabuga JSC.
120. Interestingly, the documents also reveal that there was a plan for full localization of production in Russia with minimal supply of Iranian components, which could be executed in 2023. The projected cost of each Shahed-136 under this scenario would drop to about $48,800 each, with an all-in 'transfer' price of $165,500 per unit. This gap is likely due to the mortgaged payments for linear production, additional costs, and investments in the enterprise. In other words, this would be the all-in cost of the program, including infrastructure and licenses, amortized across the production run. The more drones built, the lower this number would be as fixed costs are further offset.
121. Andrey Zlobin, "VTB Zapustil Servis Denezhnykh Perevodov v Iran [VTB Launched a Money Transfer Service to Iran]," Forbes.ru, 19 December 2022; Ekaterina Khabidulina, "Iran Soobshchil ob Otkrytii Ofisa VTB v Strane [Iran Announced the Opening of a VTB Office in the Country]," Forbes.ru, 17 May 2023, https://www.forbes.ru/finansy/489474-iran-soobsil-ob-otkrytii-ofisa-vtb-v-strane.
122. Interview with Iran-based political scientist (online), 2023.

9. RESISTANCE BY NECESSITY

1. "Deklaratsiya Rossiyskoy Federatsii i Islamskoy Respubliki Iran o Putyakh i Sredstvakh Protivodeystviya, Smyagcheniya i Kompensirovaniya Negativnykh Posledstviy Odnostoronnikh Prinuditel'nykh Mer [Declaration of the Russian Federation and the Islamic Republic of Iran on Ways and Means to Counter, Mitigate, and Compensate for the Negative Consequences of Unilateral Coercive Measures]," 5 December 2023, https://mid.ru/en/foreign_policy/news/1919257/?lang=ru.
2. Maximilian Hess, *Economic War: Ukraine and the Global Conflict between Russia and the West* (London: Hurst, 2023).
3. These restrictions come in two forms: EU bans on importing Russian crude oil and the imposition of a G7 oil price limit. Sanctions and embargos have prevented Russia from exporting oil at prices exceeding $60 USD per barrel, particularly when Western companies are involved.
4. Vladimir Yuratev, "Iran v Situatsii Transformatsii Sanktsionnogo Rezhima [Iran in the Situation of Sanction Regime Transformations]," *Kontury Global'nykh Transformatsiy: Politika, Ekonomika, Pravo* 10, no. 2 (2017); A.I. Salitskii, Xin Zhao, and V.I. Yurtaev,

"Sanktsii i Zameshchenie Importa na Primere Opyta Irana i Kitaya [Sanctions and Import Substitution as Exemplified by the Experience of Iran and China]," *Vestnik Rossiyskoy Akademii Nauk* 87, no. 3 (1 March 2017): 263-72.

5. Seyyed Ali Khamenei, "Beyanat Dar Didar Jama'i Az Karafarinan Sarasar Keshvar [Statements in a Meeting with a Group of Entrepreneurs from across the Country]," Khamenei.ir, 25 August 2010, https://farsi.khamenei.ir/speech-content?id=10077.
6. Vladimir Putin, "Meeting of the Valdai International Discussion Club," President of Russia, 24 October 2014, http://en.kremlin.ru/events/president/transcripts/46860.
7. Stanislav Olegovich Lazovskii, "Ekonomicheskaya Situatsiya v Irane v Usloviyakh Amerikanskikh Sanktsii [The Economic Situation in Iran under U.S. Sanctions]," *Analiz i Prognoz: Zhurnal Imemo Ran*, no. 1 (2020), https://doi.org/10.20542/afij-2020-1-81-93.
8. Anastasia B. Likhacheva, "Unilateral Sanctions in a Multipolar World: Challenges and Opportunities for Russia's Strategy," *Russia in Global Affairs* 17, no. 3 (30 September 2019): 109-31.
9. "Tablūr-i iqtiṣād-i muqāvamatī dar Rūsīyah dar muvājihah bā taḥrīmhā-yi Gharb[The Formation of a Resilient Economy in Russia in the Face of Western Sanctions]," Fars News, 21 March 2022.
10. "U Tegerana Bogatyi Opyt Protivodeistviya Sanktsiyam, on Predlozhil Rf Mery po Preodoleniyu Posledstvii Sanktsii Ssha—Zamglavy Tsentrobanka Irana [Tehran Has Rich Experience in Sanctions Resistance, Suggested Measures to Overcome U.S. Sanctions Consequences to Russia—Deputy Head of the Central Bank of Iran]," RIA Novosti, 1 April 2022, Integrum Digital Archive.
11. Interview with a Russia-based expert on Russian economics (online), 2023.
12. Interview with a Russia-based expert on Iran-Russia relations (online), 2023.
13. In May 2022, the former Russian ambassador to Iran argued that international sanctions imposed on Moscow after its invasion of Ukraine presented an opportunity for closer economic ties with Iran; "Rossiya i Iran Ob'edinilis' dlya Preodoleniya Bespretsedentnykh Sanktsii [Russia and Iran Joined Forces to Overcome Unprecedented Sanctions]," Pravda.ru, 16 May 2022.
14. Muḥammad Ḥasan Ma'ādī Rūdsarī and Muḥsin Ṣamadī, "Barrasī-i furṣat'hā va chālish'hā-yi ṣādirāt-i kishāvarzī va mavādd-i ghaẕāyī bih Rūsīyah [Examining the Opportunities and Challenges of Exporting Agricultural and Food Products to Russia]," Majlis-i Shūrá-yi Islāmī Markaz-i Pazhūhish'hā, 2016.
15. "Rabochiy Vizit Aleksandra Novaka v Islamskuyu Respubliku Iran 25 Maya 2022 [Working Visit of Alexander Novak to the Islamic Republic of Iran, 25 May 2022]," Pravitel'stvo Rossii, 25 May 2022, http://government.ru/news/45510.
16. Marianna Belen'kaya, "Vrag Ne Proymet [The Enemy Will Not Get Through]," *Kommersant*, 24 June 2022, Integrum Digital Archive.
17. "Sotrudnichestvo Irana i Rossii posle Ukrainskikh Sobytii i Vvedeniya Sanktsii Stalo Rasshiryat'sya [Cooperation between Iran and Russia Has Been Expanding after the Ukrainian Events and the Introduction of Sanctions]," RIA Novosti, 13 October 2022.
18. "Iz Irana v Astrakhan': Kak Sanktsii Perekroili Marshruty Importa [From Iran to Astrakhan: How Sanctions Have Redrawn Import Routes]," *RBK*, https://pro.rbc.ru/demo/64f09c0a9a79479f4015c854.
19. "Tovarooborot Rossii i Irana v 2023 Godu Snizilsya na 17,3%, do $4 mlrd [Trade

Turnover between Russia and Iran in 2023 Decreased by 17.3 percent, to $4 Billion]," Interfax, 28 February 2024, https://www.interfax.ru/russia/948210.

20. "How China, Russia and Iran Are Forging Closer Ties," *The Economist*, 18 March 2024, https://www.economist.com/finance-and-economics/2024/03/18/how-china-russia-and-iran-are-forging-closer-ties.
21. Russian exports are represented by food products and agricultural raw materials, cars, equipment and vehicles, wood and pulp and paper products, chemical industry products, metals and products made from them, etc. The import structure includes food products and agricultural raw materials, chemical industry products, pharmaceutical products, metals and products made from them, textiles and footwear, machines, equipment, and vehicles. "Statistika Vneshney Torgovli Rossii [Russian Foreign Trade Statistics]," Vneshnyaya Torgovlya Rossii, 2021, https://russian-trade.com/statistics/by-country/iran/import/2021.
22. Iman Samadi, "Tijārat-i Īrān va Rūsīyah Az Mavāni' Tā Furṣat'hā [Iran-Russia Trade: From Barriers to Opportunities]," Daftar-i Muṭāla'āt-i Dīplumāsī-i Iqtiṣādī-i, 30 November 2019, https://bit.ly/2NZdwng.
23. Mohammad Sajjad Najafi, Mohammad Qasemi, and Shima Haji, "Asār va tab'āt-i jang-i Rūsiyah va Ūkrāyn: Forsathā va tahdīdhā [The Effects and Consequences of the Russia-Ukraine War: Opportunities and Threats]," *Markaz-i Pazhūhishhā-yi Atāq-i Īrān*, 2022.
24. Nikolay Kozhanov, "Partnery po Sanktsiyam: Chego Khochet Moskva ot Novogo Prezidenta Irana [Sanctions Partners: What Moscow Wants from the New Iranian President]," Forbes.ru, 26 January 2022, https://www.forbes.ru/society/453617-partnery-po-sankciam-cego-hocet-moskva-ot-novogo-prezidenta-irana.
25. "Zasedanie Diskussionnogo Kluba 'Valdai' [Meeting of Discussion Club 'Valdai']," Press-Sluzhba Prezidenta RF, 5 October 2023, http://kremlin.ru/events/president/news/72444. Putin has frequently tied self-sufficiency with sovereignty, for example in May 2023 he stated that "self-sufficiency is an absolutely necessary condition for independence and sovereignty, this self-sufficiency must be in everything: in politics and, above all, in this case, in national politics, in the economy, in the field of defense security." "Putin Nazval Samodostatochnost' Neobkhodimym Usloviem dlya Suvereniteta [Putin Called Self-Sufficiency a Necessary Condition for Sovereignty]," RIA Novosti, 19 May 2023, https://ria.ru/20230519/samodostatochnost-1872960676.html.
26. "Mery Pravitel'stva po Povysheniyu Ustoichivosti Ekonomiki i Podderzhke Grazhdan v Usloviyakh Sanktsii [Government Measures to Increase Economic Stability and Support Citizens under Sanctions]," Pravitel'stvo Rossiiskoi Federatsii, 29 March 2022, http://government.ru/sanctions_measures/measure/110.
27. Hess, *Economic War*.
28. "Manturov Otsenil Ob'em Parallel'nogo Importa s Momenta Zapuska v $6,5 mlrd [Manturov Estimated the Volume of Parallel Imports since the Launch at $6.5 billion]," Interfax.ru, 15 August 2022, https://www.interfax.ru/business/856615; "Minpromtorg RF Podgotovil Perechen' Tovarov dlya Parallel'nogo Importa [The Ministry of Industry and Trade of the Russian Federation Has Prepared a List of Goods for Parallel Import]," Interfax, 22 April 2022, https://www.interfax.ru/business/837498.
29. "Tegeran-2022 [Tehran-2022]," *Trud: Moskva*, 19 August 2022, Integrum Digital Archive.

30. Geranmayeh and Grajewski, "Alone Together."
31. "Sih gulūgāh-i tijārat-i Īrān-Rūsīyah [Three Gateways of Iran-Russia Trade]," *Donyā-ye Eqteṣād*, 19 October 2023.
32. "Iran Ne Ustupit Zapugivaniyu so Storony SShA Prezident [Iran Will Not Yield to U.S. Intimidation, Says President]," TASS, 16 September 2022, Integrum Digital Archive.
33. Alona Mazurenko, "Russia Buys Sanctioned Parts for Aircraft through Friendly Countries: The UAE, China and Türkiye at the Top," *Pravda*, 12 September 2023, https://www.pravda.com.ua/eng/news/2023/09/12/7419552.
34. "Rossiya Prodolzhit Programmu 'Neft' v Obmen na Tovary' s Iranom, Zayavil Novak [Novak Said That Russia Will Continue the Oil-for-Goods Program with Iran]," RIA Novosti, 3 October 2018, https://ria.ru/20181003/1529923791.html.
35. "Iranskaya Neftyanaya Kompaniya i 'Gazprom' Podpisali Memorandum o Sotrudnichestve [Iranian Oil Company and Gazprom Signed a Memorandum of Cooperation],"TASS, 19 June 2022, https://tass.ru/ekonomika/15251947.
36. "Rūsīyah az Pārs Jonūbī chi mīkhāhad? [What Does Russia Want from South Pars?]," *Donya-ye Eqtesad*, 9 August 2022, https://donya-e-eqtesad.com/fa/tiny/news-3888706.
37. The largest joint investment project between Russia and Iran is still the construction of Iran's Bushehr Nuclear Power Plant. In June 2021, the implementation of another project to create a thermal power plant in Sirik, in the province of Hormozgan in southern Iran, began with Russian investment in the form of a state loan. As a result of the agreement, Russia became the largest foreign investor in Iran in 2022, contributing nearly two-thirds of the total foreign direct investment of $4.2 billion USD—an increase from the $1.45 billion USD Iran received in 2021.
38. "Economy Takes Center Stage in Budding Iran-Russia Relationship," PressTV, 4 April 2023, https://www.presstv.ir/Detail/2023/04/04/700948/Iran-Russia-strategic-partnership-economy.
39. "Rūs'hā zīr-i qarārdād'hā-yi naftī-i khvud bā Īrān zadand/Ānhā raftand va pusht-i sar'hā-yishān rā ham nigāh nakardand [The Russians Canceled Their Oil Contracts with Iran/ They Left and Didn't Look Back]," *Khabar*, 1 January 2019, khabaronline.ir/xdnp9.
40. "Pārs-i Janūbī mu'aṭṭal-i Rūsīyah [South Pars Is Subject to Russia's Suspension]," *Sharq*, 9 July 2023, https://www.sharghdaily.com/fa/tiny/news-887204.
41. "Rūznāmah-'i Jumhūrī-i Islāmī: Dawlat-i Ra'īsī faqaṭ dawlat-i jāvābīyah ast/ Dawlat bih jā-yi taqābul, bih ta'āmul rūy āvard [The Islamic Republic Newspaper: Raisi's Government Is Merely a Retaliatory One/The Government Has Chosen Cooperation over Confrontation]," Entekhab, 21 February 2024, https://www.entekhab.ir/003DCd.
42. Saeed Azimi, "Iran's Supreme Leader Blames His 'Favorite' President for Economic Woes," Stimson Center, 21 March 2024, https://www.stimson.org/2024/irans-supreme-leader-blames-his-favorite-president-for-economic-woes.
43. Umud Shokri and Brett Sudetic, "Iranian Sanctions Evasion and the Gulf's Complex Oil Trade," Middle East Institute, 11 May 2021, https://www.mei.edu/publications/iranian-sanctions-evasion-and-gulfs-complex-oil-trade.
44. Russia and Iran have a shared experience of using trade vehicles to evade sanctions. When international sanctions tightened on Iran, major Russian energy companies

like Lukoil, Rosneft, and Gazprom distanced themselves from direct involvement in Iranian projects to avoid the punitive repercussions of these sanctions. However, Zarubezhneft, a state-owned Russian oil company, found a workaround by transferring its contract with Iran to Promsyrioimport. The move was not entirely unexpected, as Promsyrioimport had already established itself as an instrument for sanctions evasion, especially under the "oil-for-goods" arrangement between Moscow and Tehran. Under this barter arrangement deal, Iran would export around 500,000 tons of oil to Russia, with half of the payment made in cash and the other half in goods and services. "Zarubezhneft' Ushla iz Irana v Preddverii Sanktsii [Zarubezhneft Left Iran ahead of Sanctions]," *Vedomosti*, 31 October 2018, https://www.vedomosti.ru/business/news/2018/10/31/785262-iz-v.

45. Iran has used a shadow banking network to serve as a conduit to access the international financial system and continue its trade activities with foreign customers, despite the sanctions in place. Iranian currency exchange houses create front companies abroad to enable trade on behalf of their Iranian clients and help them evade U.S. sanctions. See "Treasury Targets Sanctions Evasion Network Moving Billions for Iranian Regime," U.S. Department of the Treasury, 28 March 2023, https://home.treasury.gov/news/press-releases/jy1330.
46. "Iranian Nationals Charged with Conspiring to Evade U.S. Sanctions on Iran by Disguising $300 Million in Transactions over Two Decades," United States Department of Justice, 19 March 2021.
47. For example, in 2019, the Treasury Department took action against twenty-five individuals and entities, including a network of companies based in Iran, the UAE, and Turkey, for transferring over a billion dollars and euros to the IRGC and MODAFL as well as procuring millions of dollars of vehicles for MODAFL.
48. "With over 300 Sanctions, U.S. Targets Russia's Circumvention and Evasion, Military-Industrial Supply Chains, and Future Energy Revenues," U.S. Department of the Treasury, 19 May 2023, https://home.treasury.gov/news/press-releases/jy1494.
49. "Treasury Targets Sanctions Evasion Networks and Russian Technology Companies Enabling Putin's War," U.S. Department of the Treasury, 23 October 2023, https://home.treasury.gov/news/press-releases/jy0692.
50. See, for example, the case involving Turkish businessman Sitki Ayan and his ASB Group of Companies and their allegedly years-long engagement in facilitating Iran's sanctioned oil trade. ASB Group, registered in Gibraltar, was accused of leasing shipping tankers through its subsidiaries, effectively supporting the clandestine transportation of Iranian oil to various destinations, including China. Payments for these transactions were skillfully routed through a maze of shell companies across different jurisdictions in Russia, India, and the UAE, masking the true origin and destination of the funds and helping to sustain Iran's oil exports amid strict international sanctions. Tom Keatinge, "Developing Bad Habits: What Russia Might Learn from Iran's Sanctions Evasion," RUSI Occasional Paper, June 2023, https://static.rusi.org/developing-bad-habits-what-russia-might-learn-from-irans-sanctions-evasion.pdf.
51. "Russia and Sanctions Evasion," *Strategic Comments* 28, no. 4 (21 April 2022): vii-ix, https://doi.org/10.1080/13567888.2022.2107283.
52. "Chālish-i naft-i Rūsī [The Challenge of Russian Oil]," ISNA, 5 November 2022.
53. In some instances, the discounted oil sales are part of barter arrangements where Iran

receives goods, investments, or services in exchange for its oil, which helps bypass financial restrictions imposed by sanctions.

54. Armen Azizian, "Iran's Crude/Condensate Exports Reach Record-High under Sanctions—Vortexa," VORTEXA, 20 June 2023, https://www.vortexa.com/insights/crude/irans-crude-condensate-exports-reach-record-high-under-sanctions.
55. "Siyāsat'hā-yi iqtiṣādī-i Rūsīyah dar muqābalah bā taḥrīm va dars'hā-yī barā-yi Īrān [Russia's Economic Policies in Dealing with Sanctions and Lessons for Iran],"Tehran: *Majlis-i Shūrá-yi Islāmī Markaz-i Pazhūhish'hā*, November 2023.
56. Iran's reliance on Russian wheat has grown significantly, particularly after a devastating drought in 2021 that severely impacted Iran's domestic grain production. The drought forced Iran to increase its wheat imports, making Russia a major supplier. After local grain production began to recover in 2022, Iran's imports from Russia fell by 55 percent. However, in 2023, with the recovery of Iranian agriculture from drought, Iran's purchases of wheat declined—affecting the overall bilateral trade.
57. In October 2023, Russia and Iran signed an MoU on grain, but it has yet to spark a substantial change in Iranian imports. Moreover, trade between Russia and Iran, especially in wheat and grains, faces challenges related to payment and financial transactions due to sanctions. This has led to delays in discharging cargo at Iranian ports, with vessels carrying Russian wheat stranded due to documentation issues and hard currency payment delays. "Iran i Rossiya Podpisali Memorandum o Vzaimoponimanii po Dolgosrochnym Zakupkam Zerna [Iran and Russia Signed a Memorandum of Understanding on Long-Term Grain Purchases]," *Segodnya*, 12 February 2024, Integrum Digital Archive.
58. In July 2022, Russia signed the Black Sea Grain Initiative—an agreement facilitated by the United Nations and Turkey—aimed at allowing grain exports from Ukrainian ports amid the ongoing conflict. One year later, Russia withdrew from the agreement due to unmet conditions regarding its own agricultural exports.
59. "Iran Predlozhil Svoi Transportnye Koridory dlya Eksporta Rossiyskogo Zerna [Iran Offered Its Transport Corridors for the Export of Russian Grain]," RIA Novosti, 12 October 2023, https://ria.ru/20231012/zerno-1902173282.html.
60. "Aksenov Priznal, Chto Rossiya Prodaet Ukrainskoe Zerno, Zavezennoe v Krym [Aksenov Admitted That Russia Is Selling Ukrainian Grain Brought to Crimea]," Krym.realii, 15 June 2022, https://ru.krymr.com/a/news-aksenov-ukrainskoye-zerno/31899547.html.
61. "Ravand-i ṣādirāt-i ghallāt-i Rūsīyah dar ḥawzah-i Daryā-yi Siyāh [The Trend of Russia's Grain Exports in the Black Sea Region]," Muʻāvanat-i Dīplumāsī-i Iqtiṣādī Vizārat-i Umūr-i Khārijah-'i Jumhūrī-i Islāmī-i Īrān, 20 September 2023, https://economic.mfa.ir/portal/NewsView/729379.
62. "Russia's Ghost Ships and the Evolution of a Grain Smuggling Operation," Bellingcat, 21 August 2023, https://www.bellingcat.com/news/2023/08/21/russias-ghost-ships-and-the-evolution-of-a-grain-smuggling-operation.
63. "Sih gulūgāh-i tijārat-i Īrān-Rūsīyah [Three Gateways of Iran-Russia Trade]," *Donyā-ye Eqteṣād*, 19 October 2023.
64. Hamid Daraj, "Ta's̲īr-i Ittiḥādīyah-i Iqtiṣādī-i Ūrāsiyā Bar Mawqiʻīyat-i Zhi'ūikūnūmīk-i Jumhūrī-i Islāmī-i Īrān [The Impact of the Eurasian Economic Union on the Geoeconomic Position of the Islamic Republic of Iran]," *Faslnāmah-i Mutāla'āt-i Āsiyā-yi Markazī va Qafqāz* 28, no. 118 (23 August 2022): 37-60.
65. Fyodor Basov, "Antirossiyskie Sanktsii kak Test dlya Obshchey Vneshney Politiki

Evrosoyuza [Anti-Russian Sanctions as a Test for the Common Foreign Policy of the European Union]," *Mirovaya Ekonomika i Mezhdunarodnye Otnosheniya* 62, no. 10 (15 November 2018): 55-63.

66. Iman Samadi, "Tijārat-i Īrān va Rūsīyah Az Mavāniʻ Tā Furṣat'hā [Iran-Russia Trade: From Barriers to Opportunities]," Daftar-i Muṭālaʻāt-i Dīplumāsī-i Iqtiṣādī-i, 30 November 2019, https://bit.ly/2NZdwng.
67. "Chem Iran Mozhet Byt' Interesen Rossiiskomu Finansovomu Sektoru [Why Iran Might Be of Interest for the Russian Financial Sector]," *RBK*, 23 May 2023.
68. A Majlis Research Council report argued that trilateral cooperation between Russia, China, and Iran without the use of dollars and the SWIFT system limits U.S. control in international payments and oil trade, while establishing an alternative financial system between Russia, China, and its trade partners could help reduce the risks related to the sanctions that the U.S. imposed on Iran. By doing so, Iran can evade sanctions by selling its oil and perform transactions through financial institutions, futures markets, and clearing-houses through the use of Russian and Chinese payment systems. Amir Abbasi Khoshkar, "Imkān'sanjī va barāvard-i ẓarfīyat-i kharīd-i taslīḥāt-i niẓāmī az Rūsīyah va Chīn tavassut-i Īrānn [Feasibility Study and Estimation of Military Equipment Purchase Capacity from Russia and China by Iran]," *Pazhūhishkadah-i Taḥqīqāt-i Rāhburdī*, 25 August 2020, http://csr.ir/fa/news/1046.
69 Russia's SPFS was launched in 2014 primarily due to threats from Western countries about cutting off Russia's access to SWIFT as part of the sanctions imposed due to the annexation of Crimea. Elena Telegina and Gulnar Khalova, "Sanktsii i Torgovye Voiny kak Indikatory Transformatsii Mirovogo Khozyaistva: Vozmozhnosti dlya Rossii [Sanctions and Trade Wars as Indicators of the Transformation of the World Economy: Opportunities for Russia]," *Mirovaya Ekonomika i Mezhdunarodnye Otnosheniya* 63, no. 2 (26 March 2019): 13-20, https://doi.org/10.20542/0131-2227-2019-63-2-13-20.
70. "Rostekh Predstavil Blokcheyn-Platformu, Sposobnuyu Zamenit' SWIFT [Rostec Presented a Blockchain Platform That Can Replace SWIFT]," Rostec, 2 June 2022, https://rostec.ru/news/rostekh-predstavil-blokcheyn-platformu-sposobnuyu-zamenit-swift-.
71. Abdulnaser Hemmati, "Dolārīz shodan yā dolārzadāyī? [Dollarization or Dedollarization?]," *Donyā-ye Eqteṣād,* 30 May 2023.
72. "Iranskie Banki Vernulis' v Sistemu SWIFT [Iranian Banks Returned to the SWIFT System]," *RBK*, 17 January 2016, Integrum Digital Archive.
73. In September 2019, Russian presidential aide Yuriy Ushakov noted that Moscow and Tehran "are taking measures to expand direct settlements, use national currencies, and establish an interaction between the Russian financial messaging system and Iran's SEPAM, as an alternative to making payments through SWIFT." Andrei Petrov, "Rossiya i Iran Dadut Torgovyi Otvet na Sanktsii SShA [Russia and Iran Will Provide a Trade Response to U.S. Sanctions]," Rossiiskii Institut Strategicheskikh Issledovanii, 26 November 2018, Integrum Digital Archive; "Rossiya i Iran Naladyat Vzaimodeistvie Svoikh Sistem kak Al'ternativu SWIFT [Russia and Iran Facilitate Cooperation with Their Systems as an Alternative to SWIFT]," RIA Novosti, 13 September 2019, https://ria.ru/20190913/1558669383.html
74. Maria Shagina, "How Disastrous Would Disconnection from SWIFT Be for Russia?," Carnegie Endowment for International Peace, 28 May 2021, https://carnegiemoscow.org/commentary/84634.
75. "Rial-Ruble share exceeds 60% in Iran-Russia trade," Tehran Times, 24 January 2023,

https://www.tehrantimes.com/news/481213/Rial-Ruble-share-exceeds-60-in-Iran-Russia-trade.

76. "National Currencies Drive 90% of Iran-Russia Trade Transactions: Russian Senator," IRNA English, 4 October 2023, https://en.irna.ir/news/85247139/National-currencies-drive-90-of-Iran-Russia-trade-transactions. According to the Kremlin, by the end of 2024 national currencies made up 96% of Iran-Russia financial transactions, up from about 60% a year prior.
77. For example, during 2023 the ruble's value fluctuated dramatically, at one point breaching 100 rubles per U.S. dollar, while the Iranian rial's free-market rate spiraled to over 500,000 IRR per dollar amid inflation. Such volatility means that between the contract date and payment date, the ruble-rial rate can shift substantially, potentially penalizing one side.
78. "Rossiya i Iran Mogut Ob'edinit' Platezhnye Sistemy [Russia and Iran May Unite Payment Systems]," RIA Deita (Vladivostok), 25 March 2022; "Eksperty Predlagayut Sozdat' Novuyu Platezhnuyu Edinitsu v Rossii [Experts Propose Creating a New Payment Unit in Russia]," *Novye Izvestiya*, 30 March 2022, Integrum Digital Archive; "Rossiyu i Iran Sblizyat Natsional'nye Platezhnye Sistemy [Russia and Iran Will Merge National Payment Systems]," *Parlamentskaya Gazeta*, no. 3 (27 January 2023).
79. Interview with a Russia-based economic expert (online), 2023.
80. Nina Mamedova, "Mezhdunarodnyi Transportnyi Koridor 'Sever-Yug' kak Sovremennyi Analog Velikogo Volzhskogo Puti [International North-South Transport Corridor as a Modern Analogue of the Great Volga Route]," *Vostochnaya Analitika*, no. 3 (2018): 149-56; "Pashinyan: Sever-Yug Blagodarya Razblokirovke Kommunikatsii Stanovitsya Proektom Sever-Yug-Vostok-Zapad [Pashinyan: North-South Becomes a Project of North-South-East-West Thanks to the Unblocking of Communications]," Vzglyad.az, 17 February 2022; "Mezhdunarodnyi Transportnyi Koridor 'Sever-Yug' Mozhet Stat' Real'nym Konkurentom Suetskomu Kanalu [International Transport Corridor 'North-South' Could Become a Real Competitor to the Suez Canal]," Agentstvo Biznes Novostei (St. Petersburg), 3 November 2022.
81. "Sanktsii Zapada Pobuzhdayut Moskvu Diversifitsirovat' Marshruty Postavok Uglevodorodnykh Resursov [Sanctions from the West Encourage Moscow to Diversify Hydrocarbon Supply Routes]," VPS-Monitoring "Biznes-Neft'," 8 November 2022.
82. Vali Kalleji, "Sotrudnichestvo Irana i Rossii v Stroitel'stve Marshruta Resht-Astara [Cooperation between Iran and Russia in the Construction of the Rasht-Astara Route]," Valdai, 30 May 2023.
83. Interview with a Russia-based expert on Russian foreign economic investment (online), 2023.
84. "Poslanie Prezidenta Federal'nomu Sobraniyu [Address of the President to the Federal Assembly]," Prezident Rossii, 21 February 2023, http://www.kremlin.ru/events/president/transcripts/messages/70565/videos. Similarly, in 2024 he stated that "the rhythmic operation of the North-South transport corridor will connect Russia with the countries of the Middle East and Asia. It will be based not only on road routes, but also on seamless rail transport all the way from our ports on the Baltic and Barents Sea to the coast of the Persian Gulf and the Indian Ocean. We will also increase the capacity of railways in the southern direction, which will make it possible to actively use the port capacities of the Azov and Black Seas." "Poslanie Prezidenta Federal'nomu Sobraniyu [Address of the President to the Federal Assembly]," Gosudarstvennaya Duma, 29 February 2024, http://duma.gov.ru/news/58905.

85. "Mezhdunarodnyi Transportnyi Koridor 'Sever-Yug' Mozhet Stat' Real'nym Konkurentom Suetskomu Kanalu [International Transport Corridor 'North-South' Could Become a Real Competitor to the Suez Canal]."
86. Mohammad Sajjad Najafi, Mohammad Qasemi, and Shima Haji, "Asār va tab'āt-i jang-i Rūsiyah va Ūkrāyn: Forsathā va tahdīdhā [The Effects and Consequences of the Russia-Ukraine War: Opportunities and Threats]," *Markaz-i Pazhuhesh-haye Atāq-i Īrān*, 2022.
87. Ramin Farhoudi Zarnaq, "Rūsīyah-i kūchak dar dastān-i Rūsīyah-i buzurg, furṣat'hā-yī barā-yi Īrān: Furṣat'hā-yi Īrān az jang-i Rūsīyah 'alayhi-i Ūkrāyn [Small Russia in the Hands of Great Russia, Opportunities for Iran: Iran's Opportunities from Russia's War against Ukraine]," Andīsh'kadah-'i Tirind, 2022.
88 Russia's Caspian Development Strategy relies on Iranian port infrastructure and overland trade routes to expand Russian exports into the Persian Gulf and South Asian markets. Pravitel'stvo Rossiiskoi Federatsii, "Strategiya Razvitiya Rossiiskikh Morskikh Portov v Kaspiiskom Basseine, Zheleznodorozhnykh i Avtomobil'nykh Podkhodov k Nim v Period do 2030 Goda [Strategy for the Development of Sea Ports in the Caspian Sea and Rail and Road Links to Them until 2030]."
89. "Golovnoe sudno v serii konteynerovozov dlya Kaspiya planiruyut zalozhit' v mae," TASS, 30 March 2023, https://tass.ru/ekonomika/17408433.
90. IRISL has been subjected to sanctions and is known for facilitating arms shipments for the IRGC.
91. Elena Melikhova "Igor' Babushkin Predlozhil Sozdat' Sudokhodnuyu Liniyu mezhdu Portami Astrakhanskoy Oblasti i Irana [Igor Babushkin Proposed Creating a Shipping Line between the Ports of the Astrakhan Region and Iran]," *Rossiyskaya Gazeta*, 19 July 2023, https://rg.ru/2023/07/19/reg-ufo/igor-babushkin-predlozhil-sozdat-sudohodnuiu-liniiu-mezhdu-portami-astrahanskoj-oblasti-i-irana.html; "Astrakhanskiy Gubernator Predlozhil Perevozit' cherez Porty Regiona Gruzy iz Afriki [The Astrakhan Governor Proposed Transporting Cargo from Africa through the Region's Ports]," TASS, 19 September 2023, https://tass.ru/ekonomika/18786643.
92. This was articulated in Russia's Caspian Strategy: Pravitel'stvo Rossiiskoi Federatsii, "Strategiya Razvitiya Rossiiskikh Morskikh Portov v Kaspiiskom Basseine, Zheleznodorozhnykh i Avtomobil'nykh Podkhodov k Nim v Period do 2030 Goda [Strategy for the Development of Russian Sea Ports in the Caspian Basin and Rail and Road Approaches to Them until 2030]," no. 1365-⊠ (2017).
93. "Rossiya i Iran Dogovorilis' o Stroitel'stve Zheleznoi Dorogi dlya Razvitiya Mezhdunarodnogo Transportnogo Koridora 'Sever-Yug' [Russia and Iran Agreed on the Construction of a Railway for the Development of the International Transport Corridor 'North-South']," Ofitsial'nyi Internet-Resurs Ministerstva Transporta Rossiiskoi Federatsii, 17 May 2023, http://government.ru/news/45510.
94. Interview with a Russia-based expert on Russia-Iran relations (online), 2023.
95. That same year, it emerged that Iran owed 500 million euros ($591.5 million USD) for the construction of the Bushehr Nuclear Power Plant. Iran's debts for Russian agricultural products are also rising by the month.
96 A *Kommersant* article suggests that private participants in the Russian transport market have developed a number of strategies for the development of the North-South Corridor through Iran. JSC Russian Railways proposes to simply complete the missing section of the Rasht-Astara railway. GC "Delo" wants to build a combined track across the whole of Iran. But some actors do not believe in the prospects of

the railway, given the developed road network in the country and the cheapness of fuel. Some companies are pinning their hopes on the trans-Caspian route, seeing the benefit of having a direct maritime border between the Russian Federation and Iran. Calculations by Indian exporters show that it is currently more profitable to transport by land—by road through Iran, and then by rail through Azerbaijan to Russia. Natalya Skorlygina, "Koleya v Bol'shuyu Igru: Chto Zabotit Partnerov Rossii po Koridoru Sever-Yug [A Rut in the Big Game: What Worries Russia's Partners along the North-South Corridor]," *Kommersant*, 9 June 2023, https://www.kommersant.ru/doc/6030407.

97. Evgeny Vinokurov et al., "International North-South Transport Corridor: Investments and Soft Infrastructure," Almaty and Moscow: Eurasian Development Bank, 2022, https://eabr.org/upload/iblock/687/EDB_2022_Report-2_INSTC_eng.pdf.
98. "Shoygu v Tegerane Pokazali Iranskie Raketnye Kompleksy i Bespilotniki [Shoigu Was Shown Iranian Missile Systems and Drones in Tehran]," *RBK*, 20 September 2023, https://www.rbc.ru/rbcfreenews/650ac5f99a7947419a7aedcc.
99. Hanna Notte and Jim Lamson, "Iran-Russia Defense Cooperation: Current Realities and Future Horizons," CNS Occasional Paper #61 (James Martin Center for Nonproliferation Studies, August 2024), https://nonproliferation.org/wp-content/uploads/2024/08/op61-RSI_Russia-Iran_Notte-Lamson_CNS-Occasional-Paper.pdf.
100. C. Todd Lopez, "Iran Gives Russia Short-Range Missiles, While U.S., Partners Expect to Keep Bolstering Ukrainian Air Defense," DOD News, 10 September 2024, https://www.defense.gov/News/News-Stories/Article/Article/3901774/iran-gives-russia-short-range-missiles-while-us-partners-expect-to-keep-bolster/.
101. Up until 2016, Russia had been adept at expanding and sustaining its share in the international arms market, all while reducing its reliance on sales to China. Yet, the implementation of CAATSA triggered a notable decline in the value of arms exported to nearly all customers, with the exception of India and China. David Brennan and Yevgeny Kuklychev, "Russia's Arms Export Industry Is Collapsing," *Newsweek*, 12 March 2023, https://www.newsweek.com/russia-arms-export-industry-collapsing-ukraine-1786912.
102. In 2018, Cairo signed a deal with Moscow for thirty Su-35 fighters—an agreement that would have made Egypt the first customer of the Su-35S in the Middle East. Threats from the United States of sanctions against Egypt should the Su-35S be integrated into its air force posed an obstacle to the fruition of this contract. Prompted by the potential U.S. sanctions, which also carried the stern warning of ceasing maintenance support for Egypt's extensive fleet comprising over 200 F-16 aircraft, dozens of AH-64 Apache helicopters, and hundreds of M-1 Abrams tanks, the Egyptian leadership ultimately withdrew from the deal. Shifting its gaze to alternative sources, Egypt negotiated a loan agreement with France, leading to the procurement of thirty Dassault fighter jets as a substitute for the Su-35 fighters from Russia.
103. Vladimir Sazhin, "SShA Pytayutsya Prodlit' Oruzheinoe Embargo protiv Irana [The U.S. Is Trying to Extend the Arms Embargo against Iran]," *Mezhdunarodnaya Zhizn'*, 20 May 2020.
104. Interview with a Russia-based military expert (online), 2020.
105. Ibid.
106. Sayyid Mahdī, "Līst-i kharīd va furūsh-i iḥtimālī-i taslīḥāt-i Īrān [List of Potential Arms Purchases and Sales by Iran]," *Fārhīkhtigān-i Ānlāyn*, 8 July 2020.

107. "Istrebiteli Su-35C Vmesto Egipta Mozhet Poluchit' Iran—Aviatsiya Rossii [Iran May Receive Su-35C Fighters Instead of Egypt—Russian Aviation]," Aviatsiya Rossii, 6 January 2022, https://aviation21.ru/istrebiteli-su-35c-vmesto-egipta-mozhet-poluchit-iran.
108. Interview with Russia-based military analyst (online), 2023; interview with Russia-based defense expert (online), 2023; interview with Russia-based defense expert (Moscow), 2019.
109. "Rūs hā bā 12 Sukho 100 bih āsmān-i Īrān bar mī girdand [Russians Are Returning to Iranian Skies with Twelve Sukhoi 100s," *Et'emad*, 27 July 2017, https://www.magiran.com/article/3599502.
110. Courtney Kube and Carol E. Lee, "Russia Is Providing 'Unprecedented' Military Support to Iran in Exchange for Drones, Officials Say," NBC News, 9 December 2022.
111. Amir Abbasi Khoshkar, "Imkān'sanjī va barāvard-i ẓarfīyat-i kharīd-i taslīḥāt-i niẓāmī az Rūsīyah va Chīn tavassut-i Īrān [Feasibility Study and Estimation of Military Equipment Purchase Capacity from Russia and China by Iran]," *Pazhūhishkadah-i Taḥqīqāt-i Rāhburdī*, August 25, 2020, http://csr.ir/fa/news/1046.
112. "Qarārdād-i kharīd-i jangandah'hā-yi Sū-35 nahā'ī shud + Fīlm [The Purchase Agreement for Su-35 Fighter Jets Has Been Finalized + Video]," IRIBnews.ir, 11 March 2023.
113. Iran's government soon provided more confirmation through official channels. In early 2023, Iran's mission to the United Nations quietly disclosed details of the deal. Mojtaba Babaei, Iran's representative at the UN, confirmed that Tehran had finalized a contract to buy Su-35s from Russia. According to Babaei, the fighter jets met Iran's technical requirements, and the purchase agreement was signed immediately after Iran's UN arms restrictions expired in October 2020. "Namāyandah-i Īrān dar Sāzmān-i Milal kharīd-i jangandah-yi Sūkhu-35 az Rūsīyah rā taʾyīd kard [Iran's UN Representative Confirms Purchase of Su-35 Fighter Jets from Russia]," ʿAṣr-i Īrān, 25 June 2023, https://www.asriran.com/003hSs.
114. "Sūkhu-35'hāyī kih qarār būd rāhī-i Īrān shavand, sar az al-Jazāyir darāvardand [The Su-35s Intended for Iran Ended Up in Algeria]," Gadget News, 13 April 2025, https://gadgetnews.net/978479/satellite-footage-confirms-su35-algerian-base/.
115. "Farmāndih-i Nīrū-yi Havāyī-i Artish: Bih Sūkhūhā-yi Jadīd Nīyāz Dārīm [Army Air Force Commander: We Need New Sukhois]," *Donya-ye Eqtesad,* 2 June 2023, https://donya-e-eqtesad.com/fa/tiny/news-3973021.
116. "Chirā Sūkhūhā-yi Rūsī bih Īrān narasīdand? [Why Didn't the Russian Sukhois Reach Iran?]," *Tabnak*, 20 July 2023.
117. "Sukhan'gū-yi Vizārat-i Difāʿ: Dar ṣūrat-i niyāz bih kharīd-i taslīḥāt bā riʿāyat-i tamām-i javānib-i iqdam mīshavad [Spokesperson of the Ministry of Defense: If There Is a Need to Buy Weapons, It Will Be Done by Observing All Aspects]," Tasnim, 22 July 2023. Likewise, Russia apparently rebuffed Iran's request for the S-400 during Iranian Foreign Minister Javad Zarif's visit to Moscow in May 2019, which was linked to Russia's reservations about inflaming the wider tensions in the Persian Gulf between Iran and the GCC.
118. "Ikhtīṣāṣī | Kharīd-i Jangandih-i 'Sūkhū-35' va Bālgard-i 'Mīl-28' Qaṭ'ī Shud [Exclusive | Purchase of 'Su-35' Fighter and 'Mi-28' Helicopter Confirmed]," Tasnim, 28 November 2023, https://tn.ai/2996425.

119. Interview with Russia-based defense expert (online), 2023.
120. Interview with a Russia-based military analyst (online), 2023.
121. Ibid.
122. Discussion with Iran-based defense expert (online), 2023.
123. "Bībīnīd | Rivāyatī az pāygāh-i zīrzamīnī-i jangandah'hā-yi Sūkhu-35-i Īrān [Watch: A Report from Iran's Underground Base for Su-35 Fighter Jets]," Khabar Online, 17 March 2025, khabaronline.ir/xnm9R.
124. "Īn Sūkhu-35'hā-yi tāzah kay bih Īrān mī'āyand? [When Will These New Su-35s Arrive in Iran?],"Tabnāk, 29 March 2025,https://www.tabnak.ir/005RIY.
125. "Sūkhu-35'hā-yi kih qarār būd rāhī-i Īrān shavand, sar az al-Jazāyir darāvardand [The Su-35s Intended for Iran Ended Up in Algeria]," Gadget News, 13 April 2025, https://gadgetnews.net/978479/satellite-footage-confirms-su35-algerian-base/.
126. While around half of the aircraft from the original Egypt deal was reportedly completed when Russia and Iran reached their agreement, there were likely challenges in the production process related to sanctions. The Su-35's advanced systems—including navigation, missile guidance, electronic warfare, and communications—allegedly utilize Western-manufactured components, particularly from American companies. International sanctions restricting access to these components have likely impaired Russia's ability to maintain production of Su-35s destined for Iran. Additionally, Russia's wartime needs in Ukraine have strained the Russian arms industry and the ability to produce high-end technologies for export. Kyrylo Ovsyaniy, "How Russia's Warplanes Get Their 'Brain Power' from the West, despite Sanctions," RadioFreeEurope/RadioLiberty (RFE/RL, May 11, 2024), https://www.rferl.org/a/ukraine-russia-warplanes-sukhoi-sanctions-west-investigation/32939831.html.
127. "Qaṣqāvī: Rūs-hā dar Taḥvīl-i Jangandih-hā-yi Sūkhū-35 Bad'ahdī Nakardih-and [Qaṣqāvī: Russians Have Not Broken Their Promise in Delivering Su-35 Fighters]," *Ākharin Khabar*, 3 February 2025, https://akharinkhabar.ir/politics/10389469.
128. "Majvaz-i Sākht-i Jangandih-i Rūsī bih Īrān Dādih Shud?! [License for Manufacturing Russian Fighter Given to Iran?!]," *Eghtesad*, 30 October 2024, https://www.eghtesadonline.com/008Se4; "Tawlīd-i Mushtarak-i Jangandih bā Rūsīyah; Āb yā Sarāb? [Joint Fighter Production with Russia; Water or Mirage?]," *Tasnīm*, 24 August 2015, https://tn.ai/839160.
129. Bart Hendrickx "Scrutinizing the Russian-Iranian Satellite Deal,"The Space Review, 21 June 2021, https://www.thespacereview.com/article/4199/1. NPK Barl led the project on the Russia's side, overseeing ground-based infrastructure integration and development. The VNIIEM Corporation, experienced in crafting meteorological and remote sensing satellites, designed and built it.
130. Joby Warrick, "Russia Is Preparing to Supply Iran with an Advanced Satellite System That Will Boost Tehran's Ability to Surveil Military Targets, Officials Say," *Washington Post*, 10 June 2021, https://www.washingtonpost.com/national-security/iran-russia-satellite/2021/06/10/d28978f0-c9ab-11eb-81b1-34796c7393af_story.html.
131. "Iran Zainteresovan v Sovmestnykh s Rossiey Proektakh v Kosmose, Zayavil Posol [Iran Is Interested in Joint Space Projects with Russia, Ambassador Said]," *Novosti Kosmonavtiki* (Novosti-Kosmonavtiki.ru), 8 February 2022, Integrum Digital Archive; "Posol Irana v Rossii Soobshchil o Postoyannykh Peregovorakh s Rossiey

po Sotrudnichestvu v Kosmose," Aviation Explorer (Aex.ru), 14 December 2022, Integrum Digital Archive; "Rossiya i Iran Provedut Peregovory po Sotrudnichestvu v Kosmose na Vystavke Iran Air Show 2022 [Russia and Iran Will Hold Talks on Cooperation in Space at the Iran Air Show 2022]," Novosti VPK (Vpk.name), 14 December 2022, Integrum Digital Archive.

132. Ruslan Suleymanov, "Iz Tiranii: K Zvezdam [From tyranny to the stars]," *Novaya Gazeta*, 10 January 2023, https://novayagazeta.eu/articles/2023/01/10/iz-tiranii-k-zvezdam.
133. https://www.roscosmos.ru/38608/
134. Aleksandra Ganga Marokhovskaya Marina, "Rossiya Vyvela na Orbitu Iranskii Sputnik 'Khaiyam' [Russia Launched the Iranian Khayyam Satellite into Orbit]," *Izvestiya*, 9 August 2022, Integrum Digital Archive.
135. "Iran's Pars 1 satellite enters space after Russian launch," *Reuters*, February 29, 2024, https://www.reuters.com/technology/space/irans-pars-1-satellite-enters-space-after-russian-launch-2024-02-29/.
136. Beatrice Farhat, "Russia launches two Iranian satellites into orbit as ties grow," *Al-Monitor*, 5 November 2024, https://www.al-monitor.com/originals/2024/11/russia-launches-two-iranian-satellites-orbit-ties-grow.
137. "Bebīnīd | Sardār Ḥājīzādah khaṭāb bah hamtā-yi Rūs; komak konīd farmāndehī-yi fażāyī tashkīl dehīm mā ham komak mī-konīm farmāndehī-yi pehpādī ījād konīd [Watch Sardar Hajizadeh Addressed to His Russian Counterpart; Help Us Create a Space Command, We Will Also Help You Create a Drone Command]," *Et'emad*, 13 November 2023, https://www.etemadonline.com/tiny/news-640616.
138 "Fireside Chat with Director William Burns: Aspen Security Forum 2023," United States Embassy Russia, 20 July 2023, https://ru.usembassy.gov/fireside-chat-with-director-william-burns-aspen-security-forum-2023.
139. Hanna Notte and Jim Lamson, "The Uncomfortable Reality of Russia and Iran's New Defense Relationship," *War on the Rocks*, 24 July 2024, https://warontherocks.com/2024/07/the-uncomfortable-reality-of-russia-and-irans-new-defense-relationship/.
140. Mohammad Amin Ahangari, "Dastāvardhā-Yi Fanāvarāneh, Iqtisādī va Siyāsī 'Khayyām' [Technological, Economic, and Political Achievements of 'Khayyam']," *Iran*, 10 August 2022, 2.
141. Christopher Whyte, "Why Russia's Cyber Arms Transfers Are Poor Threat Predictors," CSO Online, 27 April 2023, https://www.csoonline.com/article/575175/why-russias-cyber-arms-transfers-are-poor-threat-predictors.html.
142. Gary Miller, "You Move, They Follow: Uncovering Iran's Mobile Legal Intercept System," The Citizen Lab, 16 January 2023, https://citizenlab.ca/2023/01/uncovering-irans-mobile-legal-intercept-system.

10. THE WAR CAME FULL CIRCLE

1. "Juz'īyāt-i jalsah-'i Pūtīn bā ḥuẓūr-i safīr-i Īrān dar Rūsīyah [Details of Putin's meeting with Iran's Ambassador to Russia]," Mehr News, 19 May 2024 https://mehrnews.com/x34XTx/.
2. Nicole Grajewski, "The Iran-Russia Friendship Won't Wither Under Raisi's Successor," Carnegie Endowment for International Peace, 21 May 2024,

https://carnegieendowment.org/emissary/2024/05/raisi-death-iran-russia-relationship?lang=en.

3. "Ayatolle Seyedu Ali Khamenei, Verkhovnomu rukovoditelyu Islamskoy Respubliki Iran [To Ayatollah Seyyed Ali Khamenei, Supreme Leader of the Islamic Republic of Iran]," *Kremlin*, 20 May 2024, http://kremlin.ru/events/president/letters/74069 .
4. Andrew Hanna "Raisi: Role in 1988 Massacre," Iran Primer, 21 July 2021 https://iranprimer.usip.org/blog/2021/jul/21/raisi-role-1988-massacre.
5. Arezou Rezvani "In Iran, women's resistance defies state clampdown a year after Mahsa Amini's death," NPR, 15 September 2023, https://www.npr.org/2023/09/15/1199463066/iran-mahsa-amini-anniversary-women-rights-protests.
6. Masoud Pezeshkian, "My message to the new world," *Tehran Times,* 12 July 2024, https://www.tehrantimes.com/news/501077/My-message-to-the-new-world.
7. Samer al-Ahmed and Mohammed Hassan, "Syria is where the conflict between Wagner and the Russian government began," Middle East Institute, 14 July 2023, https://mei.edu/publications/syria-where-conflict-between-wagner-and-russian-government-began.
8. Mark Katz, "Iran-Syria Air Defense Pact Could Cause Russian-Iranian Friction," Atlantic Council, 30 July 2020, https://www.atlanticcouncil.org/blogs/menasource/iran-syria-air-defense-pact-could-cause-russian-iranian-friction.
9. Martin Fornusek, "Military intelligence: Iran, Hezbollah train Russian drone operators in Syria," *The Kyiv Independent*, 12 February 2024, https://kyivindependent.com/military-intelligence-iran-hezbollah-train-russian-drone-operators-in-syria/.
10. "Lavrentyev: u RF yest' dannyye, chto spetsial'nyye podrazdeleniya Ukrainy deystvuyut v nekotorykh stranakh [Lavrentyev: Russia has data that Ukrainian special units are operating in some countries]," TASS, 29 January 2024, https://tass.ru/politika/19841631. In November 2024, Alexander Lavrentiev, Russia's special representative for Syria, told TASS, "We do indeed have information that Ukrainian specialists from the Main Intelligence Directorate of Ukraine are on the territory of Idlib." "Moskva otkryta k kontaktam s Trampom po Sirii [Moscow open to contacts with Trump on Syria]," TASS, 29 November 2024, https://tass.ru/interviews/22388825.
11. Ari Shavit, "What Israel Has Lost: And How It Can Regain Its Strategic Edge," Foreign Affairs, May/June 2025, https://www.foreignaffairs.com/middle-east/october-seven-anniversary-israel-hamas-attacks-ari-shavit.
12. Raz Zimmt, "Iran's Support for Hamas and the Risk of Multi-Front Escalation," War on the Rocks, 18 October 2023, https://warontherocks.com/2023/10/irans-support-for-hamas-and-the-risk-of-multi-front-escalation/.
13. "Vystuplenie i otvety na voprosy SMI Ministra inostrannykh del Rossiyskoy Federatsii S.V. Lavrova na press-konferentsii po itogam vizita v KNDR, Phen'yan, 19 oktyabrya 2023 goda [Statement and Answers to Media Questions by Russian Foreign Minister Sergey Lavrov at the Press Conference Following His Visit to the DPRK, Pyongyang, October 19, 2023]," Ministry of Foreign Affairs of the Russian Federation, 19 October 2023, https://mid.ru/ru/foreign_policy/news/1910193/.
14. "Izrail' Soobshchil o Namerenii Peredat' Ukraine Sistemy Preduprezhdeniya o Raketnykh Udarakh [Israel Announced Its Intention to Transfer Missile Warning Systems to Ukraine]," TASS, 26 February 2024, https://tass.ru/mezhdunarodnaya-panorama/20089873.

15. Benoit Faucon, Michael R. Gordon, Warren P. Strobel, and Alan Cullison, "Exclusive | Putin's 'Merchant of Death' Is Back in the Arms Business. This Time Selling to the Houthis," *The Wall Street Journal*, October 7, 2024, https://www.wsj.com/world/russia/putins-merchant-of-death-is-back-in-the-arms-business-this-time-selling-to-the-houthis-10b7f521.
16. Hamidreza Azizi and Hanna Notte, "Russia's Dangerous New Friends," *Foreign Affairs*, 14 February 2024, https://www.foreignaffairs.com/russian-federation/russias-dangerous-new-friends.
17. "Nebenzya vyrazil nadezhdu, chto Sovbez OON vsled za GA smozhet potrebovat' prekrashcheniya ognya v sektore Gaza [Nebenzya expressed hope that the UN Security Council, following the General Assembly, will be able to demand a ceasefire in the Gaza Strip]," TASS, 13 December 2023, https://tass.ru/politika/19521087; "Nebenzya obvinil Izrail' v tsinichnom otnoshenii k poteryam sredi grazhdanskogo naseleniya Livana [Nebenzya accused Israel of a cynical attitude towards civilian casualties in Lebanon]," TASS, 10 October 2024, https://tass.ru/politika/22096529.
18. Beatrice Farhat, "Russia sets up observation points in Syria near Golan Heights," Al-Monitor, 19 February 2024, https://www.al-monitor.com/originals/2024/02/russia-sets-up-observation-points-syria-near-golan-heights; "Russia deploys more forces in Syria's Golan Heights in message to Israel," The Jerusalem Post, 3 April 2024, https://www.jpost.com/middle-east/russia-deploys-more-forces-in-syrias-golan-heights-in-message-to-israel-732589; Nasr al-Yousef, "Why Russia deployed military posts on borders of occupied Golan Heights," Enab Baladi, November 2023, https://english.enabbaladi.net/archives/2023/11/why-russia-deployed-military-posts-on-borders-of-occupied-golan-heights; "Russia announces the establishment of two new observation points on the Syrian-Israeli border," ARK News, 6 January 2024, https://www.arknews.net/en/298412.
19. "Ḥamlah-yi shadīd-i mūshakī-yi Sipāh bih Arbīl-i ʿIrāq va Sūrīyah [Severe missile attack by the IRGC on Erbil, Iraq, and Syria]," Tabnak, 16 January 2024, https://www.tabnak.ir/fa/news/1216039.
20. "Guzārish-i ʿAmalīyātī-yi Sardār Ḥājīzādah az Mūshakbārān-i Turrūrīst'hā [Operational Report of Commander Hajizadeh on the Missile Attack Against Terrorists]," Fars News, 14 April 2024, https://farsnews.ir/politics/1705394271000861857.
21. "Ḥamlah-'i isrā'īl bih kunsulgarī-'i Īrān dar Dimashq [Israeli Airstrike on the Iranian Consulate in Damascus]," Tabnak, 1 April 2024, https://www.tabnak.ir/fa/news/1229811.
22. "ʿAks-i parbāzdīd az Sardār Ḥājīzādah dar namāz-i ʿĪd-i Fiṭr [Widely viewed photo of Commander Hajizadeh at Eid al-Fitr prayer]," Javan Online, 11 April 2024, https://www.javanonline.ir/fa/news/1223611.
23. "Sabr-i istirātizhīk dīgar tawjīhī nadārad; rūykardimān bāzdārandagī-yi fa'āl bāshad [Strategic patience is no longer justified; our approach should be active deterrence]," Mehr News, 10 April 2021, https://www.mehrnews.com/news/5191745/.
24. "Payām-i qadardānā-yi farmāndār-i Taftān az Sipāh-i Pāsdārān barā-yi pīrūzī dar 'Amaliyyāt-i Va'dah-yi Ṣādiq [Message of appreciation from the governor of Taftan to the Islamic Revolutionary Guard Corps for victory in Operation 'True Promise']," Defa Press, 14 April 2024, https://defapress.ir/fa/news/661453/.
25. Nicole Bayet Grajewski, "Iran and Israel's Dangerous Gambit," Carnegie Endowment for International Peace, 18 April 2024, https://carnegieendowment.org/emissary/2024/04/iran-and-israels-dangerous-gambit?lang=en.

26. Joedy McCreary, "Putin Didn't Pledge Russian Support for Iran If US Retaliates for Attack on Israel | Fact Check," USA Today, 22 April 2024, 2024), https://www.usatoday.com/story/news/factcheck/2024/04/22/putin-russia-support-iran-against-us-fact-check/73387608007/.
27. "Telephone Conversation with President of Iran Ebrahim Raisi," *Kremlin*, 16 April 2024, http://en.kremlin.ru/events/president/news/73869.
28. "Russian President Hails Iran's Response to Zionist Aggression," IRNA, 16 April, https://en.irna.ir/news/85447092/Russian-president-hails-Iran-s-response-to-Zionist-aggression.
29. "Zayavlenie MID Rossii v svyazi s atakoy po territorii Izrailya," Ministerstvo inostrannykh del Rossiyskoy Federatsii, 14 April 2024, https://mid.ru/ru/foreign_policy/news/1944202/.
30. "Sardār Salāmī: Maʿādilah-yi Jadīdī Raqam Khurdah; Agar Isrāʾīl Hamlah Kunad az Mabdaʾ-i Īrān Mūrad-i Tahājūm-i Mutaqābil Qarār Mīgīrad [Commander Salami: A New Equation Has Been Established; If Israel Attacks, It Will Face Reciprocal Assaults Originating from Iran]," Entekhab, 14 April 2024, https://www.entekhab.ir/fa/news/775940.
31. Michael Young, "Hezbollah Has Retaliated for Israel's Assassination of Its Senior Commander Fouad Shukr," Carnegie Endowment for International Peace, 25 August 2024, https://carnegieendowment.org/middle-east/diwan/2024/08/hezbollah-has-retaliated-for-israels-assassination-of-fouad-shukr?lang=en.
32. "Sih rūz-i ʿazā-yi ʿumūmī barā-yi shahādat-i farmāndah-yi mujāhid Isrāʾīl Haniyah [Three days of public mourning declared for the martyrdom of commander Mujahid Ismail Haniyeh]," ISNA, 31 May 2024, https://www.isna.ir/news/1403051006520; "Ismāʾīl Haniyah bih shahādat rasīd [Ismail Haniyeh was martyred]," ISNA, 31 May 2024, https://www.isna.ir/news/1403051006142; "Fawād Shukr az farmāndahān-i Ḥizb Allāh-i Lubnān bih shahādat rasīd [Fouad Shukr, one of Hezbollah's commanders in Lebanon, was martyred],"Tasnim News, 31 July 2024, https://www.tasnimnews.com/fa/news/1403/05/10/3132011.
33 Farnaz Fassihi, "Russian emissary visits Tehran at a tense moment as Iran asks for military aide," *New York Times*, 5 August 2024, https://www.nytimes.com/live/2024/08/05/world/israel-iran-hezbollah-gaza#russian-emissary-visits-tehran-at-a-tense-moment-as-iran-asks-for-military-aid:~:text=Two%20Iranian%20officials,the%20aid%20publicly.
34. "Treasury Designates Actors Facilitating Iran's Transfer of Lethal Aid to Russia," U.S. Department of the Treasury, 10 September 2024, https://home.treasury.gov/news/press-releases/jy2570.
35. "Iran Is at a Strategic Crossroads," Carnegie Endowment for International Peace, 3 October 2024, https://carnegieendowment.org/emissary/2024/10/iran-israel-missile-attack-nuclear-strategy-what-now?lang=en.
36. "Israel promises revenge after missile attack - Iran," USA Today, 2 October 2024, https://www.usatoday.com/story/news/world/2024/10/02/israel-iran-missile-attack-what-happens-next/75478676007/.
37. *Security Council, 79th Year: 9738th Meeting, Wednesday, 2 October 2024, New York*, United Nations Digital Library, https://digitallibrary.un.org/record/4064487?ln=en&v=pdf.
38. "Putin Plans to Discuss Middle East With Iran, Interfax Reports," Bloomberg, 10

October 2024, https://www.bloomberg.com/news/articles/2024-10-10/putin-plans-to-discuss-middle-east-with-iran-interfax-reports?embedded-checkout=true.

39. The meeting, which had been hastily rebranded from an informal summit of the Organization of Turkic States into an international gathering. The original plan, which included Turkish President Recep Tayyip Erdogan, had clearly gone off the rails—Erdogan bowed out at the last minute, opting instead to receive a commemorative medal in absentia.
40. "Vladimir Putin proved vstrechu s novym prezidentom Irana Masudom Pezeshkianom [Vladimir Putin held a meeting with new Iranian President Masoud Pezeshkian]," Vedomosti, 11 October 2024, https://www.vedomosti.ru/politics/articles/2024/10/11/1068114-putin-provel-vstrechu.
41. "Vtoroy den' XVI sammit BRICS [Second day of the 16th BRICS summit]," Kremlin, 23 October 2024, https://kremlin.ru/events/president/news/75373.
42. "Putin provyol peregovory s prezidentom Irana [Putin held talks with the President of Iran]," RIA Novosti, 23 October 2024, https://ria.ru/20241023/peregovory-1979596711.html.
43. "Chto izvestno ob udarakh VVS Izrailya po Iranu [What is known about Israeli Air Force strikes on Iran],"TASS, 26 October 2024, https://tass.ru/mezhdunarodnaya-panorama/22235477.
44. Sergey Strokan, "Iranskim raketam podrezali kryl'ya [Iranian Missiles Had Their Wings Clipped]," Kommersant, 27 October 2024, https://www.kommersant.ru/doc/7264936.
45. "V MID Rossii prizvali perestat' provotsirovat' Iran i vykhodit' 'iz spirali nekontroliruemoy eskalatsii' [Russian Foreign Ministry called to stop provoking Iran and exit 'the spiral of uncontrolled escalation']," RBK, 26 October 2024, https://www.rbc.ru/politics/26/10/2024/671c356c9a7947beed094140.
46. "Rossiya posle ataki Izrailya prizvala prekratit' provotsirovat' Iran [Russia after Israel's attack called to stop provoking Iran]," RBK, 26 October 2024, https://www.rbc.ru/politics/26/10/2024/671cd1cc9a7947b113ef99ed.
47. Ali Hashem and Mohammad Ali Shabani "Inside story: Hezbollah, Iran and the downfall of Assad," Amwaj, 9 December 2024, https://amwaj.media/en/article/inside-story-hezbollah-iran-and-the-downfall-of-assad.
48. "Joint Statement by the Representatives of Iran, Russia and Türkiye on the 22nd International Meeting on Syria in the Astana Format, 11-12 November 2024," Republic of Türkiye Ministry of Foreign Affairs, 12 November 2024, https://www.mfa.gov.tr/iran-rusya-ve-turkiye-temsilcileri-tarafindan-yapilan-astana-formatindaki-suriye-konulu-22-yuksek-duzeyli-toplanti-ya-iliskin-ortak-bildiri-11-12-kasim-2024.en.mfa.
49. "Siriya privetstvuet rossiyskie usiliya po ukrepleniyu mezhdunarodnoy bezopasnosti - MID [Syria welcomes Russian efforts to strengthen international security - Foreign Ministry]," TASS, 2 December 2024, https://tass.ru/mezhdunarodnaya-panorama/22529953.
50. "Rebel Groups Overrun Aleppo, Reigniting Syrian Civil War and Challenging Assad," Soufan Center, 2 December 2024, https://thesoufancenter.org/intelbrief-2024-december-2/.
51. "Goftogū-yi Sardār Bāqerī bā Vazīr-i Difā'-i Rūsīyah va Rusā-yi Artish-i 'Irāq va Sūrīyah [Conversation of Commander Bagheri with the Defense Minister of Russia

and the Chiefs of Staff of the Armies of Iraq and Syria]," Tasnim News, 3 December 2024, https://www.tasnimnews.com/fa/news/1403/09/13/3212781/.

52. "ʿArāqchī: payām-i ḥimāyat-i Īrān az Sūrīyah rā bih Bashshār Asad muntaqil kardam [Araqchi: I conveyed Iran's message of support to Bashar Assad]," Mehr News, 3 December 2024, https://www.mehrnews.com/news/6304962.
53. "Sih payām-i muhim-i nishast-i sih jānibah-'i Īrān, ʿIrāq va Sūrīyah az nigāh-i ʿArāqchī [Three key messages of the Iran-Iraq-Syria trilateral meeting from Araqchi's perspective]," Tasnim News, 6 December 2024, https://www.tasnimnews.com/fa/news/1403/09/16/3214350.
54. "V MID RF zayavili, chto SShA narushayut suverenitet Sirii i okazivayut negativnoe vliyanie na region [Russian Foreign Ministry stated that the U.S. is violating Syria's sovereignty and having a negative impact on the region]," RIA Novosti, 2 December 2024, https://ria.ru/20241202/siriya-1986902944.html.
55. "V MID: Moskva vystupaet za razvitie sotrudnichestva stran Blizhnego Vostoka i KNR [Foreign Ministry: Moscow supports the development of cooperation between Middle Eastern countries and China]," RIA Novosti, 2 December 2024, https://ria.ru/20241202/sotrudnichestvo-1986984119.html.
56. "RF i Iran vyrazili podderzhku deystviyam vlastey Sirii po vosstanovleniyu tselostnosti strany [Russia and Iran expressed support for the actions of the Syrian authorities to restore the country's integrity]," Interfax, 2 December 2024, https://www.interfax.ru/world/995542; "Guft-o-gū-yi telefonī-yi Pizishkīyān va Pūtīn dar bārah-'i waẓʿīyat-i Sūrīyah [Phone conversation between Pezeshkian and Putin about the situation in Syria]," IRNA, 2 December 2024, https://www.irna.ir/news/85677898.
57. "V Minoborony RF zayavili, chto SSHA pytayutsya zakrepostis' v Sirii dlya raskachivaniya regiona [The Russian Defense Ministry stated that the U.S. is trying to entrench itself in Syria to destabilize the region]," Gazeta.ru, 1 December 2024, https://www.gazeta.ru/army/news/2024/12/01/24518972.shtml.
58. "Ministr inostrannykh del Sirii zayavil o plane razvivat' svyazi s RF [Syrian Foreign Minister announced a plan to develop ties with Russia]," RIA Novosti, 6 December 2024, https://ria.ru/20241206/ministr-1987627889.html; "Armiya RF uspeshno protivodeystvuet terrorizmu v Sirii - postpred [Russian Army successfully counteracts terrorism in Syria - Permanent Representative]," RIA Novosti, 5 December 2024, https://ria.ru/20241205/armija-1987583672.html.
59. "Irtish-i Sūrīyah khabar-i 'aqab'nishīnī az Ḥimṣ rā takdhīb kard [Syrian Army Denies Withdrawal from Homs]," IRNA, 5 December 2024, https://www.irna.ir/news/85681674; "'Amalīyāt-i irtish-i sūrīyah dar shumāl-i Ḥmṣ [Syrian Army Operations in Northern Homs]," IRNA, 6 December 2024, https://www.irna.ir/news/85681850.
60. "Syrian insurgents have reached the gates of the capital city of Damascus, reports say," PBS, 7 December 2024, https://www.pbs.org/newshour/world/syrian-opposition-activists-say-insurgents-have-reached-suburbs-of-the-capital-city-of-damascus.
61. "Dawlat-i Asad chigūnah dar sarāshībī-yi suqūṭ qarār girift [How the Assad Government Entered the Downward Slope of Collapse]," Tasnim News, 8 December 2024, https://www.tasnimnews.com/fa/news/1403/09/18/3215150/.
62. Farnaz Fassihi and Ronen Bergman, "Iran Begins to Evacuate Military Officials and

Personnel From Syria," *The New York Times*, 6 December 2024, https://www.nytimes.com/2024/12/06/world/middleeast/iran-syria-evacuation.html.

63. Nicole Grajewski, "Why Did Iran Allow Bashar al-Assad's Downfall?," Carnegie Endowment for International Peace, 9 December 2024, https://carnegieendowment.org/middle-east/diwan/2024/12/why-did-iran-allow-assads-downfall?lang=en.
64. "V MID RF zayavili, chto zayavlenie SShA na forume v Dokhe nosit propagandistskiy kharakter [Russian Foreign Ministry stated that the U.S. statement at the Doha forum is propagandistic]," RIA Novosti, 7 December 2024, https://ria.ru/20241207/dokha-1987882589.html; "Amānī: Payāmad'hā-yi ḥavādiṣi kunūnī-yi Sūrīyah bih dushmanān-i Dimashq pīsh az dūstān-i ān khvāhad rasīd [Amani: Consequences of Current Events in Syria Will Reach Damascus's Enemies Before Its Friends]," IRNA, 7 December 2024, https://www.irna.ir/news/85682982.
65. "Asad s chlenami svoej sem'i pribyl v Moskvu, RF predostavila im ubezhishche [Assad with his family members arrived in Moscow, Russia granted them asylum]," TASS, 8 December 2024, https://tass.ru/mezhdunarodnaya-panorama/22612655; "Asad poobeshchal podrobno izlozhit' sobytiya, soputtstvovavshiye ego otezdu iz SAR [Assad promised to detail the events accompanying his departure from Syria]," RIA Novosti, 16 December 2024, https://ria.ru/20241216/asad-1989496453.html.
66. Hamidreza Azizi, "How Iran Lost Syria," *Foreign Affairs*, 18 December 2024, https://www.foreignaffairs.com/syria/how-iran-lost-syria; "Sih sinārrīū-yi pīsh-rawī-yi Īrān dar Sūrīyah-'i pasā Asad [Three scenarios ahead for Iran in post-Assad Syria]," IRNA, 21 December 2024, https://irna.ir/xjSqs4; "Dargīrī-yi gurūh-hā-yi musallaḥ-i durūzī bā nīrūhā-yi ḥukūmat-i al-Julānī dar Sūrīyah [Clashes of armed Druze groups with al-Julani government forces in Syria]," IRNA, 1 March 2025, https://irna.ir/xjT23X.

CONCLUSION

1. Farnaz Fassihi, "Iran's Most Senior General in Syria Is Killed in Israeli Airstrike, a Major Blow," *The New York Times*, 8 January 2025, https://www.nytimes.com/2025/01/08/world/middleeast/iran-general-syria-defeat.html.
2. "Tehran Appears to Criticize Moscow's Stance on Persian Gulf Islands," Radio Free Europe/Radio Liberty, 22 December 2023, https://www.rferl.org/a/iran-russia-persian-gulf-islands32743248.html
3. "Threats to Territorial Integrity of Neighbors a Red Line for Iran," IRNA, 5 September 2024, https://en.irna.ir/news/85588037/Threats-to-territorial-integrity-of-neighbors-a-red-line-for.
4. Patrick Wintour, "Iran Warns Russia Against Siding with Azerbaijan in Border Dispute,"The Guardian, 6 September 2024, https://www.theguardian.com/world/article/2024/sep/06/iran-warns-russia-against-siding-with-azerbaijan-in-border-dispute.
5. "Prezident Irana Poblagodaril Putina za Sodeistvie Vstupleniyu Tegerana v ShOS [The Iranian President Thanked Putin for Facilitating Tehran's Accession to the SCO]."
6. "Russia, Iran continuing work on cooperation agreement," Khabar Online, 12 June 2024, https://english.khabaronline.ir/news/197795/Russia-Iran-continuing-work-on-cooperation-agreement.
7. "Text of Russia-Iran comprehensive agreement fully coordinated — Lavrov," TASS, 21 June 2024, https://tass.com/politics/1802221.

8. "Rasporyazhenie o Podpisanii Dogovora o Vseob"emlyushchem Strategicheskom Partnërstve mezhdu Rossiyey i Iranom [Order on Signing the Comprehensive Strategic Partnership Treaty Between Russia and Iran]," Kremlin.ru, 18 September 2024, http://kremlin.ru/acts/news/75137.
9. "Press-konferentsiya po itogam rossiysko-iranskikh peregovorov [Press Conference Following Russian-Iranian Talks]," Kremlin.ru, 17 January 2025, http://kremlin.ru/events/president/news/76126.
10. "Dogovor o vseob″emlyushchem strategicheskom partnyorstve mezhdu Rossiyskoy Federatsiyey i Islamskoy Respublikoy Iran [Treaty on Comprehensive Strategic Partnership between the Russian Federation and the Islamic Republic of Iran]," Kremlin,ru, 17 January 2024, http://www.kremlin.ru/supplement/6258.
11. To this end, Iranian officials stress that the agreement does not establish a defense alliance. As Iranian Foreign Minister Abbas Araghchi notes, it "includes cooperation in the field of security and defense, but does not pursue the goal of creating a military alliance." Echoing this view, Iran's Ambassador to Russia has emphasized that the nature of Russian-Iranian cooperation differs from that with the DPRK or Belarus, highlighting Iran's longstanding preference for self-reliance TASS
12. Mark N. Katz, "Russia and Iran," *Middle East Policy* 19, no. 3 (1 September 2012): 54-64, https://doi.org/10.1111/j.1475-4967.2012.00547.x.

INDEX